HAZARDOUS WASTE

Third Edition

MAXINE I. LIPELES

Professor of Law and
Director of Interdisciplinary Environmental Clinic
Washington University School of Engineering & Applied Science

LexisNexis™

Matthew Bender®

ISBN#: 0820570052

Editorial Offices
744 Broad Street, Newark, NJ 07102 (973) 820-2000
201 Mission St., San Francisco, CA 94105-1831 (415) 908-3200
701 East Water Street, Charlottesville, VA 22902-7587 (804) 972-7600
www.lexis.com

(Pub.3540)

For Joel, Rachel, and Joshua
M.I.L.

Maxine Lipeles is Professor (part-time) of Environmental Regulation and Policy at Washington University, School of Engineering and Applied Science, Director of the school's Environmental Engineering Program, and Of Counsel with the law firm of Husch & Eppenberger in St. Louis, Missouri.

TABLE OF CONTENTS

PART II
THE COMPREHENSIVE ENVIRONMENTAL RESPONSE, COMPENSATION, AND LIABILITY ACT

PART III
AREAS OF OVERLAP BETWEEN
RCRA AND CERCLA

PREFACE

In comparing this Third Edition with its 1992 predecessor and the 1994-1995 Supplement, the single most striking feature is the explosion in CERCLA case law. What appeared to be black-letter principles in 1992, or even 1994, are now gray or speckled in many key respects. The rule of joint and several liability no longer applies in virtually every case; the statutory defenses are no longer wholly illusory; and the rules governing the liability of extended parties such as corporate officers and employees, parent corporations, successor corporations, and lenders, have become more subtle and complex in the past few years. This volume includes many of the seminal cases found in the prior edition (some of which have been further edited), together with newer ones that are refining, if not challenging, the earlier rules of decision. Although the CERCLA-based Problems are the same as those in the prior volume, the principles governing their resolution are somewhat different.

By contrast, the most prominent aspect of the RCRA materials is how little change of significance has transpired since the Second Edition went to press. The threshold issue of what is hazardous waste (encompassing the equally difficult question of what is solid waste) remains virtually as unsettled as it was in 1992. To be sure, some important regulatory developments have occurred—for example, the overhaul of the land ban regulations in 1994, and the expanded incentives for companies to engage in pollution prevention—but the critical, unresolved issues are strikingly similar to those in 1992.

Some features of this newer, longer edition remain constant. The book is still designed to serve a specialized course or seminar on Hazardous Waste, or to be used in tandem with other books or materials, such as Volumes 2 (Water Pollution) and 3 (Air Pollution), in a course covering several areas of pollution regulation. And we still expect the book to be of use to law students as well as engineering and business students who may have the need to be familiar with the complex and confusing world of environmental law. Finally, the several Problems interspersed through this volume can still help students to obtain the valuable experience of working through practical problems with close attention to the relevant statutory and regulatory provisions.

I remain extremely grateful to the Washington University School of Engineering, and particularly Dr. William Darby, for their ongoing support and encouragement. I am deeply indebted to Elaine Halley of the Environmental Engineering Program, and Washington University School of Law research assistants Michael Savage, Noel Oleksa, and David Czarnecki. Sean Caldwell and his team at Anderson Publishing have shepherded this project to fruition with patience and good humor.

Last but not least, I am profoundly grateful to Jack Battle, who pioneered the First Edition, worked with me on the Second Edition, and has entrusted me with the future of this volume. In fact, Jack should be credited with the creation of the Environmental Law Series. Jack envisioned a collection of focused casebooks as an alternative to the survey-style casebooks, for use in survey courses as well as in seminars. Jack's energy and insight, together with support from Anderson Publishing, brought to fruition the First Edition of the Series. With his impressive command of environmental law, and sharply-critical mind, Jack played the lead role in the Second Edition of the Water Pollution volume, and contributed invaluable to the Second Edition of this volume—notwithstanding the ever-pressing demands of his full-time law practice. Fortunately, Jack expects to play an active role in the future of the Water Pollution volume.

Maxine Lipeles   St. Louis, Missouri   August 1997

TABLE OF CASES

INTRODUCTION

Two traits that many law students strive to hone are the ability to think logically and an appreciation of the fair and equitable result. As one embarks on the study of hazardous waste law, however, the student is well-advised to keep those traits carefully in check. Federal hazardous waste law consists principally of two statutes, the Resource Conservation and Recovery Act ("RCRA") and the Comprehensive Environmental Response, Compensation, and Liability Act ("CERCLA," or the "Superfund" law), and the regulations and case law implementing and construing them. This Introduction will discuss RCRA and CERCLA in broad overview, and in relation to one another. More detailed introductory material regarding each statute is presented at the beginning of Parts I and II.

RCRA governs the day-to-day generation and handling of hazardous waste. What makes it distinctive are the complexity and density of its highly-detailed rules and regulations. The maze of regulations that has evolved, and continues to evolve, reflects detailed congressional directives, judicial constructions of statutory language, ever-changing technical developments in the identification and handling of hazardous waste, and the EPA's ever-evolving policy and technical judgments. The result is a compilation of rules so complicated that top EPA officials concede that very few people *within* the EPA actually understand the RCRA regulations. *See U.S. v. White*, 766 F.Supp. 873, 882 (E.D.Wash.1991) (in chapter 6). One can easily lose one's bearings on a "mind-numbing journey" through the RCRA regulations. *American Mining Congress v. EPA*, 824 F.2d 1177, 1189 (D.C.Cir.1987) (in chapter 2). Although the student who finds the Internal Revenue Code to be a model of logic may disagree, many who gain familiarity with the RCRA regulations find their logical component to be somewhat elusive.

CERCLA addresses the cleanup of, for the most part, previously-contaminated sites. In contrast to the excruciating detail of RCRA, CERCLA is notable for its sweeping scope. It grants the EPA an impressive array of powerful weapons to require an exceptionally broad group of parties to incur extremely high cleanup costs. The logic underpinning CERCLA is not nearly as obscure as in the RCRA context; Congress concluded that the threat posed by contaminated sites was sufficiently serious, and the prospective costs so high, that the EPA must have correspondingly powerful authority to ensure that such sites could be promptly cleaned up and that the entities responsible for the contamination, rather than the taxpayers, should bear the cleanup costs. In the interest of achieving these bold goals, traditional notions of fairness and equity do not play a prominent role in the CERCLA program. As one court noted, "CERCLA *** is not a legislative scheme which places a high priority on fairness to generators of hazardous waste." *U.S. v. Rohm & Haas*, 721 F.Supp. 666, 686 (D.N.J.1989).

It is noteworthy that these two laws—perhaps the most fearsome of the federal environmental laws —took effect within three weeks of one another, between November 19, 1980 (when the first substantive RCRA regulations became legally effective) and December 11, 1980 (when CERCLA was enacted). Although RCRA was enacted in 1976, amending the preexisting Solid Waste Disposal Act, the regulatory program necessary to implement it did not take effect until the first substantive RCRA regulations became final. Those initial regulations defined the term "hazardous waste" for the first time under federal law, and outlined the obligations of entities that generate hazardous waste and facilities that treat, store, or dispose of hazardous waste. Because RCRA operates prospectively and not retroactively (except for its cleanup programs), only those entities that generated, treated, stored, or disposed of hazardous waste after November 19, 1980 have been subject to RCRA's substantive requirements.

Almost immediately after the first RCRA regulations became final, Congress passed CERCLA to provide for the cleanup of sites that had become contaminated in the past, prior to government regulation of the handling or disposal of hazardous waste. Because, unlike RCRA, CERCLA is not a regulatory program and could be implemented without new regulations, it took effect immediately. And because of its rather extreme liability rules and its retroactive application, CERCLA promptly became the subject of considerable attention as the EPA began notifying large numbers of "potentially responsible parties" that they were required to share in the expensive investigation and cleanup of numerous Superfund sites around the nation. The relatively quick fame (or infamy) achieved by Superfund is in contrast to RCRA, its lesser-known counterpart, whose impact has been appreciated on a more gradual basis from 1980 to the present.

This volume focuses individually on RCRA and CERCLA in considerable detail, and then addresses the relationship between the two laws. The volume closes with a chapter on pollution prevention, which encompasses a variety of efforts to reduce the volume and toxicity of wastes. These efforts, many of which are voluntary, have been prompted in large part by generators' interest in reducing their compliance and liability costs under RCRA and CERCLA.

I
THE RESOURCE CONSERVATION AND RECOVERY ACT

1 OVERVIEW OF RCRA

Congress enacted the Resource Conservation and Recovery Act, 42 U.S.C. §§ 6901 *et seq.*, in 1976, midway through the period 1970-1980 during which virtually all of the principal federal environmental laws were enacted. Proceeding on a medium-by-medium basis, Congress had addressed air pollution in 1970 with the modern version of the Clean Air Act, and had tackled water pollution in 1972 with the modern version of the Clean Water Act (known then as the Federal Water Pollution Control Act). RCRA was added to the growing array of environmental laws primarily to protect the land and groundwater, the only unregulated media into which substantial volumes of hazardous waste were being disposed.

At the heart of RCRA is Subtitle C, which creates a regulatory program focused exclusively on hazardous waste. Subtitle C, 42 U.S.C. §§ 6921 - 6939b, and its implementing regulations define the universe of RCRA-regulated materials, or "hazardous waste," impose duties on entities that generate hazardous waste, typically in the course of manufacturing or other commercial activities, and prescribe standards and permit requirements for facilities that treat, store, or dispose of hazardous waste. The regulatory program under RCRA's Subtitle C is frequently described as a comprehensive, "cradle-to-grave" program that regulates the handling of hazardous waste from the moment it is generated through its ultimate disposition.

Two additional programs encompassed within the RCRA statute, although independent of the Subtitle C hazardous waste regulatory program, are Subtitle D, which calls for federal guidelines for state-run programs regulating the disposal of solid waste, and Subtitle I, which establishes a federal program governing underground tanks used to store petroleum and hazardous substances (but not hazardous waste).

As enacted in October 1976, RCRA directed the EPA to promulgate regulations within 18 months to establish the key elements of a comprehensive hazardous waste management program. Subject to the 18-month deadline were regulations: (1) specifying the criteria for identifying hazardous waste, identifying the characteristics of hazardous waste, and listing particular hazardous wastes; (2) setting standards for entities that generate or transport hazardous waste; (3) setting standards and permit requirements for existing and new facilities that treat, store, or dispose of hazardous waste; and (4) establishing guidelines for states in developing their own hazardous waste management programs.

The 18-month deadline passed without a single RCRA regulation proposed, let alone promulgated in final form. Following litigation and more missed deadlines, the EPA promulgated the first substantive RCRA regulations in final form on May 19, 1980. The regulations took effect six months later, on November 19, 1980, with the exception of regulations under § 3010(a), 42 U.S.C. § 6930(a), which require all persons subject to RCRA to notify the EPA of their existence and the nature of their activities, and which took effect on August 19, 1980. This initial package of RCRA regulations did not address all matters subject to the 18-month deadline. Most notably, regulations governing permit standards for land disposal facilities, which were receiving a large volume of hazardous waste, were not promulgated until July 1982.

The early implementation of the RCRA regulatory program was characterized by turmoil. The Reagan Administration, which assumed office in January 1981, targeted the RCRA program as excessively costly. The EPA attempted to nullify or weaken some of the regulations that had already taken effect, and in some cases was forced to reinstate the original regulations (such as when EPA lifted the ban it had shortly before imposed on placing containerized liquid waste in landfills), causing confusion, uncertainty, and the appearance of mismanagement. Ultimately, the EPA Administrator, Anne Gorsuch, resigned and her Assistant Administrator responsible for the RCRA and CERCLA programs, Rita Lavelle, was ridiculed and convicted of perjuring herself before Congress. As a result, a consensus calling for the redirection of the RCRA program emerged among members of Congress frustrated by the EPA's slow pace in fulfilling the statutory mandates of the 1976 law, those regulated entities that were trying to comply with the moving target of RCRA and suspected that some of their competitors were not, and environmentalists seeking more stringent standards for the handling of hazardous waste.

On November 8, 1984, the Hazardous and Solid Waste Amendments of 1984 ("HSWA") became law. HSWA imposed deadlines on pre-existing provisions of RCRA that the EPA had not yet implemented, most notably deadlines requiring the submission of permit applications for treatment, storage, and disposal ("TSD") facilities, and further deadlines requiring the EPA and those state agencies authorized to administer RCRA to make decisions approving or denying the permit applications. The permit-decision deadlines were November 1988 for land disposal facilities, November 1989 for incinerators, and November 1992 for all other TSD facilities. In addition, HSWA created new programs within RCRA, the two most prominent of which are known as the "land ban," which prohibits the land disposal of hazardous waste that does not meet EPA-specified treatment standards (and which was also implemented pursuant to strict statutory deadlines), and the "corrective action" program, which requires the cleanup of pre-existing contamination at TSD facilities. Further, HSWA reflected various technical judgments imposed by Congress, such as statutorily-specified minimum technology requirements for various types of land disposal facilities. For example, RCRA requires landfills and surface impoundments to have double liners, leachate collection systems, and groundwater monitoring.

This technical judgment aspect of HSWA signalled a pronounced shift in the relative roles of Congress and the EPA regarding not only RCRA, but the other principal environmental laws as well. The initial versions of the environmental laws, enacted during the 1970s through the passage of CERCLA in 1980, involved lofty congressional goals with broad delegations of authority to the EPA to develop regulatory programs to implement those goals. In contrast, when Congress returned to enact significant amendments to each of the key laws during the 1980s (beginning with HSWA in 1984 and culminating with the 1990 Amendments to the Clean Air Act), the amending laws contained numerous technical decisions made by Congress and imposed upon the EPA.

Following the enactment of HSWA, the EPA undertook with vigor the ambitious task of meeting the statutory deadlines and developing the new and modified RCRA programs. As of this writing in 1997, much has been accomplished in the implementation of RCRA and HSWA, particularly the submission and ruling upon permit applications for TSD facilities and the promulgation of treatment standards required by the land ban. On the other hand, certain significant provisions of the RCRA program remain unsettled—more than two decades after RCRA was enacted. Ironically, one of those still-unsettled areas is the threshold issue of the definition of "hazardous waste" for purposes of triggering RCRA's jurisdiction in the first place. The complex and elusive definition of hazardous waste is the subject of the next chapter.

2   DEFINITION OF HAZARDOUS WASTE

Definitions are of critical importance under RCRA. The definition of "hazardous waste" in the statute is a broadly-phrased reference to solid wastes that pose a threat to human health or the environment. RCRA § 1004(5), 42 U.S.C. § 6903(5). A more specific definition of hazardous waste for purposes of the Subtitle C regulatory program is the subject of Part 261 of the RCRA regulations, 40 C.F.R. Part 261.[1] The Part 261 regulations are among the most dense, obtuse, and significant of the vast array of RCRA regulations. In no other RCRA context is a thorough understanding of the regulations more essential, or more difficult to achieve. The authors strongly recommend that all students obtain a copy of the RCRA regulations, particularly Part 261, and work through the issues presented in the RCRA cases and problems to appreciate the complexities and subtleties of the RCRA regulations.

The RCRA definition of hazardous waste requires a two-part inquiry. First, is the material in question a "solid waste" (*i.e.,* is it a waste)? Second, if and only if the material is a "solid waste," is it a "hazardous waste" (*i.e.,* is the waste hazardous)? The balance of this chapter will address each inquiry separately.

A. Definition of Solid Waste

The statutory definition of solid waste encompasses any material, in any physical state (*i.e.,* including liquids and contained gas), that is "discarded," unless it is specifically excluded from the definition. RCRA § 1004(27), 42 U.S.C. § 6903(27). The RCRA regulations address in considerable detail the meaning of the key term

---

[1] The detailed definitions of solid and hazardous waste in the EPA's regulations at 40 C.F.R. Part 261 do not apply throughout RCRA. They apply generally to the Subtitle C hazardous waste regulatory program, except that the EPA reverts to the broader statutory definitions for purposes of (a) the corrective action program, §§ 3004(u) and 3008(h), 42 U.S.C. §§ 6924(u) and 6928(h), and (b) the enforcement-related inspection and monitoring provisions, §§ 3007 and 3013, 42 U.S.C. §§ 6927 and 6934. In addition, the EPA uses the broader statutory definition under § 7003, 42 U.S.C. § 6973, the omnibus cleanup provision which goes beyond the scope of Subtitle C. *See* 40 C.F.R. § 261.1(a) and (b).

"discarded," which is defined to include materials that are "abandoned," "recycled," or "inherently waste-like." 40 C.F.R. § 261.2(a)(1).

The EPA's decision to include recycled materials among those deemed to be discarded has generated controversy and confusion. Both results stem from the commonly-made assumptions that recycling is good for the environment, and that the recycling of hazardous waste is and/or should be free from the burdensome regulations governing the burial or destruction of hazardous waste. The EPA has been concerned, however, that mismanaged recycling activities could pose as much threat to public health and the environment as mismanaged disposal or treatment activities. Therefore, the EPA has struggled to devise regulations that encompass within RCRA those recycling activities that are more likely to pose an environmental danger, while excluding—or regulating separately, without the full force of the central hazardous waste regulations—those recycling activities that the EPA seeks most to encourage.

The first place in the RCRA program where one encounters the issue of how heavily recycling should be regulated is the definition of solid waste. As noted above, solid waste is material that is discarded, and discarded materials include those that are "recycled" within the definition of 40 C.F.R. § 261.2(c)—*except* for those recycled materials that are not solid waste, under the provisions of 40 C.F.R. §§ 261.2(e) (materials that are not solid waste when recycled) or 261.4(a)(exclusions from the definition of solid waste). As one might expect, the recycling aspect of the definition of solid waste has been the subject of considerable litigation, and as of this writing is still not entirely settled.

AMERICAN MINING CONGRESS V. ENVIRONMENTAL PROTECTION AGENCY
824 F.2d 1177 (D.C.Cir. 1987)

Before STARR and MIKVA, Circuit Judges, and McGOWAN, Senior Circuit Judge.

STARR, Circuit Judge.

These consolidated cases arise out of EPA's regulation of hazardous wastes under the Resource Conservation and Recovery Act of 1976 ("RCRA"), as amended, 42 U.S.C. §§ 6901-6933. Petitioners, trade associations representing mining and oil refining interests, challenge regulations promulgated by EPA that amend the definition of "solid waste" to establish and define the agency's authority to regulate secondary materials reused within an industry's ongoing production process. In plain English, petitioners maintain that EPA has exceeded its regulatory authority in seeking to bring materials that are not discarded or otherwise disposed of within the compass of "waste."

I

RCRA is a comprehensive environmental statute under which EPA is granted authority to regulate solid and hazardous wastes. RCRA was enacted in 1976, and amended in 1978, 1980, and 1984.

Congress' "overriding concern" in enacting RCRA was to establish the framework for a national system to insure the safe management of hazardous waste. In passing RCRA, Congress expressed concern over the "rising tide" in scrap, discarded, and waste materials. 42 U.S.C. § 6901(a)(2). As the statute itself puts it, Congress was concerned with the need "to reduce the amount of waste and unsalvageable materials and to provide for proper and economical solid waste disposal practices." Congress thus crafted RCRA "to promote the protection of health and the environment and to conserve valuable material and energy resources."

RCRA includes two major parts: one deals with non-hazardous solid waste management and the other with hazardous waste management. Under the latter, EPA is directed to promulgate regulations establishing a comprehensive management system. EPA's authority, however, extends only to the regulation of "hazardous waste." Because "hazardous waste" is defined as a subset of "solid waste," the scope of EPA's jurisdiction is limited to those materials that constitute "solid waste." That pivotal term is defined by RCRA as

> any garbage, refuse, sludge from a waste treatment plant, water supply treatment plant, or air pollution control facility *and other discarded material*, including solid, liquid, semisolid or contained gaseous material, resulting from industrial, commercial, mining, and agricultural operations, and from community activities....

42 U.S.C. § 6903(27) (emphasis added). As will become evident, this case turns on the meaning of the phrase, "and other discarded material," contained in the statute's definitional provisions.

EPA's interpretation of "solid waste" has evolved over time. On May 19, 1980, EPA issued interim regulations defining "solid waste" to include a material that is "a manufacturing or mining by-product and sometimes is discarded." 45 Fed. Reg. 33,119 (1980). This definition contained two terms needing elucidation: "by-product" and "sometimes discarded." In its definition of "a manufacturing or mining by-product," EPA expressly *excluded* "an intermediate manufacturing or mining product which results from one of the steps in a manufacturing or mining process and is typically processed through the next step of the process within a short time." *Id.*

In 1983, the agency proposed narrowing amendments to the 1980 interim rule. 48 Fed. Reg. 14,472 (1983). The agency showed especial concern over *recycling* activities. In the preamble to the amendments, the agency observed that, in light of the interlocking statutory provisions and RCRA's legislative history, it was clear that "Congress indeed intended that materials being recycled or held for recycling can be wastes, and if hazardous, hazardous wastes." The agency also asserted that "not only can materials destined for recycling or being recycled be solid and hazardous wastes, but the Agency clearly has the authority to regulate recycling activities as hazardous management."

While asserting its interest in recycling activities (and materials being held for recycling), EPA's discussion left unclear whether the agency in fact believed its jurisdiction extended to materials recycled in an industry's on-going production processes, or only to materials disposed of and recycled as part of a waste management program. In its preamble, EPA stated that "the revised definition of solid waste sets out the Agency's view of its jurisdiction over the recycling of hazardous waste.... Proposed section 261.6 then contains exemptions from regulations for those hazardous waste recycling activities that we do not think require regulation." The amended regulatory description of "solid waste" itself, then, did not include materials "used or reused as effective substitutes for raw materials in processes using raw materials as principal feedstocks." EPA explained the exclusion as follows:

> (These) materials are being used essentially as raw materials and so ordinarily are not appropriate candidates for regulatory control. Moreover, when these materials are used to manufacture new products, the processes generally are normal manufacturing operations..., The Agency is reluctant to read the statute as regulating actual manufacturing processes. ***

Id. at 14,488. This, then, seemed clear: EPA was drawing a line between discarding and ultimate recycling, on the one hand, and a continuous or ongoing manufacturing process with on-site "recycling," on the other. If the activity fell within the latter category, then the materials were not deemed to be "discarded."

After receiving extensive comments, EPA issued its final rule on January 4, 1985. 50 Fed. Reg. 614 (1985). Under the final rule, materials are considered "solid waste" if they are abandoned by being disposed of, burned, or incinerated; or stored, treated, or accumulated before or in lieu of those activities. In addition, certain recycling activities fall within EPA's definition. EPA determines whether a material is a RCRA solid waste when it is recycled by examining both the material or substance itself and the recycling activity involved. The final rule identifies five categories of "secondary materials" (spent materials, sludges, by-products, commercial chemical products, and scrap metal). These "secondary materials" constitute "solid waste" when they are disposed of; burned for energy recovery or used to produce a fuel; reclaimed; or accumulated speculatively.[1] Under the final rule, if a material constitutes "solid waste," it is subject to RCRA regulation *unless* it is directly reused as an ingredient or as an effective substitute for a commercial product, or is returned as a raw material substitute

---

[1] Under the final rule, a "use constituting disposal" is defined as direct placement on land of wastes or products containing or derived from wastes. A material is "accumulated speculatively" if it is accumulated prior to being recycled. If the accumulator can show that the materials feasibly can be recycled, and that during a one-year calendar period the amount of material recycled or transferred for recycling is 75% or more of the amount present at the beginning of the year, the materials are not considered solid wastes. A material is "reclaimed" if it is processed to recover a usable product, or if it is regenerated.

to its original manufacturing process.[2] In the jargon of the trade, the latter category is known as the "closed-loop" exception. In either case, the material must not first be "reclaimed" (processed to recover a usable product or regenerated). EPA exempts these activities "because they are like ordinary usage of commercial products."

II

Petitioners, American Mining Congress ("AMC") and American Petroleum Institute ("API"), challenge the scope of EPA's final rule. Relying upon the statutory definition of "solid waste," petitioners contend that EPA's authority under RCRA is limited to controlling materials that are *discarded or intended for discard*. They argue that EPA's reuse and recycle rules, as applied to in-process secondary materials, regulate materials that have not been discarded, and therefore exceed EPA's jurisdiction.[3]

To understand petitioners' claims, a passing familiarity with the nature of their industrial processes is required.

Petroleum. Petroleum refineries vary greatly both in respect of their products and their processes.   Most of their products, however, are complex mixtures of hydrocarbons produced through a number of interdependent and sometimes repetitious processing steps. In general, the refining process starts by "distilling" crude oil into various hydrocarbon streams or "fractions." The "fractions" are then subjected to a number of processing steps. Various hydrocarbon materials derived from virtually all stages of processing are combined or blended in order to produce products such as gasoline, fuel oil, and lubricating oils. Any hydrocarbons that are not usable in a particular form or state are returned to an appropriate stage in the refining process so they can eventually be used. Likewise, the hydrocarbons and materials which escape from a refinery's production vessels are gathered and, by a complex retrieval system, returned to appropriate parts of the refining process. Under EPA's final rule, this reuse and recycling of materials is subject to regulation under RCRA.

---

[2] Specifically, the final rule excludes materials recycled by being: "(1) (u)sed or reused as ingredients in an industrial process to make a product, *provided the materials are not being reclaimed;* or (2) (u)sed or reused as effective substitutes for commercial products; or (3) (r)eturned to the original process from which they are generated, without first being reclaimed." (emphasis added). In the third category, the material must be returned to the original manufacturing process as a substitute for raw material feedstock, and the process must use raw materials as principal feedstocks.

[3] EPA's final rule currently exempts solid wastes generated from the smelting and refining of ores and minerals pursuant to 42 U.S.C. § 6921(b)(3)(A)(ii), which provides that solid wastes from the extraction, beneficiation, and processing of ores and minerals are exempt from regulation until at least six months after EPA has completed studies of such wastes. The final rule also exempts petroleum refining wastes, or oils recovered from such wastes, that are recycled by reinserting them into the refining process along with the normal crude feedstock. Notwithstanding the exempt status of most mining and petroleum wastes, certain recycling practices of AMC and API are currently subject to substantive regulation under EPA's rules.

* * *

Mining. In the mining industry, primary metals production involves the extraction of fractions of a percent of a metal from a complex mineralogical matrix (i.e., the natural material in which minerals are embedded). Extractive metallurgy proceeds incrementally. Rome was not built in a day, and all metal cannot be extracted in one fell swoop. In consequence, materials are reprocessed in order to remove as much of the pure metal as possible from the natural ore. Under EPA's final rule, this reprocessed ore and the metal derived from it constitute "solid waste." What is more, valuable metal-bearing and mineral-bearing dusts are often released in processing a particular metal. The mining facility typically recaptures, recycles, and reuses these dusts, frequently in production processes different from the one from which the dusts were originally emitted. The challenged regulations encompass this reprocessing, to the mining industry's dismay.

Against this factual backdrop, we now examine the legal issues presented by petitioners' challenge.

III

We observe at the outset of our inquiry that EPA's interpretation of the scope of its authority under RCRA has been unclear and unsteady. As previously recounted, EPA has shifted from its vague "sometimes discarded" approach of 1980 to a proposed exclusion from regulation of all materials used or reused as effective substitutes for raw materials in 1983, and finally, to a very narrow exclusion of essentially only materials processed within the meaning of the "closed-loop" exception under the final rule. We emphasize, therefore, that we are confronted with neither a consistent nor a longstanding agency interpretation. Under settled doctrine, "(a)n agency interpretation of a relevant provision which conflicts with the agency's earlier interpretation is 'entitled to considerably less deference' than a consistently held agency view."

A

Because the issue is one of statutory interpretation, the principles enunciated in *Chevron U.S.A., Inc. v. NRDC,* 467 U.S. 837 (1984), and its progeny guide our inquiry. ***

* * *

We thus begin our inquiry with the first step of *Chevron's* analysis: did Congress clearly intend to limit EPA's regulatory jurisdiction to materials disposed of or abandoned, as opposed to materials reused within an ongoing production process? ***

* * *

B

Guided by these principles, we turn to the statutory provision at issue here. Congress, it will be recalled, granted EPA power to regulate "solid waste." Congress specifically defined "solid waste" as "discarded material." EPA then defined "discarded material" to include materials destined for reuse in an industry's ongoing production processes. The challenge to EPA's jurisdictional reach is founded, again, on the proposition that in-process secondary materials are outside the bounds of EPA's lawful authority. Nothing has been discarded, the argument goes, and thus RCRA jurisdiction remains untriggered.

1

The first step in statutory interpretation is, of course, an analysis of the language itself. As the Supreme Court has often observed, "the starting point in every case involving statutory construction is 'the language employed by Congress.'" *** Here, Congress defined "solid waste" as "discarded material." The ordinary, plain-English meaning of the word "discarded" is "disposed of," "thrown away" or "abandoned." Encompassing materials retained for immediate reuse within the scope of "discarded material" strains, to say the least, the everyday usage of that term.

Although the "ordinary and obvious meaning of the (statutory) phrase is not to be lightly discounted," *Cardoza-Fonseca*, 107 S.Ct. at 1213, we are hesitant to attribute decisive significance to the ordinary meaning of statutory language. ***

We hasten to add that this is by no means to say that language employed by a legislative body in that which we call *law* is doomed to remain inherently unclear and ambiguous. The Supreme Court has held, in a variety of contexts, that the statutory terms themselves can and do clearly express Congress' intent. *** In view of this considerable body of learning with respect to the reading of statutes, pointing in quite different directions, we are frank to admit that in our analysis we dare accord the ordinary meaning of "discarded"—i.e., disposed of—considerable, but by no means conclusive, weight in our interpretive task.

In short, a complete analysis of the statutory term "discarded" calls for more than resort to the ordinary, everyday meaning of the specific language at hand. *** The statutory provision cannot properly be torn from the law of which it is a part; context and structure are, as in examining any legal instrument, of substantial import in the interpretive exercise.

As we previously recounted, the broad objectives of RCRA are "to promote the protection of health and the environment and to conserve valuable material and energy resources...." 42 U.S.C. § 6902. But that goal is of majestic breadth, and it is difficult *** to pour meaning into a highly specific term by resort to grand purposes. Somewhat more specifically, we have seen that RCRA was enacted in response to Congressional findings that the "rising tide of scrap, discarded, and waste materials" generated by consumers and increased industrial production had presented heavily populated urban communities with "serious financial, management, intergovernmental, and technical problems in the disposal of solid wastes." *Id.* § 6901(a). *** Also animating Congress were its findings that "disposal of solid and hazardous waste" without careful planning and management presents a danger to human health and the environment; that methods to "separate usable materials from solid waste" should be employed; and that usable energy can be produced from solid waste. *Id.* § 6901(b),(c),(d).

The question we face, then, is whether, in light of the National Legislature's expressly stated objectives and the underlying problems that motivated it to enact

RCRA in the first instance, Congress was using the term "discarded" in its ordinary sense—"disposed of" or "abandoned"—or whether Congress was using it in a much more open-ended way, so as to encompass materials no longer useful in their original capacity though destined for immediate reuse in another phase of the industry's ongoing production process.

For the following reasons, we believe the former to be the case. RCRA was enacted, as the Congressional objectives and findings make clear, in an effort to help States deal with the ever-increasing problem of solid waste *disposal* by encouraging the search for and use of alternatives to existing methods of disposal (including recycling) and protecting health and the environment by regulating hazardous wastes. To fulfill these purposes, it seems clear that EPA need not regulate "spent" materials that are recycled and reused in an *ongoing* manufacturing or industrial process. These materials have not yet become part of the waste disposal problem; rather, *they are destined for beneficial reuse or recycling in a continuous process by the generating industry itself.*

* * *

2

Our task in analyzing the statute also requires us to determine whether other provisions of RCRA shed light on the breadth with which Congress intended to define "discarded." ***

* * *

*** EPA argues that § 6924(q)(1) evinces Congressional intent to include recycled in-process materials within the definition of "solid waste." We note at the outset that this provision is likewise a subsection of § 6924 and is therefore directed towards hazardous waste treatment facilities. The ever-present circularity problem thus looms here as well. But that is not all. EPA's argument is deficient in other respects too. Section 6924(q)(1) commands the agency to promulgate standards applicable to persons who produce, market, distribute, or burn fuels produced from or otherwise containing hazardous waste. The final sentence of that subparagraph states:

(F)or purposes of this subsection, the term "hazardous waste listed under section 6921 of this title" includes any commercial chemical product which is listed under section 6921 of this title and which, in lieu of its original intended use, is (i) produced for use as (or as a component of) a fuel, (ii) distributed for use as a fuel, or (iii) burned as a fuel.

Congress apparently added this language to override a then-existing EPA regulation which provided that unused commercial chemical products were solid wastes only when "discarded." 40 C.F.R. § 261.33 (1983). "Discarded" was at that time defined as abandoned (and not recycled) by being disposed, burned, or incinerated (but not burned for energy recovery). 40 C.F.R. § 261.2(c) (1983). ***

We think it likely that in this provision Congress meant only to speak to the specific problem it identified—the burning of commercial chemicals as fuels, contrary to their original intended use. Congress addressed this problem by deeming the offending materials to be "discarded" and therefore within the statutory definition of "solid waste." This specific measure did not, however, revamp the basic definitional section of the statute.

3

After this mind-numbing journey through RCRA, we return to the provision that is, after all, the one before us for examination. And that definitional section, we believe, indicates clear Congressional intent to limit EPA's authority. First, the definition of "solid waste" is situated in a section containing thirty-nine separate, defined terms. This is definitional specificity of the first order. The very care evidenced by Congress in defining RCRA's scope certainly suggests that Congress was concerned about delineating and thus cabining EPA's jurisdictional reach.

Second, the statutory definition of "solid waste" is quite specific. Although Congress well knows how to use broad terms and broad definitions, as for example, "waters of the United States" in *Riverside Bayview*, or in an altogether different setting, the term "intelligence source" in *CIA v. Sims*, 471 U.S. 159 (1985), the definition here is carefully crafted with specificity. It contains three specific terms and then sets forth the broader term, "other discarded material." *** Here, the three particular classes— garbage, refuse, and sludge from a waste treatment plant, water supply treatment plant, or air pollution control facility—contain materials that clearly fit within the ordinary, everyday sense of "discarded." It is most sensible to conclude that Congress, in adding the concluding phrase "other discarded material," meant to grant EPA authority over similar types of waste, but not to open up the federal regulatory reach of an entirely new category of materials, i.e., materials neither disposed of nor abandoned, but passing in a continuous stream or flow from one production process to another.

In sum, our analysis of the statute reveals clear Congressional intent to extend EPA's authority only to materials that are truly discarded, disposed of, thrown away, or abandoned. EPA nevertheless submits that the legislative history evinces a contrary intent. *** Although we find RCRA's statutory language unambiguous, and can discern no exceptional circumstances warranting resort to its legislative history, we will nonetheless in an abundance of caution afford EPA the benefit of consideration of those secondary materials.

4
* * *

*** [A] fair reading of the legislative history reveals intimations of an intent to regulate under RCRA only materials that have truly been discarded. Not only is the language of the legislative history fully consistent with the use of "discarded" in the sense of "disposed of," but it strains the language to read it otherwise. Most significantly, in discussing its choice of the words "discarded materials" to define "solid waste," the House Committee stated:

> Not only solid wastes, but also liquid and contained gaseous wastes, semi-solid wastes and sludges are the subjects of this legislation. Waste itself is a misleading word in the context of the committee's activity. *Much*

> *industrial and agricultural waste is reclaimed or put to new use and is therefore not a part of the discarded materials disposal problem the committee addresses.*

H.R.Rep. No. 1491, 94th Cong., 2d Sess. at 2, U.S. Code Cong. & Admin. News 1976, p. 6240 (emphasis added). ***

* * *

After all is said and done, we are satisfied that the legislative history, rather than evincing Congress' intent to define "discarded" to include in-process secondary materials employed in an ongoing manufacturing process, confirms that the term was employed by the Article I branch in its ordinary, everyday sense.

IV

We are constrained to conclude that, in light of the language and structure of RCRA, the problems animating Congress to enact it, and the relevant portions of the legislative history, Congress clearly and unambiguously expressed its intent that "solid waste" (and therefore EPA's regulatory authority) be limited to materials that are "discarded" by virtue of being disposed of, abandoned, or thrown away. While we do not lightly overturn an agency's reading of its own statute, we are persuaded that by regulating in-process secondary materials, EPA has acted in contravention of Congress' intent.

MIKVA, Circuit Judge, dissenting:

The court today strains to overturn the Environmental Protection Agency's interpretation of the Resource Conservation and Recovery Act to authorize the regulation of certain recycled industrial materials. Under today's decision, the EPA is prohibited from regulating in-process secondary materials that contribute to the ominous problem that Congress sought to eradicate by passing the RCRA. In my opinion, the EPA has adequately demonstrated that its interpretation is a reasonable construction of an ambiguous term in a statute committed to the agency's administration. We therefore are obliged to defer to the agency's interpretation under the principles of *Chevron U.S.A., Inc. v. NRDC*, 467 U.S. 837 (1984), and *INS v. Cardoza-Fonseca*, 107 S.Ct. 1207 (1987). I dissent.

* * *

In my opinion, the EPA's interpretation of solid waste is completely reasonable in light of the language, policies, and legislative history of RCRA. *See United States v. Riverside Bayview Homes*, 474 U.S. 121 (1986). Congress had broad remedial objectives in mind when it enacted RCRA, most notably to "regulat(e) the treatment, storage, transportation, and disposal of hazardous wastes which have adverse effects on the environment." 42 U.S.C. § 6902(4). The disposal problem Congress was combating encompassed more than just abandoned materials. RCRA makes this clear with its definition of the central statutory term "disposal":

> the discharge, deposit, injection, dumping, spilling, leaking, or placing of any solid waste or hazardous waste into or on any land or water so that

> such solid waste or hazardous waste or any constituent thereof may enter
> the environment or be emitted into the air or discharged into any waters,
> including ground waters.

42 U.S.C. § 6903(3). This definition clearly encompasses more than the everyday meaning of disposal, which is a "discarding or throwing away." *Webster's Third International Dictionary* 654 (2d ed. 1981). The definition is *functional*: waste is disposed under this provision if it is put into contact with land or water in such a way as to pose the risks to health and environment that animated Congress to pass RCRA. Whether the manufacturer subjectively intends to put the material to additional use is irrelevant to this definition, as indeed it should be, because the manufacturer's state of mind bears no necessary relation to the hazards of the industrial processes he employs.

Faithful to RCRA's functional approach, EPA reasonably concluded that regulation of certain in-process secondary materials was necessary to carry out its mandate. The materials at issue in this case can pose the same risks as abandoned wastes, whether or not the manufacturer intends eventually to put them to further beneficial use. As the agency explained, "(s)imply because a waste is likely to be recycled will not ensure that it will not be spilled or leaked before recycling occurs." J.A. 67. The storage, transportation, and even recycling of in-process secondary materials can cause severe environmental harm. Indeed, the EPA documented environmental disasters caused by the handling or storage of such materials. It also pointed out the risk of damage from spills or leaks when certain in-process secondary materials are placed on land or in underground product storage.

Moreover, the agency's action is carefully aligned with Congress' functional approach to problems of waste disposal. The agency is not seeking to regulate all recycled materials. Rather, it has promulgated a complicated scheme of different categories so as to regulate materials only when they present the same types of environmental risks RCRA seeks to correct. EPA stressed that "to determine if a secondary material is a RCRA solid waste when recycled, one must examine both the material and the recycling activity involved. A consequence is that the same material can be a waste if it is recycled in certain ways, but would not be a waste if it is recycled in other ways." J.A. 69. Thus, the agency has sought to regulate these materials only when they present the risks Congress was combatting in RCRA.

*   *   *

Similarly, in this case the EPA has interpreted solid waste in a manner that seems to expand the everyday usage of the word "discarded." Its conclusion, however, is fully supportable in light of the statutory scheme and legislative history of RCRA. The agency concluded that certain on-site recycled materials constitute an integral part of the waste disposal problem. This judgment is grounded in the EPA's technical expertise and is adequately supported by evidence in the record. The majority nevertheless reverses the agency because it believes that the materials at issue "have not yet become part of the waste disposal problem." This declaration is nothing more than a substitution of the majority's own conclusions for the sound technical judgment of the EPA. The EPA's interpretation is a reasonable construction of an ambiguous statutory provision and should be upheld. *Chevron* and *Cardoza-Fonseca* are totally neutered by review such as the majority today affords.

NOTES

1. Can you tell exactly what the court finds objectionable in the 1985 recycling regulations and what it finds acceptable? Perhaps the difficulty of understanding the opinion has contributed to the EPA's delay in making responsive amendments to the regulations.

2. Any attempt to comprehend the EPA's definition of solid waste, the cornerstone of the EPA's jurisdiction over hazardous waste, must involve a careful reading of the regulations at 40 C.F.R. §§ 261.2 (definition of solid waste) and 261.4(a) (exclusions from definition of solid waste). Following is the text of a substantial portion of § 261.2, as promulgated in January 1985 and then challenged in *American Mining Congress v. Environmental Protection Agency (AMC I)*.

§ 261.2 Definition of solid waste

(a) (1) A solid waste is any discarded material that is not excluded by § 261.4(a) or that is not excluded by variance granted under § 260.30 and 260.31.

(2) A discarded material is any material which is:

(i) Abandoned, as explained in paragraph (b) of this section; or

(ii) Recycled, as explained in paragraph (c) of this section; or

(iii) Considered inherently waste-like, as explained in paragraph (d) of this section.

(b) Materials are solid waste if they are abandoned by being:

(1) Disposed of; or

(2) Burned or incinerated; or

(3) Accumulated, stored, or treated (but not recycled) before or in lieu of being abandoned by being disposed of, burned, or incinerated.

(c) Materials are solid wastes if they are recycled—or accumulated, stored, or treated before recycling—as specified in paragraphs (c)(1) through (4) of this section.

(1) Used in a manner constituting disposal.

(i) Materials noted with a "*" in Column 1 of Table 1 are solid wastes when they are:

(A) Applied to or placed on the land in a manner that constitutes disposal; or

(B) Used to produce products that are applied to or placed on the land or are otherwise contained in products that are applied to or placed on the land (in which cases the product itself remains a solid waste).

(ii) However, commercial chemical products listed in § 261.33 are not solid wastes if they are applied to the land and that is their ordinary manner of use.

(2) Burning for energy recovery.

(i) Materials noted with a "*" in column 2 of Table 1 are solid wastes when they are:

(A) Burned to recover energy;

(B) Used to produce a fuel or are otherwise contained in fuels (in which cases the fuel itself remains a solid waste).

(ii) However, commercial chemical products listed in § 261.33 are not solid wastes if they are themselves fuels.

(3) Reclaimed. Materials noted with a "*" in column 3 of Table 1 are solid wastes when reclaimed.

(4) Accumulated speculatively. Materials noted with a "*" in column 4 of Table 1 are solid wastes when accumulated speculatively.

Table 1

	Use constituting disposal (§261.2(c)(1)) (1)	Energy recovery/fuel (§261.2(c)(2)) (2)	Reclamation (§261.2(c)(3)) (3)	Speculative accumulation (§261.2(c)(4)) (4)
Spent materials	(*)	(*)	(*)	(*)
Sludges (listed in 40 CFR Part 261.3 or 261.32)	(*)	(*)	(*)	(*)
Sludges exhibiting a characteristic of hazardous waste	(*)	(*)	....	(*)
By-products (listed in 40 CFR Part 261.31 or 261.32)	(*)	(*)	(*)	(*)
By-products exhibiting a characteristic of hazardous waste	(*)	(*)	....	(*)
Commercial chemical products listed in 40 CFR 261.33	(*)	(*)	....	....
Scrap metal other than excluded scrap metal (see 261.1 (c) (9))	(*)	(*)	(*)	(*)

Note: The terms 'spent materials', 'sludges', 'by-products', and 'scrap metal' are defined in §261.1

(d) Inherently waste-like materials. The following materials are solid wastes when they are recycled in any manner:

(1) Hazardous Waste Nos. F020, F021 (unless used as an ingredient to make a product at the site of generation), F022, F023, F026, and F028.

(2) Secondary materials fed to a halogen acid furnace that exhibit a characteristic of a hazardous waste or are listed as a hazardous waste as defined in subparts C or D of this part.

* * *

(e) Materials that are not solid waste when recycled.

(1) Materials are not solid wastes when they can be shown to be recycled by being:

(i) Used or reused as ingredients in an industrial process to make a product, provided the materials are not being reclaimed; or

(ii) Used or reused as effective substitutes for commercial products; or

(iii) Returned to the original process from which they are generated, without first being reclaimed. The material must be returned as a substitute for raw material feedstock, and the process must use raw materials as principal feedstocks.

(2) The following materials are solid wastes, even if the recycling involves use, reuse, or return to the original process (described in paragraphs (e)(1) (i) through (iii) of this section):

(i) Materials used in a manner constituting disposal, or used to produce products that are applied to the land; or

(ii) Materials burned for energy recovery, used to produce a fuel, or contained in fuels; or

(iii) Materials accumulated speculatively; or

(iv) Materials listed in paragraph (d)(1) of this section.

* * *

3. On January 8, 1988, the EPA proposed a two-fold revision to 40 C.F.R. §§ 261.2 and 261.4 in response to the *AMC I* decision. 55 Fed. Reg. 519. First, for sludges and by-products that are reclaimed, the proposal would have essentially eliminated the inquiry into whether they are solid wastes in favor of specifically listing—in the hazardous waste listings at §§ 261.31 and 261.32—those sludges and by-products that are deemed to be both solid and hazardous wastes when reclaimed. The proposal identified several factors to be weighed by the EPA in determining whether to list reclaimed sludges and by-products. Second, the proposal would have added slightly-expanded versions of the closed-loop exception to apply specifically to the petroleum and mining practices addressed in the litigation. The American Mining Congress filed

an unsuccessful contempt petition challenging the EPA's circumscribed, proposed response to the court's ruling.

4. Although the EPA is still working on broad-ranging changes to the recycling aspect of the definition of solid waste to address the underlying issues raised in *AMC I*, it has promulgated some piecemeal regulatory amendments in partial response to that decision.

a. In July 1994, the EPA finalized the petroleum refining exclusion proposed in January 1988. 59 Fed. Reg. 38536, 38537, 38545 (1994), *amended* 61 Fed. Reg. 13103, 13106 (1996) (codified at 40 C.F.R. § 261.4(a)(12)).

b. The EPA has also proposed a conditional exclusion for certain recycled secondary mineral processing materials, although a supplemental proposal suggested that further restrictions may be tied to this exclusion if adopted. 61 Fed. Reg. 2338, 2341, 2371-2 (1996) (to be codified as proposed 40 C.F.R. § 261.4(a)(15) and (16)), and 62 Fed. Reg. 26041 (1997) (supplemental proposal).

c. In a move not specifically limited to the petroleum and mining industries, the EPA expanded the closed-loop exclusion that the court discussed in *AMC I* to encompass the recycling of secondary as well as primary materials. As revised in regulations promulgated in September 1994 (as part of a land ban rulemaking - *see* Chapter 4), 40 C.F.R. § 261.2(e)(1)(iii) now reads as follows:

(1) Materials are not solid wastes when they can be shown to be recycled by being:

* * *

(iii) Returned to the original process from which they are generated, without first being reclaimed or land disposed. The material must be returned as a substitute for feedstock materials. In cases where the original process to which the material is returned is a secondary process, the materials must be managed such that there is no placement on the land.

See 59 Fed. Reg. 47982, 48041 (1994). The EPA explained as follows its intentions in thus amending the regulations:

Today's action addresses the second condition [of the closed-loop exclusion in 261.2(e)(1)(iii)]—that the production process to which a secondary material is returned be a primary process. This condition was part of the original exclusion due to considerations regarding jurisdiction, as it was understood in 1985, rather than to an evaluation of the potential impacts on the environment from such "closed-loop" recycling involving secondary processes. This condition thus was established without a consideration of whether such secondary materials would be part of the waste management problem. By definition, a secondary process uses waste materials as its principal feedstock. The Agency therefore concluded that the process residue, which is returned to the original process as a substitute for feedstock that is itself waste, is no less a waste than the waste material original introduced. ***

Although the Agency continues to believe that the jurisdictional logic behind this condition is sound, the judicial opinions regarding RCRA jurisdiction allow more weight to be given to environmental considerations. Thus, EPA has reevaluated this condition of the exclusion from the definition of solid waste due to its impact on the recycling of residues from secondary processes, in particular secondary lead smelters, and has determined that the condition of a closed-loop involving only primary processes is not legally compelled, and that this condition is less relevant as an environmental consideration, assuming that the secondary material is well-managed prior to reprocessing in the primary or secondary process that generated it.

Id. at 48014.

d. Broader efforts to revise the definition of solid waste to encourage hazardous waste recycling while still regulating those aspects that pose a threat to human health and the environment remain "in process". In fact, the EPA's thoughts concerning appropriate amendments to the definition of solid waste have been frequently recycled, both on-site (within EPA) and off-site (involving various stakeholders in the public domain), for the past decade. In November 1996, the EPA released for informal comment a draft proposal describing two options for redefining which secondary materials are considered solid waste under RCRA. Environmental Protection Agency, "Background Paper—Options for Redefining RCRA Jurisdiction" (Nov. 19, 1996). The "transfer-based" option would exclude from the definition of solid waste materials that are recycled on-site or intra-company, provided certain additional conditions are satisfied. The "in-commere" option would exclude almost all recycled materials from the definition of solid waste, with exceptions for recycling involving burning for energy recovery, land placement, use constituting disposal, speculative accumulation, and materials deemed inherently waste-like. Some of the distinctions presently critical to a recycling analysis under 40 C.F.R. § 261.2—based on the type of material involved and the difference between use/reuse and reclamation—would become irrelevant under the draft proposed options.

5. While the EPA continues to decide how to respond to *AMC I*, the U.S. Court of Appeals for the District of Columbia has been called upon in several subsequent cases to clarify its holding and apply it to different factual situations.

6. *American Petroleum Institute v. EPA*, 906 F.2d 729 (D.C.Cir.1990), addressed treatment standard regulations issued by the EPA for certain hazardous wastes subject to the RCRA land ban. The regulations had, among other things, prescribed high temperature metals recovery as the method of treating K061 waste, a listed hazardous waste consisting of zinc-bearing emission control dust or sludge generated from the primary production of steel in electric arc furnaces. The EPA declined to impose treatment standards for the slag residue generated by the K061 treatment process, on the ground that the K061 itself ceased being "solid waste" once it entered the treatment process.

As the agency explained in the notice of proposed rulemaking, the furnaces used for metals reclamation "are normally ... essential components of the industrial process, and when they are actually burning secondary materials for material recovery, [they] can be involved in the very act of production, an activity normally beyond the Agency's RCRA authority." 53 Fed. Reg. 11,753 (1988). Therefore, the EPA felt constrained to view K061 as no longer being "waste" within the meaning of the RCRA once the K061 enters a reclamation furnace.

An environmental group (the Natural Resources Defense Council), a waste treatment company (Chemical Waste Management, Inc.), and a waste treatment trade association (the Hazardous Waste Treatment Council) challenged the EPA's decision not to impose treatment standards for the K061 slag residues. The court vacated and remanded the regulations insofar as they exempted K061 treatment residue from the RCRA land ban.

*** EPA bases its reading of the RCRA almost entirely on our decision in *American Mining Congress v. EPA*, 824 F.2d 1177 (D.C.Cir.1987) ("*AMC*"). The issue in *AMC* was whether the EPA could, under the RCRA, treat as "solid wastes" "materials that are recycled and reused in an ongoing manufacturing or industrial process." We held that it could not because

> [these] materials have not yet become part of the waste disposal problem; rather, *they are destined for beneficial reuse or recycling in a continuous process by the generating industry itself.*

Materials subject to such a process were not "discarded" because they were never "disposed of, abandoned, or thrown away."

AMC is by no means dispositive of EPA's authority to regulate K061 slag. Unlike the materials in question in *AMC*, K061 is indisputably "discarded" *before* being subject to metals reclamation. Consequently, it *has* "become part of the waste disposal problem"; that is why EPA has the power to require that K061 be subject to mandatory metals reclamation. *See* 53 Fed. Reg. 11,752-53 (recognizing this point). Nor does anything in *AMC* require EPA to cease treating K061 as "solid waste" once it reaches the metals reclamation facility. K061 is delivered to the facility not as part of an "*ongoing* manufacturing or industrial process" within "the generating industry," but as part of a mandatory waste treatment plan prescribed by EPA. As such, the resulting slag appears to remain within the scope of the agency's authority as "sludge from a *waste treatment plant*." 42 U.S.C. § 6903(27); see also 42 U.S.C. § 6903(34) (defining "treatment" as "any method, technique, or process ... designed to change the physical [or] chemical ... character or composition of any hazardous waste so as to ... render such waste ... amenable for recovery....").

API v. EPA, 906 F.2d at 741. For the subsequent history of the land ban treatment standards for K061, see *Steel Manufacturers Ass'n v. EPA*, 27 F.3d 642 (D.C.Cir. 1994) (in chapter 4).

7. In *American Mining Congress v. EPA*, 907 F.2d 1179 (D.C.Cir.1990)(*AMC II*), the court reviewed EPA regulations listing as RCRA hazardous waste six wastes generated from metal smelting operations. The "solid waste" issue focused on three of the wastes, which the American Mining Congress claimed did not satisfy the regulatory definition of solid waste because they were "beneficially reused in mineral processing operations."

The primary smelting operations that generate these three wastes produce large volumes of wastewater that the smelting company must treat before discharging it. Many smelting operations use surface impoundments to collect, treat, and dispose of the wastewater. These impoundments continuously produce sludges, which precipitate from the wastewater.

Petitioners' basic claim is that sludges from wastewater that are stored in surface impoundments and that *may* at some time in the future be reclaimed are not "discarded." The agency, however, exercising its expert judgment, has concluded that, because these sludges are the product of wastewater and are stored in impoundments that threaten harm to the health and environs of those living nearby, these materials are "discarded."
***

To support their claim that RCRA forecloses EPA regulation of these sludges, petitioners invoke this court's decision in *AMC*, 824 F.2d 1177. At issue in *AMC* was whether EPA could, under RCRA, treat as "solid wastes" "materials that are recycled and reused in an *ongoing* manufacturing or industrial process." We held that the agency could not treat such materials as solid wastes, because they "have not yet become part of the waste disposal problem; rather, *they are destined for beneficial reuse or recycling in a continuous process by the generating industry itself." Id.* (emphasis in original). Because such materials were never "disposed of, abandoned, or thrown away," we concluded, they were not "discarded" within the meaning of RCRA.

Petitioners read *AMC* too broadly. *AMC*'s holding concerned only materials that are "destined for *immediate reuse* in another phase of the industry's ongoing production process," and that "have not yet become part of the waste disposal problem." Nothing in *AMC* prevents the agency from treating as "discarded" the wastes at issue in this case, which are managed in land disposal units that *are* part of wastewater treatment systems, which *have* therefore become "part of the waste disposal problem," and which *not* part of ongoing industrial processes. Indeed, *API* explicitly rejected the very claim that petitioners assert in this case, namely, that under

RCRA, potential reuse of a material prevents the agency from classifying it as "discarded."

AMC II, 907 F.2d at 1185-1186.

8. The Fourth Circuit employed similar reasoning in upholding the EPA's characterization of a slag processing area as a solid waste management unit (for purposes of corrective action—*see* chapter 5.A) even though the slag, after curing for six months in an outdoor pile, was sold to the construction industry for use as road aggregate. Applying *AMC I, American Petroleum Institute, AMC II,* and *U.S. v. ILCO, Inc.* (*see* note 10.a, *infra*), the Fourth Circuit analyzed the solid waste issue as follows:

> From these cases, we glean that the fundamental inquiry in determining whether a byproduct has been "discarded" is whether the byproduct is *immediately* recycled for use in the same industry; if not, then the byproduct is justifiably seen as "part of the waste disposal problem," *AMC I,* 824 F.2d at 1186, and therefore as a "solid waste." ***
>
> *** Owen's slag constitutes "discarded material" and therefore "solid waste." The slag is not immediately used in Owen's production process; rather, the slag must sit, untouched, for some six months before it is sold to other entities. The EPA is justified in finding that, where a byproduct sits untouched for six months, it cannot be said that the material was "*never* 'disposed of, abandoned, or thrown away.'" *American Petroleum Inst.,* 906 F.2d at 741 (emphasis added). The EPA is also justified to conclude that, because the slag is sold to others for use in roadbed construction, it is not "destined for beneficial reuse or recycling in a continuous process *by the generating industry itself.*" *AMC I,* 824 F.2d at 1186.

Owen Electric Steel Co. of South Carolina, Inc. v. EPA, 37 F.3d 146, 150 (4th Cir. 1994).

9. It is worth noting one exclusion from the definition of solid waste that is unrelated to recycling, but is also of great practical significance. RCRA § 1004(27) and the implementing regulations, 40 C.F.R. § 261.4(a)(2), exclude "industrial wastewater discharges that are point source discharges subject to regulation [the statute uses "permits" instead of "regulation"] under Section 402 of the Clean Water Act." The EPA estimates that this exemption takes approximately as much would-be hazardous waste out of RCRA's jurisdiction as remains subject to RCRA, notwithstanding the fact that the exclusion "applies only to the actual point source discharge. It does not exclude industrial wastewaters while they are being collected, stored or treated before discharge, nor does it exclude sludges that are generated by industrial wastewater treatment." 40 C.F.R. § 261.4(a)(2)(Comment). *See* 55 Fed. Reg. 40881, 40887 (1990).

10. The confounding complexity of the regulatory definition of solid waste was underscored by two appellate court decisions in 1993, both reversing district courts' determinations of whether the materials in question were "solid wastes" within the meaning of 40 C.F.R. Part 261.

a. In *U.S. v. ILCO, Inc.*, 996 F.2d 1120 (11th Cir. 1993), the EPA and the Alabama Department of Environmental Management brought a civil RCRA enforcement action against ILCO, which owned and operated a secondary lead smelting facility. The district court ruled in favor of the EPA and Alabama on all issues except one, and imposed civil penalties of $3.5 million for violations of RCRA, the Clean Water Act, and state law, issued an injunction requiring ILCO to attain compliance with those laws, and ordered ILCO to pay the EPA $845,000 as reimbursement for cleanup costs incurred under CERCLA. The one issue on which the EPA and the State lost, but then prevailed on appeal, was whether the lead plates and groups that ILCO reclaimed from spent car and truck batteries for recycling purposes were "discarded," as the EPA asserted, or purchased as raw materials for the purpose of recovering lead values and therefore not "discarded," as the district court had held.

The Eleventh Circuit's analysis is summarized in the following excerpt:

Pursuant to its authority, EPA has promulgated regulations which specifically address discarded lead-acid batteries. Without clarifying the meaning of "discarded," Congress defined solid waste as "any discarded material" not otherwise exempted from regulation. EPA has filled the statutory gap by defining "discarded material" as any material which is abandoned, recycled, or inherently wastelike. 40 C.F.R. § 261.2(a)(2). "Recycled material" refers to, inter alia, spent material which has been reclaimed. 40 C.F.R. § 261.2(c)(3). A material is "'reclaimed' if it is processed to recover a usable product, or if it is regenerated. Examples are recovery of lead values from spent batteries...." 40 C.F.R. § 261.1(c)(4). "Reclaimed material" clearly includes lead values derived from the plates and groups at issue here. Furthermore, these battery components fall within the § 261.1(c)(4) definition of recycled material because ILCO runs the plates and groups through a smelting process to recover a usable product, lead, which is then cast into ingots and sold. Thus, having met the definition of "recycled," the lead components are discarded material as defined in 40 C.F.R. § 261.2(a)(2).

The regulations also specify those recycled materials which are solid wastes. They include "spent materials" that are recycled by "reclamation," or are "accumulated, stored, or treated before recycling" by reclamation. 40 C.F.R. § 261.2(c). A "spent material" is "any material that has been used and as a result of contamination can no longer serve the purpose for which it was produced without processing." 40 C.F.R. § 261.1(c)(1). Thus, the applicable regulations are unambiguous with respect to spent lead components used in a recycling process: spent materials "are solid wastes when reclaimed." 40 C.F.R. § 261.2(c)(3) and Table 1.

ILCO argues that it has never "discarded" the plates and groups and, therefore, the material it recycles is not "solid waste" as defined in RCRA § 6903(27). The lead plates and groups are, no doubt, valuable feedstock for a smelting process. Nevertheless, EPA, with congressional authority, promulgated regulations that classify these materials as "discarded solid waste." *Somebody* has discarded the battery in which these components are found. This fact does not change just because a reclaimer has purchased or finds value in the components.

The regulations reflect EPA's policy decision that spent batteries, including their lead components, became "part of the waste disposal problem," *AMC I*, 824 F.2d at 1186, when the original consumer discarded the battery. It is unnecessary to read into the word "discarded" a congressional intent that the waste in question must finally and forever be discarded, as ILCO seems to argue. It is perfectly reasonable for EPA to assume Congress meant "discarded once." Were we to rule otherwise, waste such as these batteries would arguably be exempt from regulation under RCRA merely because they are potentially recyclable. Previously discarded solid waste, although it may at some point be recycled, nonetheless remains solid waste. *** Therefore, we find these batteries and their contents are "discarded" within the everyday sense of the word. Their secondary character as recyclable material is irrelevant to that determination.

Id., 996 F.2d at 1131-1132.

b. In *U.S. v. Self*, 2 F.3d 1071 (10th Cir. 1993), Steven Self was convicted of violating RCRA (and other federal laws) for, among other things, the diversion of a shipment of natural gas condensate destined for his hazardous waste treatment, storage, and disposal facility to a gas station, blending it with gasoline, and selling it to the public as automotive fuel. In appealing his conviction regarding these actions, Self argued that the natural gas condensate, when burned for energy recovery, is not a hazardous waste under RCRA. The Tenth Circuit agreed. Presented below are those portions of the case relevant to the definition of solid waste.

UNITED STATES V. SELF
2 F.3d 1071 (10th Cir. 1993)

Before LOGAN, SEYMOUR and BALDOCK, Circuit Judges.
BALDOCK, Circuit Judge.

Defendant Steven M. Self appeals his convictions on four counts of violating the Resource Conservation and Recovery Act ("RCRA"), 42 U.S.C. § 6928(d), one count of mail fraud, and one count of conspiracy to violate RCRA, the Clean Air Act ("CAA"), and the Clean Water Act ("CWA"). Three of the four substantive RCRA counts (counts 2, 3 and 4) and the mail fraud count (count 7) relate to the diversion of a shipment of natural gas condensate destined for a hazardous waste treatment, storage and disposal facility to a gas station, blending it with gasoline and selling it to the public as automotive fuel. The remaining substantive RCRA count (count 8) relates to the storage of twenty-nine drums of waste material in violation of a RCRA permit. The conspiracy count (count 1) relates to the activity supporting the other counts as well as unpermitted burning of waste and unpermitted dumping of waste water. ***

I.

The record reveals the following facts. In 1981, Defendant and Steven Miller formed EkoTek, Inc. *** EkoTek purchased an industrial facility in Salt Lake City, Utah. Using Miller's technical expertise, EkoTek began re-refining used oil into marketable products. Defendant and Miller managed EkoTek on a day-to-day basis with Defendant primarily responsible for the financial aspects of the business, and Miller primarily responsible for the technical aspects.

The facility purchased by EkoTek was an authorized RCRA interim status treatment, storage and disposal facility. *** In November 1986, EkoTek began marketing itself as a hazardous waste recycling facility. *** In April 1987, a representative of Southern California Gas Company ("SCGC"), met with Miller at EkoTek and discussed EkoTek disposing of SCGC's natural gas pipeline condensate. The parties agreed that the condensate was hazardous waste and should, therefore, be transported and handled under a RCRA manifest. Miller indicated that EkoTek could dispose of the natural gas condensate by burning it as fuel in EkoTek's onsite process heaters or boilers. SCGC subsequently contracted with and agreed to pay EkoTek "to transport, burn, and/or dispose of natural gas condensate for $2.50 per gallon."

Shortly thereafter, an EkoTek tanker truck driver picked up a shipment of natural gas condensate from a SCGC facility in Los Angeles, California. The driver had been instructed by his supervisor to pick up the shipment and bring it back to EkoTek. As was his routine practice, the driver stopped at a gas station in Barstow, California, which was owned by Defendant, and telephoned his supervisor. On instructions from Defendant, the supervisor told the driver to leave the trailers containing the natural gas condensate at the gas station and return to Los Angeles to pick up an unrelated shipment. Defendant telephoned the gas station manager and instructed him to blend the natural gas condensate with gasoline in a 5-10% mixture and add an octane booster. The gasoline and condensate mixture was then sold to the public as automotive fuel. On Defendant's instructions, Miller told EkoTek's Refinery Operations Manager to sign the manifest to indicate that the natural gas condensate shipment had been received at EkoTek and to falsify EkoTek's operating log accordingly. A copy of the manifest was mailed to SCGC.

II.

With regard to the substantive RCRA counts and the mail fraud count relating to the diversion of the natural gas condensate to the Barstow gas station Defendant argues that natural gas condensate, when burned for energy recovery, is not a hazardous waste subject to regulation under RCRA. Therefore, Defendant claims the district court erred by denying Defendant's pretrial motion to dismiss, by denying Defendant's motion for a judgment of acquittal, and in its instruction to the jury defining hazardous waste. ***

A.

RCRA defines "hazardous waste," in relevant part as "a solid waste, or combination of solid wastes, which because of its quantity, concentration, or physical, chemical, or infectious characteristics may ... pose a substantial present or potential hazard to human health or the environment when improperly treated, stored, transported, or disposed of, or otherwise managed." 42 U.S.C. § 6903(5)(B). Natural gas condensate is a relatively volatile substance, having a flash point of less than 140 degrees F and, therefore, is "hazardous" as contemplated by RCRA. *See* 40 C.F.R. §§ 261.3(a)(2)(i), 261.21(a)(1) (1992). Nonetheless, "for a waste to be classified as hazardous, it must first qualify as a solid waste under RCRA." *Connecticut Coastal Fishermen's Ass'n v. Remington Arms Co., Inc.*, 989 F.2d 1305, 1313 (2d Cir.1993). *** RCRA regulations narrow the definition of "solid waste" to "any discarded material that is not excluded by § 261.4(a) or that is not excluded by a variance granted under §§ 260.30 and 260.31." 40 C.F.R. § 261.2(a)(1). As there is no contention that natural gas condensate is subject to the § 261.4(a) exclusion, or that it has been granted a variance under § 260.30 and 260.31, whether natural gas condensate is a solid waste turns on whether it is a discarded material.

RCRA regulations define "discarded material" to include material which is "[a]bandoned" or "[r]ecycled." *Id.* § 261.2(a)(2). A material is abandoned, inter alia, by being "[b]urned or incinerated." *Id.* § 261.2(b)(2). A material is recycled, inter alia, by being "[b]urn[ed] for energy recovery" or "[u]sed to produce a fuel or are otherwise contained in fuels." *Id.* § 261.2(c)(2). Any material that is abandoned by being burned or incinerated is considered a solid waste. *See id.* § 261.2(b). However, we note only certain types of materials that are recycled by being burned for energy recovery are considered solid wastes. *See id.* § 261.2(c). ***

The only type of material which is considered solid waste when it is recycled by being burned for energy recovery and which might encompass natural gas condensate is a "[b]y-product exhibiting a characteristic of hazardous waste." *See* 40 C.F.R. § 261.2 (Table 1). As noted earlier, natural gas condensate exhibits the ignitability characteristic of hazardous waste; thus, the issue turns on whether natural gas condensate is a "by-product" as defined by RCRA regulations. RCRA regulations define "by-product" as "a material that is not one of the primary products of a production process and is not solely or separately produced by the production process" exclusive of "co-product[s]." 40 C.F.R. § 261.1(c)(3). While RCRA's definition of "by-product" is certainly subject to reasonable interpretation, the EPA directly addressed the issue of whether natural gas condensate is a by-product in its 1985 comment to its current regulatory definition of "solid waste":

> Off-specification fuels burned for energy recovery ... are not by-products, and so would not be considered to be wastes under this provision. An example [is] natural gas pipeline condensate. The condensate contains many of the same hydrocarbons found in liquefied natural gas, and certain higher hydrocarbons that also have energy value. It is generated in the

> pipeline transmission of natural gas. This condensate is not considered to
> be waste when burned for energy recovery.[6]

50 Fed. Reg. 630 n. 18 (Jan. 4, 1985). Relying on this EPA statement, Defendant argues that so long as natural gas condensate is burned for energy recovery, it is not a by-product and, therefore, not a discarded material by virtue of being recycled, and, therefore, not a solid waste, and, therefore, not a hazardous waste under RCRA.

The government argued below and continues to argue on appeal that natural gas condensate is hazardous waste if it is used in a manner which was not the original intended manner or normal intended use for that material within the industry. In support of this argument, the government first directs us to the EPA's long-standing distinction between legitimate and sham burning for energy recovery. The government then points to an EPA comment stating that commercial chemical products when burned for energy recovery are considered solid wastes because this is a manner of recycling which differs from their normal manner of use. *See* 50 Fed. Reg. 618 (Jan. 4, 1985). Next, the government relies on an EPA statement that the status of "non-listed commercial chemical products ... would be the same as those listed in § 261.33—[t]hat is, they are not considered solid wastes when recycled except when they are recycled in ways that differ from their normal manner of use." 50 Fed. Reg. 14,216, 14,219 (Apr. 11, 1985).

By focusing on the EPA distinction between legitimate and sham burning for energy recovery, the government appears to be arguing that the natural gas condensate was not recycled within the meaning of the regulations and, therefore, was abandoned by being burned or incinerated. This distinction would undermine Defendant's argument because any abandoned material is considered solid waste. On the other hand, by focusing on the EPA's rationale for classifying commercial chemical products which are burned for energy recovery as solid waste, the government's argument also suggests that natural gas condensate is a non-listed commercial chemical product, and, therefore, must be recycled in a normal manner in order to not be considered a hazardous waste. This argument would also undermine Defendant's argument because recycling commercial chemical products by burning them for energy recovery is not a normal manner of use and, therefore, the natural gas condensate, to the extent it is a commercial chemical product, is a solid waste. The government does not distinguish between these two alternative arguments but rather collapses the EPA's distinction between legitimate and sham burning for energy recovery with the EPA's rationale for classifying commercial chemical products which are burned for energy recovery as solid wastes.

---

[6] In its 1983 proposed rule defining "solid waste," only listed by-products were considered solid wastes when recycled. However, the 1985 final rule "determined that all by-products ... are solid wastes when burned as fuels or used to produce a fuel." 50 Fed. Reg. 629 (Jan. 4, 1985). In adopting this final rule, the EPA stated that by-products are "unlike commercial fuels" and are "significantly different in composition from fossil fuels." Distinguishing between by-products and fossil fuels, the EPA noted that by-products "are waste-like because they are residual materials containing toxic constituents not ordinarily found in fossil fuels." It was in this context that the EPA singled out natural gas condensate as an example of an off-specification fuel that is not a by-product.

In doing so, the government combines otherwise unrelated EPA comments concerning distinct provisions within the regulatory definition of "solid waste" and misapplies these EPA comments to the facts of this case, as we discuss below.

1.

The legitimate versus sham distinction first arose in 1980 when the EPA defined "solid waste" to include "materials which have served their original intended purpose and are sometimes discarded." 45 Fed. Reg. 33,093 (May 19, 1980). Under this definition, "virtually all ... secondary materials" were considered solid wastes. 50 Fed. Reg. 618 (Jan. 4, 1985). However, the EPA exempted from regulation all recycling activity and the transportation and storage of non-sludges and non-listed hazardous waste which were recycled, and recognized that "burning of hazardous wastes as fuels can be a type of recycling activity exempted from regulation." 48 Fed. Reg. 11, 157-58 (Mar. 16, 1983). Expressing concern about, inter alia, the "burning of organic wastes that have little or no heat value in industrial boilers under the guise of energy recovery," 45 Fed. Reg. 33,093 (May 19, 1980), the EPA adopted a policy that in order to fall within the exemption, the burning must "constitute legitimate, and not sham, recycling." 48 Fed. Reg. 11,158 (Mar. 16, 1983).

In 1985, the EPA amended its regulatory definition of "solid waste" to substantially its present form which asks "both what a material is and how it is being recycled before knowing whether it is a solid waste." 50 Fed. Reg. 616 (Jan. 4, 1985). Following the 1985 amendment, the EPA's distinction between legitimate and sham burning became significant, not only by continuing to determine the applicability of the recycling exemption, but also by determining whether a material is being burned or incinerated—i.e. burned for destruction—and, therefore, abandoned, or is being burned for energy recovery and, therefore, recycled.

Contrary to the government's argument, the EPA has never distinguished legitimate from sham burning for energy recovery based on whether the burning was the original intended use or normal manner of use of the material within the industry. The "primary" factor in distinguishing legitimate from sham burning for energy recovery is "the energy value of the hazardous waste being ... burned." 48 Fed. Reg. 11,158 (Mar. 16, 1983). As the EPA stated, "[i]f the wastes being burned have only *de minimus* energy value, the burning cannot recover sufficient energy to characterize the practice as legitimate recycling.... [T]he wastes, for practical purposes are being burned to be destroyed." 48 Fed. Reg. 11,158 (Mar. 10, 1983). Natural gas condensate has a relatively high energy value, and the government conceded at oral argument that the natural gas condensate could have been burned for legitimate energy recovery in the boiler or industrial furnace at EkoTek.

The government's reliance on the EPA statement that commercial chemical products, when burned for energy recovery, are solid wastes because this manner of recycling differs from their normal manner of use is completely misplaced. In this statement, the EPA was not distinguishing legitimate from sham recycling methods. Rather, the EPA was explaining its rationale for classifying commercial chemical products as solid waste when they are recycled by being burned for energy recovery. Specifically, the EPA stated that

> Although [commercial chemical products] ... ordinarily are not wastes when recycled ... we are including them as wastes when they are recycled in ways that differ from their normal manner of use, namely, when they are used in a manner constituting disposal, or when they are burned for energy recovery (assuming these materials are neither a pesticide nor a commercial fuel).

50 Fed. Reg. 618 (Jan. 4, 1985). This EPA comment merely explains why the EPA considers commercial chemical products which are legitimately recycled by being burned for energy recovery to be solid wastes even though commercial chemical products which are recycled by other methods, namely reclamation and speculative accumulation, are not considered solid wastes. *** Indeed, it is implicit in this EPA statement of why commercial chemical products are solid wastes when burned for energy recovery that the commercial chemical product has been legitimately recycled. Contrary to the government's argument, this EPA comment has nothing to do with whether a particular manner of burning for energy recovery is legitimate or sham.

2.

Alternatively, the government suggests that natural gas condensate is a commercial chemical product (albeit an unlisted one), and, under the EPA's policy treating unlisted commercial chemical products like listed commercial chemical products, is a solid waste even if it is legitimately burned for energy recovery. This argument fails for several reasons.

First, only listed commercial chemical products are considered solid wastes when burned to recover energy, *see* 40 C.F.R. § 261.2 (Table 1), and natural gas condensate is not listed. We recognize that the EPA has stated that it is "implicit" in the statutory and regulatory scheme that the "status" of "non-listed commercial chemical products ... would be the same as those listed in § 261.33—[t]hat is, they are not considered solid wastes when recycled except when they are recycled in ways that differ from their normal manner of use." 50 Fed. Reg. 14,216, 14,219 (Apr. 11, 1985). However, such an implicit construction of the regulations is certainly not clear from the regulations themselves. To the contrary, the regulations define "commercial chemical products" by reference to a specific list of materials, which suggests that non-listed materials are not subject to regulation as commercial chemical products.

In addition to natural gas condensate not being listed as a commercial chemical product, the government's own expert testimony at trial belies the government's contention on appeal that natural gas condensate is a commercial chemical product. The EPA has defined "commercial chemical product" as "a chemical substance which is manufactured or formulated for commercial or manufacturing use which consists of the commercially pure grade of the chemical, any technical grades of the chemical that are produced or marketed, and all formulations in which the chemical is the sole active ingredient." 40 C.F.R. § 261.33(d) (comment). The government's expert testified that natural gas condensate is an unintended by-product of the transportation of natural gas through pipelines. Notably, the government never asserted below that natural gas condensate was a commercial chemical product; rather, the government responded to Defendant's motion to dismiss by claiming that natural gas condensate "is a by-product of a manufacturing process." In light of the government expert's description of natural gas condensate and the government's contention below that natural gas condensate is a by-product, the government cannot seriously argue that natural gas condensate is manufactured or formulated for commercial or manufacturing use.

The government's characterization of natural gas condensate as a commercial chemical product cannot be reconciled with other EPA interpretations of the regulatory definition of solid waste. Notably, the EPA stated that burning commercial chemical products for energy recovery is never the normal use of such products. 50 Fed. Reg. 618 (Jan. 4, 1985). Accordingly, commercial chemical products which are burned for energy recovery are always considered solid wastes. *See* 40 C.F.R. § 261.2 (Table 1). If natural gas condensate is a commercial chemical product, as the government's argument suggests, it would always be a solid waste when burned for energy recovery. Yet, this very same EPA comment cites natural gas condensate as an example of an off-specification fuel which is not considered to be a waste when burned for energy recovery. The EPA specifically qualified its statement that burning commercial chemical products for energy recovery is never their normal manner of use by "assuming [that] these materials are [not] a commercial fuel." Thus, the government's construction is inconsistent with the EPA's interpretation.

* * *

*** [W]e agree with Defendant that, under the EPA's interpretation of the regulations in effect as of 1987, natural gas condensate is not a hazardous waste subject to RCRA regulation when it is burned for energy recovery, which includes burning it as automotive fuel.

* * *

NOTES

1. How could the government have lost this case? The defendant's actions suggest that he believed he was improperly handling the natural gas condensate; the condensate was clearly hazardous; and the customers who bought the surreptitiously-blended fuel were defrauded. Might the court have been more deferential to the EPA's regulatory interpretation if this had been a civil, rather than criminal, enforcement action?

2. One subtle theme among the EPA's various arguments in *Self* is the concern that to exclude from RCRA regulation the burning of hazardous waste for energy recovery would create a huge loophole for "sham recycling," where hazardous waste could be burned for destruction under the guise of burning it for recycling purposes. On the other hand, the EPA has been constantly reminded by the fuel blenders and

hazardous waste burners that many hazardous wastes constitute suitable fuels that may be burned with less air pollution than is attributable to conventional fossil fuels. After considering the competing arguments, the EPA in April 1996 proposed excluding from the definition of solid waste certain hazardous waste-derived fuels that share critical specifications of conventional fossil fuels.

    *** The Agency believes that many fuels produced from hazardous wastes are more waste-like than fuel- or product-like, and must be regulated as such. We are aware, however, of certain fuels and products produced from hazardous waste that are more appropriately classified and managed as products rather than wastes. EPA believes this syngas [synthesis gas] meeting the requirements of the proposed exclusion is such a material. Syngas is a commercial product which has important uses in industry as both a feedstock and commercial fuel, and it may be used as both a feedstock and commercial fuel at a manufacturing facility. ***

* * *

    To ensure that any excluded syngas meets *** low levels of hazardous compounds relative to levels in fossil fuels in order to be excluded from the definition as a solid waste, the Agency is proposing the following syngas specifications:

    — Minimum Btu value of 5,000 Btu/lb;

    — Less than 1 ppmv of each hazardous constituent listed in Appendix VIII of Part 261 (that could reasonably be expected to be in the gas) ***;

    — Less than 1 ppmv of total chlorine; and

    — Less than 1 ppmv of total nitrogen, other than diatomic nitrogen.

***

    We also note that conditions imposed for exclusion of syngas fuels in no way precludes the use of syngas as an ingredient in manufacturing, which is evaluated under a different set of criteria, when the syngas is produced from hazardous waste. In other words, if the syngas were to be used as either a product in manufacturing or burned as a fuel, it would be excluded as a product when it met the criteria for use as a product and was used for that purpose and excluded as a fuel when burned.

61 Fed. Reg. 17358, 17465 (1996). *See also* Barry S. Neuman and Bill Schofield, *EPA's Proposed Comparable Fuels Exemption Under RCRA: Does It Spell Relief?* 27 Env't Rep. (BNA) 1664 (1996).

Problem #1: DEFINITION OF SOLID WASTE

Would a "solid waste within the terms of the current definition at 40 C.F.R. § 261.2 exist in any of the following situations?

A. Bob's Energy Service buys "slop oil" containing "emulsion solids" (a refinery byproduct) from an oil refinery to recycle it to produce naptha and heating oil. Is the slop oil solid waste?

B. Evercell, Inc., a battery manufacturer, sells scrap cadmium generated from its manufacturing operation to an overseas recycler. Is the scrap cadmium solid waste?

C. Compucycle, Inc. is in the business of recycling computers and computer parts. It uses solvents to clean circuit boards, and now wants to try to recycle the spent solvents, too. It arranges to sell the spent solvents for use as metal degreasers. Are the spent solvents solid waste?

D. Brash Brass Co. operates a brass furnace that employs a baghouse to trap the air pollutants it generates. The trapped dust, known as baghouse dust, is processed in a metals recovery unit to recover high-grade zinc metal and zinc alloys. Is the baghouse dust solid waste?

B. Definition of Hazardous Waste

The statutory definition of hazardous waste is relatively broad, subject to ambiguity, and requires the exercise of professional judgment:

> The term "hazardous waste" means a solid waste, or combination of solid wastes, which because of its quantity, concentration, or physical, chemical, or infectious characteristics may—
>
> (A) cause, or significantly contribute to an increase in mortality or an increase in serious irreversible, or incapacitating reversible, illness; or
>
> (B) pose a substantial present or potential hazard to human health or the environment when improperly treated, stored, transported, or disposed of, or otherwise managed.

RCRA § 1004(5), 42 U.S.C. § 6903(5).

Although the EPA employs the statutory definition for purposes of RCRA's two cleanup programs (*i.e.*, the corrective action program under Subtitle C, and the omnibus cleanup authority under Subtitle G, § 7003), the governing definition of hazardous waste for all other RCRA Subtitle C purposes is that set forth in Part 261 of the regulations.

The RCRA regulations define hazardous waste as a material that is (1) a solid waste and (2) either (a) exhibits one of the four characteristics specified in Part 261, Subpart C—reactivity, corrosivity, ignitability, and toxicity, or (b) is listed in one of the EPA's four lists of hazardous wastes in Part 261, Subpart D, or (c) is deemed to be a listed hazardous waste under the "mixture" or "derived-from" rules.

The regulations in Subpart C of Part 261 reference tests, in most but not all cases, that may be performed to determine whether a solid waste exhibits a particular hazardous waste characteristic. For example, most liquid wastes exhibit the characteristic of ignitability if, when tested under one of the specified test methods, they have a flash point of less than 140 degrees Fahrenheit. 40 C.F.R. § 261.21. As is true throughout the RCRA regulations, common sense or intuitive understandings of certain terms should not be used. One must consult the regulations to determine precisely what tests are prescribed, or what descriptive features are identified, to determine whether a solid waste exhibits one or more of the hazardous waste characteristics. This is particularly true with respect to the toxicity characteristic, 40 C.F.R. § 261.24. Whether a solid waste exhibits the characteristic of toxicity depends solely upon whether, when tested by the analytical method known as the Toxicity Characteristic Leaching Procedure ("TCLP"), it contains any of the 39 specified contaminants (metals, pesticides, and certain organics) in concentrations equal to or greater than the specified "regulatory level." Thus, if a waste does not contain any of the 39 contaminants, or contains them in concentrations below the TCLP regulatory levels, it does not exhibit the toxicity characteristic notwithstanding the professional judgment of any number of toxicologists that it may be toxic.

Although several challenges were leveled at the EPA's adoption of the TCLP test to determine whether a solid waste exhibits the toxicity characteristic, the D.C. Circuit Court of Appeals rejected all claims but one. *Edison Electric Institute v. EPA*, 2 F.3d 438 (D.C. Cir. 1993). A controversial aspect of the TCLP test is that it is based on a "generic mismanagement scenario" (*i.e.*, it assumes that the wastes in question will be disposed of in municipal solid waste landfills, with other types of wastes, and then leach out into the environment); the court held the EPA's use of the mismanagement scenario to be a "reasonable interpretation of the statutory language." The D.C. Circuit also ruled, however, that the EPA had not established a factual basis for applying the generic mismanagement scenario to certain mineral processing wastes and electric utility wastes. *See* 61 Fed. Reg. 2338 (1996) and 62 Fed. Reg. 26041 (1997) for the EPA's proposed rule in response to *Edison Electric Institute*.

In addition to the four characteristics, a solid waste may be considered a hazardous waste under RCRA if it appears on one of the four lists in Subpart D of Part 261. EPA makes an individual determination with respect to each waste so listed, and then promulgates the listing as an amendment to the Part 261, Subpart D regulations. The four lists contain (1) wastes from nonspecific sources, (2) wastes from specific sources, (3) commercial chemical products listed because of acute toxicity, and (4) commercial chemical products listed for reasons other than acute toxicity. 40 C.F.R. §§ 261.31-.33. Although most of the listed hazardous wastes were listed because of toxicity or acute toxicity, this listing criterion must be distinguished from the toxicity characteristic, which is based solely on the TCLP test.

The mixture and derived-from rules apply essentially to listed hazardous wastes. They are described, and successfully challenged, in the following case.

SHELL OIL CO. v. ENVIRONMENTAL PROTECTION AGENCY
950 F.2d 741 (D.C.Cir. 1991)

Before BUCKLEY, WILLIAMS, and THOMAS, Circuit Judges. (Former Circuit Judge THOMAS, now an Associate Justice of the Supreme Court of the United States, was a member of the panel when the case was argued but did not participate in this opinion.)

PER CURIAM.

In these consolidated cases, petitioners challenge both the substance of several rules promulgated by the Environmental Protection Agency pursuant to the Resource Conservation and Recovery Act of 1976 and its compliance with the Administrative Procedure Act's rulemaking requirements.

Consolidated petitioners challenge two rules that categorize substances as hazardous wastes until a contrary showing has been made: the "mixture" rule, which classifies as a hazardous waste any mixture of a "listed" hazardous waste with any other solid waste, and the "derived-from" rule, which so classifies any residue derived from the treatment of hazardous waste. They argue that the EPA failed to provide adequate notice and opportunity for comment when it promulgated the mixture and derived-from rules, and that the rules exceed the EPA's statutory authority.

* * *

I. Background

The EPA promulgated the disputed rules in order to implement the Resource Conservation and Recovery Act ("RCRA"). RCRA created a "cradle-to-grave" system for tracking wastes from their generation to disposal. The statute consists of two main parts: one governs the management of non-hazardous solid waste; the other, hazardous waste. *See American Mining Congress v. EPA*, 824 F.2d 1177, 1179 (D.C.Cir.1987) ("*AMC I*").

As enacted, Subtitle C of RCRA required the EPA to establish a comprehensive national system for safely treating, storing, and disposing of hazardous wastes. It defined "hazardous waste," in part, as a "solid waste" which may "pose a substantial present or potential hazard to human health or the environment when improperly treated, stored, transported, or disposed of, or otherwise managed." 42 U.S.C. § 6903(5) (1976). It gave the EPA until April 21, 1978 to develop and promulgate criteria for identifying characteristics of hazardous waste and to list particular wastes as hazardous. *See id.* § 6921(a), (b). It further required the EPA to promulgate regulations "as may be necessary to protect human health and the environment" respecting the practices of generators, transporters, and those who own or operate hazardous waste treatment, storage, or disposal facilities. *Id.* §§ 6922-6924. RCRA prohibited treatment, storage, or disposal of hazardous waste without a permit and required the EPA to promulgate standards governing permits for facilities performing such functions. *Id.* § 6925.

On February 17, 1977, the EPA published a Notice of Intent to Develop Rulemaking, 42 Fed. Reg. 9,803 (1977); and on May 2, 1977, it published an Advance Notice of Proposed Rulemaking, 42 Fed. Reg. 22,332 (1977), which set forth detailed questions on each of the subsections of Subtitle C. In addition, it circulated for comment several drafts of regulations, met with experts and representatives of interested groups, and held public hearings. This process culminated in the publication, on December 18, 1978, of proposed regulations covering most of the statutorily required standards. *See* 43 Fed. Reg. 58,946-59,022 (1978).

This proposal elicited voluminous comment, and the EPA held five large public hearings. The EPA failed to issue final regulations by the April 1978 statutory deadline; several parties sued the Agency to compel it to do so. Although the district court initially ordered the EPA to promulgate the regulations by December 31, 1979, the complexity of the task led the court to modify the order to require, instead, that the EPA use its best efforts to issue them by April 1980. The EPA published its "revisions to final rule and interim final rule" on May 19, 1980. 45 Fed. Reg. 33,066 (1980). It noted that time pressures had had an effect on the new regulations. Because of limited information, the Agency was unable to avoid underregulation and overregulation. It complained that the demands of developing a national, comprehensive system of hazardous-waste management made precise tailoring to individual cases impossible. *See id.* 33,088.

More than fifty petitions were brought to challenge these final rules. In 1982, we deferred briefing on these challenges to allow the parties to pursue settlement discussions and ordered the EPA to file monthly status reports. We did not stay the rules, however, which have remained in effect. Most of the issues have been resolved by settlement, by subsequent statutory or regulatory revision, or by the failure of petitioners to pursue them. The issues presented here are those that the EPA identified in January 1987 as unlikely to be settled, and that were subject to the briefing schedule established by this court on June 12, 1989.

* * *

II. Discussion

A. Principles Governing Judicial Review

The Administrative Procedure Act ("APA") governs judicial review of final regulations promulgated under RCRA. In issuing regulations, the EPA must observe the notice-and-comment procedures of the APA, and the public-participation directive of RCRA. The relationship between the proposed regulation and the final rule determines the adequacy of notice. A difference between the two will not invalidate the notice so long as the final rule is a "logical outgrowth" of the one proposed. If the deviation from the proposal is too sharp, the affected parties will not have had adequate notice and opportunity for comment. RCRA defines the scope of the EPA's regulatory discretion: In formulating rules, the clearly expressed intent of Congress binds agencies as it binds courts. Where congressional intent is ambiguous, however, an agency's interpretation of a statute entrusted to its administration is entitled to deference, so long as it is reasonable.

B. The Mixture and Derived-From Rules

The mixture and derived-from rules are to be found in the definition of "hazardous waste" that appears in the final rules. That definition includes as hazardous all wastes resulting from mixing hazardous and other wastes and from treating, storing, or disposing of hazardous wastes, until such time as the wastes are proven nonhazardous. Petitioners protest that these provisions had no counterpart in, and were not a logical outgrowth of, the proposed regulations; thus, the promulgation of the rules violated the notice-and-comment requirements of RCRA and the APA. We agree.

1. *Statutory Background*

To become subject to RCRA's comprehensive regulatory system, a material must be a hazardous waste, which RCRA defines, in part, as:

a solid waste, or combination of solid wastes, which because of its quantity, concentration, or physical, chemical, or infectious characteristics may—

*   *   *   *   *   *

(B) pose a substantial present or potential hazard to human health or the environment when improperly treated, stored, transported, or disposed of, or otherwise managed.

42 U.S.C. § 6903(5) (1976). To determine what materials fall within that definition, the EPA must promulgate criteria for the identification and listing of hazardous wastes. The statute provides the EPA with specific instructions for identifying and listing hazardous waste. *** *Id.* § 6921 (a), (b).

2. *The Proposed Regulations*

In its proposed regulations, the EPA adopted the following definition of "hazardous waste":

"Hazardous waste" has the meaning given in [RCRA, 42 U.S.C. § 6903(5)] *as further defined and identified in this Subpart.*

43 Fed. Reg. 58,955 (*emphasis added*). The regulations then set forth the following scheme for identifying and listing hazardous wastes:

(a) *Criteria for identifying the characteristics of hazardous waste.* A characteristic of hazardous waste will be established under § 250.13

where, based on information from damage incidents or scientific and technical information, the Administrator determines that:

(1) The characteristic can be defined in terms of specific physical, chemical, toxic, infectious, or other properties of a solid waste that will cause the waste to be a hazardous waste pursuant to the definition in [42 U.S.C. § 6903(5)], and

(2) The properties defining the characteristic are measurable by standardized and available testing protocols applicable to waste.

(b) *Criteria for listing hazardous waste.* A solid waste, or source or class of solid waste, will be listed as a hazardous waste in § 250.14 if the Administrator determines that the solid waste:

(1) Possesses any of the characteristics defined in § 250.13, and/or

(2) Meets the definition of hazardous waste found in [42 U.S.C. § 6903(4)].

43 Fed. Reg. 58,955.

Although the EPA initially identified nine possible characteristics as potentially hazardous, it decided to rely on only four of them—ignitability, corrosivity, reactivity, and toxicity—in its proposed section 250.13, because only these could be tested reliably and inexpensively. Because solid wastes that present a hazard but do not display one of these four characteristics remained subject to RCRA, the EPA proposed to list such wastes specifically, and to treat any waste once listed as hazardous until a person managing the waste filed a delisting petition and demonstrated to the EPA that the waste did not pose a hazard.

3. *The Final Rules*

The final rules defined a hazardous waste more broadly than did the proposed regulations. Under the final rules, a hazardous waste is a solid waste that is not specifically excluded from regulation and meets any one of the following criteria:

(i) It is listed in Subpart D and has not been excluded from the lists in Subpart D under §§ 260.20 and 260.22 of this Chapter.

(ii) It is a mixture of solid waste and one or more hazardous wastes listed in Subpart D and has not been excluded from this paragraph under §§ 260.20 and 260.22 of this Chapter.

(iii) It exhibits any of the characteristics of hazardous waste identified in Subpart C.

45 Fed. Reg. 33,119 (40 C.F.R. § 261.3(a)(2)). In addition, a solid waste generated from the treatment, storage, or disposal of a hazardous waste is considered a hazardous waste. *Id.* 33,120 (40 C.F.R. § 261.3(c)(2)).

In establishing criteria for identifying and listing hazardous wastes in its final rules, the EPA relied heavily on the dangers that such wastes pose. *See* 45 Fed. Reg. 33,121 (40 C.F.R. §§ 261.10-.11). Thus the EPA compiled a list of toxic constituents as a starting point and required that a waste be listed as hazardous if it (1) exhibits one of the four characteristics of hazardous waste identified in Subpart C of the regulations ("hazardous characteristics"), (2) meets certain toxicity criteria, or (3) contains any of the toxic constituents listed in Appendix VIII unless, after considering any of the following factors, the Administrator concludes that the waste is not capable of posing a substantial present or potential hazard to human health or the environment when improperly treated, stored, transported or disposed of, or otherwise managed. *Id.* 33,121 (40 C.F.R. § 261.11(a)(1)-(3)). *****

A number of interested parties had challenged the listing of classes of wastes in the proposed regulations as an unwarranted expansion of the statutory phrase "particular wastes," which, they asserted, required the listing of specific wastes only. The EPA nevertheless retained the proposed scheme in its final rules, stating that its use of classes was justified by the complexity of the factors bearing on hazard and the impossibility of defining a numerical threshold level for hazardous characteristics.

4. *The Mixture Rule*

The mixture rule requires that a waste be treated as hazardous
if [i]t is a mixture of solid waste and one or more hazardous wastes listed in Subpart D and has not been excluded from this paragraph under §§ 260.20 and 260.22 of this Chapter.

45 Fed. Reg. 33,119 (40 C.F.R. § 261.3(a)(2)(ii)). Once classified as hazardous, then, a mixture must be so treated until delisted.[4]

The EPA acknowledged at the outset that the mixture rule was "a new provision," and that it had no "direct counterpart in the proposed regulations." 45 Fed. Reg. 33,095. Nevertheless, it added the rule
for purposes of clarification and in response to questions raised during the comment period concerning waste mixtures and when hazardous wastes become subject to and cease to be subject to the Subtitle C hazardous waste management system.

Id.

Although admitting that it had failed to say so in the proposed regulations, the EPA stated that it had "intended" to treat waste mixtures containing Subpart D wastes as hazardous. It then presented the mixture rule as necessary to close "a major loophole in the Subtitle C management system." *Id.* 33,095. Otherwise, generators of hazardous waste "could evade [those] requirements simply by commingling [Subpart D] wastes with nonhazardous solid waste" to create a waste that did not demonstrate any of the four testable characteristics but that posed a hazard for another reason. *Id.* The Agency explained that although the mixture rule might include waste with concentrations of Subpart D wastes too low to pose a hazard, the delisting process and the possibility of

---

[4] The EPA notes that subsequent regulatory action limits petitioners' challenge of the mixture rule to listed wastes, because a mixture that does not exhibit any of the four testable characteristics is no longer classified as hazardous. *See* Brief for Respondent at 37 n.28 (citing 40 C.F.R. § 261.3(a)(2)(iii)(1988)).

segregating waste to avoid the problem mitigated the burden of the rule. Finally, the EPA invoked the practical difficulties of its task to justify the rule's adoption:

> Because the potential combinations of listed wastes and other wastes are infinite, we have been unable to devise any workable, broadly applicable formula which would distinguish between those waste mixtures which are and are not hazardous.

Id.

While the EPA admits that the mixture rule lacks a clear antecedent in the proposed regulations, it nonetheless argues that the rule merely clarifies the intent behind the proposal that listed wastes remain hazardous until delisted. As industry could not have reasonably assumed that a generator could bring a listed waste outside the generic listing description simply by mixing it with a nonhazardous waste, the rule cannot be seen as a "bolt from the blue." *Cf. WJG Telephone Co., Inc. v. FCC*, 675 F.2d 386, 388-90 (D.C.Cir.1982).

5. *The Derived-From Rule*

The derived-from rule provides as follows:

> any solid waste generated from the treatment, storage or disposal of a hazardous waste, including any sludge, spill residue, ash, emission control dust or leachate (but not including precipitation run-off), is a hazardous waste.

45 Fed. Reg. 33,120 (40 C.F.R. § 261.3(c)(2)). Subpart D wastes continue to be regulated as hazardous until delisted; a solid waste derived from Subpart C wastes may emerge from regulation if it does not itself display a hazardous characteristic. *See id.* 33,120 (40 C.F.R. § 261.3(d)).

The EPA's justifications for the derived-from rule resemble those for the mixture rule. Arguing that the products of treatment, storage, or disposal of listed hazardous wastes usually continue to pose hazards, the EPA defends the rule as "the best regulatory approach we can devise," given the fact that "we are not now in a position to prescribe waste-specific treatment standards which would identify those processes which do and do not render wastes or treatment residues nonhazardous." 45 Fed. Reg. 33,096. The EPA acknowledged, however, that the rule was a new provision, "added both in response to comment and as a logical outgrowth of [§ 261.3(b)]." *Id.*

6. *Adequacy of Notice*

Although the EPA acknowledges that neither of the two rules was to be found among the proposed regulations, it nevertheless argues that they were foreseeable—and, therefore, the notice adequate—because certain of the comments received in response to the rulemaking appeared to anticipate both the mixture and the derived-from rules. We are unimpressed by the scanty evidence marshaled in support of this position.

* * *

The EPA's argument also fails to take into account a marked shift in emphasis between the proposed regulations and the final rules. Under the EPA's initial regulatory strategy, the

> EPA planned to identify and quantitatively define all of the characteristics of hazardous waste. Generators would be required to assess their wastes in accordance with these characteristics and EPA would list hazardous wastes where it had data indicating the wastes exhibited one of the identified characteristics.

45 Fed. Reg. 33,106. As a consequence, listing was to "play [the] largely supplementary function" of increasing the "certainty" of the process. *Id.* Listing was also to have relieved generators of listed wastes of the burden of testing for characteristics "unless they wish to demonstrate that they are not subject" to Subtitle C regulation. 43 Fed. Reg. 58,951. Thus, the proposed regulations imposed, as a generator's principal responsibility, the duty to test wastes for hazardous characteristics and suggested that if the required tests failed to reveal a hazard, the waste would not need to be managed as hazardous.

The final rules, however, place a heavy emphasis on listing. As a consequence, the final criteria for listing are "considerably expanded and more specific" than those proposed. The EPA justified this "change in emphasis in [its] regulatory strategy," on the basis that it was "not fully confident that it can suitably define and construct testing protocols for [several] characteristics."

Whatever the basis for this shift in strategy, it erodes the foundation of the EPA's argument that the mixture rule was implicit in the proposed regulations. A system that would rely primarily on lists of wastes and waste-producing processes might imply inclusion of a waste until it is formally removed from the list. The proposed regulations, however, did not suggest such a system. Rather, their emphasis on characteristics suggested that if a waste did not exhibit the nine characteristics originally proposed, it need not be regulated as hazardous. We conclude, therefore, that the mixture rule was neither implicit in nor a "logical outgrowth" of the proposed regulations.

Similarly, while the derived-from rule may well have been the best regulatory approach the EPA could devise, it was not a logical outgrowth of the proposed regulations. The derived-from rule is not implicit in a system based upon testing wastes for specified hazardous characteristics—the system presented in the proposed regulations. To the contrary, the derived-from rule becomes counterintuitive as applied to processes designed to render wastes nonhazardous. Rather than presuming that these processes will achieve their goals, the derived-from rule assumes their failure.

* * *

Because the EPA has not provided adequate notice and opportunity for comment, we conclude that the mixture and derived-from rules must be set aside and remanded to the EPA. In light of the dangers that may be posed by a discontinuity in the regulation of hazardous wastes, however, the agency may wish to consider reenacting the rules, in whole or part, on an interim basis under the "good cause" exemption of 5 U.S.C. § 553(b)(3)(B) pending full notice and opportunity for comment.

As we vacate them on procedural grounds, we do not reach petitioners' argument that the mixture and derived-from rules unlawfully expand the EPA's jurisdiction under Subtitle C of RCRA.

* * *

NOTES

1. On March 3, 1992, the EPA reinstated the mixture and derived-from rules, temporarily until April 28, 1993, and requested public comment on possible revisions to the rules. 57 Fed. Reg. 7628 (1992). The EPA also announced its view that the *Shell Oil* decision applied prospectively only, an issue which the D.C. Circuit had declined to clarify.

2. On May 20, 1992, the EPA published a package of proposed revisions to the definition of hazardous waste. 57 Fed. Reg. 21450 (1992). Apparently desirous of avoiding the notice defect that invalidated the 1980 publication of the mixture and derived-from rules, the EPA's proposal contained a smorgasbord of options, any combination of which might have been adopted. The proposal featured two principal options, each of which had several variations.

One of the principal options under consideration would have maintained the existing system of listed and characteristic wastes, mixture and derived-from rules, and delisting petitions, and grafted onto it another means of exiting RCRA regulation. If a listed hazardous waste (or a waste considered to be a listed waste by virtue of the mixture and derived-from rules) did not contain specified constituents in concentrations greater than specified limits, then that waste would no longer be subject to RCRA. The EPA anticipated limits based on health risk, with widely varying margins of safety under consideration.

The second principal option was more far-reaching in scope and would have ultimately supplanted the existing scheme of listed, characteristic, mixture and derived-from rules. This option would have relied solely upon characteristics as a means of determining entry into as well as exit from RCRA regulation. It would have vastly increased the number of constituents for which toxicity characteristic levels exist, and these regulatory levels would have determined whether a waste is subject to RCRA regulation, without regard to whether it is a mixture or treatment residue.

Finally, the EPA also proposed applying different numerical criteria, using either option, to determining whether a waste is subject to RCRA regulation depending on the method by which it is managed. The EPA described this "contingent management option" as follows:

> The basic reasoning is that if a waste is managed safely, the criteria against which it is judged can be less stringent. Proven safe disposal can allow more concentrated waste out of subtitle C without increasing risk to human health and the environment so long as the waste is disposed of in accord with the contingent management criteria.

57 Fed. Reg. at 21459-60. The contingent management option was illustrative of a rather dramatic shift in the EPA's approach to RCRA regulation, reflected throughout the May 20, 1992 proposal package. The EPA explained:

> Since 1980, EPA has implemented the section 1004(5) definition by considering the plausible types of mismanagement that a waste could be subject to and determining the hazards presented by the waste under that scenario. Thus, in analyzing whether a waste should be identified as "hazardous" EPA has not generally determined whether that waste is in fact mismanaged under the scenario, but only whether it could be. Thus, EPA's hazardous waste definitions capture wastes which could be hazardous if mismanaged, not wastes which are necessarily hazardous under all circumstances.
>
> *** EPA does not believe that the statute requires that the hazardous waste designation always assume mismanagement of the waste in question. Moreover, because the Agency has acquired 12 years of experience in implementing the hazardous waste program and a more detailed knowledge concerning actual waste management practices, the Agency believes that it is appropriate to begin tailoring the scope of its hazardous waste program to reflect how wastes are actually managed, rather than how they might be managed under a worst-case analysis.

57 Fed. Reg. at 21455.

3. On September 25, 1992, Congress tacked onto an appropriations bill a provision stating that the interim mixture and derived-from rules "shall not be terminated or withdrawn until revisions are promulgated and become effective." The provision also barred the EPA from issuing revised rules before October 1993, and required the agency to issue final regulations by October 1994. H.R. 5679, *in* 138 CONG. REC. H9450, H9455, H9484 (daily ed. Sept. 25, 1992).

4. On October 30, 1992, the EPA deleted the April 1993 expiration date from the reinstated mixture and derived-from rules, 57 Fed. Reg. 49278 (1992), and withdrew the May 1992 proposal for revising the definition of hazardous waste. 57 Fed. Reg. 49280 (1992). The EPA indicated that it was overwhelmed by the negative comments it had received regarding the May 1992 proposal.

5. After suit was brought to enforce the (missed) statutory deadline for issuing revised rules, the EPA entered into a consent decree establishing yet another rulemaking schedule. *Environmental Technology Council v. Browner*, C.A. No. 94-2119 (TFH) (D.C.Cir. 1994). That resulted in two proposed rulemakings, one to address process-generated hazardous waste, 60 Fed. Reg. 66344 (1995), and one to address contaminated media, 61 Fed. Reg. 18780 (1996), *corrected* 61 Fed. Reg. 41111 (1996).

A. Proposal For Process-Generated Wastes

The proposal regarding process-generated hazardous waste would retain the mixture and derived-from rules, but provide an alternative to the costly, time-consuming delisting procedure whereby hazardous waste rendered innocuous could escape RCRA jurisdiction. In the agency's words:

The Environmental Protection Agency (EPA) today is proposing to amend its regulations under *** RCRA by establishing constituent-specific exit levels for low-risk solid wastes that are designated as hazardous because they are listed, or have been mixed with, derived from, or contain listed hazardous wastes. Under this proposal, generators of listed hazardous wastes that meet the self-implementing exit levels would no longer be subject to the hazardous waste management system under Subtitle C of RCRA as listed hazardous wastes. ***

Many of the exit levels are established using an innovative risk assessment which evaluates potential exposure pathways, both direct and indirect, from a variety of sources, such as waste piles and surface impoundments. This assessment focuses on both human and environmental receptors ***. ***

* * *

For 191 of the 376 constituents of concern, EPA conducted a detailed human health risk analysis to develop risk-based levels for either the wastewater or nonwastewater form of a constituent (or both). To conduct this analysis, EPA identified five types of units actually and rather frequently used to manage nonhazardous wastes that covered the full range of environmental releases needing analysis. The May 1992 proposal of exit levels for listed wastes, like many previous RCRA rules, assessed only risks from releases to groundwater. In response to complaints that such an assessment would not protect human health and the environment from other types of releases, EPA also assessed potential releases to air, surface water and soil in this proposal.

For each category of releases, EPA evaluated both relatively simple pathways (such as direct human ingestion of contaminated groundwater) and more complex pathways (such as the deposition of windblown waste particles on agricultural land, followed by crop uptake, consumption of the crop by cattle, and consumption of contaminated beef or milk by humans). EPA assessed approximately 8 to 27 release pathways depending on the type of waste management unit.

Additionally, EPA screened the same group of 191 constituents to identify the highest priorities for assessment of ecological receptors. In addition, EPA considered for its assessment the toxicological effects of silver on ecological receptors. EPA conducted a specific assessment of ecological risks for 47 constituents using the same five units and the same pathways (modified to reflect ecological exposures) for each unit. ***

Data limitations and resource constraints prevented EPA from conducting a risk analysis for the remaining constituents of concern. For each of these constituents, EPA extrapolated exit levels from levels derived-from the risk assessment for similar chemicals. ***

60 Fed. Reg. 66344, 66349-50.

Shortly before the consent decree deadline for promulgating final regulations, the EPA announced that the innovative, multi-pathway risk assessment methodology developed to establish proposed exit levels was sufficiently flawed that the agency required substantial additional time to revise the methodology and publish a revised proposal before any final regulatory package could be published. *Agency to Revise Risk Assessment Model, Repropose HWIR For Process Waste, Official Says,* 27 Env't Rep. (BNA) 1615 (Dec. 6, 1996). The parties negotiated a revised consent decree, allowing the EPA until October 31, 1999 to issue a revised, proposed definition of hazardous waste, and until April 30, 2001 to issue the final rule. *Accord Reached on HWIR Reproposal For Revising Multipathway Risk Model,* 27 Env't Rep. (BNA) 2509 (April 18, 1997).

B. Proposal for Contaminated Media

(1) Contained-in Policy

As a prelude to considering the EPA's proposal for redefining when contaminated media are hazardous waste, it is necessary to become familiar with the EPA's "contained-in policy," which provides that contaminated media (groundwater, soil, and/or sediment) containing listed hazardous waste should be treated as if they are hazardous waste until they either no longer contain the listed hazardous waste or are delisted. This policy is premised on the assumption that media are not solid waste because, although they have become contaminated, they are not discarded as long as they remain in place. Therefore, the mixture rule would not apply to the contaminated media because it applies to the mixture of a solid waste with a listed hazardous waste. Although neither the RCRA statute nor the Part 261 regulations would define contaminated media as hazardous waste, the EPA nonetheless believes that, as a matter of policy, they should be handled in accordance with RCRA standards.

The EPA enunciated the contained-in policy in a number of memoranda and letters known generically as "guidance documents." The guidance documents appear in a wide variety of forms, ranging from thick, printed manuals to short letters to private attorneys. They are not subject to any of the notice and comment or publication requirements applicable to regulations. They nonetheless indicate the EPA's interpretation of the RCRA statute and regulations as applied to fact situations that may not be addressed in either the regulations or the Federal Register preambles that accompany the publication of the regulations. The guidance documents pertaining to the contained-in policy include a November 13, 1986 memorandum from the Director of the EPA's Office of Solid Waste to the Director of the Waste Management Division at the EPA's Region IV (OSWER Policy Directive 9481.00-6), an April 8, 1987 letter from the Chief of the EPA's Waste Characterization Branch to the State of Washington's Department of Ecology, and a June 19, 1989 letter from the EPA's Acting Assistant Administrator to the Commissioner of the New York State Department of Environmental Conservation.

In what situations would the contained-in policy trigger the application of RCRA where it would not otherwise be triggered? In those situations, is one legally required to apply RCRA standards to contaminated media that do not meet the Part 261 definition of hazardous waste? Once the contaminated media are removed for treatment and/or disposal, does the contained-in policy still apply or does RCRA jurisdiction attach directly under the Part 261 regulations? You may wish to revisit these questions in light of *Chemical Waste Management, Inc. v. Environmental Protection Agency*, 869 F.2d 1526 (D.C.Cir.1989) (in chapter 4).

(2) 1996 Contaminated Media Proposal

The EPA's 1996 contaminated media proposal would, in effect, codify the contained-in policy by creating a new set of provisions (proposed 40 C.F.R. Part 269) governing "hazardous contaminated media," defined as media containing listed or characteristic hazardous waste. The hazardous contaminated media would be further defined according to a "bright-line" test, based on concentration levels for some 200 constituents, to differentiate higher risk from lower risk contaminated media. Media falling above the bright line would remain subject to RCRA regulation as hazardous waste, although the full impact of the regulatory program would be mitigated by creating soil-specific land disposal treatment standards (rather than using the land disposal treatment standards designed for process-generated wastes) and by waiving the facility-wide corrective action requirement (*see* chapter 5.A) for sites where hazardous waste treatment, storage, or disposal is being conducted solely for clean-up purposes. For media falling below the bright line, the EPA and authorized states could establish site-specific management standards in lieu of Subtitle C RCRA requirements. 61 Fed. Reg. 18780 (1996).

6. Consistent with this apparent trend toward removing lower-risk wastes from RCRA regulatory jurisdiction is the EPA's "universal waste" rule published May 11, 1995. 60 Fed. Reg. 25492 (1995). The rule applies to specified materials that are generated by a wide variety of commercial, industrial, and even consumer activities and that—by virtue of hazardous waste exclusions for certain types of generators (households and conditionally-exempt small quantity generators)—are disposed of in significant quantities in non-hazardous waste facilities such as municipal landfills. The universal waste rule establishes management standards mandatorily applicable to non-exempt commercial or industrial entities and potentially applicable to exempt entities. As an initial matter, the rule applies to batteries, recalled and unused pesticides, and mercury-containing thermostats. These materials are not excluded from the definition of hazardous waste, but are subject to different, and less stringent management standards pursuant to newly-created 40 C.F.R. Part 273. *See* 40 C.F.R. § 261.9. The EPA anticipates that with relaxed management standards, retail outlets and other businesses will encourage exempt entities (consumers and small quantity generators) to recycle—rather than landfill or incinerate—their used batteries, unused or recalled pesticides, and mercury-containing thermometers.

7. The exclusion from the definition of hazardous waste for materials generated by households, 40 C.F.R. § 261.4(b)(1), has also attracted attention in the context of municipal trash-to-energy facilities. Although such facilities are statutorily exempt from RCRA regulation, 42 U.S.C. § 6921(i), a conflict between circuits necessitated Supreme Court resolution of the question whether ash generated by such facilities is also exempt from the definition of hazardous waste. *See City of Chicago v. Environmental Defense Fund*, 511 U.S. 328 (1994) (in chapter three).

8. While the EPA has been struggling to adopt regulatory changes in response to *Shell Oil* and the underlying substantive concerns regarding the over-inclusive scope of the mixture and derived-from rules, the courts have faced difficult issues arising from the sudden disruption of a program that had been in place on the federal and state levels for over a decade. One issue was whether the D.C.Circuit's 1991 invalidation of the EPA's 1980 mixture and derived-from rules was effective retroactively, whereby the rules were never validly in effect until "reinstated" on March 3, 1992, or prospectively only, which would have preserved the status quo as it existed from 1980 until 1991.

Shortly after *Shell Oil*, the Eighth Circuit held that the invalidation applied retroactively. In *United States v. Goodner Brothers Aircraft*, 966 F.2d 380 (8th Cir. 1992), *cert. denied*, 506 U.S. 1049 (1993), the court vacated the RCRA convictions of an aircraft repainting company and its owner on the ground that the jury verdicts against them could have been based on the mixture rule, which had not been lawfully in effect at the time of the defendants' actions.

The EPA's efforts to establish that *Shell Oil* applied only prospectively were rejected not only by the courts, but also by the agency's Environmental Appeals Board. *In re Hardin County*, 1994 WL 157572 (EPA Env. App. Bd., Apr. 12, 1994).

Once it seemed settled that the mixture and derived-from rules were void *ab initio*, parties looked to state law counterparts to those rules and to other provisions of the EPA's hazardous waste rules to attempt to fill the regulatory gap created by *Shell Oil*. Regarding state versions of the mixture and derived-from rules, the EPA's Environmental Appeals Board determined that the EPA could not enforce state regulations that are "broader in scope" than the federal rules, and found that a state regulatory program that incorporates the mixture and derived-from rules was broader in scope than the federal program prior to the "reinstatement" of those rules. *Ibid.*

The following cases represent divergent responses to the EPA's arguments that other provisions of the hazardous regulations brought certain mixtures under RCRA jurisdiction, without resort to the mixture rule.

UNITED STATES V. BETHLEHEM STEEL CORP.
38 F.3d 862 (7th Cir. 1994)

Before ESCHBACH, RIPPLE, and KANNE, Circuit Judges.
KANNE, Circuit Judge.

The United States brought this penal enforcement action on behalf of the United States Environmental Protection Agency ("EPA") against Bethlehem Steel Corporation to enforce hazardous waste requirements under the Resource Conservation and Recovery Act ("RCRA") and the Safe Drinking Water Act ("SDWA").

Bethlehem Steel Corporation owns and operates an integrated steelmaking facility at Burns Harbor, Indiana. The United States alleges that a series of environmental violations have occurred (and continue to occur) at Burns Harbor. More specifically, the government's complaint asserts six claims for injunctive relief and civil penalties in connection with two types of "solid" waste generated by the facility. The government's first claim concerns the plant's generation of waste ammonia liquor. Bethlehem disposes of waste ammonia liquor by channelling it through pipes, then forcing it down under pressure into two Class I underground injection wells at the plant site. The government's second through sixth claims pertain to sludges the plant previously generated from the treatment of electroplating and other wastewaters. These sludges are currently stored or disposed of in two finishing lagoons and a landfill, also at the plant site.

Both parties moved for partial summary judgment on the six claims. The district court granted partial summary judgment in favor of the United States on all the claims and denied Bethlehem's motions. In its Memorandum Opinion and Order, the district court issued a permanent injunction, ordering Bethlehem to comply with its hazardous waste obligations under the two statutes. Bethlehem appeals from the district court's decision.

I. BACKGROUND

*** Section 3005(a) of RCRA generally prohibits the operation of hazardous waste management facilities or units, except in accordance with a RCRA permit or with established interim status requirements. All of Bethlehem's problems in this case arise either from the company's alleged failure to follow the conditions of a valid permit or to comply with interim status regulations.

* * *

B. United States' Second through Sixth Claims for Relief

In its second through sixth claims for relief, the United States alleges that Bethlehem violated RCRA by failing to comply with RCRA "interim status performance standards" for its landfill and two terminal polishing lagoons.

From the mid-1960's until June 16, 1983, Bethlehem conducted tin and chromium electroplating at its Burns Harbor facility, generating electroplating wastewater as a by-product. Bethlehem treated this electroplating wastewater by, among other things, mixing it with other kinds of wastewaters, then adding a flocculent or thickener and allowing the resulting solids to settle to the bottom as sludge. After the clarified water was drawn off, the sludge was filtered. The clarified water was sent to two terminal polishing lagoons to allow further settling and to allow the temperature and chemical composition of the water to equilibrate. The filtered sludge was disposed of in the landfill. The United States contends that because 40 C.F.R. § 261.31 lists "wastewater treatment sludges from electroplating operations" as F006 hazardous waste, Bethlehem's landfill and lagoons are "hazardous waste management units" subject to 42 U.S.C. § 6925(a)'s permit requirements.

In enacting RCRA, Congress recognized that the EPA could not issue permits to all applicants before RCRA's effective date. Thus, RCRA provides that facilities already in existence on November 19, 1980, could continue to manage hazardous waste without a permit on an "interim status" basis, until the EPA made a final administrative disposition of their submitted permit applications. To obtain interim status, existing facilities were required to submit a "Part A application" by a certain date and then were to be "treated as having been issued [a] permit."

Such facilities nonetheless were required to conduct their hazardous waste management in compliance with the "interim status standards" set forth at 40 C.F.R. Pt. 265. In the last five counts of its complaint, the government alleges that Bethlehem did not meet its interim status obligations to (1) comply with closure and post-closure requirements, (2) implement a groundwater monitoring system, (3) establish financial assurance for closure and post-closure care of each of its units, (4) implement a run-on control system for the landfill, and (5) submit a Part B application as requested by the Indiana Department of Environmental Management.

The district court agreed with the government and granted partial summary judgment on all six of the United States' claims, holding Bethlehem liable for injunctive relief and civil penalties not to exceed $25,000 per day of violation for each of Bethlehem's violations. The court's memorandum opinion contained an injunction ordering Bethlehem to comply with the corrective action requirements of its UIC permit, and with the interim status requirements for its terminal polishing lagoons and landfill.

II. DISCUSSION
* * *

B. Landfill and Polishing Lagoons
* * *

As we previously discussed, RCRA section 3005's permit requirements apply to the treatment, storage, and disposal of hazardous wastes. Wastes are considered hazardous, and therefore subject to RCRA's subtitle C permit requirements, if they fit one of two categories. First, they may be "characteristic" hazardous wastes, meaning they possess one of the four hazardous characteristics of ignitability, corrosivity, reactivity, or toxicity. Second, the EPA may deem wastes hazardous by rulemaking. These wastes are known as "listed wastes." Listed wastes remain hazardous waste until the EPA approves a petition for its "delisting."

The United States maintains that the settled sludge at the bottom of Bethlehem's finishing lagoons and the filtered sludge disposed of in its landfill are F006 listed waste, because the sludges are properly classified as "wastewater treatment sludges from electroplating operations." See 40 C.F.R. § 261.31. The government advances two bases under which Bethlehem's sludges should be considered regulated F006 waste.

First, it argues that the language of the F006 listing itself—"wastewater treatment sludges from electroplating operations"—contemplates "mixed" sludges like Bethlehem's (i.e., those resulting from the treatment of wastewaters which came in part from electroplating operations). Second, it argues that even if the language of the F006 listing does not cover "mixed" electroplating sludges, the regulation should still be read consistently with the "general principle [underlying RCRA] that a hazardous waste does not lose its hazardous character simply because it changes form or is combined with other substances." To fail to do so, the government warns, would effectively gut RCRA.

If Bethlehem's sludges are listed waste, they would be considered hazardous until delisted. Bethlehem's sludges were not delisted; therefore, Bethlehem's lagoons and landfill would be subject to RCRA's section 3005 interim status requirements, if indeed they contain F006. (Recall that Bethlehem was a pre- November 19, 1980 facility with a permit application pending with the EPA and was thus qualified to be an interim status facility). Bethlehem has failed to meet a slew of the EPA's interim status standards, 40 C.F.R. § 265; thus, if the government's arguments are correct, Bethlehem would potentially be liable for injunctive relief and penalties.

Bethlehem attempts to refute the government's arguments by (1) asserting that the F006 listing, by its terms, applies only to sludge from pure electroplating wastewaters; and (2) referring us to *Shell Oil v. EPA*, 950 F.2d 741 (D.C.Cir.1991), to support the proposition that its wastewater treatment sludge is not F006 listed waste because it has been mixed with other solid wastes.

We agree with Bethlehem on both points. We must first acknowledge that the plain language of the F006 listing is not particularly instructive in this case. Although the district court notes that "the term 'wastewater treatment sludges from electroplating operations' does not have the words 'solely', 'only', or 'exclusively' in it, to imply that only wastewater treatment sludges from electroplating operations and not a mixture thereof is hazardous waste," we are equally persuaded by Bethlehem's observation that the listing also "does not contain the words, 'partly,' 'mixed with,' or 'in trace amount' either."

Similarly, we find it significant that the F006 listing lacks the phrase "mixtures/blends," or any mention of a threshold concentration percentage (for instance, ten percent or more electroplating wastewater). The F001-F005 listings immediately preceding F006 contain both.[12] A facility may reasonably infer that when the EPA intends to include waste mixtures in its listings, it knows how to do so, and that in the F006 listing, such mixture language is conspicuously absent. Subsequently, the EPA explicitly "amend [ed] ... [the F001-F005] spent solvent listings to include solvent mixtures," 40 C.F.R. § 271.1 (table 1); 50 Fed. Reg. 53318 (December 31, 1985) ("Today's amendment will close a major regulatory loophole which allows toxic solvent mixtures to remain unregulated.") but did not amend the F006 listing to include electroplating wastewater mixtures.

Finally, the EPA's statement at 45 Fed. Reg. 33095 (May 19, 1980), with regard to its promulgation of the "mixture rule," provides the last clue that tips our construction of the F006 listing in Bethlehem's favor. The EPA there stated:

1. *What is hazardous waste?*

---

[12]For example, the F004 listing specifies "the following spent non-halogenated solvents: Cresols and cresylic acid, and nitrobenzene; all spent solvent mixtures/blends containing, before use, a total of ten percent or more (by volume) of one or more of the above non-halogenated solvents or those solvents listed in F001, F002, and F005; and still bottoms from the recovery of these spent solvents and spent solvent mixtures."

Paragraph (a) of this section defines what a hazardous waste is. It provides that a solid waste is a hazardous waste if ... it either (1) is listed as a hazardous waste in Subpart D, (2) is a waste mixture containing one or more hazardous wastes listed in Subpart D....

* * * * * *

Although it was not expressly stated in the proposed regulation, EPA intended waste mixtures containing listed hazardous wastes to be considered a hazardous waste and managed accordingly. *Without [the mixture] rule, generators could evade Subtitle C requirements simply by commingling listed wastes with nonhazardous solid waste....* Obviously, this would leave a major loophole in the Subtitle C management system and create inconsistencies in how wastes must be managed under that system.

45 Fed. Reg. 33095 (May 19, 1980) (emphasis added). Thus, the EPA itself seems to concede that although it meant to include waste mixtures in the Subpart D listings, without a separate rule specifying that such mixtures are hazardous, the language of the listing itself fails to reach such mixtures. We conclude that the F006 listing does not, independent of the mixture rule, include Bethlehem's mixed wastewater treatment sludges.

Bethlehem is also correct that its sludges are not listed F006 waste because the *Shell Oil* case invalidated the mixture rule. ***

* * *

In its brief, the United States argues to this court the very theory explicitly rejected by *Shell Oil.* The government states, "The regulation of these [mixed wastes] is not a result of the application of specific rules such as the 'mixture rule,' but a result of application of the more general principles and provisions embodied in these rules." And further, "The RCRA 'continuing jurisdiction' principle means only that the hazardous waste portion of the mixture is subject to regulation—i.e., that one cannot hide waste or change its hazardous character by mixing it into a pile of non-hazardous waste." The government, in essence, urges us to reach a conclusion directly at odds with the reasoning in *Shell Oil;* namely, that the EPA may reach mixed wastes without relying on the mixture rule, because the principles underlying the rule are implicit in the Subpart D listings and the final rule, stripped of the invalidated mixture provision.

This we decline to do. We find the reasoning of the *Shell Oil* opinion persuasive on the point that the regulation of waste mixtures is simply not a logical outgrowth of the proposed definition of hazardous waste, and that without the explicit mixture rule, the definition leaves a major loophole through which waste mixtures could slip. Therefore, we must reject the notion that the policy behind the mixture rule is "embodied" as a general principle within the definition and that such a principle may operate to reach wastes that would have been covered by the mixture rule, but for its invalidation.

Finally, we determine that no "principle of continuing jurisdiction" is applicable to this case. The principle of continuing jurisdiction applies not to mixtures of hazardous and nonhazardous solid wastes, but to mixtures of hazardous waste and environmental media, such as soil and groundwater. *See Chemical Waste Management, Inc. v. EPA*, 869 F.2d 1526 (D.C.Cir.1989). In *Chemical Waste Management*, the court adopted the agency's position regarding environmental media contaminated by hazardous waste. The agency's position was "that hazardous waste cannot be presumed to change character when it is combined with an environmental medium, and that the hazardous waste restrictions therefore continue to apply to waste which is contained in soil or groundwater." *Id*. at 1539. The court went on to state, however, that "[t]he EPA's approach to contaminated soil is also ... entirely consistent with the agency's general regulatory framework, which emphasizes that a continuing presumption of hazardousness attaches to hazardous waste which changes form or is combined with other substances." *Id*. at 1540-41.

Ironically, the court deduced that such a "coherent regulatory framework" existed, partly because of the now-invalid mixture and "derived-from" rules. It noted that "[p]recisely the same logic" that underlies the mixture and derived-from rules applies to the conclusion that the EPA has continuing jurisdiction over combinations of hazardous waste and environmental media.

Because the mixture and derived-from rules were invalidated in *Shell Oil*, the government's attempt to use the principle of continuing jurisdiction here to buttress its claim regarding Bethlehem's mixed wastes constitutes bootstrapping. We conclude that Bethlehem's wastewater treatment sludges cannot be F006 listed waste by virtue of the principle of continuing jurisdiction.

CONCLUSION
* * *

*** Bethlehem's wastewater treatment sludges do not fall within the listing for F006 hazardous waste. The parties agree that the sludges are a mixture of F006 and non-hazardous waste, and the government does not allege that Bethlehem's sludges are hazardous waste by virtue of any theory other than its listing as F006 waste. As such, the sludges in Bethlehem's two lagoons and landfill are not subject to RCRA subtitle C requirements as a listed hazardous waste. ***

RIPPLE, Circuit Judge, concurring in part and dissenting in part.

* * *

I believe that the sludge at the bottom of Bethlehem's finishing lagoons and the filtered sludge in its landfill are properly classified as F006 listed waste because these sludges are "wastewater treatment sludges from electroplating operations." 40 C.F.R. § 261.31. In my view, the agency's description is very clear and further specificity is not required. I note that the F006 listing specifically eliminates from its scope sludges produced by certain processes. If the agency believed that other exclusions, based for instance on the percentage of the sludge attributable to hazardous waste, were appropriate, it would have included such a specification.

In the following case, the Fifth Circuit reached a different conclusion from the Seventh Circuit without disagreeing with the latter's analysis in *Bethlehem Steel*. The excerpt below is from one of three cases, all of which are examined in chapter three, concerning a hazardous waste facility charged with "sham recycling." Presented below are the portions addressing the mixture rule issue. A more complete statement of the facts is included in the chapter three excerpts.

UNITED STATES V. MARINE SHALE PROCESSORS
81 F.3d 1329 (5th Cir. 1996)

Before GARZA, KING and HIGGINBOTHAM.
HIGGINBOTHAM, Circuit Judge.

This case, along with Nos. 94-30419 and 95-60228, concerns the past actions and future fate of Marine Shale Processors, Inc., a hazardous waste treatment facility. The cases involve multiple aspects of each of the federal environmental laws as affecting disputes between the Environmental Protection Agency and MSP. We provide a brief explanation of the three cases in this opinion before discussing the specific issues raised by this appeal.

I

In 1985, Marine Shale Processors, Inc. opened a facility in Amelia, Louisiana purporting to recycle hazardous waste through its newly acquired rotary kiln, a mechanism 275 feet long and 11 feet in diameter with the capacity to heat materials to temperatures in excess of 2000 degrees Fahrenheit. MSP's treatment process began with placement of materials in its kiln. From there, most material traveled through oxidizers and slag boxes. The process generated significant quantities of smoke, flue gases, and air particles. Carcinogenic heavy metals tended to concentrate in these air particles. The air pollutants passed through baghouses, which collected some of the material in the form of caked dust. The dust dropped off the bags to the bottom of the baghouses, where it was collected, run through the oxidizers and slag boxes, then combined with the rest of the material produced from the primary process. The nature of MSP's operation made it subject to federal and state laws limiting pollution of water, air, and land. These laws required MSP to obtain permits specifying the type and amount of pollutants that it could discharge into the environment.

* * *

III

The district court decided all RCRA issues relevant to this appeal by summary judgment. In particular, the district court held that MSP had violated land ban regulations on numerous occasions. In addition, the district court held that MSP had stored K-listed wastes without a permit or interim status, but ruled that MSP had interim status to store F-listed wastes. Both the United States and MSP appeal the district court's RCRA rulings. ***

* * *

Shortly after opening, MSP began accepting D- and U-listed wastes. It also began receiving material manifested as "K001" from two customers, Colfax Creosoteing Co. and Durawood Treating Co. *** Colfax and Durawood had hired MSP to clean up large wastewater treatment ponds. These ponds contained primarily water, creosote, and pentachlorophenol. Also present were trace amounts of chrome, copper, and arsenic, along with unspecified quantities of debris. MSP pumped the water from these ponds and removed it to MSP's rotary kiln site. MSP added absorbent materials, composed in part of material previously generated from MSP's rotary kiln, to solidify what remained and removed the entirety of the pond site material by bulldozer. Materials arriving at MSP's rotary kiln site from Colfax and Durawood remained there partially on a cement pad.

MSP's treatment of the Colfax and Durawood materials led the United States four years later to file an information alleging that MSP "did knowingly store and cause to be stored hazardous wastes identified or listed pursuant to Title 42, United States Code, Section 6921, namely, bottom sediment sludge from the treatment of wastewaters from wood preserving facilities using creosote and/or pentachlorophenol." The United States' indictment covered MSP's activities only in 1985. MSP pled guilty to this charge.

* * *

In this action, the United States alleged that MSP stored K- and F-listed wastes without a permit or interim status. ***

[T]he district court fined MSP $1,000,000 for storing K-listed wastes without a permit. ***

2

MSP urges that the district court erred in reading the ban on the storage of K-listed wastes to cover the Colfax and Durawood materials, and that in fact these materials were waste mixtures covered only by the Mixture Rule regulations declared invalid in *Shell Oil*. ***

* * *

3

a

We reject MSP's contention that the materials manifested K001 were waste mixtures subject to regulation only under the Mixture Rule invalidated in *Shell Oil*. MSP contends that the material ultimately stored at its facility as a result of the Colfax and Durawood cleanups included soil, debris, creosote, copper, chrome, arsenic, wastewater, and the absorbent material it added to the bottom of the pond before bulldozing. Accordingly, MSP argues, these materials contained matter not included in K001 definition, and thus constituted matter subject to regulation only pursuant to the Mixture Rule.

Excepting the absorbent material, all other results of the Colfax and Durawood cleanup operations easily meet the definition of a K-listed waste. A K001 waste is a "[b]ottom sediment sludge from the treatment of wastewaters from wood preserving processes that use creosote and/or pentachlorophenol." 40 C.F.R. § 261.32. The evidence established that the materials in the pond came from the treatment of wastewaters from wood preserving processes that used creosote. For instance, Clyde M. Norton, the Vice-President of the corporation that owned Colfax and Durawood, stated in an affidavit that the materials originally in the pond before MSP began its cleanup had been generated from the two companies' wood treating operations.

MSP's primary argument is that extraneous matter in the materials it received prevented those materials from falling within the regulatory definition of a "sludge." We do not agree. The regulations define a "sludge" as "any solid, semi-solid, or liquid waste generated from a[n] ... industrial wastewater treatment plant." 40 C.F.R. § 260.10. Thus, the definition of a sludge, like the definition of a K001 waste, focuses primarily on the origin of the material at issue, not, as MSP contends, on its composition. Moreover, a sludge is a waste generated from a wastewater plant, not as MSP contends, from a wastewater operation. "The word 'plant' denotes an entire facility, a collection of units, machines, land, buildings, and fixtures used in a trade or business, not a single intermediate unit in the treatment process." *In re Brown Wood Preserving Co.*, 1989 WL 253215, at * 6 (EPA May 3, 1989). MSP's own evidence established that the entirety of the material, except for the absorbent material MSP added to the bottom of the ponds after removing the wastewater itself, came from the industrial wastewater treatment plants located on the Colfax and Durawood sites.

We have more difficulty characterizing the results of MSP's bulldozing, after it had added absorbent materials to the Colfax and Durawood wastewater ponds, but we ultimately agree with the district court that the addition of these absorbent material did not cause the Colfax and Durawood wastes to lose their K-listed character. As the district court noted, MSP's interpretation of the definition of K001 waste leads to absurd results. Under its interpretation, MSP could have transformed the Colfax and Durawood materials into mixtures, regulable only by the Mixture Rule invalidated in *Shell Oil*, by adding a drop of water or a speck of dust to every barrel of waste it received, so long as the drop or speck did not come from a wastewater treatment facility. Indeed, although MSP repeatedly contends that the K001 listing applies only to "pure" substances of the nature described in that regulation, such purity exists only in theory. Rudimentary chemical principles establish that a liquid absorbs gases from the surrounding air and trace amounts of impurities from the container in which the liquid resides. Thus, had MSP added nothing at all to the soils it bulldozed from the Colfax and Durawood sites, the resulting material would still not have been pure K001 waste within MSP's use of the phrase. Instead, the arriving material would have consisted of a mixture of K001 waste, dissolved gas molecules from the air, trace amounts of whatever metal or ceramic or synthetic housed the waste in transit, and impurities stuck to the inside of the container. MSP's brand of purity exists only in the hypotheticals of chemistry classrooms, and its interpretation of the regulations would render them meaningless.

We hold that a substance does not lose its character as a K-listed waste, and thus does not become regulable only by the previously invalid Mixture Rule, unless the materials added to it change its basic composition in some significant way. We draw support from the D.C. Circuit's decision in *Chemical Waste Management, Inc. v. Environmental Protection Agency*, 869 F.2d 1526, 1539 (D.C.Cir.1989). In upholding EPA's "contained-in" policy, the D.C. Circuit rejected the argument that "an agglomeration of soil and hazardous waste is to be regarded as a new and distinct substance" and instead accepted EPA's position that "hazardous waste cannot be presumed to change character when it is combined with an environmental medium." 869 F.2d at 1539. Under the circumstances of this case, we decline MSP's invitation to hold that the addition of an absorbing agent or other inert debris to a K001 waste transforms the waste into a new and distinct substance regulable only through the Mixture Rule. We hold that a K001 waste remains a K001 waste after the addition of a substance that results in no significant change in composition.

We need not specify exactly where the line between a significant and insignificant alteration lies. The addition of the absorbent agent did not cause a significant alteration of the Colfax and Durawood materials for several reasons. First, from the standpoint of their toxic composition, these materials were in the heart of the definition of the K001 listing. As the district court observed, "[i]f these wastes fail to qualify as K001 wastes, I cannot envision what wastes would." Second, evidence in the record strongly suggested that at the time these wastes were being shipped, those in the industry considered them K001 sludges. Huey Stockstill, the MSP officer in charge of the Colfax and Durawood cleanup, repeatedly characterized the material brought to MSP's kiln site as sludge. The materials were manifested as K001 wastes. The contract between Colfax and Marine Shale described the wastes as "creosote waste that has been generated during wood treating operations at the Colfax wood preserving facility." Third, MSP pled guilty to storing K-listed waste on its premises without a permit as a result of charges focusing on its storage of the Colfax and Durawood materials, suggesting that it too thought these materials constituted K001 waste, although in the face of litigation it has changed its position. MSP argues that its guilty plea was also based on the Mixture Rule, but the charges to which MSP pled recite the definition of a K001 waste without mentioning this rule. Fourth, the addition of the absorbent was entirely incidental to a cleanup operation, and thus resembles the impurities a waste might absorb from its container during transport and storage.

We reject MSP's contention that our decision places us in conflict with the Seventh Circuit's holding in *United States v. Bethlehem Steel Corp.*, 38 F.3d 862, 865, 868-71 (7th Cir.1994). In *Bethlehem Steel*, the defendant had mixed an F006 waste with "other kinds of wastewater," 38 F.3d at 865, before the addition of a thickener allowed a sludge to precipitate to the bottom. The addition of these other wastewaters so changed the basic composition of the substance at issue that EPA resorted to arguments found unpersuasive in Shell Oil in an attempt to place the wastewaters within the F006 listing. We find no conflict between our holding and that of *Bethlehem Steel*.

* * *

NOTES

1. Do you think that the Fifth Circuit would have reached the same conclusion if the EPA had never promulgated the mixture rule? The Fifth Circuit bases its holding on the D.C. Circuit decision upholding the contained-in policy; that decision (*see* chapter 4), which predated *Shell Oil*, found the contained-in policy to be a reasonable interpretation by the EPA of its mixture and derived-from rules. Is it appropriate for the Fifth Circuit to rely on the contained-in decision to reach mixtures after the mixture rule was found to be void?

2. Do you agree with the Fifth Circuit that this decision does not conflict with the Seventh Circuit's decision in *Bethlehem Steel?*

3. If you were the Administrator of the EPA, would you want this issue resolved? Why or why not? Given that the EPA is required to revise the Part 261 regulations (now by April 2001), would you retain, modify, or eliminate the mixture and derived-from rules? Would you codify the contained-in policy? Does the definition of solid waste as discarded material constrain the EPA's legal authority to codify the contained-in policy?

4. Few wastes have caused more decisionmaking dilemmas for the EPA under RCRA than used oil. In May 1980, when the EPA published its initial regulations defining hazardous waste, it deferred listing used oil as a hazardous waste, but it did list certain petroleum refining wastes (K048 - K052). Although most used oil was treated the same as any other waste under the four hazardous waste characteristics, little used oil exhibited a characteristic as then defined. In addition, RCRA expressly deferred from Subtitle C regulation oilfield wastes, such as drilling fluids and produced waters, but not the produced crude oil. RCRA § 3001(b)(2), 42 U.S.C. § 6921(b)(2); 40 C.F.R. § 261.4(b)(4). After Congress passed the Used Oil Recycling Act in October 1980, the EPA reported to Congress, as required by that Act, its intention to list used oil as hazardous waste. When that intention had not been implemented as of the 1984 RCRA amendments, Congress directed the EPA to make a final determination regarding the hazardous waste status of used oil by November 1986. Although the EPA proposed in November 1985 to list used oil as hazardous waste, it reversed course in the final regulations, published November 1986, and decided not to list used oil as hazardous waste. That decision was overturned on the ground that the EPA had erroneously relied on the stigma that would attach to used oil if classified as hazardous waste, and the anticipated effect of that stigma to discourage the responsible handling and recycling of used oil. *Hazardous Waste Treatment Council v. EPA,* 861 F.2d 270 (D.C. Cir.1988).

In March 1990, when the EPA substantially revised the toxicity characteristic component of the definition of hazardous waste, it brought benzene as a contaminant within the toxicity characteristic. The result was to render a considerable amount of used oil hazardous waste under the TCLP test. At the same time, however, the EPA deferred the application of the new toxicity characteristic to media and debris contaminated by petroleum from underground storage tanks.

In May 1992, the EPA announced that it would not list used oil destined for disposal as hazardous waste. 57 Fed. Reg. 21524 (1992). That decision was based, at least in part, on the facts that some used oil would be hazardous waste anyway under the toxicity characteristic, and that the phaseout of lead in gasoline had reduced the concentration of lead in used oil. The D.C. Circuit upheld the EPA's decision not to list used oil destined for disposal over challenges by the National Resource Defense Council that RCRA requires the EPA to list the oils as hazardous waste. *NRDC v. EPA*, 25 F.3d 1063 (D.C. Cir. 1994).

In August 1992, the EPA announced its decision not to list as hazardous waste used oil that is recycled or burned for energy recovery. Instead, the EPA promulgated the used oil mixture rule, featuring a separate set of less stringent management standards for recycled or burned used oil, and allowing dilution as a method of treatment. 57 Fed. Reg. 41566 (1992). After the rule was challenged, the EPA tried first to vacate, and then to stay it. Both times, the D.C. Circuit held that the EPA lacked the authority to do so without complying with notice and comment requirements. *Appeals Court Vacates EPA Stay of Used Oil Mixture Rule Under RCRA*, 26 Env't Rep. (BNA) 1797 (1996). As a result, the used oil mixture rule remains in effect in states without an authorized RCRA program, and in states that have adopted the rule. For states with an authorized RCRA program that had not implemented the rule, RCRA Subtitle C remains the authority for regulating used oil. As this history suggests, the regulatory status of used oil under RCRA remains a moving target.

Problem #2: DEFINITION OF HAZARDOUS WASTE

Pay close attention to the provisions of 40 C.F.R. Part 261 in working through these Problems.

A. The Clever Cleaver Company ("CCC") is a utensil manufacturer that generates several hazardous wastes, some listed and some characteristic. CCC incinerates the hazardous wastes, all mixed together, in an on-site incinerator. The operation of the incinerator (a form of "thermal treatment") produces the following materials: (1) gases, which are released into the air; (2) ash, which is disposed of as a hazardous waste; and (3) baghouse dust, which is generated by the incinerator's air pollution control equipment and is the focus of CCC's request for your legal advice.

Applying the Toxicity Characteristic Leaching Procedure, the baghouse dust contains 1.5 mg/L of cadmium. CCC had been handling the baghouse dust as a hazardous waste and sending it off-site to a nearby hazardous waste landfill. The RCRA land ban regulations now require CCC to arrange for treatment of the baghouse dust prior to landfilling, further increasing the company's RCRA compliance costs.

CCC has an incentive program offering employees 10% of the cost savings the company achieves as the result of an employee proposal. In response to the incentive program, one of CCC's environmental engineers has proposed that instead of paying others to transport, treat, and dispose of the baghouse dust off-site as hazardous waste, CCC could actually use the baghouse dust in place of the lime that it has long been purchasing for use (in adjusting pH) in its on-site wastewater treatment plant.

CCC seeks your considered legal advice as to whether the baghouse dust would be a hazardous waste under RCRA if used as proposed by the employee. The company is eager to obtain the tremendous cost savings at stake by not treating the dust as a RCRA waste, and by buying less lime, but it is equally interested in steering clear of costly civil or criminal RCRA enforcement proceedings.

B. Big Bang Company ("BBC") is a diversified manufacturer whose product lines include, among other things, certain explosives used by municipal governments for Fourth of July and other festivities. BBC's explosives production process generates a reddish-colored liquid that contains trace amounts of TNT, is reactive, and is also within the RCRA waste code K047. BBC's manufacturing plant generates approximately 1,500 kilograms per month of this "red water." The red water is piped directly from the production process to an on-site storage tank and then shipped to a hazardous waste incinerator.

A minor mishap recently occurred, and BBC has come to you for legal advice. While some K047 red water was being piped from the production line into the storage tank, a valve began leaking and a fair amount of K047 spilled onto the soil before plant personnel eventually noticed the leak and stopped the flow. The plant personnel then dug up the contaminated soil and placed it in drums. They tested the drummed soil and found that it exhibited none of the four hazardous waste characteristics under RCRA. They then sealed the drums and placed them in a secure staging area and asked you for legal advice in order to decide how to dispose of the contaminated soil.

Please advise BBC whether the contaminated soil, as presently stored on-site in drums, is a (a) solid waste and/or (b) hazardous waste under RCRA Subtitle C.

3 ENTITIES REGULATED BY RCRA: GENERATORS AND TREATMENT, STORAGE, AND DISPOSAL FACILITIES

A. Generators

Although RCRA's regulatory requirements are more heavily oriented toward treatment, storage, and disposal ("TSD") facilities, the number of entities that generate hazardous waste is severalfold the number of TSD facilities. From a regulatory standpoint, the crucial distinction between the two categories is that TSD facilities must have a permit (or "interim status") to operate, whereas generators need only an identification number.

The RCRA statute does not define the term generator; the regulations provide that a generator is "any person whose act or process produces hazardous waste under Part 261 or whose act first causes a hazardous waste to become subject to regulation." 40 C.F.R. § 260.10. The regulations require generators to: (1) determine, by testing or by their knowledge of the waste, whether any solid wastes they generate are hazardous waste; (2) obtain an identification number; (3) ensure, by means of a "manifest" document that must accompany their wastes from cradle to grave, that any hazardous wastes sent off-site are handled by permitted hazardous waste transporters, treatment, storage, and/or disposal facilities; (4) comply with various Department of Transportation regulations regarding packaging, labeling, marking, and placarding of hazardous waste prior to off-site shipment; (5) comply with various recordkeeping and reporting requirements; and (6) ensure that their wastes are treated to applicable standards prior to being land disposed. 40 C.F.R. Part 262.

The regulations further provide that a generator may store its own hazardous waste for up to 90 days without becoming a storage facility (which would entail a TSD permit), provided that the generator complies with certain personnel training, preparedness, and contingency plan provisions in the TSD facility regulations. *See* 40 C.F.R. § 262.34. Pursuant to the 1984 amendments to RCRA, the EPA in 1985 extended generator requirements to previously-exempt entities that generate less than 1,000 kilograms of hazardous waste per month. The current threshold for being "conditionally exempt" from RCRA is 100 kilograms of hazardous waste per month; generators of less than that volume may send their hazardous waste to permitted solid waste facilities and are not subject to RCRA's generator regulations. 40 C.F.R. § 261.5. Generators of between 100 and 1,000 kilograms of hazardous waste per month are subject to most, but not all, of the requirements applicable to large quantity generators. They may store waste on-site for 180 days before triggering storage facility status, and their reporting requirements are less burdensome than those applicable to larger quantity generators. 40 C.F.R. §§ 262.34(d) and 262.44.

From the generator's vantage point, the most critical aspects of RCRA are keeping track of the ever-changing definition of regulated "hazardous waste" and complying with the land ban requirements. A significant, emerging area of interest to generators is hazardous waste minimization, or pollution prevention. This is spurred both by public pressure to reduce the volume and toxicity of hazardous waste before, rather than after, it is generated, and by generators' desire to reduce their compliance costs and potential liabilities. (See chapter 19.)

Presently, RCRA only requires each generator to certify on its manifests that it has a program in place to reduce the volume and toxicity of the waste it generates to the extent "economically practicable," and that the method of treatment, storage, or disposal being used for the waste shipment is the "practicable method currently available to the generator which minimizes the present and future threat to human health and the environment." RCRA. § 3002(b). In May 1993, the EPA published guidance to help hazardous waste generators reduce the volume of waste they produce. Interim Final Guidance on Waste Minimization for Hazardous Waste Generators, 58 Fed. Reg. 31114 (1993). The waste minimization guidance adds some detail to the vaguely-worded statutory requirement for hazardous waste generators to implement waste minimization programs.

> EPA believes waste minimization programs should incorporate, in a way that meets individual organizational needs, the following basic elements: (1) top management support; (2) characterization of waste generation and waste management costs; (3) periodic waste minimization assessments; (4) appropriate cost allocation; (5) encouragement of technology transfer, and (6) program implementation and evaluation.

58 Fed. Reg. at 31114. Although the guidance offers some general suggestions for generators in designing waste minimization programs, it is questionable whether generators can be required to adopt such suggestions in light of the statutory language permitting each generator to determine the economical practicability of potential waste minimization efforts.

Every two years, the EPA publishes data concerning hazardous waste management. The preliminary data for 1995 showed an *increase* in the volume of hazardous waste generated in the United States, from 258 million tons in 1993 to 279 million tons in 1995—notwithstanding the EPA's emphasis on waste minimization since 1993. Some 19,900 generators produced this volume of hazardous waste, ninety-six percent of which was in the form of wastewater. The 1993-1995 increase in hazardous waste generation broke a pattern of decreasing volumes from 1985 to 1989 and then again from 1991 to 1993. (The increase from 1989 to 1991 was attributable to the revised definition of the toxicity characteristic, which brought more constituents within the scope of toxicity-characteristic hazardous waste.) To a large extent, the 1993-1995 increase was caused by an 80 million ton increase in the State of Texas. *Hazardous*

Waste Generation and Management on the Increase? 15 HAZ. WASTE CONSULTANT (Elsevier Science), May/June 1997, at 2.18.

Of the 279 million tons of hazardous waste generated in 1995, some 277 tons were managed by some 1,800 RCRA-regulated TSD facilities. Although the volume of RCRA-managed waste rose by 40 million tons from 1993 to 1995, the number of TSDs managing that waste dropped by 800. The methods of hazardous waste management included aqueous treatment units (53 percent), land-based disposal or treatment (landfills, underground injection, surface impoundments) (eight percent), thermal treatment (incineration and fuel substitution in boilers and industrial furnaces) (two percent), recovery operations (one percent), and other treatment techniques, such as sludge treatment and stabilization (36 percent). *Ibid.* Over the period 1985-1996, less than five percent of the total hazardous waste generated was sent off-site for treatment, storage, or disposal at commercial TSDs; nearly all of the rest was managed at on-site, "captive" TSD facilities. *Commercial Hazardous Waste Management Facilities: 1997 Survey of North America*, 15 HAZ. WASTE CONSULTANT (Elsevier Science), March/April 1997, at 4.6.

The next subchapter addresses the RCRA provisions regulating such TSD facilities, whether commercial or captive.

B. Treatment, Storage, and Disposal Facilities

As enacted in 1976, RCRA required all facilities that treat, store, or dispose of hazardous waste to obtain an operating permit from the EPA or, if so authorized, the state. Not intending to force the immediate closure of facilities that were already treating, storing, or disposing of hazardous waste, Congress anticipated that existing facilities could obtain interim authorization, or "interim status," to operate pending the promulgation of regulations governing TSD permits, and pending the submission and review of such permit applications. Once the initial RCRA regulations took effect on November 19, 1980, any facility that thereafter, treated, stored, or disposed of hazardous waste was required to obtain interim status by filing a notice of hazardous waste activity, pursuant to RCRA § 3010, and a "Part A" application. Dissatisfied with the pace at which the EPA and the states were processing more comprehensive, or "Part B," permit applications, Congress in the 1984 RCRA amendments specified a series of deadlines for all then-existing TSD facilities to submit their Part B applications (or lose interim status), and for the EPA or state to grant or deny the applications. RCRA regulations at 40 C.F.R. Parts 265 and 264 set forth detailed operating, reporting, and closure requirements for interim status and Part B facilities, respectively. The balance of this subchapter will focus largely on the threshold issues of which facilities are subject to regulation as TSDs.

The following case serves as a segue from the issue of which materials are RCRA hazardous wastes to the issue of which facilities are subject to RCRA regulation as hazardous waste treatment, storage, and disposal facilities—all in the context of a statutory exclusion.

CITY OF CHICAGO V. ENVIRONMENTAL DEFENSE FUND
511 U.S. 328 (1994)

JUSTICE SCALIA delivered the opinion of the Court.

We are called upon to decide whether, pursuant to § 3001(i) of the Solid Waste Disposal Act (Resource Conservation and Recovery Act of 1976 (RCRA)), 42 U.S.C. § 6921(i), the ash generated by a resource recovery facility's incineration of municipal solid waste is exempt from regulation as a hazardous waste under Subtitle C of RCRA.

I

Since 1971, petitioner the city of Chicago has owned and operated a municipal incinerator, the Northwest Waste-to-Energy Facility, that burns solid waste and recovers energy, leaving a residue of municipal waste combustion (MWC) ash. The facility burns approximately 350,000 tons of solid waste each year and produces energy that is both used within the facility and sold to other entities. The city has disposed of the combustion residue—110,000 to 140,000 tons of MWC ash per year—at landfills that are not licensed to accept hazardous wastes.

In 1988 respondent Environmental Defense Fund (EDF) filed a complaint against the petitioners, the city of Chicago and its Mayor, under the citizen suit provisions of RCRA, 42 U. S. C. § 6972, alleging that they were violating provisions of RCRA and of implementing regulations issued by the Environmental Protection Agency (EPA). Respondent alleged that the MWC ash generated by the facility was toxic enough to qualify as a "hazardous waste" under EPA's regulations, 40 CFR pt. 261. It was uncontested that, with respect to the ash, petitioners had not adhered to any of the requirements of Subtitle C, the portion of RCRA addressing hazardous wastes. Petitioners contended that RCRA § 3001(i), excluded the MWC ash from those requirements. The District Court agreed with that contention, and subsequently granted petitioners' motion for summary judgment.

The Court of Appeals reversed, concluding that the "ash generated from the incinerators of municipal resource recovery facilities is subject to regulation as a hazardous waste under Subtitle C of RCRA." The city petitioned for a writ of certiorari, and we invited the Solicitor General to present the views of the United States. On September 18, 1992, while that invitation was outstanding, the Administrator of EPA issued a memorandum to EPA Regional Administrators, directing them, in accordance with the agency's view of § 3001(i), to treat MWC ash as exempt from hazardous waste regulation under Subtitle C of RCRA. Thereafter, we granted the city's petition, vacated the decision, and remanded the case to the Court of Appeals for the Seventh Circuit for further consideration in light of the memorandum.

On remand, the Court of Appeals reinstated its previous opinion, holding that, because the statute's plain language is dispositive, the EPA memorandum did not affect its analysis. Petitioners filed a petition for writ of certiorari, which we granted.

II

RCRA is a comprehensive environmental statute that empowers EPA to regulate hazardous wastes from cradle to grave, in accordance with the rigorous safeguards and waste management procedures of Subtitle C, 42 U.S.C. §§ 6921-6934. (Nonhazardous wastes are regulated much more loosely under Subtitle D, 42 U.S C. §§ 6941-6949.) Under the relevant provisions of Subtitle C, EPA has promulgated standards governing hazardous waste generators and transporters, and owners and operators of hazardous waste treatment, storage, and disposal facilities (TSDF's). Pursuant to § 6922, EPA has directed hazardous waste generators to comply with handling, record-keeping, storage, and monitoring requirements. TSDF's, however, are subject to much more stringent regulation than either generators or transporters, including a 4-to-5 year permitting process, burdensome financial assurance requirements, stringent design and location standards, and, perhaps most onerous of all, responsibility to take corrective action for releases of hazardous substances and to ensure safe closure of each facility. "[The] corrective action requirement is one of the major reasons that generators and transporters work diligently to manage their wastes so as to avoid the need to obtain interim status or a TSD permit." 3 Environmental Law Practice Guide § 29.06[3][d] (M. Gerrard ed. 1993) (hereinafter Practice Guide).

RCRA does not identify which wastes are hazardous and therefore subject to Subtitle C regulation; it leaves that designation to EPA. When EPA's hazardous-waste designations for solid wastes appeared in 1980, they contained certain exceptions from normal coverage, including an exclusion for "household waste," defined as "any waste material ... derived from households (including single and multiple residences, hotels and motels)," codified as amended at 40 CFR § 261.4(b)(1). Although most household waste is harmless, a small portion—such as cleaning fluids and batteries—would have qualified as hazardous waste. The regulation declared, however, that "[h]ousehold waste, including household waste that has been collected, transported, stored, treated, disposed, recovered (e.g., refuse-derived fuel) or reused" is not hazardous waste. Moreover, the preamble to the 1980 regulations stated that "residues remaining after treatment (e. g. incineration, thermal treatment) [of household waste] are not subject to regulation as a hazardous waste." 45 Fed. Reg. 33099. By reason of these provisions, an incinerator that burned only household waste would not be considered a Subtitle C TSDF, since it processed only nonhazardous (i.e., household) waste, and it would not be considered a Subtitle C generator of hazardous waste and would be free to dispose of its ash in a Subtitle D landfill.

The 1980 regulations thus provided what is known as a "waste stream" exemption for household waste, i.e., an exemption covering that category of waste from generation through treatment to final disposal of residues. The regulation did not, however, exempt MWC ash from Subtitle C coverage if the incinerator that produced the ash burned anything *in addition to* household waste, such as what petitioner's facility burns:

nonhazardous industrial waste. Thus, a facility like petitioner's would qualify as a Subtitle C hazardous waste generator if the MWC ash it produced was sufficiently toxic —though it would still not qualify as a Subtitle C TSDF, since all the waste it took in would be characterized as nonhazardous. (An ash can be hazardous, even though the product from which it is generated is not, because in the new medium the contaminants are more concentrated and more readily leachable.)

Four years after these regulations were issued, Congress enacted the Hazardous and Solid Waste Amendments of 1984, which added to RCRA the "Clarification of Household Waste Exclusion" as § 3001(i). The essence of our task in this case is to determine whether, under that provision, the MWC ash generated by petitioner's facility —a facility that would have been considered a Subtitle C generator under the 1980 regulations—is subject to regulation as hazardous waste under Subtitle C. We conclude that it is.

Section 3001(i), entitled "Clarification of household waste exclusion," provides:

"A resource recovery facility recovering energy from the mass burning of municipal solid waste shall not be deemed to be treating, storing, disposing of, or otherwise managing hazardous wastes for the purposes of regulation under this subchapter, if—

"(1) such facility—

"(A) receives and burns only—

"(i) household waste (from single and multiple dwellings, hotels, motels, and other residential sources), and

"(ii) solid waste from commercial or industrial sources that does not contain hazardous waste identified or listed under this section, and

"(B) does not accept hazardous wastes identified or listed under this section, and

"(2) the owner or operator of such facility has established contractual requirements or other appropriate notification or inspection procedures to assure that hazardous wastes are not received at or burned in such facility."

The plain meaning of this language is that so long as a facility recovers energy by incineration of the appropriate wastes, *it* (the *facility*) is not subject to Subtitle C regulation as a facility that treats, stores, disposes of, or manages hazardous waste. The provision quite clearly does *not* contain any exclusion for the *ash itself.* Indeed, the waste the facility produces (as opposed to that which it receives) is not even mentioned. There is thus no express support for petitioners' claim of a waste-stream exemption.

Petitioners contend, however, that the practical effect of the statutory language is to exempt the ash by virtue of exempting the facility. If, they argue, the facility is not deemed to be treating, storing, or disposing of hazardous waste, then the ash that it treats, stores, or disposes of must itself be considered nonhazardous. There are several problems with this argument. First, as we have explained, the only exemption provided by the terms of the statute is for the *facility.* It is the facility, *not the ash*, that 'shall not be deemed' to be subject to regulation under Subtitle C. *Unlike* the preamble to the 1980 regulations, which had been in existence for four years by the time § 3001(i) was enacted, § 3001(i) does not explicitly exempt MWC ash generated by a resource recovery facility from regulation as a hazardous waste. In light of that difference, and given the statute's express declaration of national policy that "[w]aste that is ... generated should be treated, stored, or disposed of so as to minimize the present and future threat to human health and the environment," 42 U.S.C. § 6902(b), we cannot interpret the statute to permit MWC ash sufficiently toxic to qualify as hazardous to be disposed of in ordinary landfills.

Moreover, as the Court of Appeals observed, the statutory language does not even exempt the *facility* in its capacity as a *generator* of hazardous waste. RCRA defines "generation" as "the act or process of producing hazardous waste." 42 U.S.C. § 6903(6). There can be no question that the creation of ash by incinerating municipal waste constitutes "generation" of hazardous waste (assuming, of course, that the ash qualifies as hazardous under 42 U.S.C. § 6921 and its implementing regulations, 40 CFR pt. 261). Yet although § 3001(i) states that the exempted facility "shall not be deemed to be treating, storing, disposing of, or otherwise managing hazardous wastes," it significantly omits from the catalogue the word "*generating*." Petitioners say that because the activities listed as exempt encompass the full scope of the facility's operation, the failure to mention the activity of generating is insignificant. But the statute itself refutes this. Each of the three specific terms used in § 3001(i)—"treating," "storing," and "disposing of"—is separately defined by RCRA, and none covers the production of hazardous waste. The fourth and less specific term ("otherwise managing") is also defined, to mean "collection, source separation, storage, transportation, processing, treatment, recovery, and disposal," 42 U.S.C. § 6903(7)—just about every hazardous waste-related activity *except* generation. We think it follows from the carefully constructed text of section 3001(i) that while a resource recovery facility's management activities are excluded from Subtitle C regulation, its generation of toxic ash is not.

Petitioners appeal to the legislative history of § 3001(i), which includes, in the Senate Committee Report, the statement that "[a]ll waste management activities of such a facility, including the *generation*, transportation, treatment, storage and disposal of waste shall be covered by the exclusion." S. Rep. No. 98-284, p. 61 (1983) (emphasis added). But it is the statute, and not the Committee Report, which is the authoritative expression of the law, and the statute prominently *omits* reference to generation. ***
Petitioners point out that the activity by which they "treat" municipal waste is the very same activity by which they "generate" MWC ash, to wit, incineration. But there is nothing extraordinary about an activity's being exempt for some purposes and nonexempt for others. The incineration here is exempt from TSDF regulation, but subject to regulation as hazardous waste generation. ***

Our interpretation is confirmed by comparing § 3001(i) with another statutory exemption in RCRA. In the Superfund Amendments and Reauthorization Act of 1986, Congress amended 42 U.S.C. § 6921 to provide that an "owner and operator of equipment used to recover methane from a landfill shall not be deemed to be managing, generating, transporting, treating, storing, or disposing of hazardous or liquid wastes within the meaning of" Subtitle C. This provision, in contrast to § 3001(i), provides a complete exemption by including the term "generating" in its list of covered activities.

*** We agree with respondents that this provision "shows that Congress knew how to draft a waste stream exemption in RCRA when it wanted to."

Petitioners contend that our interpretation of § 3001(i) turns the provision into an "empty gesture," since even under the pre-existing regime an incinerator burning household waste and nonhazardous industrial waste was exempt from the Subtitle C TSDF provisions. If § 3001(i) did not extend the waste-stream exemption to the product of such a combined household/nonhazardous-industrial treatment facility, petitioners argue, it did nothing at all. But it is not nothing to codify a household waste exemption that had previously been subject to agency revision; nor is it nothing (though petitioners may value it as less than nothing) to *restrict* the exemption that the agency previously provided—which is what the provision here achieved, by withholding all waste-stream exemption for waste processed by resource recovery facilities, even for the waste stream passing through an exclusively household-waste facility.[4]

We also do not agree with petitioners' contention that our construction renders § 3001(i) ineffective for its intended purpose of promoting household/nonhazardous-industrial resource recovery facilities by subjecting them "to the potentially enormous expense of managing ash residue as a hazardous waste." It is simply not true that a facility which is (as our interpretation says these facilities are) a hazardous waste "generator," is also deemed to be "managing" hazardous waste under RCRA. Section 3001(i) clearly exempts these facilities from Subtitle C TSDF regulations, thus enabling them to avoid the "full brunt of EPA's enforcement efforts under RCRA." Practice Guide § 29.05[1].

RCRA's twin goals of encouraging resource recovery and protecting against contamination sometimes conflict. It is not unusual for legislation to contain diverse purposes that must be reconciled, and the most reliable guide for that task is the enacted text. Here that requires us to reject the Solicitor General's plea for deference to the EPA's interpretation, which goes beyond the scope of whatever ambiguity § 3001(i) contains. Section 3001(i) simply cannot be read to contain the cost-saving waste stream exemption petitioners seek.

* * *

[Dissenting opinion of Justices Stevens and O'Connor omitted.]

NOTES

1. Assume that, after this decision, the City of Chicago tests the ash generated by its resource recovery facility, and finds that it routinely exhibits the toxicity characteristic. The ash is now considered to be hazardous waste, and must therefore be

---

[4] We express no opinion as to the validity of EPA's household waste regulation as applied to resource recovery facilities *before* the effective date of § 3001(i). Furthermore, since the statute in question addresses only resource recovery facilities, not household waste in general, we are unable to reach any conclusions concerning the validity of EPA's regulatory scheme for household wastes not processed by resource recovery facilities.

treated in accordance with the land ban regulations before it can be land disposed. Assume further that the plant manager determines that the city can treat the ash on-site for significantly less than it would cost the city to send the ash off-site for comparable treatment. Is the city required to obtain a RCRA treatment permit for the facility in order to treat the ash, or is it exempt under § 3001(i) of the statute?

2. If the facility is exempt under § 3001(i) but the ash is not, at what point in the generation and handling of the ash does it become subject to RCRA regulation if it is hazardous? In the EPA's view, RCRA jurisdiction attaches when an ash stream exits the combustion building. 60 Fed. Reg. 6666 (1995).

3. When you study CERCLA, consider whether a municipality that sent its incinerator ash to a solid waste landfill prior to *City of Chicago v. Environmental Defense Fund* now faces clean-up liability as a CERCLA generator for having arranged for the disposal of a hazardous substance (the ash) at the (now-leaking) landfill.

4. Because the permit process for treatment, storage, and disposal facilities is so time-consuming and costly, the substantive provisions of RCRA are so complex and extensive, and the need for a permit triggers the EPA's authority to require facility-wide clean-up (see chapter 5.A. regarding RCRA's corrective action provisions), entities potentially subject to RCRA TSD regulation have painstakingly explored the nooks and crannies of the various statutory and regulatory exemptions. *See* Richard Stoll, *Coping With the RCRA Hazardous Waste System: A Few Practical Points for Fun and Profit,* 1 ENVTL. HAZARDS 6 (July 1989). The following case addresses a widely-invoked exclusion, designed to harmonize RCRA permitting with the extensive NPDES permit program administered under the Clean Water Act.

UNITED STATES V. ALLEGAN METAL FINISHING CO.
696 F.Supp. 275 (W.D.Mich. 1988)

ENSLEN, District Judge.

Plaintiff United States of America ("plaintiff") brings this action pursuant to provisions of the federal Resource Conservation and Recovery Act ("RCRA"). Presently before me is defendant Allegan Metal Finishing Company's ("defendant" or "Allegan") motion for immediate consideration of certain threshold liability issues which were previously set forth in the parties' cross-motions for summary judgment. The cross-motions for summary judgment address defendant's alleged RCRA liability with respect to two "holding ponds" which process wastewaters that were discharged from Allegan's metal finishing facility. ***

Allegan, a Michigan corporation, has operated its Michigan facility since 1959. Allegan performs its electroplating process for a variety of industries including the automobile and appliance industries. As a part of its electroplating process, Allegan produces various wastewaters as by-products including zinc-cyanide, zinc-chloride, chromate and acid and alkali rinses. Allegan's wastewater treatments system, as of

November 18, 1980, and prior to the use of its current wastewater treatment plan, included separate chemical treatment of wastewater from the zinc electroplating process and of wastewater from all rinses and related chromate post-treatments. After this separate chemical treatment, the treated wastewaters were then combined and treated physically. Since 1972, Allegan has maintained the two holding ponds at issue here on a parcel of property which is situated between its manufacturing site and the Kalamazoo River.

It is also undisputed that Allegan began using its two holding ponds pursuant to a 1972 State of Michigan Stipulation No. V-00250. Until October 1987, Allegan discharged wastewaters, treated according to the process described above, from its Allegan, Michigan facility into the two holding ponds. This discharge is characterized by the U.S. Environmental Protection Agency ("EPA") as wastewater treatment sludges from electroplating operations designated by the EPA as listed hazardous waste F006 pursuant to RCRA regulations described at 40 C.F.R. Part 261, Subpart D.

These holding ponds act as "large sand filters" through which the treated wastewaters pass. Treated precipitated solids are allowed to collect within the ponds and are characterized as "sludge." At the end of 1985, Allegan was generating approximately 0.25 tons of ("dried") sludge per day. Until approximately 1981, Allegan periodically dredged the sludge from the ponds and placed it on the banks of the ponds to dry. Allegan would then have the sludge transported to a properly licensed off-site disposal facility. Allegan last transported such sludges from the ponds in 1983.

* * *

On June 23, 1980, Allegan submitted to the EPA a notification of hazardous waste activity identifying F006 as a waste by-product which was generated at the Allegan facility. On November 15, 1982, Allegan submitted to the EPA an amended notification of hazardous waste activity which identified waste F008 and deleted waste F006 as waste generated by Allegan.

On December 10, 1984, the EPA issued to Allegan an administrative complaint pursuant to § 3008 of RCRA, 42 U.S.C. § 6928. The administrative complaint alleged that Allegan failed to comply with the RCRA permitting requirements and interim status standards for the holding ponds. It is apparently now undisputed that Allegan submitted a RCRA Part A interim status permit application for the ponds on February 21, 1985 and that the EPA accepted the application as if timely filed. Further, in its memorandum in response to defendant's reply brief in opposition to its motion for partial summary judgment, plaintiff asserts that the issue of whether defendant has interim status at all is not an issue in this case because the Allegan facility failed to comply with section 3005(e) in order to maintain authority to operate. ***

The EPA and Allegan settled the RCRA claims at issue in the administrative complaint by entering into a Consent Agreement and Final Order ("CAFO") entered by the EPA Regional Administrator on June 28, 1985. On May 15, 1985, Allegan submitted a contingency plan to EPA and the Michigan Department of Natural Resources ("MDNR"). That plan was revised for EPA and MDNR approval on June 15, 1985. On April 5, 1985, Allegan submitted its Closure Plan for the holding ponds to the

EPA. *** On September 27, 1985, the EPA approved Allegan's Closure Plan pursuant to further revisions as defined by the EPA.

On August 15, 1985, Allegan submitted to the EPA satisfactory hazardous waste personnel training records. On April 23, 1985, Allegan submitted to the EPA a groundwater assessment plan. *** Finally, on January 20, 1986, the EPA approved Allegan's revised groundwater assessment plan.

On January 31, 1986, Allegan submitted to the EPA an irrevocable letter of credit with standby trust which satisfied the RCRA financial assurance for closure requirements. It is undisputed that Allegan has not demonstrated that it has obtained insurance for bodily injury and personal damage to third-parties caused by non-sudden accidental occurrences arising from the operation of the holding ponds. ***

*   *   *

Discussion

The "Threshold Issues"

Defendant first argues that RCRA applies only to "solid waste." See 42 U.S.C. §§ 6902 & 6903. Defendant argues that under § 1004(27) of RCRA the term "solid waste" does not include "solid or dissolved materials in ... industrial discharges which are point sources subject to permits under section 402 of the Federal Water Pollution Control Act, ..." 42 U.S.C. § 6903(27). Plaintiff claims, however, that *the wastewaters discharged into defendant's holding ponds constitute "solid waste"* which is further characterized as "hazardous" under RCRA.

Defendant asserts that the wastewater discharged by it to the holding ponds at issue here has at all relevant times been subject to regulation by the State of Michigan Water Resources Commission under wastewater discharge permits. Defendant asserts further that in 1972 it was permitted to discharge this treated wastewater to the holding ponds pursuant to a Michigan Water Resources Commission Stipulation. In 1982, defendant argues, pursuant to the National Pollutant Discharge Elimination System ("NPDES") program under § 402 of the Federal Water Pollution Control Act (33 U.S.C. § 1342), and the federally authorized State permit system administered under the Michigan Water Resources Commission Act Rules, Part 21, it was issued a discharge permit which superseded the 1972 stipulation. Finally, defendant asserts that the 1982 NPDES permit required upgrading defendant's wastewater treatment system for discharge to the surface water, and then closure of the holding ponds which would be bypassed by the NPDES discharge.

In sum, defendant is arguing that it is the NPDES regulatory scheme rather than the RCRA program which controls the wastewater discharge which, defendant asserts, is at issue here. Defendant concludes that based upon the NPDES permit regulation, defendant's wastewater discharge to the holding ponds at issue is not "solid waste" regulated under RCRA and that plaintiff's complaint must therefore be dismissed.

*** Plaintiff argues that defendant's reading and application of the definition of "solid waste" is flawed. I agree. The definition of "solid waste" provides in pertinent part:

> The term "solid waste" means any garbage, refuse, sludge from a waste supply treatment plant, or air pollution control facility and other discarded material, including solid, liquid, semisolid, or contained gaseous material resulting from industrial, commercial, mining, and agricultural operations, and from community activities, *but does not include ... industrial discharges which are point sources subject to permits under section 1342 of Title 33 ....*

Section 1004(27) of RCRA, 42 U.S.C. § 6903 (emphasis added).

It is clear that the exclusion enshrined in the definition of solid waste is for those *actual discharges from point sources* which are made pursuant to and authorized by a NPDES permit. Further, the regulation that defines "solid waste" states that "(t)his exclusion applies only to the *actual permit discharges.*" 40 C.F.R. § 261.4(2) (emphasis added).

It is also clear that defendant was not authorized and in fact, did not discharge wastewater from its facility pursuant to a NPDES permit until October 1987. Further, defendant was issued a NPDES permit October 1982. The permit required defendant to construct a wastewater treatment system which was to be operational by 1984. Defendant thus had no permit to discharge wastewater from its facility into the Kalamazoo River until the wastewater treatment was operational. It was not until late 1987 that defendant started actually discharging wastewater pursuant to that permit. Prior to October 1987, it appears that defendant discharged wastewater from its facility to the two on-site holding ponds at issue here. Accordingly, I find no merit in defendant's argument that a NPDES permit—which did not authorize discharges into the Kalamazoo River until October 1987 —somehow precludes RCRA regulation with respect to the disposal of hazardous waste to its on-site ponds that occurred continuously from 1980 until October 1987. This is especially so in the face of the above-cited "Comment" attached to the regulation defining solid waste exclusions. *See* 40 C.F.R. § 261.4(2).

Moreover, I am persuaded by plaintiff's argument that even allowing that defendant has discharged wastewater from its facility since October 1987 *under the NPDES permit,* that facility is nevertheless still subject to regulation under RCRA to the extent that the facility generates, treats and stores hazardous waste. Plaintiff points out that the regulation that defines solid waste based on discharges pursuant to a NPDES permit states that "(t)his exclusion ... does not exclude industrial wastewaters while they are being collected, stored or treated before discharge, *nor does it exclude sludges that are generated by industrial wastewater treatment.*" 40 C.F.R. § 261.4(2) (emphasis added). It is clear that the pond sludge at issue here falls into the latter category.

* * *

Because defendant has not satisfied all the requirements of the CAFO in a timely manner, plaintiff has brought an action to enforce the CAFO. Moreover, plaintiff alleges that defendant is presently in violation of RCRA. ***

Plaintiff's First Claim for Relief

Plaintiff's first claim for relief alleges that defendant is liable under § 3008(a) of RCRA for violation of the permitting requirements of § 3005(a) and (e) of RCRA, 42 U.S.C. § 6925(a) and (e). *****

Defendant's liability for violations of § 3005(a) and (e) can be established either by proving that defendant did not achieve interim status on November 18, 1980, or, in the alternative, even if defendant is construed to have met the requirements for interim status, it lost that status on November 8, 1985 when it *failed to certify compliance* with the financial assurance requirements. *****

*   *   *

I am not wholly unsympathetic to defendant's arguments that it was commercially impracticable to fulfill the financial responsibility requirements by November 8, 1985. However, it appears to me that it was the intent of Congress that interim status cannot be maintained beyond November 8, 1985 unless an operator *certifies* compliance with the financial responsibility requirements by that date. Moreover, it is clear that an "operator cannot certify compliance if the facility is not actually in compliance." *Vineland*, 810 F.2d at 409 n.4 (3d Cir. 1987).

*   *   *

I will now discuss further the four specific elements which must be established in order to make out a violation of section 3005(a) & (e).

1) *Defendant is an operator of a hazardous waste facility.*

Defendant's admissions establish that defendant is the owner or operator of a facility which produces wastewaters which are hazardous wastes.   Moreover, defendant's own waste analysis indicates that its ponds contain "characteristic" hazardous wastes in that they contain levels of chromium in excess of the EPA regulatory requirements.

(2) *Defendant's facility is a land disposal facility.*

*   *   *

I reject defendant's argument that the term "land disposal facility" used in section 3005(e)(2) of RCRA is constrained by the regulatory definition of "disposal facility" found at 40 C.F.R. § 261.10 [sic—§ 260.10].   The regulatory definition limits a "disposal facility" to a location where hazardous waste is "intentionally placed" and will remain after closure.   Plaintiff argues that this definition is at odds with the broad definition of "land disposal" and "disposal" contained in the statute and that it is the statutory definition which must control. *****

The statutory definition of "land disposal" appears to me to include "any placement" in a surface impoundment—whether or not the material is intended to remain there after the facility is closed.   To adopt defendant's definition would appear to frustrate the intent of Congress in enacting section 3005(e)(2). It is clear that the intent of Congress was to ensure that all facilities where hazardous wastes are placed on the ground—and for that reason threaten to contaminate the groundwater—have a groundwater monitoring program and will make assurance of financial capability to remedy environmental damage. ***

* * *

Here, defendant argues that while it intended to place its wastewaters in the holding ponds, it did so "without the knowledge or understanding that they would subsequently be characterized as 'hazardous' and certainly with no intent that they would remain in the ponds after closure." Defendant argues further that its EPA-approved closure plan is characterized as a "clean-close" which apparently means that the wastes in the ponds are to be completely excavated and transported off-site for disposal.

I simply cannot accept defendant's crabbed definition of "land disposal facility" drawn from the regulatory definition of "disposal facility" found at 40 C.F.R. § 261.10 [sic]. Again, such a definition would defeat the intent of section 3005 and would also conflict with the *statutory* definitions of "land disposal" and "disposal." Nor will I read into the statute some "state of mind" requirement as to whether the waste and/or wastewater at issue is "hazardous" or whether the defendant intended the waste to remain (after closure). It is clear that a facility is subject to regulations as a "disposal facility," and/or a "land disposal facility" where the facility is "intentionally used" to discharge hazardous waste. Even more important, the civil violations of RCRA provisions are properly characterized as strict liability offenses.

* * *

Accordingly, I find that the two ponds at the Allegan facility are surface impoundments within the meaning of RCRA and as such were subject to the November 8, 1985 LOIS deadline.

3) Defendant failed to certify compliance or comply with the requirements of § 3005(e)(2).

I have previously discussed in some detail the financial responsibility requirements and concluded that defendant failed to certify on or before November 8, 1985 that it had obtained the required liability insurance coverage and financial assurance for closure. Defendant admits that it did not obtain an irrevocable standby letter of credit which satisfied the financial assurance for closure requirement until January 31, 1986.

Further, I reject in this enforcement action, defendant's assertion of the viability of an "impossibility" defense. ***

4) Defendant operated the facility without a permit and without the benefit of "interim status" beyond the November 8, 1985 cut-off date.

Defendant's admissions establish that it continued to place listed hazardous waste F006 into at least one of the holding ponds after November 8, 1985. Further, it appears that this hazardous waste disposal continued until October, 1987.

I conclude that partial summary judgment is appropriate on plaintiff's first claim, in that it has satisfied the requisite elements to make out a violation of section 3005(a) & (e).

* * *

NOTES

1. Regarding the EPA's statement that the point source exclusion "does not exclude industrial wastewaters while they are being collected, stored or treated before discharge," compare the exemption from both the interim status standards and the final standards which applies to, *inter alia*, "wastewater treatment units." *See* 40 C.F.R. §§ 264.1(g)(6), 265.1(c)(10), and the definition in § 260.10. Throughout RCRA, it is critical to distinguish between exemptions from the definition of solid or hazardous waste and exemptions from various regulatory requirements that otherwise apply to the generation, treatment, storage, and/or disposal of hazardous waste.

2. The 1984 amendments to RCRA reflected Congress' concern that many pre-RCRA land disposal facilities were leaking, causing soil and groundwater contamination. The amendments sought expressly to discourage land disposal of hazardous waste, to impose stringent design and monitoring requirements upon those land disposal facilities that do exist, and to reduce the volume and toxicity of hazardous waste that is sent to landfills. *See, e.g.,* RCRA §§ 1002(b)(7) (congressional finding that land disposal should be minimized or eliminated), 3004(c)-(m) land ban provisions, 3004(o) and (p) (minimum technology and groundwater monitoring requirements), and 3005(e)(2), (i), and (j) (upgrade requirements for land disposal facilities and surface impoundments). The cited provisions of § 3005 required interim status land disposal facilities and surface impoundments to upgrade various aspects of their design and/or operations as a condition of retaining interim status. Congress did not want to wait until land disposal facilities underwent Part B permit review to determine whether they were operating safely.

According to EPA figures, two-thirds of the nation's 1600 land disposal facilities went out of business on November 8, 1985, rather than try to meet the loss of interim status ("LOIS") requirements of § 3005(e)(2). By November 8, 1988, when the EPA was required to grant or deny all Part B permit applications for land disposal facilities, only 168 land disposal facility permits had been issued. Of these 168 permitted operating facilities, most were run by companies for their own on-site waste disposal operations. *See* 19 Env't Rep. (BNA) 1460-61 (1988). By 1996, only 23 commercial hazardous waste landfills were in operation, with two expanding, two applying for expansion permits, and ten new landfill proposals in under consideration. *Commercial Hazardous Waste Management Facilities: 1997 Survey of North America*, 15 HAZ. WASTE CONSULTANT (Elsevier Science), March/April 1997, at 4.6, 4.58.

3. According to a 1988 report by the General Accounting Office, the inability to obtain insurance was the reason for ceasing operations most often given by companies, particularly smaller ones, that left the hazardous waste land disposal business after 1982.

Also according to the GAO report, the average premium for pollution liability insurance in 1986 was eleven times higher than in 1982. The number of insurance companies writing pollution coverage dropped markedly over the same time period. Sudden accidental insurance that would satisfy the requirements of 40 C.F.R. §§ 264.147(a) and 265.147(a) for all hazardous waste treatment, storage, or disposal facilities was written by only 31 companies in 1986. Coverage for nonsudden accidental occurrences that would comply with the requirements for *land disposal* facilities in sections 264.147(b) and 265.147(b) was written by only 12 companies in 1986. Reports to GAO revealed only 17 "nonsudden" policies written in 1986. The clear indication of the GAO report was that hazardous waste facility managers increasingly had been forced to rely on the other financial assurance mechanisms allowed by the RCRA regulations, particularly the "financial test" option, 40 C.F.R. §§ 264.147(f) and 265.147(f). *See* 19 Env't Rep. (BNA) 1869-70 (1989).

A GAO update report in 1994, reflecting 1990 and 1991 data, painted a similar picture.

> The majority of companies operating treatment, storage, and disposal facilities in 1991 that attempted to obtain pollution insurance found that it was difficult to obtain. GAO identified 24 insurance companies that provided pollution liability insurance in some form. *** GAO found that closure and post-closure insurance was available to treatment, storage, and disposal facilities only under exception circumstances.

> About one third of treatment, storage, and disposal companies are are subject to the financial responsibility requirements of the act use liability insurance to cover accidental occurrences. ***

> The difficulty experienced by land disposal companies in obtaining pollution insurance in 1991 has not significantly lessened since 1986.

GENERAL ACCOUNTING OFFICE, HAZARDOUS WASTE: AN UPDATE ON THE COST AND AVAILABILITY OF POLLUTION INSURANCE (1994) (GAO/PEMD-94-16).

4. Any TSD facility that was in operation at any time after RCRA took effect in 1980 is subject to the following closure process when it ceases operation: All TSD facilities must have closure plans, approved by the EPA or authorized state, while still in operation. (Part B permits will not be issued unless an acceptable closure plan is part of the permit application.) When a TSD, or any unit thereof, ceases operations, it must implement its closure plan. If the closure removes all hazardous waste from the site (known as a "clean closure"), then the facility need not obtain a post-closure permit. If hazardous waste remains on-site following closure, then the facility must obtain a post-closure permit, which requires continued operation and maintenance activities for a 30-year period. Before they even commence operations, newly-permitted TSD facilities are required to demonstrate financial responsibility for implementing closure and post-closure activities. *See* 40 C.F.R. Part 264, Subparts G and H (for Part B-permitted facilities) and Part 265, Subparts G and H (for interim status facilities).

5. In what circumstances does passive treatment, storage, or disposal trigger RCRA's requirements for the operation and/or closure of a TSD facility? In what circumstances is intentional treatment, storage, or disposal necessary to invoke the TSD

requirements? In *In re Consolidated Land Disposal Regulation Litigation*, 938 F.2d 1386 (D.C.Cir. 1991), the D.C. Circuit upheld the EPA's position that although a facility that ceased receiving hazardous waste prior to the implementation of RCRA regulations was not a disposal facility under the EPA's regulations requiring operating facility permits, it was nonetheless a disposal facility under the statutory definitions and must therefore obtain a post-closure permit to ensure proper maintenance of the closed facility.

7.   One subset of treatment, storage, and disposal facilities—combustion facilities—has attracted close scrutiny and generated considerable controversy. After the following introductory Note, attention focuses on a combustion facility that the EPA accused of "sham recycling."

NOTE REGARDING COMBUSTION FACILITIES

Although combustion was earlier viewed as a promising and less-polluting alternative to the land disposal of hazardous waste, in May 1993 the EPA signaled a policy shift reflecting growing concerns about the environmental and health impacts of hazardous waste combustion. The EPA's Draft Strategy for Combustion of Hazardous Waste in Incinerators and Boilers (May 18, 1993) called for an 18-month moratorium on the permitting of new combustion capacity, the performance of site-specific risk assessments at combustion facilities, more stringent restrictions on air emissions from combustion facilities, enhanced public participation in the permitting process, and enhanced inspection and enforcement. The EPA announced its draft combustion strategy simultaneously with its waste minimization guidance for hazardous waste generators, reflecting a goal of reducing the need for additional combustion capacity by reducing the volume of hazardous waste generated in the first instance.

Much of the "draft" strategy remains in effect, except that the EPA usually drops the term "draft" from the title. The strategy applies to hazardous waste incinerators, which have been subject to RCRA's Subtitle C requirements from the outset, as well as boilers and industrial furnaces ("BIFs") burning hazardous waste, which did not come under comparable RCRA regulation until 1991, 56 Fed. Reg. 7134 (1991) ("the BIF rules"). The BIF rules have been the subject of controversy and litigation. A multiparty suit challenging the BIF rules resulted in the settlement of many issues in October 1993; the settlement included a series of deadlines requiring the EPA to initiate various rulemakings concerning possible amendments to the BIF rules and to the regulations governing hazardous waste incinerators. In *Horsehead Resource Development Co. v. EPA*, 16 F.3d 1246 (D.C. Cir. 1994), *cert. denied*, 513 U.S. 816 (1994), the D.C. Circuit resolved the issues that had not been settled, upholding the EPA's regulatory authority and the content of all but one aspect of the challenged regulations. The opinion provides a concise history of the regulation of BIF facilities under RCRA:

Hazardous waste is burned for three purposes: to destroy the waste (incineration), to serve as fuel (energy recovery), and to recover usable materials such as metals (materials recovery). Hazardous waste often has a great deal of heat value when used as fuel; and this use also has the benefit of destroying or at least reducing the volume of the waste, thereby reducing reliance on landfilling. In its early attempts to implement Subtitle C, the EPA was particularly concerned that its regulations not discourage beneficial uses of hazardous wastes, such as energy recovery and recycling. For this reason, in 1981, the EPA deferred regulating air emissions from BIFs burning hazardous waste as fuel or for materials recovery, but did adopt rules controlling emissions from hazardous waste incinerators, which burn waste primarily in order to destroy it.

Exempting facilities that burned hazardous waste for energy recovery from Subtitle C's requirements created a regulatory "loophole" by means of which over half of the hazardous waste generated in the United States came to be burned in BIFs not subject to RCRA. Congress closed this loophole by enacting RCRA section 3004(q) as part of the Hazardous and Solid Waste Amendments of 1984. Section 3004(q) set a deadline of November 8, 1986 for the EPA to promulgate regulations governing the burning of hazardous waste for energy recovery.

In 1985, in response to section 3004(q), the EPA imposed its first controls on the marketing and burning of hazardous waste fuels. These regulations provide that hazardous waste or fuels containing hazardous waste are subject to transportation and storage controls under Subtitle C prior to being burned as fuel or being blended or processed for use as fuel.

In 1987, again pursuant to section 3004(q), the EPA published its proposed BIF Rule for public comment. *** The final BIF Rule *** was published in the Federal Register in 1991.

Id. at 1253.

In April 1996, the EPA proposed controversial emission standards for three categories of hazardous waste combustors: hazardous waste incinerators; hazardous waste-burning cement kilns; and lightweight aggregate kilns. 61 Fed. Reg. 17358 (1996). In May 1997, the EPA made available revised data regarding the proposed regulations, announced that it is considering significant changes to the proposed standards, and requested public comment. 62 Fed. Reg. 24212 (1997). When ultimately issued, the regulations will jointly implement RCRA and the Clean Air Act with respect to air emissions from these hazardous waste facilities. Plans to consolidate the permit requirements under the two statutes appear to be foundering on concerns that the statutes have different permit renewal and modification procedures, as well as separate and potentially duplicative enforcement and citizen suit provisions.

In August 1996, the EPA issued the first permit to burn hazardous waste as fuel under the 1991 BIF rule. The BIF permit, issued to Ash Grove Cement Co. of Chanute, Kansas, was challenged by incinerator interests, environmentalists, a group of citizens, and the permittee itself. *In re Ash Grove Cement Co.*, RCRA Appeal No. 96-4 (EPA Env. App. Bd., filed Sept. 13, 1996).

In addition to new regulations, the EPA's combustion strategy is also reflected in a vigorous enforcement effort directed at hazardous waste combustion facilities. Since the EPA issued its Draft Combustion Strategy in 1993, it has commenced at least three clusters of enforcement actions against some 80 hazardous waste combustion facilities. *BIFs Hardest Hit by EPA's Combustion Strategy,* 13 HAZ. WASTE CONSULTANT (Elsevier Science), March/April 1995, at 3.4.

One of the EPA's most aggressive and most visible enforcement actions was against Marine Shale Processors, a hazardous waste combustion facility sued for violations of RCRA, the Clean Water Act, and the Clean Air Act. On April 18, 1996, the Fifth Circuit handed down a trilogy of decisions, all concerning Marine Shale Processors, which collectively constitute a crash course in RCRA. The first decision is the enforcement action brought by the EPA; an excerpt concerning the mixture rule issue is included in chapter 2.B. The District Court assessed $8 million in penalties against Marine Shale for violations of RCRA, the Clean Air Act, and the Clean Water Act. In portions of the opinion not included below, the Fifth Circuit upheld the RCRA and Clean Air Act penalties and remanded the Clean Water Act penalty for recalculation. The second decision features a claim by a Marine Shale customer that the facility is exempt from RCRA regulation. The third decision addresses the EPA's denial of Marine Shale's application for a Boiler and Industrial Facility Permit under the BIF regulations described above.

UNITED STATES V. MARINE SHALE PROCESSORS
81 F.3d 1329 (5th Cir. 1996)

Before REYNALDO G. GARZA, KING and HIGGINBOTHAM.
HIGGINBOTHAM, Circuit Judge.

This case, along with Nos. 94-30419 and 95-60228, concerns the past actions and future fate of Marine Shale Processors, Inc., a hazardous waste treatment facility. The cases involve multiple aspects of each of the federal environmental laws as affecting disputes between the Environmental Protection Agency and MSP. We provide a brief explanation of the three cases in this opinion before discussing the specific issues raised by this appeal.

I

In 1985, Marine Shale Processors, Inc. opened a facility in Amelia, Louisiana purporting to recycle hazardous waste through its newly acquired rotary kiln, a mechanism 275 feet long and 11 feet in diameter with the capacity to heat materials to temperatures in excess of 2000 degrees Fahrenheit. MSP's treatment process began with placement of materials in its kiln. From there, most material traveled through oxidizers and slag boxes. The process generated significant quantities of smoke, flue gases, and air particles. Carcinogenic heavy metals tended to concentrate in these air particles. The air pollutants passed through baghouses, which collected some of the material in the form of caked dust. The dust dropped off the bags to the bottom of the baghouses, where it was collected, run through the oxidizers and slag boxes, then combined with the rest of the material produced from the primary process. The nature of MSP's operation made it subject to federal and state laws limiting pollution of water, air, and land. These laws required MSP to obtain permits specifying the type and amount of pollutants that it could discharge into the environment.

RCRA regulations divide facilities using heat to process hazardous waste into three basic types: incinerators, boilers, and industrial furnaces. *See* 40 C.F.R. § 260.10 (defining all three terms). From 1980 to 1991, the regulations required only facilities engaged in incineration to obtain permits before operating. *See* Final Rule, Burning of Hazardous Wastes in Boilers and Industrial Furnaces, 56 Fed.Reg. 7134, 7138 (1991); 40 C.F.R. pt. 264 subpt. O. In 1991, EPA amended the regulations to require all facilities using thermal processes to treat hazardous waste to obtain one of two types of permits. Incinerators needed Subpart O permits, and boilers and industrial furnaces were required to obtain BIF permits. See 40 C.F.R. pt. 266 subpt. H. Since opening operations in 1985, Marine Shale has claimed that its kiln system constitutes an industrial furnace under the RCRA regulations. When EPA amended the regulations to require all thermal treatment facilities to acquire permits, MSP filed a six volume permit application with EPA Region VI. Four years later, EPA finally denied this permit application. Invoking our authority to set aside final agency action under the Administrative Procedures Act, MSP appealed the permit denial. In number 95-60228, we address that appeal.

In 1990, the United States sued MSP under RCRA, alleging that MSP was an incinerator of hazardous waste operating without the required Subpart O permit and was illegally disposing incinerator ash on the ground. The United States later amended its complaint to allege violations of the CWA [Clean Water Act], the CAA [Clean Air Act], and other provisions of RCRA. Southern Wood Piedmont Company, the entity sending the largest volume of hazardous waste to Marine Shale, intervened and sought a declaration that all material resulting from the processing of its waste was exempt from RCRA regulation. ***

Early in the litigation, District Court Judge Haik granted the United States' motion for a preliminary injunction prohibiting MSP from transporting the material resulting from its process away from grounds owned by MSP or its sister corporation, Recycling Park, Inc. After allegations that representatives of MSP attempted to bribe Judge Haik, Fifth Circuit Chief Judge Politz ordered the case transferred to Judge Adrian Duplantier, who has presided since.

Judge Duplantier divided the litigation into phases. In the first phase, the United States and SWP tried their RCRA claims to a jury. After a five-week trial, the jury was unable to agree to answers to four of thirteen interrogatories. Judge Duplantier declared a mistrial on the claims prosecuted by the United States and granted SWP's motion for partial judgment under Fed.R.Civ.P. 54(b). Dissatisfied with the scope of this judgment, SWP appealed to this court. Contending that the district court erred in entering the Rule

54(b) judgment, the United States cross-appealed. In number 94-30419 [81 F.3d 1361], we address the appeals from this judgment.

After this unsuccessful attempt to resolve RCRA issues, Judge Duplantier proceeded to the later phases of the case. The court conducted a bench trial on the CWA and CAA issues. It also resolved certain outstanding RCRA claims by summary judgment. The sum of the district court's rulings was that MSP had violated several provisions of all three environmental statutes. The district court fined MSP for each violation and granted the United States' request for injunctive relief. *** Judge Duplantier entered a second Rule 54(b) judgment incorporating all matters decided at the later phase of the litigation. In this case, we address issues arising from this second Rule 54(b) judgment.

* * *

III

The district court decided all RCRA issues relevant to this appeal by summary judgment. In particular, the district court held that MSP had violated land ban regulations on numerous occasions. In addition, the district court held that MSP had stored K-listed wastes without a permit or interim status, but ruled that MSP had interim status to store F-listed wastes. Both the United States and MSP appeal the district court's RCRA rulings. ***

* * *

Congress passed the current version of RCRA in 1976. 42 U.S.C. § 6925(a) directed EPA to promulgate regulations governing the issuance of permits to store hazardous wastes on the ground. Realizing that EPA could not issue permits to all existing facilities simultaneously with the promulgation of these regulations, Congress created a grandfathering scheme granting interim status to certain facilities. In order to achieve interim status, a facility must have (1) existed at the time it was rendered subject to a storage regulation, (2) filed a hazardous waste notification form and, (3) filed a permit application with either EPA or the relevant state regulatory body. RCRA treated facilities that had taken these three steps as though they had been issued permits until EPA had finally resolved the pending permit application.

In 1980, EPA promulgated regulations requiring certain facilities to obtain permits covering storage before storing F- or K-listed wastes, but not for certain other types of waste. ***

In 1984, EPA certified LDEQ's state hazardous waste program, allowing LDEQ to regulate the storage of hazardous waste on its own and placing primary responsibility for RCRA enforcement with LDEQ. MSP asserts, and EPA does not dispute, that Louisiana's regulations initially allowed recycling facilities to store wastes other than those included in the K- and F-listings without permits. MSP began operations in 1985 without a RCRA storage permit.

Shortly after opening, MSP began accepting D- and U-listed wastes. It also began receiving material manifested as "K001" from two customers, Colfax Creosoteing Co. and Durawood Treating Co. ***

* * *

Sometime in 1985, LDEQ and MSP entered into discussions concerning whether MSP's activity constituted "storage" under the relevant regulations. In these discussions, LDEQ suggested that MSP apply for a storage permit under forthcoming regulations requiring facilities to obtain a permit to store all listed wastes, as opposed to just K- and F-listed wastes. MSP and EPA agree that on January 1, 1986, LDEQ promulgated these storage regulations, which required all facilities to obtain RCRA permits before storing any type of listed waste. In response, MSP submitted to LDEQ a notification form and Part I of a permit application to store U- and D-listed wastes in early January, 1986. On January 31, 1986, MSP amended its application to include a request for permission to store F- and K-listed wastes. Two months later, MSP began accepting F-listed wastes. On June 9, 1986, LDEQ wrote MSP a letter stating its view that MSP had obtained interim status and could store any hazardous waste listed in its application form until LDEQ ruled on the application. ***

In this action, the United States alleged that MSP stored K- and F-listed wastes without a permit or interim status. *** [T]he district court fined MSP $1,000,000 for storing K-listed wastes without a permit. In assessing this fine, the court considered as a mitigating factor LDEQ's communications to MSP in 1986 and thereafter ***.

* * *

We hold that a facility may not achieve interim status under RCRA if it has illegally stored listed waste without a permit prior to the time it seeks to achieve interim status. Such a facility was not in existence at the time it was required to have a permit, and the facility has rendered itself subject to the permit requirement. Accordingly, we affirm the district court's K-listed waste ruling and reverse its decision that MSP possessed interim status to store F-listed waste.

> The interim status dispute in this case centers on the following statutory language:
>
> Any person who owns or operates a facility required to have a permit under this section which facility ... is in existence on the effective date of statutory or regulatory changes under this chapter that render the facility subject to the requirement to have a permit ... shall be treated as having been issued a permit until such time as final administrative disposition of [the permit] application has been made.

42 U.S.C. § 6925(e).

Three concepts from this portion of the statute resolve the case before us. First, section 6925(e) refers to "a permit." Under RCRA, EPA issues a particular facility one permit only. If a facility treats, stores, and disposes of hazardous waste, a single permit covers all of these activities. If it engages in any of these activities with respect to more than one type of waste, a single permit covers all wastes specified in that permit.

Second, section 6925(e) grants interim status to persons operating a "facility." As we will explain, the district court's holding implies that the statute grants interim status on a wastestream by wastestream basis, but the statute's plain language contemplates a grant or denial of interim status on a facility by facility basis.

Third, section 6925(e) focuses on whether a facility was in existence at the time it was "render[ed] ... subject" to the statutory requirement that it obtain a permit. The crucial point in time under RCRA is the moment at which the law required the facility to have a permit. Section 6925(e) grants interim status only to facilities that were "in existence" at this moment.

With these three concepts firmly in mind, we conclude that MSP's storage of K-listed wastes rendered it unable to achieve interim status to store any type of waste. In 1980, EPA required that all facilities, including recycling facilities, have RCRA permits before storing K-listed waste. When Louisiana took over the administration of its own RCRA program in 1984, it also required facilities storing K-listed waste to obtain a RCRA permit. In 1985, MSP stored the K-listed wastes from the Colfax and Durawood cleanup operations. MSP had no RCRA permit at this time. It could not obtain interim status because it was not in existence in either 1980 or 1984, the promulgation dates for the regulations requiring a permit for the storage of K-listed wastes, and because it had no pending permit application. In 1985, therefore, MSP lacked interim status.

An alternative application of the statute to these facts yields an identical result. The section 6925(e) exception to the permit requirement applies only when "statutory or regulatory changes ... render the facility subject" to the necessity that the facility obtain a permit. In this case, statutory and regulatory changes did not render MSP subject to the permit requirement; rather, MSP rendered itself subject to this requirement by storing a listed waste for which it needs a permit. Either way, because the section 6925(e) exception does not apply, MSP needed a permit to store waste, and its failure to procure one prior to its storage activity resulted in a RCRA violation.

Our difficulty with the district court's holding lies in its assumption that MSP could achieve interim status by applying for a permit to store F-listed waste when it became subject to regulations corresponding to that type of waste. This holding presumes that MSP was rendered subject to the requirement that it obtain a permit in 1986. In essence, the district court held that RCRA operates on a wastestream by wastestream basis. But MSP needed a permit to cover its storage of K-listed waste several months before. MSP did not need one permit to store K-listed wastes and a second to store F-listed wastes. RCRA contemplates that a facility will receive a single permit to cover storage of all types of waste, and that this permit will govern the storage at the entire facility. RCRA permitting does not operate on a wastestream by wastestream basis.

* * *

NOTES

1. Upon reading RCRA § 3005(c), which prescribes deadlines (ending in 1988) for interim status facilities to have their Part B permit applications granted or denied, one might assume that the concept of interim status became irrelevant in 1988. That is not the case, notwithstanding Marine Shale's unsuccessful attempt to invoke the concept in the foregoing case, because the universe of materials considered to be "hazardous waste" is constantly changing. For example, when the EPA amended the toxicity

characteristic in 1990 (by replacing the extraction procedure, which addressed 14 constituents, with the toxicity characteristic leaching procedure, which addresses 39 constituents), many facilities that were already operating but not previously handling hazardous waste automatically became TSD facilities. In addition, whenever the EPA adds new substances to the four lists of hazardous waste, facilities handling those materials may automatically change status from non-RCRA facilities to RCRA TSDs. *See* RCRA § 3005(e)(1)(A)(ii).

The BIF regulations, described above and applied in the Marine Shale decision in this set, exemplify another means by which existing facilities can become interim status facilities by means of changes in EPA regulations.

2. Relying on a 1986 letter from the Louisiana Department of Environmental Quality, stating that MSP had obtained interim status, Marine Shale raised an estoppel defense in the foregoing enforcement action. The Fifth Circuit rejected the defense, explaining that Marine Shale's reliance on the letter was not reasonable. 81 F.3d at 1348-51.

UNITED STATES V. MARINE SHALE PROCESSORS
81 F.3d 1361 (5th Cir. 1996)

Before GARZA, KING and HIGGINBOTHAM.
HIGGINBOTHAM, Circuit Judge.

This is an appeal and cross-appeal from a Rule 54(b) judgment in favor of a company attempting to clean up its hazardous waste sites. *** We vacate the judgment and remand.

I

From 1923 to 1985, Southern Wood Piedmont Company [SWP] operated several wood treatment facilities designed primarily to manufacture railroad ties and telephone poles. These facilities treated wood with preservatives such as creosote and pentachlorophenol, leaving behind acres of soil contaminated with toxic wastes. Facing slackening demand, SWP in 1985 decided to close its facilities and clean up its waste sites. It sought to avoid regulation under the Resource Conservation and Recovery Act, and liability under The Comprehensive Environmental Response, Compensation & Liability Act, by recycling its contaminated soil into a product covered by an EPA regulation known as the Product Rule. *See* 40 C.F.R. § 266.20(b). If SWP were successful in recycling its hazardous waste into a product covered by the Product Rule, the resulting material could be placed on the ground without violating RCRA. Relying in part on its own investigation and in part on letters from the Louisiana Department of Environmental Quality stating that Marine Shale Processors, Inc. was a legitimate recycler of hazardous waste, SWP contracted with MSP to dispose of SWP's contaminated soil.

From 1986 to 1989, ninety-five percent of the material SWP sent to MSP arrived in shipments called "campaign runs." In a campaign run, MSP earmarked one to two weeks of kiln time to process SWP's soil exclusively. Until 1989, MSP processed the other five percent of SWP's material together with whatever other material happened to be available at the time. In 1989, SWP and MSP modified their contract so as to require MSP to process SWP's material separately from all other materials. Before beginning a campaign run pre-1989 or any SWP processing post-1989, MSP purged its kiln but not its baghouses or its oxidizers.

This appeal concerns SWP's intervention in the *** [action below]. SWP's complaint in intervention alleged that "MSP has taken delivery of certain material from [SWP] ... and, using its thermal process, has made a product from that material." The complaint in intervention further alleged that SWP's soil "[was] and at all times has been processed by MSP separately from material from other sources." SWP sought a declaratory judgment that the Product Rule exempted the material produced from its contaminated soil from RCRA regulation.

The district court submitted interrogatories to the jury. The jury returned answers to some of these questions and found itself unable to agree on others. The interrogatories relevant to this appeal, together with the jury's answer if any, are set out below:

1. Was MSP entitled to a recycler exemption from the requirement of a permit as an operator of an incinerator of hazardous waste? (unable to answer)

2. Were all of the hazardous wastes accepted by MSP beneficially used or reused or legitimately recycled? (unable to answer)

2(a). Were all of the hazardous wastes accepted by MSP prior to August 21, 1991, beneficially used or reused or legitimately recycled? (unable to answer)

3. Was the material produced by MSP from Southern Wood Piedmont Company's waste a "product" produced for the general public's use? (yes)

4. Did the waste material received by MSP from Southern Wood Piedmont Company undergo a chemical reaction in the course of processing the material so as to become inseparable by physical means? (yes)

5. Was the material produced by MSP from waste other than Southern Wood Piedmont Company's waste a "product" produced for general public's use? (unable to answer)

6. Did the waste material produced by MSP from waste other than Southern Wood Piedmont Company's waste undergo a chemical reaction in the course of processing the material so as to become inseparable by physical means? (unable to answer)

Because the jury found itself unable to answer interrogatories 1, 2, 2(a), 5 and 6, among others, the district court declared a mistrial. Based on the jury's affirmative answers to interrogatories 3 and 4, SWP moved for the entry of judgment under Fed.R.Civ.P. 54(b). District court judge Duplantier obliged and entered an order stating in relevant part:

[A]ll material produced by Marine Shale Processors, Inc. from Southern Wood Piedmont Company materials *processed separately from other materials* satisfies all criteria of 40 C.F.R. § 266.20(b) and corresponding Louisiana regulations, and, as such, is not subject regulation as a hazardous waste.... (emphasis added)

SWP objects to the emphasized portion of the district court's judgment. On appeal, SWP asks this court to modify the judgment to read as follows:

[A]ll material produced by Marine Shale Processors, Inc. from Southern Wood Piedmont Company materials satisfies all criteria of 40 C.F.R. § 266.20(b) and corresponding Louisiana regulations, and, as such, is not subject to regulation as a hazardous waste....

The dispute on this issue focuses on the fact that MSP often mixed metal-bearing baghouse dust with material emerging from its kiln in a slagging process. Because MSP did not clean its baghouses before processing SWP waste, the material produced from the processing of SWP's contaminated soil was mixed with quantities of toxic metals from other sources.

On cross appeal, the United States contends that the district court erred in entering a Rule 54(b) judgment for several reasons. The United States first attacks the judgment in favor of SWP on the ground that the district court improperly entered judgment when the jury had been unable to answer the question of whether MSP was engaged in a process of legitimate recycling. Second, the United States contends that the district court erred in holding that MSP had obtained an express exemption from the Louisiana Department of Environmental Quality as required by Louisiana Regulations operating in lieu of the federal Product Rule. Third, the United States argues that the court gave erroneous jury instructions addressed to interrogatory 3. Finally, the United States contends that the district court abused its discretion on certain evidentiary rulings.

We discuss the issues raised by the United States' cross appeal first. Because we agree with the United States on some of the contentions in its cross-appeal, we vacate and remand. Given our disposition of the United States' cross-appeal, we do not reach the questions posed by SWP's appeal. ***

II

The United States argues that the district court improperly entered a Rule 54(b) judgment in the absence of a jury resolution on the question of whether MSP was engaged in a process of legitimate recycling. According to the United States, the federal Product Rule exempts a product produced for the general public's use only if the product emerges from a process of legitimate, as opposed to sham, recycling. Because the jury failed to answer interrogatories 1, 2, and 2(a), the United States argues, it failed to determine the analytically prior issue of whether MSP was engaged in legitimate recycling. Thus, the district court abused its discretion by entering a Rule 54(b) judgment when the jury had not decided all issues relating to the SWP declaratory judgment.

40 C.F.R. § 261.6(a)(2) declares that "recyclable materials used in a manner constituting disposal" are "not subject to [regulation as listed or characteristic wastes]

but are regulated under subpart[ ] C ... of part 266." The Product Rule appears in Subpart C of part 266; this regulation provides,

> Products produced for the general public's use that are used in a manner that constitutes disposal and that contain recyclable materials are not presently subject to regulation if the recyclable materials have undergone a chemical reaction in the course of producing the products so as to become inseparable by physical means and if such products meet the [treatment standards for land disposal] for each recyclable material (i.e. hazardous waste) that they contain.

40 C.F.R. § 266.20 (alterations added). Accordingly, in order to be exempt from regulation under the Product Rule, a substance must (1) be produced for the general public's use, (2) [be] used in a manner that constitutes disposal, (3) contain recyclable materials, (4) have undergone a chemical reaction during the production process so as to be inseparable by physical means, and (5) meet land ban standards for each hazardous waste it contains. The United States focuses on the third element.

The third element of the Product Rule requires that the substance at issue contain recyclable materials. "Hazardous wastes that are recycled will be known as 'recyclable materials.'" 40 C.F.R. § 261.6(a)(1). "A material is "recycled" if it is used, reused, or reclaimed." 40 C.F.R. § 261.1(c)(7). "A material is 'used or reused' if it is ... [e]mployed as an ingredient (including use as an intermediate) in an industrial process to make a product." 40 C.F.R. § 261.1(c)(5)(I). Accordingly, in order for its substance to meet the third element of the product rule, a facility must have employed the hazardous waste as an ingredient in an industrial process to make a product. Mercifully, the regulatory definitions end here; the regulations do not define the terms "ingredient" or "industrial process."

The United States points out that EPA has consistently interpreted the Product Rule to include a requirement that the substance at issue be produced from a process of legitimate, as opposed to sham, recycling. According to these documents, sham recycling, as opposed to legitimate recycling, occurs when the hazardous waste purportedly recycled contributes in no significant way to the production of the product allegedly resulting from the recycling. One EPA publication, in the midst of discussing an example involving the recycling of hazardous waste to produce aggregate in an aggregate kiln, states that legitimate recycling is occurring if "the prohibited hazardous wastes and their hazardous constituents do contribute legitimately to producing aggregate."[4] In other words, the sham versus legitimate recycling inquiry focuses on the purpose or function the hazardous waste allegedly serves in the production process. If the waste does not in fact serve its alleged function in the process, then sham recycling is occurring.

Although the text of 40 C.F.R. § 266.20(b) itself does not mention sham or legitimate recycling, the distinction is inherent in the language "[e]mployed as an

---

[4]Proposed Rules, *Land Disposal Restrictions*, 53 Fed.Reg. at 17,606 ***

ingredient ... in an industrial process to make a product" in 40 C.F.R. § 261.1(c)(5)(I). A hazardous waste is not "employed as an ingredient" if it contributes in no legitimate way to the product's production. EPA's interpretation of its own regulation as including a distinction between sham and legitimate recycling is entitled to deference. In this case, the interpretative exercise is fairly straightforward. A substance cannot be an ingredient in making something if it is merely along for the ride.

We agree with the United States that the district court should not have entered a Rule 54(b) partial judgment without deciding whether MSP was engaging in sham versus legitimate recycling. To illustrate our reasoning, we provide the following examples. Hypothetical Facility A generates a large amount of liquid organic waste. In order to rid itself of the waste, Facility A heats the liquid to very high temperatures in the presence of oxygen, causing the carbon and hydrogen in the organic waste to burn away. The temperatures in the heating device are so high as to make irrelevant any heat contribution from the burning of the organic waste. Facility A has incinerated, not recycled, its organic waste. To the extent that Facility A has made a product, it has done so without using its hazardous waste.

Hypothetical Facility B also generates a large amount of liquid organic waste. In order to rid itself of the waste, the facility dumps the substance into soil. Facility B then digs up the soil containing the waste and heats it to very high temperatures in the presence of oxygen, causing the carbon and hydrogen in the organic waste to burn. The temperatures in the heating device are so high as to make irrelevant any heat contribution from the burning of the organic waste. The soil, however, conglomerates together and forms something that Facility B calls "aggregate." Under such circumstances, Facility B has not recycled its hazardous waste. The only difference between Facilities A and B is that Facility B dumped its waste in soil first. If the organic waste provides neither energy nor materials, then the organic material contributes nothing to the production of the "aggregate." Facility B could have manufactured the exact same "aggregate" by dumping virgin soil into its heating device.

SWP argues that producing a product is recycling. This contention ignores the fact that the hazardous waste in MSP's "feedstocks" may simply be along for the ride. At bottom, SWP's argument depends on the idea that soil contaminated with organic waste is a fundamentally distinct substance from the organic waste itself. We do not agree. *See Chemical Waste Management, Inc. v. Environmental Protection Agency*, 869 F.2d 1526, 1539 (D.C.Cir.1989) (holding that EPA could reasonably reject the argument that "an agglomeration of soil and hazardous waste is to be regarded as a new and distinct substance"). Incineration does not cease to be incineration when one dumps the waste to be incinerated into a temporary medium like soil.

In *Marine Shale Processors, Inc. v. United States Environmental Protection Agency*, 81 F.3d 1329, 1339-44, we held that EPA could conclude that MSP is burning its organic wastes for destruction, and thus that the waste is not recycled or reclaimed or reused. This holding supports our conclusion that, at minimum, an issue of fact exists as to whether SWP's organic waste is a legitimate ingredient in the production of any Marine Shale product. Accordingly, we vacate the district court's Rule 54(b) judgment and remand for further proceedings. We express no view as to the sufficiency of the evidence to support a jury finding in favor of or against SWP, nor regarding any possible preclusive effect of EPA's conclusions in number 95-60228.

* * *

NOTES

1. If you were responsible for enforcing the EPA's Product Rule, how would you distinguish between legitimate and sham recycling? Do you agree with the result in this case? Why or why not?

2. Does the Fifth Circuit's decision regarding SWP's claims require it to uphold the EPA's denial of MSP's BIF permit? That case follows.

MARINE SHALE PROCESSORS, INC. v. UNITED STATES ENVIRONMENTAL PROTECTION AGENCY
81 F.3d 1371 (5th Cir. 1996)
cert. denied, 117 S.Ct. 682 (1997)

Before GARZA, KING and HIGGINBOTHAM.
HIGGINBOTHAM, Circuit Judge.

This case is an appeal of Marine Shale Processors, Inc. from final agency action of the Environmental Protection Agency. Specifically, MSP challenges EPA's decision to deny MSP's application for a Boiler and Industrial Furnace Permit required by the Resource Conservation and Recovery Act. This case is one of the trio described in *United States v. Marine Shale Processors, Inc.*, 81 F.3d 1329 (5th Cir.1996). We affirm.

I

In 1980, EPA promulgated regulations pursuant to RCRA governing the treatment, storage, and disposal of hazardous waste. These regulations defined two methods of processing waste, incineration and recycling. The rules required facilities engaged in incineration to procure a permit called a Subpart O permit, a reference to 40 C.F.R. pt. 264 subpt. O. Facilities engaged in recycling could operate without permits. *See* 45 Fed.Reg. at 33,120 (promulgating 40 C.F.R. § 261.6).

In 1985, EPA defined a new category of hazardous waste processing devices called "industrial furnaces," a term defined to include "aggregate kilns" having certain characteristics. Industrial furnaces could engage in either incineration or burning for energy recovery. If the industrial furnace facility engaged in incineration, then it needed a Subpart O permit. If the industrial furnace engaged in recycling, no permit was necessary. MSP began operations in 1985, claiming an exemption from the Subpart O permit requirement on the grounds that its kiln was an aggregate kiln and that its facility was an industrial furnace engaged in recycling.

On August 14, 1990, the United States sued MSP in United States District Court for the Eastern District of Louisiana in the action giving rise to Nos. 94-30419 and 94-30664, claiming among other things that MSP had incinerated hazardous waste without a Subpart O permit since it opened for business in 1985. In 1991, EPA promulgated new rules requiring that all devices using thermal combustion to treat hazardous wastes have either a Subpart O permit or a new form of permit for recycling facilities called a Boiler and Industrial Furnace permit. Final Rule, *Burning of Hazardous Wastes in Boilers and Industrial Furnaces*, 56 Fed.Reg. 7134, 7138 (1991). These regulations ended the exception from the permit requirement for facilities engaged in recycling. MSP submitted a BIF permit application and a Certification of Compliance with BIF regulations. On the basis of these filings and its contention that it fit within the previously existing recycling exemption, MSP claimed interim status to operate while EPA considered the permit application. EPA's internal consideration of MSP's application for a BIF permit proceeded simultaneously with litigation of the United States' action in Louisiana District Court.

On January 31, 1994, EPA issued a tentative decision denying MSP's BIF permit application. EPA rested its tentative denial upon its conclusions that MSP did not produce aggregate and that its system did not use thermal treatment to accomplish recovery of materials or energy within the meaning of 40 C.F.R. § 260.10. EPA opened its decision for public comment.

A jury trial on the United States' claim in district court that MSP had incinerated waste without a permit began in April, 1994. At the end of a five-week trial, the court submitted 13 interrogatories to the jury. In late May, the jury found itself able to agree to answers to only nine of the questions. The questions relevant to this appeal, together with the jury's answer if any, were as follows:

1. Was MSP entitled to a recycler exemption from the requirement of a permit as an operator of an incinerator of hazardous waste? (unable to answer)

2. Were all of the hazardous wastes accepted by MSP beneficially used or reused or legitimately recycled? (unable to answer)

2(a). Were all of the hazardous wastes accepted by MSP prior to August 21, 1991, beneficially used or reused or legitimately recycled? (unable to answer)

10. Is MSP's rotary kiln an aggregate kiln? (yes)

13. Are the rotary kiln, oxidizers Nos. 1 and 2, and slag box part of a kiln system that produces aggregate? (yes)

Because the jury failed to answer four of the interrogatories, the district court declared a mistrial.

In September, 1994, EPA issued a final decision denying MSP's application for a BIF permit. EPA rested upon its finding that MSP's rotary kiln system did "not meet the definition of aggregate kiln and, therefore, does not meet the definition of industrial furnace." EPA also cited MSP's poor history of compliance with the environmental laws, as well as its finding that MSP could not qualify as an aggregate kiln because it destroyed hazardous waste. MSP appealed to the Environmental Appeals Board, relying on principles of Article III, the seventh amendment, collateral estoppel, due process, and the Administrative Procedures Act.

In March, 1995, after a review of the record, the EAB affirmed EPA's denial. The EAB stated that MSP did not produce "commercial-grade aggregate" from its system and thus that its facility could not qualify as an aggregate kiln. The EAB questioned EPA's reliance on MSP's compliance history and on MSP's destruction of hazardous waste, but ultimately affirmed the decision in its entirety. In April, 1995, EPA finally denied MSP's BIF permit application on all grounds stated in its September, 1994 ruling. MSP appeals the denial of its permit application, invoking our authority under 5 U.S.C. § 706(2) to set aside final agency action. We affirm.

* * *

III

MSP argues that EPA's findings of fact and conclusions of law were arbitrary and capricious. We do not agree.

* * *

*** [W]e focus our discussion here on the evidence underpinning the finding that MSP's system does not use thermal processes to accomplish recovery of energy or materials and on certain determinations EPA made in deciding that MSP's material does not qualify as aggregate within the meaning of 40 C.F.R. § 260.10.

A

EPA's finding that MSP has not designed or used its facility to accomplish recovery of material products and thus that MSP does not use thermal treatment to accomplish recovery of materials or energy is not arbitrary or capricious. As our discussion will make clear, EPA's decisions are highly technical and scientific and are not readily susceptible to lay review. Most of these findings are factual. We bear these considerations firmly in mind when considering MSP's request that we upset EPA's conclusions in an area in which Congress has chosen to trust the experts.

Throughout this section, we assume that MSP produces something it calls aggregate and that its kiln system is an integral component of the process for this aggregate's production. We focus entirely on the question of whether EPA could conclude that MSP does not use thermal treatment to accomplish recovery of materials or energy, or that the design and use of MSP's device is not primarily to accomplish recovery of material products.

1

EPA considered evidence that MSP processed quantities of "lab packs" containing wastes that could contribute nothing to the production of a product. The lab packs were packages of kitty litter and other absorbent material surrounding glass or plastic containers of toxic chemicals. For example, Dr. Douglas Kendall, an EPA chemist, used MSP's manifests and Material Characterization Data Sheets to determine that MSP processed sulfur, toluene solution, ammonium hydroxide, hydrochloric acid solutions and mixtures, nitric acid, and sulfuric acid. Dr. Kendall confirmed that these wastes do not release significant energy when burned and, because they react to form gases at high temperatures, could not provide bulk for MSP's product. EPA considered similar evidence regarding such materials as poisons, pesticides, other acids, and bases; specific substances included methylene chloride, trichlorotrifluoroethane, chloroform, perchloroethylene, trichloroethylene, nitric oxide, fluorotrichloromethane, pentachlorophenol, ethylenediamine, formaldehyde, carbon tetrachloride, and phosgene. MSP's experts could not specify how many of these substances contributed to a manufacturing process. MSP's handling of these substances also suggests that they contribute nothing to production. MSP employee Annika Keslick told EPA that MSP normally opened ten percent of these lab packs, and MSP's examination upon opening was limited to matching the name on the glass or plastic container within the pack to the information contained on the MCDS or manifest.

EPA could find that MSP was not accomplishing recovery of energy or materials from these wastes. The composition of the wastes themselves did not allow their combustion to contribute to any production process, and we cannot understand how MSP could have recovered energy or materials from these wastes without sampling them to verify their contents. MSP's only defense of its treatment of the lab pack wastes was that the kitty litter and other packaging provided mass for its aggregate. EPA could conclude that this argument misconstrues the regulations and is wrong as a matter of law. One does not recycle hazardous waste by placing that waste into a container and then recycling the container.

MSP correctly points out that the lab packs constituted only around one percent of the total volume of wastes processed at its facility. Nevertheless, the amount of material was significant in absolute terms in that MSP processed an average of three to four hundred of the lab packs per week, and MSP's cavalier treatment of these "feedstocks" gives us pause when we consider the remainder of MSP's claim that all of its wastes contributed in some way to its process.

2

EPA considered evidence that MSP processed large quantities of waste with metal contaminants that contribute in no legitimate way to any manufacturing process and thus that MSP's use of these wastes did not constitute recovery of energy or materials. The metallic composition of these wastes spanned the periodic table and included highly variable quantities of lead, barium, cadmium, iron, silicon, aluminum, manganese, copper, zinc, bromine, strontium, calcium, and chromium. MSP's kiln did not destroy these metals. The residue from the process of metal-bearing waste, which MSP calls primary aggregate, normally required slagging to reduce leaching potential.

MSP suggests that it used these metals for two purposes. First, all provided mass for the ultimate product. Second, some compounds from these metals had other properties useful to the manufacturing process or the ultimate product. Dr. Paul Queneau, a metallurgical engineer, told EPA that iron oxide and alumina and titanium are "chain formers, and they very much enhance the environmental stability of the slag."

Other metallic oxides lowered the melting point of the mixture and decrease its "melt viscosity."

EPA's disbelief of these justifications was not arbitrary or capricious. EPA scientists stated that the metal content of the waste necessitated slagging before the ultimate product could be legally placed on the ground and that the slagging process significantly reduced the mass produced. Dr. Terrance McNulty, an expert in extractive metallurgy, also provided evidence that many of these metals impeded production of the slag. Barium, for instance, which at times constituted fourteen to sixteen percent of the slag mass, impeded production because the high melting points of its compounds made liquification more difficult. Most importantly, EPA considered evidence suggesting that while many of the metal compounds do exhibit some of the desirable properties that Dr. Queneau identified, they do so only when present in certain concentrations. Chemist Stanley Wrobleski confirmed that Marine Shale made no attempt to control the metallic composition of its primary or slagged material and that metal concentrations varied widely. Moreover, EPA considered evidence such as a letter from Woodward-Clyde Consultants, MSP's primary environmental consultant, to George Eldredge, an MSP officer, stating that many of the metal compounds "are not introduced specifically or purposefully into the raw product in order to incorporate a particular physical characteristic into the produced aggregate but are inherent elements of the raw materials used in the manufacture of the aggregate." Under such circumstances, EPA could conclude that MSP's process did not recover these metal-bearing wastes or their metallic constituents.

3

The largest percentage of MSP's wastes consisted of soil contaminated by organic compounds. MSP contends that the soil provided raw material, or mass, for its aggregate and that the organic compounds released heat when burned. Accordingly, MSP argues that both the soil and the waste contributed to its aggregate production process.

EPA's rejection of these arguments was not arbitrary or capricious. EPA considered evidence that some of these wastes consisted of soil contaminated with pentachlorophenol, which it specifically labeled a low energy hazardous waste constituent. In addition, EPA could conclude that MSP's process generated heat far in excess of that needed to make its product. Ronald Corwin, an EPA expert witness, suggested that the vast majority of the heat MSP produced from its burning travels in non-contact cooling water through MSP's facility and out into Bayou Boeuf. While MSP correctly points out that no recycling process is one hundred percent efficient, EPA's assessment of whether this heat is used or wasted is a particularly technical judgment about the overall efficiency of MSP's process. We will not disturb this judgment in this case.

4

At oral argument, MSP strenuously contended that EPA's permit denial decision rested on the conclusion that EPA could reject the application if MSP burned a thimbleful of hazardous waste for destruction, and thus that EPA had imposed an unreasonable burden in requiring a potential BIF to prove that it was recovering every atom or every bit of heat from waste in order to claim entitlement to a BIF permit. We make no comment on this argument; this is simply not a thimbleful case. EPA has concluded that the overwhelming majority of MSP's wastes are burned for destruction, not used for recovery of energy or materials. The findings of fact and conclusions of law underlying these decisions are not arbitrary or capricious. EPA could conclude that to the extent that MSP produced a product, it did so in spite of the wastes it purported to recycle.

5

MSP's final attack on this analysis is that a focus upon recovery of energy or materials constitutes an analysis of the role that each material plays in the manufacturing process and of the purpose the particular facility serves. After the promulgation of the BIF regulations, MSP argues, a focus on purpose is improper. In particular, MSP quotes the EAB's statement that "we have serious doubts as to whether after promulgation of the BIF rule the purpose for which MSP is burning hazardous waste at the facility is relevant to the determinant of whether MSP's facility meets the industrial furnace definition." *In re Marine Shale Processors, Inc.*, 1995 WL 135572, at *25 n. 32 (EPA 1995). MSP also notes that 40 C.F.R. § 266.100 establishes that the BIF rules regulate BIFs without regard to whether the particular facility is burning for destruction or is recycling.

MSP's argument fails to separate two analytically distinct issues and regulations. 40 C.F.R. § 260.10 governs whether a facility definitionally qualifies as a BIF. Once a facility has definitionally qualified as a BIF, 40 C.F.R. pt. 266 subpt. H governs most aspects of its operations, including burning for destruction. Although we note that some tension might arise if EPA were to interpret section 260.10's definition of BIF to exclude a facility that burns a thimbleful of waste for destruction, EPA has not done so here, as is made clear by EPA's focus on whether MSP used its kiln system *"primarily to accomplish recovery of material products."* 40 C.F.R. § 260.10 (emphasis added). We cannot conceive of an interpretation of "to accomplish recovery of materials or energy" and other similar phrases in section 260.10 that does not focus on purpose.

An analysis of the preambles to the regulations defining BIFs supports our conclusion. In distinguishing between boilers and incinerators, EPA did seek to shift the initial focus of the definitional inquiry from primary purpose to structural design. Thus, EPA considered and eventually adopted a definition of boiler depending on whether the facility "achieve[s] heat transfer within the combustion chamber itself, generally by exposing the heat recovery surface to the flame." Proposed Rule, *Hazardous Waste Management System: General*, 48 Fed.Reg. 14,472, 14,483 (1983); *see* Final Rule, *Hazardous Waste Management System; Definition of Solid Waste*, 50 Fed.Reg. 614, 626-27 (1985). But EPA recognized that some facilities normally engaging in recycling lacked this distinguishing characteristic of boilers, and therefore chose to rely in part upon the primary purpose test in defining *industrial furnaces*. 50 Fed.Reg. at 626-27. Thus, the language of the rules and of the preambles supports our conclusion that EPA may interpret 40 C.F.R. § 260.10 to include a focus on the primary purpose of the facility or the role played by wastes processed within it.

B

We hold that EPA's refusal to label MSP's kiln an aggregate kiln was not arbitrary or capricious. MSP's primary attack upon this portion of EPA's reasoning is that EPA erred by narrowing its definition of "aggregate" to "commercial grade aggregate." In particular, MSP disputes EPA's reliance upon standards promulgated by the Louisiana Department of Transportation in reaching its decision that MSP's material does not constitute commercial grade aggregate. EPA's interpretations of its own regulations are entitled to substantial deference. We find no error.

In making its adjudicative decision, EPA had to employ some set of standards to distinguish aggregate from any material, such as cigarette ash, capable of occupying space. The history of EPA's focus on recycling of hazardous wastes to produce a commercial product, as well as the use of commercial terms like "manufacturing" process and "industrial" furnace, suggests that EPA's decision to employ commercial criteria in its decision was reasonable at least.

EPA considered factual evidence from witnesses knowledgeable in the construction field that aggregate purchasers typically employ at least some specifications for the product they purchase. In addition, EPA heard evidence that a material must meet LaDOT specifications before the State of Louisiana will buy it for state construction projects and that many private commercial contractors adopt these specifications as well. In the face of this legal history, regulatory language, and factual evidence, we cannot fault EPA's choice to rely on common commercial specifications to define the term "aggregate kiln" in 40 C.F.R. § 261.10 [sic - §260.10].

* * *

Given EPA's legal interpretation of its own regulation, we find nothing arbitrary or capricious in its application of this interpretation to the facts at hand, and we refuse to upset its conclusion that MSP's material is not commercial grade aggregate. MSP concedes that its material, and substances made from it, could not meet many of the LaDOT standards. In addition, MSP concedes that it conducts no tests at all on its material to determine strength, size, shape, specific gravity, absorbency, durability, compaction, or texture. Although MSP presented expert studies suggesting that its slagged and primary material could be useful in the production of certain concrete and asphaltic products, other experts disagreed. The choice of which expert opinions to credit belongs to the EPA permitting staff. Like the Environmental Appeals Board, we are struck by the fact that MSP has never field tested any of the products that its experts testified might possibly be manufactured in part from its slagged and primary material and that none of MSP's product has ever been commercially used for these purposes. Under such circumstances, EPA's application of the law to the facts is not arbitrary or capricious.

* * *

NOTES

1. While MSP's *certiorari* petition was pending before the Supreme Court, the company sought to remain in operation. In the enforcement action (the first of the three foregoing cases), the District Court had issued three injunctions (one under each of the statutes found to be violated), but stayed them pending appeal. The Fifth Circuit left the injunctions in place, but also kept the stay in effect pending an explanation by the District Court of its reasons for issuing the permanent injunctions. During this time, the EPA's response to inquiries from MSP's customers was that anyone sending hazardous waste to MSP after April 18, 1996 (the date of the Fifth Circuit's three decisions) was violating RCRA.

MSP then asked the District Court to extend the stay of the injunctions while it pursued a RCRA incinerator permit, and to direct the EPA not to initiate enforcement actions against any generator sending waste to MSP while the stay was in effect. The District Court denied MSP's requests, stating that only the EPA or the Louisiana Department of Environmental Quality could authorize MSP to operate in the absence of a permit, and that it had no power to enjoin the EPA from undertaking enforcement activities. The Fifth Circuit denied MSP's request for a writ of mandamus. *Marine Shale Processors, Inc. v. EPA,* 91 F.3d 16 (1996).

On June 18, 1996, the EPA directed MSP immediately to stop accepting hazardous waste, and to complete burning the hazardous waste already on-site by July 5. *Summary of Recent Legal Cases,* 15 HAZ. WASTE CONSULTANT (Elsevier Science) March/April 1997, at 3.11.

2. If you were the environmental consultant to MSP, with a substantial investment in hazardous waste treatment technology and large bills, what would you advise at this point? MSP has signed an option to sell its assets and liabilities to a third party, GTX, contingent upon obtaining all permits necessary to operate the facility. Upon other permits, GTX has applied for a hazardous waste incinerator permit under RCRA. *Ibid.*

Problem #3: TSD Status

TO: Peter Partner, Rick & Ruh, P.C.

FROM: Carlin Counsel, Klean & Mean, Inc.

RE: Request for Prompt, Accurate, Wise, and Inexpensive Legal Advice

As you know, Klean & Mean, Inc. is a small company in the commercial printing business. It was incorporated and commenced operations in 1977. It has operated continuously at a 25-acre site, which it leases, within a 150-acre industrial park. Numerous entities have conducted various manufacturing activities at the industrial park since approximately 1947. Since 1977, Klean and Mean has generated waste solvents, inks, and dyes disposed of as hazardous wastes at off-site facilities.

In order to undertake a long-overdue facility renovation, Klean & Mean applied to Prudent Bank and Trust for a large loan. Prudent Bank commissioned a thorough environmental audit, which identified the existence of a fairly large pit, some 100 yards behind the printing shop, that was presumably used for dumping purposes at times during the site's long industrial history. Klean & Mean was previously unaware of the pit, and has never used it. Soil in the pit and groundwater beneath it were sampled and found to contain a variety of spent solvents listed as hazardous wastes under RCRA, including but not limited to the solvent wastes generated by Klean & Mean. The consultants suspect that the solvents were spilled onto the soil and then leaked, and are continuing to leak, into the underlying groundwater.

I am anxious to obtain your prompt, accurate, and wise legal advice regarding the following questions. Please keep your bill to a minimum.

1. Klean & Mean has not submitted any notifications to the EPA pursuant to RCRA § 3010. (a) Was Klean & Mean required to have done so in August 1980 (90 days after the initial hazardous waste definition regulations were promulgated)? (b) Is it now required to do so regarding the pit?

2. Is Klean & Mean required by any other provision of the RCRA statute or regulations (*e.g.*, 40 C.F.R. Part 262) to report the existence of the pit?

3. Klean & Mean has not filed either a "Part A" interim status or a "Part B" permit application. Was it, or is it now, required to do so?

4. Can the EPA require Klean & Mean to conduct a RCRA closure of, and/or to obtain a post-closure permit for, the contaminated pit?

C. Role of State Regulation Regarding Hazardous Waste

Although the RCRA statute and regulations comprise the heart of the regulatory program, and the EPA's guidelines and policies set the framework for its implementation, the individual states also play a substantial role regarding RCRA. That role is, or can be, multi-dimensional. First, the statute provides for EPA to "authorize" states to administer and enforce the RCRA program within their borders. States are eligible to be so authorized upon submittal to the EPA of a program that (1) is equivalent to the federal program, (2) is consistent with the federal program and with other states' RCRA programs, and (3) provides for adequate enforcement. RCRA § 3006(b), 42 U.S.C. § 6926(b). Although most states were authorized to implement those provisions of RCRA that were in effect prior to the 1984 amendments, the states had to apply again for authorization to implement the provisions added by HSWA, most notably the corrective action requirements.

A second aspect of the states' RCRA role is their authority to impose requirements that are more—but not less—stringent than comparable RCRA requirements. RCRA § 3009, 42 U.S.C. § 6929. Pursuant to this authority, many states have elected to regulate as hazardous waste materials that are not deemed hazardous under RCRA, or to impose more stringent operating requirements than are imposed under RCRA (provided that such requirements are not inconsistent with RCRA).

The following case challenges New Jersey's authority to implement a hazardous waste program of broader scope than the federal RCRA program.

OLD BRIDGE CHEMICALS, INC. V. NEW JERSEY DEPARTMENT OF ENVIRONMENTAL PROTECTION
965 F.2d 1287 (3d Cir. 1992)
cert. denied, 506 U.S. 1000 (1992)

Before GREENBERG, SCIRICA, and ROSENN, Circuit Judges.
ROSENN, Circuit Judge.

This appeal presents questions arising from a state's regulatory scheme for the disposition and management of toxic wastes within its jurisdiction and a potential conflict with the commerce clause of the federal constitution and congressional legislation. The New Jersey Department of Environmental Protection (NJDEP), the agency charged with the promulgation and enforcement of regulations governing waste management in the State of New Jersey, enacted a regulatory program governing the management of hazardous wastes. Old Bridge Chemicals, Inc. (OBC) claims that the regulations relating to recyclable by-product hazardous wastes violate the commerce clause and the Resource Conservation and Recovery Act (RCRA). OBC sought relief in the United States District Court for the District of New Jersey to enjoin NJDEP from using RCRA hazardous waste codes to identify this class of hazardous wastes. OBC also sought a declaration that New Jersey's definition of solid waste, without state-specific waste codes, violates the commerce clause. The district court entered summary judgment for the New Jersey Department of Environmental Protection. OBC appealed and we affirm.

I.

OBC is a chemical manufacturing company chartered under New Jersey laws with gross annual sales approaching $20 million. For twenty years, it has purchased chemicals, including zinc oxide, sulfuric acid, copper sulfate solution and crystals, copper chloride, and copper ammonium chloride, from out-of-state companies. These out-of-state companies produce the chemicals as necessary adjuncts to the manufacture of primary marketable commodities. OBC uses them in the production of pure, basic chemicals for sale to agriculture, water treatment, dry cell battery and textile industries.

Under the New Jersey Solid Waste Management Act, NJDEP has the responsibility to promulgate and update rules and regulations concerning the State's waste management. In 1987, NJDEP adopted a revised definition of "solid waste," which made its definition of solid waste more expansive and stringent than the federal definition. Although the federal definition excludes any materials recycled "as effective substitutes for commercial products," 40 C.F.R. § 261.2(e)(1)(ii), New Jersey's amended definition includes "by-product" materials that are recycled. As a consequence of the new regulations, many of the raw materials used by OBC are now classified as solid wastes under the New Jersey definition notwithstanding their exemption from federal regulation. In addition, under both the federal and state regulations, a substance considered a "hazardous waste" must first classify as a solid waste. See 40 C.F.R. § 261.3; N.J.A.C. 7:26-1.4. Because NJDEP's definition of "solid waste" includes by-product materials that are recycled, such materials may be hazardous only under the New Jersey scheme.

On January 11, 1990, NJDEP notified OBC that virtually all of OBC's imported raw materials were by-product solid wastes subject to New Jersey's hazardous waste regulations. Under NJDEP's expanded regulations, OBC's imported raw chemicals, copper chloride and copper ammonium chloride, further classify as by-product solid wastes exhibiting hazardous waste characteristics and are thus hazardous wastes. OBC concedes that these raw materials are of a hazardous nature.

Under the New Jersey scheme, these recyclable hazardous wastes must be labelled and identified for record keeping and recording purposes by their characteristic EPA hazardous waste code, even if they originate from out-of-state sources. In addition, although RCRA does not require shipments of such recyclable hazardous wastes to be done "under manifest," New Jersey requires that shipments of these wastes to and from the State be made pursuant to the State's manifest system, modelled after RCRA's. A manifest is a document used to identify the quantity, composition, and the origin, routing, and destination of hazardous wastes during their transportation. It provides a "cradle to grave" means for tracking hazardous wastes through a paper trail from the point of generation to the point of treatment, storage, or disposal.

* * *

OBC does not object to New Jersey's more expansive definition of "solid waste," but argues that New Jersey's use of the RCRA hazardous waste codes creates a detrimental impact upon interstate commerce because it appears that such coding *ipso facto* renders New Jersey-only hazardous wastes subject to nationally restrictive RCRA hazardous waste regulations in interstate shipment. OBC asserts that as a consequence, its out-of-state suppliers are refusing to continue to sell such recyclable by-product materials to OBC or are threatening to withdraw as suppliers because they do not wish to be burdened by New Jersey's requirements for manifesting, labelling, and transporting, non-federally designated hazardous wastes. They fear that identifying their routinely marketed products as federal hazardous wastes could subject them to federal regulatory liability as unlicensed hazardous waste generators or transporters. OBC claims that these potential losses to its sources of supply may force it to close its operations.

II.

In deciding this case, we recognize the serious difficulties inherent in hazardous waste management, particularly in the State of New Jersey. As we have previously noted, the disposition of solid waste in New Jersey "has been in a state of crisis since the midseventies, and continues to be 'one of [the] state's most severe problems.'" *J. Filiberto Sanitation, Inc. v. New Jersey Dep't of Envtl. Protection*, 857 F.2d 913, 918 (3rd Cir.1988) (quoting *A.A. Mastrangelo, Inc. v. Commissioner of Dep't of Envtl. Protection*, 90 N.J. 666, 670-71 (1982)). However, solid waste is an increasingly common commodity of interstate commerce; therefore, New Jersey's regulations must be consistent with the dictates of the commerce clause. In addition, although the State is understandably driven to correct the public health and safety problems posed by hazardous wastes, New Jersey, in its efforts to do so, must not contravene RCRA.

In interpreting the applicable federal legislation and regulations to determine Congress's intent, and in interpreting New Jersey's regulations to determine whether they comport with the Constitution and the federal environmental scheme, our role is not to pass judgment on the effectiveness and wisdom of the particular state regulations at issue, but only to apply the law as we find it. ***

A. Commerce Clause Claim
* * *
1. Heightened Scrutiny
* * *

The commerce clause prohibits states from regulating subjects that "are in their nature national, or admit only of one uniform system, or plan of regulation." *CTS Corp. v. Dynamics*, 481 U.S. at 88-89. Therefore, as stated, we apply the heightened scrutiny test as a standard of review when a regulation undermines uniformity in an area of particular federal importance.

It is undisputed that hazardous waste management is an area of national importance. Congress passed RCRA in 1976 as the principal federal statute regulating the generation, transportation, and disposal of hazardous wastes, stating that the problems of waste disposal had "become a matter national in scope and in concern and necessitat[ed] federal action." 42 U.S.C. § 6901(a)(4). However, although waste management may be an area of overriding national importance, in legislating in this field Congress has set only a floor, and not a ceiling, beyond which states may go in regulating the treatment, storage, and disposal of solid and hazardous wastes.

RCRA expressly allows states to adopt more stringent "requirements" than those imposed by the EPA regulations, although states may not impose any regulations less stringent than the floor set by RCRA. The "savings clause" of RCRA states:

> [N]o State ... may impose any requirements less stringent than those authorized under this subchapter respecting the same matter as governed by such regulations.... Nothing in this chapter shall be construed to prohibit any State ... thereof from imposing any requirements, including those for site selection, which are more stringent than those imposed by such regulations.

This express provision of RCRA reveals a congressional intent that hazardous waste is not an area of particular federal importance requiring one, uniform, national system or plan of regulation. In fact, although Congress recognized the need for federal regulation, it stated that "the collection and disposal of solid wastes should continue to be primarily the function of the State." Id. § 6901(a)(4).

The structure of EPA's Form 8700-12 is further evidence that RCRA envisions a dual federal-state system of hazardous waste regulation, with states able to categorize additional wastes as hazardous. This form specifically designates a space reserved for listing state regulated wastes, and advises originators of hazardous waste that "[m]any States have requirements that vary from the Federal regulations [which] *may be more strict than the federal requirements by identifying additional wastes as hazardous.*" (Emphasis added). The form reveals that the EPA contemplates that RCRA enables states to designate wastes as hazardous beyond those RCRA designates as hazardous.

Moreover, there is no congressional intent to preempt the entire field of interstate waste management or transportation. This provides further evidence that Congress did not intend RCRA to assume overriding federal importance at the expense of the states' sovereign power to enact more stringent, but not conflicting, state regulation. Thus, the heightened scrutiny applied to state statutes undermining uniformity in areas of particular federal importance is not implicated because the federal statutory and regulatory framework affords states the option to adopt their own, more stringent hazardous waste regulations so long as they do not discriminate against out-of-state interests or favor in-state interests.

* * *

OBC also argues that we should apply heightened scrutiny because NJDEP's regulations subject recyclable by-product materials like copper chloride and copper aluminum chloride to conflicting commands from different states. The Supreme Court has invalidated state statutes where a state has "projected" its legislation into other states and directly regulated commerce therein, thereby either forcing individuals to abandon commerce in other states or forcing other states to alter their regulations to conform with the conflicting legislation. The Court has acted similarly where a state statute created contradictory and inconsistent state regulation of vehicles which burdened interstate transportation.

For several reasons, the regulations at issue here do not pose such problems. First, OBC has not pointed to regulations of other states which *conflict* with the New Jersey solid waste regulations. OBC merely asserts that unlike New Jersey, other states do not define the above mentioned by-product materials as solid wastes. *** As there is no actual conflict among state regulations, NJDEP's regulations do not burden interstate commerce with "*inconsistent* regulations." In addition, New Jersey is not "projecting" its legislation into other states. Nor does OBC claim that NJDEP's regulations require out-of-state companies to abandon commerce in other states or require other states to alter their waste management schemes to conform with New Jersey's.

Thus, we conclude, as did the district court, that the appropriate test for evaluating NJDEP's regulations is not heightened scrutiny, but rather the balancing test from *Pike v. Bruce Church, Inc.*, 397 U.S. 137 (1970). ***

* * *

2. The Balancing Test

* * *

A challenged regulation is discriminatory when it confers advantages upon in-state economic interests, either directly or through imposition of a burden upon out-of-state interests, as against out-of-state competitors. The district court reasoned that the challenged regulations burdened all commerce, not just interstate commerce, inasmuch as both New Jersey producers and OBC's out-of-state producers of the solid waste hazardous materials were required to abide by the manifest requirements. The court concluded that because the need for uniformity was not at issue and the challenged regulations applied even-handedly to all, the regulations imposed no burden on interstate commerce. ***

We agree with the district court's analysis. ***

* * *

B. RCRA Claim

OBC next argues that NJDEP's regulation classifying the recyclable by-product materials as solid waste is facially inconsistent with RCRA and therefore disrupts the uniform federal regulatory scheme pertaining to hazardous wastes management. We disagree. RCRA's "savings clause" expressly provides that a state is not precluded from adopting more stringent requirements than those imposed by the EPA regulations. 42 U.S.C. § 6929. In explaining this clause, Congress stated that the regulations promulgated by the EPA were to be "the minimum standards applicable to hazardous waste management." 1976 U.S.C.C.A.N. 6238, 6269. Thus, RCRA sets a floor, not a ceiling, for state regulation of hazardous wastes. Accordingly, NJDEP regulations are consistent with the clear language and intent of RCRA.

In addition, state regulations that differ from federal regulations do not necessarily violate the federal act because RCRA expressly permits more stringent state regulations. Therefore, a mere inconsistency between the state and federal schemes does not constitute a violation of RCRA. *Accord General Electric Co. v. Flacke*, 461 N.Y.S.2d 138 (1982) (state environmental regulation's definition of "waste" which included reused or recycled materials was not inconsistent with RCRA because RCRA "allows states to require stricter and more stringent standards than the federal program.")

Moreover, OBC's assertion that the regulations pose a threat to the uniformity of the RCRA identification system is suspect in light of the availability of two spaces on the manifest form for identifying the transported wastes as "New Jersey special wastes not subject to federal RCRA requirements," thereby simply removing any doubt that the materials are RCRA wastes and any consequent threat to the uniformity of RCRA. Further, as we observed earlier, use of the RCRA codes actually enhances the uniformity of the federal codes because the New Jersey-only wastes contain the same chemical composition and inherent dangers as the corresponding RCRA wastes. Finally, out-of-state manufacturers solely shipping recyclable by-product materials to New Jersey need not fear federal liability for shipping non-federally designated wastes because they may inform the EPA on their Form 8700-12 that they will be shipping New Jersey-only hazardous wastes.

III.

In summary, NJDEP's hazardous waste regulations defining recyclable by-products as solid wastes and requiring such wastes, if hazardous, to be marked with EPA codes, do not violate the commerce clause. OBC fails to make the showing of discrimination or threat to uniformity in an area of particular federal importance necessary to implicate heightened scrutiny. Under the *Pike* balancing test, the New Jersey scheme is constitutional as it does not burden interstate commerce. Further, there has been no showing of a violation of RCRA stemming from New Jersey's use of the federal waste codes. Accordingly, the district court's summary judgment will be affirmed.

NOTES

1. The principle that state laws may be more stringent than, provided not inconsistent with, RCRA applies as well to local ordinances. Close questions may arise, however, where a state or local ordinance is so stringent as to undermine RCRA policy. For example, the owner of a cement kiln seeking to burn hazardous waste as fuel challenged a local zoning ordinance requiring a conditional use permit, claiming that the requirement frustrates RCRA's policy of encouraging hazardous waste recycling. In *Blue Circle Cement, Inc. v. Board of County Commissioners of the County of Rogers*, 27 F.3d 1499 (10th Cir. 1994), the Tenth Circuit summarized the relevant case law as follows:

> *** First, ordinances that amount to an explicit or de facto total ban of an activity that is otherwise encouraged by RCRA will ordinarily be preempted by RCRA. Second, an ordinance that falls short of imposing a

total ban on encouraged activity will ordinarily be upheld so long as it is supported by a record establishing that it is a reasonable response to a legitimate local concern for safety or welfare. Significant latitude should be allowed to the state of local authority, However, if the ordinance is not addressed to a legitimate local concern, or if it is not reasonably related to that concern, then it may be regarded as a sham and nothing more than a naked attempt to sabotage federal RCRA policy of encouraging the safe and efficient disposition of hazardous waste materials.

Id. at 1508.

2. As *Old Bridge Chemicals* indicates, the states' flexibility in adopting hazardous waste programs is bounded in part by the federal RCRA program and in part by the Constitution. Constitutional issues are at the forefront concerning state hazardous and solid waste laws that, while not implicating RCRA, may affect the transport of hazardous or solid waste across state or county lines. In the past few years, the Supreme Court has addressed several cases involving constitutional challenges to state and local laws regulating hazardous and solid waste handling.

3. In *Chemical Waste Management, Inc. v. Hunt*, 504 U.S. 334 (1992), the Supreme Court ruled unconstitutional an Alabama statute imposing a hazardous waste disposal fee on wastes generated outside the state, based on a violation of the dormant Commerce Clause.

No State may attempt to isolate itself from a problem common to the several States by raising barriers to the free flow of interstate trade. ***

* * *

The State, however, argues that the additional fee imposed on out-of-state hazardous waste serves legitimate local purposes related to its citizens' health and safety. Because the additional fee discriminates both on its face and in practical effect, the burden falls on the State "to justify it both in terms of the local benefits flowing from the statute and the unavailability of nondiscriminatory alternatives adequate to preserve the local interests at stake." *Hunt v. Washington Apple Advertising Comm'n*, 432 U.S. 333, 353 (1977). ***

The State's argument here does not significantly differ from the Alabama Supreme Court's conclusions on the legitimate local purposes of the additional fee imposed, which were: "The Additional Fee serves these legitimate local purposes that cannot be adequately served by reasonable nondiscriminatory alternatives: (1) protection of the health and safety of the citizens of Alabama from toxic substances; (2) conservation of the environment and the state's natural resources; (3) provision for compensatory revenue for the costs and burdens that out-of-state waste generators impose by dumping their hazardous waste in Alabama; (4) reduction of the overall flow of wastes traveling on the state's highways, which flow creates a great risk to the health and safety of the state's citizens." 584 So.2d, at 1389. These may all be legitimate local interests, and petitioner has not attacked them. But only rhetoric, and not explanation, emerges as to why Alabama targets only interstate hazardous waste to meet these goals. As found by the Trial Court, "[a]lthough the Legislature imposed an additional fee of $72.00 per ton on waste generated outside Alabama, there is absolutely no evidence before this Court that waste generated outside Alabama is more dangerous than waste generated in Alabama. The Court finds under the facts of this case that the only basis for the additional fee is the origin of the waste." App. to Pet. for Cert. 83a-84a. In the face of such findings, invalidity under the Commerce Clause necessarily follows, for "whatever [Alabama's] ultimate purpose, it may not be accomplished by discriminating against articles of commerce coming from outside the State unless there is some reason, apart from their origin, to treat them differently." *Philadelphia v. New Jersey*, 437 U.S., at 626-627. ***

Ultimately, the State's concern focuses on the volume of the waste entering the Emelle facility. Less discriminatory alternatives, however, are available to alleviate this concern, not the least of which are a generally applicable per-ton additional fee on all hazardous waste disposed of within Alabama, or a per-mile tax on all vehicles transporting hazardous waste across Alabama roads, or an evenhanded cap on the total tonnage landfilled at Emelle, which would curtail volume from all sources. To the extent Alabama's concern touches environmental conservation and the health and safety of its citizens, such concern does not vary with the point of origin of the waste, and it remains within the State's power to monitor and regulate more closely the transportation and disposal of all hazardous waste within its borders. Even with the possible future financial and environmental risks to be borne by Alabama, such risks likewise do not vary with the waste's State of origin in a way allowing foreign, but not local, waste to be burdened. In sum, we find the additional fee to be "an obvious effort to saddle those outside the State" with most of the burden of slowing the flow of waste into the Emelle facility. *Philadelphia v. New Jersey*, 437 U.S., at 629. "That legislative effort is clearly impermissible under the Commerce Clause of the Constitution." *Ibid.*

Id. at 339, 342-346.

4. On the same day as it handed down the *Chemical Waste Management* decision, the Court struck down as violative of the Commerce Clause a Michigan law that prohibited private landfill operators from accepting solid waste originating outside the county in which their facilities were located. *Fort Gratiot Sanitary Landfill, Inc. v. Michigan Department of Natural Resources*, 504 U.S. 353 (1992).

Michigan and St. Clair County assert that the Waste Import Restrictions are necessary because they enable individual counties to make adequate plans for the safe disposal of future waste. Although accurate forecasts about the volume and composition of future waste flows may be an indispensable part of a comprehensive waste disposal plan, Michigan could attain that objective without discriminating between in- and out-of-state waste. Michigan could, for example, limit the amount of waste that landfill operators may accept each year. There is, however, no valid health and safety reason for limiting the amount of waste that a landfill operator may accept from outside the State, but not the amount that the operator may accept from inside the State.

Id. at 366-67. See also *Oregon Waste Systems, Inc. v. Department of Environmental Quality of Oregon*, 511 U.S. 93 (1994) (holding unconstitutional an Oregon surcharge on the in-state disposal of solid waste generated in other states, notwithstanding Oregon's contention that the surcharge reflected the fact that Oregonians—but not out-of-state waste generators—were already paying waste disposal costs through other fees or taxes.)

5. In May 1994, the Supreme Court held that a New York "flow control" ordinance—one of many laws that have been enacted across the nation to attempt to enhance solid waste recycling and resource recovery—ran afoul of the dormant Commerce Clause. The ordinance at issue, requiring all nonhazardous waste to be deposited at a designated transfer station, was enacted by the Town of Clarkstown as part of a financing plan for a new solid waste transfer station, which the town had agreed to build as part of an earlier consent decree with the New York State Department of Environmental Conservation. *C & A Carbone, Inc. v. Town of Clarkstown*, 511 U.S. 383 (1994).

While the immediate effect of the ordinance is to direct local transport of solid waste to a designated site within the local jurisdiction, its economic effects are interstate in reach. The Carbone facility in Clarkstown receives and processes waste from places other than Clarkstown, including from out of State. By requiring Carbone to send the nonrecyclable portion of this waste to the Route 303 transfer station at an additional cost, the flow control ordinance drives up the cost for out-of-state interests to dispose of their solid waste. Furthermore, even as to waste originant in Clarkstown, the ordinance prevents everyone except the favored local operator from performing the initial processing step. The ordinance thus deprives out-of-state businesses of access to a local market. These economic effects are more than enough to bring the Clarkstown ordinance within the purview of the Commerce Clause. ***

* * *

The flow control ordinance does serve a central purpose that a nonprotectionist regulation would not: It ensures that the town-sponsored facility will be profitable, so that the local contractor can build it and Clarkstown can buy it back at nominal cost in five years. In other words, as the most candid of amici and even Clarkstown admit, the flow control ordinance is a financing measure. By itself, of course, revenue generation is not a local interest that can justify discrimination against interstate commerce. Otherwise States could impose discriminatory taxes against solid waste originating outside the State. ***

Clarkstown maintains that special financing is necessary to ensure the long-term survival of the designated facility. If so, the town may subsidize the facility through general taxes or municipal bonds. But having elected to use the open market to earn revenues for its project, the town may not employ discriminatory regulation to give that project an advantage over rival businesses from out of State.

Id. at 389, 393-94.

In a concurring opinion, Justice O'Connor noted:

It is within Congress' power to authorize local imposition of flow control. Should Congress revisit this area, and enact legislation providing a clear indication that it intends States and localities to implement flow control, we will, of course, defer to that legislative judgment. Until then, however, Local Law 9 cannot survive constitutional scrutiny. ***

Id. at 410.

6. As a result of *Carbone*, the bond ratings of some 17 solid waste authorities across the country were downgraded, making it much more difficult for local governments to borrow money for their solid waste management facilities. Various interests pertaining to local government operations and solid waste handling are lobbying Congress for legislation granting flow control authority to municipalities. *Flow-Control Proponents Urge Congress to Provide Relief from High Court Ruling,* 27 Env't Rep. (BNA) 2204 (March 7, 1997).

7. Construing *Carbone*, the Third Circuit has held that municipal flow control ordinances are not inherently unconstitutional, provided that in-state and out-of-state entities have equal opportunities to compete to deliver solid waste disposal services. *Harvey & Harvey, Inc. v. Chester County,* 68 F.3d 788 (3rd Cir. 1995), *cert. denied,* 116 S.Ct. 1265 (1996).

8. Historically, facilities that treat, store, or dispose of non-hazardous solid waste were regulated at the local level. During the 1970s, most states imposed regulatory requirements on solid waste landfills. The EPA's role was limited to general permitting guidelines, set forth at 40 C.F.R. Part 257, and did not extend to any regulatory or enforcement authority. The 1984 Amendments to RCRA required the EPA to play a more active role in setting minimal national standards for solid waste disposal facilities. RCRA § 4010, 42 U.S.C. § 6949a. The EPA's initial response to this directive was the promulgation of national standards for the design and operation of municipal solid waste landfills. 40 C.F.R. Part 258; *see* 56 Fed. Reg. 50978 (1991).

In *Sierra Club v. EPA,* 992 F.2d 337 (D.C. Cir. 1993), the D.C. Circuit addressed various challenges to the EPA's RCRA Subtitle D regulations governing municipal solid waste landfills. The court upheld the EPA's approach—*i.e.*, setting location, design and operating requirements rather than specific numeric limits for toxic constituents of sludge disposed of with other solid waste in municipal landfills—rejecting claims that such approach violated the Clean Water Act. The court, however, vacated and remanded the exemption of small landfills from the general groundwater monitoring requirements, as inconsistent with the Subtitle D provisions of RCRA, specifically § 4010(c), 42 U.S.C. § 6949a(c). In 1996, the EPA promulgated two sets of regulations responding to the remand. First, the EPA ruled that hazardous waste from conditionally-exempt small quantity generators (which is conditionally exempt from RCRA regulation pursuant to 40 C.F.R. § 261.5) may be sent to non-municipal, non-hazardous waste disposal facilities only if they meet standards specified in the regulations. 61 Fed. Reg. 34252 (1996). Second, the EPA codified statutory provisions exempting certain small landfills—those accepting less than 20 tons of municipal solid waste per day, without evidence of groundwater contamination, and located in dry or remote areas—from groundwater monitoring requirements. 61 Fed. Reg. 50410 (1996) (implementing the Land Disposal Program Flexibility Act, Pub. L. No. 104-119, §3, 109 Stat. 830 (1996), which legislatively overruled the D.C. Circuit as to the *Sierra Club* decision regarding small landfills, and as to the *Chemical Waste Management* decision (second decision so titled in chapter 4) regarding land ban requirements for decharacterized wastes handled in Clean Water Act units and underground injection wells).

4 THE LAND BAN

The central objective of the Hazardous and Solid Waste Amendments of 1984 (*i.e.*, the 1984 amendments to RCRA) was to minimize or eliminate the land disposal of hazardous waste. That objective is summarized in the congressional finding added to the introductory provisions of RCRA:

> [C]ertain classes of land disposal facilities are not capable of assuring long-term containment of certain hazardous wastes, and to avoid substantial risk to human health and the environment, reliance on land disposal should be minimized or eliminated, and land disposal, particularly landfill and surface impoundment, should be the least favored method for managing hazardous wastes.

RCRA § 1002(b)(7), 42 U.S.C. § 6901(b)(7).

The bias against land disposal is manifested in "minimum technology requirements" for the design and operation of land disposal facilities, (*i.e.,* double liners, leachate collection systems, and groundwater monitoring), first-priority deadlines for existing land disposal facilities to submit Part B permit applications (November 8, 1985) and for the EPA or state to decide whether to grant or deny those applications (November 8, 1988), and the LOIS (loss of interim status) provisions discussed in the preceding chapter. Of greatest impact, for the policy disfavoring land disposal as well as for the RCRA program in general, are the land ban provisions, also known as the land disposal restrictions ("LDRs" in RCRA-speak). *See* RCRA §§ 3004(o), 3005(e)(2)(A), 3005(c)(2)(A)(i), and 3004(c)-(m), respectively.

Underlying a complex array of land ban rules and exceptions, codified at 40 C.F.R. Part 268, is the principle that hazardous waste may not be land disposed unless it meets specified treatment standards. Land disposal is broadly defined to include virtually any "placement" of hazardous waste in or on the land. RCRA § 3004(k), 42 U.S.C. § 6924(k). The 1984 amendments established a series of deadlines by which the EPA was required to (and did) promulgate treatment standards for all hazardous wastes. There are three types of treatment standards: (1) a concentration level, which requires that a waste be treated, using any lawful method, until its hazardous constituents are present in concentrations at or below the treatment standard; (2) a treatment method, which prescribes certain technologies or technology options that must be used to treat certain hazardous wastes; and (3) no land disposal, which prohibits the land disposal of certain wastes under any circumstances.

In order to develop treatment standards, the EPA first determines the best demonstrated available technology ("BDAT") for each waste or group of wastes. The EPA then uses the BDAT to specify a treatment standard. It is important to recognize that only where the treatment standard is a specified method must the BDAT actually be employed. Otherwise, for example where the treatment standard is a concentration level, the waste may be treated by any lawful means so long as the resulting concentration level is as least as low as that achieved by the BDAT. The following case addresses the analytical approach employed by the EPA in developing BDAT as the benchmark for setting land ban treatment standards. (In response to the second of the decisions in this chapter styled *Chemical Waste Management, Inc. v. U.S.E.P.A*, the EPA adopted a supplemental method for setting treatment standards, known as universal treatment standards. They will be addressed later in the chapter.)

HAZARDOUS WASTE TREATMENT COUNCIL V. U.S. ENVIRONMENTAL PROTECTION AGENCY

886 F.2d 355 (D.C.Cir. 1989), *cert. denied,* 498 U.S. 849 (1990)

PER CURIAM.

In 1984, Congress amended the Resource Conservation and Recovery Act ("RCRA") to prohibit land disposal of certain hazardous solvents and wastes containing dioxins except in narrow circumstances to be defined by Environmental Protection Agency ("EPA") regulations. In these consolidated cases, petitioners seek review of EPA's final "solvents and dioxins" rule published pursuant to Congress' 1984 mandate. We conclude that the rule under review is consistent with RCRA, but remand one aspect of the rulemaking to the agency for further explanation.

I.

A. *Statutory Scheme.*

The Hazardous and Solid Waste Amendments of 1984 ("HSWA"), substantially strengthened EPA's control over the land disposal of hazardous wastes regulated under RCRA's "cradle to grave" statutory scheme. In preambular language to the HSWA, Congress, believing that "land disposal facilities were not capable of assuring long-term containment of certain hazardous wastes," expressed the policy that "reliance on land disposal should be minimized or eliminated." 42 U.S.C. § 6901(b)(7). In order to effectuate this policy, HSWA amended section 3004 of RCRA to prohibit land disposal of hazardous waste unless the waste is "pretreated" in a manner that minimizes "short-term and long-term threats to human health and the environment," or unless EPA can determine that the waste is to be disposed of in such a fashion as to ensure that "there will be no migration of hazardous constituents from the disposal [facility]...."

As amended, RCRA requires EPA to implement the land disposal prohibition in three phases, addressing the most hazardous "listed" wastes first.[1] In accordance with strict statutory deadlines, the Administrator is obligated to specify those methods of land disposal of each listed hazardous waste which "will be protective of human health and the environment." In addition, "[s]imultaneously with the promulgation of regulations ... prohibiting ... land disposal of a particular hazardous waste, the Administrator" is required to

> promulgate regulations specifying those levels or methods of treatment, if any, which substantially diminish the toxicity of the waste or substantially reduce the likelihood of migration of hazardous constituents from the waste so that short-term and long-term threats to human health and the environment are minimized.

Id. § 6924(m).

Respecting two categories of hazardous wastes, including the solvents and dioxins at issue here Congress, however, declined to wait for phased EPA implementation of the land disposal prohibition. For these wastes, Congress imposed earlier restrictions, prohibiting land disposal after dates specified in the HSWA except in accordance with pretreatment standards or pursuant to regulations specifying "protective" methods of disposal. These prohibitions, as applied to the solvents and dioxins listed in the HSWA, were to take effect November 8, 1986. In order to further RCRA's basic purpose of mandating treatment of hazardous wastes in lieu of land disposal, Congress further provided that storage of wastes falling within the land disposal prohibition would be "prohibited unless such storage is solely for the purpose of the accumulation of such quantities of hazardous waste as are necessary to facilitate proper recovery, treatment or disposal." *Id.* § 6924(j). Congress believed that permitting storage of large quantities of waste as a means of forestalling required treatment would involve health threats equally serious to those posed by land disposal, and therefore opted in large part for a "treat as you go" regulatory regime.

B. *The Rulemaking Under Review.*

In January 1986, EPA issued a notice of proposed rulemaking announcing its draft implementation of the land disposal prohibition for solvents and dioxins. *See* 51 Fed. Reg. 1602 (1986) (hereinafter "Proposed Rule"). Approximately ten months later, after receiving extensive public commentary on the draft blueprint, EPA published a final solvents and dioxins rule differing in some respects from its draft approach. *See* 51 Fed. Reg. 40,572 (1986) (hereinafter "Final Rule"). These differences were especially

---

[1] EPA was given the task of dividing the wastes presently "listed" as hazardous under RCRA into thirds according to their "intrinsic hazard," 42 U.S.C. §6924(g)(2). In keeping with RCRA's deadline, the resulting schedule, promulgated in 1986, required EPA to implement the land disposal prohibition and promulgate treatment standards for each third by no later than 45, 55, and 66 months after enactment of the HSWA, respectively. *See* 42 U.S.C. §6924(g)(4).

striking in EPA's implementation of section 3004(j) and section 3004(m) of RCRA, governing the storage prohibition and *treatment* standards, respectively, for solvents and dioxins. These portions of the rule, together with other discrete portions of the rulemaking faulted by petitioners, are summarized below.

1. *Section 3004(m) Treatment Standards.*

In the Proposed Rule, EPA announced its tentative support for a treatment regime embodying both risk-based and technology-based standards. The technology-based standards would be founded upon what EPA determined to be the Best Demonstrated Available Technology ("BDAT"); parallel risk-based or "screening" levels were to reflect "the maximum concentration [of a hazardous constituent] below which the Agency believes there is no regulatory concern for the land disposal program and which is protective of human health and the environment." Proposed Rule at 1611. The Proposed Rule provided that these two sets of standards would be melded in the following manner:

First, if BDAT standards were more rigorous than the relevant health-screening levels, the latter would be used to "cap the reductions in toxicity and/or mobility that otherwise would result from the application of BDAT treatment[.]" Thus, "treatment for treatment's sake" would be avoided. Second, if BDAT standards were less rigorous than health-screening levels, BDAT standards would govern and the screening level would be used as "a goal for future changes to the treatment standards as new and more efficient treatment technologies become available." Finally, when EPA determined that the use of BDAT would pose a greater risk to human health and the environment than land disposal, or would provide insufficient safeguards against the threats produced by land disposal, the screening level would actually become the 3004(m) treatment standard.

EPA invited public comment on alternative approaches as well. The first alternative identified in the Proposed Rule (and the one ultimately selected by EPA) was based purely on the capabilities of the "best demonstrated available technology." Capping treatment levels to avoid treatment for treatment's sake, according to EPA, could be accomplished under this technology-based scheme by "the petition process":

> Under this approach, if a prescribed level or method of treatment under section 3004(m) resulted in concentration levels that an owner/operator believed to be overly protective, the owner/operator could petition the Agency to allow the use of an alternative treatment level or method or no treatment at all by demonstrating that less treatment would still meet the petition standard of protecting human health and environment.

Id. at 1613. And the function served by health-screening levels of providing a default standard when the application of BDAT technology would itself pose a threat to human health and the environment could likewise be fulfilled by the petition process: "an owner operator could petition the Agency ... to allow continued land disposal of the waste upon a demonstration that land disposal of the waste would not result in harm to human health and the environment." *Id.*

The Agency received comments supporting both approaches, but ultimately settled on the pure-technology alternative. Of particular importance to EPA's decision were the comments filed by eleven members of Congress, all of whom served as conferees on the 1984 RCRA amendments. As EPA recorded in the preamble to the Final Rule:

> [These] members of Congress argued strongly that [the health screening] approach did not fulfill the intent of the law. They asserted that because of the scientific uncertainty inherent in risk-based decisions, Congress expressly directed the Agency to set treatment standards based on the capabilities of existing technology.
>
> The Agency believes that the technology-based approach adopted in [the] final rule, although not the only approach allowable under the law, best responds to the above stated comments.

Final Rule at 40,578.

EPA also relied on passages in the legislative history supporting an approach under which owners and operators of hazardous waste facilities would be required to use "'the best [technology] that has been demonstrated to be achievable.'" *Id.* (quoting 103 CONG.REC. S9178 (daily ed. July 25, 1984) (statement of Senator Chaffee). And the agency reiterated that the chief advantage offered by the health-screening approach—avoiding "treatment for treatment's sake"—could "be better addressed through changes in other aspects of its regulatory program." *Id.* As an example of what parts of the program might be altered, EPA announced that it was "considering the use of its risk-based methodologies to characterize wastes as hazardous pursuant to section 3001 [of RCRA]."

Petitioner CMA challenges this aspect of the rule as an unreasonable construction of section 3004(m)'s mandate to ensure that "short-term and long-term threats to human health and the environment are minimized." 42 U.S.C. § 6924(m). In the alternative, CMA argues that EPA has failed to explain the basis—in terms of relevant human health and environmental considerations—for its BDAT regime, which allegedly requires treatment in some circumstances to levels far below the standards for human exposure under other statutes administered by EPA. Thus, CMA claims that EPA's action in promulgating a technology-based rule is arbitrary and capricious.

* * *

II. SECTION 3004(M) TREATMENT STANDARDS

CMA challenges EPA's adoption of BDAT treatment standards in preference to the approach it proposed initially primarily on the ground that the regulation is not a reasonable interpretation of the statute. CMA obliquely, and Intervenors Edison Electric and the American Petroleum Institute explicitly, argues in the alternative that the agency did not adequately explain its decision to take the course that it did. We conclude, as to CMA's primary challenge, that EPA's decision to reject the use of screening levels is a reasonable interpretation of the statute. We also find, however, that EPA's justification of its choice is so fatally flawed that we cannot, in conscience, affirm it. We therefore grant the petitions for review to the extent of remanding this issue to the agency for a fuller explanation.

A. The Consistency of EPA's Interpretation with RCRA.

Our role in evaluating an agency's interpretation of its enabling statute is as strictly circumscribed as it is simply stated: We first examine the statute to ascertain whether it clearly forecloses the course that the agency has taken; if it is ambiguous with respect to that question, we go on to determine whether the agency's interpretation is a reasonable resolution of the ambiguity. *Chevron*, 467 U.S. at 842-45.

1. Chevron *Step I: Is the Statute Clear?*

We repeat the mandate of § 3004(m)(1): the Administrator is required to promulgate "regulations specifying those levels or methods of treatment, if any, which substantially diminish the toxicity of the waste or substantially reduce the likelihood of migration of hazardous constituents from the waste so that short-term and long-term threats to human health and the environment are minimized." 42 U.S.C. § 6924(m)(1).

CMA reads the statute as requiring EPA to determine the levels of concentration in waste at which the various solvents here at issue are "safe" and to use those "screening levels" as floors below which treatment would not be required. CMA supports its interpretation with the observation that the statute directs EPA to set standards only to the extent that "threats to human health and the environment are minimized." We are unpersuaded, however, that Congress intended to compel EPA to rely upon screening levels in preference to the levels achievable by BDAT.

The statute directs EPA to set treatment standards based upon either "levels or methods" of treatment. Such a mandate makes clear that the choice whether to use "levels" (screening levels) or "methods" (BDAT) lies within the informed discretion of the agency, as long as the result is "that short-term and long-term threats to human health and the environment are minimized." To "minimize" something is, to quote the Oxford English Dictionary, to "reduce [it] to the smallest possible amount, extent, or degree." But Congress recognized, in the very amendments here at issue, that there are "long-term uncertainties associated with land disposal," 42 U.S.C. § 6924(d)(1)(A). In the face of such uncertainties, it cannot be said that a statute that requires that threats be minimized unambiguously requires EPA to set levels at which it is conclusively presumed that no threat to health or the environment exists.

Nor are we at all persuaded by CMA's interpretation of *NRDC v. EPA*, 824 F.2d 1146, 1163 (D.C.Cir.1987) *(en banc)*, in which we held that EPA was not permitted to "substitute technological feasibility for health as the primary consideration under Section 112 [of the Clean Air Act]." That provision requires the Administrator to set air pollution standards "at the level which in his judgment provides an ample margin of safety to protect the public health." 42 U.S.C. § 7412(b)(1)(B). EPA had set emission standards for vinyl chloride, however, "based solely on the level attainable by the best available control technology," 824 F.2d at 1149, despite its finding that such levels would create health risks. It had neither stated that the risks it found were insignificant, nor explained how the risks it accepted were consistent with its statutory duty to provide "an ample margin of safety." *Id.* This court held that EPA had erred in failing to consider whether the best available technology was sufficient to provide the statutorily mandated margin of safety.

* * *

2. Chevron *Step II: Is EPA's Interpretation Reasonable?*

The screening levels that EPA initially proposed were not those at which the wastes were thought to be entirely safe. Rather, EPA set the levels to reduce risks from the solvents to an "acceptable" level, and it explored, at great length, the manifest (and manifold) uncertainties inherent in any attempt to specify "safe" concentration levels. The agency discussed, for example, the lack of any safe level of exposure to carcinogenic solvents, 51 Fed. Reg. at 1,628; the extent to which reference dose levels (from which it derived its screening levels) understate the dangers that hazardous solvents pose to particularly sensitive members of the population; the necessarily artificial assumptions that accompany any attempt to model the migration of hazardous wastes from a disposal site; and the lack of dependable data on the effects that solvents have on the liners that bound disposal facilities for the purpose of ensuring that the wastes disposed in a facility stay there. Indeed, several parties made voluminous comments on the Proposed Rule to the effect that EPA's estimates of the various probabilities were far more problematic than even EPA recognized.

CMA suggests, despite these uncertainties, that the adoption of a BDAT treatment regime would result in treatment to "below established levels of hazard." It relies for this proposition almost entirely upon a chart in which it contrasts the BDAT levels with (1) levels EPA has defined as "Maximum Contaminant Levels" (MCLs) under the Safe Drinking Water Act; (2) EPA's proposed "Organic Toxicity Characteristics," threshold levels below which EPA will not list a waste as hazardous by reason of its having in it a particular toxin; and (3) levels at which EPA has recently granted petitions by waste generators to "delist" a particular waste, that is, to remove it from the list of wastes that are deemed hazardous. CMA points out that the BDAT standards would require treatment to levels that are, in many cases, significantly below these "established levels of hazard." If indeed EPA had determined that wastes at any of the three levels pointed to by CMA posed no threat to human health or the environment, we would have little hesitation in concluding that it was unreasonable for EPA to mandate treatment to substantially lower levels. In fact, however, none of the levels to which CMA compares the BDAT standards purports to establish a level at which safety is assured or "threats to human health and the environment are minimized." Each is a level established for a different purpose and under a different set of statutory criteria than concern us here; each is therefore irrelevant to the inquiry we undertake today.

The drinking water levels, for example, are established under a scheme requiring EPA to set "goals" at a level at which "no known or anticipated adverse effects on the health of persons occur." 42 U.S.C. § 300g-1(b)(4). EPA is then to set MCLs as close to its goals as "feasible," taking into account, among other things, treatment costs. 42

U.S.C. §§ 300g-1(b)(4), (5). Since SDWA goals are set only to deal with "known or anticipated" adverse health effects, a mere "threat" to human health is not enough in that context. Moreover, SDWA levels are set without reference to threats to the environment. Finally, EPA must consider costs in setting its MCLs; there is no similar limitation in § 3004 of RCRA.

Similarly, in promulgating the OTC levels, EPA made clear that, "[in] establishing a scientifically justifiable approach for arriving at [OTC levels], EPA wanted to assure a *high degree of confidence* that a waste which releases toxicants at concentrations above the [OTC level] would pose a hazard to *human health*." EPA Hazardous Waste Management System; Identification and Listing of Hazardous Waste ..., Proposed Rule, 51 Fed. Reg. 21,648, 21,649 (1986) (emphases added). Thus it is clear that wastes with toxicant levels below the OTC thresholds may still pose *"threats* to human health [or] *the environment." Id.* at 21,648 (emphases added).

Finally, CMA points to the "delisting levels" as appropriate points of comparison. The term is a bit misleading, however. EPA delists particular wastes in response to individual petitions, and it has not adopted formal, or even *de facto*, levels below which any waste will be delisted. That EPA has delisted, in particular circumstances, wastes containing concentrations of solvents higher than those called for by the BDAT standards adds nothing to CMA's argument. The treatment standards establish a generic approach, requiring that all wastes deemed to be hazardous be treated to a set level in order to minimize threats to health and to the environment. If a waste is listed as hazardous, and an individual generator wants to dispose of it without meeting the BDAT standards, it may petition to have its particular waste delisted. If the agency grants the delisting petition, only the petitioner is affected; the generally required level of treatment remains the same. Hence, there is no inconsistency between a "delisting level," accepted in particular circumstances, that permits a higher level of a particular contaminant then the BDAT level otherwise generally applicable.

In sum, EPA's catalog of the uncertainties inherent in the alternative approach using screening levels supports the reasonableness of its reliance upon BDAT instead. Accordingly, finding no merit in CMA's contention that EPA has required treatment to "below established levels of hazard," we find that EPA's interpretation of § 3004(m) is reasonable.

Our concurring colleague suggests that our discussion of the reasonableness of the BDAT standard is unnecessary, if not "perhaps analytically impossible." Contrary to the impression given in his separate opinion, however, the basis upon which we find EPA's interpretation reasonable here is not one that we have supplied, but the one EPA itself put forth. In its Initial Rule document discussing BDAT as well as screening levels, and in its briefs to this court, EPA has presented precisely the arguments we find persuasive here. While, as we shall see, those arguments are inadequate to justify the choice made, in the Final Rule, in favor of BDAT as against screening levels—which also seem to present a reasonable approach—they do demonstrate that the BDAT approach is reasonable.

B. *Was EPA's Explanation Adequate?*

The Supreme Court has made it abundantly clear that a reviewing court is not to supplement an agency's reasons for proceeding as it did, nor to paper over its plainly defective rationale: "The reviewing court should not attempt itself to make up for such deficiencies [in the agency's explanation]; we may not supply a reasoned basis for the agency's action that the agency itself has not given." *Motor Vehicles Manufacturers Ass'n v. State Farm Mut. Auto Ins. Co.,* 463 U.S. 29, 43 (1983). Accordingly, in order to determine whether we can affirm EPA's action here, we must parse the language of the Final Rule to see whether it can be interpreted to make a sensible argument for the approach EPA adopted. We find that it cannot.

As we have said, EPA, in its Proposed Rule, expressed a tentative preference for an approach that combined screening levels and BDAT. It indicated that it thought either that approach or BDAT alone was consistent with the statute, and recognized that there were myriad uncertainties inherent in any attempt to model the health and environmental effects of the land disposal of hazardous wastes. It initially concluded, however, that despite those uncertainties, the better approach was to adopt the combination of screening levels and BDAT. Nevertheless, in the Final Rule, it rejected its earlier approach, and adopted a regime of treatment levels defined by BDAT alone.

In order fully to convey the inadequacy of EPA's explanation, we quote the relevant portion of the Final Rule at length:

Although a number of comments on the proposed rule favored the first approach; that is, the use of screening levels to "cap" treatment that can be achieved under BDAT, several commenters, including eleven members of Congress, argued strongly that this approach did not fulfill the intent of the law. They asserted that because of the scientific uncertainty inherent in risk-based decisions, Congress expressly directed the Agency to set treatment standards based on the capabilities of existing technology.

The Agency believes that the technology-based approach adopted in today's final rule, although not the only approach allowable under the law, best responds to the above-stated comments. Accordingly, the final rule establishes treatment standards under RCRA section 3004(m) based exclusively on levels achievable by BDAT. The Agency believes that the treatment standards will generally be protective of human health and the environment. Levels less stringent than BDAT may also be protective.

* * *

51 Fed. Reg. at 40,578.

To summarize: after EPA issued the Proposed Rule, some commenters, including eleven members of Congress, chastised the agency on the ground that the use of screening levels was inconsistent with the intent of the statute. They stated that because of the uncertainties involved, Congress had mandated that BDAT alone be used to set treatment standards. EPA determined that the "best [response]" to those comments was to adopt a BDAT standard. It emphasized, however, that either course was consistent with the statute (and that it was therefore not *required* to use BDAT alone). Finally, it asserted, without explanation, that its major purpose in initially proposing screening levels "may be better addressed through changes in other aspects of its regulatory program," and gave an example of one such aspect that might be changed.

This explanation is inadequate. It should go without saying that members of Congress have no power, once a statute has been passed, to alter its interpretation by post-hoc "explanations" of what it means; there may be societies where "history" belongs to those in power, but ours is not among them. In our scheme of things, we consider legislative history because it is just that: *history*. It forms the background against which Congress adopted the relevant statute. Post-enactment statements are a different matter, and they are not to be considered by an agency or by a court as legislative history. An agency has an obligation to consider the comments of legislators, of course, but on the same footing as it would those of other commenters; such comments may have, as Justice Frankfurter said in a different context, "power to persuade, if lacking power to control." *Skidmore v. Swift & Co.*, 323 U.S. 134, 140 (1944).

It is unclear whether EPA recognized this fundamental point. On the one hand, it suggested that the adoption of a BDAT-only regime "[best-responded]" to the comments suggesting that the statute required such a rule. On the other hand, EPA went on at some length to establish that the comments were in error, in that screening levels are permissible under the statute. EPA's "rationale," in other words, is that several members of Congress (among others) urged upon it the claim that Proposition X ("Congress mandated BDAT") requires Result A ("EPA adopts BDAT"), and that although Proposition X is inaccurate, the best response to the commenters is to adopt Result A.

Nor is anything added by EPA's bald assertion that its reason for initially preferring Result B (screening levels) "may be" better served by other changes in the statutory scheme. In its Proposed Rule, EPA had, after extensive analysis of the various alternatives, come to the opposite conclusion. It is insufficient, in that context, for EPA to proceed in a different direction simply on the basis of an unexplained and unelaborated statement that it might have been wrong when it earlier concluded otherwise.

In the entire relevant text of the Final Rule, EPA neither invokes nor discusses the uncertainties inherent in the land disposal process in support of its determination to use BDAT. EPA's only mention of the concept is in its description of the commenters' argument that, because of such uncertainties, Congress mandated BDAT—an argument that EPA rejected. While it may be that EPA intended that reference to act as an incorporation of all the uncertainties it outlined in its Proposed Rule, or all the many challenges to its assumptions that commenters submitted in response to the Proposed Rule, that intent, if indeed it exists, is so shrouded in mist that for this court to say that we could discern its outlines would be as illogical as the agency's explanation in the Final Rule itself.

* * *

NOTES

1. The EPA subsequently published a revised explanation of its use of BDAT, rather than risk levels, in setting land ban treatment standards. 55 Fed. Reg. 6640 (1990). The EPA's revised explanation followed the reasoning set forth by the D.C. Circuit, focusing on the uncertainties inherent in predicting health risks and selecting technology-based standards as a more objective means of minimizing risk than predictive, risk-based standards.

2. The preceding case challenged the first set of land ban regulations promulgated by the EPA, regarding certain solvent and dioxin wastes that Congress had directed the EPA to address first. RCRA § 3004(e). The second set of land ban regulations pertained to the so-called "California list" wastes, which were also specified in the statute and were borrowed from a list used by the State of California. RCRA § 3004(d)(2). Then the EPA divided the universe of RCRA-listed hazardous wastes (as of November 1984) into thirds, and addressed each third in a series of three rulemakings. The so-called "third-third" also included land ban treatment standards for the characteristic hazardous wastes.

The treatment standards for characteristic wastes represent a notable exception to the Agency's use of BDAT to set treatment standards. Although the EPA initially proposed several BDAT-based treatment standards that would have required treatment beyond the levels at which the wastes triggered the RCRA characteristic in the first place, 54 Fed. Reg. 48372 (1989), the final regulation primarily used characteristic levels as treatment standards for most (but not all) characteristic wastes. 55 Fed. Reg. 22520 (1990). As usual, a suit was filed challenging the third-third regulations. In a significant decision (set forth later in this chapter), the D.C. Circuit held that the EPA had not demonstrated that a treatment standard based solely on removal of the hazardous characteristic satisfied the requirement in RCRA § 3004(m) to minimize threats to human health and the environment. *Chemical Waste Management, Inc. v. U.S.E.P.A.*, 976 F.2d 2 (D.C.Cir. 1992), *cert. denied*, 507 U.S. 1057 (1993). The EPA responded with another set of treatment standards—universal treatment standards—that supplement the removal-of-characteristic standard with BDAT-based concentration levels. (*See* Notes following that *Chemical Waste Management* case later in this chapter.)

3. The EPA's approach to setting universal treatment standards builds on the strategy earlier devised by the agency to address multi-source leachate (*i.e.*, the seepage from wastes that had been buried or placed on or in the ground, typically in a landfill or waste pile) and for contaminated media. The following case challenged the EPA's initial handling of hazardous waste leachate and contaminated media (in the "first-third" set of treatment standards).

CHEMICAL WASTE MANAGEMENT, INC. v. ENVIRONMENTAL PROTECTION AGENCY
869 F.2d 1526 (D.C.Cir. 1989)

Before WALD, Chief Judge and MIKVA, Circuit Judge, and REVERCOMB, District Judge of the District of Columbia.
    WALD, Chief Judge.

* * *

I. FACTS

A. *Applicable Statute and Regulations*

* * *

The RCRA was recently modified by the Hazardous Solid Waste Amendments of 1984 (the "1984 Amendments"), which established sweeping restrictions on the land disposal of hazardous wastes. The EPA was required to establish a schedule dividing the hazardous wastes into "thirds"; the agency promulgated the schedule in May of 1986. The division of the schedule into thirds was designed as a means of phasing in the land disposal restrictions. By August 8, 1988, the EPA was required to promulgate treatment standards for each of the first-third scheduled wastes; these wastes may not be land disposed unless they have been treated to meet the applicable standards or the disposal unit is one from which there will be no migration of hazardous constituents for as long as the waste remains hazardous. ***

The present dispute concerns the rulemaking in which the EPA established treatment standards for first-third wastes. The new regulations were submitted for public comment in two Notices of Proposed Rulemaking, which were published in the Federal Register on April 8, 1988 and May 17, 1988. The final rule was published in the Federal Register on August 17, 1988, with an effective date of August 8, 1988. In these public notices the EPA issued treatment standards for the various wastes; in lengthy preambles to the notices, the agency discussed the interpretive principles which would guide its application of the standards. Three such principles merit discussion here.

One of these principles concerns the treatment standards applicable to leachate produced from hazardous waste. Leachate is produced when liquids, such as rainwater, percolate through wastes stored in a landfill. The resulting fluid will contain suspended components drawn from the original waste. Proper leachate management involves the storage of wastes in lined containers so that leachate may be collected before it seeps into soil or groundwater. The leachate will periodically be pumped out of the container and subsequently treated.

An EPA regulation promulgated in 1980, known as the "derived-from rule," provided that "any solid waste generated from the treatment, storage, or disposal of a hazardous waste, including any sludge, spill residue, ash, emission control dust, or leachate (but not including precipitation run-off) is a hazardous waste." 40 C.F.R. § 261.3(c)(2)(i). Thus, for some years prior to the 1988 rulemaking, it had been understood that leachate derived from a hazardous waste was itself a hazardous waste. In the 1988 preambles, the agency stated that leachate derived from multiple hazardous wastes would be deemed to contain each of the wastes from which it was generated, and that it must therefore be treated to meet the applicable treatment standards for each of the underlying wastes.[5] This is known as the "waste code carry-through" principle.

The second interpretive principle at issue in this proceeding also involves the treatment requirements for hazardous waste leachate. In its preamble to the August rule, the agency stated that "(h)azardous waste listings are retroactive, so that once a particular waste is listed, all wastes meeting that description are hazardous wastes no matter when disposed." 53 Fed. Reg. 31,147 (August 17, 1988). The implications of that statement center around wastes which were not deemed hazardous at the time they were disposed but which are subsequently listed as hazardous wastes. The RCRA does not require that such wastes be cleaned up or moved from the landfill, nor does the agency impose any retroactive penalty on the prior disposal of the waste. Under the August rule, however, the agency announced that leachate which is actively managed after the underlying wastes have been listed as hazardous will itself be deemed a hazardous waste and must be treated to the applicable standards. Under this approach, the fact that the original waste was not deemed hazardous at the time of disposal is simply irrelevant in determining the treatment requirements for the leachate.

Finally, the agency discussed the applicability of the treatment standards to contaminated environmental media such as soil and groundwater. The preamble stated that "[i]n these cases, the mixture is deemed to be the listed waste." 53 Fed. Reg. 31,142 (August 17, 1988). Thus, when a listed hazardous waste (or hazardous waste leachate) is mixed with soil or groundwater—as may occur, for example, through spills or leaking —the soil or groundwater is subject to all the treatment standards or restrictions that would be applicable to the original waste.

B. *The Present Litigation*

*   *   *

Petitioners in this case raised a host of substantive and procedural challenges to the August rulemaking. First, the petitioners contested the agency's determination that "derived-from" wastes (such as leachate) will be subject to the standards applicable to each of the underlying wastes. The petitioners' position was in essence that the EPA should establish separate treatment standards for leachate, based on a leachate treatability study, rather than assuming that leachate can be treated to the standards for all of the wastes from which it is generated. The petitioners also challenged the application of the treatment standards to leachate derived from wastes which were not deemed hazardous at the time they were disposed; their claim was that such a regulation would constitute improper "retroactive" rulemaking. They also contested the agency's

---

[5] Since different wastes will typically be stored together in a landfill, it is not uncommon for leachate to be derived from many different wastes.

statement that environmental media contaminated by listed hazardous wastes would themselves be considered hazardous wastes and would be required to meet the treatment standards. Finally, the petitioners contended that the challenged regulations had been promulgated in violation of the notice and comment requirements of the APA.

Shortly before oral argument, however, the posture of the case changed dramatically. ***[S]ettlement negotiations *** produced agreement on some preliminary issues, and *** a negotiated settlement seemed likely on all issues pertaining to the waste code carry-through principle. Under the terms of the proposed settlement, all multiple-waste leachate would be rescheduled to the third-third, and a leachate treatability study would be undertaken so that appropriate treatment standards could be determined.

The issues argued to the court, and the issues that we decide today, are therefore limited to the following. First, did the agency improperly engage in retroactive rulemaking in ordering that its leachate regulations be made applicable to leachate derived from wastes which were not deemed hazardous at the time they were disposed? Second, did the agency act in an arbitrary and capricious manner by mandating that environmental media contaminated by hazardous wastes must themselves be treated as hazardous wastes? Finally, did the EPA fail to provide interested parties with adequate notice of and opportunity to comment on the foregoing regulatory principles?

II. ANALYSIS

A. *"Retroactive" Hazardous Waste Listings*

* * *

3. Merits

* * *

In discussing the presumption against retroactive lawmaking, this court has noted that "the Supreme Court's teaching in this area is, upon analysis, decidedly unfriendly to statutory interpretations that would effect a latter-day burdening of a completed act —lawful at the time it was done—with retroactive liability." *Ralis*, 770 F.2d at 1127. It is plain, however, that the regulation with which we are confronted here is not retroactive as that term was used in *Ralis*. The agency has made no effort to impose a legal penalty on the disposal of waste which was not deemed hazardous at the time it was disposed. Nor, in fact, does this regulation require the cleanup of any newly listed hazardous wastes. The preamble to the final rule expressly provides that "these residues could become subject to the land disposal restrictions for the listed waste from which they derive *if they are managed actively after the effective date of the land disposal prohibition for the underlying waste.*" 53 Fed. Reg. 31,148 (August 17, 1988) (emphasis supplied). The rule has prospective effect only: treatment or disposal of leachate will be subject to the regulation only if that treatment or disposal occurs after the promulgation of applicable treatment standards.

As a practical matter, of course, a landfill operator has little choice but to collect and manage its leachate. Active management of leachate is sound environmental practice, and a panoply of regulations require it. A landfill operator therefore finds its present range of options constrained by its own past actions (the decision to accept certain wastes) even though it could not have foreseen those consequences when the actions occurred. This does not, however, make the rule a retroactive regulation. It is often the case that a business will undertake a certain course of conduct based on the current law, and will then find its expectations frustrated when the law changes. This has never been thought to constitute retroactive lawmaking, and indeed most economic regulation would be unworkable if all laws disrupting prior expectations were deemed suspect.

Moreover, we find this aspect of the agency's interpretation of the derived-from rule to be eminently reasonable. The derived-from rule establishes a presumption: leachate generated from hazardous waste will be presumed hazardous unless it is proved nonhazardous or treated to applicable standards. The reasonableness of that presumption does not vary depending upon the time when the underlying waste was disposed. In fact, the view of the rule urged by the petitioners would seem to create serious enforcement problems. No doubt there are many landfills which have accepted certain listed hazardous wastes both before and after the wastes were listed. Under petitioners' approach, leachate generated from the wastes disposed after listing would be deemed hazardous and would be subject to the treatment standards; leachate derived from previous shipments of the same waste would not. There is, however, no possible way of determining which portions of the collected leachate were generated from particular shipments of the underlying waste.

In upholding the EPA rule as a nonretroactive regulation, we do not believe that we have impermissibly sustained the agency's decision on a basis other than that relied upon by the agency itself. The EPA did, it is true, state repeatedly that "hazardous waste listings are retroactive." Read in context, however, these statements mean only that the hazardousness of leachate will depend on the composition of the underlying wastes, not on the time at which those wastes were disposed. The agency emphasized that its action would apply only to the future active management of leachate. *** Although the EPA did use the word "retroactive" in a way that careful lawyers would not, we believe that the basis on which the agency acted was congruent in substance (if not in phrasing) with the rationale which we uphold today.

B. *Contaminated Environmental Media*

1. Notice and Comment

Petitioners also challenge the EPA's assertion that environmental media (*e.g.*, soil or groundwater) which are contaminated with hazardous wastes will themselves be considered hazardous wastes, and thus will be subject to the land disposal restrictions. Although petitioners appear to press their argument that this measure was adopted in violation of the APA's notice and comment requirements, we believe that the notice and comment argument actually adds nothing to their position. The EPA makes no attempt to defend the contaminated soil rule as a new regulation; the agency does not purport to have weighed the pros and cons of the policy within the course of the 1988 rulemaking. Rather, the agency relies exclusively on the contention that the challenged rule is simply the application to environmental media of regulations adopted in 1980. If the EPA is correct in this assertion, then it was not required to provide notice or to consider comments in 1988. ***

* * *

3. Did the Agency Reasonably Interpret the 1980 Regulations?

In reviewing the EPA's application of its 1980 rules to contaminated soil, we are guided by two fundamental principles. The first is that "[a]n agency's interpretation of its own regulations will be accepted unless it is plainly wrong." *General Carbon Company v. Occupational Safety and Health Review Commission*, 860 F.2d 479, 483 (D.C.Cir.1988). The second is that on "a highly technical question ... courts necessarily must show considerable deference to an agency's expertise." *MCI Cellular Telephone Company v. FCC*, 738 F.2d 1322, 1333 (D.C.Cir.1984). Taken together, these principles counsel extreme circumspection in our review of the agency's action.

The agency's rule, adopted in 1980, provides that "[a] hazardous waste will remain a hazardous waste" until it is delisted.[16] *See* [40 C.F.R.] §§ 261.3(c)(1), 261.3(d)(2). The petitioners argue in essence that an agglomeration of soil and hazardous waste is to be regarded as a new and distinct substance, to which the presumption of hazardousness no longer applies. The agency's position is that hazardous waste cannot be presumed to change character when it is combined with an environmental medium, and that the hazardous waste restrictions therefore continue to apply to waste which is contained in soil or groundwater. Certainly the EPA's position appears plausible on its face. Moreover, several other factors support the agency's interpretation of its rules.

In its preamble to the 1980 regulations, the agency sought to explain the circumstances under which a hazardous waste would cease to be a hazardous waste. The agency stated that a waste, once deemed hazardous, would ordinarily be presumed to retain its hazardous character. The EPA explained: "As a practical matter, this means that facilities which store, dispose of or treat hazardous waste must be considered hazardous waste management facilities for as long as they continue to contain hazardous waste and that any wastes removed from such facilities—including spills, discharges or leaks—must be managed as hazardous wastes." 45 Fed. Reg. 33,096 (May 19, 1980). The preamble did not specifically refer to contaminated environmental media, and it is certainly true that hazardous wastes may spill or leak into solid waste rather than into soil or groundwater. Clearly, though, the EPA's current treatment of contaminated soil is entirely consistent with the 1980 preamble's insistence that hazardous wastes will ordinarily be presumed to remain hazardous.

---

[16] In filing a delisting petition, a petitioner seeks to convince the EPA that its particular form of the waste, although it falls within the regulatory definition of hazardous waste, does not in fact pose a hazard. *See* 40 C.F.R. §§ 260.20, 260.22.

The EPA's approach to contaminated environmental media is also consistent with the derived-from and mixture rules established in 1980. *See* 40 C.F.R. §§ 261.3(c)(2)(i), 261.3(a)(2)(iv). These rules provide that a hazardous waste will continue to be presumed hazardous when it is mixed with a solid waste, or when it is contained in a residue from treatment or disposal. The derived-from and mixture rules do not, it is true, apply by their own terms to contaminated soil or groundwater. They nevertheless demonstrate that the agency's rule on contaminated soil is part of a coherent regulatory framework. It is one application of a general principle, consistently adhered to, that a hazardous waste does not lose its hazardous character simply because it changes form or is combined with other substances. In promulgating the mixture rule, the agency did not presume that every mixture of listed wastes and other wastes would in fact present a hazard. Rather, the agency reasoned that "(b)ecause the potential combinations of listed wastes and other wastes are infinite, we have been unable to devise any workable, broadly applicable formula which would distinguish between those waste mixtures which are and are not hazardous." 45 Fed. Reg. 33,095 (May 19, 1980). The EPA therefore concluded that it was fair to shift to the individual operator the burden of establishing (through the delisting process) that its own waste mixture is not hazardous. Precisely the same logic applies to combinations of hazardous waste and soil or groundwater.

* * *

*** We do believe *** that, given the agency's broad discretion to interpret its own rules, it was entirely reasonable for the EPA to arrive at that conclusion. We therefore must sustain the agency's position.

* * *

NOTES

1. Treating leachate as hazardous waste if it is generated from a listed hazardous waste is an application of the "derived-from rule" discussed in chapter 2.B. As indicated above in *Chemical Waste Management*, the EPA's first-third land ban regulations required that leachate be treated, prior to land disposal, to meet all treatment standards for each of the wastes from which it was generated. Although this approach to setting treatment standards for leachate was one of the issues raised in the *Chemical Waste Management* litigation, the parties reached a settlement prior to oral argument and the EPA agreed to conduct a leachate treatability study and revisit the issue of appropriate treatment standards for multi-source leachate.

The EPA promulgated revised treatment standards for multi-source leachate in the third-third set of treatment standards. 55 Fed. Reg. 22520 (1990). As revised, the land ban regulations treat multi-source leachate as a particular hazardous waste, rather than a derivative of numerous other wastes. The regulations establish a separate waste code (F039) for multi-source leachate, and prescribe fixed treatment standards for wastewater and nonwastewater forms of leachate and residues derived from leachate treatment. The treatment standards consist of maximum concentration levels for more than 200 constituents that might be found in the leachate. *Id.* at 22532, 22619-25.

2. Does the portion of the *Chemical Waste Management* opinion regarding contaminated media effectively elevate the EPA's "contained-in policy" to the status of a regulation? If so, on what basis can the court do that? Does it undermine the notice and comment requirements in the Administrative Procedure Act? Would the panel that decided *Shell Oil Co. v. EPA* (chapter 2.B) have reached the same result as did the *Chemical Waste Management* panel in the case above? If that case did not, in effect, convert the contained-in policy into a regulation, what is the practical difference between the policy and regulations, such as the mixture and derived-from rules? On August 18, 1992, the EPA promulgated additional treatment standards for "newly listed wastes" (*i.e.*, wastes listed as hazardous after HSWA was enacted in November 1984) and contaminated debris. 57 Fed. Reg. 37194 (1992). In addition to codifying the contained-in policy regarding contaminated debris, the regulations expanded the options for handling contaminated debris under the land disposal restrictions. Generators may, as before, treat the debris until it achieves the treatment standards applicable to all wastes contaminating the debris, an often-costly undertaking. Alternatively, the EPA established treatment standards for contaminated debris *per se*; it can be treated by specified technologies (various forms of extraction, destruction, or immobilization) until it meets certain performance standards.

3. Is the contained-in policy based directly on (or "derived from") the mixture and derived-from rules? If so, what is the status of the contained-in policy after *Shell Oil*? What is the effect of the *Chemical Waste Management* holding regarding contaminated media after *Shell Oil*?

4. Since at least 1990, the EPA has maintained that it is "generally inappropriate or unachievable for soils contaminated with hazardous waste" (deemed hazardous waste under the contained-in policy) to be subject to the same treatment standards as "as-generated" wastes. 55 Fed. Reg. 8759 (1990). However, although the agency indicated its intention to set soil-specific treatment standards, 58 Fed. Reg. 48154 (1993), it has not yet done so. As of July 1997, contaminated media are subject to the treatment standards for the various hazardous wastes that are contained-in the media. *See* 59 Fed. Reg. 47982, 47986 (1994).

The EPA's April 1996 proposal for identifying hazardous waste in the context of contaminated media has again employed soil-specific land ban treatment standards, which would be tied to the criteria for determining whether or not contaminated media are considered to be hazardous waste. 61 Fed. Reg. 18780 (1996) (see chapter 2.B. above).

5. There are several potential means of complying with the RCRA land ban. The most widely applicable—and frequently the only—option is to comply with the treatment standard(s) specified in 40 C.F.R. Part 268, Subpart D (*i.e.*, a concentration level, a treatment method, or no land disposal). The following exemptions may also be available although, with the exception of the surface impoundment treatment option, they may not be claimed by any particular generator or for any particular waste unless specifically so authorized by the EPA.

a. *Surface impoundment treatment exemption*: If specified design and operation requirements are satisfied, hazardous wastes may be placed in surface impoundments for treatment purposes without violating the land ban. 40 C.F.R. § 268.4.

b. *Treatment standard variance*: Where a waste is sufficiently different from those used by the EPA in setting treatment standards, one may seek the EPA's approval to adopt an alternative treatment standard that is more appropriate to the waste. 40 C.F.R. §§ 268.42(b), 268.44(a), and 268.44(h).

c. *Capacity variance*: The EPA may grant nationwide variances based on the unavailability of treatment capacity, RCRA §3004(h)(2), as well as individual, waste-specific and generator-specific variances where treatment capacity is not available, notwithstanding the generator's diligent efforts to obtain access to such capacity and provided that the generator has a binding commitment for such treatment to be made available. 40 C.F.R. § 268.5. Both types of variances are time-limited.

d. *No-migration exemption*: Land disposal of wastes that do not satisfy the applicable treatment standard may take place if the EPA grants a no-migration petition for that particular disposal location. The EPA will not grant any such petition unless it is shown, to a reasonable degree of certainty, that there will be no migration of hazardous constituents from the disposal unit for as long as the wastes remain hazardous. *See* RCRA § 3004(d)(1), (e)(1), (f)(2), and (g)(5); 40 C.F.R. § 268.6. The following case addresses the EPA's implementation of the no-migration exemption.

NATURAL RESOURCES DEFENSE COUNCIL V. UNITED STATES ENVIRONMENTAL PROTECTION AGENCY
907 F.2d 1146 (D.C.Cir. 1990)

Before WALD, Chief Judge, and RUTH B. GINSBURG and WILLIAMS, Circuit Judges.

PER CURIAM.

This case concerns the disposal of hazardous waste by "deep injection"; that is, the injection of hazardous waste into "wells" located thousands of feet beneath the surface of the earth. The Environmental Protection Agency ("EPA") has issued regulations under the Resource Conservation and Recovery Act ("RCRA") governing this method of hazardous waste disposal, and various petitioners challenge them. Industry petitioners claim the regulations are too stringent; environmental petitioners claim they are too lenient. We hold that the regulations are reasonable exercises of the EPA's authority and discretion under RCRA except insofar as they relate to the disposal of hazardous waste in "geologic repositories," that is, salt domes, salt beds, underground mines, and caves. We believe the EPA has ignored its statutory duty to promulgate standards for these repositories and has not adequately defended its permitting process against NRDC's statutory challenges, and so we remand these issues for further agency consideration. In all other respects, we deny the petitions for review.

I. BACKGROUND
* * *

    * * * HSWA [the Hazardous and Solid Waste Amendments of 1984] ***
legislated new "land ban" provisions governing the land disposal of hazardous waste,
§ 6924(d)-(g). Subsection (d) governs all methods of land disposal, except disposal by
deep injection, of certain, specified wastes (mostly toxic metals), popularly known as
the "California list" wastes. Subsection (e) governs all methods of land disposal, except
disposal by deep injection, of solvents and dioxins. Subsection (f) governs disposal by
deep injection of the wastes specified in subsections (d) and (e). Finally, subsection (g)
governs all methods of land disposal, including disposal by deep injection, of all
hazardous wastes other than the "California list" or solvents and dioxins covered by
subsections (d), (e), and (f). In toto, subsections (d) through (g) of § 6924 govern all
methods of land disposal of all hazardous wastes.

    In 1988, the EPA promulgated final rules pursuant to subsections (f) and (g)
governing the disposal of hazardous wastes by deep injection. 53 Fed. Reg. 28,118
(1988). These rules supplemented the EPA's Underground Injection Control ("UIC")
program, which governed underground injection of solid waste, to take into account
injection of hazardous waste. The general scheme adopted by the EPA provided that
underground injection of hazardous wastes would be prohibited unless the would-be
injector obtained a permit from the EPA for a particular underground injection well.
New rules located at 40 C.F.R. Part 148 identified the wastes otherwise prohibited from
underground injection and specified the procedures for obtaining a permit to allow their
injection. New Subpart G of 40 C.F.R. Part 146 set out technical criteria that
underground injection wells must satisfy before they could be approved for hazardous
waste disposal. In sum, the EPA's regulatory scheme for deep well injection of
hazardous waste contained two important components: (1) the substantive standard that
a hazardous waste injection well must meet, and (2) the permit procedures by which an
injector must demonstrate that a well meets that standard.

    The new rules also presented the EPA's interpretations of several key statutory
terms. The permissibility of a land disposal method under subsections (d) through (g)
of § 6924 turns on whether the method will be "protective of human health and the
environment for as long as the waste remains hazardous." Subsections (d), (e), and (g),
but not (f), state that to meet this standard, an applicant must demonstrate to the
Administrator, to a reasonable degree of certainty, that "there will be no migration of
hazardous constituents from the disposal unit or injection zone for as long as the wastes
remain hazardous." With regard to these safety standards, the EPA made the following
interpretations: First, the EPA decided to apply the "no migration" standard to waste
disposal governed by subsection (f) (deep injection of the "California list" wastes and
solvents and dioxins) as well as to disposal governed by the other subsections.

    Second, it decided that the term "the wastes" in the statutory no migration
standard refers to the wastes that migrate out of the injection zone, and that the no
migration standard is therefore satisfied if the injector demonstrates that no hazardous
waste will migrate out of the injection zone.

Third, it decided that the term "migration" encompasses not only fluid migrations, but also migrations by molecular diffusion.

Fourth, it decided that in demonstrating that there will be no improper migration, an injector must show that there will be no migration for as long as the wastes remain hazardous, or for 10,000 years, whichever period is shorter.

Finally, the EPA decided that the term "injection zone," which is not defined in the statute, means any geological formation, group of formations, or part of a formation, that can meet RCRA's safety standards for containing waste.

In the preamble to its regulations, the EPA stated that the regulations might apply to the disposal of waste in geologic repositories. The EPA would, however, use individualized permit proceedings to determine whether the new regulations could appropriately govern disposal of hazardous waste in geologic repositories.

The Chemical Manufacturers Association and other industry groups (collectively referred to as "CMA" or "industry petitioners") claim that the EPA's rules impose unreasonably strict requirements that are unrelated to protection of human health and the environment. The Natural Resources Defense Council and other environmental groups (collectively referred to as "NRDC" or "environmental petitioners") claim the rules are not as protective of human health and the environment as the statute requires. The environmental petitioners also claim that the EPA cannot, consistent with the statutory directives of § 6924(b), apply the regulations to the injection of waste into geologic repositories.

In passing on the claims of the petitioners, we are guided, as always, by *Chevron U.S.A., Inc. v. NRDC*, 467 U.S. 837 (1984). With respect to each claim, we inquire "whether Congress has directly spoken to the precise question at issue." *Id.* at 842. In determining the intent of Congress, we must look to "the particular statutory language at issue, as well as the language and design of the statute as a whole," *K Mart Corp. v. Cartier, Inc.*, 108 S. Ct. 1811, 1817 (1988), and we must employ traditional tools of statutory construction, including, where appropriate, legislative history. If the intent of Congress is clear, we must give it effect. If, however, the statute is silent or ambiguous on a particular issue, we must defer to the agency's interpretation of the statute so long as it is reasonable and consistent with the statutory purpose.

II. INDUSTRY CLAIMS
* * *

C. The Content of the "No Migration" Standard —Industry Challenges

1. RCRA and SDWA

The industry petitioners claim that as a matter of statutory interpretation the no migration standard of RCRA is identical to the safety standard of the Safe Drinking Water Act ("SDWA"), 42 U.S.C. § 300h(b)(1). We disagree.

The texts of RCRA and SDWA provide no support for the CMA's identity argument. SDWA protects sources of drinking water; RCRA protects human health and the environment. SDWA states that underground injection must not endanger drinking water sources; RCRA states that there must be no migration of hazardous constituents from the injection zone for as long as the wastes remain hazardous; it makes no reference to anything outside the injection zone that might be threatened by such a migration. The statutory texts provide no evidence whatsoever that Congress intended that the RCRA and SDWA standards be identical.

* * *

The only question remaining is whether the EPA's interpretation of RCRA as imposing a stricter standard on deep well injection of hazardous waste than SDWA is reasonable and consistent with RCRA's purposes. We believe that it is. RCRA's facially stronger text, requiring "no migration of hazardous constituents from the ... injection zone for as long as the wastes remain hazardous," subsection (g)(5), makes the EPA's tougher stance entirely reasonable. Its unstinting interpretation is consistent with RCRA's expressly stated purpose of minimizing the land disposal of hazardous waste.

* * *

3. Ten Thousand Years

Did the EPA abuse its discretion in requiring injectors to show that there will be no migration of hazardous constituents from the injection zone for 10,000 years? CMA claims both that Congress intended a shorter period, and that 10,000 years is longer than the hazardous life of the wastes.

First, Congress never decided for itself that a shorter period than 10,000 years was adequate for keeping hazardous wastes in the injection zone. CMA can point to no decisive support for its less than 10,000 year claim in the statutory text or history. It is true that the legislative reports speak of the decomposition time of hazardous waste in terms of centuries rather than millennia. See S.Rep. No. 284, 98th Cong., 1st Sess. 15 (1983) ("Wastes chemically decompose in a land disposal facility, although often this decomposition occurs very slowly stretching over centuries."); H.R.Rep. No. 198, 98th Cong., 1st Sess. 33 ("land disposal of wastes ... might be appropriate if there is a reasonable certainty that wastes will be contained in the very long-term (i.e., at least several hundred years)."). However, the statute mandates containment "for as long as the wastes remain hazardous." Subsection (g)(5). Congress could hardly have desired the EPA to regulate waste disposal only for centuries even if scientific predictions project that the waste could remain hazardous for a much longer period. The EPA chose 10,000 years as a time limit because it would be long enough to insure that the "no migration" standard would be met, and yet short enough to come within the limitations of predictability. The EPA's choice was reasonable and consistent with the statutory purpose of preventing migration of hazardous constituents for as long as the wastes remain hazardous.

CMA may be correct that some injected wastes will cease to be hazardous in less than 10,000 years; in such a case the regulations specifically allow the injector to seek relief on the basis of such a showing. The regulations require the injector to show that there will be no migration so long as the wastes remain hazardous, or for 10,000 years, whichever period is shorter. The EPA's regulation properly places its emphasis on the statutory requirement of preventing migration for as long as the wastes remain hazardous. It does not require injectors to control the wastes for a longer period.

* * *

III. NRDC CLAIMS

A. *EPA's Interpretation of the "No Migration" Standard.*

Subsections (d), (e) and (g) of § 6924 ban the land disposal of hazardous wastes unless, for each of three specified methods, it has

> been demonstrated to the Administrator, to a reasonable degree of certainty, that there will be *no migration of hazardous constituents* from the disposal unit or injection zone *for as long as the wastes remain hazardous.*

42 U.S.C. § 6924(d), (e), (g) (emphasis added). As we noted above, EPA read this "no migration" standard into subsection (f) as well, in the interests of uniform treatment. *See* 53 Fed. Reg. at 28,120 (col. 3). The issue here is whether the "no migration" standard would be violated if hazardous constituents seeped out of the storage area at a time where *some* of the stored wastes were still hazardous, but *not* those actually leaving.

"Hazardous constituent" is a term of art referring to a list of chemical compounds compiled at 40 C.F.R. Part 261, Appendix VIII. Since these are defined by molecular formulae without reference to concentrations, a single molecule of such a chemical is a "hazardous constituent." A hazardous waste, by contrast, is such only if various factors, including the *concentration* of hazardous constituents, actually make it hazardous to human health or the environment. 40 C.F.R. § 261.11(a)(3)(ii); 42 U.S.C. § 6921(b) (requiring the Administrator to list wastes as hazardous if they contain "certain constituents (such as identified carcinogens, mutagens, or teratagens) at levels in excess of levels which endanger human health."). Thus, read literally, the "no migration" standard would seem to prohibit the migration of even a single molecule (or perhaps an appropriate de minimis amount) for the statutory time period, even though the migrating waste is itself not hazardous at all.

There is, however, an ambiguity in the statutory definition of the period—"as long as *the wastes* remain hazardous." To which "wastes" does the clause refer? Since the consistency of wastes may vary throughout an injection zone (or a disposal unit), wastes in one part, particularly near the perimeter, may no longer be hazardous while wastes in another part still are. Can hazardous constituents in such non-hazardous wastes migrate without violating the "no migration" standard? Or must the operator assure no migration of constituents until all wastes throughout the injection zone are no longer hazardous? Noting this textual ambiguity, the EPA interpreted "the wastes" to refer to the wastes containing the hazardous constituents that are leaving the injection zone. Under this reading, hazardous constituents may migrate so long as "the wastes" immediately surrounding them at the border are no longer hazardous, or, putting it slightly differently, so long as they do not migrate in high enough concentrations to be hazardous wastes.

NRDC's most powerful argument is then that EPA has artfully transformed the standard "no migration of hazardous *constituents*" into a quite different standard—"no migration of hazardous *wastes*." We find this challenge quite close, but the ambiguity is serious enough to allow EPA under *Chevron* to resolve the issue in the way it has.

The EPA rests in part on a structural contention that "[ordinarily] the term 'hazardous constituents' has no regulatory effect unless concentrations are also considered." This is true in the sense that RCRA "ordinarily" regulates "hazardous wastes," which of course are defined (in part) in terms of concentrations of hazardous constituents, but it is obviously not a basis for reading "constituents" as "wastes" when Congress chooses the former. Nonetheless the exceptional character of the usage may suggest a need to be on guard against facile literalism.

The parties agree that we can learn something from § 6925(j), one of the rare other places in RCRA where Congress used the term "constituents" with a material regulatory effect. Section 6925(j) conditions a variance from certain technological control requirements for certain surface impoundments on the operator's proving that there will be "no migration of any hazardous constituent into ground water or surface water at any future time." 42 U.S.C. § 6925(j)(4). Even the EPA assumes that this other "no migration" standard prohibits migration of *any* hazardous constituent (down to a single molecule or an appropriate de minimis level). Nonetheless, § 6925(j) does not contain the ambiguous "for so long as the wastes remain hazardous" clause. Furthermore, it contains an additional, if not earth-shattering, textual difference. While § 6924 prohibits "migration of hazardous constituents," § 6925(j) prohibits "migration of *any* hazardous constituent." If Congress had wanted § 6924's "no migration" standards to cover a single molecule, it could have expressed the point as aggressively as in § 6925. And of course the context suggests a reason for a difference: § 6925(j)(4) protects water resources, which are not directly implicated under the controlling language of § 6924, and its "no migration" requirement works only as a condition for a variance. Overall, however, we find the statutory language and structure ambiguous and so turn to the legislative history.   *   *   *

Finding no clear congressional determination in § 6924 that hazardous constituents must not migrate regardless of hazard, and the reasonableness of the EPA's policy choice being unquestioned, we affirm its decision.

*   *   *

NOTES

1. The EPA subsequently proposed amending the land ban regulations to reflect the *NRDC* court's interpretation of the "no migration" test. The EPA explained:

[T]he Agency proposes to clarify and amend § 268.6(a) to define the term "no migration of hazardous constituents from the disposal unit or injection zone" *** to mean that concentrations of hazardous constituents do not and shall not exceed Agency-approved health-based or environmental-based levels, in any environmental medium, at the boundary of the unit or injection zone. Under this approach, possible migration pathways for each medium are as follows: Concentrations of hazardous constituents in ground water in the vicinity of the unit could not exceed the appropriate ingestion health-based levels for drinking water. Surface water concentrations, both in surface water bodies in the vicinity of the unit and in storm runoff from the unit, likewise could not exceed appropriate health-based levels for drinking water or ambient water quality criteria. Similarly, concentrations in soil *** outside the unit could not exceed health-based levels for ingestion. Finally, air emissions of hazardous constituents from the unit *** could not exceed the appropriate health-based levels for inhalation exposure.

57 Fed. Reg. 35940, 35941 (1992). Is this proposal consistent with the *NRDC* opinion? Is it consistent with the other provisions of the land ban program?

2. The land ban regulations contain two significant provisions that modify and tighten, for land ban purposes, rules that apply less stringently in the rest of the RCRA program.

a. *Storage prohibition:* Whereas hazardous waste generators are allowed to store on-site the waste that they generate for up to 90 days (or 180 days, for small quantity generators) without requiring a storage facility permit, the land ban regulations impose a prohibition on any storage of hazardous waste subject to land ban, unless for the sole purpose of accumulating sufficient quantities to facilitate proper recovery, treatment, or disposal of the waste. 40 C.F.R. § 268.50.

The D.C. Circuit upheld the storage prohibition regulation, rejecting claims that it was inconsistent with RCRA and unreasonable to apply the land ban storage prohibition to mixed hazardous-radioactive wastes for which adequate treatment methods are not yet available. *Edison Electric Institute v. EPA*, 996 F.2d 326 (D.C. Cir. 1993).

> *** As amended in 1984 by the HSWA, RCRA was clearly intended to provide draconian incentives—such as the prohibition of all forms of land disposal for specified wastes—for the rapid development of adequate treatment and disposal capacity. These incentives would be significantly diminished to the extent that generators could rely on the possibility of storing their wastes indefinitely in the event that capacity was not developed in a timely fashion. ***
>
> *   *   *
>
> Petitioners make several other arguments to support their position that section 3004(j) authorizes the indefinite storage of mixed wastes, or at the very least, that the statute is ambiguous. Most prominently, petitioners stress that the EPA's interpretation of section 3004(j) imposes requirements that are impossible for mixed waste generators to meet. According to petitioners, even if generators were to cease their operations entirely—an action that would entail massive disruption of the national economy—they would remain in violation with respect to mixed wastes

that have already been generated and wastes that would be produced during the shutdown process. Petitioners contend that statutory constructions yielding such "absurd" or "impossible" results are to be avoided.

There are two responses to petitioners' "impossibility" argument. As an initial matter, the impossibility of compliance with section 3004(j) emerges only if one adopts petitioners' *ex post* perspective on the statute. That is, petitioners look only at the situation as it stands currently, after the relevant LDR deadlines have passed. Given the technology-forcing nature of the statute, however, it is more reasonable to adopt an *ex ante* view and ask whether, if sufficient resources were devoted to the problem, it was possible to develop the required treatment and disposal technologies between 1986, when it became clear that RCRA applied to mixed wastes, and the present.

Moreover, even though it may have proven impossible for generators to develop the required treatment and disposal options within the statutory period, courts have not shrunk from adopting onerous interpretations of statutory provisions where required by the clear intent of Congress. ***

Id. at 335-36.

b. *Dilution prohibition:* Whereas it is permissible to dilute a characteristic hazardous waste such that it no longer exhibits a characteristic, and ceases to be a RCRA hazardous waste, the land ban prohibits (with some exceptions) the dilution of any hazardous waste subject to the land ban, or any treatment residue, as a substitute for adequate treatment to meet applicable treatment standards. 40 C.F.R. § 268.3.

In promulgating land ban treatment standards for characteristic wastes (as part of the third-third rulemaking), the EPA amended the regulations to allow for dilution of characteristic wastes treated in Clean Water Act units or disposed of in underground injection wells. Moreover, the EPA stated in the Preamble that it would allow dilution as a means of achieving a "deactivation" treatment standard—treatment to remove the hazardous waste characteristic—for most corrosive, ignitable, and reactive characteristic wastes. These and other aspects of the third-third rulemaking regarding characteristic wastes were challenged in the following case.

CHEMICAL WASTE MANAGEMENT, INC. V. UNITED STATES ENVIRONMENTAL PROTECTION AGENCY
976 F.2d 2 (D.C. Cir. 1992), *cert. denied,* 507 U.S. 1057 (1993)

Before EDWARDS, BUCKLEY, and HENDERSON, Circuit Judges.
PER CURIAM.

* * *

The regulations under review implement the land-ban program for the last third of the ranked list of wastes, the "third-third." They largely consist of treatment standards for characteristic wastes. The final rule also modifies regulations governing characteristic wastes that are managed in treatment systems regulated through National Pollutant Discharge Elimination System permits issued under the Clean Water Act as well as regulations affecting those disposed of in underground injection wells regulated under the Safe Drinking Water Act. The rule establishes a variety of compliance requirements as well.

Fourteen petitions for review were filed and consolidated into this proceeding. Petitioners divided the case into three groups of issues for purposes of briefing and argument. The first focuses on industry petitioners' challenge to standards mandating treatment of characteristic wastes beyond the point at which they cease to display hazardous characteristics and on NRDC petitioners' challenge to dilution as a method of treatment. The second centers on the Clean Water Act and underground injection well questions. The third consists of the remaining issues. This opinion adopts the same approach.

II. TREATMENT STANDARDS FOR CHARACTERISTIC WASTES

A. Proposed Rule

As described above, at the outset of the RCRA program, the EPA identified four characteristics as hazardous: ignitability, corrosivity, reactivity, and EP toxicity. In its proposed rules, and in the final regulations, the Agency divided characteristic wastes into subcategories, suggesting treatment standards or levels for each subcategory. For some of these, the EPA proposed treatment to reduce the presence of the characteristic below the level at which the waste was defined as hazardous. For example, a waste is considered corrosive, and therefore hazardous, if it is aqueous and has a pH of less than two or greater than 12.5. The proposed rule required treatment that would result in a pH between six and nine. For other subcategories, however, the EPA suggested treatment to the characteristic level and no further.

The Agency stated that it possessed the authority to compel treatment below characteristic levels. It took note of the argument that the characteristic levels represent the limit of subtitle C authority—that the Agency had no power to regulate a waste where the characteristic had been brought below the level deemed hazardous. The Agency believed, however, that section 3004(m) extended its authority beyond that point. *** The EPA concluded that it was directed by the statute to require a waste that is hazardous at the point of generation and is destined for land disposal to "be treated by methods which substantially reduce toxicity and minimize threats to human health and the environment." *Id*. [54 Fed. Reg. at 48,490.]

As to methods of treatment, the proposed rule largely followed the judgment made by the EPA in previous land-ban program rulemakings. In those earlier rules, the EPA determined that treatment would be accomplished through the use of "best demonstrated available technologies." The proposed rule specified the particular technology to be used in the treatment of most ICR wastes. For a handful of others, the Agency offered a measure of flexibility by creating a "deactivation" category of treatment. According to the proposal, the EPA had "determined that within [several ICR subcategories] there appear to be a further variety of different waste groups, each with a certain degree of uniqueness with respect to hazard and handling requirements." *Id.* at 48,419. Therefore, while the Agency recommended a number of methods, it proposed to allow generators or treaters of those wastes to select the appropriate method of treatment. *Id.* at 48,419-20.

In implementing the land-ban program for solvents and wastes containing dioxins, the EPA barred dilution as an alternative for "adequate treatment." ***

At several points in the proposed third-third rule, the EPA reaffirmed its decision that a generator or treater might not dilute wastes to escape the dictates of the land disposal program. In its discussion of ignitable wastes, the Agency stated that "a prohibited form of dilution that is used to remove a characteristic from a prohibited hazardous waste would be a violation of the dilution prohibition in [40 C.F.R.] section 268.3." 54 Fed. Reg. at 48,422. Among the EPA's concerns was the possibility that dilution of ignitable wastes would lead to dangerous emissions of volatile organic compounds, a problem that could be avoided by using other treatment methods.

The EPA proposed a similar bar with regard to reactive wastes: "[D]ilution of reactive wastes should not automatically be considered to be a legitimate form of treatment." *Id.* at 48,426. It proposed that reactive cyanides and sulfides be treated like any toxic waste; "[w]ith respect to other reactive wastes, most cannot be diluted without violent reaction so that dilution is not a viable management alternative[.]" *Id.*

Finally, the EPA suggested that corrosives be treated by neutralization, not dilution, to alter their pH. According to the Agency, dilution would require the use of large amounts of water and would create a greater volume of waste; moreover, dilution "does not treat or remove hazardous constituents in the wastes." *Id.* at 48,423.

* * *

B. Final Rule

In the final rule, the EPA revised many of its proposed treatment standards for ICR and toxic characteristic wastes. The EPA, however, did not back away from its basic position that it could require treatment below characteristic levels. Because "Congress has given apparently conflicting guidance on how the Agency should address land disposal prohibitions for characteristic wastes," the EPA "believes it has authority to reconcile these potential conflicts and to harmonize statutory provisions to forge a coherent regulatory system." 55 Fed. Reg. at 22,651. The EPA agreed with many participants in the comment period that "one permissible construction of the language in section 3004(g)" (which requires the promulgation of regulations "prohibiting ... methods of land disposal of the [listed] hazardous wastes") is that subtitle C rules applied only to hazardous wastes, and therefore the applicability of the land disposal regulations must be judged at the moment of disposal. 55 Fed. Reg. at 22,652. Ultimately, the EPA concluded that Congress did not state when the status of the waste should be evaluated for purposes of the ban on land disposal; therefore, the EPA could choose to regulate the waste "at the point of generation or at the point of disposal (and possibly at some other point or combination of the two)." *Id.*

While viewing its authority broadly, the EPA decided to exercise it sparingly:

Today's rule reflects a decision to take limited, but nonetheless significant, steps within the point of generation framework. As a general matter, the Agency believes that the goals of [the program] may require application of standards which go beyond the characteristic level ... in some future cases.

Id. at 22,654. The final regulations call for treatment below characteristic levels for only a handful of wastes. ***

The EPA determined that for most ICR wastes, treatment to characteristic levels would be sufficient. The Agency found upon review that

[t]he environmental concerns from the properties of ignitability, corrosivity, and reactivity are different from the environmental concern from EP toxic wastes. Toxic constituents can pose a cumulative impact on land disposal even where waste is below the characteristic level. Where wastes pose an ascertainable toxicity concern ... the Agency has developed treatment standards that address the toxicity concern and (in effect) require treatment below the characteristic level.... Otherwise, treatment that removes the properties of ignitability, corrosivity, and reactivity, fully addresses the environmental concern from the properties themselves.

Id. at 22,655.

The EPA also retreated from its emphasis on technology-based treatment in the final regulations, altering its position on the use of dilution as a method of treatment:

In all cases, the Agency has determined that for non-toxic hazardous characteristic wastes, it should not matter how the characteristic property is removed so long as it is removed. Thus, dilution is an acceptable treatment method for such wastes.

Id. at 22,532. The Agency included dilution within the ambit of the "deactivation" treatment standard. The final rule defined the standard as "[d]eactivation to remove the hazardous characteristics of a waste due to its ignitability, corrosivity, and/or reactivity." As long as these characteristics are removed, any method can be employed under the final regulations. The EPA allowed full discretion among specified technological methods of treatment (such as neutralization or incineration) as well as dilution with water or other wastes. For toxic wastes, the prohibition on dilution remained.

*** Only in three subcategories of ICR wastes did the EPA mandate the use of technological treatment: reactive sulfides; reactive cyanides; and ignitable liquid nonwastewater wastes containing more than ten percent total organic compounds. For all corrosive wastes, other ignitable liquid wastes (nonwastewaters with low total organic compounds and ignitable wastewaters), ignitable compressed gases, ignitable reactive wastes, explosive wastes, water reactives, and other reactives dilution would be acceptable.

* * *

D. Industry Petitioners' Challenge to the Treatment Standards

Industry petitioners contend that RCRA does not provide authority for the EPA to mandate treatment of characteristic wastes after their ignitability, corrosiveness, reactivity, or EP toxicity has been addressed. They make a straightforward argument:

Subtitle C regulations attach to a waste only when it is hazardous. The moment a waste ceases to meet the regulatory definition of a hazardous waste, the EPA loses its authority to regulate further. ***

Industry petitioners point to a welter of provisions in RCRA where the words "hazardous waste" are used as proof that the statute applies only to waste defined as hazardous. Subtitle C, they explain, is entitled "Hazardous Waste Management," and the entire subtitle addresses that problem—the management of *hazardous* waste. ***

In their view, the 1984 Amendments did not change this boundary. They point out that land disposal is defined in part as "any placement of such hazardous waste in a landfill, [or] surface impoundment," RCRA § 3004(k); that section 3004(g) similarly "prohibit[s] one or more methods of land disposal of hazardous wastes," and, finally, that section 3004(m) authorizes land disposal of hazardous waste that has been treated, suggesting to industry petitioners that the provision specifically authorizes only the disposal of wastes that remain hazardous after treatment. Thus, they conclude, the disposal restrictions can apply only to wastes that are hazardous at the moment of disposal.

In its brief, the EPA reiterates the rationales stated in its final rule: The key provisions of the land-ban program, sections 3004(g)(5) and (m), can be read as allowing the Agency to apply land disposal restrictions at any time it wishes; those provisions at a minimum contemplate activity that occurs before land disposal; section 3004(m)(1) requires treatment to avoid the prohibition on land disposal; and treatment must take place, by definition, before disposal occurs. *** The Agency reasons that the subtitle C program can attach at the point of generation, and the broad language of section 3004(m)(1) allows additional treatment to remove risks posed by wastes beyond those inherent in the characteristic.

*** We find little support in the statute or our prior decisions for the notion that Congress mandated the line industry petitioners draw. These petitioners believe that the definition of a hazardous waste acts as a revolving regulatory door, allowing continual entrance and egress from RCRA's requirements. The key provisions of the statute support a contrary view—that hazardous waste becomes subject to the land disposal program as soon as it is generated.

RCRA directs the Administrator to "promulgate regulations identifying the characteristics of hazardous waste ... which shall be subject to the provisions of this subchapter." RCRA § 3001(b)(1). This appears to bring a waste within the statutory scheme once it is identified as hazardous. Under the dictates of the 1984 Amendments, the Administrator "shall promulgate regulations ... [banning land disposal for] any hazardous waste identified or listed under section 6921 of this title." RCRA § 3004(g)(4). Again, the focus is on the identification of a waste as hazardous.

* * *

The 1984 Amendments also provide the EPA with the authority to mandate treatment past the point at which a characteristic is removed. Section 3004(g)(5) requires the Administrator to promulgate regulations prohibiting land disposal of hazardous wastes "except with respect to a hazardous waste which has complied with the pretreatment regulations promulgated under subsection (m) of this section." Subsection (m)(1), in turn, calls on the Administrator to

> specify those levels or methods of treatment, if any, which substantially diminish the toxicity of the waste or substantially reduce the likelihood of migration of hazardous constituents from the waste so that short-term and long-term threats to human health and the environment are minimized.

The requirement that treatment "substantially diminish the toxicity" or substantially reduce the likelihood of migration of hazardous constituents suggests concerns that go beyond the characteristics identified in 40 C.F.R. Part 261, subpart C. Similarly, in concluding that the EPA had the authority to require technologies that go beyond the elimination of hazardous characteristics, we have noted that "minimize" offers a broad mandate: "To 'minimize' something is, to quote the Oxford English Dictionary, to 'reduce [it] to the smallest possible amount, extent, or degree.'" *HWTC III*, 886 F.2d at 361.

*   *   *

E. NRDC Petitioners' Challenge to Deactivation Treatment Standard

NRDC petitioners ask this court to vacate the deactivation treatment standard as applied to ICR wastes because it authorizes the dilution of these wastes to eliminate their ignitability, corrosiveness, or reactivity rather than mandating use of technological treatment. NRDC petitioners rely on the language of section 3004(m)(1), statements in the legislative history of the 1984 Amendments, and the overall structure of the RCRA program as support for their position that treatment does not include dilution. They claim that some form of technology must be used to treat wastes in all instances.

They also contend that dilution fails to satisfy the statutory requirement that treatment minimize short-term and long-term threats to human health and the environment, or to substantially diminish the toxicity of the waste. In their view, the removal of these characteristics through dilution only affects the short-term risk that the waste will manifest that property; it does not address the threats posed by the hazardous organic and inorganic constituents of those wastes. ***

We believe that dilution can, in principle, constitute an acceptable form of treatment for ICR wastes. We do not read the 1984 Amendments as mandating the use of the best demonstrated available technologies ("BDAT") in all situations. *** NRDC petitioners insist that under the plain terms of *** [§ 3004(m)(1)], the deactivation standard fails because dilution is not a "method of treatment." Although they acknowledge that the statutory definition of "treatment" is broad enough to encompass dilution, they maintain that Congress had a more exacting criterion in mind when it enacted section 3004(m).

We agree that the section imposes an exacting standard: It requires that treatment prior to land disposal "substantially diminish the toxicity of the waste or substantially reduce the likelihood of migration of hazardous constituents from the waste so that short-term and long-term threats to human health and the environment are minimized." RCRA 3004(m)(1). But this provision does not bar dilution as a means of treating ICR wastes; instead, it defines the purposes that a method of treatment must achieve. Any treatment that meets those objectives is permissible. When read against RCRA's broad definition of treatment, we cannot say Congress clearly barred dilution as an acceptable methodology.

* * *

We are more troubled by the question whether the dilution of certain ICR wastes will satisfy section 3004(m). Treatment must meet the standards established by that section, and its requirements are clear: It must remove the characteristic and reduce the presence of hazardous constituents when those constituents are present in sufficient concentrations to pose a threat to human health or the environment. *** We find it unclear whether dilution is fully consistent with section 3004(m)'s treatment standards for all of the subcategories of ICR wastes for which the EPA has proscribed [*sic*] deactivation.

As we have explained, the proposed rule pointed to significant problems that could arise if dilution was accepted as a means of treating ICR wastes. In the final regulations, the Agency found that deactivation "addresses the environmental concern from the properties themselves." The EPA admitted, however, that "the characteristic level is only one indicator of hazard and, thus, removal of the specific characteristic is not the same as assuring that the waste is safe." It then acknowledged "that this approach does not fully address the potential problem of toxic constituents that may be present in [ICR] wastes, nor encourage minimization ... of non-toxic characteristic hazardous wastes." ***

Unfortunately, these confessions are not a substitute for a rule conforming to the statute's command. We conclude that the deactivation standard, in its present form, is permissible only in the case of corrosive wastes; and then only so long as they do not contain hazardous constituents that, following dilution, would themselves present a continuing danger to human health or the environment.

1. *Ignitable Wastes*

At oral argument, counsel for the EPA conceded that some ignitable wastes subject to the deactivation standard include hazardous or toxic constituents that will remain after dilution, perhaps at sufficient levels to pose a risk to human health and the environment. Further, in the proposed rule, the EPA barred dilution of all ignitable wastes because of the risk of emissions of volatile organic compounds during dilution and the possibility that the waste would regain its ignitability after dilution. ***

The final regulations suggested a number of technology-based treatment methods that might be used for ignitable wastes, but in the end authorized dilution if it would remove the characteristic alone, except for ignitable wastes including more than ten percent total organic compounds. ***

In view of the EPA's position that treatment pursuant to section 3004(m) requires the removal of a waste's hazardous characteristic and the reduction of other hazardous constituents, and the Agency's concessions that constituents are present in some ignitable wastes subject to the deactivation standard, we vacate this part of the rule. To conform with its own reading of section 3004(m), the Agency must identify the ignitable wastes that include, after dilution, sufficiently high levels of hazardous constituents to pose a risk to human health or the environment, and propose a method of treatment that will deal with these threats. In addition, the Agency must address the problem of VOC emissions from ignitable wastes during dilution. The EPA's statement that it believes that VOC emissions can be controlled by changes in operating parameters is inadequate. It must state, with evidentiary support, that the risk of VOC emissions during dilution is minimal for ignitable wastes now subject to the deactivation standard, or it must require actions to minimize that risk.

2. Corrosive Wastes

The EPA asserts in its brief that the sole problem posed by corrosive wastes is their corrosiveness: "[T]here are no hazardous constituents in the waste." *** But NRDC petitioners come to a different conclusion. They point to the proposed rule, *** and a statement from the EPA's BDAT Background Document stating that some corrosive wastes do in fact possess hazardous constituents beyond their potential for corrosion. *** NRDC petitioners acknowledge that corrosive wastes can be treated effectively by mixing acid and alkaline wastes; but they object to dilution with water because it will not treat the toxic constituents they claim are present in corrosive wastes. ***

The final regulations themselves are somewhat ambiguous on the question of the presence of hazardous constituents. ***

We agree with the EPA that dilution can be an acceptable form of treatment of corrosive wastes. But in the face of this record, we cannot rely on the assertions made in the EPA's brief and oral argument that corrosive wastes pose no hazards other than those presented by this characteristic. If, however, the facts will support these assurances, the EPA may cure this defect and meet the requirements of section 3004(m) with a statement, backed by evidence, that the corrosive wastes subject to the deactivation standard do not contain hazardous constituents that pose a threat to human health and the environment. If such a statement may be made, the Agency should be able to revise its rulemaking prior to the issuance of the mandate in this case.

3. Reactive Wastes

With regard to reactive wastes, we have a problem of a different kind. Although, in the final regulations and in its brief, the EPA spoke of ICR wastes generally when it confessed that hazardous constituents might remain in some wastes following deactivation, we find nothing in the proposed or final regulations to suggest that reactive wastes contain such constituents, other than reactive cyanides and sulfides for which the EPA ordered technological treatment. Nor have NRDC petitioners identified any. Therefore, we have no basis for vacating the use of the deactivation standard for the remaining subcategories of reactive wastes because of the threat of migration of hazardous constituents.

The EPA, however, has only partially addressed the problem, raised in the proposed rule, of the effect of dilution on reactive wastes—that those wastes could display their reactive characteristic in the process of dilution. ***

The final regulations thus offer no assurance that dilution of explosive, water reactive, or other reactive wastes will not create a risk of violent reaction. The final regulations state that the Agency will not prohibit the practice of diluting wastes with other materials to reduce the risk of reaction, and suggest that this might be a useful step to take prior to technological treatment. This ignores the reality of the EPA's deactivation standard: Dilution of these wastes by any method is permissible if it removes the characteristic.

We grant, on narrow grounds, the petition for review as to reactive wastes. The Agency must limit dilution to methods that will curb the risk of violent reactions, mandate preliminary steps to prevent such reactions, require a technological treatment, or find, with the backing of evidence, that there is no significant risk of reaction present for any of the three subcategories of reactive wastes for which deactivation is a permissible form of treatment.

* * *

III. THE EPA'S DILUTION RULES

The issues that we next face focus on challenges to the EPA's new dilution permissions, formulated to integrate RCRA requirements with Clean Water Act ("CWA") treatment systems and deep injection wells regulated pursuant to the Safe Drinking Water Act ("SDWA"). Contemporaneously with the promulgation of the third-third rule, the EPA amended a rule that had prohibited dilution of wastes in lieu of treatment. Pursuant to the amended rule, centralized CWA treatment systems may aggregate certain characteristic waste streams; the aggregation results in dilution that purportedly removes the hazardous characteristic without treatment. Under this new rule, dilution is allowed where the EPA has not specified a particular treatment method and where the CWA system includes a treatment protocol addressed to the types of characteristic wastes being aggregated. As a consequence of this rule, CWA treatment facilities may continue to use unlined surface impoundments as part of their treatment trains. The EPA also promulgated a new rule that permits the operators of deep injection wells to dilute all characteristic wastes, in lieu of treatment, prior to underground injection.

NRDC petitioners contend that aggregation and dilution of characteristic wastes in CWA facilities, in lieu of treatment, is inconsistent with the requirements for hazardous waste management under RCRA. *** Similarly, NRDC petitioners assert that the rule permitting dilution in lieu of treatment prior to deep well injection violates RCRA because it allows land disposal of untreated hazardous wastes. ***

* * *

A. Clean Water Act Treatment Systems

1. *Background*

* * *

Treatment facilities operating pursuant to the CWA often receive waste streams from many sources, and generally these streams are combined for centralized treatment. Following aggregation, the facilities sometimes place the combined stream in unlined surface impoundments as part of the CWA treatment train. These impoundments do not meet RCRA subtitle C standards and they are regulated solely under RCRA subtitle D (solid wastes). However, as the EPA noted in the final rule, the use of surface impoundments for solid wastes clearly implicates the land ban under RCRA. The CWA treatment facilities at issue here do not handle listed hazardous wastes; thus, prior to the third-third proceeding, which classified and identified the characteristic hazardous wastes, the use of an unlined surface impoundment did not implicate RCRA at all.

In addition, under RCRA rules prior to the third-third proceeding, the EPA prohibited dilution of any hazardous waste. Thus, once a waste was determined to be hazardous, it had to be "treated" under RCRA; dilution was not a form of treatment, nor could it be used to avoid RCRA's treatment rules ***. The EPA specifically noted, however, that it did not intend to prohibit "legitimate aggregation of waste streams (*e.g.,* wastewaters) to facilitate centralized treatment."

Although CWA treatment facilities handled characteristic wastes before the adoption of the third-third rule, there were no land-ban requirements under RCRA directed at these wastes. *** After promulgation of the third-third rule, however, CWA facilities handling characteristic wastes became subject to potential regulation under RCRA's subtitle C impoundment and land-ban requirements. ***

To meet its concern over forcing CWA facilities to meet RCRA's subtitle C requirements, the EPA amended section 268.3. The amendment provides that CWA treatment facilities do not violate section 268.3 when they aggregate characteristic wastes for which no specific treatment method has been detailed with other waste streams and thereby dilute the wastes to below the characteristic level. *** [D]ilution is permitted only for those waste streams that the EPA has otherwise permitted to be "treated" by dilution, that is, ICR wastes, *and* those EP toxic metal wastes for which the EPA has required treatment to a specific level (as opposed to by a specific method). Because this dilution removes the characteristic prior to placement in the unlined surface impoundment, the EPA claims that RCRA is satisfied—no land disposal of "hazardous waste" occurs.

NRDC petitioners challenge the amendment permitting dilution before wastes are placed in CWA surface impoundments. Because RCRA requires treatment before any land disposal (unless the land disposal facility wins a no-migration finding) and because CWA surface impoundments are "land disposal facilities," merely diluting the characteristic wastes to remove the characteristic does not satisfy the statute.

2. Analysis

We already have held that RCRA section 3004(m)(1) requires treatment both to remove the characteristic *and* to substantially reduce the toxicity of *all* hazardous constituents present in the characteristic waste. The treatment standards are the core of RCRA's hazardous waste management scheme, and nothing in RCRA or the CWA permits the EPA to establish different treatment standards when wastewaters are treated in CWA systems instead of facilities operated solely to RCRA standards. Nevertheless, Congress, when enacting RCRA, was cognizant of the substantial development of CWA systems, and, thus, permitted regulatory "accommodation" of RCRA and CWA systems. Thus, we agree with the EPA that, under RCRA, diluted formerly characteristic wastes may be placed in subtitle D surface impoundments which are part of an integrated CWA treatment train. However, in order for true "accommodation" to be accomplished, we find that RCRA treatment requirements cannot be ignored merely because CWA is implicated; that is, the CWA does not *override* RCRA. Thus, we hold that, whenever wastes are put in CWA surface impoundments before they have been treated pursuant to RCRA to reduce the toxicity of all hazardous constituents, these wastes must be so treated before exiting the CWA treatment facilities. In other words, CWA facilities handling characteristic wastes must remove the characteristic and decrease the toxicity of the waste's hazardous constituents *to the same degree* that treatment outside a CWA system would.

* * *

We wish to make explicit the impact of our holding because we find merit in significant parts of both parties' positions. First, where dilution to remove the characteristic *meets* the definition of treatment under section 3004(m)(1), nothing more is required. Second, where dilution removes the characteristic but does not "treat" the waste by reducing the toxicity of hazardous constituents, then the decharacterized waste may be placed in a surface impoundment *if and only if* the resulting CWA treatment fully complies with RCRA § 3004(m)(1). In other words, the material that comes out of CWA treatment facilities that employ surface impoundments must remove the hazardous constituents to the same extent that any other treatment facility that complies with RCRA does.

* * *

In sum, section 3004(m)(1)'s treatment standards lie at the core of RCRA subtitle C and require that any hazardous waste be treated in such a way that hazardous constituents are removed from the waste before it enters the environment. Nonetheless, RCRA section 1006(b)(1) contemplates some accommodation with existing CWA systems; to strictly apply each RCRA prohibition would nullify section 1006(b)(1) and, we think, would be untrue to Congress's intent. Thus, allowing temporary deposit of decharacterized wastes is a reasonable accommodation so long as complete circumvention of the treatment standards does not occur. Finally, we emphasize that the result here is unique to CWA systems. Nothing herein permits the placement (temporarily or otherwise) of hazardous wastes or formerly hazardous wastes which have not yet met section 3004(m)(1) treatment standards into non-subtitle C surface impoundments except in existing CWA treatment systems which ultimately treat the streams to full section 3004(m)(1) standards.[10]

B. Deep Injection Wells Regulated Under the Safe Drinking Water Act

1. *Generally*

In the final third-third rule, the EPA promulgated a dilution rule for deep injection well facilities similar to the CWA treatment facilities rule just considered. Under new 40 C.F.R. § 148.1(d)(1991), operators of deep injection wells[11] are permitted to dilute characteristic wastes to remove the characteristic prior to injecting those wastes. Unlike the CWA dilution permission, operators of deep injection wells may dilute all characteristic hazardous wastes, *including* those for which a specific treatment method is required (for example, high total organic compound ignitable wastes, which otherwise must be incinerated or utilized as fuel substitute). *** NRDC petitioners again charge that the rule violates RCRA because hazardous wastes are land disposed before being treated to section 3004(m)(1) standards; the EPA argues that the rule meets RCRA because no "hazardous" wastes are injected and that the rule is a necessary accommodation with the SDWA, which governs deep well injection generally. Consistent with our resolution of the Clean Water Act systems issue, we hold that dilution followed by injection into a deep well is permissible only where dilution itself fully meets section 3004(m)(1) standards or where the waste will subsequently meet section 3004(m)(1) standards. Because deep well injection is permanent land disposal, our holding in effect permits diluted decharacterized wastes to be deep well injected only when dilution meets the section 3004(m)(1) standard or where the deep well secures a no-migration variance.

Before the third-third rule, many deep injection wells handled characteristic wastes without being subject to subtitle C requirements. Therefore, the EPA promulgated section 148.1(d) for reasons similar to those it offered to support section 268.3(b). In general, the EPA claimed that the rule was required to protect existing SDWA systems. "The large facilities that have these wells often mix waste streams and through this mixing remove the characteristic prior to disposal. A dilution prohibition would require restructuring of these facilities." 55 Fed. Reg. at 22,658.

---

[10] Furthermore, as the EPA concedes in its brief, if the stream entering the surface impoundment is not decharacterized, then RCRA requires the impoundment to meet the subtitle C requirements. Similarly, any hazardous precipitate or other hazardous material generated during CWA treatment must be managed in accord with subtitle C.

[11] The deep injection wells at issue here, Class I deep wells, inject wastewaters into geologic formations below the lowest formation containing a source of drinking water.

The EPA also argued that treatment to RCRA standards would provide no environmental benefit over dilution and injection. The "EPA believes that the application of dilution rules to these wastes would not further minimize threats to human health and the environment. Specifically, EPA believes that disposal of these metals by underground injection at the characteristic level is as sound as the treatment option." *Id.* The EPA additionally concluded that all injection wells would meet the no-migration requirement, and the Agency therefore held that it would not require individual no-migration showings.

We reject each of the EPA's proffered justifications. Unlike the CWA system context, where the hazardous wastes can be eventually treated to RCRA standards, injected wastes are not treated further. Section 1006(b)(1) cannot be used to wholly circumvent RCRA. To permit deep well injection operators to dilute all characteristic wastes to below the characteristic level and then to inject them would completely avoid the balance Congress struck in RCRA. Specifically, Congress required that any land disposal of hazardous waste be preceded by treatment to section 3004(m)(1) standards *or* by a site-specific no-migration finding. Although we have found the temporary placement of decharacterized wastes in CWA surface impoundments, which admittedly are land disposal facilities, to be a reasonable accommodation with the CWA, that holding turns on the prospect for future treatment so that the core of RCRA is not voided. Here, no treatment follows decharacterization.

* * *

*** Congress decided that no-migration showings were the only alternative to treatment under section 3004(m)(1). The EPA's claim that its experience showed, in general, that deep injection wells would win no-migration variances is not relevant under Congress's requirement that each site be certified, see RCRA § 3004(g), and is belied by the EPA's record evidence.

* * *

NOTES

1. This decision set the EPA on another course of regulatory decisions that raise not only land ban issues, but also threshold issues regarding the definition of hazardous waste. *See* Kenneth M. Kastner, *RCRA At a Crossroads—Whether to Regulate Hazardous Waste Based on Risk or Technological Controls*, 24 Env't Rep. (BNA) 247 (June 4, 1993).

2. In response to this decision, the EPA adopted substantial revisions to the land ban treatment standards. In September 1994, the EPA established "universal treatment standards" (UTS pursuant to the Letter Conservation Program), which are technology-based concentration limits for more than 200 hazardous constituents. 59 Fed. Reg. 47982 (1994). For most of the characteristic wastes that exhibit the corrosivity, ignitability, or reactivity characteristic, the UTS supplement the deactivation standard, requiring that the waste be treated not only to remove the characteristic, but also to

ensure that none of the specified constituents is present in concentrations greater than prescribed in the UTS. For toxicity characteristic wastes, where dilution has always been impermissible, the UTS supplement many of the treatment standards stated as concentration levels (rather than methods), requiring that treatment address all UTS constituents present in the waste.

For listed wastes, the UTS replace any previously-inconsistent concentration levels for UTS constituents. Prior to the UTS, the treatment standards for several constituents varied depending on the particular waste in which the constituent was present. UTS eliminates such discrepancies and, in the case of 41 percent of all constituent/treatability group combinations, replaced the previous concentration levels with the UTS concentration levels. *See* Bob Van Voorhees, Ken Kastner, and Barton Day, *'Universal Treatment Standards' Adopted; Restrictions Imposed for Toxicity Characteristic Organics, Newly Listed Wastes*, 25 Env't Rep. (BNA) 1231 (Oct. 21, 1994).

3. Characteristic wastes treated in Clean Water Act-regulated units or disposed of in underground injection wells were not subject to the universal treatment standards when published in 1994. Just as the EPA was publishing treatment standards for such wastes, pursuant to a court-ordered deadline, Congress passed and President Clinton signed a "rifle shot" amendment to RCRA, exempting such wastes from additional treatment standards provided the hazardous characteristic is removed prior to land placement. Land Disposal Program Flexibility Act of 1996, Pub. L. 104-119, §2, 109 Stat. 830 (1996). The law also requires the EPA to conduct a study to determine whether the risks posed by such wastes should be subject to further treatment standards, under RCRA or under other federal or state programs.

4. For any wastes identified or listed as hazardous after the 1984 amendments, RCRA § 3004(g)(4) directs the EPA to set land ban treatment standards within six months after the listing or identification takes effect. Thus, the EPA periodically issues additional treatment standards; for example, land disposal standards for newly-listed wood preserving wastes were published in May 1997. 62 Fed. Reg. 25998 (1997).

5. Perhaps the most significant anticipated changes in the land ban program will occur in tandem with the ultimate promulgation of the Hazardous Waste Identification Rule, presently slated for April 2001. The EPA has repeatedly indicated its intention to cap land disposal restrictions for as-generated listed wastes at the exit levels it expects to set in that rule. *See* Notes following *Shell Oil* in chapter 2.B. above.

6. The following case addresses land disposal treatment standards set by the EPA after losing the hazardous waste identification issue in *American Petroleum Institute v. EPA*, 906 F.2d 729 (D.C.Cir. 1990) (*see* Notes following *American Mining Congress* in chapter 2.A. above).

STEEL MANUFACTURERS ASSOCIATION V. ENVIRONMENTAL PROTECTION AGENCY

27 F.3d 642 (D.C.Cir. 1994)

Before MIKVA, Chief Judge, SENTELLE and RANDOLPH, Circuit Judges.
PER CURIAM.

These consolidated petitions for review challenge a final rule promulgated by the Environmental Protection Agency ("EPA" or "agency") under the authority of section 3004 of the Resource Conservation and Recovery Act ("RCRA"), 42 U.S.C. § 6924 (1988). The rule, entitled "Land Disposal of Electronic Arc Furnace Dust (K061)," 56 Fed. Reg. 41,164 (Aug. 19, 1991), establishes numerical treatment standards for thirteen metals contained in residual slag after hazardous waste K061 is processed in high temperature metals recovery ("HTMR") facilities. Representatives of the iron and steel industry assert that the final rule fails to provide a reasoned explanation for the agency's assertion of authority to regulate contaminant levels in K061 slag. Petitioners also contend that EPA acted arbitrarily and capriciously and contrary to RCRA by establishing a treatment standard for zinc, which the agency does not currently consider a "hazardous constituent."

We hold that EPA adequately explained its decision to bring K061 slag within the regulatory scope of RCRA. The agency met its explanatory burden by adopting this court's position in *American Petroleum Institute v. EPA*, 906 F.2d 729 (D.C.Cir.1990), that regulating K061 slag furthers the "cradle to grave" regulatory philosophy established in the RCRA statute and is consistent with prior agency rules. We also conclude that the agency's decision to set a zinc treatment standard was authorized by RCRA and supported by evidence in the record. Accordingly, we deny the petitions for review.

I. STATUTORY AND REGULATORY BACKGROUND

* * *

B. Treatment Standards for K061 Electric Arc Furnace Dust

Electric arc furnace dust, which is also known by its hazardous waste designation code "K061," is collected by emission control devices when steel is manufactured. EPA listed K061 as a hazardous waste under RCRA primarily because it contains high concentrations of hexavalent chromium, lead, and cadmium. However, K061 also contains substantial quantities of other metals, including antimony, arsenic, barium, beryllium, mercury, nickel, selenium, silver, thallium, vanadium, and zinc.

Some of those metals can be extracted from K061 dust, and the mobility of the other metals can be limited, by subjecting the dust to high temperature metals recovery ("HTMR"). High concentrations of valuable metals such as zinc create strong incentives for steel manufacturers and others to reprocess K061 dust. EPA estimates that approximately 90% of high-zinc K061 currently is reprocessed using HTMR and that most of this metals recovery is performed by commercial facilities designed for that purpose. Once the valuable metals have been extracted from K061 dust, the rock-like slag product that remains is also put to further use, principally as road base material in highway construction, or as an anti-skid material applied directly to road surfaces.

In its First-Third rulemaking, 53 Fed. Reg. 31, 138 (1988), EPA identified HTMR as the BDAT for treatment of high-zinc K061 hazardous wastes because it believed that mandatory recycling of recoverable metals would reduce the amount of hazardous wastes ultimately treated and disposed. However, EPA declined to extend its treatment standards to K061 slag residues. EPA noted that HTMR furnaces used for metals recovery "'are normally ... essential components of the industrial process ... [and] involved in the very act of production, an activity normally beyond the Agency's RCRA authority.'" 53 Fed. Reg. 11,753 (1988). Relying on its "indigenous principle," which stated that "[a] secondary material burned in an industrial furnace exclusively for materials recovery is not a solid ... waste ... if it is indigenous to the process in which the industrial furnace is used, in the sense of being generated by the same type of industrial furnace as that in which burning occurs," 52 Fed. Reg. 16,982, 17,034 (1987), EPA concluded that it had no jurisdiction over K061 slag residues under RCRA. According to EPA, "K061 ceases to be a 'solid waste' when it arrives at a metals reclamation facility because at that point it is no longer 'discarded material.'" *API*, 906 F.2d at 740.

This court reversed and remanded the K061 rule to EPA in *American Petroleum Institute v. EPA*, 906 F.2d 729 (D.C. Cir.1990). The court explained that neither case law nor RCRA unambiguously foreclosed EPA's power to prescribe treatment standards for K061 slag, and that by declining to regulate on that basis the EPA had unlawfully exempted K061 slags from RCRA's land disposal provisions. The court also made clear that "the scope of the agency's interpretive discretion on remand is far from unbounded," and any decision not to extend treatment standards to K061 slag would have to be reconciled with RCRA's cradle-to-grave regulatory structure and EPA's derived-from rule.

On remand, EPA adopted the final rule that is the subject of this appeal. The rulemaking established concentration-based treatment standards for high-zinc K061 dust and identified permissible quantities of thirteen metals in K061 dust following HTMR, although not all of these metals (in particular, zinc) are currently listed as "hazardous constituents" under RCRA.

EPA also specified that K061 slag residues from HTMR would be subject to the treatment standards established in the rule. The agency first acknowledged the need to act promptly, given the possibility that K061 residues might be subject to a complete land ban under RCRA's hard-hammer provisions due to the pending lapse of existing treatment standards for K061 on August 8, 1991. While EPA noted that it was engaged in a "comprehensive reevaluation of its rules" regarding the solid waste status of recycled materials such as K061, it concluded that it would defer to later rulemakings "any definitive determination on some of the broader issues ... regarding which materials are and are not solid wastes when destined for recycling." EPA accordingly stated its intention to retain "existing Agency rules" that "K061 destined for metals reclamation is a solid waste ... [and n]on-product residues from the metals reclamation process remain hazardous wastes under the K061 code by virtue of the derived-from rule in 40 C.F.R. 261.2(c)(3)." ***

* * *

II. DISCUSSION

A. K061 Slag Treatment Standards

* * *

In *API*, we held that because K061 itself is "indisputably 'discarded' before being subject to metals reclamation," EPA could not disavow its authority to regulate K061 slag by reliance on our decision in *American Mining Congress v. EPA*, 824 F.2d 1177 (D.C. Cir.1987), which held that RCRA does not apply to *non-discarded* materials used in ongoing industrial processes. While recognizing RCRA's jurisdictional bar against regulating non-discarded materials, *API* in effect rejected EPA's use of the "indigenous principle" as a rational means of distinguishing discarded wastes from non-wastes. EPA was thus left with two choices on remand: It could have again refused to regulate K061 slag under a reconstituted indigenous principle; or, as the court strongly urged, it could have set K061 slag treatment standards based on the existing "derived from" rule. Petitioners do not challenge EPA's reading of its own rules, and in *API* we noted that under those rules "it would appear EPA must prescribe treatment standards for the disposal of K061 slag." *API*, 906 F.2d at 742. EPA chose the latter course, but noted that it was doing so only in the interim to avoid the "hard hammer" of an absolute ban on K061 slag disposal should EPA's existing treatment standards lapse. Because of this exigency, the agency deferred making "any definitive determination on some of the broader issues raised by the court's opinion regarding which materials are and are not solid wastes when destined for recycling."

We are satisfied that EPA's course was reasoned and proper. Initially, we do not share petitioners' view that in establishing K061 slag treatment standards, EPA "abandon[ed] its longstanding prior rule not to intrude into production processes," and therefore was required to provide greater than customary justification for the final rule. EPA did not "abandon" the view expressed in *AMC I* that materials used in ongoing production processes are not subject to RCRA. Rather, the agency jettisoned only the indigenous principle as the method of determining whether or not a material is a component of the production process. The agency believed, and we agree, that this result was a natural consequence of our decision in *API*. Read correctly, *API* held that the indigenous principle was not the product of reasoned decisionmaking and that EPA therefore could not rely on the principle in exempting K061 slag from RCRA land disposal restrictions. As the agency chose on remand not to attempt another justification for its nonregulation, but rather to set K061 slag standards, its only burden was to explain why treatment standards are consistent with both the derived-from rule and the broad purposes of RCRA. *** The agency clearly met its burden.

RCRA's jurisdictional bar against regulating the production process still stands, and as EPA acknowledged in its final rule, the agency is currently engaged in making "waste/non-waste determinations" that will bear on the classification of recycled materials such as K061 slag. Until such definitive determinations are made, operation of existing agency rules define the contours of the jurisdictional bar. Accordingly, EPA did not deviate from longstanding policy any more than was required by *API*, and no higher justification for the final rule was necessary.

* * *

B. The Zinc Treatment Standard

As discussed above, EPA's final rule limits concentration levels for thirteen metals, including zinc, found in K061 dust. EPA promulgated the concentration standards pursuant to RCRA section 3004(m), which directs EPA to:

> promulgate regulations specifying those levels or methods of treatment, if any, which substantially diminish the toxicity of the waste or substantially reduce the likelihood of migration of *hazardous constituents* from the waste so that short-term and long-term threats to human health and the environment are minimized.

42 U.S.C. § 6924(m)(1) (emphasis added). A separate regulation lists the "hazardous constituents" referred to in section 3004(m). 40 C.F.R. Part 261, appendix VIII. Zinc is not on the list. Petitioners claim that the absence of zinc from the list prohibits EPA from setting zinc treatment standards. We disagree. Employing the familiar analysis of *Chevron U.S.A., Inc. v. Natural Resources Defense Council*, 467 U.S. 837 (1984), we find that petitioners' position is not mandated by the plain directive of § 3004(m), and we therefore bow to the EPA's interpretation of the section, which we find reasonable.

Section 3004(m) authorizes EPA to establish treatment standards "which substantially reduce the likelihood of migration of hazardous constituents." It does not, as petitioners' reading would suggest, command EPA to set standards *for* hazardous constituents that will reduce the likelihood of their migration. Therefore, if setting a treatment standard for zinc "substantially reduces the migration" of materials that *are* listed in Appendix VIII—as EPA claims it does—we see nothing in § 3004(m) that unambiguously prevents EPA from doing so.

* * *

Petitioners argue in the alternative that even if a zinc standard is permissible under RCRA, the present one is not supported by evidence in the record and therefore is arbitrary and capricious. We reject this argument as well. EPA established a zinc treatment standard in order to insure proper operation of HTMR processes by maximizing zinc recovery. The agency found that high zinc recovery lowers both the overall volume of slag and the mobility of toxic metals in the slag residue—results consistent with RCRA's broad goals of minimizing the amount of waste and reducing the likelihood of hazardous materials leaching onto the land. Petitioners concede that maximizing zinc recovery would lower the volume of zinc in the slag—and, logically, the overall volume of slag itself—but they dispute EPA's finding that maximizing zinc recovery will reduce the mobility of hazardous constituents.

We conclude that minimizing the overall volume of slag that is to be disposed is, by itself, a sufficient justification for the zinc treatment standard, and therefore we do not reach petitioners' claim that EPA failed to demonstrate that zinc is an accurate predictor of leachate levels of other constituents found in K061 slag. Minimizing the volume of K061 slag—which is a hazardous waste under current EPA regulations notwithstanding the fact that all of its constituents may not themselves be "hazardous"—promotes RCRA's abiding goal of reducing or eliminating the generation of hazardous wastes. *****

* * *

NOTES

1. Do you find it ironic that RCRA's waste minimization policy was deemed sufficiently strong to support treatment standards for an element that is not even listed as a hazardous constituent? What is the difference between a hazardous waste and a hazardous constituent?   Why are constituents significant under the land disposal restrictions program?

2. The next chapter addresses RCRA's two cleanup programs. The first, known as corrective action, involves hazardous constituents as well as hazardous waste. RCRA § 3004(u).   The second, pertaining to situations of imminent and substantial endangerment, involves solid waste and hazardous waste. Both programs invoke the broader, more indefinite, statutory definitions of hazardous and solid waste than the more painstakingly complex definitions in the Part 61 regulations.

Problem #4: LAND BAN

INFL8, Inc., ("II") an air bag manufacturer, has undertaken a rush project to dismantle its existing air bags and replace them with a redesigned version that will inflate less forcefully. II is trying to recycle as much of the material in the dismantled air bags as possible, particularly the initiator, which contains ZPP which is reactive under 40 C.F.R. § 261.33(a)(1) [waste code D003 if "hazardous waste"]. During the course of this rush project, II learns of a substitute for ZPP that is so much less costly than ZPP, and so much easier to handle, that II intends to dispose of all ZPP remaining at the facility and purchase the substitute in its place. ZPP plans to treat the ZPP on-site to remove its reactivity and then send it to a solid waste landfill.

1. What questions must you answer in order to determine whether II's proposed treatment will satisfy applicable land disposal restrictions?

2. For review, does II need a RCRA TSD permit for any of these activities?

5   CLEANUP PROVISIONS UNDER RCRA

Two unrelated sets of RCRA provisions authorize the EPA to require the cleanup of hazardous waste and, in some cases, solid waste: (1) the corrective action provisions apply to releases of hazardous waste and hazardous constituents at facilities that treated, stored, or disposed of hazardous waste at any time after RCRA took effect in November 1980; and (2) the omnibus cleanup provisions pertain to imminent and substantial endangerments posed by the past or present handling of solid or hazardous waste.

A. Corrective Action Requirements

The corrective action provisions address the cleanup of preexisting contamination at hazardous waste treatment, storage, and disposal facilities. The EPA's early experience under the Superfund law (CERCLA, or Comprehensive Environmental Response, Compensation, and Liability Act) had revealed that a significant number of the contaminated sites posing a threat to human health or the environment were those at which hazardous waste had been treated, stored, or disposed, whether before or after RCRA took effect. *See, e.g., United States v. Chem-Dyne*, 572 F.Supp. 802 (S.D.Ohio 1983), in chapter 10.A. The corrective action provisions were then added to RCRA in the 1984 amendments, partially to shift responsibility for at least some of those sites from the massive CERCLA program into the RCRA program. Using RCRA's corrective action provisions to compel TSDs (or at least those that remain in operation) to clean up their sites is more efficient and effective, from the EPA's perspective, than using CERCLA because the EPA can use its regulatory and permitting leverage over RCRA TSDs to require them to conduct cleanup activities as a condition of remaining in business.

Congress differentiated between corrective action at permitted TSDs, RCRA § 3004(u), 42 U.S.C. § 6924(u), and corrective action at interim status TSDs, RCRA § 3008(h), 42 U.S.C. § 6928(h). Corrective action requirements apply to permitted TSDs via conditions in their Part B permits, and they are imposed on interim status TSDs by means of administrative or judicial orders. In addition, corrective action requirements can also be applied to facilities that had, or should have had, interim status after November 19, 1980, but which subsequently closed rather than pursue formal interim status and/or Part B status. Such facilities must proceed through closure and, unless the closure leaves the site free from hazardous waste contamination, post-closure, which requires a permit. The post-closure permit will, under § 3004(u), trigger corrective action requirements.

The statutory language authorizing the EPA to require corrective action at permitted and interim status TSDs suggests different conditions triggering the application of corrective action requirements. Permitted TSDs may be required to remediate "all releases of hazardous waste *or constituents* from any *solid waste management unit* [at the TSD] ***, regardless of the time at which waste was placed in such unit." RCRA § 3004(u) (emphasis supplied). Interim status TSDs are subject to corrective action orders whenever "there is or has been a release of hazardous waste into the environment" from the facility. RCRA § 3008(h). Notwithstanding the differences in statutory language, the EPA has interpreted the two provisions coterminously, extending to the widest reaches of both. *See* John C. Chambers, Jr., *Overview of RCRA Corrective Action Requirements,* 20 Chem. Waste Lit. Rep. (Computer L. Rep.) 723 (Oct. 1990). The EPA has accomplished this by (1) implying into the interim status provisions the more expansive aspects of § 3004(u), encompassing releases of hazardous constituents as well as hazardous waste, *see United States v. Clow Water Systems*, 701 F.Supp. 1345 (S.D. Ohio 1988), and (2) invoking supplementary RCRA authorities to circumvent the limitation in § 3004(u) that corrective action at permitted facilities pertain to releases from "solid waste management units." *See In the Matter of Amerada Hess Corp. Port Reading Refinery*, RCRA App. No. 88-10 (EPA Aug. 15, 1989)(in this chapter).

Although RCRA § 3004(u) directs the EPA to adopt implementing regulations, regulatory authority for at least the first 13 years of the program has been spotty. Shortly after the program was statutorily adopted, the EPA issued two sets of "codification" regulations, which incorporated into regulation form the statutory corrective action provisions and stated the EPA's general approach to their implementation. (Challenges to the first codification regulation are addressed in the *United Technologies* case immediately below.) In 1990 (after a two-year impasse between the EPA and the Office of Management and Budget), the EPA issued proposed corrective action regulations that would create a new Subpart S in Part 264, governing permitted TSDs. 55 Fed. Reg. 30798 (1990). The proposed Subpart S regulations specify the procedures by which decisions are to be made and actions undertaken concerning the investigation, assessment, and cleanup of hazardous waste contamination. Issues regarding the scope of the program and the extent of cleanup required, among others, have generated such controversy that the EPA has still (as of July 1997) not finalized the Subpart S proposal. Rather, the EPA has been using the proposed regulations as "guidance." *See* 58 Fed. Reg. 8658-8659 (1993).

The EPA has, however, promulgated one aspect of the proposed regulations, regarding corrective action management units ("CAMUs") and temporary units ("TUs"). *Ibid.* Both concepts apply only to remediation wastes, and not to "as-generated" wastes. The designation of a CAMU enables the entity conducting a cleanup (whether under RCRA or under CERCLA) to move contaminated materials from one part of a site to another without triggering the land ban requirement that such material be treated before being placed on the land. A temporary unit is an area used for the treatment or storage of remediation wastes, for which unit the EPA decides to apply alternative requirements instead of the standard RCRA Subtitle C requirements regarding design, operation, or closure. 40 C.F.R. §§ 264.3, 264.101, 264.552-553. The fact that the CAMU and TU concepts are expected to facilitate CERCLA (as well as RCRA) cleanup activities explains why the EPA promulgated this aspect of the corrective action regulations before finalizing the rest of the regulatory package.

> The proposed subpart S [corrective action] regulations contained several key remediation waste management provisions. These provisions were designed to reduce or eliminate certain waste management requirements of the current RCRA subtitle C regulations which, when applied to remediation wastes, impede the ability of the Agency to select and implement reliable, protective and cost-effective remedies at RCRA facilities. These impediments also occur at sites being remediated under CERCLA authorities, since RCRA requirements are often applicable or relevant and appropriate requirements (ARARs), as defined in CERCLA and in the CERCLA National Contingency Plan.

> Therefore, EPA believes that pending the promulgation of the comprehensive subpart S rules, it is useful and necessary to expedite the promulgation of these key provisions of subpart S, and thereby realize the benefits that they will provide in an accelerated time frame.

58 Fed. Reg. at 8658. Two environmental organizations and the Hazardous Waste Treatment Council sought judicial review of the CAMU/TU regulations. *Environmental Defense Fund v. EPA*, No. 93-1316 (D.C.Cir., filed May 14, 1993), but the parties agreed to stay the litigation pending the promulgation of a final rule on the definition of hazardous waste for contaminated media (see chapter 2.B). *Action on Suit Over CAMU Provisions Stayed Pending Issuance of Contaminated Media Rule*, 25 Env't Rep. (BNA) 1216 (Oct. 21, 1994).

In May 1996, the EPA issued an Advanced Notice of Proposed Rulemaking, inviting public comment on which portions of the 1990 proposed regulations should be finalized, which modified and re-proposed, and which addressed by guidance rather than regulation. 61 Fed. Reg. 19432 (1996). In the absence of comprehensive regulations, the case law addressing the statutory provisions has also remained somewhat sparse. Many issues have been resolved on a case-by-case basis in administrative proceedings.

The following case examines the first codification regulations, focusing on the EPA's expansive interpretation of some key terms not defined in the statute.

UNITED TECHNOLOGIES CORP. V. ENVIRONMENTAL PROTECTION AGENCY
821 F.2d 714 (D.C. Cir. 1987)

Before EDWARDS and STARR, Circuit Judges, and SWYGERT, Senior Circuit Judges for the Seventh Circuit.
EDWARDS, Circuit Judge.

These consolidated cases involve various challenges to a final rule promulgated by the Environmental Protection Agency ("EPA" or the "Agency") to conform its hazardous waste regulations to new statutory provisions enacted in the Hazardous and Solid Waste Amendments of 1984 (the "1984 Amendments"). ***

* * *

I. BACKGROUND
* * *

The EPA has promulgated several sets of regulations implementing Subtitle C of the RCRA. The section 3004 standards applicable to facilities with permits are set forth in [40 C.F.R.] Part 264. Part 265 sets forth the standards applicable to facilities operating under interim status.

Although the RCRA, as originally enacted, imposed a regulatory scheme on the active management of hazardous wastes, it did not require permittees to take significant remedial action to correct past mismanagement of hazardous waste. In 1980, however, Congress enacted the Comprehensive Environmental Response, Compensation, and Liability Act ("CERCLA") to provide for the cleanup of hazardous releases not addressed by other statutory programs. Included in CERCLA was a "Superfund" to pay for such corrective action pending recovery of the cleanup costs from the owner or operator who was responsible for the release.

Congress comprehensively amended the RCRA in 1984, when it enacted the 1984 Amendments. The 1984 Amendments imposed additional section 3004 requirements on permittees. Of particular relevance here is section 3004(o)(1)(A), 42 U.S.C. § 6924(o)(1)(A), which requires every landfill or surface impoundment unit for which an application for a final determination regarding the issuance of a permit is received after November 8, 1984 to conform with certain design and monitoring requirements. Also, under section 3004(u), 42 U.S.C. § 6924(u), owners and operators must take corrective action for all releases of hazardous waste or constituents from any solid waste management unit at a facility regardless of the time at which waste was placed in the unit.

The Agency then proceeded to promulgate regulations to implement the 1984 Amendments. On July 15, 1985, it issued the Final Rule, the purpose of which was "to incorporate into the existing Subtitle C regulations a set of requirements from the new RCRA amendments that became effective as a matter of statute in the short term." 50 Fed. Reg. at 28,703. The Final Rule was made effective immediately and was promulgated without prior notice or an opportunity for comment by interested parties.

Thereafter, the Agency promulgated other regulations implementing other aspects of the 1984 Amendments, which were subjected to notice and comment procedures before adoption as a final rule. As of this date, the Agency is considering petitions seeking the promulgation of additional regulations to flesh out portions of the 1984 Amendments.

Several groups of petitioners have asked this court to review various aspects of the Final Rule. One group, hereafter referred to as "Industry Petitioners," is composed of industrial concerns that, as a by-product of their production processes, generate hazardous waste that they manage on-site. Several utilities and utility associations (including the Edison Electric Institute), hereinafter referred to as "EEI," have also challenged certain of the regulations. Finally, the Environmental Defense Fund and the Natural Resources Defense Council (collectively "EDF") have filed a petition for review.

* * *

III. THE MERITS

A. *Interpretation of "Facility"*

Section 3004(u) of the Act requires owners and operators to take "corrective action for all releases of hazardous waste or constituents from any solid waste management unit at a treatment, storage or disposal facility ... regardless of the time at which waste was placed in such unit." To implement section 3004(u) in its regulatory scheme, the EPA promulgated 40 C.F.R. § 264.101 (1986), which provides in pertinent part that "(t)he owner or operator of a facility seeking a permit for the treatment, storage or disposal of hazardous waste must institute corrective action ... for all releases of hazardous waste or constituents from any solid waste management unit at the facility, regardless of time at which waste was placed in such unit." In its preamble to the Final Rule, the EPA stated that, based on its examination of congressional intent underlying section 3004(u), it would be interpreting the term "facility" as used in section 264.101 as "not limited to those portions of the owner's property at which units for the management of solid or hazardous waste are located, but rather extend(ing) to *all contiguous property under the owner or operator's control." 50 Fed. Reg. at 28,712 (emphasis added).

The Industry Petitioners challenge this definition of "facility." They claim that the Agency's definition is incompatible with the plain language of section 3004(u) and is inconsistent with congressional intent. Alternatively, they contend that, in the absence of congressional intent to the contrary, the Agency is "bound" to employ the definition of "facility" it promulgated in 1980, codified at 40 C.F.R. § 260.10 (1986). We disagree. ***

1. *The Plain Language of Section 3004(u)*

The Industry Petitioners first urge that the EPA's definition of "facility" is inconsistent with the directive in section 3004(u) to take corrective action "*at a treatment, storage or disposal facility.*" They argue that the word "at" clearly shows an intent to limit the duty to take corrective action only to "contiguous land ... used for treating, storing, or disposing of hazardous waste." 40 C.F.R. § 260.10 (1986). However, this would virtually nullify the requirement, to take corrective action for releases from any *solid waste* management unit. Under the Industry Petitioners' view, the only way a duty would attach to take corrective action for releases from a solid waste unit would be if that solid waste unit happened to be on the "contiguous land ... used for ... hazardous waste."

We fail to see how the use of the word "at" in section 3004(u) clarifies, in any way, the meaning to be placed on the word "facility." It certainly does not *require* the use of the Industry Petitioners' definition. Moreover, looking at section 3004(u) as a whole, it appears that employing the Industry Petitioners' definition would render the duty to take corrective action for releases from solid waste management units virtually meaningless. Absent some affirmative showing that Congress intended to achieve such an anomalous result, we are not persuaded that the EPA misconstrued the statutory language.

2. *Congressional Intent*

The Agency argues that its interpretation of the word "facility" in this context, if not mandated by the plain wording of section 3004(u), is consistent with the congressional scheme underlying the 1984 Amendments. It notes first that the broad purpose underlying this aspect of the 1984 Amendments was to relieve future burdens on the "Superfund" program. *See* H.R. REP. NO. 198, 98th Cong., 1st Sess. 20, 61 ("House Report"). As the House Report stated: "Unless all ... releases ... at permitted facilities are ... cleaned up ... many more sites will be added to the future burdens of the Superfund program.... The responsibility to control such releases lies with the facility owner and operator and should not be shifted to the Superfund program, particularly when a final permit has been requested by the facility." The Agency also reasons that, since section 3004(v), 42 U.S.C. § 6924(v), clearly employs a broader concept of a "facility" than does the section 260.10 definition, one can reasonably assume a similarly broad meaning of "facility" was intended in section 3004(u).

Section 3004(u) was enacted out of congressional concern "that current EPA regulations do not address all releases of hazardous constituents from solid waste management units at facilities receiving permits under section 3005(e). This could likely result in a situation of EPA issuing a final permit to a facility which is causing ground water contamination from inactive units, without the permit addressing that contamination in any way." House Report at 60. Section 3004(u), in essence, creates the broad duty to take corrective action as a *quid pro quo* to obtaining a permit. Given this purpose, it appears that the EPA's construction of "facility" is fully consistent with congressional intent.

This view is further confirmed by section 3004(v), which requires an owner or operator to use best efforts to take corrective action "beyond the facility boundary." The provision is satisfied if the owner or operator is "unable to obtain the necessary permission to undertake such action." Clearly, "facility" is used in section 3004(v) to describe all of the property under the control of the owner or operator. We have no reason to assume that Congress intended a different meaning of facility in section 3004(u).

We can find no basis for overturning the EPA's interpretation of "facility" in this case. Indeed, even if we were "unable to discern congressional intent after employing traditional tools of statutory construction," *UAW v. Brock*, 816 F.2d at 765 n.5 (D.C.Cir.1987), we would still uphold the Agency's interpretation. It is clear to us that, to the extent there is "'any gap left, implicitly or explicitly, by Congress,'" *Chevron U.S.A., Inc. v. Natural Resources Defense Council, Inc.*, 467 U.S. 837, 843, (1984), the Agency has acted to fill that gap in a way that is rational and not inconsistent with the 1984 Amendments. *******

3.   *The Agency is Not Required to Employ its Prior Definition in Construing a New Congressional Enactment*

The Industry Petitioners next contend that, in any event, *i.e.*, without regard to the reasonableness of the EPA's current interpretation, the Agency is bound by its prior rulemaking to employ the initial definition of facility. This argument is wholly without merit.

The Industry Petitioners apparently have failed to recognize that the Agency has not "changed" its prior definition of facility; the EPA will continue to use the section 260.10 definition in construing other regulatory and statutory provisions under the RCRA. ******* Here, the Agency has interpreted *newly* enacted statutory language, so it is hardly surprising that EPA officials did not feel constrained by the previously existing definition of facility. Furthermore, and most importantly, the EPA adequately explained its reasons for departing from the section 260.10 definition, thus making clear the reasonableness of its position.

* * *

NOTES

1. The implications of the corrective action definition of "facility" are further described in the EPA's 1990 proposed regulations:

> Clearly, property that is owned by the owner/operator that is located apart from the facility (i.e., separated by land owned by others) is not part of the

"facility." EPA does intend, however, to consider property that is separated only by a public right-of-way (such as a roadway or power transmission right-of-way) to be contiguous property. The term "contiguous property" also has significant additional meaning when applied to a facility where the owner is a different entity from the operator. For example, if a 100-acre parcel of land were owned by a company that leases five acres of it to another company that, in turn, engages in hazardous waste management on the five acres leased, the "facility" for purposes of corrective action would be the entire 100-acre parcel.

55 Fed. Reg. at 30808.

2. The *United Technologies* case highlights one of several situations where a key term is defined more expansively for some RCRA purposes than for others. Have you read other cases in which such a dichotomy has arisen? Look for additional examples in the context of RCRA § 7003 actions, addressed in the second part of this chapter.

3. Perhaps the most notable aspect of the corrective action program is its far-reaching jurisdictional scope. Whereas all other provisions of RCRA Subtitle C apply only to hazardous waste, as defined in the 40 C.F.R. Part 261 regulations, the corrective action provisions require the cleanup of substances that may not be hazardous waste under the Part 261 regulations.

First, as previously noted, § 3004(u) expressly extends to the cleanup of hazardous constituents (as well as hazardous waste), and § 3008(h) has been construed by the EPA to apply to hazardous constituents as well. Second, the EPA's definition of hazardous waste in the proposed corrective action regulations employs the statutory definition of hazardous waste, RCRA § 1004(5), which is potentially broader in scope than the Part 261 regulations. 55 Fed. Reg. at 30809. According to one commentator, "EPA is in effect proposing to reserve the right to unilaterally classify wastes not heretofore subject to the RCRA regulatory program as 'hazardous waste' for purposes of § 3004(u) without going through the normal notice and comment rulemaking proceedings." Chambers, 20 Chem. Waste Lit. Rep. at 729.

4. Another significant term for corrective action purposes is "solid waste management unit" (or "SWMU," one of the more challenging RCRA acronyms), which appears in § 3004(u) but in no other RCRA provision. Left undefined by Congress, the EPA defined it as follows in the 1990 proposed corrective action regulations:

Any discernible unit at which solid wastes have been placed at any time, irrespective of whether the unit was intended for the management of solid or hazardous waste. Such units include any area at a facility at which solid wastes have been routinely and systematically released.

55 Fed. Reg. at 30874. The EPA explained in the preamble to the proposed regulations that releases (including spills and leaks) from process areas and product storage facilities would not be considered SWMUs unless they were "routine and systematic in nature." *Id.* at 30809.

The following SWMU decision was rendered by the EPA Administrator during the administrative review (which must be pursued before judicial review may be sought) of a Part B permit whose corrective action provisions required the cleanup of contamination associated with an underground product storage tank.

IN THE MATTER OF:
AMERADA HESS CORP. PORT READING REFINERY
RCRA Appeal No. 88-10 (U.S.E.P.A., Aug. 15, 1989)

WILLIAM K. REILLY, Administrator

Before me is a petition filed by Amerada Hess Corporation under 40 CFR § 124.19 requesting review of a permit issued by U.S. EPA Region II under the 1984 Hazardous and Solid Waste Amendments to the Resource Conservation and Recovery Act ("RCRA"), 42 U.S.C.A. §§ 6901-6991i. The permit is for Hess's oil refinery in Port Reading, New Jersey. ***

Hess's petition raises a single issue. In 1986, Hess removed a 500-gallon underground storage tank from its facility. The permit characterizes the excavated area as a solid waste management unit ("SWMU"), and requires Hess to conduct soil analysis under RCRA § 3004(u) to determine whether the area is contaminated. Hess asserts that the tank stored only product and feedstock, not solid waste. *Cf.* 42 U.S.C.A. § 6903(27) ("'solid waste' means any garbage, refuse * * * and other discarded material"). Hess therefore concludes that the excavated area is not a SWMU subject to RCRA § 3004(u), which by its terms is limited to releases from SWMUs.

Analysis

The Region does not dispute Hess's assertion that the tank stored only product and feedstock. Despite the original status of the stored materials, however, a spill or release in the excavated area would be "solid waste" under RCRA because the spilled materials would be unquestionably discarded. Hess is correct that the Agency's RCRA jurisdiction does not extend to product or feedstock which is not otherwise solid waste. The disputed soil sampling requirements, however, are not directed toward the storage of product or feedstock, but instead address a potential release of solid waste to the environment.

Although a release in the excavated area would be solid waste, there would still be some question under RCRA § 3004(u) as to whether the area is a "solid waste *management* unit."[4] Regardless of whether this area is a SWMU subject to RCRA §

---

[4] The term "solid waste management unit" includes areas contaminated by routine and systematic releases, but not by a one-time, accidental spill. *See* 50 Fed. Reg. 28712-13 (July 15, 1985); Memorandum from Marcia E. Williams, Office of Solid Waste, to Hazardous Waste Division Directors, Regions I-X (July 24, 1987) (Attachment 3 to Region Response). The Region argues that soil analysis

3004(u), however, adequate legal authority for the disputed requirements exists under RCRA § 3005(c)(3). This "omnibus provision" allows the Agency to impose any permit term and condition necessary to protect human health and the environment.[5] In my view, this authority provides a sufficient legal predicate for requiring soil sampling for a suspected release from a non-SWMU. For an interim status facility, the statute expressly authorizes corrective action without regard to whether the release originated from a SWMU or a non-SWMU. For a permitted facility, the omnibus provision may likewise be used to address a suspected release of solid waste, regardless of its source, where necessary to protect human health and the environment.

Release detection in the form of groundwater monitoring is routinely required for most units that manage hazardous waste, irrespective of whether there is a suspicion of a release. The Agency has not found it necessary to require such routine monitoring for SWMUs, but a RCRA permit applicant may be required to conduct soil sampling and other preliminary detection activities where necessary to determine whether a suspected release from a SWMU requires a more complete investigation. For a suspected release from a non-SWMU, the threshold showing needed to justify such soil sampling should be derived from the language of the omnibus provision itself. In other words, such a requirement may be imposed for a suspected release from a non-SWMU if, in the words of the omnibus provision, it is "necessary to protect human health and the environment."

Region II plainly believes that such necessity exists in this case. Although the Region initially justified the requirements at issue under RCRA § 3004(u), the same determination of necessity is required under that provision as under the omnibus provision. Hess challenges Region II's determination in this respect by asserting that the tank was structurally intact when it was removed. It fails, however, to provide any contemporaneous documentation to support this assertion. Even assuming this contention to be true, it would not rule out the possibility of spills while the tank was in use. Hess also asserts that it visually inspected the surrounding soil when the tank was removed, and that the excavated area was backfilled with clean soil. The Region was aware of these contentions, but it nevertheless concluded that a "no release" confirmation by soil analysis is necessary to protect human health and the environment due to the age of the tank and the absence of relevant historical records and field data. This decision is supported by the RCRA Facility Assessment conducted by the New Jersey Department of Environmental Protection, which characterizes the area as having a "suspected release" and concludes that "[s]oil sampling is warranted to determine

---

might reveal that the excavated area is a SWMU, but fails to explain how such analysis could demonstrate a history of routine and systematic (as opposed to isolated and sporadic) spills.

[5]*See* 42 U.S.C.A. § 6925(c)(3) ("Each permit issued under this section shall contain such terms and conditions as the Administrator (or the State) determines necessary to protect human health and the environment"); *see also* 40 CFR § 270.32(b)(2); ***.

whether or not a release may have occurred in the area." Region Response, Attachment 1 at Revised Narrative pp. 3-4, Preliminary Assessment at p.3.

* * *

Conclusion

For the reasons set forth above and in the Region Response, and based on the record before me, Hess's petition for review is denied. The Region is directed to revise the permit to provide that the conditions at issue are being imposed under RCRA § 3005(c)(3), not Section 3004(u).

NOTES

1. Since *Amerada Hess*, the scope of the EPA's authority to require corrective action investigation and cleanup of areas that do not qualify as solid waste management units ("SWMUs") has been addressed in several other permit appeal proceedings before the EPA Administrator and, after its creation, the EPA's Environmental Appeals Board.

2. In *In re Morton International, Inc. (Moss Point, Mississippi)*, 1992 WL 83771 (EPA RCRA Appeal 90-17, Feb. 28, 1992), former EPA Administrator William Reilly addressed the non-SWMU issue as well as other significant jurisdictional issues that frequently arise in the corrective action context. As in *Amerada Hess*, the *Morton* proceeding involved the company's appeal of the corrective action provisions in its Part B permit for a chemical manufacturing plant.

Morton challenged the permit's definition of the term "SWMU," which included any unit "which has been used for the treatment, storage, or disposal of solid waste at any time, irrespective of whether the unit is or ever was intended for the management of solid waste." The Administrator upheld the definition:

> At present, there is no unitary definition of the term "SWMU" in the statute or regulations. The terms "solid waste management" and "unit" are, however, defined. RCRA defines "solid waste management" as "the systematic administration of activities which provide for the collection, source separation, storage, transportation, transfer, processing, treatment, and disposal of solid waste." 42 U.S.C. § 6903(28). The term "unit" refers to any contiguous area of land on or in which waste is placed. See 47 Fed. Reg. 32,289 (July 26, 1982). Based upon these definitions, the term "SWMU" plainly includes any unit (contiguous area of land on or in which waste is placed) used for solid waste management (the systematic collection, source separation, storage, transportation, transfer, processing, treatment or disposal of solid waste).

> Morton's suggestion to the contrary notwithstanding, a determination that waste management activities are "systematic" need not be based on a finding that the permittee subjectively intended or deliberately sought to

manage the waste. Rather, operations or activities that inevitably lead to routine waste handling are sufficiently "systematic" to constitute "solid waste management" as defined in RCRA. ***

The Administrator also rejected Morton's challenge to the designation of a latex recovery pit as a SWMU requiring investigation. Morton argued that the latex recovery pit was not used to manage solid waste, but was instead part of a continuous production process because it captured upsets of latex and returned them to the production process. Finding that the pit was designed and intended not only to recover latex, but also to store and discard process wastewater, the Administrator upheld its classification as a SWMU.

Morton's claim that the EPA was not authorized to require corrective action for "areas of concern" that were admittedly not SWMUs invited the Administrator to expound upon his *Amerada Hess* ruling regarding the interplay between RCRA's corrective action provisions and its "omnibus provision."

*** Morton argues that only § 3004(u) expressly authorizes corrective action beyond hazardous waste management units by requiring corrective action for releases from SWMUs. Morton maintains that § 3005(c)(3), the RCRA "omnibus provision," does not extend this authorization, that is, that § 3005(c)(3) "only allows conditions within the scope of the permit as delineated by other statutory provisions." ***

I am not persuaded by Morton's argument that § 3004(u) (or any other Subtitle C provision) expressly or implicitly limits the broad grant of authority contained in § 3005(c)(3). Such an interpretation would render § 3005(c)(3) superfluous in the corrective action context. Moreover, § 3004(u) is not the only provision in Subtitle C allowing corrective action beyond hazardous waste management units; § 3008(h)(1) allows corrective action for any release of hazardous waste at an interim status facility if necessary to protect human health and the environment regardless of whether the release is from a SWMU or non-SWMU area.[16] *** Section 3004(u) is best read not as a limit on § 3005(c)(3), but as a mandatory minimum requirement that the Agency must fulfill. The legislative history of § 3005(c)(3) shows an intent to authorize the Administrator to impose permit conditions beyond those mandated by the applicable regulations (i.e., those implementing § 3004(u)) as required to address situations at each permitted facility that threaten human health or the environment. Accordingly, the Agency has repeatedly held that § 3005(c)(3) authorizes corrective action permit requirements, such as soil sampling or other preliminary detection activities, for non-SWMU areas when necessary to protect human health and the environment.

---

[16] Beyond Subtitle C, RCRA § 7003 also allows corrective action from non-SWMU areas by authorizing the Administrator to initiate a suit against any person who has contributed to the handling, storage, treatment, transportation or disposal of any solid or hazardous waste that presents an imminent and substantial endangerment to health or the environment.

Although § 3005(c)(3) provides authority to require corrective action for non-SWMU areas, this authority is not unlimited. The statutory context of RCRA "makes clear that the omnibus provision should not be used as a blank check for unbridled regulation without an adequate nexus to solid or hazardous waste." *In re BP Chemicals America, Inc.*, RCRA Appeal No. 89-4, p. 7 (Aug. 20, 1991). By its own terms, § 3005(c)(3) authorizes only those permit conditions necessary to protect human health and the environment.   Unwarranted uses of this provision are checked on a case-by-case basis through petitions for review of final permit decisions. For these reasons, there is no merit to Morton's contention that the Region's interpretation of § 3005(c)(3) will allow unbridled regulatory access to production processes. The Region has not attempted to use § 3005(c)(3) to regulate Morton's production processes, but to require corrective action for releases associated with those production processes that threaten human health and the environment.

Because § 3005(c)(3) authorizes corrective action for non-SWMU areas, the Region's characterization of the area as an "area of concern" is not determinative of whether corrective action is appropriate. Rather, the issue is whether the Region's decision to require the type of corrective action detailed in the permit for this AOC meets the test detailed in § 3005(c)(3), that is, whether it is necessary to protect human health and the environment.

In this case, the Region's exercise of the authority granted by § 3005(c)(3) is appropriate. As described in the RFA, the AOC encompasses

all process areas ... where storage and manufacturing operations take place. Prior to approximately 1975, these areas lacked any secondary containment, or contained inadequate secondary containment ... . Prior to this date, wastewater was carried by Ditches interlacing this AOC. Additional ditches, trenches, and sumps may have existed (some presumably in the present-day concreted areas) since the [Morton] plant started operation in 1955. An old underground pipe ... was removed from service in 1983 or 1984. It had been in service for 18 years; the facility could not provide information/documentation on the structural integrity of the pipe when it became inactive.

RFA, pp. 33-34. *** These findings and recommendations in the RFA support the limited type of corrective action immediately required by the permit, namely, the preparation of a workplan to confirm the existence of a suspected release of hazardous wastes or constituents requiring corrective action. ***

3. Administrator Reilly's analysis of the interplay between the SWMU concept in RCRA § 3004(u) and the agency's omnibus permit authority under RCRA § 3005(c)(3) has been embraced by the Environmental Appeals Board in subsequent

corrective action permit appeals. *See, e.g., In re Sandoz Pharmaceuticals Corp.*, 24 Envtl. L. Rep. (Envtl. L. Inst.) 40019 (EPA Env. App. Bd., July 9, 1992) (remanding permit to Region to determine whether the inclusion of corrective action permit conditions for non-SWMU "areas of concern"—former underground product storage tank locations, where remediation had already occurred—was "necessary to protect human health or the environment" so as to invoke the agency's omnibus authority under § 3005(c)(3)).

4. The process by which hazardous waste and hazardous constituent contamination is investigated and cleaned up under RCRA is modeled upon the CERCLA program. The first phase is a RCRA facility assessment, involving a review of records concerning the history of and conditions at the site, and a site investigation. The second step is a RCRA facility investigation, which is an extensive sampling and testing program to determine the precise nature and extent of suspected contamination. The third step is a corrective measures study, which assesses the risks posed by the contamination and evaluates options for reducing or eliminating those risks. Finally, the EPA selects an option and the corrective action is implemented.

5. One of the most difficult aspects of the RCRA corrective action (and the CERCLA "response action") process is determining the appropriate extent of cleanup, or "how clean is clean." The 1990 proposed corrective action regulations would resolve that issue on a case-by-case basis, setting site-specific cleanup standards for each contaminated medium. This approach differs from that currently employed, pursuant to statutory directive, under CERCLA. (See chapter 14.)

6. The following case provides some insight into the practical ramifications of the corrective action program.

INLAND STEEL CO. V. ENVIRONMENTAL PROTECTION AGENCY
901 F.2d 1419 (7th Cir. 1990)

Before POSNER, FLAUM, and RIPPLE, Circuit Judges.
POSNER, Circuit Judge.

Two steel companies challenge orders by the Environmental Protection Agency requiring them to take corrective action under section 3004(u) of the Resource Conservation and Recovery Act, as amended by the Hazardous and Solid Waste Amendments Act of 1984, 42 U.S.C. § 6924(u). The legal and technical matrix in which this challenge is embedded is immensely complex, but the complexities are irrelevant, so we shall simplify ruthlessly. ***

The companies manufacture steel in northern Indiana, producing as an unwanted by-product liquid wastes containing ammonia and other hazardous chemicals. Pipes carry these wastes to five deep injection wells on the companies' property. Drilled fifteen years ago, these wells range in depth from 2,500 to more than 4,000 feet. They end in porous rock. The wastes are forced down the wells and into the rock under pressure, and fill the pores in the rock. The bottoms of the wells are more than a quarter mile below the lowest aquifer from which drinking water is obtained and below any other ground waters known to be connected to surface waters. *** [A]bove [the zone in which the wells terminate] is a layer of impermeable rock so that the wastes cannot seep back up. The wells are elaborately sheathed to prevent leakage before the wastes reach the bottom.

There have been no complaints of leakage from the companies' wells and—as yet anyway—no complaints of harm or even danger to health (or to other good things) from the wastes that have been disposed of down these wells. Not that they have really been "disposed of"; in effect they are being stored in the porous rock at the bottom of the wells. The EPA has no plans to restrict the operation of the wells and one may wonder therefore why it insists that the wells are disposing of "solid wastes" *** [under RCRA]. The answer appears to be that under section 3004(u) of the Act no one may obtain a permit to dispose of solid wastes without taking corrective action with respect to *all* solid waste management units on the property, even inactive units. True, the statutory term is "facility," not "property," but, with support from section 3004(v), 42 U.S.C. § 6924(v), the EPA has interpreted the term to include "all contiguous [to the actual solid waste disposal facilities] property under the owner or operator's control." *Hazardous Waste Management System: Final Codification Rule*, 50 Fed. Reg. 28702, 28712 (1985). The interpretation has been upheld. *United Technologies Corp. v. EPA*, 821 F.2d 714, 721-23 (D.C.Cir.1987). The steel companies have several inactive waste management units on the same properties that the deep injection wells are on, so if the wells are disposing of solid wastes within the meaning of the Act the companies will be required to take corrective action with respect to the inactive units even though the EPA seeks no change in the operation of the wells. The costs of cleaning up inactive solid waste management units—units in which wastes may have been stored for many years and become highly toxic—can be immense. It is these costs that the companies seek to avoid by arguing that their deep injection wells are not solid waste disposal facilities within the meaning of the Resource Conservation and Recovery Act and hence that the EPA's orders directing corrective action are invalid.

*** [W]hile contesting the EPA's determination that their deep injection wells are solid waste disposal facilities, the companies no longer contest the proposition that if they are they are subject to the Resource Conservation and Recovery Act. Nor do the companies suggest that the fact that the EPA is more interested in their inactive waste management units than in their deep injection wells precludes interpreting the Resource Conservation and Recovery Act to cover such wells, or that the wells could not be "solid waste" disposal facilities because they are disposing of liquid wastes. We are in a statutory Cloud Cuckoo Land in which "solid waste" expressly includes liquid wastes. 42 U.S.C. § 6903(27). This same subsection, however, contains the statutory language on which the companies do rely: "The term 'solid waste' ... does not include ... solid or dissolved materials in ... industrial discharges which are point sources subject to permits under" section 402 of the Clean Water Act, 33 U.S.C. § 1342. The companies argue that the wastes that they pump into their deep injection wells are industrial discharges and that a deep injection well is a point source within the meaning of the Clean Water Act because pollutants might be discharged from them. 33 U.S.C. § 1362(14). If they are right on both counts and therefore subject to the permit requirements of section 402 of the Clean Water Act, then the wells are not solid waste disposal facilities and are not regulable under the Resource Conservation and Recovery Act.

Section 402 of the Clean Water Act authorizes the states to administer a system of required permits for the discharge of pollutants into navigable waters, defined as waters of the United States, 33 U.S.C. § 1362(7), subject to a variety of conditions including that the state's permit program must "control the disposal of pollutants into wells." 33 U.S.C. § 1342(b)(1)(D). Indiana has issued permits to Inland and Bethlehem that both limit the total volume of wastes that they may pump down the wells and require adherence to the wells' design parameters, although the permits do not limit the amounts of any specific pollutants that may be sent down the wells. The existence of these permits may seem to make the companies' case, but it does not. The exemption in the Resource Conservation and Recovery Act is for discharges subject to the permit requirements of section 402 of the Clean Water Act, not for possession of a permit as such. The companies have *begged* Indiana to continue including the deep injection wells in the permits that it periodically renews, though the state has no desire to include them because it does not think that these particular wells pose any menace to navigable waters, however broadly defined. The companies argue that with a permit they are exempt from the Resource Conservation and Recovery Act. They are wrong. They must be *required* by the Clean Water Act to have a permit.

In arguing that they are not required to have such a permit, the EPA urges a distinction between "discharge" and "disposal." The exemption in the Resource Conservation and Recovery Act is for "discharges," and the EPA argues that what deep injection wells do is better described as "disposal," which the Act defines as "the *discharge*, deposit, *injection*, dumping, spilling, leaking, or placing of any solid waste." 42 U.S.C. § 6903(3) (emphasis added). The argument is that all "discharges" are "disposals," but not all "disposals" are "discharges"; some are "injections." The Act does not exempt disposals that are not discharges. The agency also relies on a new provision in the 1984 amendments to the Act. This provision defines "land disposal" to include "any placement of hazardous waste in ... [an] injection well," 42 U.S.C. § 6924(k), but does not authorize corrective action under section 3004(u), and that is the provision under which the challenged orders were issued. So the agency's second strut collapses, and we must consider whether deep well injections are disposals, but not discharges; only if the answer is "yes" can the EPA prevail.

The Clean Water Act seeks to protect navigable waters by limiting discharges into them. A well that injects wastes more than a quarter mile below the lowest known aquifer is not discharging wastes into navigable waters. There is some water in the rocks into which the wells pump, but the companies do not suggest that it is connected to any navigable waters. It is true, as we noted earlier, that the Act requires the states, as a condition of being allowed to administer the permit program, to control the disposal of pollutants *through wells*, and nothing in the Act limits the depth of the wells subject to it. But as far as we are able to determine, the Act was not intended to authorize the regulation of *all* wells used to dispose of pollutants, regardless of absence of any effects on navigable waters. We must therefore consider the possibility of such effects from the disposal of pollutants through deep injection wells.

Three such effects can be conjectured. First, a well might end in navigable waters, but these wells do not. Second, since the legal concept of navigable waters might include ground waters connected to surface waters—though whether it does or not is an unresolved question—a well that ended in such connected ground waters might be within the scope of the Act. But the waters at the bottom of these wells are not connected to surface waters.

Third, wastes leaking through the (upper) casing of even the deepest injection well could pollute navigable waters. This is possible, of course, but in the EPA's current view the connection with navigable waters is too tenuous to bring deep injection wells under the Clean Water Act. It is, however, the EPA's former view, and the one we accepted in *United States Steel Corp. v. Train*, 556 F.2d 822, 851-53 (7th Cir.1977). At issue in *United States Steel Corp.* was the EPA's authority to regulate steelmakers' deep injection wells under the Clean Water Act. (This was before Indiana had taken up the congressional invitation for states to administer the clean water permit program as the EPA's surrogates.) The principal basis of our conclusion was the breadth of the provision requiring control of wells, a breadth we thought underscored by the exclusion of oil and gas wells only. We noted in passing that too little was known about deep injection of wastes to require the EPA to disregard the possibility that those wastes might find their way into navigable waters after all.

Suppose we now know (or we defer to the EPA's present view) that this possibility is nil. This would weaken *United States Steel Corp. v. Train*—how badly we need not decide—but would not dictate the outcome of the present case. If *United States Steel Corp.* is all wet, then the steel companies are not required to obtain permits for deep injection wells under the Clean Water Act and the exemption in the Resource Conservation and Recovery Act is inapplicable. Yet even if the decision stands and Clean Water Act permits are required for these wells, this would not invalidate the EPA's orders in the present case, because the exemption in the Resource Conservation and Recovery Act is limited to discharges; it does not extend to all activities that the state might regulate under the Clean Water Act. *United States Steel Corp.* did not hold that deep injection wells are subject to the Clean Water Act because they are point sources of industrial *discharges*, but if they are not then the exemption does not come into play.

The fact that our decision in *United States Steel Corp.* may have exaggerated the danger that deep injection wells pose to navigable waters can only strengthen the EPA's position in the present case, paradoxical as this may seem. The Clean Water Act is designed for the protection of navigable waters. To use that Act to exempt from the Resource Conservation and Recovery Act a form of waste disposal that if it poses any environmental hazard poses it to a part of the environment other than the navigable waters of the United States would itself be paradoxical. The purpose of the exemption in section 1004(27) of the Resource Conservation and Recovery Act, so far as we can discern it, is to avoid duplicative regulation, not to create a regulatory hole through which billions of gallons of hazardous wastes can be pumped into the earth without any controls provided they are pumped deeply enough to endanger neither navigable waters nor the supply of drinking water, the latter being protected by the Safe Drinking Water Act, 42 U.S.C. §§ 300f *et seq.*

But if deep injection endangers neither navigable waters nor drinking water, does this not mean that it must be harmless, and if so why worry that it might fall between regulatory stools? It may not be harmless. Deep injection could have adverse effects on navigable waters or drinking water that were too indirect or long run to fall under the mantle of these statutes, and in addition it could contaminate mineral resources in the injection zone. A subtler objection to the EPA's interpretation is that although there may be a regulatory gap if the Resource Conservation and Recovery Act is held inapplicable, it may be small relative to the costs of cleaning up the properties containing deep injection wells. As we suggested at the outset of this opinion, it appears that what the EPA is really up to is using the wells as an excuse for forcing the companies to clean up—at great expense—other waste disposal sites on the properties containing the wells. This may be, but the companies do not argue that the EPA's ulterior motives invalidate an objectively reasonable interpretation of the statute.

We reach the conclusion that deep well injection is subject to the Resource Conservation and Recovery Act not because the dictionary requires us to distinguish between discharge and disposal, as of course it does not. We reach it because a failure to make the distinction would create a senseless regulatory gap, though at the moment, given what is known about properly sited deep injection wells—and there is no argument that these companies' wells are not property sited—not a particularly ominous one. Regulation is not a seamless whole, and when the seam reflects a compromise we are duty-bound to honor it if constitutional. But we can find no indication that Congress intended to exempt the owners of deep injection wells from regulation under the Resource Conservation and Recovery Act, and the language of the Act does not so compellingly prescribe such a result that we must do or die without reasoning why. If the language does not compel, neither is it deformed by, the EPA's interpretation, to which we owe some, perhaps considerable, deference, and which is supported by the policies that appear to animate the Act and rebutted by no other sources of interpretive wisdom.

NOTES

1. Not long after losing its challenge to the EPA's RCRA jurisdiction over the company's underground injection wells, Bethlehem Steel faced an enforcement action for alleged violations of both RCRA and the Safe Drinking Water Act concerning, among other things, its alleged failure to satisfy its corrective action obligations under

its RCRA permits. The District Court found that Bethlehem Steel had violated the two statutes, in part because it had not fulfilled its corrective action obligations, and ordered the company to pay a civil penalty of $6 million ($4.2 million of which was related to violations of the underground injection well permits). *U.S. v. Bethlehem Steel,* 829 F.Supp. 1023 (N.D.Ind. 1993) (partial summary judgment and injunction granted for EPA), *aff'd in part and vacated in part,* 38 F.3d 862 (7th Cir. 1994), and 829 F.Supp. 1047 (N.D.Ind. 1993) (civil penalty imposed).

2. As will be more evident after you study CERCLA, there are many similarities between the RCRA corrective action program and the broader CERCLA cleanup program. One of the distinctive features of CERCLA is the EPA's authority to issue an administrative order directing private parties to conduct a cleanup, CERCLA § 106(a), and the inability of the recipients of the order to challenge its content or applicability to them unless and until it is enforced against them. CERCLA § 113(h). At least one court has applied the CERCLA rule against pre-enforcement review to attempts to challenge administrative corrective action orders under RCRA § 3008(h).

*** [S]ection 3008(h) of RCRA provides two enforcement options when the EPA determines that there has been a release of hazardous waste into the environment from certain RCRA regulation facilities. The EPA may: (1) "issue an order requiring corrective action," or (2) "commence a civil action ... for appropriate relief, including a temporary or permanent injunction." 42 U.S.C.A. § 6928(h)(1). Violation of a section 3008(h) order may subject the violator to civil or administrative penalties of up to $25,000 per day. To obtain civil penalties, the EPA must institute a civil action. If the EPA seeks to impose administrative penalties, the violator is entitled to an administrative hearing before such penalties may be imposed.

* * *

As an initial matter, I note that no provision of RCRA expressly addresses pre-enforcement review of section 3008(h) orders. ***   I therefore *** determine whether there is a fairly discernible intent to preclude judicial review.

* * *

In 1986 Congress amended CERCLA to expressly preclude pre-enforcement judicial review of administrative orders, codifying existing case law which barred pre-enforcement judicial review. *** Prior to Congress's express rejection of pre-enforcement judicial review under CERCLA, however, various courts concluded that the statutory scheme and purpose of CERCLA enforcement provisions indicated that pre-enforcement judicial review was not available for administrative orders. *See, e.g., Lone Pines Steering Committee v. United States EPA,* 777 F.2d 882, 886-87 (3d Cir. 1985) ***. The *Lone Pines Steering Committee* court stated:

The statutory approach to the problem of hazardous waste is inconsistent with the delay that would accompany pre-enforcement review. Thus, although not explicitly stated in the statute, we find in (CERCLA) an implicit disapproval of pre-enforcement judicial review. That policy decision is not limited to emergency situations but applies to remedial actions as well.

Id. at 886-87.

Those same considerations apply to RCRA. Congress designed the enforcement options of section 3008(h) of RCRA to enable the EPA to avoid the slowness of the permit process and determine how best to achieve compliance with RCRA. To allow judicial review of an administrative order before the EPA seeks to enforce that order would take away from the EPA the ability to avoid the judicial process and interfere with the regulatory scheme Congress established.

Amoco Oil Co. v. United States Environmental Protection Agency, 959 F.Supp. 1318 (D.Colo. 1997).

B. RCRA § 7003 Cleanup Actions

Prior to the 1984 enactment of RCRA's corrective action provisions, § 7003, 42 U.S.C. § 6973, was the only provision from the original 1976 version of the Act that expressly authorized the EPA to compel the cleanup of hazardous waste contamination. That provision empowers the EPA to seek a court order or issue an administrative order when the "handling, storage, treatment, transportation or disposal of any solid waste or hazardous waste may present an imminent and substantial endangerment to health or the environment." Not only is § 7003 located outside of RCRA Subtitle C (*i.e.,* in Subtitle G, Miscellaneous Provisions), but the EPA's jurisdictional reach under it is as broad as the statutory definitions of the terms in § 7003, without being limited by the exceptions and exclusions in the regulatory definitions in the 40 C.F.R. Part 261 regulations implementing RCRA Subtitle C. The EPA's authority under RCRA § 7003 extends even beyond its authority under RCRA's Subtitle C corrective action provisions in that it applies to solid waste contamination, and it applies to sites regardless of whether they are or ever were RCRA TSD facilities.

During the years between the 1976 enactment of RCRA and the 1984 amendments, a number of issues arose concerning the jurisdictional reach of § 7003. The following case addresses several of those issues, as to which the courts expressed conflicting views.

UNITED STATES V. WASTE INDUSTRIES, INC.
734 F.2d 159 (4th Cir. 1984)

Before WIDENER and SPROUSE, Circuit Judges, and BUTZNER, Senior Circuit Judge.

SPROUSE, Circuit Judge.

After the Environmental Protection Agency (EPA) investigated the Flemington landfill waste disposal site in New Hanover County, North Carolina (the Flemington landfill) for possible water pollution in the surrounding area, the United States of America for the Administrator of the EPA initiated this action against Waste Industries, Inc.; Waste Industries of New Hanover County, Inc.; the New Hanover County Board of Commissioners; and the individual owner-lessors of land used for the Flemington landfill (all defendants will be referred to collectively as the landfill group). The EPA demanded affirmative action by the landfill group under section 7003 of the Resource Conservation and Recovery Act of 1976 (Act), 42 U.S.C. § 6973, to abate alleged threats to public health and the environment posed by hazardous chemicals leaking from the Flemington landfill, to monitor the area for further contamination, to reimburse the EPA for money spent on the area, and to provide residents with a permanent potable water supply. The district court granted the landfill group's motion to dismiss under Federal Rule of Civil Procedure 12(b)(6) for failure to state a cause of action and the EPA brought this appeal. We reverse.

I

The district court, before ruling on the motion to dismiss, referred the case to a United States magistrate for factual development by order filed April 10, 1980. The magistrate issued lengthy factual findings which were taken as true by the district court for purposes of the motion. Essentially, the findings of fact showed that before 1968, New Hanover County, North Carolina (County) had no trash or solid waste disposal programs or facilities. Private trash and garbage dumps existed throughout the County, but most were simply the result of the public's disposal of garbage and waste on private property without the permission of the property owners. The County first began to address the problem in 1968 when it contracted with the city of Wilmington to use its landfill facilities. The County negotiated leases for two other landfill sites after finding that use of the Wilmington facility did not alleviate the problem. The County's experience with landfill operations was unsatisfactory, however, and in the fall of 1971, the County began looking for other solutions to its disposal problems. After some investigation, the County Board granted Waste Industries, Inc. and Waste Industries of New Hanover County, Inc. (referred to collectively as Waste Industries) an exclusive license to dispose of solid waste generated in the County.

Under the terms of the license, Waste Industries was to establish and operate landfills for the sanitary disposal of solid waste generated within the County on sites

Waste Industries owned. Waste Industries was to obtain all licenses and permits for operation of the landfills. The license agreement contained several provisions common to County contracts at that time: it required (a) that Waste Industries hold the County harmless for claims arising out of Waste Industries' actions; (b) that Waste Industries provide a performance bond; and (c) that Waste Industries observe state and local regulations. It also, among other things, required Waste Industries to provide the County with a review of the volume of the material disposed. In return, Waste Industries gained an exclusive franchise to operate sanitary landfills within the County to provide sanitary disposal of solid waste, such as inflammable or toxic materials and industrial, commercial, and agricultural by-products. The Waste Industries-County agreement was renewed, rewritten, or amended in 1975, 1977, and 1978.

After signing the initial agreement in 1972, Waste Industries obtained several landfill sites, including the seventy-acre Flemington site leased from private owners. The Flemington leases granted Waste Industries sole use and control of the premises. The landfill Waste Industries then established on the site is situated in a hole from which sand has been removed, known as a "sand barrow pit"; the surrounding soil is composed of highly permeable sand. The Flemington landfill is within a mile of both the Cape New Fear and Northeast Cape New Fear Rivers. During the operation of the landfill, unknown quantities of solid and hazardous waste were buried at the site. These wastes began leaching through the sandy soil beneath them and into the groundwater aquifer below. Before Waste Industries began operating the landfill, the residents of the Flemington community had high quality groundwater. Flemington area residents first noticed a decline in water quality in autumn 1977, when their water became foul in color, taste, and smell. Some residents suffered illnesses or side effects such as blisters, boils, and stomach distress they attribute to their use of well water. Residents complained to the County Board and demanded help.

In response to residents' demands, the County in 1978 placed surplus water tanks that it still operates in the Flemington area. Many residents, however, had found it difficult to use these tanks because of infirmity or disability. Many families wash their clothes at laundromats and drive to the homes of friends or relatives elsewhere to bathe. Others have abandoned their homes because of the contaminated water.

In addition to constructing the water tanks, the County in August 1978 referred the question of groundwater quality in and near the Flemington community to the North Carolina Department of Natural Resources and Community Development. The Department directed Waste Industries to cease disposing of waste at the Flemington landfill, which it did on June 30, 1979.

Meanwhile, the water contamination problem was brought to the attention of the EPA's regional office, which conducted hydrologic investigations of Flemington groundwater and well water in April, July, and September 1979. The September investigation was the broadest undertaken by the EPA and was designed to determine what landfill wastes were contaminating area groundwater and in what direction the contaminated aquifer groundwater was moving beneath the Flemington area. Analysis of Flemington area groundwater samples taken by the EPA revealed a large number of toxic, organic, and inorganic contaminants, including known carcinogens, resulting from improper disposal of waste at the Flemington landfill. The contaminants found beneath the landfill and in residential wells include tetrachloroethylene, benzene, trichloroethylene; 1,2-dichloroethane; vinyl chloride, methylene chloride, and lead. These chemicals, migrating from the Flemington landfill, have been detected in residential wells at levels sufficient to affect adversely human health and the environment.   The presence of chlorides, dichlorophenol, chlorobenzene, iron, manganese, phenol, and zinc has rendered the water in the wells unfit for human consumption because some of these chemicals are suspected carcinogens and all of them are a source of extremely bad taste or odor in water. Concentrations of lead, benzene, tetrachloroethylene, trichlorethylene, 1,2-dichloroethane, and vinyl chloride found in three residential wells pose an unacceptably high risk of neurological damage in children and cancer in humans of any age.

After conducting its July 1979 tests, the EPA warned many local residents that continued use of their wells for any purpose would endanger their health, and informed the County that additional water tanks were needed to meet local residents' needs. *** Finally, after the September 1979 testing established the landfill as a source of groundwater contamination, the EPA demanded that the County provide an adequate water supply to Flemington residents. A water system funded with federal, state, and local money is now in operation.

The new water system, however, has not solved the problem of escaping waste. As precipitation infiltrates the landfill waste and transports contaminants through permeable soil, the contaminants reach the local aquifer and move laterally through the aquifer in the direction of groundwater flow to the south and east. Tests indicate that the process of leaching and migration of contaminants will continue indefinitely unless remedial action is taken.

II

The EPA, in its initial complaint, requested preliminary and permanent injunctive relief requiring the appropriate parties: (1) to supply affected residents with a permanent and potable source of water; (2) to develop and implement a plan to prevent further contamination; (3) to restore the groundwater; (4) to monitor the area for further contamination; and (5) to reimburse the EPA for money spent in connection with the Flemington landfill. ***

The district court, in a thorough opinion, found that the EPA's claim for permanent injunctive relief failed to state a cause of action. It concluded that Waste Industries' failure to abate the leaching of contaminants was not actionable under section 7003 of the Act, because the provision was not intended to apply to past conduct that terminated before enforcement was sought. ***

On appeal, the EPA contends that the district court relied on erroneous premises to support its conclusion and argues that the broad remedial purposes of section 7003 can only be served by permitting actions such as this requiring malfeasant polluters to correct their past abuses of the environment. The landfill group, relying on the district court's reasoning, reads the statute restrictively.   We disagree with this limited interpretation of section 7003 as restraining only active human conduct, and reverse. The stated rules of statutory construction simply do not apply and comparison to other statutes cited by the district court sheds no light on congressional purpose in enacting section 7003.

III

* * *

The landfill group contends, and the district court held, that this section does not authorize an action to correct hazardous conditions because it only regulates the wastes themselves before or as they are produced, not the conditions they later create.   The fallacy of that contention is demonstrated by the indication of Congress that section 7003 remedies exist apart from the other provisions in the Act's structure.   In addition, section 7003 stands apart from the other sections of the Act defining the EPA's regulatory authority.   The regulatory scheme for hazardous wastes appears in subtitle C of the Act; the scheme for solid wastes, in subtitle D.   In contrast, section 7003 appears in subtitle G, and it is designed to deal with situations in which the regulatory schemes break down or have been circumvented.

We do not attach the same significance to the location of section 7003 in the miscellaneous subtitle of the statute as did the lower court.   This section is logically placed in the statutory structure to provide a remedy for environmental endangerment by hazardous or solid waste, whether or not those engaging in the endangering acts are subject to any other provision of the Act. Its application "notwithstanding any other provision of this chapter" indicates a congressional intent to include a broadly applicable section dealing with the concerns addressed by the statute as a whole.

The operative language of section 7003 authorizes the administrator to bring an action against any person contributing to the alleged disposal to stop such disposal "*or to take such other action as may be necessary.*" 42 U.S.C. § 6973(a) (emphasis added). "Disposal" is defined in 42 U.S.C. § 6903(3) as follows:

> The term "disposal" means the discharge, deposit, injection, dumping, spilling, leaking, or placing of any solid waste or hazardous waste into or on any land or water so that such solid waste or hazardous waste or any constituent thereof may enter the environment or be emitted into the air or discharged into any waters, including ground waters.

The district court held, after a contextual analysis, that this language means only disposal by "active human conduct." We cannot agree.   The term "disposal," it is true, is used throughout subtitle C in the sense that the Administrator can regulate current disposal of hazardous waste.   In this way, the Act regulates current conduct of would-be polluters.   But a strained reading of that term limiting its section 7003 meaning to active conduct would so frustrate the remedial purpose of the Act as to make it meaningless. Section 7003, unlike the provisions of the Act's subtitle C, does not regulate conduct but regulates and mitigates endangerments.   The Administrator's intervention authorized by section 7003 is triggered by evidence that the "disposal of ... hazardous waste *may present* an imminent and substantial endangerment." (emphasis added).

The inclusion of "leaking" as one of the diverse definitional components of "disposal" demonstrates that Congress intended "disposal" to have a range of meanings, including conduct, a physical state, and an occurrence. Discharging, dumping, and injection (conduct), hazardous waste reposing (a physical state) and movement of the waste after it has been placed in a state of repose (an occurrence) are all encompassed in the broad definition of disposal. "Leaking" ordinarily occurs when landfills are not constructed soundly or when drums and tank trucks filled with waste materials corrode, rust, or rot. Thus "leaking" is an occurrence included in the meaning of "disposal."

The district court's statutory analysis relied heavily upon the present-tense definition of "disposal" as indicative of an intent to restrain only ongoing human conduct. The Act, however, permits a court to order a responsible party to "stop" activities "*or* to take such other action as may be necessary" (emphasis added) to abate the endangerment. Such grammatical niceties as tense may be useful in arriving at a narrowly-sculpted meaning, but they are of little help in interpreting remedial statutes in which actions such as "may be necessary" are contemplated in order to abate gross dangers to a community. Since the term "disposal" is used throughout the Act, its definition in section 6903(3) must necessarily be broad and general to encompass both routine regulatory and the less common emergency situations. Thus it includes such diverse characteristics as "deposit, injection, dumping, spilling, leaking, or placing" wastes. We must assume that Congress included "leaking" as a definitional component of "disposal" for a purpose. We conclude that Congress made "leaking" a part of the definition of "disposal" to meet the need to respond to the possibility of endangerment, among other reasons.

Congress expressly intended that this and other language of the Act close loopholes in environmental protection. Limiting the government's enforcement prerogatives to cases involving active human conduct would open a gaping hole in the overall protection of the environment envisioned by Congress, a protection designed to be responsive to unpredictable occurrences. Without a means to respond to disasters precipitated by earlier poor planning, our nation's resources could be "conserved" from further harm, as the title of the Resource Conservation and Recovery Act suggests, but never "recovered" to their former wholesome condition.

IV

The landfill group argues that section 7003 was designed to control pollution only in emergency situations. The district court agreed, concluding that it was similar to other statutes designed by Congress solely to eliminate emergency problems. We find this position unsupportable, for the section's language stands in contrast to "emergency" type statutes. The language of section 7003 demonstrates that Congress contemplated circumstances in which the disposal of hazardous waste "*may present* an imminent and substantial endangerment" (emphasis added); therefore, the section's application is not specifically limited to an "emergency."

The Third Circuit, in its recent interpretation of the Act's section 7003, reached the same conclusion. It described section 7003 as having "enhanced the courts' traditional equitable powers by authorizing the issuance of injunctions when there is but a risk of harm, a more lenient standard than the traditional requirement of threatened irreparable harm." *United States v. Price*, 688 F.2d 204, 211 (3d Cir. 1982). Thus the Third Circuit's interpretation of section 7003, far from limiting its application to emergency situations, gave full effect to this expansion of the courts' traditional powers.

V

Although strictly speaking there is little legislative history to assist us in our quest for exact congressional intent, the history of the Act's amendments is enlightening. The legislative history of the Act as originally enacted contains no specific discussion of the reach of section 7003 and no mention of the reasons for its insertion. The hastiness of the Act's passage in the final days of a congressional session has been well-documented. That the Act was intended to eliminate any remaining loopholes in statutory protection from toxic pollution, however, is plain from a consideration of the legislative history of the statute as a whole.

The focus of our attention, then, is not on the Act's legislative history, but on the legislative history of its 1980 amendments, in which various congressional committees addressed the issues of EPA authority under section 7003 and the purposes of this section. Later congressional ratification of the availability of section 7003 as a tool for abating hazards created by inactive solid and hazardous waste disposal sites such as the Flemington landfill has been consistent and authoritative. Although this is not legislative history as such, the views of subsequent Congresses on the same or similar statutes are entitled to some weight in the construction of previous legislation. ***

*** For example, a congressional report on hazardous waste disposal issued when the 1980 amendments were being drafted observed:

> Imminence in this section [7003] applies to the nature of the threat rather than identification of the time when the endangerment initially arose. The section, therefore, may be used for events which took place at some time in the past but which continue to present a threat to the public health or the environment.

Subcommittee on Oversight and Investigation of the Committee on Interstate and Foreign Commerce, Report on Hazardous Waste Disposal, H.R.Comm. Print No. 96-IFC 31, 96th Cong., 1st Sess. 32 (1979) (Eckhardt Report). After noting that "RCRA is basically a prospective act designed to prevent improper disposal of hazardous wastes in the future," the Eckhardt Report points out: "The only tool that [the Act] has to remedy the effects of past disposal practices which are not sound is its imminent hazard authority [section 7003]." Accordingly, the authority to abate waste hazards is expansive:

> Section 7003 is designed to provide the Administrator with overriding authority to respond to situations involving a substantial endangerment to

health or the environment, regardless of other remedies available through the provisions of the Act.

Id. at 32.

It is true that some confusion has been created in the interpretation of section 7003 by the EPA's own earlier interpretation—since abandoned—of its authority under this section. The EPA at first took the position that because of its present tense language the statute was not intended to apply to inactive disposal facilities. 43 Fed. Reg. 58,984 (December 18, 1978). This narrow reading by the agency led the House Committee on Interstate and Foreign Commerce, one of the committees which had developed the original Act, to rebuke the EPA for its lack of vigor in using section 7003 and admonish the agency that section 7003 "should be used for abandoned sites as well as active ones." H.R.Rep. No. 96-191, 96th Cong., 1st Sess. 5 (1979). Not only did Congress reject the EPA's narrow view of its own authority, but the EPA later reversed its own early interpretation of section 7003. *See* 45 Fed. Reg. 33,170 (May 19, 1980). The agency's current view is, of course, entitled to substantial deference. *See Andrus v. Sierra Club*, 442 U.S. 347, 356-61 (1979) (Supreme Court defers to Council on Environmental Quality's later reversal of earlier interpretation of regulations).

VI

The landfill group next contends, and the district court held, that section 7003 is solely jurisdictional, authorizing remedies or proceedings, not creating liabilities. Those liabilities, in this view, come only from the earlier, regulatory, portions of the Act. The district court took this view of the section for various reasons, some of which we have already discussed and discarded, including the location of section 7003 within the Act and its broad wording. Again, we cannot agree.

Congress intended section 7003 to function both as a jurisdictional basis and a source of substantive liability. The Eckhardt Report states:

§ 7003 is essentially a codification of the common law public nuisance....

However, § 7003 should not be construed solely with respect to the common law. Some terms and concepts, such as persons "contributing to" disposal resulting in a substantial endangerment, are meant to be more liberal than their common law counterparts.

Eckhardt Report at 31. Congress's intent, then, was to establish a standard of liability by incorporating and expanding upon the common law.

* * *

Section 7003 is a congressional mandate that the former common law of nuisance, as applied to situations in which a risk of harm from solid or hazardous wastes exists, shall include new terms and concepts which shall be developed in a liberal, not a restrictive, manner. This ensures that problems that Congress could not have anticipated when passing the Act will be dealt with in a way minimizing the risk of harm to the environment and the public.

VII

The landfill group accurately states that although the Act was passed in 1976, regulations promulgated under it were, in fact, not finally adopted until May 1980, some four months after this action was filed and eleven months after the Flemington landfill closed. It argues, therefore, that to grant the requested relief would be a retroactive application of the Act. Section 7003 does not, however, depend on regulations for its application. It became operative upon enactment without need for the promulgation of regulations. In fact, the regulations issued under the Act pertain to subtitle C and establish rules for safe management practices for persons handling hazardous wastes, not for situations covered by section 7003. The Flemington landfill was in operation for three years after the effective date of section 7003, so applying it to the landfill group has no retroactive effect.

VIII

Contrary to the district court holding, we conclude on the peculiar facts of this case that permanent mandatory injunctive relief is an appropriate remedy. The landfill group argues that no emergency exists and that CERCLA provides an adequate remedy at law. The EPA need not prove that an emergency exists to prevail under section 7003, only that the circumstances may present an imminent and substantial endangerment. It has been alleged that an imminent and substantial endangerment exists. We make no finding on whether the EPA will be able to meet its burden at trial. Since this case came to us in the posture of an appeal from the grant of a Rule 12(b)(6) motion to dismiss, we have viewed all the evidence in the light most favorable to the party opposing the motion, the EPA.

Finally, the landfill group contends that an injunction cannot issue because CERCLA provides an adequate remedy at law. This lawsuit was not brought in common-law equity, however, but pursuant to an express statutory command giving the EPA an injunctive remedy. Congress chose to enhance the courts' traditional equitable powers in order to protect the public and the environment. Any other decision would, in effect, interpret CERCLA as repealing the Act—a result obviously not intended by Congress.

For the reasons stated we reverse the district court's grant of the landfill group's motion to dismiss and remand for further proceedings consistent with this opinion.

NOTES

1. Six months after the Fourth Circuit decided *Waste Industries*, Congress enacted the Hazardous and Solid Waste Amendments of 1984. In addition to requiring substantial changes in RCRA Subtitle C, Congress amended § 7003 to make clear that it applied to past as well as present conduct, and that liability was not based on negligence.

2. The following case was originally filed in August 1980, well before the 1984 HSWA amendments to RCRA and four months before the enactment of the Comprehensive Environmental Response, Compensation, and Liability Act ("CERCLA"), the principal federal law governing hazardous waste cleanup. It initially alleged claims under RCRA § 7003, but was amended to include CERCLA claims as well. The portion of the Eighth Circuit's decision that pertains to the elements of an action under RCRA § 7003 is reprinted below; it expressly considers the 1984 amendments. The portion of the decision that pertains to the liability of individual corporate officers or employees thereunder is quoted in chapter 6.A, and the portions that pertain to CERCLA are not included in this casebook.

United States v. Northeastern Pharmaceutical & Chemical Co.

810 F.2d 726 (8th Cir. 1986), *cert. denied,* 484 U.S. 848 (1987)

Before McMILLIAN, JOHN R. GIBSON and BOWMAN, Circuit Judges. McMILLIAN, Circuit Judge.

Northeastern Pharmaceutical & Chemical Co. (NEPACCO), Edwin Michaels and John W. Lee appeal from a final judgment entered in the District Court for the Western District of Missouri finding them and Ronald Mills jointly and severally liable for response costs incurred by the government after December 11, 1980, and all future response costs relative to the cleanup of the Denney farm site that are not inconsistent with the national contingency plan (NCP) pursuant to §§ 104, 107 of the Comprehensive Environmental Response, Compensation, and Liability Act of 1980 (CERCLA). For reversal, appellants argue the district court erred in (1) applying CERCLA retroactively, (2) finding Michaels and Lee individually liable, (3) failing to dismiss NEPACCO as a party defendant, (4) awarding response costs absent affirmative proof that the response costs were consistent with the NCP, (5) refusing to reduce the award of response costs by the amount of a prior settlement, and (6) denying appellants a jury trial.

The United States cross-appeals from that part of the district court judgment denying recovery of response costs incurred before December 11, 1980, and finding appellants and Mills were not liable for response costs pursuant to § 7003(a) of the Resource Conservation and Recovery Act of 1976 (RCRA), 42 U.S.C.A. § 6973(a). For reversal the government argues the district court erred in (1) finding the government could not recover response costs incurred before the effective date of CERCLA, December 11, 1980, and (2) finding appellants and Mills were not liable for response costs under RCRA § 7003(a).

For the reasons discussed below, we affirm in part, reverse in part, and remand for further proceedings consistent with this opinion.

I. FACTS

The following statement of facts is taken in large part from the district court's excellent memorandum opinion, *United States v. Northeastern Pharmaceutical & Chemical Co.*, 579 F.Supp. 823 (W.D.Mo.1984)(*NEPACCO*). NEPACCO was incorporated in 1966 under the laws of Delaware; its principal office was located in Stamford, Connecticut. Although NEPACCO's corporate charter was forfeited in 1976 for failure to maintain an agent for service of process, NEPACCO did not file a certificate of voluntary dissolution with the secretary of state of Delaware. In 1974 its corporate assets were liquidated, and the proceeds were used to pay corporate debts and then distributed to the shareholders. Michaels formed NEPACCO, was a major shareholder, and was its president. Lee was NEPACCO's vice-president, the supervisor of its manufacturing plant located in Verona, Missouri, and also a shareholder. Mills was employed as shift supervisor at NEPACCO's Verona plant.

From April 1970 to January 1972 NEPACCO manufactured the disinfectant hexachlorophene at its Verona plant. NEPACCO leased the plant from Hoffman-Taff, Inc.; Syntex Agribusiness, Inc. (Syntex), is the successor to Hoffman-Taff. Michaels and Lee knew that NEPACCO's manufacturing process produced various hazardous and toxic byproducts, including 2,4,5-trichlorophenol (TCP), 2,3,7,8-tetrachlorodibenzo-p-dioxin (TCDD or dioxin), and toluene. The waste byproducts were pumped into a holding tank which was periodically emptied by waste haulers. Occasionally, however, excess waste byproducts were sealed in 55-gallon drums and then stored at the plant.

In July 1971 Mills approached NEPACCO plant manager Bill Ray with a proposal to dispose of the waste-filled 55-gallon drums on a farm owned by James Denney located about seven miles south of Verona. Ray visited the Denney farm and discussed the proposal with Lee; Lee approved the use of Mills' services and the Denney farm as a disposal site. In mid-July 1971 Mills and Gerald Lechner dumped approximately 85 of the 55-gallon drums into a large trench on the Denney farm (Denney farm site) that had been excavated by Leon Vaughn. Vaughn then filled in the trench. Only NEPACCO drums were disposed of at the Denney farm site.

In October 1979 the Environmental Protection Agency (EPA) received an anonymous tip that hazardous wastes had been disposed of at the Denney farm. Subsequent EPA investigation confirmed that hazardous wastes had in fact been disposed of at the Denney farm and that the site was not geologically suitable for the disposal of hazardous wastes. Between January and April 1980 the EPA prepared a plan for the cleanup of the Denney farm site and constructed an access road and a security fence. During April 1980 the EPA conducted an on-site investigation, exposed and sampled 13 of the 55-gallon drums, which were found to be badly deteriorated, and took water and soil samples. The samples were found to contain "alarmingly" high concentrations of dioxin, TCP and toluene.

In July 1980 the EPA installed a temporary cap over the trench to prevent the entry and run-off of surface water and to minimize contamination of the surrounding soil and groundwater. The EPA also contracted with Ecology & Environment, Inc., for the preparation of a feasibility study for the cleanup of the Denney farm site. Additional on-site testing was conducted. In August 1980 the government filed its initial complaint against NEPACCO, the generator of the hazardous substances; Michaels and Lee, the corporate officers responsible for arranging for the disposal of the hazardous substances; Mills, the transporter of the hazardous substances; and Syntex, the owner and lessor of the Verona plant, seeking injunctive relief and reimbursement of response costs pursuant to RCRA § 7003. In September 1983 the feasibility study was completed.

In the meantime the EPA had been negotiating with Syntex about Syntex's liability for cleanup of the Denney farm site. In September 1980 the government and Syntex entered into a settlement and consent decree. Pursuant to the terms of the settlement, Syntex would pay $100,000 of the government's response costs and handle the removal, storage and permanent disposal of the hazardous substances from the Denney farm site. The EPA approved Syntex's proposed cleanup plan, and in June 1981 Syntex began excavation of the trench. In November 1981 the site was closed. The 55-gallon drums are now stored in a specially constructed concrete bunker on the Denney farm. The drums as stored do not present an imminent and substantial endangerment to health or the environment; however, no plan for permanent disposal has been developed, and the site will continue to require testing and monitoring in the future.

In August 1982 the government filed an amended complaint adding counts for relief pursuant to CERCLA §§ 104, 106, 107. CERCLA was enacted after the filing of the initial complaint. In September 1982 the district court granted partial summary judgment in favor of the government, holding NEPACCO had the capacity to be sued under Delaware law. In September 1983 the district court denied the defense demand for a jury trial, holding the government's request for recovery of its response costs was comparable to restitution and thus an equitable remedy. The trial was conducted during October 1983. The district court filed its memorandum opinion in January 1984.

II. DISTRICT COURT DECISION

The district court found that dioxin, hexachlorophene, TCP, TCB (1,2,3,5-tetrachlorobenzene, also found at the Denney farm site), and toluene have high levels of toxicity at low-dose levels and are thus "hazardous substances" within the meaning of RCRA § 1004(5), and CERCLA § 101(14). The district court also found there was a substantial likelihood that the environment and human beings would be exposed to the hazardous substances that had been disposed of at the Denney farm site. A state geologist testified the Denney farm site is located in an area in which substances rapidly move through the soil and into the groundwater and, although no dioxin had been found in the water in nearby wells, dioxin had been found as far as 30 inches beneath the soil in the trench.

A. RCRA Findings

The district court held that RCRA § 7003(a) requires a finding of negligence in order to hold past off site generators and transporters liable for response costs, and thus RCRA did not apply to past non-negligent off-site generators and transporters of hazardous substances.

* * *

IV. RCRA

A. Standard and Scope of § 7003 Liability

*** [T]he government argues on cross-appeal that it can also recover its response costs pursuant to RCRA § 7003(a). The district court did not reach the recovery issue because it held that under RCRA § 7003(a) (prior to 1984 amendments discussed below), proof of fault or negligence was required in order to impose liability upon past off-site generators and transporters. Because the government did not allege or prove negligence, the district court found no liability under RCRA § 7003(a) (prior to 1984 amendments). The government argues that the standard of liability under RCRA § 7003(a), as initially enacted and as amended in 1984, is strict liability, not negligence, and that liability under RCRA can be imposed even though the acts of disposal occurred before RCRA became effective in 1976. We agree.

RCRA was initially enacted in 1976, and was amended in 1978 and 1980. In November 1984, after the district court's January 1984 decision in the present case, RCRA was again amended by the Hazardous and Solid Waste Amendments of 1984 (1984 amendments). We have considered the 1984 amendments and the accompanying legislative history and, for the reasons discussed below, we believe the 1984 amendments support the government's arguments about RCRA's standard and scope of liability and retroactivity.

The critical issue is the meaning of the phrase "contributing to." Before its amendment in 1984, RCRA § 7003(a) imposed liability upon any person "contributing to" "the handling, storage, treatment, transportation or disposal of any solid or hazardous waste" that "may present an imminent and substantial endangerment to health or the environment." ***

* * *

Then, in November 1984, Congress passed and President Reagan signed the 1984 amendments, which were described as "clarifying" amendments and specifically addressed the standard and scope of liability of § 7003(a). As amended in 1984, RCRA § 7003(a) (new language in italics; deleted language in brackets), now provides in pertinent part:

> Notwithstanding any other provision of this chapter, upon receipt of evidence that the *past or present* handling, storage, treatment, transportation or disposal of any solid waste or hazardous waste may present an imminent and substantial endangerment to health or the environment, the Administrator may bring suit on behalf of the United

States in the appropriate district court [to immediately restrain any person] *against any person (including any past or present generator, past or present transporter, or past or present owner or operator of a treatment, storage, or disposal facility) who has contributed or who is* contributing to such handling, storage, treatment, transportation or disposal [to stop] *to restrain such person from* such handling, storage, treatment, transportation, or disposal [or to take such other action as may be necessary], *to order such person to take such other action as may be necessary, or both.*

As amended, RCRA § 7003(a) specifically applies to *past* generators and transporters.

Congress' intent with respect to the standard of liability under RCRA § 7003(a), as amended by the 1984 amendments, is clearly set forth in the accompanying House Conference Report. The House Conference Report also expressly disapproved of the *Wade* and *Waste Industries* [district court] cases, which were relied upon by the *NEPACCO* court, as well as the *NEPACCO* decision itself. The House Conference Report stated:

> Section 7003 focuses on the abatement of conditions threatening health and the environment and not particularly human activity. Therefore, it has *always reached those persons who have contributed in the past or are presently contributing to the endangerment, including but not limited to generators, regardless of fault or negligence.* The amendment, by adding the words "have contributed" is merely intended to clarify the existing authority. Thus, for example, *non-negligent generators whose wastes are no longer being deposited or dumped at a particular site may be ordered to abate the hazard to health or the environment posed by the leaking of the wastes they once generated and which have been deposited on the site.* The amendment reflects the long-standing view that generators and other persons involved in the handling, storage, treatment, transportation or disposal of hazardous wastes must share in the responsibility for the abatement of the hazards arising from their activities. The section was intended and is intended to abate conditions resulting from past activities.
> ***

H.R. Conf. Rep. No. 1133, 98th Cong., 2d Sess. 119 (1984) (emphasis added).

Thus, following the 1984 amendments, past off-site generators and transporters are within the scope of RCRA § 7003(a). From the legislative history of the 1984 amendments, it is clear that Congress intended RCRA § 7003(a), as initially enacted and as amended, to impose liability without fault or negligence and to apply to the present conditions resulting from past activities. In other words, RCRA § 7003(a), as initially enacted and as amended, applies to past non-negligent off-site generators like NEPACCO and to non-negligent past transporters like Mills.

* * *

B. Retroactivity

This argument is closely related to the question of the scope of § 7003(a) liability discussed above. Appellants argue that because RCRA, unlike CERCLA, is prospective in focus and was not enacted until 1976, RCRA cannot be retroactively applied to impose liability on them for acts that occurred in 1971. A similar retroactivity argument was raised in *United States v. Price*, 523 F.Supp. at 1071-72. The defendants in *United States v. Price* had argued that RCRA could not be applied retroactively to impose liability on them for disposing of toxic wastes in 1972. The *Price* court rejected the retroactivity argument, stating

> [t]he gravamen of a section 7003 action ... is not defendants' dumping practices, which admittedly ceased with respect to toxic wastes in 1972, but the present imminent hazard posed by the continuing disposal [which is defined by RCRA § 1003(3) to include "[t]he ... leaking ... of any solid waste or hazardous waste into or on any land or water,"] of contaminants into the groundwater [or into the environment]. Thus, the statute neither punishes wrongdoing nor imposes liability for injuries inflicted by past acts. Rather, as defendants themselves argue, its orientation is essentially prospective. When construed in this manner, the statute is simply not retroactive. It merely relates to current and future conditions.

Id. at 1071. We hold RCRA is not retroactive because it imposes liability for the *present and future* conditions resulting from past acts.

In summary, we hold that RCRA § 7003(a), as initially enacted and as clarified by the 1984 amendments, imposes strict liability upon past off-site generators of hazardous waste and upon past transporters of hazardous waste. We reverse that part of the district court judgment holding that RCRA does not apply to past non-negligent off-site generators and transporters.

* * *

NOTES

1. As the EPA prevailed both in the courts and in the Congress (with the enactment of the 1984 amendments) regarding the liability rules under RCRA § 7003, it was also realizing its awesome powers to accomplish cleanup actions under CERCLA. Where the EPA discovers contamination at a site, and the contamination includes a "hazardous substance" (see chapter 8), the agency would typically prefer to exercise its CERCLA authority to force the private parties to conduct the cleanup. The scope of parties subject to CERCLA liability is at least as broad as, if not broader than, under RCRA § 7003; for some categories of parties, the EPA does not even have to prove that they "contributed" to the contamination, as it must prove under RCRA § 7003; and the EPA can use the additional threat of cleaning up the site with Superfund money and suing the responsible parties for reimbursement (as well as treble damages, if the

responsible parties have failed to comply with an EPA cleanup order) as further leverage to force a cleanup. Thus, where jurisdiction exists under both RCRA § 7003 and CERCLA, RCRA § 7003 is likely to make an appearance in the pleadings, but not to play a key role in the litigation.

2. The EPA continues to use RCRA § 7003 for sites where the contamination does not include a hazardous substance—most notably, sites involving petroleum contamination, because petroleum is excluded from the definition of hazardous substance. CERCLA § 101(14). The *Aceto Agricultural Chemicals* case in chapter 10.D illustrates the EPA's ongoing use of RCRA § 7003. That case involved various pesticide wastes, most of which were hazardous substances and therefore covered under CERCLA. Although some of the wastes were not hazardous substances and therefore not subject to CERCLA, they still qualified as solid waste under RCRA § 7003. Where the EPA finds contamination at a RCRA TSD facility, it generally prefers to use its corrective action authorities rather than CERCLA. RCRA/NPL Listing Policy, 51 Fed. Reg. 21054 (1986).

3. Of perhaps greater ongoing significance is the citizen suit analog of RCRA § 7003, which authorizes "any person" (including a state or locality, a corporation, partnership, or association, as well as an individual) to sue any other person or entity "who has contributed or who is contributing to the past or present handling *** of any solid or hazardous waste which may present an imminent and substantial endangerment to health or the environment." RCRA § 7002(a)(1)(B), 42 U.S.C. § 6972(a)(1)(B). The language of this provision is identical in all relevant respects to the § 7003 provision authorizing the EPA to bring suit to obtain a cleanup order; it naturally omits any authority for a citizen to issue an administrative cleanup order, which EPA is empowered to do.

4. The remaining cases in this chapter involve citizen suits addressing solid waste or hazardous waste contamination under RCRA § 7002(a)(1)(B). The first case contrasts the citizen suit enforcement action under § 7002(a)(1)(A), which addresses violations of RCRA regulatory provisions (the citizen suit counterpart to the EPA enforcement actions examined in the next chapter) with the citizen suit cleanup action under RCRA § 7002(a)(1)(B).

5. Before bringing suit or issuing an administrative order under RCRA § 7003(a), the EPA must notify the affected state. The prerequisites for filing a citizen suit under RCRA § 7002(a)(1)(B) are more extensive. The prospective plaintiff must give notice of the endangerment, 90 days before filing suit, to the EPA, the affected state, and any person alleged to have contributed or to be contributing to the endangerment, except that the 90-day waiting period does not apply to endangerment actions based on violations of Subtitle C. § 7002(b)(2)(A). In addition, a citizen suit may not be brought under § 7002(a)(1)(B) if the EPA or state is undertaking specified actions to redress the endangerment. RCRA § 7002(b)(2)(B) and (C).

CONNECTICUT COASTAL FISHERMEN'S ASS'N V. REMINGTON ARMS CO.
989 F.2d 1305 (2d Cir. 1993)

Before CARDAMONE, WINTER and MAHONEY, Circuit Judges.
CARDAMONE, Circuit Judge.

Critical on this appeal is the meaning of the terms "solid waste" and "hazardous waste," as these terms are defined in the Solid Waste Disposal Act, 42 U.S.C. §§ 6901-6992k, as amended by the Resource Conservation and Recovery Act of 1976 (RCRA), and the Hazardous and Solid Waste Amendments of 1984. Defining what Congress intended by these words is not child's play, even though RCRA has an "Alice in Wonderland" air about it. We say that because a careful perusal of RCRA and its regulations reveals that "solid waste" plainly means one thing in one part of RCRA and something entirely different in another part of the same statute.

"When I use a word," Humpty Dumpty said in a rather scornful tone, "it means just what I choose it to mean—neither more nor less."

"The question is," said Alice, "whether you *can* make words mean so many different things."

"The question is," said Humpty Dumpty, "which is to be master— that's all."

Lewis Carroll, Through the Looking-Glass ch. 6 at 106-09 (Schocken Books 1987) (1872). Congress, of course, is the master and in the discussion that follows, we undertake to discover what meaning Congress intended in its use of the words solid and hazardous waste.

Remington Arms Co., Inc. (Remington or appellant) has owned and operated a trap and skeet shooting club—originally organized in the 1920s—on Lordship Point in Stratford, Connecticut since 1945. Trap and skeet targets are made of clay, and the shotguns used to knock these targets down are loaded with lead shot. The Lordship Point Gun Club (the Gun Club) was open to the public and it annually served 40,000 patrons. After nearly 70 years of use, close to 2,400 tons of lead shot (5 million pounds) and 11 million pounds of clay target fragments were deposited on land around the club and in the adjacent waters of Long Island Sound. Directly to the north of Lordship Point lies a Connecticut state wildlife refuge at Nells Island Marsh, a critical habitat for one of the state's largest populations of Black Duck. The waters and shore near the Gun Club feed numerous species of waterfowl and shorebirds.

Plaintiff, Connecticut Coastal Fishermen's Association (Coastal Fishermen or plaintiff) brought suit against defendant Remington alleging that the lead shot and clay targets are hazardous wastes under RCRA and pollutants under the Clean Water Act (Act). Remington has never obtained a permit under § 3005 of RCRA for the storage and disposal of hazardous wastes, or a National Pollutant Discharge Elimination System (pollution discharge) permit pursuant to § 402 of the Clean Water Act. Plaintiff insists that Remington must now clean up the lead shot and clay fragments it permitted to be scattered on the land and in the sea at Lordship Point. Because the debris constitutes an imminent and substantial endangerment to health and the environment under RCRA, we agree.

BACKGROUND

In response to citizens' concerns regarding the impact of the Gun Club operations on the surrounding environment, the Connecticut Department of Environmental Protection (DEP or the Department) began an investigation in May 1985 into possible contamination. Concluding that the Gun Club's activities "reasonably can be expected to cause pollution," the DEP issued an administrative order (Order WC4122) on August 19, 1985, requiring Remington to:

1) Investigate the extent and degree of lead contamination of sediments and aquatic life as a result of past and present activities of the Remington Gun Club....

2) Perform a study to evaluate the potential for lead poisoning of waterfowl as a result of past and present activities at the Remington Gun Club.

3) Take remedial measures as necessary to minimize or eliminate the potential for contamination of aquatic life and waterfowl.

Order WC4122 required that remedial action *be completed* in a year or by August 31, 1986, "except as may be revised by the recommendations of [a] detailed engineering study and agreed to by" the DEP. It did not order Remington to cease discharging lead shot or targets or to obtain a pollution discharge permit. The DEP did not then have authority to issue RCRA permits.

Meanwhile, pursuant to the DEP's August 1985 order, Remington commissioned a study by Energy Resources Company. The scope of the study was approved by the DEP on February 3, 1986. *** The completed Energy Resources study was submitted to the DEP on July 2, 1986—one month before the August deadline for complete remediation. Based on the results of this study, the Department modified Order WC4122 on October 24, 1986 (modified order). The modified order required Remington to cease all discharges of lead shot at the Gun Club by December 31, 1986 and to submit a plan detailing remediation options by April 30, 1987. It did not prohibit Remington from continuing to operate the Gun Club after December 31, 1986, if steel shot was used in place of lead shot.

In response to the modified order, Remington commissioned a study by Battelle Ocean Sciences (Battelle) to look into remediation alternatives. Again, the DEP approved the scope of the Battelle study, though the study did not address remediation of the clay target fragments. Remington submitted the results of the Battelle study to the DEP on January 1, 1988. ***

In September 1988 the DEP *** directed Remington to investigate the effect of the clay targets on the environment. Remington asked Battelle to conduct a further study, which it submitted to the Department in February 1990. The DEP approved

Battelle's latest report on June 8, 1990. As a result, but well over a year later, the DEP ordered Remington to supplement the proposed remediation plan to include removal of visible clay target fragments from the beach surface above the mean low water mark of Long Island Sound and to study the possible removal of targets from the water. Remington has now submitted the ordered supplemental report, and is awaiting its approval by the Department. It will have six months after the DEP approves the remediation plan to submit final engineering plans and a construction schedule. Because the proposed remediation plan involves dredging navigable waters of the United States, Remington will have to obtain permits from the U.S. Army Corps of Engineers. To date, none of the lead shot or the clay target fragments has been removed from Lordship Point or the surrounding waters of Long Island Sound.

PRIOR PROCEEDINGS

The Coastal Fishermen's Association filed its original complaint on April 24 and amended it on October 21, 1987. The amended complaint alleges that the operation of the Gun Club involved the discharge of pollutants from a point source without a pollution discharge permit in violation of the Clean Water Act, and that because the lead shot and clay targets are hazardous wastes, the Gun Club is a hazardous waste storage and disposal facility subject to RCRA requirements. Plaintiff sought a declaration that Remington had violated and was violating both the Act and the RCRA orders compelling it to remedy the accumulations of shot and target debris. Plaintiff sought civil penalties and attorney's fees, but it did not ask to have the Gun Club's future activities enjoined.

*** On September 11, 1991, the United States District Court for the District of Connecticut ruled that it lacked jurisdiction over plaintiff's Clean Water Act causes of action because the DEP was "diligently prosecuting an action under a [comparable] State law," as provided in § 309(g)(6)(A)(ii) of the Act, precluding citizen suits. Turning to the RCRA claims, the district court held that the lead shot and clay targets were "discarded material" under 42 U.S.C. § 6903(27), were "solid waste" under that statute, and therefore were subject to regulation under RCRA. It further stated that the lead shot was a "hazardous waste," but believed there were genuine issues of material fact as to whether the clay targets were "hazardous waste" under RCRA.

*** We now affirm the district court's Clean Water Act ruling, though we do so on different grounds. With respect to the RCRA holding, we reverse in part and affirm in part.

DISCUSSION
* * *

II. *RESOURCE CONSERVATION AND RECOVERY ACT*

A. *Overview*

Turning now to Remington's appeal from the district court's RCRA ruling, plaintiff asserts that Remington has been operating an unpermitted facility for the treatment, storage or disposal of hazardous wastes in violation of 42 U.S.C. § 6925 (a citizens suit claim under § 6972(a)(1)(A)) and has created an "imminent and substantial endangerment" to human health and the environment under § 6972(a)(1)(B). The district court did not distinguish between these causes of action in granting plaintiff summary judgment. Remington, as noted, never obtained a RCRA permit for the operation of its Gun Club facility, but contends that because lead shot and clay target debris are not "solid wastes"—and hence cannot be "hazardous wastes" regulated by RCRA—it is not subject to a permit requirement. In essence, Remington contends that RCRA does not apply to the Gun Club because any disposal of waste that occurred there was merely incidental to the normal use of a product.

*** Under RCRA "hazardous wastes" are a subset of "solid wastes." Accordingly, for a waste to be classified as hazardous, it must first qualify as a solid waste under RCRA. We direct our attention initially therefore to whether the lead shot and clay targets are solid waste.

B. *Chevron Analysis*

Our analysis of the definition of solid waste entails statutory interpretation as outlined in *Chevron, U.S.A., Inc. v. Natural Resources Defense Council*, 467 U.S. 837, 842-43 (1984). First, the reviewing court must address "whether Congress has directly spoken to the precise question at issue" by focusing on the language and structure of the statute itself, and then—if necessary—examine congressional purpose expressed in legislative history. A clear legislative purpose ends our inquiry, but if "the statute is silent or ambiguous with respect to the specific issue, the question for the court is whether the agency's answer is based on a permissible construction of the statute." ***

We consider first the statutory definition of solid waste. RCRA defines solid waste as:

> any garbage, refuse, sludge from a waste treatment plant, water supply treatment plant, or air pollution control facility *and other discarded material* ... resulting from industrial, commercial, mining and agricultural operations, and from community activities ...

42 U.S.C. § 6903(27) (emphasis added). Remington admits that its Gun Club is a "commercial operation" or a "community activity;" it challenges the district court's finding that the lead shot and clay target debris are "discarded material." The statute

itself does not further define "discarded material," and this creates an ambiguity with respect to the specific issue raised by Remington: At what point after a lead shot is fired at a clay target do the materials become discarded? Does the transformation from useful to discarded material take place the instant the shot is fired or at some later time?

The legislative history does not satisfactorily resolve this ambiguity. It tells us that RCRA was designed to "eliminate the last remaining loophole in environmental law" by regulating the "disposal of discarded materials and hazardous wastes." H.R.Rep. No. 1491, 94th Cong., 2d Sess. 4 (1976). Further, the reach of RCRA was intended to be broad.

> It is not only the waste by-products of the nation's manufacturing processes with which the committee is concerned: *but also the products themselves once they have served their intended purposes and are no longer wanted by the consumer.* For these reasons the term discarded materials is used to identify collectively those substances often referred to as industrial, municipal or post-consumer waste; refuse, trash, garbage and sludge.

Id. at 2 (emphasis added). Yet, the legislative history does not tell us at what point products have served their intended purposes. The statutory definition of "disposal" as "the discharge, deposit, injection, dumping, spilling, leaking, or placing of any solid waste or hazardous waste into or on any land or water," 42 U.S.C. § 6903(3), while broad, sheds little light on this question. *** Thus, we proceed to the second step of the *Chevron* analysis and consider the EPA's interpretation.

The RCRA regulations create a dichotomy in the definition of solid waste. The EPA distinguishes between RCRA's regulatory and remedial purposes and offers a different definition of solid waste depending upon the statutory context in which the term appears. In its *amicus* brief, the EPA tells us that the regulatory definition of solid waste—found at 40 C.F.R. § 261.2(a)—is narrower than its statutory counterpart. ***

The regulations further state that the statutory definition of solid waste, found at 42 U.S.C. § 6903(27), applies to "imminent hazard" lawsuits brought by the United States under § 7003. This statement recognizes the special nature of the imminent hazard lawsuit under RCRA. Currently, RCRA authorizes two kinds of citizen suits. The first, under § 7002(a)(1)(A), enables private citizens to enforce the EPA's hazardous waste regulations and—according to 40 C.F.R. § 261.1(b)(1)—invokes the narrow regulatory definition of solid waste. The second type of citizen suit, under § 7002(a)(1)(B), authorizes citizens to sue to abate an "imminent and substantial endangerment to health or the environment." While the regulations do not specifically mention this second category of citizen suit, regulatory language referring to § 7003 must also apply to § 7002(a)(1)(B) because the two provisions are nearly identical. Consequently, the broader statutory definition of solid waste applies to citizen suits brought to abate imminent hazard to health or the environment.

We recognize the anomaly of using different definitions for the term "solid waste" and that such view further complicates an already complex statute. Yet, we believe on balance that the EPA regulations reasonably interpret the statutory language. Hence, we defer to them. Dual definitions of solid waste are suggested by the structure and language of RCRA. Congress in Subchapter III isolated hazardous wastes for more stringent regulatory treatment.   Recognizing the serious responsibility that such regulations impose, Congress required that hazardous waste—a subset of solid waste as defined in the RCRA regulations—be clearly identified. The statute directs the EPA to develop specific "criteria" for the identification of hazardous wastes as well as to publish a list of particular hazardous wastes. By way of contrast, Subchapter IV that empowers the EPA to publish "guidelines" for the identification of problem solid waste pollution areas, does not require explanation beyond RCRA's statutory definition of what constitutes solid waste. Hence, the words of the statute contemplate that the EPA would refine and narrow the definition of solid waste for the sole purpose of Subchapter III regulation and enforcement.

C. *Regulatory Definition of Solid Waste*

The EPA, as *amicus*, concludes that the lead shot and clay targets discharged by patrons of Remington's Gun Club do not fall within the narrow regulatory definition of solid waste. Again, this issue is one we need not resolve because plaintiff has failed to allege a valid claim, brought under the § 7002(a)(1)(A) citizen suit provision, that Remington violated § 6925 of RCRA.

Plaintiff first alleges that Remington is operating a hazardous waste *disposal* facility without a permit, in violation of § 6925. This claim alleges a "wholly past" RCRA violation and is dismissed under *Gwaltney*. The Supreme Court acknowledged that the language in the citizen suit provisions of the Clean Water Act and § 7002(a)(1)(A) of RCRA is identical, yielding the same requirement that plaintiff allege an ongoing or intermittent violation of the relevant statute. *** Because we find no valid allegation of a present violation with respect to Coastal Fishermen's Clean Water Act suit, we must reach the same result with respect to its first claim under § 7002(a)(1)(A) of RCRA.

Second, plaintiff alleges that Remington owns or is operating a hazardous waste *storage* facility without a permit in violation of § 6925. Because plaintiff's alleged "violation" would continue as long as the lead shot and clay targets are "stored" in the waters of Long Island Sound, *Gwaltney* does not bar this claim. But RCRA and its regulations do. RCRA defines "storage" as "the containment of hazardous waste, either on a temporary basis or for a period of years, in such a manner as not to constitute disposal of such hazardous waste."   § 6903(33).   Neither the statute nor its accompanying regulations define "containment," but "storage" is further defined in the regulations as "the holding of hazardous waste for a temporary period, at the end of which the hazardous waste is treated, disposed of, or stored elsewhere." The lead shot and clay targets now scattered in the waters of Long Island Sound at no time have been contained or held.

Moreover, the very essence of Coastal Fishermen's complaint is that Remington left the debris in the Sound with no intention of taking additional action. Hence, the alleged storage of the waste logically may not be an interim measure as the regulations require. Coastal Fishermen therefore failed to state a valid claim that Remington owns or operates a hazardous waste storage facility or that it violated § 7002(a)(1)(A). Because only such a violation would trigger application of the regulatory definition of solid waste, it is unnecessary to decide whether the lead shot and clay targets fall within RCRA's regulatory scope.

D. *Statutory Definition of Solid Waste*

Coastal Fishermen's allegation that the lead shot and clay target debris in Long Island Sound creates an "imminent and substantial endangerment" under § 7002(a)(1)(B) of RCRA need not meet the present violation hurdle. An imminent hazard citizen suit will lie against any "past or present" RCRA offender "who has contributed or who is contributing" to "past or present" solid waste handling practices that "may present an imminent and substantial endangerment to health or the environment." Therefore, under an imminent hazard citizen suit, the endangerment must be ongoing, but the conduct that created the endangerment need not be.

As already noted, RCRA regulations apply the broader statutory definition of solid waste to imminent hazard suits. The statutory definition contains the concept of "discarded material," 42 U.S.C. § 6903(27), but it does not contain the terms "abandoned" or "disposed of" as required by the regulatory definition. 40 C.F.R. §§ 261.2(a)(2), (b)(1). Amicus interprets the statutory definition of solid waste as encompassing the lead shot and clay targets at Lordship Point because they are "discarded." Specifically, the EPA states that the materials are discarded because they have been "left to accumulate long after they have served their intended purpose." Without deciding how long materials must accumulate before they become discarded—that is, when the shot is fired or at some later time—we agree that the lead shot and clay targets in Long Island Sound have accumulated long enough to be considered solid waste.

E. *Hazardous Waste*

Having resolved that the lead shot and clay targets are discarded solid waste, we next analyze whether they are hazardous waste. RCRA defines "hazardous waste" as

a solid waste, or combination of solid wastes, which because of its quantity, concentration, or physical, chemical, or infectious characteristics may—

. . .

(B) pose a substantial present or potential hazard to human health or the environment when improperly treated, stored, transported, or disposed of, or otherwise managed.

42 U.S.C. § 6903(5)(B).

Certain wastes have been listed by the EPA as hazardous pursuant to 40 C.F.R. § 261.30. Alternatively, a waste is considered hazardous if it exhibits any of the characteristics identified in 40 C.F.R. §§ 261.20 through 261.24: ignitability, corrosivity, reactivity, or toxicity. The district court granted summary judgment in favor of plaintiff on the issue of whether the lead shot qualified as a hazardous waste, but at the same time stated there were genuine issues of material fact as to whether the clay targets were hazardous waste. Remington objects to both rulings.

1. *Lead Shot*

The district court concluded that the lead shot was hazardous waste as a matter of law because it satisfied the requirements of 40 C.F.R. § 261.24 for toxicity. That regulation provides that a solid waste is toxic, and therefore hazardous if, using appropriate testing methods, an "extract from a representative sample of the waste contains any of the contaminants listed ... at the concentration equal to or greater than" that specified. 40 C.F.R. § 261.24(a). For lead, the concentration threshold is 5.0 mg/L. *Id.* table 1.

The Battelle study commissioned by defendant outlines the test method utilized as in accordance with EPA procedures, and was of the view that

> Forty-five percent of the sediment samples analyzed exceeded the [applicable limits for lead]. On the basis of these results, upland disposal of the sediments as they currently exist in the environment at Lordship Point would require use of a RCRA-certified hazardous waste disposal site.

Remington does not challenge the accuracy or methodology of the Battelle study that clearly demonstrates that both the sediment at Lordship Point and the lead shot itself are toxic within the meaning of 40 C.F.R. § 261.24. The Battelle study further opines that "the accumulation of lead in the tissues of mussels and ducks [is] sufficient to indicate a lead contamination problem requiring remediation at Lordship Point." As a matter of law, the lead shot is a solid waste which, due to its toxicity and the fact that it poses a substantial threat to the environment, is a hazardous solid waste subject to RCRA remediation and regulation.

Amicus, National Rifle Association (NRA), contends that because RCRA must be "integrated" with other environmental statutes, *see* 42 U.S.C. § 6905(b), and because the Toxic Substances Control Act exempts from the definition of "toxic substance" shells and cartridges for use in firearms, the lead shot should not be classified as a hazardous waste (presumably because it should not be considered "toxic") under RCRA.

NRA misreads the Toxic Substances Control Act. The section relied on, 15 U.S.C. § 2602(2), does not purport to define "toxic" substances, but rather defines "chemical" substances. Again, the "integration" is designed "for purposes of administration and enforcement and [to] avoid duplication," not, as NRA urges, for the perilous purpose of engaging in a far-ranging search through the United States Code for exemptions from particular provisions of one environmental statute in order to apply them to another.

In fact, were RCRA to be integrated with other environmental statutes, it would seem more appropriate to look to the Migratory Bird Treaty Act, pursuant to which the Secretary of the Interior has approved regulations promulgated by the Fish and Wildlife Service, prohibiting the use of lead shot in 12 gauge or larger shotguns when duck hunting. More fundamentally, the distinction between "substances" and "wastes" is "a substantial one [which] should be preserved, absent a clear legislative intent to the contrary." *Murtha*, 958 F.2d at 1202.

2. *Clay Targets*

Remington declares the clay targets cannot be hazardous waste merely because they contain hazardous wastes listed in 40 C.F.R. § 261.33(f). Regardless of whether this assertion properly interprets 40 C.F.R. § 261.33(d) (comment), it is irrelevant. The district court did not decide that there was a genuine issue as to whether the clay targets were hazardous because it was not yet determined whether they contain hazardous wastes listed in 40 C.F.R. § 261.33(f). Rather, it ruled this issue remained undecided because the appropriate tests to determine toxicity under 40 C.F.R. § 261.24 had not yet been completed.

* * *

NOTES

1. Just when you thought you had mastered the "mind-numbing" regulatory definitions of solid and hazardous waste, the broader, more vague, statutory definitions take precedence.

2. The contrast between the use of the 40 C.F.R. Part 261 definitions for the day-to-day regulatory program, and the use of the statutory definitions for the cleanup provisions (under both corrective action and §§ 7003 and 7002(a)(1)(B)) is highlighted in *Comite Pro Rescate de la Salud v. Puerto Rico Aqueduct and Sewer Authority*, 888 F.2d 180 (1st Cir. 1989), *cert. denied*, 494 U.S. 1029 (1990). That case involved a citizen suit against a sewer authority, and industries discharges wastes thereto, for the alleged leaking of solid and hazardous waste from the sewer system, presenting an imminent and substantial endangerment.

The statutory definition of solid waste excludes "solid or dissolved material in domestic sewage." RCRA § 1004(27). The court concurred in the EPA's view that that statutory exclusion is limited to sewage emanating from residences, and does not extend to sanitary sewage from industries.

The industries then contended that the EPA's statutory construction was inconsistent with the agency's regulations:

> The defendants reply to these arguments by pointing to a specific EPA regulation, written in respect to other parts of the RCRA statute, which says

(a) *Materials which are not solid wastes.* The following materials are not solid wastes for purposes of this part: (1)(i) Domestic sewage; and (ii) Any mixture of domestic sewage and other wastes that passes through a sewer system to a publicly-owned treatment works for treatment. *"Domestic sewage" means untreated sanitary wastes that pass through a sewer system.*

40 C.F.R. § 261.4 (emphasis added). The defendants note that the last sentence of this regulation defines "domestic sewage" by referring only to the *type* of waste, not to its *source*; they infer that the definition includes as "domestic sewage" sanitary wastes originating at the workplace; and they argue that EPA is bound by this definition.

We do not accept this argument for two reasons. First, EPA denies that this definition includes sanitary wastes originating in factories; it says that the definition simply refers to the kind of *residential* waste at issue; the regulation's silence about source does not mean that source is irrelevant. EPA's reading of its regulation is not totally unreasonable; and, in light of an agency's considerable legal authority to interpret its own regulations, this argument is dispositive. ***

Second, as we just mentioned, the definitional regulation applies "only to wastes that also are hazardous *for purposes of* the regulations implementing *Subtitle C* of RCRA." 40 C.F.R. § 261.1(b)(1) (emphasis added). Sections 7002 and 7003 are not part of Subtitle C. Indeed, the regulation goes on to say

A material which is not defined as a solid waste in this part, or is not a hazardous waste identified or listed in this part, *is still a solid waste* ... if ... in the case of section 7003, the statutory elements are established.

40 C.F.R. § 261.1(b)(2) (emphasis added). (Since Congress had not yet enacted § 7002(a)(1)(B) when EPA wrote this regulation, we take § 7003 to stand for the nearly identical § 7002(a)(1)(B) as well.) Defining "solid waste" more narrowly for purposes of Subtitle C than for purposes of §§ 7002 and 7003 may make sense. Subtitle C contains highly detailed recordkeeping, notification, and permit requirements; to ease administrative burdens, EPA may want to include those factory pipes that contain only a little sanitary waste, but exclude those that contain little else. Sections 7002 and 7003, on the other hand, are invoked only to respond to imminent and substantial endangerments to health or the environment; in such a context, involving a present threat to public welfare and no ongoing administrative duties, EPA may want to include even those factory pipes that contain a relatively small proportion of industrial wastes.

In any event, why, given the general broad language of the entire definitional section, could not EPA define the exception's scope somewhat differently for purposes of different parts of the RCRA statute? We concede that a court might find it difficult to uphold even minor variations in an agency's interpretation and application of the same statutory words if the *reason* for the court's "deference to administrative interpretations," *Chevron*, 467 U.S. at 844, were the court's belief that historical or administrative circumstances mean that the agency *likely knew better* what Congress had in mind, *see Mayburg*, 740 F.2d 100 at 105-06. The court might ask how Congress, using a single set of words in a single statutory sentence, could have meant several different things. However, where the *reason* for the court's "deference" reflects its belief that Congress, in effect, *delegated* to the agency a degree of interpretive power, it does not seem odd to find the agency interpreting the same words somewhat differently as they apply to different parts of the statute in order better to permit that statute to fulfill its basic congressionally determined purposes. Had the statute *expressly* delegated the authority to the EPA to decide the precise scope of the various parts of the statutory definition under different parts of the statute, it would not seem at all odd to find the EPA tailoring its scope to fit the needs and objectives of the statute's different parts. Why should the EPA not have somewhat similar authority, at least to create minor differences, where the delegation is *implicit*, where the courts infer a congressional delegatory intent from the nature of the overall regulatory scheme, its heavy dependence upon sensible administration for its success, and the rather interstitial nature of the particular legal question—where such are the reasons for what the Supreme Court in *Chevron* calls "deference?" ***

Id. at 186-87.

3. In *Connecticut Coastal Fishermen's Ass'n* and *Comite Pro Rescate de la Salud*, the courts did not assess whether the facts "may present an imminent and substantial endangerment to health or the environment" for purposes of § 7002(a)(1)(B). In *Lincoln Properties, Ltd. v. Higgins*, 23 Envtl. L. Rep. (Envtl. L. Inst.) 20665 (E.D. Cal. 1993), the court summarized the relevant case law concerning the meaning of the key terms in § 7002(a)(1)(B):

In order to succeed on its RCRA claim, Lincoln must establish (1) that the conditions at Lincoln Center may present an imminent and substantial endangerment to health or the environment; (2) that the endangerment stems from the handling, storage, treatment, transportation or disposal of any solid or hazardous waste; and (3) that the dry cleaners have contributed or are contributing to such handling, storage, treatment, transportation or disposal. The court now turns to these elements.

1. *Imminent and Substantial Endangerment*. Section 6972(a)(1)(B) authorizes injunctive relief where the site conditions "may present an imminent and substantial endangerment to health or the environment." *** First, it is significant that the word "may" precedes the standard of liability: "[t]his is 'expansive language,' which is 'intended to confer upon the

courts the authority to grant affirmative equitable relief to the extent necessary to eliminate any risk posed by toxic wastes.'" *Dague v. City of Burlington*, 935 F.2d 1343, 1355 (2d Cir. 1991) (*quoting United States v. Price*, 688 F.2d 204, 213-14 (3d Cir. 1982)), *rev'd in part on other grounds*, 112 S. Ct. 2638 (1992). Thus, § 6972's application is not limited to emergency situations.

Second, "endangerment" means a threatened or potential harm and does not require proof of actual harm. As one court recognized in construing the phrase "will endanger" in the Clean Air Act, "[t]he meaning of 'endanger' is not disputed. Case law and dictionary definition agree that endanger means something less than actual harm. When one is endangered, harm is threatened; no actual injury need ever occur." *Ethyl Corp. v. Environmental Protection Agency*, 541 F.2d 1, 13 (D.C. Cir. 1976), *cert. denied*, 96 S. Ct. 2662 (1976).

Third, a finding of "imminence" does not require a showing that actual harm will occur immediately so long as the risk of threatened harm is present. *** An endangerment is "imminent" if factors giving rise to it are present, even though the harm may not be realized for years.

Finally, the word "substantial" does not require quantification of the endangerment (e.g., proof that a certain number of persons will be exposed, that 'excess deaths' will occur, or that a water supply will be contaminated to a specific degree). Instead, the decisional precedent demonstrates that an endangerment is substantial if there is some reasonable cause for concern that someone or something may be exposed to a risk of harm by a release or a threatened release of a hazardous substance if remedial action is not taken.

However, injunctive relief should not be granted "where the risk of harm is remote in time, completely speculative in nature, or de minimis in degree." *United States v. Reilly Tar & Chemical Corp.*, 546 F. Supp. 1100, 1109 (D. Minn. 1982).

Id. at 20671.

4. Following are excerpts from one case where the court found the requisite endangerment, and one where the court did not.

(a) In the *Lincoln Properties* decision excerpted above, a number of dry cleaners presently or previously located in the Lincoln Center shopping center had discharged dry cleaning chemicals into the sewer system, from which they leaked into the groundwater in the vicinity of the shopping center. Applying the principles set forth in the preceding excerpt, the court found an imminent and substantial endangerment:

Here, Lincoln has established by undisputed evidence that the contamination at Lincoln Center may present an imminent and substantial threat of harm ("endangerment") to the environment. RCRA does not define the term "environment." However, it presumably encompasses the air, soil and water, including groundwater. In this case, the environment has already been degraded significantly by the contaminants' invasion of the water table. The groundwater in Zones A and B now contains PCE, TCE and DCE in concentrations far exceeding federal and state standards. Zone C water may have been contaminated by mixing in the wells with water from other Zones. There may be a "pocket" or "pool" of pure PCE, which continues to release PCE, beneath the site. The PCE plume now occupies a substantial area of the Lincoln Center subsurface. The plume is unstable: while its rate of movement is in dispute, it is undisputed that PCE, TCE and DCE have migrated vertically and laterally in the subsurface, and may continue to so migrate. This movement presents a threat of further endangerment to the environment.

The dry cleaners contend that the reported cases that found "imminent and substantial endangerment" to the environment involved a threat that living organisms would be exposed to contaminants, or something more than "mere" groundwater contamination. The court is not persuaded. The statute speaks of endangerment to health or the environment. The term "environment" appears to include air, soil and water. *** Neither the statute nor the case law interposes an additional requirement that humans or other life forms be threatened.

Furthermore, here, the contamination is not isolated. Contamination of an isolated region far from human or other life may not present the possibility of "imminent and substantial endangerment of the environment" within the meaning of RCRA. Lincoln Center, however, is located in a populated area. The beneficial uses of the water beneath Lincoln Center include domestic, municipal, agricultural and industrial supply. Over time, the City of Stockton and San Joaquin County have chosen to locate municipal supply wells in the Lincoln Center area. Several County wells have already been closed at least in part as a result of the contamination. In addition, there are numerous private wells in the area, some of which draw from (contaminated) Zone B. It is unclear how many of these wells are now in use. However, it is clear that a substantial measure of Stockton groundwater has been removed from public use.

The extent of the threat of harm to human health is vigorously disputed by the parties. According to plaintiff's own expert, the water in City Well No. 11 will not exceed the federal MCL levels for PCE until at least 2007. This does not appear to establish a sufficient possibility of imminent and substantial endangerment to health to warrant injunctive relief. However, the possible health effects are relevant to the question of environmental endangerment, and provide further support for the court's finding that the conditions at Lincoln Center may present a substantial and imminent endangerment to the environment.

In sum, there is present harm to the environment which is both imminent and substantial. Certainly a substantial risk of endangerment may be presented.

The dry cleaners argue that injunctive relief is not warranted because they are no longer discharging PCE. RCRA, however, "authorizes the cleanup of a site, even a dormant one, if that action is necessary to abate a present threat to the public health or the environment." *U.S. v. Price*, 688 F.2d 204, 214 (3d Cir. 1982). The environment at Lincoln Center is presently threatened.

Id. at 20671-72.

(b) In contrast, where state authorities had cleaned up lead and asbestos contamination in a residential neighborhood, the court dismissed a citizen suit attempt to have additional cleanup performed under RCRA § 7002(a)(1)(B). *Price v. United States Navy*, 818 F.Supp. 1323 (S.D. Cal. 1992).

*** The court agrees with the defendant that the language of the statute implies that there must be a threat which is present now, although the impact of the threat may not be felt until later. The court also agrees that the endangerment must be substantial or serious and that there must be some necessity for the action.

Witnesses who were employees of the State of California, Mr. Vitale and Mr. Scandura, as well as Dr. Levy, the State's toxicologist, agreed that for an imminent and substantial endangerment to exist (1) there must be a population at risk, (2) the contaminants must be listed as hazardous waste under RCRA, (3) the level of contaminants must be above levels that are considered acceptable by the State, and (4) there must be a pathway of exposure.

There is no dispute that 6025 Edgewater is in a residential neighborhood. Although asbestos was found on the site, it was the presence of hazardous levels of lead at 6021 and 6025 Edgewater that caused State officials to be concerned. Moreover, lead rather than asbestos is a listed contaminant under RCRA.

The State invested more than $300,000.00 to perform a cleanup of the properties located at 6021, 6025, 6035 and 6045 Edgewater. Soil from the front and back yards at 6025 Edgewater was removed to a depth of three feet and replaced with clean fill. Additionally, the side yards were capped with concrete. The purpose of the cleanup was to eliminate the only possible pathway to exposure-ingestion since there was no threat of migration of contaminants through ground or surface water or air.

* * *

Prior to the cleanup, the State determined that soil under the homes at the site or beneath cement or asphalt posed no threat to public health or the environment and would be left undisturbed. Witnesses for the State testified that concrete slab foundations and driveways act as effective barriers or caps to any possible contamination. The State's toxicologist, Dr. Levy, agreed that a concrete barrier blocks the only pathway to lead contamination.

Although Mr. Vitale and Mr. Scandura testified that contaminants probably remain underneath the home at 6025 Edgewater, they both agreed that there is no imminent and substantial endangerment at the present time because of the concrete barriers. Moreover, the State certified that all appropriate response actions had been completed and that no further removal/remedial action is necessary.

Under RCRA, the court has jurisdiction "to restrain" or to order "such other action as may be necessary" or "both". In other words, the court can grant affirmative relief, if necessary, to abate an imminent and substantial endangerment. Here, plaintiffs have failed to meet their burden that an imminent and substantial endangerment to health or environment presently exists.

Plaintiffs argue that necessity is not a requirement for this court to order abatement under RCRA. Plaintiffs rely on testimony that there continues to be contamination underneath the foundation and that plaintiffs cannot make repairs, renovations or upgrades without disturbing the concrete slabs and causing a release. This would also constitute a violation of the deed restrictions.

The court is not convinced that, even if contaminants remain beneath the house, that the levels of contaminants are hazardous. In addition, repairs and/or renovations might not cause a release of contaminants. Mr. Vitale testified that the State knew before its cleanup about the cracks in the slab and did not think they were significant.

Plaintiffs assert that they have lost all equity in their property, that no bank will lend money with the property as security and that plaintiffs will never be able to sell the home. However, plaintiffs offered absolutely no evidence to support this contention.

The court concludes that there is no imminent nor substantial endangerment and that there is no necessity for an abatement order. Whatever threat existed prior to the cleanup has been eliminated. No further action is needed now nor may any action ever be needed to abate contamination.

Id., at 1324-26.

5. For a notable limitation on the use of citizen suits alleging an imminent and substantial endangerment under RCRA § 7002(a)(2)(B), see *Greenpeace, Inc. v. Waste Technologies Industries*, 9 F.3d 1174 (6th Cir. 1993), upholding the dismissal of a citizen suit challenging a hazardous waste incinerator that was operating pursuant to a RCRA permit.

We therefore conclude that the only method Congress provided in the RCRA to challenge permitted activity is a challenge to the permit itself through § 6976(b). *** A hazardous waste operator's compliance with the terms of its RCRA permit precludes district court jurisdiction under § 6972(a)(1)(B) to challenge properly permitted activity.

Id. at 1181-82. The Sixth Circuit held that the citizens' group's invocation of § 7002(a)(1)(B) was, in effect, an improper collateral attack on the permitting process, which could only be challenged through prescribed procedures (which did not encompass imminent and substantial danger actions under that 7002(a)(1)(B)). *See also Chemical Weapons Working Group Inc. v. Army Department*, 111 F.3d 1485 (10th Cir. 1997).

6. For an analysis of the various applications of a citizens' suit alleging an imminent and substantial endangerment under RCRA § 7002(a)(1)(B), see Adam Babich, *RCRA Imminent Hazard Authority: A Powerful Tool for Businesses, Governments, and Citizen Enforcers*, 24 Envtl. L. Rep. (Envtl. L. Inst.) 10122 (Mar. 1994).

7. A "person" seeking to force another person to clean up a contaminated site has only RCRA § 7002(a)(1)(B) (as well as any common law claims that may be available); the EPA's alternative of issuing a cleanup order under RCRA § 7003(a) or CERCLA § 106 is not an option for non-EPA parties. A person seeking to clean up a contaminated site directly, and then sue the responsible parties for reimbursement, will typically look first to CERCLA § 107(a)(4)(B). Because CERCLA does not cover petroleum cleanups, private parties who clean up leaking underground petroleum storage tanks have sought to use RCRA § 7002(a)(1)(B) to abate the endangerment and then sue for restitution. After a conflict between the circuits arose as to the availability of this procedure, the Supreme Court ruled that the statute does not authorize such remedy. *Meghrig v. KFC Western Inc.*, 116 S.Ct. 1251 (1996) (in chapter 17).

8. After learning more about CERCLA, return to these materials regarding RCRA § 7003 and consider the post-CERCLA significance of RCRA §§ 7003 and 7002(a)(1)(B). Why did Congress take the time and effort to amend RCRA § 7003 in 1984, four years after it had enacted CERCLA? Under what circumstances might a contaminated site be redressable only under RCRA §§ 7002 and 7003, and not under CERCLA?

6 ENFORCEMENT ACTIONS UNDER RCRA

A. Civil Enforcement

RCRA's provisions are enforceable through a variety of mechanisms. The EPA may bring civil and criminal proceedings, states that are authorized to administer the RCRA program may similarly commence enforcement proceedings under state law, and any other person or entity may bring suit, under certain circumstances, pursuant to RCRA's citizen suit provisions.

When the EPA learns of a RCRA violation, it may pursue civil enforcement proceedings of an administrative or judicial nature. The EPA, in its discretion, "may issue an [administrative] order assessing a civil penalty for any past or current violation, requiring compliance immediately or within a specified time period, or both." RCRA § 3008(a)(1), 42 U.S.C. § 6928(a)(1). Alternatively, the EPA may file suit in federal court seeking "appropriate relief, including a temporary or permanent injunction." *Ibid.* Regardless of whether an enforcement order is issued by the EPA or by a court, it may impose civil penalties of up to $25,000 per day for each violation and it may suspend or revoke the violator's RCRA permit. RCRA § 3008(a)(3). For the benefit of and to promote consistency among the various EPA regional offices and the authorized states, the EPA has developed guidance documents that address the types of enforcement actions to be undertaken in different circumstances, and the calculation of civil penalties to be assessed in administrative orders or requested in court proceedings. *See* EPA, HAZARDOUS WASTE CIVIL ENFORCEMENT RESPONSE POLICY (1996) and EPA, RCRA CIVIL PENALTY POLICY (1990).

Where the EPA has authorized a state to implement the RCRA program (or portions thereof) within that state, the state generally has the primary responsibility for enforcement, but the EPA retains enforcement authority as well. *See, e.g., In re Harmon Electronics, Inc.,* 1997 WL 133778 (EPA Env.. App. Bd., March 24, 1997) (excerpted at the end of this subchapter).

Any person may commence a citizen suit against any other person allegedly "in violation of any permit, standard, regulation, condition, requirement, prohibition, or order" in effect under RCRA, provided that they give 60 days' prior notice and that neither the EPA nor the state is diligently prosecuting the violation in question. RCRA § 7002(a)(1)(A) and (b)(1), 42 U.S.C. § 6972(a)(1)(A) and (b)(1). Finally, a citizen suit may also be brought against the EPA for failure to perform a nondiscretionary duty. RCRA § 7002(a)(2) and (c).

The following case is a hybrid between an EPA enforcement action and a citizen suit, and the remedies imposed by the court are collectively among the most severe ones to date resulting from a litigated (rather than settled) RCRA enforcement proceeding.

UNITED STATES ENVIRONMENTAL PROTECTION AGENCY v. ENVIRONMENTAL WASTE CONTROL, INC.
917 F.2d 327 (7th Cir. 1990), *cert. denied*, 499 U.S. 975 (1991)

Before WOOD, JR., CUDAHY and COFFEY, Circuit Judges.
CUDAHY, Circuit Judge.

The Environmental Protection Agency, together with an environmental intervenor, Supporters to Oppose Pollution, Inc., brought suit against Environmental Waste Control (and its owners and operators) in connection with a hazardous waste landfill operated by Environmental Waste Control in Indiana. The district court found against Environmental Waste Control, ordered the offending landfill permanently closed (along with certain other corrective measures) and assessed civil fines amounting to almost $3,000,000. Environmental Waste Control appeals. We affirm.

I. FACTUAL BACKGROUND

This appeal arises from an enforcement action brought by the United States, on behalf of the Environmental Protection Agency (the "EPA"), to enforce hazardous waste requirements under the Resource Conservation and Recovery Act ("RCRA") at Environmental Waste Control's Four County Landfill (the "Landfill") in Fulton County, Indiana. The United States brought this action against Environmental Waste Control, James Wilkins, and the West Holding Company as the Landfill's owners, and against Environmental Waste Control and Steven Shambaugh as the Landfill's operators. (All are referred to collectively as "EWC.") RCRA establishes a comprehensive federal program governing the generation, transportation, storage and treatment of hazardous wastes "to minimize the present and future threat to human health and the environment." 42 U.S.C. § 6902(b). 42 U.S.C. § 6925(a) requires that a hazardous waste facility be operated only in accordance with a permit. Recognizing that the EPA could not issue permits to all applicants before RCRA's effective date, Congress provided that a facility in existence as of November 19, 1980, could obtain "interim status," allowing it to continue operating until final action on its permit application. 42 U.S.C. § 6925(e). To obtain interim status, a facility is required to file a limited "Part A application," and is then "treated as having been issued a permit." 42 U.S.C. § 6925(e). An interim status facility must comply with the standards set forth in 40 C.F.R. pt. 265, which, among other things, mandates that such a facility have a "ground-water monitoring program capable of determining the facility's impact on the quality of ground water in the uppermost aquifer underlying the facility" and also requires that an interim status facility meet certain financial responsibility requirements.

Following the submission of the "Part A application," a facility must file a "Part B application" to obtain a permit. Upon successful completion of the Part B process, a hazardous waste permit is issued, and the facility must comply with this permit and the regulatory standards set forth in 40 C.F.R. pt. 264.

In 1984, Congress passed the Hazardous and Solid Waste Amendments (the "HSWA") to RCRA. The HSWA were adopted in response to concerns about widespread groundwater contamination from interim status facilities. The HSWA provide, in part, that all land disposal facilities granted interim status before November 8, 1984, would automatically lose that status on November 8, 1985, unless the facility: (A) applied for a final Part B permit determination before November 8, 1985; and (B) certified that it was "in compliance with applicable groundwater monitoring and financial responsibility requirements." 42 U.S.C. § 6925(e)(2). RCRA also requires the owners and operators of hazardous waste landfills to comply with minimum technology requirements which mandate the installation of two or more liners and a leachate collection system for the lateral expansion of interim status landfills with respect to waste received after May 8, 1985. 42 U.S.C. §§ 6924(o)(1)(A) and 6936(b). When the EPA determines that there has been a release of hazardous waste from an interim status facility, the EPA may seek corrective action. 42 U.S.C. § 6928(h)(1). Accordingly, the EPA filed suit against EWC in federal court, alleging basically: (1) that the Landfill had lost its interim status by failing to comply with the applicable financial responsibility and groundwater monitoring requirements; (2) that EWC had violated RCRA's minimum technology requirements between May 8, 1985 and August 16, 1986; (3) that the Landfill's groundwater monitoring system did not comply with the applicable regulations; and (4) that hazardous waste or hazardous waste constituents had been released at the Landfill, thereby permitting the court to order a corrective measure study. The EPA sought civil penalties and an order closing the Landfill, at least temporarily. The Supporters to Oppose Pollution ("STOP"), the environmental intervenor, joined the EPA's claims, but asked for a permanent, instead of temporary, closing of the Landfill. STOP also brought additional claims relating to the Landfill's alleged release of hazardous waste into the environment.

A month-long trial was held. In its Memorandum Opinion and Order, the district court noted its shock and dismay at EWC's conduct, explaining that EWC, while "afforded repeated opportunities to comply with RCRA requirements ... has responded by developing a dismal history of delay, mis-performance, and noncompliance." The district court essentially found: that the Landfill had lost its interim status as of November 8, 1985 because, as of that date, it had not fully complied with the required financial assurance and groundwater monitoring standards; that EWC had failed to maintain an adequate monitoring system and had illegally disposed of hazardous wastes in cells lacking liners; and that, as a result of EWC's violations, there was a release of hazardous wastes which contaminated groundwater underlying the Landfill and which had the potential for contaminating nearby private drinking wells. The district court assessed civil penalties of nearly $3,000,000 against EWC. The district court also ordered EWC to undertake certain corrective measures and, most importantly, permanently enjoined the operation of the Landfill.

EWC appeals on the grounds that: (1) a permanent injunction was improper; (2) the Four County Landfill should not have lost its interim status; (3) its current groundwater monitoring system is fully adequate, and (4) the corrective action plan mandated by the district court was inappropriate for the conditions existing at the Four County Landfill. We affirm the judgment of the district court in all respects.

II. LEGAL ANALYSIS

A. The Propriety of the Permanent Injunction

EWC claims that the enforcement of a permanent injunction against its landfill is improper because: (1) RCRA does not authorize permanent closure in interim enforcement cases; (2) the district court did not adequately consider, or properly weigh, the competing equities; and (3) the evidence adduced at trial showed that there had been no substantial harmful effects on the environment. None of EWC's claims has merit.

EWC first contends that RCRA does not authorize permanent closure in *interim status* cases. We are puzzled how EWC can seriously advance this argument. First, it should be noted that the district court held that EWC "has not argued that permanent closure is not an available remedy." Hence, in all likelihood, EWC has waived this argument. Regardless, the text of the relevant statute plainly allows for a permanent injunction in interim status cases such as this one.

42 U.S.C. section 6928(h)(1) is entitled "Interim status corrective action" and provides:

> Whenever on the basis of any information the Administrator [of the EPA] determines that there is or has been a release of hazardous waste into the environment from a facility authorized to operate under section 6925(e) of this title, the Administrator may issue an order requiring corrective action or such other response measure as he deems necessary to protect human health or the environment or the Administrator may commence a civil action in the United States district court in the district in which the facility is located for appropriate relief, *including a temporary or permanent injunction.* (emphasis supplied).

Hence, it is clear from the language of this section that a permanent injunction is an available remedy in interim status cases. When the text and meaning of a statute are clear, we will not look to legislative history.

EWC's next contention, that the district court did not properly balance the competing equities, is simply incorrect. The record shows that the district court, in fact, went to great pains to outline the reasons (which included threats to the environment) for its decision to permanently enjoin the operation of EWC's landfill. Moreover, it is clear that the district court specifically undertook to balance the benefit to the public against the harm to the public in this case. ("The risk to the public of any continued operation of the Four County Landfill by EWC greatly outweighs any harm from permanent closure.") In addition, we think it beyond question, given the district court's findings, that a remedy at law would have been inadequate in this case. As the Supreme Court noted in *Amoco Production Co. v. Gambell*, 480 U.S. 531, 545 (1987):

> Environmental injury, by its nature, can seldom be adequately remedied by money damages and is often permanent or at least of long duration, *i.e.,* irreparable. If such injury is sufficiently likely, therefore, the balance of harms will usually favor the issuance of an injunction to protect the environment.

Hence, the record shows that the district court did balance the competing equities both thoroughly and correctly in this case—notwithstanding that it may not have even been required to undertake such a balance. It is an accepted equitable principle that a court does not have to balance the equities in a case where the defendant's conduct has been willful. As noted earlier, the district court essentially found that EWC's conduct had been willful. Moreover, as the Fourth Circuit noted, relying on an opinion of ours:

> the law of injunctions differs with respect to governmental plaintiffs (or private attorneys general) as opposed to private individuals. Where the plaintiff is a sovereign and where the activity may endanger the public health, "injunctive relief is proper, without resort to balancing." *Illinois v. Milwaukee*, 599 F.2d 151, 166 (7th Cir. 1979), *rev'd on other grounds*, 451 U.S. 304 (1981). Second, in cases of public health legislation, the emphasis shifts from irreparable injury to concern for the general public interest....

Environmental Defense Fund, Inc. v. Lamphier, 714 F.2d 331, 337-38 (4th Cir. 1983).

For all the foregoing reasons, we find that the district court's decision to issue a permanent injunction against EWC was correct and was supported by the potential danger to the environment and to public health.[2]

B. The Loss of Environmental Waste Control's "Interim Status"

EWC contends that the Four County Landfill never lost its interim status, despite the contrary finding of the district court, because (1) EWC's insurance complied with all applicable regulations as of November 8, 1985, or, in the alternative, because the district court should have considered good faith a defense to the failure to carry the required amount of insurance; and (2) because EWC was actually in compliance with the applicable hazardous waste groundwater monitoring requirements as of November 8, 1985.

Under RCRA's interim status provision, 42 U.S.C. § 6925(e)(2), the failure of a landfill to meet either the applicable financial responsibility or groundwater monitoring requirements, as of November 5, 1985, automatically results in the loss of interim status.

---

[2] Our conclusion is in no way changed by the fact that it was STOP, and not the EPA, that asked for permanent closure of the Landfill. The right to intervene, codified at 42 U.S.C. § 9613(i)(1987 Supp.), permits citizens to press the same procedural and substantive claims that the United States may pursue.

Because we find that EWC failed to carry the required amount of insurance and because good faith is not an adequate defense to compliance with these financial regulations, EWC lost its interim status as of November 8, 1985. We therefore need not address EWC's allegations concerning whether the Landfill met the groundwater monitoring standards required of interim status facilities as of November 8, 1985.

With respect to RCRA's financial responsibility requirements for interim status facilities, EWC makes five arguments (all of which were rejected by the district court): (1) that the applicable insurance regulations did not expressly require that the prescribed amounts of required coverage be aggregated (and EWC, which had not aggregated, therefore had enough); (2) that EWC's coverage was adequate because it was approved by the Indiana Department of Environmental Management;[3] (3) that the EPA was estopped from asserting that a higher amount of insurance was necessary because an operator of the EPA's "hot line" assured EWC's insurance broker that $3,000,000/$6,000,000 was adequate; (4) that an endorsement on EWC's primary policy was in force which provided an assurance that EWC's policy complied with RCRA's requirements; and (5) that another policy was in force which, coupled with EWC's primary policy, met the statutory requirements. EWC initially challenges the district court's ruling that the EPA's interim status regulations required total coverage for sudden and nonsudden occurrences of $4,000,000 per occurrence and $8,000,000 in the aggregate. The relevant financial responsibility regulations are set forth in 40 C.F.R. § 265.147. Subpart (a) requires, with respect to hazardous waste treatment, storage or disposal facilities, that:

> [t]he owner or operator must have and maintain liability coverage for sudden accidental occurrences in the amount of at least $1 million per occurrence with an annual aggregate of at least $2 million, exclusive of legal defense costs.

Subpart (b) applies to surface impoundments, landfills or land treatment facilities and requires that:

> [t]he owner or operator must have and maintain liability coverage for nonsudden accidental occurrences in the amount of at least $3 million per occurrence with an annual aggregate of at least $6 million, exclusive of legal defense costs.

The district court held that because both subparts applied to the operations of EWC, EWC was required to comply with the financial strictures of both, totaling $4,000,000 per occurrence with an annual aggregate of $8,000,000.

EWC contends that the requirements "nowhere expressly stated that a total of $4 million per occurrence and $8 million annual aggregate was required for a combined limits policy." (EWC carried an insurance policy which covered only $3,000,000 per occurrence and had an annual aggregate of $6,000,000.) But we think that the requirements were clear. The separate subparts applied to different types of occurrences.

---

[3] Given that the federal government has not delegated enforcement of the strictures of the HSWA to the states, EWC cannot rely on Indiana's approval of its insurance policy as proof that it complied with federal law.

Each subpart had to be satisfied. Aggregation was therefore required. As noted previously, we will not look past statutory or regulatory language when the text is clear.

EWC argues, however, that the 1988 amendment to these regulations, which explicitly calls for aggregation of the interim status insurance requirements, and the 1981 draft of the regulations (which also contained an aggregation provision that was later deleted) support its theory that aggregation was not required *until* the 1988 amendment. We do not agree. Perhaps Congress, or the EPA, thought that the regulation was clear without a specific aggregation provision—clear, that is, until interim status facilities' operators tried to avoid the requirement by arguing that aggregation was not required. In sum, we think that the language of this regulation was sufficiently clear to preclude a presumption that the 1988 amendments were meant to change, rather than clarify, existing law. Indeed, the 1988 rule states that it is merely "specifying more clearly" the aggregate coverage mechanisms required by combined coverage mechanisms (53 Fed. Reg. at 33,939); that the EPA decided "to maintain the present scope of coverage" (*id.* at 33,946); and that the modification "does not add any compliance requirements" (*id.* at 33,949).

EWC's other arguments pertaining to the insurance requirements applicable to interim status facilities can be similarly rejected. Information provided by a government hot line cannot be enough to estop the government from enforcing violations of federal law. Moreover, we hold that reliance on such a hot line here was not reasonable, given the clarity of the regulations. With respect to EWC's claims regarding the endorsement and the additional insurance policy, we find that the district court was correct in rejecting these arguments. The endorsement, for example, clearly states that it does not modify the policy, the terms of which were only $3,000,000 per occurrence and $6,000,000 in the aggregate. And, the district court expressly excluded evidence regarding EWC's second insurance policy, a policy which had probably expired and which was never identified to the EPA (or to the district court until 169 weeks into the instant lawsuit) as a source of coverage. Given the facts, this exclusion was clearly appropriate. We therefore reject EWC's claims that it complied with the applicable financial responsibility regulations. Accordingly, the Four County Landfill lost its interim status as of November 8, 1985.[4]

---

[4] EWC asserts that its good faith should be a defense to noncompliance with the groundwater monitoring and financial responsibility requirements imposed upon interim status facilities. The district court rejected this argument on the grounds that EWC's "good faith"—while relevant to the scope of relief and penalties—was not relevant to whether EWC actually complied with the federal requirements. We agree. The fact that EWC attempted to comply with the insurance regulations and that no harm resulted from EWC's under-insurance is simply irrelevant. The fact still remains that EWC failed to meet federal standards, a failure which deprived EWC of its interim status. Given the environmental problems facing the world today and the federal laws in question, we think that it would be counterproductive to read a "good faith" defense where none exists. We will not excuse EWC from failing to satisfy the requirements of our environmental laws. Hence, we think that the district court's decision not to recognize a "good faith" defense here was eminently sound.

C. The Adequacy of EWC's Groundwater Monitoring System

The district court held that the groundwater monitoring system at the Landfill did not meet the required standards as of November 8, 1985, and also held that, even at the start of trial, the Landfill did not have a compliant groundwater monitoring system. In this regard, the district court noted that

> [t]he purpose of a hazardous waste landfill's groundwater monitoring system is to detect immediately the migration of hazardous waste or hazardous waste constituents from the waste management area into the environment so that any necessary corrective or remedial action can be taken. Among the major threats a hazardous waste landfill may pose to public health and the environment is the potential that hazardous constituents may escape and contaminate the groundwater beneath the facility.
>
> *   *   *   *   *   *
>
> The design, construction, and depth of [the Landfill's] groundwater monitoring wells have prevented EWC and its consultants from learning the extent and permeability of the uppermost aquifer, which precludes confident assessment of the groundwater flow's horizontal and vertical direction and velocity. One cannot design a meaningful groundwater monitoring system without knowing the location of the uppermost aquifer and direction of the groundwater flow. EWC has not acquired that knowledge.

Environmental Waste Control, 710 F.Supp. at 1222. Hence, the district court found that EWC was in continuing violation of 40 C.F.R. section 265.90(a), which requires that an interim status facility have a groundwater monitoring program that is "capable of determining the facility's impact on the quality of ground water in the uppermost aquifer."[5] *Id.* at 1225.

The thrust of EWC's complaint on appeal seems to be that the district court erred in not admitting newly obtained data into evidence or, in the alternative, that the district court erred in finding EWC's groundwater monitoring system to be inadequate. Whether EWC's groundwater monitoring system complied with federal law is a question of fact which will not be disturbed unless clearly erroneous.

Our review of the record leads us to the conclusion that there was no clear error here. The new data proffered by EWC came too late for its probative value to outweigh its prejudice. Moreover, the evidence in the record was sufficient to sustain the court's

---

[5] The district court explained that

> [a]n aquifer is a geological formation, group of formations, or part of a formation capable of yielding a significant amount of groundwater to wells or springs. The uppermost aquifer is that nearest the natural ground surface and includes the lower aquifers that are hydraulically interconnected to that aquifer within the facility's property boundary.

Environmental Waste Control, 710 F.Supp. at 1213 n.33.

extensive findings. We therefore affirm the district court's decision as to the inadequacy of EWC's groundwater monitoring system.

D. The District Court's Corrective Action Plan

Finally, EWC contends that the corrective action plan imposed by the district court was inappropriate for the conditions existing at the Landfill. Again, we disagree. The assessment of penalties is committed to the informed discretion of the trial court, and will be reversed only upon a showing that the district court abused its discretion. EWC has offered us no sound reason which would justify a finding that the district court abused its discretion in deciding on the corrective action plan and other remedies, remedies which were clearly imposed only after thoughtful examination and assessment of the evidence and applicable law.

* * *

NOTES

1. Perhaps the most notable aspect of *Environmental Waste Control* is the breadth of the remedies imposed, and readily upheld by the Seventh Circuit: the permanent closure of the landfill; a civil penalty of $2.8 million; and the obligation to undertake extensive site investigation and cleanup (corrective action). The corrective action obligation was explored in the previous chapter; the following notes will address the injunctive relief and penalty issues.

2. There are at least two distinct issues raised by the court's discussion of injunctive relief: (1) the proof necessary to support injunctive relief in environmental cases; and (2) the contours of the permanent injunction issued in this case.

    a. One of the traditional prerequisites for the issuance of injunctive relief is the determination that legal remedies are inadequate to prevent irreparable harm. *Amoco Production Co. v. Village of Gambell*, 480 U.S. 531 (1987). In *Environmental Waste Control*, the Seventh Circuit suggests that environmental injury is presumptively irreparable, particularly where the government is the plaintiff. The Seventh Circuit reiterated this approach in *U.S. v. Bethlehem Steel Corp.*, 38 F.3d 862 (7th Cir. 1995) (excerpted for other purposes in chapter 2.B). In *Environmental Waste Control*, although the EPA was a plaintiff, it was not seeking a permanent closure of the landfill; that relief was requested by the plaintiff-intervenor citizens' group. The Seventh Circuit states in footnote 2 that the same exception to the general rules regarding injunctive relief is available in such circumstances. Does that effectively mean that in any case seeking to enforce alleged violations of RCRA, whether the enforcement action is brought by the EPA (or state) or, under the citizen suit provision, by anyone else, the plaintiffs are presumptively entitled to injunctive relief once they establish an environmental violation? *See Amoco Production Co. v. Gambell*, 480 U.S. at 541-546.

b. Does the Seventh Circuit distinguish between the availability of a permanent injunction (*i.e.*, an injunction issued at the end of a case, remaining in effect indefinitely under its terms) and a permanent injunction that permanently shutters a facility? Could not the court have issued a permanent injunction that precluded EWC from operating unless and until the EPA granted a Part B permit to operate a hazardous waste disposal facility? In fact, although the EPA had denied EWC's application for a Part B permit, that decision was under administrative review at the time of the enforcement litigation. *U.S.E.P.A. v. Environmental Waste Control,* 710 F.Supp. 1172, 1205 (N.D.Ind. 1989). Should it not be the EPA's role, at least in the first instance, to determine whether EWC meets the technical criteria to operate a hazardous waste disposal facility? Does the Seventh Circuit's permanent injunction preclude the EPA from deciding, at the close of the administrative appeal, that EWC should receive a permit?

2. In *Environmental Waste Control,* the Seventh Circuit affirmed in a two-sentence analysis the imposition of $2.8 million in civil penalties. How does the EPA determine the amount of civil penalties to impose in an administrative proceeding, under RCRA § 3008(a)(3), and how does a court determine the amount of civil penalties to impose in a judicial proceeding, under RCRA § 3008(g)?

a. Both provisions authorize civil penalties in an amount not to exceed $25,000 per violation per day. However, as a result of the Federal Civil Penalties Inflation Adjustment Act of 1990, Pub. L. No. 101-410, 104 Stat. 890 (1990), and the Debt Collection Improvement Act of 1996, Pub. L. No. 104-134, 110 Stat. 1321 (1996), the EPA is required to adjust upward its maximum statutory penalties to account for inflation. Effective January 31, 1997, the EPA increased the maximum statutory penalties under all statutes it administers (except the Safe Drinking Water Act, which was amended in 1996), by the maximum possible adjustment of 10 percent. Civil Monetary Penalty Inflation Adjustment Rule, 61 Fed. Reg. 69360 (1996). The new maximum civil penalties under RCRA are $27,500.

b. The statute directs the EPA to "take into account the seriousness of the violation and any good faith efforts to comply with applicable requirements" in setting the amount of the penalty. RCRA § 3008(a)(3). Although the provision authorizing judicial imposition of civil penalties does not specify any particular factors to be taken into account, courts have adopted the factors applicable to administratively-set penalties. *See, e.g., United States v. Ekco Housewares, Inc.,* 62 F.3d 806 (6th Cir. 1995), and cases cited therein. In exercising its discretion to set civil penalties under RCRA, the district court may consider other factors, as well.

> Numerous other factors are relevant, including the harm caused by the violation, any economic benefit derived from noncompliance, the violator's ability to pay, the government's conduct, and the clarity of the obligation involved.

Id. at 814.

c. In *Ekco Housewares,* the Sixth Circuit considered at some length the defendant's claims that mitigating factors were given insufficient weight in setting a $4.6

million penalty for noncompliance with RCRA regulations requiring hazardous waste disposal facilities to demonstrate financial responsibility for third-party claims and for closure and post-closure costs.

In determining whether the court gave Ekco short shrift in its treatment of the numerous alleged mitigating factors, we first examine the purpose of the financial responsibility regulations, which is to require the owner/operator of a hazardous waste facility to document that it has secured the resources required to close the facility in an appropriate and safe manner, and to pay third-party claims that may arise from its operations. The timing of these obligations is critical. The regulations require that the owner/operator secure the necessary funds, and document that it has done so, prior to closure. This requirement is imposed to reduce the risk that insufficient funds will be available after the facility is shut down, when the owner/operator may not have the economic ability or incentive to devote resources to a defunct operation. ***

Mindful of these significant regulatory goals, we reject Ekco's contention that the $1000 per day penalty was excessive because AHP [American Home Products Corporation, Ekco's parent company] always had the financial resources to close the impoundment and satisfy third-party claims, and ultimately provided the necessary documentation. Ekco's "no harm-no foul" theme, recurrent throughout this appeal, simply misses the mark. Ekco was required to have secured the funds and documented their existence on each day of each year in question. It cannot escape the consequences of its inaction by pointing to its eventual, and untimely, compliance.

We are persuaded, however, that the district court gave too little weight to the fact that Ekco substantially complied with its closure and post-closure care obligations on June 25, 1990, when it submitted AHP's letter of credit; and with its third-party claims obligations on September 29, 1992, when it submitted AHP's guarantee. The court found the technical defects existed in both instruments, leading it to continue the $1000 per day penalty for each violation until final abatement. The penalty imposed for the period following Ekco's substantial compliance is significant, as the time period involved exceeds two years for two violations, and five months for the third violation.

The EPA legitimately may require that financial responsibility requirements be satisfied in the manner specified in the regulations, and an owner/operator's failure to comply with those requirements renders it subject to the imposition of penalties. In assessing the seriousness of a violation of this type, however, the court should consider principally whether the defects threaten the availability of the funds. Other relevant factors include the violator's attempt to cure the defects, whether there are impediments to cure that are outside the violator's direct control, and the timeliness of the violator's response.

    We conclude that the amount of the penalty imposed here is excessive, because the record does not reflect that the defects in the letter of credit and guarantee in any way impaired the availability of the funds. There is no indication that the defects in the letter of credit, e.g., the failure to provide a duplicate trust agreement and to name Ekco in the letter of credit itself, had any bearing on the bank's obligation to pay Ohio EPA upon presentment. Likewise, there is no evidence that AHP's guarantee was invalid when originally submitted, and its sole "defect" was in having an effective date of 1988 rather than the date on which it was executed. Ekco documented that secured funds were available in amounts that were satisfactory to Ohio EPA. The principal purpose of the regulations thus was fulfilled, and Ekco should not be required to pay the same amount in penalties for the period following its substantial compliance as it must pay for the period when it was in complete default. We therefore remand to permit the district court to re-assess the proper penalty to be imposed for the periods noted above.

Id at 815-16.

The court rejected Ekco's claim that the penalty should be set aside because it was significantly higher than penalties imposed in similar cases.

    Ekco acknowledged that significantly higher penalties have been imposed in RCRA cases [footnote cites cases imposing penalties amounting to $1500, $200, and $2500 per day], but contends that these cases are inapposite because the violations involved conduct that actively caused environmental harm. In contrast, argues Ekco, its violations merely involved a failure to provide the EPA with financial documentation. Ekco's assessment of the relative seriousness of a violation of the financial responsibility regulations is questionable. These regulations are not mere paperwork requirements, and a party cannot comply by submitting a financial statement or other indicators of its net worth. The purpose of these regulations is to ensure that adequate funds are secured (through, e.g., a letter of credit, guarantee or liability policy) in the present to meet the future financial needs for closing a hazardous waste site and satisfying any third-party claims that might arise therefrom. A present violation of these regulations may significantly impair the ability to close and remediate the site when needed and to protect third parties from harm. This risk of future harm posed by a hazardous waste facility such as that owned by Ekco, found by the district court to present serious risks to human health and the environment, is no less important a consideration than the risk of present harm caused by activities causing contamination.

Id. at 817.

3. Another notable aspect of RCRA enforcement is the imposition of liability on individuals, such as corporate officers and employees, as well as the corporations on whose behalf they were acting. Individual liability is most stark in the context of criminal charges, where conviction will result in jail time. But it also arises in the civil context.

a. After the Seventh Circuit's decision in *Environmental Waste Control*, the two individuals who had been sued as owners and operators of the company and the site filed for bankruptcy. The cleanup of the site became a Superfund matter, and the individuals ultimately entered into a settlement with the EPA whereby the two individuals agreed to turn over all of their available assets and remain liable for future cleanup costs. *Indiana Landfill Owners Lose Assets, Retain Liability*, 24 Env't Rep. (BNA) 2114 (Apr. 15, 1994).

b. One important case regarding the standard for imposing liability on individual corporate officers is *U.S. v. NEPACCO*, 810 F.2d 726 (8th Cir. 1986), *cert. denied*, 484 U.S. 848 (1987), portions of which were reprinted in chapter 5 concerning RCRA § 7003. The Eighth Circuit's analysis of the individual liability of the company president, who neither participated in nor approved of the dioxin disposal, and the vice president, who did, is as follows:

*** Because NEPACCO's assets have already been liquidated and distributed to its shareholders, *** it is unlikely that the government will be able to recover anything from NEPACCO.

* * *

The government argues *** that Lee and Michaels can be held individually liable as "contributors" under RCRA § 7003(a). For the reasons discussed below, we agree with the government's liability arguments.

* * *

RCRA § 7003(a) imposes strict liability upon "any person" who is contributing or who has contributed to the disposal of hazardous substances that may present an imminent and substantial endangerment to health or the environment. As defined by statute, the term "person" includes both individuals and corporations and does not exclude corporate officers and employees. *See* RCRA § 1004(15), 42 U.S.C. § 6903(15). *** Congress could have limited the RCRA definition of "person" but did not do so. More importantly, imposing liability upon only the corporation, but not those corporate officers and employees who actually make corporate decisions, would be inconsistent with Congress' intent to impose liability upon the persons who are involved in the handling and disposal of hazardous substances.

*** Lee and Michaels can be held individually liable if they were personally involved in or directly responsible for corporate acts in violation of RCRA. ***

We hold Lee and Michaels are individually liable as "contributors" under RCRA § 7003(a). Lee actually participated in the conduct that violated RCRA; he personally arranged for the transportation and disposal of hazardous substances that presented an imminent and substantial endangerment to health and the environment. Unlike Lee, Michaels was not personally involved in the actual decision to transport and dispose of the hazardous substances. As NEPACCO's corporate president and as a major NEPACCO shareholder, however, Michaels was the individual in charge of and directly responsible for all of NEPACCO's operations, including those at the Verona plant, and he had the ultimate authority to control the disposal of NEPACCO's hazardous substances.

Id. at 742, 745.

c. To what extent, if any, did the fact that NEPACCO no longer existed affect the imposition of liability on Lee and Michaels?

d. When there is a corporate violation of RCRA, how might one determine whether individual corporate officers or employees are also subject to liability? In what circumstances could you advise a corporate officer or employee who has some responsibility for environmental compliance that he or she is not exposed to RCRA liability regarding a corporate RCRA violation? These issues will be revisited in chapter 11.A. concerning individual liability under CERCLA.

4. Yet another noteworthy aspect of *Environmental Waste Control* was the significant role played by the plaintiff-intervenor citizens' group. In RCRA as in other areas of environmental law, citizen suits play a significant enforcement role.

One issue that has been the subject of some confusion is whether a citizen suit may be brought, under the RCRA citizen suit provision and in federal court, when the EPA has authorized the state to administer RCRA by means of state law. It is well settled that state authorization does not impair the right to bring a citizen suit endangerment action under RCRA § 7002(a)(1)(B) (addressed in chapter 5.B above). The conflict centers on the effect of state authorization on the right to bring a citizen suit enforcement action under RCRA § 7002(a)(1)(A), and it arises typically where an authorized state does not provide for citizen suits under the state law counterpart to RCRA. There is considerable, although not complete, consensus that RCRA § 7002(a)(1)(A) may be invoked in such circumstances to enforce state law, regulations, and permits.

In *Acme Printing Ink Co. v. Menard, Inc.,* 881 F.Supp. 1237, 1244 (E.D. Wis.1995), the court explained as follows:

*** While it is certainly true that a plaintiff "may only sue for violations of the state regime and not for violations of the federal regime," subsection (a)(1)(A) explicitly permits a citizen suit to enforce any regulation "which has become effective pursuant to this Act." The approved state regulations embodied in the WHWMP [Wisconsin Hazardous Waste Management Plan] have "become effective" under section 6972 of RCRA and thus remain enforceable under RCRA's citizen suit provision.

See also Murray v. Bath Iron Works Corp., 867 F.Supp. 33, 42-43 (D.Me. 1994); *Glazer v. American Ecology Environmental Services Corp.*, 894 F.Supp. 1029 (E.D.Tex.1995); and *Sierra Club v. Chemical Handling Corp.*, 824 F.Supp. 195 (D.Colo.1993). *But see Coalition for Health Concern v. LWD, Inc.*, 60 F.3d 1188, 1194 (6th Cir. 1995) (dismissing RCRA citizen suit in authorized state under Burford abstention doctrine, in light of state's "overriding interest in the protection of its environment from the effects of unregulated hazardous waste ***. [T]he exercise of federal review at this juncture would be disruptive of Kentucky's efforts to establish a coherent policy with respect to the licensing of hazardous waste facilities.").

The EPA's view, however, is that a RCRA § 7002(a)(1)(A) citizen suit may also assert violations of the federal scheme: "Under RCRA, Section 7002, *** any person, whether in an authorized or unauthorized State, may sue to enforce compliance with statutory and regulatory standards." 45 Fed. Reg. 85016, 85020-21 (Dec. 24, 1980). *See also Long Island Soundkeeper Fund, Inc. v. New York Athletic Club*, 42 E.R.C. 1421 (S.D.N.Y. 1996).

NOTE REGARDING ENFORCEMENT MITIGATION

Thus far (and hereafter), the enforcement material highlights the harshness of the RCRA enforcement provisions. Before concluding the civil enforcement subchapter, it would be well to note two incentives that the EPA offers to enhance environmental protection while reducing enforcement burdens.

First, when settling an administrative or judicial civil enforcement action, the EPA will agree to reduce the penalty assessment where the defendant agrees to undertake a "supplemental environmental project," defined by the agency as "environmentally beneficial projects which a defendant/respondent agrees to undertake in settlement of an enforcement action, but which the defendant/respondent is not otherwise legally required to perform." EPA, INTERIM REVISED POLICY ON THE USE OF SUPPLEMENTAL ENVIRONMENTAL PROJECTS IN EPA ENFORCEMENT SETTLEMENTS (June 1997). The EPA justifies this initiative as follows:

> In settling enforcement actions, EPA requires alleged violators to promptly cease the violations and, to the extent feasible, remediate any harm caused by the violations. EPA also seeks substantial monetary penalties in order to deter noncompliance. Without penalties, companies would have an incentive to delay compliance until they are caught and ordered to comply. Penalties promote environmental compliance and help protect public health by deterring future violations by the same violator and deterring violations by other members of the regulated community. Penalties help ensure a national level playing field by ensuring that violators do not obtain an unfair economic advantage over their

competitors who made the necessary expenditures to comply on time. Penalties also encourage companies to adopt pollution prevention and recycling techniques, so that they minimize their pollutant discharges and reduce their potential liabilities.

Statutes administered by EPA generally contain penalty assessment criteria that a court or administrative law judge must consider in determining an appropriate penalty at trial or a hearing. In the settlement context, EPA generally follows these criteria in exercising its discretion to establish an appropriate settlement penalty. In establishing an appropriate penalty, EPA considers such factors as the economic benefit associated with the violations, the gravity or seriousness of the violations, and prior history of violations. Evidence of a violators commitment and ability to perform a SEP [supplemental environmental project] is also a relevant factor for EPA to consider in establishing an appropriate settlement penalty. All else being equal, the final settlement penalty will be lower for a violator who agrees to perform an acceptable SEP compared to the violator who does not agree to perform a SEP.

The Agency encourages the use of SEPs. While penalties play an important role in environmental protection by deterring violations and creating a level playing field, SEPs can play an additional role in securing significant environmental or public health protection and improvement. SEPs may not be appropriate in settlement of all cases, but they are an important part of EPA's enforcement program. SEPs may be particularly appropriate to further the objectives in the statutes EPA administers and to achieve other policy goals, including promoting pollution prevention and environmental justice.

The EPA's calculated dollar value of SEPs in RCRA actions was $4.5 million in fiscal year 1995, and $14.2 million in fiscal year 1996. The 1996 figures compare with $8.1 million in criminal penalties assessed, $9.1 million in civil judicial penalties assessed, $7.8 million in administrative penalties assessed, and injunctive relief valued at $60.9 million. EPA, FY 1995 ENFORCEMENT AND COMPLIANCE ASSURANCE ACCOMPLISHMENTS REPORT (July 1996); EPA, FY 1996 ENFORCEMENT AND COMPLIANCE ASSURANCE ACCOMPLISHMENTS REPORT (May 1997). It is clear that SEPs now play an important role in settlement negotiations.

Second, the EPA has offered to mitigate penalties for environmental violations where companies undertake voluntary self-audits and promptly disclose and correct the violations detected. Final Policy Statement: Incentives for Self-Policing: Discovery, Disclosure, Correction and Prevention of Violations, 60 Fed. Reg. 66706 (1995) ("EPA Audit Policy").

Under the EPA Audit Policy, the agency will not, under specified conditions, seek civil penalties for violations which are discovered through voluntary environmental audits or documented, systematic procedures or practices which reflect due diligence in detecting, preventing, and correcting violations. In addition, the EPA will generally refrain from recommending criminal prosecution of violations so discovered. Further, the EPA will reduce civil penalties by 75 percent for violations that meet the above requirements even if not discovered through an audit or compliance management system. However, the EPA expressly reserves its authority to recoup economic benefits that the company gained by noncompliance.

The EPA Audit Policy stipulates the following nine conditions for complete penalty reduction eligibility; the EPA allows for a 75 percent penalty reduction where all but the first are met:

The violation must have been discovered through either (a) an environmental audit that is systematic, objective, and periodic *** or (b) a documented, systematic procedure or practice which reflects the regulated entity's due diligence in preventing, detecting, and correcting violations.

* * *

*** The violation must have been identified voluntarily, and not through a monitoring, sampling, or auditing procedure that is required by statute, regulation, permit, judicial or administrative order, or consent agreement. *** Disclosure (must be) prompt and in writing.

* * *

*** In order to be "voluntary", the violation must be identified and disclosed by the regulated entity prior to: the commencement of a federal, state, or local agency inspection, investigation, or information request; notice of a citizen suit; legal complaint by a third party; the reporting of the violation to EPA by a "whisteblower" employee; and imminent discovery of the violation by a regulatory agency.

This condition means that regulated entities must have taken the initiative to find violations and promptly report them, rather than reacting to knowledge of a pending enforcement action or third-party complaint. ***

* * *

The regulated entity must agree to take steps to prevent a recurrence of the violation, including but not limited to improvements to its environmental auditing or due diligence efforts. ***

* * *

*** The same or closely-related violation must not have occurred previously within the past three years at the same facility, or be part of a pattern of violations on the regulated entity's part over the past five years. This provides companies with a continuing incentive to prevent violations. ***

The term "violation" includes any violation subject to a federal or state civil, judicial, or administrative order, consent agreement, conviction or plea agreement *** and *** any act or omission for which the regulated entity has received a penalty reduction in the past. ***

* * *

*** Penalty reductions are not available under this policy for violations that resulted in serious actual harm or which may have presented an imminent and substantial endangerment to public health or the environment. Such events indicate a serious failure (or absence) of a self-policing program, which should be designed to prevent such risks, and it would seriously undermine deterrence to waive penalties for such violations. ***

The final policy also excludes penalty reductions for violations of the specific terms of any order, consent agreement, or plea agreement. ***

* * *

*** The regulated entity must cooperate as required by EPA and provide information necessary to determine the applicability of the policy. *** Cooperation includes assistance in determining the facts of any related violations suggested by the disclosure, as well as of the disclosed violation itself. ***

Id. at 66707-10.

The Audit Policy provides no relief for violations which cause actual harm or which may present imminent and substantial endangerment. Further, the EPA retains the right to pursue criminal prosecution against any culpable individual, including high level corporate officials or managers who are consciously involved or willfully blind to the violations.

The EPA Audit Policy elicited ambivalent responses from the regulated community and various states. As of 1997, approximately 20 states provided some form of environmental audit immunity and/or audit privilege. 34 Toxics Law Rep. (BNA) 943 (Jan. 29, 1997). Such statutes typically grant a qualified privilege to environmental audit information providing, with variations, protection for audit information from disclosure to enforcement officials or from discovery in court action. Many statutes require that regulated entities self-evaluate, correct, and voluntarily report violations to regulators in order to invoke the privileges. Proponents contend that audit statutes remove disincentives to conducting compliance audits by mitigating fears that audit documentation might be used against the company in an enforcement proceeding. The state audit privilege laws, however, have sparked considerable controversy between the EPA and several states. The EPA stated its views in the Audit Policy:

> The Agency remains firmly opposed to the establishment of a statutory evidentiary privilege for environmental audits for the following reasons: Privilege, by definition, invites secrecy, instead of the openness needed to build public trust in industry's ability to self-police. ***

* * *

> EPA rarely uses audit reports as evidence. ***

* * *

Further, a privilege would invite defendants to claim as "audit" material almost any evidence the government needed to establish a violation or determine who was responsible. *****

60 Fed. Reg. at 66709.

Moreover, the EPA has threatened to withhold approval of state regulatory programs where state audit privilege statutes impair the enforceability of the state scheme. *See* 62 Fed. Reg. 1387, 1398 (1997) (Michigan) and 61 Fed. Reg. 32693, 32697 (1996) (Texas).

Apart from the recent wave of state statutory privileges for environmental audits, companies also rely on the attorney-client, work product, and critical self-analysis privileges to shield environmental audits from disclosure.

The attorney-client privilege protects confidential disclosures made by a client to an attorney in order to obtain legal advice. In *Olen Properties Corp. v. Sheldahl, Inc.*, 1994 WL 212135 (C.D.Cal., Apr. 14, 1994), Sheldahl successfully asserted the attorney-client privilege to shield environmental audits prepared by the company to assist attorneys in evaluating its compliance with relevant laws and regulations and in rendering a legal opinion.

The work product privilege shields documents created in preparation for or in anticipation of litigation. Documents prepared in the ordinary course of business of investigating environmental problems may fall outside the protection. In *Louisiana Environmental Action Network, Inc. v. Evans Industries, Inc.*, 1996 WL 325588 (E.D.La., June 11, 1996), the court rejected a work product claim regarding memoranda addressing management's concerns over possible litigation, prepared after an EPA investigation. The court also refused to shield a document detailing results of biomonitoring tests and concerns over potential future legal consequences.

The self-critical analysis privilege is asserted more often than it is judicially recognized. Even where the privilege is recognized, the party asserting it must satisfy at least three criteria: first, the information must result from a self-critical analysis undertaken by the party seeking the protection; second, the public must have a strong interest in preserving the free flow of information sought; and third, the information must be of the type whose flow would be curtailed if discovery was allowed. See *Dowling v. American Hawaii Cruises*, 971 F.2d 423 at 426 (9th Cir. 1992). In *Evans Industries*, the court found persuasive the EPA's Audit Policy and the plaintiff's arguments against the privilege of self-critical analysis for voluntary environmental self-analyses:

> As correctly noted by the plaintiff,
> [t]he consequences of failure to comply with state and federal environmental laws and regulations—including the possibility of criminal sentences, substantial civil penalties, debarment from entering into government contracts and public disapproval—make it essential that corporations constantly evaluate their compliance with those laws and regulations.

Thus, there is no reason to believe that the possibility of disclosure during discovery would deter such evaluations.

Second, it is not clear that such environmental reviews are always performed with the expectation that they will be kept confidential. Indeed, the EPA has agreed to waive a portion of the penalties for violations that are promptly disclosed and corrected through environmental compliance management systems. 60 Fed. Reg. 66707.

1996 WL 325588 at *2.

To the contrary is *Reichhold Chemicals, Inc. v. Textron, Inc.*, 157 F.R.D. 522 (N.D. Fla. 1994), which recognized a self-critical analysis privilege for the retrospective analysis of past conduct and the resulting environmental consequences.

*** It allows individuals or businesses to candidly assess their compliance with regulatory and legal requirements without creating evidence that may be used against them by their opponents in future litigation. The rationale for the doctrine is that such critical self-evaluation fosters the compelling public interest in the observance of law. The privilege protects an organization or individual from the Hobson's choice of aggressively investigating accidents or possible regulatory violations, ascertaining the causes and results, and correcting any violations or dangerous conditions, but thereby creating a self-incriminating record that may be evidence of liability, or deliberately avoiding making a record on the subject (and possibly leaving the public exposed to danger) in order to lessen the risk of civil liability. ***

*   *   *

*** Instead, I conclude that the self-evaluation privilege promotes the interests of justice and should be applied in appropriate environmental cases. *** This privilege in this case applies only to reports which were prepared after the fact for the purpose of candid self-evaluation and analysis of the cause and effect of past pollution, and of Reichhold's possible role, as well as other's, in contributing to the pollution at the site. Such reports are privileged only if they have in fact been kept confidential. Moreover, this is a privilege which can be overcome if one or more *** (parties) can demonstrate extraordinary circumstances or special need.

Id. at 524, 527.

Should Congress enact federal legislation establishing a privilege or immunity for environmental audits? The question remains the subject of some debate.

The following case involves the application of the EPA's Audit Policy to an enforcement proceeding, and it underscores the dual nature of enforcement under RCRA, where states and the EPA play significant, although not always consonant, roles.

IN RE HARMON ELECTRONICS, INC.
1997 WL 133778 (E.P.A. Env. App. Bd., March 24, 1997)

Before Environmental Appeals Judges McCALLUM, REICH and STEIN.
Judge McCALLUM.

Before us is an appeal of an administrative enforcement action brought pursuant to the Resource Conservation and Recovery Act ("RCRA"). Respondent Harmon Electronics, Inc. ("Harmon") has appealed an Initial Decision issued by Administrative Law Judge Frank W. Vanderheyden ("Presiding Officer") assessing a civil penalty against Harmon for various violations of the requirements of Missouri's authorized RCRA program.[6] In its appeal, Harmon raises the following issues: (1) whether the Region's enforcement action against Harmon is precluded by the language of RCRA and by principles of res judicata, because the State of Missouri has already taken action with respect to the same violations; (2) whether the Region's action against Harmon is barred by the general statute of limitations at 28 U.S.C. § 2462 because all of the violations charged in the First Amended Complaint first accrued more than five years before the Region commenced its action against Harmon; (3) whether, in light of the Agency's self-policing policy,[3] the gravity component of the penalty assessed against Harmon should be eliminated, given that Harmon discovered and voluntarily reported its own violations and worked cooperatively with the State of Missouri to remedy the violations; (4) whether Harmon is liable for failing to obtain liability insurance after it ceased its hazardous waste management operations in 1987, and, if Harmon is liable, whether a penalty is appropriate; (5) whether the Presiding Officer's penalty assessment for Harmon's violation of the financial responsibility requirements, including an upward adjustment for bad faith, is appropriate; and (6) whether the Region failed to meet its burden of proof on the seriousness of the violations alleged in all the counts of the Region's First Amended Complaint.

For the reasons set forth below, Harmon's appeal is dismissed.

I. BACKGROUND

Harmon operates a facility in Grain Valley, Missouri ("the facility") where it assembles signal equipment for the railroad industry. From 1973, when Harmon began operating the facility, until November of 1987, Harmon's employees used organic solvents (specifically, 1,1,1-trichloroethane ("TCA"), freon, trichloroethylene ("TCE"), toluene, xylene and methylene chloride) to clean flux from the equipment being

---

[6]The State of Missouri has received authorization from EPA to administer a hazardous waste management program in lieu of the federal program, pursuant to RCRA § 3006(b), 42 U.S.C. § 6926(b), and 40 C.F.R. part 271, subpart A.

[3]60 Fed. Reg. 66706 (Dec. 22, 1995)(Incentives for Self-Policing: Discovery, Disclosure, Correction and Prevention of Violations).

assembled. These solvents, when discarded, are classified as hazardous wastes under RCRA. Every one to three weeks, one of Harmon's maintenance workers would dispose of the unused solvents by throwing them out the back door of the facility onto the ground.

This disposal practice came to the attention of Harmon's management sometime in November of 1987, when Harmon's personnel manager was performing a routine Occupational Safety and Health Act ("OSHA") safety walk-through of the facility. Harmon's management ordered an immediate halt to the disposal practice, and in December of 1987, Harmon changed its assembly process so that it could use a nonhazardous cleaning material, rather than solvents. As a consequence, Harmon ceased generating hazardous waste.

Soon after learning of the disposal practice, Harmon's management initiated an investigation of the disposal site, and over the next six months, hired several consultants to investigate the effects of the disposal practice. From these investigations, Harmon learned that there was contamination at the immediate disposal area. In May of 1988, one of those consultants, International Technology Corporation ("IT"), analyzed the previously collected data, and issued what is called the "Phase I Report." This report indicates that the soil at the site was contaminated with freon, TCA, toluene, methyl chloride, and xylene.

On June 27, 1988, representatives of the Missouri Department of Natural Resources ("MDNR") met with representatives of Harmon and IT at Harmon's request. During this meeting, Harmon's representatives disclosed Harmon's practice of disposing of unused solvents out the back door of the facility. They also provided MDNR with a copy of the Phase I Report. Subsequently, on August 1, 1988, a compliance inspection of Harmon's facility was conducted. As a result of this inspection, on August 9, 1988, MDNR sent a Notice of Violation ("NOV") to Harmon. It also sent a letter explaining that:

> The violations cited pertain to the improper disposal of hazardous waste onto the ground, the hazardous waste storage area, and the failure to comply with all standards applicable to generators of hazardous waste.

On November 1, 1989, MDNR sent Harmon a letter stating that Harmon's disposal site "is a hazardous waste land disposal facility, as defined in the state and federal hazardous waste laws and regulations." In the letter, MDNR informed Harmon that, as a hazardous waste land disposal facility, Harmon was subject to the requirements of 40 C.F.R. part 265, which are incorporated by reference into Missouri's RCRA program. *** MDNR explained that its standard procedure was to issue an administrative order requiring a facility to comply with applicable standards. However, because of Harmon's voluntary disclosure and its cooperation in completing work to characterize the site, MDNR proposed that Harmon enter into a consent decree with MDNR, which would allow for more flexibility than an administrative order.

On February 27, 1990, Harmon submitted a legal memorandum to MDNR, conceding that MDNR had legal authority to classify its facility as a hazardous waste land disposal facility under RCRA, but arguing that MDNR, as a matter of discretion, should forgo such a classification as a way of rewarding Harmon for voluntarily reporting its violations and encouraging other facilities to self-report. By letter dated May 16, 1990, however, MDNR rejected Harmon's arguments, noting that it was already rewarding Harmon for its voluntary disclosure by forgoing pursuit of monetary penalties and by offering Harmon the opportunity to enter into a consent decree. The letter also stated that Harmon must come into compliance with RCRA and other laws and regulations governing hazardous waste disposal within 60 days.

By letter dated May 29, 1990, U.S. EPA Region VII, which has an oversight role in State RCRA programs, informed MDNR that the EPA considered Harmon a high priority class I violator under EPA's RCRA Enforcement Response Policy, and that it expected MDNR to expedite its enforcement of Harmon's violations, including the assessment of monetary penalties. The letter concluded that if MDNR did not initiate an enforcement action within 30 days, the Region would consider initiating its own enforcement action against Harmon. ***

Finally, on September 30, 1991, the Region did bring the instant action against Harmon, filing an administrative complaint consisting of four counts and alleging the following violations: (1) operation of a hazardous waste landfill without a permit or interim status, in violation of section 3005 of RCRA, 42 U.S.C. § 6925, and 40 C.F.R. part 270 (Count I); (2) failure to have a groundwater monitoring program for a hazardous waste landfill, in violation of 40 C.F.R. part 265, subpart F (Count II); (3) failure to establish and maintain financial assurance for closure and post-closure and liability coverage for sudden and non-sudden accidental occurrences at a landfill, in violation of 40 C.F.R. part 265, subpart H (Count III); and (4) failure to provide timely notification and/or register as a hazardous waste generator, in violation of section 3010(a) of RCRA, 42 U.S.C. § 6930(a) (Count IV).

After the Region had filed its complaint, a Missouri Circuit Court judge entered a consent decree, dated March 5, 1993, approving a settlement agreement between Harmon and the State of Missouri. The Consent Decree provides in part as follows:

WHEREAS, Harmon specifically denies the allegations of fact and conclusions of law contained in plaintiff's petition; and

WHEREAS, Harmon, without adjudicating or admitting any issue of fact or law herein, agrees with plaintiff to the entry of this Consent Decree in settlement of the petition.

* * * * * * *

In addition, the provisions of this Consent Decree shall apply to all persons, firms, corporations and other entities who are or will be acting in concert and in privity with, or on behalf of, the parties to this Decree or their servants, employees, successors and assigns.

EPA was not a party to either the settlement agreement or the consent decree.

* * *

*** At the conclusion of the hearing, the Presiding Officer issued an Initial Decision, in which he rejected the proposed penalty of $2,343,706 and assessed a much lower penalty of $586,716. The Presiding Officer reduced the multi-day penalties for all four counts of the First Amended Complaint to reflect Harmon's self-reporting and cooperation with MDNR in the investigation and remediation of the site.

* * *

II. DISCUSSION

A. The Overfiling Issue

On appeal, Harmon challenges the Region's authority "to assess penalties and issue a compliance order when the State of Missouri has issued a consent decree concerning the same RCRA violations and determined not to assess penalties because of Harmon's voluntary disclosure." In support of its challenge, Harmon makes two separate arguments, one based on the language of RCRA and one based on principles of res judicata. The argument based on the language of RCRA is as follows:

> [I]n bringing this action, EPA disregards the plain language of RCRA § 3006, which provides that authorized State programs operate "in lieu of" the federal program and that any action taken by a State under its authorized hazardous waste program "shall have the same force and effect" as actions taken by EPA. RCRA § 3006(b) and (d). Consequently, when an authorized state has taken action to enforce its hazardous waste laws, as MDNR took against Harmon, § 3006 requires EPA to give "force and effect" to such action. EPA's action against Harmon and the Initial Decision violate the plain language of § 3006 by giving Missouri's actions no force or effect.

> * * * * * * *

> Thus, when reading § 3006 together with § 3008, EPA may not overfile when the state has taken actions to enforce its hazardous waste program which must be given full force and effect. EPA may overfile when the state had taken no enforcement actions. If EPA believes the state's enforcement actions are inadequate, then EPA must withdraw authorization pursuant to § 3006(b) and (e).

We need not dwell for long on this statutory argument. It is well settled that, even when the authorized State has taken action, RCRA nevertheless authorizes the Agency to take its own action. Harmon has not offered any persuasive reasons to reopen this well-established reading of the statute, and we decline to do so.

We turn therefore to Harmon's second argument, which is based on principles of res judicata. Harmon contends that the Region's enforcement action is precluded by principles of res judicata because "MDNR's enforcement actions against Harmon included a Missouri Consent Decree which was signed by the Honorable David W. Shinn, Jackson County, Missouri Circuit Court Judge, on March 5, 1993." ***

* * *

Missouri law provides that "[r]es judicata prevents a party or privy from relitigating facts or questions in issue in a former action between the same parties which has been settled by judgment on the merits." *Clements v. Pittman*, 765 S.W.2d 589, 591

(Mo. 1989). Res judicata applies to a non-party only if the non-party is in privity with a party. *Id.* "Privity connotes those who are so connected with the party to the judgment as to have an identity of interest that the party to the judgment represented the same legal right." *Id.* ***

In its appeal brief, Harmon bases its claim of privity on the State authorization relationship between the Agency and the State of Missouri. Harmon contends that State authorization, in and of itself, creates a relationship of privity for purposes of res judicata.

It is undoubtedly clear under the RCRA statutory framework, that the State of Missouri, when administering its hazardous waste program pursuant to authority granted to it by EPA under RCRA § 3006, acts as EPA's agent and representative and, consequently, the parties are in privity. ***

Under RCRA § 3006(b), EPA and Missouri, as an authorized state, have identical interests in enforcing the RCRA regulations as incorporated by reference in Missouri. For a state to receive authorization under RCRA § 3006(b), it must demonstrate that the state program is equivalent to the federal program and that the state program will provide adequate enforcement of hazardous waste regulations. By virtue of the authorization provisions of RCRA, both EPA and Missouri have the same interest in enforcing compliance with the state hazardous waste program.

The Region counters that, for a number of reasons, State authorization alone does not ensure that the Agency's interests will be identical to those of the authorized State. First, the Region points out that EPA has an interest in national uniformity in the enforcement of RCRA requirements. This concern is reflected in the imposition of national minimum standards for hazardous waste management in RCRA and in the requirement that a State adopt "equivalent" state standards as a prerequisite for authorization. The Region points out that some States might not share the Agency's concern for nationwide uniformity and in fact might be far less interested in enforcing strict, nationally-consistent hazardous waste management standards than in encouraging regulated industries to remain in or relocate to the State, thereby preserving or bolstering the State's economy.

The Region also contends that EPA has an interest in deterring non-compliance through the assessment of penalties in a manner consistent with EPA's 1990 RCRA Civil Penalty Policy. Under that policy, some types of violations call for $20,000-25,000 per day of violation. The Region points out, however, that in significant, high priority cases a State may not share EPA's interest in imposing penalties at or approaching this level, and in some cases, a State may not even have the authority to assess such penalties, since it is possible for a State to obtain authorization under RCRA § 3006 with a maximum civil penalty authority of only $10,000 per day per violation.

The Region also points out that EPA may have national enforcement priorities that differ from those of an authorized State, and that even when EPA and an authorized State have common enforcement interests, economic and resource considerations may make it difficult or impossible for an authorized State to represent EPA's interests adequately or as well as EPA would represent such interests in its own enforcement action.

Based on the Region's arguments, we are persuaded that State authorization alone does not ensure an identity of interests between the Agency and the State for purposes of establishing privity. Although the Agency and an authorized State are charged with enforcing the same regulatory scheme, and often share common interests, to assume that the Agency and the State government will always have identical interests and concerns in the enforcement of individual matters within that regulatory scheme would ignore political barriers and fiscal realities. For example, there are instances where compliance problems within a State may go unaddressed or be inadequately addressed for resource or other reasons. There may also be cases where environmental violations within a State pose problems in other States, or across the nation as a whole (e.g., where a single company has violated federal environmental laws in many States). Thus, the interests of a State will often differ from those of the Agency. Because many enforcement decisions are a matter of discretion, it is important that the possibility of EPA enforcement be available as a backstop to ensure that wrongdoing is properly addressed and to fully vindicate federal interests.[14] Further, the reservation of overfiling authority to EPA where a State has not taken adequate action would be rendered meaningless if res judicata automatically (by virtue of State authorization alone) operated to preclude EPA action. We conclude, therefore, that State authorization alone cannot ensure an identity of interests between the Agency and the authorized State, even where the State has taken some action against the same respondent.

That conclusion, however, does not end our inquiry. It remains to be determined whether, in the particular circumstances of this case, an identity of interests existed between the Region and the State of Missouri with respect to the consent decree.

At oral argument, Harmon emphasized that the Region did not have significant involvement in the State's dealings with Harmon. The implication Harmon wishes us to draw from this argument is that, if the Region had believed that its interests were not being represented by the State, it would have intervened to a much greater extent than it did. The Region's lack of involvement, Harmon believes, suggests that it was satisfied with the State's handling of the case.

This argument, however, ignores the Region's repeated communications to MDNR concerning the assessment of penalties against Harmon. For example, on May 29, 1990, the Region sent a letter to MDNR, stating that the Region considered Harmon a high priority class I violator under EPA's RCRA Enforcement Response Policy. The letter further stated that the Region expected MDNR to expedite its enforcement of the violations including the assessment of monetary penalties. The letter concluded that if

---

[14]We note that our conclusion in this regard only addresses the narrow issue of whether State authorization, by itself, precludes EPA from overfiling. In concluding that it does not, we do not mean to imply that it is necessary or appropriate for EPA to exercise its overfiling authority in all cases where the State has not sought precisely the same relief as EPA would have. On the contrary, this is a policy determination that must be made on a case-by-case basis.

MDNR did not initiate an enforcement action within 30 days, seeking both compliance and the assessment of a penalty, the Region might initiate its own enforcement action against Harmon. The Region sent another letter to MDNR on October 15, 1990, this time stating that if MDNR did not initiate an enforcement action within 30 days, the Region would take its own action. Despite these communications from the Region, the State of Missouri signed the consent decree, which does not require Harmon to pay any penalties.

Thus, before the entry of the consent decree, the Region unequivocally expressed its interest in having substantial penalties assessed against Harmon (later proposing a penalty in excess of $2.3 million). The State, on the other hand, expressed its interest in rewarding Harmon for what the State viewed as Harmon's self-reporting of the violations charged in this action by settling the matter without penalties. Given this clash of interests over the propriety and amount of penalties, we conclude that no identity of interests existed between the Region and the State of Missouri with respect to the entry of the consent decree. In other words, the particular circumstances of this case do not establish a relationship of privity between the Region and the State.

* * *

In sum, the Board is of the view that EPA was not in privity with Missouri when that State took action against Harmon, either by virtue of State authorization alone or by virtue of the particular circumstances of this case. EPA is not bound under the doctrine of res judicata by the results of that State's actions and is therefore not precluded from bringing the challenged action.

B. The Statute of Limitations

As previously stated, after an evidentiary hearing on the issue of an appropriate penalty, the Presiding Officer assessed a penalty of $586,716. In so doing, the Presiding Officer held that the violations at issue in this case were continuing ones. Nevertheless, the Presiding Officer stated that the general five-year statute of limitations at 28 U.S.C. § 2462[21] is "germane to the assessment of penalties in this proceeding," and he only assessed penalties for violations occurring within five years from the date the initial complaint was filed, September 30, 1991.

---

[21]28 U.S.C. § 2462 provides as follows:

> Except as otherwise provided by Act of Congress, an action, suit or proceeding for the enforcement of any civil fine, penalty, or forfeiture, pecuniary or otherwise, shall not be entertained unless commenced within five years from the date when the claim first accrued if, within the same period, the offender or the property is found within the United States in order that proper service may be made thereon.

After the evidentiary hearing in this case, the United States Court of Appeals for the District of Columbia issued a decision in *3M Co. v. Browner*, 17 F.3d 1453, 1461 (D.C. Cir. 1994), holding that the five-year statute of limitations at 28 U.S.C. § 2462 is applicable to an administrative enforcement action for the assessment of a penalty, unless Congress has specifically provided for a different limitations period for the type of administrative action at issue.

The statute of limitations requires that an action such as this one be commenced within five years from the date the claims raised in the action "first accrued." Harmon argues that the violations it is charged with committing "first accrued" for purposes of 28 U.S.C. § 2462 between 1980-82, when Harmon first became subject to RCRA's permitting and other requirements but neglected to file the required notifications necessary to obtain interim status and a permit or to comply with Act's groundwater monitoring or financial assurance requirements. Because EPA did not institute the instant enforcement action until more than five years after Harmon first became subject to RCRA's permitting and other requirements, Harmon argues that the action must now be dismissed in its entirety as untimely.

Harmon does not dispute the fact that the elements establishing the violations in 1980-82 were equally present in 1987. In other words, there is no dispute in the record that Harmon was the owner and operator of an active hazardous waste management facility in 1980-82, and that Harmon was still the owner and operator of the same active facility in 1987. In fact, the record demonstrates that these elements existed continuously throughout the entire 1980-87 period and that at no time during that period did Harmon ever have interim status or a permit for the facility.

Harmon argues that all four counts of the First Amended Complaint are nevertheless barred under the statute of limitations because each alleged violation was "complete and instantaneous," and therefore had accrued, the moment Harmon first became subject to the applicable requirements. ***

* * *

Under this statute of limitations, the government is barred from maintaining an action to enforce a civil penalty or fine, inter alia, unless the action is commenced within five years of "the date when the claim first accrued." 28 U.S.C. § 2462. Stated in its simplest terms, "[a] cause of action 'accrues' when a suit may be maintained thereon." Black's Law Dictionary 21 (6th Ed. 1990). "A claim normally accrues when the factual and legal prerequisites for filing suit are in place." *3M Co. v. Browner*, 17 F.3d 1453, 1459 (D.C. Cir. 1994) (case of an alleged violation of a regulatory requirement under the Toxic Substances Control Act (TSCA), 15 U.S.C. § 2601, et seq.) ***

* * *

A continuing violation accrues when the course of illegal conduct is complete, not when an action to enforce the violation can first be maintained. *** Several courts have held that the continuing violations doctrine applies to civil penalty cases subject to the general five-year statute of limitations in 28 U.S.C. § 2462. ***

Given that a continuing violation tolls the running of the five-year limitation period in 28 U.S.C. § 2462, it is readily apparent that the date when a violation "first accrues" is not to be confused with the date when a violation "first occurs." Because of the tolling effect, a claim for civil penalties in a case to which the continuing violations doctrine applies may be maintained at any time beginning when the illegal course of conduct first occurs and ending five years after it is completed. Harmon is guilty of either not understanding or obfuscating the distinction between these dates, for it cites *3M* for the proposition that accrues "means the point in time at which a cause of action *first exists ***.*" Harmon's Brief at 28 (emphasis added). If this proposition were true for all situations (which plainly is not the case) then there would be a clear inconsistency in the case law between cases applying the doctrine of continuing violations and those applying the rule of accrual in *3M*. In point of fact, however, there is no inconsistency; the continuing violations doctrine is simply a recognized exception to the general rule. ***

Having shown that the date when a violation first accrues under the general five-year statute of limitations is not to be confused with the date when the violation first occurs, we next turn to a consideration of whether RCRA itself contemplates the existence of continuing violations and whether the specific violations alleged are continuing in nature.

Although RCRA does not contain any explicit language stating that violations under the Act are continuing, it does contain language that clearly contemplates the *possibility* of continuing violations. This language appears in two separate enforcement provisions, both found within § 3008 of RCRA:

> Any person who violates any requirement of this subchapter shall be liable to the United States for a civil penalty in an amount not to exceed $25,000 for each such violation. *Each day of such* violation shall, for purposes of this subsection, constitute a separate violation.

RCRA § 3008(g), 42 U.S.C. § 6928(g) (emphasis added), and:

> Any penalty assessed in the order shall not exceed $25,000 *per day of noncompliance* for each violation of a requirement of this subchapter.

RCRA § 3008(a)(3), 42 U.S.C. § 6928(a)(3) (emphasis added). As a matter of statutory interpretation, it seems inescapable that these provisions are intended to encompass violations that either continue without interruption from one day to the next or are repeated on a regular or intermittent basis. In either event, the important point for our purposes is that the language of these two provisions, by expressly contemplating daily penalties for a violation of the Act, clearly assumes the possibility of continuing violations.

A review of RCRA's legislative history also indicates that such violations were contemplated by the Act; it suggests that the RCRA regulatory scheme was expected to give rise to continuing violations. As first enacted in 1976, section 3008(a) of RCRA required the Administrator to provide notice to violators of any violation. If, after such notice, the violation *continued* for more than 30 days, the Administrator was authorized to issue an order requiring compliance within a specified time period. Pursuant to section 3008(a)(3), a penalty would be imposed only if the offender failed to take corrective action within the time referenced in the order. In 1980, section 3008(a) was amended to authorize the Administrator to issue compliance orders immediately, instead of waiting for 30 days. A Senate Report explains the amendment as being "aimed at stopping so-called 'midnight dumping' which may not continue at any location for more than 30 days, and to seek penalties for single occurrences, rather than just *continuing offenses.*" S. Rep. No. 172, 96th Cong., 2nd Sess. 1 (1980). By thus contrasting the special case of midnight dumping with that of "continuing offenses," the report tacitly assumes that continuing offenses represent the type of offense normally encountered under RCRA. At the very minimum, this report strongly implies that at least some RCRA violations must be considered continuing ones. Thus, the legislative history of RCRA, as well as the language of the statute, supports the conclusion that Congress clearly contemplated the possibility of continuing violations under RCRA. We now turn to an analysis of the specific violations alleged in the First Amended Complaint.

1. *First Amended Complaint*

a. *Count I: Operating Without a Permit*

Count I of the First Amended Complaint alleges that Harmon operated a hazardous waste disposal facility without first achieving interim status or obtaining a permit, in violation of section 3005(a) of RCRA, 42 U.S.C. § 6925. ***

* * *

*** [I]n the present case we conclude that Congress intended the violation of RCRA's permitting requirements to be a continuing violation. *** [B]oth RCRA and its implementing regulations require owners and operators of hazardous waste facilities to "have" a permit during the active life of the facility, including the applicable closure period. This clearly includes the period during which the facility is used for the treatment, storage, or disposal of hazardous waste. Unlike *** obligations *** which are complete upon the occurrence of the date specified, the obligation under § 3005(a) of RCRA to have a permit cannot be considered complete where the facility continues to be used for the treatment, storage, or disposal of hazardous waste; in short, the obligation is continuing. This is underscored in RCRA by the additional language that "upon and after" the date permitting regulations become effective the disposal of hazardous waste is prohibited except in accordance with a permit. Given the language of RCRA, as well as the legislative history discussed above, it is clear that Congress intended the permitting requirement to be continuing in nature. Thus, we conclude that the violations alleged in Count I of the First Amended Complaint consist of the failure to meet a continuing obligation.

b. *Count II: Groundwater Monitoring*

Count II alleges Harmon's failure to have a groundwater monitoring program for its hazardous waste landfill, in violation of regulations set forth at 40 C.F.R. part 265, subpart F. As discussed infra, the First Amended Complaint alleged that prior to 1989 Harmon did not have any ground water monitoring system in place. Based on our analysis of both the statutory and regulatory provisions governing the ground water monitoring requirements, we conclude that the violation alleged in Count II arises from the failure to meet a continuing obligation.

Several provisions of RCRA § 3004 require the Administrator to promulgate and implement ground water monitoring requirements for landfills and surface impoundments as well as other regulated units. See, e.g., RCRA §§ 3004(a), (o), and (p); see also §§ 3005(e)(2)(B), 3005(i), and 3015(b). Although these provisions do not explicitly state that the obligation to comply with ground water monitoring requirements is ongoing, the nature of the requirements is such that Congress must assuredly have contemplated continuing obligations. As early as 1976, Congress recognized ground water contamination from hazardous wastes as "perhaps the most pernicious effect" of unregulated waste disposal. H.R. Rep. No. 94-1461, 94th Cong., 2d Sess. 89. Many provisions of RCRA, including several new amendments added in 1984, reflect Congress' continuing concern about ground water monitoring. For example, in 1984 Congress added RCRA § 3005(e)(2)(B), providing that interim status to operate would terminate for an affected facility unless the facility certified by a specified date that it "is in compliance with all applicable groundwater monitoring and financial responsibility requirements." As noted by EPA in codifying these amendments into its regulations, "Congress asserted that since EPA's ground-water monitoring requirements have been in effect since November 1981, there is no excuse for noncompliance at this late date. 129 Cong. Rec. H8142 (October 6, 1983)." 50 Fed. Reg. 28,702, 28,724 (July 15, 1985) (EPA's Final Codification rule for the 1984 Amendments to RCRA). Given these provisions and legislative history, as well as the nature of the underlying requirements, it is simply unimaginable that the Congress would have viewed the ground water monitoring violation Harmon is charged with as anything other than a continuing violation.

Further, the ordinary meaning of the word "monitoring" connotes an ongoing activity. ***

This conclusion is supported by the language of the regulations implementing the ground water monitoring requirements. For example, the regulations state, in part, that properly installed monitoring wells must,

> [I]mmediately detect any statistically significant amounts of hazardous waste or hazardous waste constituents that migrate from the waste management area to the upper most aquifer.

40 C.F.R. § 265.91(a)(2). It is difficult to imagine how a monitoring activity could "immediately" detect this type of movement unless the monitoring is conducted on an ongoing basis. ***

*   *   *

c. Count III: Financial Responsibility

Count III alleges Harmon's failure to obtain, establish, or maintain financial assurance for closure and post-closure at its facility, and its failure to obtain and maintain insurance coverage for sudden and non-sudden accidental occurrences. As was true for the ground water monitoring requirements, both the language of RCRA and the nature of the requirements are such that Congress surely contemplated continuing obligations. The failure to comply with these obligations, therefore, resulted in continuing violations.

The statutory provision dealing with financial responsibility is section 3004 of RCRA. This section expressly requires the Administrator to promulgate regulations requiring financial responsibility. *** Subsection (t)(1) of section 3004 lists the financial mechanisms by which a person may comply with the financial responsibility requirements. *** Each of the specified means in section 3004(t) for establishing financial responsibility contemplates an ongoing contractual relationship or ability to assure the availability of funds. *** Congress must have intended that they be treated as continuing obligations, for the need for financial responsibility continues throughout the life of the facility and any applicable post-closure period. Indeed, these provisions were designed to assure that monies would be available for closure and post-closure whether or not the owner or operator were available or solvent.

* * *

d. *Count IV: Notification Under RCRA § 3010*

Count IV alleges a violation of Section 3010 of RCRA, 42 U.S.C. § 6930. *** The first sentence of section 3010(a) requires notification of specified hazardous waste activities "[n]ot later than ninety days after promulgation of regulations" that make such hazardous wastes subject to RCRA regulation. At first glance, this notification requirement resembles the draft registration requirement at issue in *Toussie [v. United States*, 397 U.S. 112 (1970)] in that it requires action within a particular time frame and does not expressly provide that the obligation to take such action continues beyond that time frame. If section 3010 only contained the 90-day notification requirement, Harmon's reliance on *Toussie* and similar cases might well be persuasive. Section 3010, however, also contains a prohibition. Specifically, it states that, absent such notification, hazardous waste may not be "transported, treated, stored, or disposed of." This prohibition distinguishes section 3010 from the draft registration requirement at issue in *Toussie*. By prohibiting the act of disposal without having complied with the notification provision, section 3010 describes two separate requirements, the violation of which could result in two different but often interrelated violations, one consisting solely of a failure to file a notification within 90 days and the other consisting of hazardous waste activities that violate the prohibition. At least with respect to the latter violation, Harmon continued to violate the prohibition until at least November 1987 by repeatedly disposing of hazardous waste without having filed the required notification. No such notification was filed until 1988. This continuous course of prohibited conduct is a continuing violation. ***

e. *The Illegal Conduct Continued into the Limitations Period*

As discussed above, RCRA and its implementing regulations provide that the obligations to have a permit, to have a groundwater monitoring system in place, and to maintain financial responsibility are continuing obligations. The failure to fulfill those obligations, therefore, results in continuing violations. In addition, RCRA imposes a prohibition on hazardous waste disposal activities where notification under § 3010(a) has not been given. Continuously engaging in the disposal of hazardous waste when notification has not been given, therefore, results in a continuing violation. For the following reasons, we also conclude that Harmon's illegal conduct continued into the limitations period preceding the filing of the complaint in this action.

Harmon actively disposed of hazardous waste onto the ground behind its building from the time the applicable RCRA requirements became effective until the end of 1987. This disposal took place approximately once every one to three weeks. By reason of these activities, Harmon was the owner and operator of a hazardous waste management facility. Even after Harmon had ceased its active disposal of hazardous waste at the end of 1987, it continued to be the owner of a hazardous waste management facility and retained that status at the time of the filing of the complaint. As an owner and operator of a hazardous waste disposal facility, Harmon was subject to: (1) the obligation to have a permit; (2) the obligation to have a groundwater monitoring system in place; and (3) the obligation to maintain financial responsibility. From the time those obligations became effective in 1980 and 1982, until the filing of the complaint, Harmon failed to comply with either the permit, financial responsibility requirements, or groundwater monitoring requirements. As for count IV, by continuing to dispose of hazardous waste at least until November of 1987 without having filed the required notification, Harmon engaged in a continuous course of conduct whereby it continued to violate the prohibition in section 3010 at least until that date.

* * *

3. Conclusions Relating to the Statute of Limitations

In view of the foregoing discussion, we reach the following conclusions with regard to Harmon's statute of limitations challenge: (1) The violations alleged in counts I, II, and III of the First Amended Complaint each arose from the failure to comply with a continuing obligation, and the violation alleged in count IV arose from a continuous course of prohibited conduct; (2) The violations alleged were continuing violations that continued into the limitations period; and (3) The First Amended Complaint adequately alleges that Harmon committed continuing violations and that such violations continued into the limitations period. We therefore reject Harmon's statute of limitations challenge.

C. Self-Reporting

Harmon discovered the violations charged in the First Amended Complaint during a routine OSHA walk-through investigation of its facility in November 1987. It then reported those violations to the MDNR on June 27, 1988. Harmon argues that the Agency should forgo assessing penalties against Harmon as a way of rewarding Harmon for its good conduct. Harmon contends that by so rewarding it, the Agency will create an incentive for others to follow Harmon's example.

The Presiding Officer shared the belief that Harmon should be rewarded for discovering and voluntarily disclosing its violations. He therefore reduced by 66% the multi-day penalties sought by the Region in the First Amended Complaint. In addition, because he concluded that Harmon discovered and voluntarily disclosed the violations, the Presiding Officer increased the Region's recommended downward adjustment for good faith with respect to two of the counts in the First Amended Complaint. Harmon argues, however, that the Presiding Officer erred by not completely eliminating the gravity-based penalties for its violations.

In support of its argument, Harmon points to EPA's policy statement on self-reporting of violations. This policy statement was issued in final form on December 22, 1995, under the title "Incentives for Self-Policing: Discovery, Disclosure, Correction and Prevention of Violations." 60 Fed. Reg. 66706 (Dec. 22, 1995). The new policy provides that:

> [W]here violations are found through voluntary environmental audits or efforts that reflect a regulated entity's due diligence, and are promptly disclosed and expeditiously corrected, EPA will not seek gravity-based (i.e., non-economic benefit) penalties and will generally not recommend criminal prosecution against the regulated entity. EPA will reduce gravity-based penalties by 75% for violations that are voluntarily discovered, and are promptly disclosed and corrected, even if not found through a formal audit or due diligence.

60 Fed. Reg. 66706. The new policy lists nine conditions that a regulated entity must meet in order for the Agency to reduce, or forgo seeking, gravity-based penalties under the policy. If the entity meets all nine conditions, the Agency will not seek gravity-based civil penalties, and generally will not seek criminal prosecution. If the entity meets all of the conditions except the first—requiring the violation to have been discovered through an environmental audit or due diligence—the Agency will reduce its recommended gravity-based penalties by 75%.

*** Harmon *** concedes that it does not meet all (or even all but the first) of the nine conditions set out in the final form of the new policy. Nevertheless, Harmon still maintains that it satisfies the "spirit" and "essence" of the new policy, if not all nine conditions set out in that policy.

The Region, on the other hand, correctly points out that the policy is specifically intended as guidance in a settlement context and was never meant for use in an adjudicatory context. ***

After careful consideration of the arguments, we conclude that the Presiding Officer did not err by failing to eliminate all of the gravity-based penalties for Harmon's violations. We agree with Harmon that its disclosure of its RCRA violations is relevant to consider in the penalty context. We believe, however, that the Presiding Officer adequately rewarded such conduct by reducing Harmon's multi-penalties by 66% for all counts in the complaint, and increasing the Region's proposed penalty reductions for good faith. The nature of the violations involve critically important requirements that go to the heart of the RCRA program. We are unwilling to grant any further downward adjustments beyond that which the Presiding Officer has already awarded.

Harmon's invocation of the "spirit" of the new self-policing, self-reporting policy, so as to credit it with even greater penalty reductions than the Presiding Officer has already allowed, is rejected. Harmon downplays one critically important aspect of the "spirit," as well as the terms, of the policy, which is to encourage settlements rather than allow a case to run its full course through expensive and time-consuming litigation. This important aspect of the policy would be undermined if the penalty reduction provisions of the policy were applied in full here.

* * *

D. *The Financial Responsibility Requirements*

Harmon raises three issues relating to Count III of the First Amended Complaint, which alleges violations of the financial responsibility requirements.

* * *

3. *The Missouri Consent Decree*

Harmon argues that it is not liable for its failure to obtain liability insurance coverage because it "is specifically excused by the State of Missouri from such performance as long as it continues to fulfill the requirements of the Consent Decree." Harmon contends that: "In paragraph 6 [of the consent decree], the State agrees to forgo enforcement actions based upon the liability insurance requirements as long as Harmon continues to make a semi-annual demonstration of its attempts to comply with the regulations at 40 C.F.R. § 265.147."

Harmon's argument is rejected. It is true that the State, in an exercise of its enforcement discretion, agreed to forgo enforcement actions, provided Harmon made an effort to comply with section 265.147; however, the consent decree did not relieve Harmon of its obligation to comply with section 265.147. Moreover, this exercise of enforcement discretion on the part of the State does not prevent the Region from taking its own enforcement action against Harmon. As the Board observed in a similar situation:

> [A] State's exercise of its enforcement discretion is certainly not binding on the Region. Indeed, EPA's statutory right to overfile is founded on the notion that EPA is entitled to bring enforcement actions in an authorized State whenever the State, in EPA's opinion, has not exercised its enforcement discretion properly.

In re Gordon Redd Lumber Co., 4 E.A.D. 301, 317-318 (EAB 1994). We conclude that the existence of the consent decree did not make it inappropriate for the Presiding Officer to order Harmon to obtain liability insurance coverage, as is required by the express terms of the regulations, and to assess a penalty against Harmon for its failure to obtain such coverage.

* * *

III. CONCLUSION

For all the foregoing reasons, we come to the following conclusions. With respect to the first issue discussed above, we hold that: (1) RCRA authorizes EPA to bring an action in an authorized State even if the State has taken action against the same respondent for the same violations; (2) State authorization in and of itself does not establish a relationship of privity between EPA and the authorized State, such that under the doctrine of res judicata, EPA is bound by the results of a State enforcement action just as the State is bound; and (3) The particular dealings between the Region and the State of Missouri in this case did not establish a relationship of privity, such that EPA is bound by the consent decree just as the State of Missouri is bound. With respect to the other issues raised in this appeal, we hold that: (1) The Region's action against Harmon is not barred by the applicable statute of limitations; (2) The Presiding Officer's penalty assessment need not be reconsidered in light of the new policy on self-policing; (3) Even though Harmon ceased active hazardous waste management operations in 1987, it was required to maintain liability insurance coverage and its failure to do so violated the RCRA financial responsibility requirements; (4) The Presiding Officer's penalty assessment for Harmon's violation of the financial responsibility requirements, including an upward adjustment for bad faith, is appropriate; and (5) The Presiding Officer's determinations on the seriousness of the violations charged in the First Amended Complaint are supported by the preponderance of the evidence.

* * *

NOTES

1. In light of the Environmental Appeals Board's discussion of continuing violations, what RCRA violations would not fall into that category? For what violations does the five-year statute of limitations apply? How does the five-year statute of limitations apply to continuing violations?

2. Although Harmon apparently believed it had resolved its RCRA problems by means of negotiations with the State of Missouri, that did not preclude the EPA from taking civil enforcement action. The remainder of this chapter focuses on criminal enforcement. To what extent would Harmon's agreement with the State affect the EPA's ability to take criminal enforcement action against the company and its employees?

B. Criminal Enforcement

RCRA subjects a broad range of "knowing" violations to criminal prosecution. RCRA § 3008(d) and (e), 42 U.SC. § 6928(d)(and (e). Knowing violation of RCRA's various regulatory requirements, such as knowingly transporting or causing to be transported any RCRA hazardous waste to a facility that lacks a RCRA permit, is punishable by a fine of up to $50,000 per day of violation, imprisonment for up to two or five years (depending on the particular violation), or both. RCRA § 3008(d). Conviction for knowingly violating RCRA in a manner that knowingly "places another person in imminent danger of death or serious bodily injury" is punishable by a fine of up to $250,000 ($1 million for organizations), imprisonment for up to 15 years, or both. RCRA § 3008(e).

A crucial and controversial issue in the RCRA criminal enforcement arena is what the government must prove in order to establish a "knowing" violation. An early authority on this issue was *United States v. Johnson & Towers, Inc.*, 741 F.2d 662 (3d Cir. 1984), *cert. denied,* 469 U.S. 1208 (1985). Without obtaining a RCRA TSD permit, Johnson & Towers pumped hazardous wastes from its truck cleaning operations into a trench that flowed into a nearby creek. The government charged the company, a foreman, and a service manager in the trucking department with knowingly treating, storing, or disposing of hazardous waste without a permit, in violation of RCRA § 3008(d)(2)(A).

First, the Third Circuit addressed the individuals' argument that because only facility owners and operators are required to apply for RCRA permits, only they are subject to criminal prosecution for handling hazardous waste without such permit:

*** [I]f we view the statutory language in its totality, the congressional plan becomes more apparent. First, "person" is defined in the statute as "an individual, trust, firm, joint stock company, corporation (including a government corporation), partnership, association, State, municipality, commission, political subdivision of a State, or any interstate body." 42 U.S.C. § 6903(15). Had Congress meant in section 6928(d)(2)(A) to take aim more narrowly, it could have used more narrow language. Since it did not, we attribute to "any person" the definition given the term in section 6903(15).

Second, under the plain language of the statute the only explicit basis for exoneration is the existence of a permit covering the action. Nothing in the language of the statute suggests that we should infer another provision exonerating persons who knowingly treat, store or dispose of hazardous waste but are not owners or operators.

Finally, though the result may appear harsh, it is well established that criminal penalties attached to regulatory statutes intended to protect public health, in contrast to statutes based on common law crimes, are to be construed to effectuate the regulatory purpose.

* * *

Although Congress' concern may have been directed primarily at owners and operators of generating facilities, since it imposed upon them in section 6925 the obligation to secure the necessary permit, Congress did not explicitly limit criminal liability for impermissible treatment, storage, or disposal to owners and operators. The House Committee's discussion of enforcement contains several references relevant only to owners and operators, but it says, in addition: "This section *also* provides for criminal penalties for the person who ... disposes of any hazardous waste without a permit under this title...." H.R.Rep. No. 1491, *supra* at 31, 1976 U.S.Code Cong. & Ad.News at 6269 (emphasis added). The "also" demonstrates that the reach of section 6928(d)(2) is broader than that of the rest of the statute, particularly the administrative enforcement remedies. The acts that were made the subject of the criminal provision were distinguished in the House Report from the other conduct subject to administrative regulation because they were viewed as more serious offenses. As the Report explained, "[the] justification for the penalties section is to permit a broad variety of mechanisms so as to stop the illegal disposal of hazardous wastes." *Id*.

We conclude that in RCRA *** Congress endeavored to control hazards that, "in the circumstances of modern industrialism, are largely beyond self-protection." *United States v. Dotterweich*, 320 U.S. at 280. It would undercut the purposes of the legislation to limit the class of potential defendants to owners and operators when others also bear responsibility for handling regulated materials. The phrase "without having obtained a permit *under section 6925*" (emphasis added) merely references the section under which the permit is required and exempts from prosecution under section 6928(d)(2)(A) anyone who has obtained a permit; we conclude that it has no other limiting effect. ***

Id. at 665-67.

Next, the Third Circuit turned to the government's burden on remand in proving a "knowing" violation of RCRA § 3008(d)(2)(A):

If the word "knowingly" in section 6928(d)(2) referred exclusively to the acts of treating, storing or disposing, as the government contends, it would be an almost meaningless addition since it is not likely that one would treat, store or dispose of waste without knowledge of that action. At a minimum, the word "knowingly", which introduces subsection (A), must also encompass knowledge that the waste material is hazardous. Certainly, "[a] person thinking in good faith that he was [disposing of] distilled water when in fact he was [disposing of] some dangerous acid would not be covered." *United States v. International Minerals & Chemical Corp.*, 402 U.S. 558, 563-64 (1971).

Whether "knowingly" also modifies subsection (A) presents a somewhat different question. ***

Treatment, storage or disposal of hazardous waste in violation of any material condition or requirement of a permit must be "knowing," since the statute explicitly so states in subsection (B). It is unlikely that Congress could have intended to subject to criminal prosecution those persons who acted when no permit had been obtained irrespective of their knowledge (under subsection (A)), but not those persons who acted in violation of the terms of a permit unless that action was knowing (subsection (B)). Thus we are led to conclude either that the omission of the word "knowing" in (A) was inadvertent or that "knowingly" which introduces subsection (2) applies to subsection (A).

* * *

[I]n light of our interpretation of section 6928(d)(2)(A), it is evident that the district court will be required to instruct the jury, *inter alia*, that in order to convict each defendant the jury must find that each knew that Johnson & Towers was required to have a permit, and knew that Johnson & Towers did not have a permit. Depending on the evidence, the district court may also instruct the jury that such knowledge may be inferred.

Id. at 668-69.

In the years following *Johnson & Towers*, virtually all of the other circuits to face this knowledge issue have begged to differ with the Third Circuit. The following case articulates the current majority view.

UNITED STATES V. DEAN
969 F.2d 187 (6th Cir. 1992), *cert. denied*, 507 U.S. 1033 (1993)

Before NELSON and NORRIS, Circuit Judges; and JOINER, Senior District Judge for the Eastern District of Michigan.
JOINER, Senior District Judge.

Defendant Gale E. Dean appeals his convictions on one count of conspiracy to violate the Resource Conservation and Recovery Act (RCRA) ***; one count of failure to file documentation of hazardous waste generation, storage, and disposal as required by 42 U.S.C. § 6928(d)(4); and one count of storage of spent chromic acid without a permit, one count of storage and disposal of chromic acid rinse water and wastewater sludges in a lagoon without a permit, and one count of disposal of paint sludge and solvent wastes in a pit without a permit, all in violation of 42 U.S.C. § 6928(d)(2)(A).

I.

Defendant's convictions arose out of the operation of the General Metal Fabricators, Inc. (GMF) facility in Erwin, Tennessee, which engaged in metal stamping, plating, and painting. The facility utilized hazardous chemicals and generated hazardous waste. The owners of GMF, Joseph and Jean Sanchez; as well as Dean, the production manager; and Clyde Griffith, the plant manager; were indicted for conspiracy to violate RCRA, and, individually, for violations of various sections of the statute. The district court granted defendant's motion to sever his trial from that of the other defendants.

RCRA provides a comprehensive system of oversight of hazardous materials, a system centered upon requirements that facilities utilizing such materials obtain permits, and maintain proper records of the treatment, storage, and disposal of hazardous substances. No permit was sought for the GMF facility. The hazardous waste disposal practices at GMF were discovered by chance by state waste-management authorities whose attention was caught, while driving to an appointment at another facility, by two 55-gallon drums abandoned among weeds on GMF's property.

As production manager, Dean had day-to-day supervision of GMF's production process and employees. Among his duties was the instruction of employees on hazardous waste handling and disposal. Numerous practices at GMF violated RCRA. GMF's plating operations utilized rinse baths, contaminated with hazardous chemicals, which were drained through a pipe into an earthen lagoon outside the facility. In addition, Dean instructed employees to shovel various kinds of solid wastes from the tanks into 55-gallon drums. Dean ordered the construction of a pit, concealed behind the facility, into which 38 drums of such hazardous waste were tossed. The contents spilled onto the soil from open or corroded drums. Chemical analyses of soil and solid wastes, entered by stipulation at trial, revealed that the lagoon and the pit were contaminated with chromium. In addition, the pit was contaminated with toluene and xylene solvents. All of these substances are hazardous. Drums of spent chromic acid solution were also illegally stored on the premises.

Defendant was familiar with the chemicals used in each of the tanks on the production lines, and described to authorities the manner in which the contents of the rinse tanks were deposited in the lagoon. Material Safety Data Sheets (MSDS) provided to GMF by the chemical manufacturer clearly stated that various chemicals in use at GMF were hazardous and were subject to state and federal pollution control laws. The MSDS were given to investigators by Dean, who demonstrated his knowledge of their contents. The MSDS delivered with the chromic acid made specific reference to RCRA and to related EPA regulations. Dean informed investigators that he "had read this RCRA waste code but thought it was a bunch of bullshit."

II.

A.

Dean assigns as error numerous aspects of the proceedings in the trial court. We shall address first a number of contentions going to the scope and elements of RCRA's criminal provisions, which we think of primary importance among the issues raised by defendant. The first of these issues arises in connection with defendant's contention that the trial court erred in denying his motion for an acquittal on Count 4, because there was no evidence that defendant knew of RCRA's permit requirement. Defendant's characterization of the evidence is inaccurate; but moreover, we see no basis on the face of the statute for concluding that knowledge of the permit requirement is an element of the crime. The statute penalizes:

> Any person who—
>
> ....
>
> > (2) knowingly treats, stores, or disposes of any hazardous waste identified or listed under this subchapter—
> >
> > > (A) without a permit under this subchapter or pursuant to title I of the Marine Protection, Research, and Sanctuaries Act (86 Stat. 1052); or
> > >
> > > (B) in knowing violation of any material condition or requirement of such permit; or
> > >
> > > (C) in knowing violation of any material condition or requirement of any applicable interim status regulations or standards
>
> ....

42 U.S.C. § 6928(d)(2). Defendant was convicted of violating subsection 6928(d)(2)(A).

The question of interpretation presented by this provision is the familiar one of how far the initial "knowingly" travels. Other courts of appeals have divided on this question. In *United States v. Johnson & Towers, Inc.*, 741 F.2d 662 (3d Cir.1984), *cert. denied*, 469 U.S. 1208 (1985), the Court of Appeals for the Third Circuit concluded that knowledge of the permit requirement was an element of the crime, observing:

> Treatment, storage or disposal of hazardous waste in violation of any material condition or requirement of a permit must be "knowing," since the statute explicitly so states in subsection (B). It is unlikely that Congress could have intended to subject to criminal prosecution those persons who acted when no permit had been obtained irrespective of their knowledge (under subsection (A)), but not those persons who acted in violation of the terms of a permit unless that action was knowing (subsection (B)). Thus we are led to conclude either that the omission of the word "knowing" in (A) was inadvertent or that "knowingly" which introduces subsection (2) applies to subsection (A).

Id. at 668 (footnote omitted).

The Court of Appeals for the Ninth Circuit disagreed with the Third Circuit in *United States v. Hoflin*, 880 F.2d 1033 (9th Cir.1989), *cert. denied*, 493 U.S. 1083 (1990). The Ninth Circuit noted first the well-established principle of statutory construction that courts will "give effect, if possible, to every clause and word of a statute," ***, pointing out that the Third Circuit's reading of subsection 6928(d)(2)(A) would render mere surplusage the word "knowing" in subsections 6928(d)(2)(B) and

(C). *Hoflin*, 880 F.2d at 1038. The Ninth Circuit also disagreed with the Third Circuit that there was anything illogical about reading subsections 6928(d)(2)(B) and (C) to have a knowledge requirement but subsection 6928(d)(2)(A) to have none. The Ninth Circuit observed that the permit requirement is intended to give the EPA notice that oversight of a facility is necessary (and, by implication, the force of the statutory scheme would be greatly diminished by exempting all who claimed ignorance of the statute's requirements). The difference in *mens rea* between the subsections signifies the relative importance, in the estimation of Congress, of the twin requirements of obtaining a permit and complying with the permit. This ranking is consistent with the greater likelihood that compliance *with* the permit will be monitored. The Court of Appeals for the Fourth Circuit agreed with the Ninth Circuit in *United States v. Dee*, 912 F.2d 741 (4th Cir.1990), *cert. denied*, 111 S.Ct. 1307 (1991).

All of the courts to address this question have reasoned by analogy from the holding of the Supreme Court in *United States v. International Minerals & Chemical Corp.*, 402 U.S. 558 (1971). In that case, the indictment was brought under 18 U.S.C. § 834(f), which penalizes knowing violation of any regulation. The regulation at issue, enacted by the Interstate Commerce Commission, required shipping papers to reflect certain information concerning corrosive liquids being shipped. The question before the Supreme Court was whether knowledge of existence of the regulation was an element of the crime. The Court held that it was not, turning its decision upon the maxim that ignorance of the law is no excuse. The Court concluded its opinion by stating, with equal force here, that when "dangerous or deleterious devices or products or obnoxious waste materials are involved, the probability of regulation is so great that anyone who is aware that he is in possession of them or dealing with them must be presumed to be aware of the regulation." *Id.* at 565. The Court of Appeals for the Third Circuit mitigated its holding in *Johnson & Towers* somewhat in light of *International Minerals*, holding that knowledge of RCRA would be imputed to employees above a certain level of responsibility (no guidance was given concerning the level of responsibility required, on grounds that there was insufficient evidence in the record on the responsibilities of the employees at issue).

We agree with the reasoning of the Court of Appeals for the Ninth Circuit in *Hoflin*. The "knowingly" which begins § 6928(d)(2) cannot be read as extending to the subsections without rendering nugatory the word "knowing" contained in subsections 6928(d)(2)(B) and (C). Subsection 6928(d)(2)(A) requires knowing treatment (or knowing storage, or knowing disposal) of hazardous waste. It also requires proof that the treatment, or storage, or disposal, was done without a permit. It does not require that the person charged have known that a permit was required, and that knowledge is not relevant.

As to subsections 6928(d)(2)(B) and (C), the requirements are different. Here, the statute clearly requires in addition that if one is to be charged under 6928(d)(2)(B) with violating the terms of a permit or under 6928(d)(2)(C) with violating regulations then one must be aware of the additional requirements of the permit or regulation. To us the statute is clear, makes sense and does not contain the ambiguities or inconsistencies found by others.

The Court of Appeals for the Third Circuit hypothesized in the alternative that Congress inadvertently omitted the word "knowing" from subsection 6928(d)(2)(A), because, the court opined, the plain language reading of section 6928(d)(2) to which we adhere resulted in an "unlikely" statutory scheme.   A general review of the reasonableness of legislative choices, however, is not among our statutory construction tools. The inquiry ends with a cogent means of reading the plain language of the statute. The *Hoflin* court, moreover, adequately addressed the reasons Congress might have had for crafting the statute in this manner. Finally, we note that statutes which are designed to protect the public health and safety (as is RCRA, *Johnson & Towers*, 741 F.2d at 668) have consistently been distinguished in Supreme Court precedent as more likely candidates for diminished *mens rea* requirements.

We do not agree with the suggestion in *Johnson & Towers* that section 6928(d)(2)(A) is in fact a strict liability crime if knowledge of the permit requirement need not be shown. The provision applies by its terms to any person who "*knowingly* treats, stores or disposes of hazardous waste." 42 U.S.C. § 6928(d)(2) (emphasis ours). The Supreme Court's pronouncement in *International Minerals*, quoted above, stands for the proposition that persons involved in hazardous waste handling have every reason to be aware that their activities are regulated by law, aside from the rule that ignorance of the law is no excuse. In this case, the documentation provided by the chemical manufacturer abundantly illustrates one means by which knowledge of hazardous waste laws is communicated. Accordingly, even absent the requirement of proof that the defendant knew of RCRA's permit provisions, the statute does not impose strict liability. The district court did not err in declining to grant defendant's motion for acquittal based on his alleged ignorance of RCRA's permit requirement.

B.

Defendant also contends that the district court should have granted his motion for acquittal because subsection 6928(d)(2)(A) was not intended to reach employees who are not "owners" or "operators" of facilities. By its terms, the provision applies to "any person." "Person" is a defined term meaning "an individual, trust, firm, joint stock company, corporation (including a government corporation), partnership, association, State, municipality, commission, political subdivision of a State, or any interstate body." 42 U.S.C. § 6903(15).

Defendant would be hard pressed to convince the court that he is not an "individual." He argues, however, that because only owners and operators of facilities are required to obtain permits, 42 U.S.C. § 6925, the penalty imposed for hazardous waste handling without a permit by subsection 6928(d)(2)(A) must apply only to owners and operators.

This contention is unpersuasive for numerous reasons. Of primary importance is the fact that it is contrary to the unambiguous language of the statute. We agree with the Third Circuit that "[h]ad Congress meant in § 6928(d)(2)(A) to take aim more narrowly, it could have used more narrow language." *United States v. Johnson & Towers, Inc.*, 741 F.2d 662 (3d Cir.1984). Second, while defendant's argument at first glance has logical appeal in relation to subsection 6928(d)(2)(A), the relevant language "any person" prefaces § 6928(d) generally. A number of separate crimes are set out in § 6928(d), several of them having nothing to do with the permit requirement (e.g., failure to maintain requisite documentation or to comply with regulations). Defendant's argument would accordingly impose a limitation on all of the crimes set out in § 6928(d) on a ground relevant to few of them. Third, even the logical appeal of the assertion does not withstand scrutiny. The fact that Congress chose to impose the permit requirement upon owners and operators does not undercut the value of further assuring permit compliance by enacting criminal penalties which would lead others to make inquiry into the permit status of facilities. Given that "[s]uch wastes typically have no value, yet can only be safely disposed of at considerable cost," *United States v. Hoflin*, 880 F.2d 1033, 1038 (9th Cir.1989), *cert. denied*, 493 U.S. 1083 (1990), facilities generating hazardous waste have a strong incentive to evade the law. Moreover, clean-up of the resulting environmental damage almost always involves far greater cost than proper disposal would have, and may be limited to containing the spread of the harm. Defendant argues that employees are the least likely persons to know facilities' permit status. However, employees of a facility are more able to ascertain the relevant facts than the general public, which the statute is intended to protect. In light of these factors, it was entirely reasonable for Congress to have created broad criminal liability. Fourth, it is far from clear that defendant is in fact not an "operator" of GMF, a term defined in the regulations to mean "the person responsible for the overall operation of a facility." 40 C.F.R. § 260.10 (1991). Finally, we agree with the Court of Appeals for the Third Circuit that this result is also supported by the decision of the Supreme Court in *United States v. Dotterweich*, 320 U.S. 277 (1943), and by the legislative history. We conclude that employees may be criminally liable under § 6928(d).

C.

Defendant contends that he should have been acquitted on Count 3 because the chromic acid at issue was not "hazardous waste" as required by 42 U.S.C. § 6928(d)(2)(A), set out above. The term "hazardous waste" is defined as:

> [A] solid waste, or combination of solid wastes, which because of its quantity, concentration, or physical, chemical, or infectious characteristics may—
>
> > (A) cause, or significantly contribute to an increase in mortality or an increase in serious irreversible, or incapacitating irreversible, illness; or
> >
> > (B) pose a substantial present or potential hazard to human health or the environment when improperly treated, stored, transported, or disposed of, or otherwise managed.

42 U.S.C. § 6903(5). Count 3 involved spent chromic acid solution which was being stored in drums at the facility. Dean contends that the chromic acid was not "hazardous"

within the meaning of § 6903(5), apparently on the ground that the chromic acid did not pose a danger to human health in the conditions under which it was being stored at GMF. *American Mining Congress v. EPA*, 907 F.2d 1179, 1191 (D.C.Cir.1990), upon which defendant relies, contains nothing supporting this proposition, and is directed at an inapposite question of law.

Defendant does not deny that the "chemical ... characteristics" of chromic acid involve a threat to human health, as was prominently stated in the MSDS provided by its vendor. It is not apparent from the plain language of the statute that it requires, as defendant would read it, that a hazardous waste present a threat to human health as a result of the manner in which it is being stored. We note that the definitions of "disposal" and "storage" under the statute are distinguished by the fact that the former is defined to mean placing the waste in a location where environmental contamination may result, while the latter is defined as "containment" of waste in a manner not constituting disposal, *i.e.,* such that environmental contamination will not result. A substance contained in a manner which does not threaten environmental contamination presumably would not present a threat to human health. Substances being "stored" would accordingly not be "hazardous," therefore storage could never be a predicate for a RCRA violation. This result is clearly contrary to the terms of the statute, and highlights the fallacy in defendant's argument.

Moreover, construing the statute to penalize storage of hazardous substances without a permit, without regard to whether the means of storage is itself unsafe, is in keeping with the statute's purposes. The requirement of a permit is intended to remedy the danger to the public health (underscored by the events in this case) presented by facilities whose generation of hazardous waste is unknown to authorities charged with monitoring the handling of wastes, for the protection of the environment.

* * *

NOTES

1. If this knowledge issue goes to the Supreme Court, should it adopt the *Johnson & Towers* approach, the *Dean* approach, or some other view?

The cases in the *Dean* camp include *United States v. Wagner*, 29 F.3d 264 (7th Cir. 1994); *United States v. Laughlin*, 10 F.3d 961 (2d Cir. 1993), *cert. denied*, 511 U.S. 1071 (1994); *United States v. Dee*, 912 F.2d 741 (4th Cir. 1990), *cert. denied*, 499 U.S. 919 (1991); and *United States v. Hoflin*, 880 F.2d 1033 (9th Cir. 1989), *cert. denied*, 493 U.S. 1083 (1990). *Cf. United States v. Speach*, 968 F.2d 795 (9th Cir. 1992), distinguishing the knowledge requirement under RCRA § 3008(d)(1)(knowingly transporting hazardous waste to an unpermitted facility) from that under § 3008(d)(2)(A).

2. Courts have routinely held that a RCRA criminal defendant need "know" that the material in question was a "hazardous waste" as defined in the RCRA statute or regulations (see chapter 2). The defendant must know that she is handling hazardous

waste, but that knowledge is readily established. The Ninth Circuit upheld a jury instruction requiring proof that the defendant "knew that the chemical wastes had the potential to be harmful to others or the environment." *United States v. Hoflin,* 880 F.2d at 1039. The Fourth Circuit (and others) have quoted the Supreme Court for the proposition that:

> [W]here, as here ... , dangerous *** or obnoxious waste materials are involved, the probability of regulation is so great that anyone who is aware that he is in possession of them or dealing with them must be presumed to be aware of the regulation.

United States v. Dee, 912 F.2d at 745, *quoting United States v. International Minerals & Chemical Corp.,* 402 U.S. 558, 565 (1971).

3. As crucial as is the element of knowledge, the courts have been less-than-exacting in terms of the means whereby knowledge can be proven. Even in *Johnson & Towers,* which requires as much proof of knowledge as any case, the Third Circuit underscored that such proof may be inferred.

In light of the fact that knowledge of the law need not be proven or, as in the Third Circuit, it may be proven by circumstantial evidence, what is the difference between a civil and a criminal violation of RCRA? How would you advise a Vice President for Environmental Affairs, for example, of his or her potential criminal liability for RCRA violations committed by employees under his or her supervision? Of what significance is prosecutorial discretion in determining whether to pursue a matter civilly, criminally, or both? Why might the government decide to invoke both civil and criminal enforcement authorities in some situations?

4. *U.S. v. MacDonald & Watson Waste Oil Co.* addresses several key issues regarding criminal enforcement under RCRA and CERCLA. The portions of the opinion excerpted below focus principally on the applicability of the "responsible corporate officer doctrine" to RCRA prosecutions. The excerpt also illustrates the sort of facts sufficient to sustain a conviction for the knowing violation of RCRA's criminal provisions.

Footnotes 15-18 and associated text refer to several of the other leading cases construing RCRA's knowledge requirement, and how it may or must be proven.

Portions of the opinion not included in this excerpt concern the EPA's residual authority to enforce RCRA violations in states authorized to implement the RCRA program (an issue addressed in *Harmon Electronics*), the elements necessary to prove a criminal violation of RCRA, and the reporting requirement under CERCLA § 103 regarding releases of hazardous substances. The CERCLA portion of the opinion appears in chapter 16.

UNITED STATES v. MACDONALD & WATSON WASTE OIL CO.
933 F.2d 35 (1st Cir. 1991)

Before CAMPBELL, Circuit Judge, TIMBERS, Senior Circuit Judge of the Second Circuit, and CYR, Circuit Judge.
CAMPBELL, Circuit Judge.

This appeal concerns the criminal liability of individuals and corporations under hazardous waste disposal laws.

Following a jury trial in the district court, appellants were convicted, *inter alia*, of having violated criminal provisions of the Resource Conservation and Recovery Act ("RCRA") and the Comprehensive Environmental Response, Compensation and Liability Act ("CERCLA").

The indictment originally contained 53 counts. By September 11, 1989, when the trial began, 16 counts had been dismissed and eight severed; and, during trial 12 more counts were dismissed on the government's motion, leaving 17 for submission to the jury. The submitted counts all related to the transportation and disposal of toluene waste from the Master Chemical Company. Appellants were convicted on all 17 counts, as follows: MacDonald & Watson Waste Oil Co. ("MacDonald & Watson"), Faust Ritarossi, Frances Slade and Eugene K. D'Allesandro were convicted, on two counts each, of knowingly transporting and causing the transportation of hazardous waste, namely toluene and soil contaminated with toluene, to a facility which did not have a permit, in violation of RCRA, § 3008(d)(1), 42 U.S.C. § 6928(d)(1). MacDonald & Watson and Narragansett Improvement Co. ("NIC") were convicted of knowingly treating, storing and disposing of hazardous waste, namely toluene and soil contaminated with toluene, without a permit, in violation of RCRA, § 3008(d)(2)(A), 42 U.S.C. § 6928(d)(2)(A).

MacDonald & Watson and NIC were convicted of failing to report the release of a hazardous substance into the environment in violation of CERCLA, § 103(b)(3), 42 U.S.C. § 9603(b)(3).

MacDonald & Watson was convicted of making false statements in violation of 18 U.S.C. § 1001 and of mail fraud in violation of 18 U.S.C. § 1341.

I. FACTS

Located in Boston, Massachusetts, Master Chemical Company manufactured chemicals primarily for use in the shoe industry. Master Chemical had been owned by the Estate of Moses Weinman (hereinafter "the Estate"), which was the principal in transactions with appellants. Among the chemicals Master Chemical used was toluene, which it stored in a two thousand gallon underground storage tank. When Master Chemical personnel discovered in the late fall or early winter of 1982 that water was entering the tank and contaminating the toluene, the tank was emptied and its use discontinued. In 1984, Master Chemical Company was sold, and the toluene tank was excavated and removed. A Master Chemical employee testified that he found a small hole in the tank, and that the soil surrounding the tank appeared black and wet and smelled of toluene.

An environmental consulting firm, Goldberg-Zoino & Associates, Inc. ("GZA"), was retained to assist in the cleanup. GZA prepared a study of the site and solicited a bid from MacDonald & Watson for the excavation, transportation, and disposal of the toluene-contaminated soil. MacDonald & Watson, a company with offices in Johnstown, Rhode Island, was in the business of transporting and disposing of waste oils and contaminated soil. MacDonald & Watson operated a disposal facility on land in Providence, Rhode Island, known as the "Poe Street Lot," leased from appellant NIC. MacDonald & Watson operated the Poe Street Lot under NIC's Rhode Island RCRA permit, which authorized the disposal at the lot of *liquid* hazardous wastes and soils contaminated with non-hazardous wastes such as petroleum products. Neither NIC nor MacDonald & Watson held a RCRA permit authorizing them to dispose of *solid* hazardous wastes such as toluene-contaminated soil at the lot. At the Rhode Island administrative hearing held when NIC sought its permit, appellant D'Allesandro, president of MacDonald & Watson, testified that hazardous waste operations at the Poe Street Lot would be managed by MacDonald & Watson and that he would be the manager of the facility there. According to the terms of NIC's lease of the Poe Street Lot to MacDonald & Watson, NIC retained responsibility for compliance with state and federal law with respect to permitting and operating the hazardous waste treatment and storage facilities.

The Estate accepted MacDonald & Watson's bid to remove and clean up the contaminated soil. The Estate's attorney, Deborah Shadd, discussed the proposed arrangement with appellant Slade, MacDonald & Watson's employee, and sent Slade a contract under which MacDonald & Watson would remove "contaminated soil and toluene." Shadd asked Slade to review the contract. Shadd also asked Slade to have it signed for MacDonald & Watson, which she did. Thereafter, appellant Ritarossi, another employee of MacDonald & Watson, supervised the transportation of the toluene-contaminated soil from Master Chemical to the Poe Street Lot in nine 25-yard dump truck loads and one 20-yard load. A Massachusetts hazardous waste manifest accompanied each truckload, bearing the Massachusetts hazardous waste code M-001.[2] Four of the manifests bore Ritarossi's signature. Prior to acceptance of the waste at the Poe Street Lot, MacDonald & Watson employees received an "Authorization to Accept Shipment of Spill Cleanup Material" form bearing Slade's typed name, describing the spilled material as "toluene," and describing the "petroleum product and the material spilled into" as "toluene and gravel." At this point, a MacDonald & Watson employee stamped the manifests "Non-hazardous in Rhode Island, Accepted for Processing at Asphalt Production Plant." ***

---

[2] "M-001" is a Massachusetts code designating waste oil, which is considered hazardous under Massachusetts law but not under RCRA or Rhode Island law. No RCRA hazardous waste identification number was assigned to the waste.

A. *Sufficiency of the Evidence*
* * *

With respect to the convictions under RCRA, appellants contend that the evidence was insufficient to establish that the Master Chemical contaminated soil was a "hazardous waste" for purposes of RCRA.[3] They argue that petroleum constituents other than toluene were detected in the soil, (including benzene and methyl tert-butyl ether), and that another tank containing non-hazardous petroleum derivatives toluene and benzene was located near the site of the toluene tank. They also argue that testimony regarding water entering the toluene tank and the hole discovered when the tank was removed did not establish that the toluene tank leaked, because the water could have entered through a pipe and the hole could have resulted during tank removal. These arguments are not persuasive. Contamination with other non-hazardous chemicals would not render soil that was also contaminated with toluene a non-hazardous waste. Groundwater in the toluene tank excavation pit showed toluene at 360,000 parts per million, vastly greater than levels of any other chemical. This sample data, along with testimony regarding the soil's toluene smell, and other testimony, was plainly sufficient to enable the jury to find that the soil was contaminated with toluene and was a hazardous waste as defined in the relevant regulations implementing RCRA.

Appellant Frances Slade challenges the sufficiency of the evidence to convict her under § 3008(d)(1) of RCRA, which penalizes, "Any person who ... (1) *knowingly* transports or causes to be transported any hazardous waste identified or listed under this subchapter to a facility which does not have a permit under this subchapter...." (Emphasis supplied). She contends that the evidence was insufficient to prove that her actions on behalf of MacDonald & Watson were taken with knowledge that the material involved was a RCRA hazardous waste. She complains that the prosecution relied "exclusively" on the testimony of the Estate's lawyer, Deborah Shadd, who dealt with Slade and sent her the contract covering transportation and disposal of the Master Chemical waste. This evidence, Slade contends, does not establish that Slade actually reviewed the contract and specifications, or would have learned from these the specific nature of the contaminated soil. Further, she argues that neither the contract nor the attached specifications identified the contaminating substance as commercially pure toluene.

We disagree that the evidence was insufficient for the jury to infer Slade's knowledge concerning soil contaminated with commercial chemical product toluene, the hazardous waste charged. There was testimony from a former MacDonald & Watson employee that Slade was "in charge of material coming in and coming out of

---

[3] Under the relevant regulation, 40 C.F.R. § 261.33(d), the following are hazardous wastes when they are discarded or intended to be discarded:

> Any ... contaminated soil ... resulting from the cleanup of a spill into or on any land or water of any commercial chemical product ... having the generic name listed in paragraph ... (f) of this section.

Commercial toluene is one such listed chemical product. Rhode Island's regulations, by incorporation of 40 C.F.R. § 261.33(d) and (f), similarly list commercial chemical product toluene and soil contaminated therewith as hazardous wastes.

MacDonald & Watson to Narragansett Improvement." There was evidence that Slade had attended state compliance inspections. The jury could infer that she was knowledgeable as to what substances were allowed, and what were disallowed under NIC's permit. It could also infer from her responsibilities and her dealings with Deborah Shadd that she reviewed the contract and specifications Shadd sent to her, and learned therefrom the nature of the substance. Attorney Shadd's May 29, 1986, letter of transmission to Slade requested her to "review the enclosed agreement, particularly the first four pages," and then arrange for it to be signed before a Notary Public by an authorized representative of MacDonald & Watson. Shadd's letter to Slade also requested her to send copies of MacDonald & Watson's licenses to transport and dispose of hazardous waste, further indicating that hazardous waste was involved and that the question of legality and a proper permit was critical. The first page of the enclosed agreement recited that the contractor "agrees to remove and dispose of contaminated soil and toluene," and would do so "in accordance with all applicable federal, state, and local laws, regulations, and requirements." The specifications attached stated that soil "contaminated with toluene and lesser amounts of other volatile organic compounds has been identified ... at the site of a formerly existing 2,000 gallon underground storage tank used *for the storage of toluene*." (Emphasis supplied.) Clearly, Slade was on notice that more than a mere petroleum by-product was involved. The specifications also conditioned disposal of the contaminated soil at MacDonald & Watson's facility upon soil characteristics meeting "criteria for disposal at this facility." The jury could reasonably infer that Slade received Shadd's letter and the enclosed contract, and followed Shadd's directions, including her directions to review it, especially since the contract was thereafter executed by the firm's controller, Naples, who returned it to Shadd. We find the evidence sufficient, therefore, for the jury to have inferred that Slade knew the material was the hazardous waste in question.[4]

Ritarossi contends that the evidence was insufficient to prove that he either knew that the material shipped to NIC was subject to RCRA regulation as toluene-contaminated soil or to prove he knew the substance and limitations of NIC's permit. However, Ritarossi could be found to have signed several of the "Authorization to Accept Shipment" forms which describes the "spilled material" as toluene and provides "toluene and gravel" as the "Description of petroleum product spilled and material spilled into." Joseph Weinman (son of Moses Weinman) testified that he discussed the circumstances surrounding the leaking toluene tank with Ritarossi during excavation of the tank. Moreover, a GZA environmental consultant testified that he

---

[4] Slade also contends that the evidence was insufficient to prove that she *caused* the transportation of the material under 42 U.S.C. § 6928(d)(1). Based on her position of responsibility with MacDonald & Watson (in particular her being, as testified, in charge of material coming into the NIC facility), and the fact that the contract she reviewed and handled with Master Chemical called for MacDonald & Watson to remove and dispose of contaminated soil and toluene from the original site to the MacDonald & Watson facility, the jury could reasonably conclude that Slade's role in negotiating, reviewing and facilitating the contract on behalf of MacDonald & Watson directly assisted in causing the transportation of the material. Additionally, Slade's typed name appeared on documents in connection with the shipment and delivery.

asked Ritarossi to include options in MacDonald & Watson's bid both for disposal at MacDonald & Watson's facility and for disposal at an out-of-state RCRA secure landfill because the consultant did not know whether MacDonald & Watson had the proper permits to dispose of the material at their facility. We find sufficient evidence from which the jury could determine that Ritarossi knew the material was toluene-contaminated soil and also to infer that he either knew that NIC's permit did not permit acceptance of such material or, at very least, willfully failed to determine the material's status under NIC's permit.

* * *

C. *RCRA Violations*

MacDonald & Watson, D'Allesandro, Slade and Ritarossi were convicted of knowingly transporting, or causing the transportation of hazardous waste, i.e., toluene-contaminated soil, to a facility which does not have a permit, under 42 U.S.C. § 6928(d)(1). MacDonald & Watson and NIC were convicted of knowingly treating, storing and disposing of a hazardous waste without a permit, under § 6928(d)(2)(A). They now argue that their convictions were illegal because NIC did in fact have a Rhode Island RCRA permit, albeit one that did not allow disposal into its facility of toluene-contaminated soil. NIC's permit, instead, authorized acceptance of liquid RCRA hazardous wastes and non-hazardous solids, such as petroleum-contaminated solid materials. While NIC's permit, therefore, provided no authority to dispose of the hazardous waste in question, appellants contend they did not violate either prong of § 6928(d) because the statute only penalizes transportation "to a facility which does not have a permit under this subchapter," and disposal "without a permit under this subchapter."

We find this argument entirely unpersuasive. Sections (d)(1) and (d)(2)(A) both penalize unpermitted transportation and disposal of "*any* hazardous waste identified or listed under this subchapter" (emphasis supplied), thus embracing the hundreds of different noxious substances described and listed in EPA regulations. *See* 40 C.F.R. [Part 261] Subparts C and D. As these toxic wastes vary enormously in levels of toxicity and other characteristics, they require different kinds of facilities for safe disposal. In order to channel each waste to a proper disposal facility, Congress established a system of permits, with each permit indicating what wastes that particular facility may legally accept. Thus the statutory phrase "which does not have a permit" naturally conveys the meaning: "which does not have a permit for that substance." Having a permit for some different substance would frequently offer no more protection to the public than having no permit at all. Just as a deer hunting license does not imply a license to hunt duck, a facility "which does not have a permit" clearly implies, in this context, a facility which does not have a relevant permit. Any other construction would ignore the central object of the permit program, which is to limit the disposal of any given waste to an appropriate facility. ***

To construe subsection (d)(1) and subsection (d)(2)(A) as appellants urge would not only involve reading the word "permit" abnormally (i.e., as meaning an irrelevant permit as well as a relevant one), but would significantly weaken the protection against the danger that most concerned Congress, namely the improper disposal of toxic wastes.

* * *

D. *The Responsible Corporate Officer Doctrine*

D'Allesandro, the President and owner of MacDonald & Watson, contends that his conviction under RCRA, § 3008(d)(1), must be vacated because the district court incorrectly charged the jury regarding the element of knowledge in the case of a corporate officer. Section 3008(d)(1) penalizes "Any person who .... (1) *knowingly* transports or causes to be transported any hazardous waste identified or listed under this subchapter .... to a facility which does not have a permit ...." (Emphasis supplied.) In his closing, the prosecutor conceded that the government had "no direct evidence that Eugene D'Allesandro actually knew that the Master Chemical shipments were coming in," i.e., were being transported to the Poe Street Lot under contract with his company. The prosecution did present evidence, however, that D'Allesandro was not only the President and owner of MacDonald & Watson but was a "hands-on" manager of that relatively small firm. There was also proof that that firm leased the Poe Street Lot from NIC, and managed it, and that D'Allesandro's subordinates had contracted for and transported the Master Chemical waste for disposal at that site. The government argued that D'Allesandro was guilty of violating § 3008(d)(1) because, as the responsible corporate officer, he was in a position to ensure compliance with RCRA and had failed to do so even after being warned by a consultant on two earlier occasions that other shipments of toluene-contaminated soil had been received from other customers, and that such material violated NIC's permit. In the government's view, any failure to prove D'Allesandro's actual knowledge of the Master Chemical contract and shipments was irrelevant to his criminal responsibility under § 3008(d)(1) for those shipments. The court apparently accepted the government's theory. It instructed the jury as follows:

> When an individual Defendant is also a corporate officer, the Government may prove that individual's knowledge in either of two ways. The first way is to demonstrate that the Defendant had actual knowledge of the act in question. The second way is to establish that the Defendant was what is called a responsible officer of the corporation committing the act. In order to prove that a person is a responsible corporate officer three things must be shown.
>
> First, it must be shown that the person is an officer of the corporation, not merely an employee.
>
> Second, it must be shown that the officer had direct responsibility for the activities that are alleged to be illegal. Simply being an officer or even the president of a corporation is not enough. The Government must prove that the person had a responsibility to supervise the activities in question.
>
> And the third requirement is that the officer must have known or believed that the illegal activity of the type alleged occurred.

The court's phrasing of the third element at first glance seems ambiguous: it could be read to require actual knowledge of the Master Chemical shipments themselves. We are satisfied, however, that the court meant only what it literally said: D'Allesandro must have known or believed that illegal shipments *of the type* alleged had previously occurred. This tied into evidence that D'Allesandro had been advised of two earlier shipments of toluene-contaminated waste, and was told that such waste could not legally be received. For the court to require a finding that D'Allesandro knew of the alleged shipments themselves (i.e., the Master Chemical shipments), would have duplicated the court's earlier instruction on actual knowledge, and was not in accord with the government's theory.

D'Allesandro challenges this instruction, contending that the use of the "responsible corporate officer" doctrine is improper under § 3008(d)(1) which expressly calls for proof of knowledge, i.e., requires *scienter*. The government responds that the district court properly adapted the responsible corporate officer doctrine traditionally applied to strict liability offenses to this case, instructing the jury to find knowledge "that the illegal activity of the *type alleged* occurred,"—a finding that, together with the first two, made it reasonable to infer knowledge of the particular violation. We agree with D'Allesandro that the jury instructions improperly allowed the jury to find him guilty without finding he had actual knowledge of the alleged transportation of hazardous waste on July 30 and 31, 1986, from Master Chemical Company, Boston, Massachusetts, to NIC's site, knowledge being an element the statute requires. We must, therefore, reverse his conviction.

The seminal cases regarding the responsible corporate officer doctrine are *United States v. Dotterweich*, 320 U.S. 277 (1943), and *United States v. Park*, 421 U.S. 658 (1975). These cases concerned misdemeanor charges under the Federal Food, Drug, and Cosmetic Act, relating to the handling or shipping of adulterated or misbranded drugs or food. The offenses alleged in the informations failed to state a knowledge element, and the Court found that they, in fact, dispensed with a *scienter* requirement, placing "the burden of acting at hazard upon a person otherwise innocent but standing in responsible relation to a public danger." *Dotterweich*, 320 U.S. at 277. The Court in *Park* clarified that corporate officer liability in that situation requires only a finding that the officer had "authority with respect to the conditions that formed the basis of the alleged violations." But while *Dotterweich* and *Park* thus reflect what is now clear and well-established law in respect to public welfare statutes and regulations lacking an express knowledge or other *scienter* requirement, we know of no precedent for failing to give effect to a knowledge requirement that Congress has expressly included in a criminal statute. *Park*, 421 U.S. at 674. Especially is that so where, as here, the crime is a felony carrying possible imprisonment of five years and, for a second offense, ten.

The district court, nonetheless, applied here a form of the responsible corporate officer doctrine established in *Dotterweich* and *Park* for *strict liability* misdemeanors, as a substitute means for proving the explicit knowledge element of this RCRA felony, 42 U.S.C. § 6920(d)(1). As an alternative to finding actual knowledge, the district court permitted the prosecution to constructively establish defendant's knowledge if the jury found the following: (1) that the defendant was a corporate officer; (2) with responsibility to supervise the allegedly illegal activities; and (3) knew or believed "that the illegal activity of the type alleged occurred." As previously stated, the third element did not necessitate proof of knowledge of the Master Chemical shipments charged in the indictment, but simply proof of earlier occasions when D'Allesandro was told his firm had improperly accepted toluene-contaminated soil.

Contrary to the government's assertions, this instruction did more than simply permit the jury, if it wished, to infer knowledge of the Master Chemical shipments from relevant circumstantial evidence including D'Allesandro's responsibilities and activities as a corporate executive. With respect to circumstantial evidence, the district court properly instructed elsewhere that knowledge did not have to be proven by direct evidence but could be inferred from the defendant's conduct and other facts and circumstances. The court also instructed that the element of knowledge could be satisfied by proof of willful blindness.[15] These instructions allowed the jury to consider whether relevant circumstantial evidence established that D'Allesandro actually knew of the charged Master Chemical shipments. These would have sufficed had it merely been the court's purpose to point out that knowledge could be established by circumstantial evidence, although the court could, had it wished, have elaborated on the extent to which D'Allesandro's responsibilities and duties might lead to a reasonable inference that he knew of the Master Chemical transaction.

Instead, the district court charged, in effect, that proof that D'Allesandro was a responsible corporate officer would conclusively prove the element of his knowledge of the Master Chemical shipments. The jury was told that knowledge could be proven "in either of two ways." Besides demonstrating actual knowledge, the government could simply establish the defendant was a responsible corporate officer—the latter by showing three things, none of which, individually or collectively, necessarily established his actual knowledge of the illegal transportation charged. Under the district court's instruction, the jury's belief that the responsible corporate officer lacked actual knowledge of, and had not willfully blinded himself to, the criminal transportation alleged would be insufficient for acquittal so long as the officer knew or even

---

[15] The court instructed the jury generally regarding the element of knowledge as follows:

> An act is said to be done knowingly if it is done voluntarily and intentionally and not because of ignorance, mistake, accident or some other reason. The requirement that an act be done knowingly is designed to insure that a Defendant will not be convicted for an act that he did not intend to commit or the nature of which he did not understand. Proof that a Defendant acted knowingly or with knowledge of a particular fact does not require direct evidence of what was in that Defendant's mind. Whether a Defendant acted knowingly or with knowledge of a particular fact may be inferred from that Defendant's conduct, from that Defendant's familiarity with the subject matter in question or from all of the other facts and circumstances connected with the case.
>
> In determining whether a Defendant acted knowingly, you also may consider whether the Defendant deliberately closed his eyes to what otherwise would have been obvious. If so, the element of knowledge may be satisfied because a Defendant cannot avoid responsibility by purposefully avoiding learning the truth. However, mere negligence or mistake in not learning the facts is not sufficient to satisfy the element of knowledge.

erroneously believed that illegal activity of the same type had occurred on another occasion.

We have found no case, and the government cites none, where a jury was instructed that the defendant could be convicted of a federal crime *expressly requiring knowledge as an element,* solely by reason of a conclusive, or "mandatory" presumption of knowledge of the facts constituting the offense. The government's primary reliance on the Third Circuit's more limited decision in *Johnson & Towers,* 741 F.2d 662, 670, is misplaced. There, the court of appeals concluded that "knowingly" applies to all elements of the offense, including permit status, in RCRA § 3008(d)(2)(A). The court of appeals advised that proof of knowledge of the permit requirement and the nonexistence of the permit did not impose a great burden because such knowledge might, in a proper case, be inferred. Relying on the Supreme Court's decision in *United States v. International Minerals & Chemical Corp.,* 402 U.S. 558, 563 (1971),[16] the court of appeals emphasized "that under certain regulatory statutes requiring 'knowing' conduct, the government need prove only knowledge of the actions taken and not of the statute forbidding them." *Johnson & Towers,* 741 F.2d at 669,[17] *see also United States v. Dee,* 912 F.2d 741, 745-46 (4th Cir. 1990), *cert. denied,* 111 S. Ct. 1307 (1991) (knowledge of RCRA's prohibitions may be presumed; instruction that defendants had to know substances involved were chemicals, without requiring knowledge they were hazardous, was harmless error)***. Thus, this case supports only the position that knowledge of the law may be inferred,[18] and does not address knowledge of acts.

* * *

We agree with the decisions discussed above that knowledge may be inferred from circumstantial evidence, including position and responsibility of defendants such as corporate officers, as well as information provided to those defendants on prior

---

[16] In that case, the Supreme Court held that a statute regarding failure to record shipment of chemicals, and specifically proscribing "knowing violation of regulations" did not require knowledge of the regulations. The Court clearly stated that "knowledge of the shipment of the dangerous materials is required." 402 U.S. at 560. Thus, the Court reasoned that handlers of dangerous materials may be subject to different standards than others; it was only *knowledge of the regulations* that the Court found could be presumed. 402 U.S. at 565.

[17] The government also cites the *Hayes* and *Hoflin* decisions in support of its position. In *Hoflin,* as discussed above, the Ninth Circuit disagreed with the *Johnson & Towers* court and decided that knowledge of the nonexistence of a permit was not necessary for conviction under RCRA, § 3008(d)(2)(A). The *Hoflin* court, however, found that knowledge of the hazardous nature of the material disposed must be proven, and did not suggest that such knowledge could be irrebuttably presumed for corporate officers as the court instructed here. In *Hayes,* also discussed above, the Eleventh Circuit found knowledge of the nonexistence of a permit a required element under RCRA, § 3008(d)(1). There, the court of appeals simply found, "in this regulatory context a defendant acts knowingly if he willfully fails to determine the permit status of the facility." *Hayes,* 786 F.2d at 1504.

[18] Further, the court of appeals in *Johnson & Towers* did not indicate how knowledge may be inferred. To the extent the fact of permit nonexistence may be inferred, such inference may be from willful blindness or other circumstantial evidence. The court of appeals did not indicate that such facts could be irrebuttably presumed based on corporate position and facts unrelated to the specific alleged illegal activity charged.

occasions. Further, willful blindness to the facts constituting the offense may be sufficient to establish knowledge. However, the district court erred by instructing the jury that proof that a defendant was a responsible corporate officer, as described, would suffice to conclusively establish the element of knowledge expressly required under § 3008(d)(1). Simply because a responsible corporate officer believed that on a prior occasion illegal transportation occurred, he did not necessarily possess knowledge of the violation charged. In a crime having knowledge as an express element, a mere showing of official responsibility under *Dotterweich* and *Park* is not an adequate substitute for direct or circumstantial proof of knowledge.

NOTES

1. Compare the First Circuit's refusal in *MacDonald & Watson* to impose criminal liability on a corporate president who did not personally participate in the unlawful activities with the Eighth Circuit's affirmation of such liability for civil enforcement purposes in *United States v. NEPACCO*, 810 F.2d 726, *cert. denied,* 484 U.S. 848 (1987) (quoted in notes following *Environmental Waste Control* in subchapter A, above).

2. Although many aspects of RCRA enforcement are typical of the enforcement schemes under the other federal environmental regulatory statutes, significant differences in the statutory language should be noted. For example, the Clean Water Act expressly authorizes responsible corporate officer liability for criminal violations of the Act. 33 U.S.C. § 1319(c)(6).

C. Notice

Related to the concept of knowledge, for criminal liability purposes, is the concept of notice, which has both civil and criminal applications. In a regulatory environment characterized by mind-numbing regulatory provisions and reams (and gigabytes) of uncompiled, unindexed, guidance materials, to what extent must a regulated entity be able to discern the rules before being exposed to civil or criminal liability?

In the civil context, the most significant decision on this issue arose not under RCRA, but under an analogous regulatory scheme governing the handling of polychlorinated biphenyls (PCBs) under the Toxic Substances Control Act (TSCA).

GENERAL ELECTRIC CO. V. UNITED STATES ENVIRONMENTAL PROTECTION AGENCY
53 F.3d 1324 (D.C.Cir. 1995)

Before WALD, SILBERMAN, and TATEL, Circuit Judges.
TATEL, Circuit Judge.

The Environmental Protection Agency fined the General Electric Company $25,000 after concluding that it had processed polychlorinated biphenyls in a manner not authorized under EPA's interpretation of its regulations. We conclude that EPA's interpretation of those regulations is permissible, but because the regulations did not provide GE with fair warning of the agency's interpretation, we vacate the finding of liability and set aside the fine.

I.

GE's Apparatus Service Shop in Chamblee, Georgia decommissioned large electric transformers. Inside these transformers was a "dielectric fluid" that contained high concentrations of polychlorinated biphenyls ("PCBs"), which are good conductors of electricity. PCBs are also dangerous pollutants. *** Recognizing the dangers of PCBs, Congress has required their regulation under the Toxic Substances Control Act. 15 U.S.C. §§ 2601- 29 (1988 & Supp. V 1993) ("TSCA"); *id.* at § 2605(e). Pursuant to TSCA, the EPA promulgated detailed regulations governing the manufacture, use, and disposal of PCBs.

Because GE's transformers were contaminated with PCBs, the company had to comply with the disposal requirements of 40 C.F.R. § 761.60. Section 761.60(b)(1) requires the disposal of transformers by either incinerating the transformer, 40 C.F.R. § 761.60(b)(1)(i)(A), or by placing it into a chemical waste landfill after the PCB-laced dielectric fluid has been drained and the transformer rinsed with a PCB solvent, *id.* at (B). GE chose the "drain-and-landfill" option of section 761.60(b)(1)(i)(B).

The drain-and-landfill alternative required GE to dispose of the liquid drained from the transformer "in accordance with" the terms of section 761.60(a). Since the dielectric fluid contained extremely high concentrations of PCBs, the relevant provision of section 761.60(a) was section (1), a catch-all section applicable to liquids contaminated with more than 500 parts per million ("ppm") of PCBs. This section required those disposing of these particularly dangerous materials to do so solely by incineration in an approved facility. 40 C.F.R. § 761.60(a). In accord with that requirement, GE incinerated the dielectric fluid after draining it from the transformers. It then soaked the transformers in a PCB solvent—in this case, freon—for 18 hours, drained the contaminated solvent, and immediately incinerated it as well.

In March, 1987, GE changed these procedures, beginning a process that ultimately led to the EPA complaint in this case. While GE continued to incinerate the dielectric fluid, it began a recycling process that recovered a portion of the dirty solvent through distillation. ***

GE and EPA agree that the regulations require the incineration of the solvent. They disagree about whether the intervening distillation and recycling process violated the regulations. EPA argues that section 761.60(b)(1)(i)(B) required GE to dispose of all the dirty solvent "in accordance with the requirements of [section 761.60(a)(1)]"—i.e., by immediate incineration. GE did not think that section prohibited it from taking intermediate steps like distillation prior to incinerating the PCBs. To GE, distillation was permitted by section 761.20(c)(2), which allows the processing and distribution of PCBs "for purposes of disposal in accordance with the requirements of § 761.60." GE believed that this section authorized intermediate processing "for purposes of disposal"—processing such as distillation—as long as it complied with the other requirements of the PCB regulations like those relating to the management of spills, storage, and labelling of PCB materials. EPA has not alleged that GE's distillation process failed to comply with those requirements. In fact, as the ALJ later concluded, distillation reduced the amount of contaminated materials, thus producing environmental benefits.

Despite those benefits, EPA charged the company with violating the PCB disposal regulations. After a hearing, an ALJ agreed and assessed a $25,000 fine. On appeal, the Environmental Appeals Board modified the ALJ's reasoning, but agreed with the disposition of the complaint and upheld the $25,000 penalty. In other proceedings, the agency found the company liable for distillation it performed in six other locations, but suspended the fines for those violations pending the outcome of this appeal.

II.

GE argues that EPA's complaint is based on an arbitrary, capricious, and otherwise impermissible interpretation of its regulations. See 5 U.S.C. § 706(2)(A) (1988). To prevail on this claim, GE faces an uphill battle. We accord an agency's interpretation of its own regulations a "high level of deference," accepting it "unless it is plainly wrong." *General Carbon Co. v. OSHRC*, 860 F.2d 479, 483 (D.C.Cir.1988). ***

* * *

In this case, EPA's Appeals Board concluded that section 761.60(b)(1)(i)(B) of the regulations required GE to dispose of the dirty solvent "in accordance with" a disposal method approved under section 761.60(a). Because distillation was not such a method, it concluded that GE had violated the regulations. GE argues that EPA's reading of the regulations is impermissible because all the solvent was eventually incinerated, because distillation is not a means of disposal but merely pre-disposal processing, and because the regulations explicitly allow pre-disposal processing to occur prior to the ultimate incineration. While GE's claims have merit, they do not demonstrate that the agency's interpretation of this highly complex regulatory scheme is impermissible.

* * *

Particularly in the context of this comprehensive and technically complex regulatory scheme, EPA's interpretation of the regulations is permissible. Although

GE's interpretation may also be reasonable, at stake here is the proper disposal of a highly toxic substance. We defer to the reasonable judgment of the agency to which Congress has entrusted the development of rules and regulations to ensure its safe disposal.

Had EPA merely required GE to comply with its interpretation, this case would be over. But EPA also found a violation and imposed a fine. Even if EPA's regulatory interpretation is permissible, the company argues, the violation and fine cannot be sustained consistent with fundamental principles of due process because GE was never on notice of the agency interpretation it was fined for violating. It is to this issue that we now turn.

III.

Due process requires that parties receive fair notice before being deprived of property. The due process clause thus "prevents ... deference from validating the application of a regulation that fails to give fair warning of the conduct it prohibits or requires." *Gates & Fox Co. v. OSHRC*, 790 F.2d 154, 156 (D.C.Cir.1986). In the absence of notice—for example, where the regulation is not sufficiently clear to warn a party about what is expected of it—an agency may not deprive a party of property by imposing civil or criminal liability. ***

Although the agency must always provide "fair notice" of its regulatory interpretations to the regulated public, in many cases the agency's pre-enforcement efforts to bring about compliance will provide adequate notice. If, for example, an agency informs a regulated party that it must seek a permit for a particular process, but the party begins processing without seeking a permit, the agency's pre-violation contact with the regulated party has provided notice, and we will enforce a finding of liability as long as the agency's interpretation was permissible. In some cases, however, the agency will provide no pre-enforcement warning, effectively deciding "to use a citation [or other punishment] as the initial means for announcing a particular interpretation"—or for making its interpretation clear. This, GE claims, is what happened here. In such cases, we must ask whether the regulated party received, or should have received, notice of the agency's interpretation in the most obvious way of all: by reading the regulations. If, by reviewing the regulations and other public statements issued by the agency, a regulated party acting in good faith would be able to identify, with "ascertainable certainty," the standards with which the agency expects parties to conform, then the agency has fairly notified a petitioner of the agency's interpretation.

* * *

In *Rollins Environmental Services, Inc. v. EPA*, as in this case, the EPA accused the petitioner of failing properly to incinerate a solvent that it had used to rinse out containers—in that case, concrete basins—that had once contained PCBs. 937 F.2d at 651. The relevant rule for rinsing basins stated that "[t]he solvent may be reused for decontamination until it contains 50 ppm PCB. The solvent shall then be disposed of as a PCB in accordance with § 761.60(a)." *Id.* Rollins reused the solvent several times, but it never reached a concentration of 50 ppm PCBs, and so Rollins disposed of the solvent in a way that was not TSCA-approved. An ALJ found a violation of the regulation, but a second ALJ assessed no financial penalty because he thought the regulations "unclear" and that Rollins' interpretation "had a definite plausibility." *Id.* On appeal within the agency, the reviewing officer concluded that the regulation was clear and imposed a $25,000 fine. *Id.* at 652.

Although we held that EPA's interpretation of the regulations was permissible, we agreed with the second ALJ that the language of the regulation was ambiguous and that both interpretations were reasonable. We also pointed out that "significant disagreement" existed among EPA's various offices regarding the proper interpretation of the language. *Id.* at 653. But Rollins had failed to raise the due process issue in his briefs or before the agency, so we allowed the violation to stand. Nonetheless, we concluded that the ambiguity of the regulation justified rescinding the fine against Rollins under TSCA's mitigation provision, which required the agency to take into account the "extent, and gravity of the violation ... the degree of culpability, and such other matters as justice may require" in setting the amount of the penalty. *Id.* at 654 (citing 15 U.S.C. § 2615(a)(2)(B)). ***

Unlike in *Rollins*, GE has clearly raised the due process "notice" issue in this case. Although we defer to EPA's interpretation regarding distillation because it is "logically consistent with the language of the regulation[s]," *Rollins*, 937 F.2d at 652, we must, because the agency imposed a fine, nonetheless determine whether that interpretation is "ascertainably certain" from the regulations. *** [W]e conclude that the interpretation is so far from a reasonable person's understanding of the regulations that they could not have fairly informed GE of the agency's perspective. We therefore reverse the agency's finding of liability and the related fine.

On their face, the regulations reveal no rule or combination of rules providing fair notice that they prohibit pre-disposal processes such as distillation. To begin with, such notice would be provided only if it was "reasonably comprehensible to people of good faith" that distillation is indeed a means of "disposal." *McElroy Electronics Corp. v. FCC*, 990 F.2d 1351, 1358 (D.C.Cir.1993). While EPA can permissibly conclude, given the sweeping regulatory definition of "disposal," that distillation is a means of disposal, such a characterization nonetheless strays far from the common understanding of the word's meaning. A person "of good faith," would not reasonably expect distillation—a process which did not and was not intended to prevent the ultimate destruction of PCBs—to be barred as an unapproved means of "disposal."

Not only do the regulations fail clearly to bar distillation, they apparently permit it. Section 761.20(c)(2) permits processing and distribution of PCBs "for purposes of disposal." This language would seem to allow parties to conduct certain pre-disposal processes without authorization as long as they facilitate the ultimate disposal of PCBs and are done "in compliance with the requirements of this Part"—i.e., in accordance with other relevant regulations governing the handling, labelling, and transportation of PCBs. § 761.20(c)(2). EPA argues—permissibly, as we concluded above—that the section allows parties to "use" PCBs in the described manner, but that those uses must still comply with the disposal requirements of section 761.60, including the requirement that unauthorized methods of disposal receive a disposal permit from the agency. This permissible interpretation, however, is by no means the most obvious interpretation of the regulation, particularly since, under EPA's view, section 761.20(c)(2) would not need to exist at all. If every process "for purposes of disposal" also requires a disposal permit, section 761.20(c)(2) does nothing but lull regulated parties into a false sense of security by hinting that their processing "for purposes of disposal" is authorized. While the mere presence of such a regulatory trap does not reflect an irrational agency interpretation, it obscures the agency's interpretation of the regulations sufficiently to convince us that GE did not have fair notice that distillation was prohibited.

* * *

Our concern about the regulations' lack of clarity is heightened by several additional factors. First, GE and EPA have had considerable difficulty even identifying which portion of section 761.60(a) applied to the disposal of the dirty solvent. ***

Second,*** it is unlikely that regulations provide adequate notice when different divisions of the enforcing agency disagree about their meaning. Such is the case here. In 1984, one EPA regional office concluded that companies could distill PCB materials without seeking additional authorization from the EPA. Although GE never proved it, the company asserted in its initial replies to the agency that a second regional office had told it the same thing. While we accept EPA's argument that the regional office interpretation was wrong, confusion at the regional level is yet more evidence that the agency's interpretation of its own regulation could not possibly have provided fair notice.

Finally, EPA's position regarding the basis for GE's liability has subtly shifted throughout this case. ***

Notwithstanding the lack of clarity in the regulations themselves, the agency argues that GE was nevertheless on notice of its interpretation. It begins by pointing to a policy statement on PCB "separation activities" issued in 1983, claiming that it provided a sufficiently clear statement of its belief that distillation required agency approval. We disagree. Although some language in that policy statement does appear to address activities like distillation, requiring further approval for "activities that can be construed to be part of, or an initiation of a disposal activity," the statement's primary focus is on preventing parties from using such processes to circumvent the disposal requirements. EPA, TSCA Compliance Program Policy No. 6-PCB-2 at 1 (August 16, 1983). As the statement notes, "it is possible to physically separate PCBs from liquids ... without EPA approval as long as these liquids ... are treated (used, stored, disposed of, etc.) as if they still contain their original PCB concentration." *Id.* at 3. A reasonable interpretation of this language is that a physical separation process that is neither intended to avoid nor actually avoids the disposal requirements for PCBs is permissible "without EPA approval" as long as it is handled in a manner consistent with the PCB regulations. GE's distillation was such a process, since the solvent was at all times handled as if it contained high concentrations of PCBs. EPA's contrary understanding of the policy statement's language is not so obvious that we consider GE to have had fair notice of the agency's reading.

* * *

We thus conclude that EPA did not provide GE with fair warning of its interpretation of the regulations. Where, as here, the regulations and other policy statements are unclear, where the petitioner's interpretation is reasonable, and where the agency itself struggles to provide a definitive reading of the regulatory requirements, a regulated party is not "on notice" of the agency's ultimate interpretation of the regulations, and may not be punished. EPA thus may not hold GE responsible in any way—either financially or in future enforcement proceedings—for the actions charged in this case. ***

NOTES

1. Although *GE* thus far lacks progeny under RCRA, the TSCA regulatory structure governing PCBs is so similar to the RCRA regulatory structure that the case is worth noting. The Ninth Circuit adopted a similar analysis, without citing *GE*, in determining that a company's Clean Air Act violation was a one-time, rather than a continuous, violation. *United States v. Trident Seafoods Corp.*, 60 F.3d 556 (9th Cir. 1995).

2. Given the extraordinary complexity of the RCRA regulations defining hazardous waste (40 C.F.R. Part 261), a notice defense was perhaps inevitable. Such defense was raised in the following criminal action. What more fitting way to conclude the RCRA materials than a criminal enforcement action that returns to the threshold RCRA issue, the definition of solid waste?

UNITED STATES V. WHITE
766 F.Supp. 873 (E.D.Wash. 1991)

McDONALD, District Judge.

* * *

I.

The instant indictment charges five defendants (Jack D. White, Robert Dickman, Gary McCourt, Steven Steed, and Puregro, Inc.) in four separate counts involving the alleged illegal storage, transportation, and disposal of hazardous waste under The Resource Conservation and Recovery Act (hereinafter RCRA), one count of knowing endangerment under RCRA, and one count of applying a pesticide in a manner inconsistent with its labelling under The Federal Insecticide, Fungicide, and Rodenticide Act (hereafter FIFRA).

* * *

II.

In late 1982 an evaporator tank was installed on the Puregro facility near Pasco, Washington. With the advent of stricter regulations regarding pesticides and other hazardous wastes in the early 1980's, disposal of waste pesticide materials and rinseates had become more difficult and expensive. Purportedly the purpose of the evaporator tank was to reduce the volume of pesticide rinseates which were produced at the facility from washing out various equipment and containers so that disposal of those rinseates would be less expensive.

The tank was used as a repository for many different types of pesticide rinseates over approximately five years, from late 1982 to May, 1987. Accordingly [sic] to the government, Puregro employees were instructed to place pesticide rinseates into the tank until it was full. Moreover, the government contends that Puregro kept no records of what was put into the tank. Some of these rinseates were allegedly contaminated with Telone II (1,3-Dichloropropene).

Sometime in 1986, the defendants contacted Crosby & Overton, Inc., referred to by the government as a hazardous waste disposal company and by the defendants as an environmental consulting firm, regarding the material in the evaporator tank. After analyzing the material Crosby & Overton advised that the material would not have to be handled as a hazardous waste if Puregro could find a use for the rinsate consistent with its intended use and also in a manner consistent with Department of Agriculture guidelines. Crosby & Overton further advised that if the material is declared waste, it must be handled as a hazardous waste.

On May 9, 1987 the defendants loaded the material from the tank into a truck and on May 12, 1987, sprayed the material on a field. The spraying allegedly resulted in endangering many citizens in the area.

Count 1 alleges a conspiracy to violate RCRA by storing, transporting, and disposing of hazardous waste without a permit, specifically 1,3-Dichloropropene. Counts 2, 3, and 4 allege violations of RCRA with respect to storage, transportation, and disposal of hazardous waste without a permit, specifically 1,3-Dichloropropene. Count 5 alleges a knowing endangerment under RCRA with respect to hazardous waste, specifically 1,3-Dichloropropene. Count 6 alleges application of the pesticides Dyfonate and Telone II in a manner inconsistent with their labelling.

III.

JOINT MOTION TO DISMISS FOR DENIAL OF DUE PROCESS, BASED ON THE VOID FOR VAGUENESS DOCTRINE OR, ALTERNATIVELY, BASED ON EPA'S UNAUTHORIZED EXTENSION OF THE RCRA REGULATIONS TO MATERIALS NOT "WASTE"

The defendants move to dismiss counts 1 through 5 of the Indictment on the grounds that the regulations that define "solid waste" and "hazardous waste" are impermissibly vague.

* * *

The standards for evaluating vagueness were set forth in *Grayned v. City of Rockford*, 408 U.S. 104, 108-109 (1972):

> Vague laws offend several important values. First, because we assume that man is free to steer between lawful and unlawful conduct, we insist that laws give the person of ordinary intelligence a reasonable opportunity to know what is prohibited, so that he may act accordingly. Vague laws may trap the innocent by not providing fair warning. Second, if arbitrary and discriminatory enforcement is to be prevented, laws must provide explicit standards for those who apply them. A vague law impermissibly delegates basic policy matters to policemen, judges, and juries for resolution on an *ad hoc* and subjective basis, with the attendant dangers of arbitrary and discriminatory applications.

* * *

The defendants' 44-page memorandum is not only lengthy, but appears to have been written in an intentionally confusing manner to lend support to their vagueness argument. *** The defendants admit that there is nothing unusually complex or vague about the language of the charging statute itself. Instead, they contend that the problem is with the regulations promulgated to identify and list particular hazardous wastes. Specifically, that the regulatory scheme created under RCRA, defining the relevant terms "solid waste" and "hazardous waste," has rendered these terms unintelligible to the ordinary person and vague as applied in this case. The defendants contend that Puregro's personnel believed that the contents of the evaporator tank were a "product" beneficially used and not a "waste" subject to the federal hazardous waste regulations. While framing their argument as "vague as applied in this case," the defendants' memorandum reads more like a challenge to the entire regulatory scheme. However, based upon the defendants' unequivocal assertion that their challenge is limited to the regulations as they are applied in this case, the court shall so limit its inquiry.

* * *

Defendants *** refer to the regulations where they argue that the language becomes impermissibly vague. Pages 18-43 of their memorandum is not only an attempt to explain why the regulations are vague but also a demonstration as to the difficulty in weeding through them. After reading and rereading the regulations several times, the court recognizes, as do the defendants, that the regulations are in fact dense, turgid, and a bit circuitous.

Appendix I to 40 C.F.R. § 260 is "designed to help those who are unfamiliar with the hazardous waste control program to determine with which, if any, of the regulations they should comply." It is essentially a road map for the regulations as they relate to hazardous waste. Appendix I first directs its reader to section 40 C.F.R. § 261.2 for a definition of solid waste.

> (a)(1) A *solid waste* is any discarded material that is not excluded by § 261.4(a) or that is not excluded by variance granted under §§ 260.30 and 260.31.

> (2) A *discarded* material is any material which is:

(i) *Abandoned*, as explained in paragraph (b) of this section; or

(ii) *Recycled*, as explained in paragraph (c) of this section; or

(iii) Considered *inherently wastelike*, as explained in paragraph (d) of this section.

40 C.F.R. § 261.2(a)(1) & (2). The defendants repeatedly question the clarity of the definition of discarded. Apparently this supports the defendants' contention that they did not discard the material, but instead used or applied it in a beneficial manner, and corresponding conclusion that the material could not have been a solid waste. Section 261.2 sets forth a list of materials that are to be considered discarded. The list includes materials which are abandoned, recycled and those materials considered inherently wastelike. These terms are further defined in section 261.2. As the government and this court both readily recognize, the series of definitions creates an organization which progresses from more general terms to more specific terms.

Once solid waste is defined under the regulations one must refer to 40 C.F.R. § 261.3 which defines hazardous waste ***.

The regulations provide, in part, that 1,3-Dichloropropene is a hazardous waste if and when it is discarded or intended to be discarded by being disposed of, burned or incinerated, or accumulated, stored, or treated (but not recycled) before being abandoned by being disposed of, burned, or incinerated. 1,3-Dichloropropene is also considered a hazardous waste if it is otherwise applied to the land in lieu of its original intended use or when it is contained in products that are applied to the land in lieu of their original intended use.

The defendants argue that the repetition of the words "disposed of" and "discarded" makes the definition of solid waste circular and, therefore, vague. However, the defendants never afford the words their common meanings. While contending the regulations are vague as applied, defendants' motion actually appears to be a disguised argument that it was not their *intent* to *discard* or *dispose* of the material in the evaporator tank, and thus, under the regulations the material could not be considered a solid waste and consequently, not a hazardous waste. This determination, however, is a question of fact for the jury.

The court's conclusion is further supported by the defendants' own memorandum which states that the government is "seeking to apply serious criminal penalties to materials *not* 'truly discarded or disposed of,' but rather held until they could be put to a beneficial use." Apparently the defendants understand the regulations well enough to recognize that they were not permitted to "truly discard or dispose of" the material in the tank. They also appear to understand the regulations well enough to conclude that spraying the material on the field was not discarding or disposing of it.

In determining whether the regulations are vague as applied, the court must consider the facts as charged in the Indictment. The purported purpose of the evaporator tank was to reduce the volume of pesticide rinseates for disposal. Allegedly, for a five year period the defendants placed different rinseates (apparently the "washings out" of other containers which held pesticides) in the evaporator tank and kept no record of what was emptied into the tank. The defendants contacted Crosby & Overton, a hazardous waste disposal company, to determine what to do with the material in the tank. In fact, a letter from Crosby & Overton to Puregro begins, "this letter is in response to our telecon of 2/19/87. Regarding *waste pesticide residue*...." (emphasis added). At least Crosby & Overton referred to the material as waste at one time. Moreover, it is undisputed that the defendants emptied the tank and sprayed the material on a field. Whether the material [was] "beneficially used" or "discarded" or "disposed of" is a question of fact that the jury must resolve.

* * *

Finally, the defendants would have this court consider comments made by officials within the EPA which indicate that the regulations are difficult and complex. Specifically, comments by Don R. Clay, EPA Assistant Administrator for the EPA Office of Solid Waste and Emergency Response, who stated:

RCRA is a regulatory cuckoo land of definition. * * * [The] Resource Recovery and Conservation Act [sic] ... is *very* complex. I believe we have five people in the agency who understand what "hazardous waste" is. What's hazardous one year isn't—wasn't hazardous yesterday, is hazardous tomorrow, because we've changed the rules.

* * * * * *

You have a waste that in one state is hazardous and in another isn't because they haven't adopted a rule yet. It is a legal statutory framework rather than logical, based on concentration and threat type of thing.

(Ct.Rec. 22, pp. 5-6) *** The defendants have attached a copy of The RCRA Implementation Study which indicates that the definitions of "solid waste" and "hazardous waste" are difficult to understand and implement. While helpful, these opinions are not determinative of the vagueness issue.

As the regulations are applied in this case, they are not vague. What is at issue is a factual dispute whether the defendants "truly discarded or disposed of" the material in the evaporator tank or whether they stored it until it could be put to beneficial use. ***

Problem #5: ENFORCEMENT

Takeover Tom is interested in acquiring Little Kem, which is a small company engaged primarily in the business of blending specialty chemicals. Little Kem was formed in 1970 by Lester Little and Karla Kem, who continue to be the sole owners of the company. Little is the President and Kem is the Vice President, and together they supervise a staff of 35, including 15 professional engineers and chemists. Little Kem conducts its operations on a 25-acre parcel of land leased from Little Old Lady, Inc. ("LOL"). LOL owns a total of 100 contiguous acres, and leases the remaining 75 acres to a variety of commercial enterprises, many of which use the chemicals produced by Little Kem.

Neither Little nor Kem is a whiz at regulatory compliance. Kem, however, is a Ph.D. chemist and chemical engineer. She designed the company's unique facility, and is well aware of the hazardous nature of some of the raw materials and chemical products handled by Little Kem. Kem knows nothing about chemistry, but he is a great "people person," and he handles the company's marketing and overall management.

Takeover Tom has assigned his environmental swat team to evaluate the RCRA compliance status of Little Kem prior to making his takeover bid. The team finds the following:

Little Kem receives raw materials and chemicals in containers provided by their suppliers. All incoming containers are stored at a gravel-covered area of the site, next to the main chemical blending unit. Occasionally, the containers have been knocked over or punctured, spilling various raw materials (including arsenic pentoxide and brucine, among others) onto the ground. To keep the area looking clean, Little Kem digs up any contaminated gravel and moves it to a gravel pit on one of the neighboring LOL parcels. Although Little Kem has no records of this activity, Little tells the swat team that it has occurred approximately once or twice a month for the past 21 years. The swat team observes the gravel pit, located approximately 150 feet from the Little Kem facility, and observes substantial discoloration not only in the pit itself, but also along the soil bordering the pit. The swat team suspects that rain water has gradually moved the waste chemicals through the gravel pit, possibly into the groundwater that the swat team has reason to believe is quite close to the surface, and probably through the soil adjacent to the pit.

The chemical blending aspect of Little Kem's operations generates an assortment of waste solvents within the designation F002 of listed hazardous wastes. Little Kem had been sending these wastes off-site to a hazardous waste incinerator until last year, when Little devised an ingenious method of burning the solvent wastes in the blending tanks after each batch of new chemicals is blended. This burning technique produces a sludge-like residue which, Kem determines on the basis of her expert knowledge, does not exhibit any of the characteristics of hazardous waste. In light of this information, Little reviewed the land ban regulations and discussed them with his college pal, a locally-celebrated divorce lawyer. He thereupon decided to send the sludge-like residue to the nearby solid waste landfill. Little Kem has been sending the residue to that landfill for the past eight months. The burning technique has greatly reduced the total volume of wastes shipped off-site by Little Kem. Whereas in the past the company typically generated 1100 kilograms per month of F002 hazardous waste solvents, the burning technique yields only 250 kilograms of residue per month.

Little Kem also generates 1200 kilograms per month of waste brucine (nonwastewater form). With a little bit of research and experimentation, Kem developed a chemical treatment process that renders the waste brucine nonhazardous such that it does not exhibit any of the four chracteristics of hazardous waste. Just to be on the safe side, Little Kem still sends the treated waste brucine to a hazardous waste landfill.

Question No. 1: Please advise Takeover Tom of any RCRA violations suggested by the above facts.

Question No. 2: Please inform Takeover Tom of the powers that the EPA may utilize under RCRA:
(a) to address or redress each of the above-described violations; and
(b) to require Little Kem to undertake any investigation and/or clean-up activities concerning (i) the container spillage area and (ii) the gravel pit.

Question No. 3: If the deal goes through, Takeover Tom would like to hire Little and Kem to run the facility for him. He is concerned, however, that they not spend their first year or two on his payroll in defending lawsuits seeking to hold them personally liable, under RCRA's civil or criminal enforcement provisions, for prior RCRA violations. Tom asks you to evaluate whether Little or Kem faces personal liability for the RCRA violations you have identified.

II
THE COMPREHENSIVE ENVIRONMENTAL RESPONSE, COMPENSATION, AND LIABILITY ACT ("CERCLA" or "SUPERFUND")

7   OVERVIEW OF CERCLA

One means of moving from RCRA to CERCLA is to ride the Magic School Bus, which is featured in a wonderfully entertaining and informative series written by Joanna Cole for children of all ages. In each book, Ms. Frizzle ("The Friz") takes her grade school class on an adventure- and fact-filled field trip, on the Magic School Bus, to learn first-hand some basic science subjects. The children are amazed and amused as they accompany The Friz to the center of the earth, for example, or through the solar system. Well-informed, if shaken as well, the class always returns to the school yard, and reality, in time for the afternoon bell.

The study of RCRA and CERCLA, the two principal federal hazardous waste laws, is not unlike a trip on the Magic School Bus. As one learns about the laws, their implementing regulations, and policy guidance generated by the EPA to supplement the laws and regulations, one enters a world that often seems more surreal than real. In that respect, RCRA and CERCLA are similar. They differ, however, in the nature of their surrealism.

A Magic School Bus ride through RCRA would be painstakingly slow, with frequent slams on the brakes as complex and barely-comprehensible regulations are posted in fine print at virtually every turn of the road. In contrast, a Magic School Bus ride through CERCLA would be breathtakingly fast, employing a super-large, super-powerful, previously-unknown type of bus, which would careen through the countryside and crush all obstacles in its way. As the reader moves into the CERCLA part of this volume, this would be a good opportunity to make sure that his or her seat belt is securely fastened.

Congress enacted the Comprehensive Environmental Response, Compensation, and Liability Act ("CERCLA" or the "Superfund" law) in December 1980, during the waning hours of the lame duck congressional session. The enactment of CERCLA was spurred primarily by the Love Canal case. Hooker Chemical and Plastics Company had used a 16-acre site in Niagara Falls, New York for the burial of some 21,800 tons of industrial wastes between 1942 and 1953, at which point it covered the chemicals with a layer of clay as was typical for that time. Hooker then sold the site to the Niagara Falls Board of Education for $1. Schools and homes were built on and near the site, and in the mid 1970s, chemicals began seeping into residential basements. In 1978, the New York Commissioner of Health declared a health emergency in the vicinity of the site. In 1979, he ordered all families with pregnant women and children under two years old to relocate from a portion of the site.

The EPA discovered that, notwithstanding the passage of many new and far-reaching environmental laws during the 1970s, none of those laws enabled the federal government to respond to and clean up such environmental contamination posing a threat to human health. The Clean Water Act authorized the Coast Guard to respond to spills of oil and hazardous substances into the navigable waters, 33 U.S.C. § 1321, but that provided no assistance for the Love Canal situation, where the contamination involved soil and groundwater. And although RCRA § 7003 authorized the EPA to respond to "imminent and substantial endangerments" involving solid or hazardous waste, it was uncertain until the 1984 RCRA amendments whether it reached parties whose contribution to the endangerment occurred wholly in the past, and it provided no mechanism for the EPA to act immediately to conduct a cleanup itself, where the cleanup could not await a lawsuit against responsible parties who might be recalcitrant, absent, or insolvent. Thus, Congress drafted CERCLA in order to provide the EPA with powerful means of responding promptly and effectively to cases of environmental contamination.

CERCLA is as straightforward as RCRA is complex. CERCLA empowers the EPA to respond to the actual or threatened release of a hazardous substance either by conducting the cleanup itself and suing a wide range of responsible parties for reimbursement, CERCLA §§ 104 and 107, 42 U.S.C. §§ 9604 and 9607, or by issuing an administrative order or seeking a court order requiring the responsible parties to conduct the cleanup themselves, CERCLA § 106, 42 U.S.C. § 9606. A party that receives an administrative order requiring it to clean up a CERCLA site cannot challenge the order until an enforcement action is brought against it, § 113(h), 42 U.S.C. 9613(h), and if it fails at that time to prove that it had "sufficient cause" for not complying with the order, it is liable for up to $25,000 per day in civil penalties for such noncompliance, § 106(b)(1), as well as treble damages if the EPA proceeds to conduct the cleanup and sues for reimbursement, § 107(c)(3).

The parties (known as potentially responsible parties, or "PRPs") that may be required to clean up, or pay for the cleanup, of CERCLA sites include: (1) the current owner and operator of the site; (2) any past owners or operators where hazardous substances were disposed of on the site during their ownership or operation; (3) parties that arranged for the disposal or treatment of hazardous substances at the site ("generators"); and (4) transporters who selected the site for the disposal or treatment of the hazardous substances they transported there. § 107(a). Liability is strict—without regard to fault—subject only to narrow defenses for releases caused solely by acts of war, God, or a third party in no employment, agency, or direct or indirect contractual relationship with the PRP. § 107(b). In short, parties who placed or caused others to place hazardous substances at a site in the past, in a manner that was then lawful, may nonetheless be required to clean up or pay for the cleanup of the site any number of years or decades later. Similarly, parties whose only involvement with a site is that they currently own or lease the property, or conduct activities there, but who had no connection whatever with any hazardous substances on the site, are also liable for site cleanup.

Sites subject to CERCLA response actions and abatement orders include virtually anyplace where hazardous substances have come to be located. A subset of this expansive universe of CERCLA sites is subject to EPA-funded cleanup activity. Any site that has been listed, by means of a rulemaking proceeding, on the National Priorities List ("NPL") under § 105, 42 U.S.C. § 9605, may be the subject of a "removal" (short-term, generally emergency-spurred) action or a "remedial" (longer-term, permanent) action conducted by the EPA using monies from the Superfund, an $8.5 billion fund created by taxes and fees and administered by the EPA for the purpose of cleaning up CERCLA sites. Even if a site is not listed on the NPL, the EPA may nonetheless use Superfund monies to conduct a removal, but not remedial, action at the site. Regardless of whether a site is on the NPL, and regardless of whether the EPA undertakes to clean it up or to order the PRPs to clean it up, a CERCLA site may be cleaned up by *any* party, including but not limited to a state, a locality, a corporation, or an individual, who may then sue the PRPs for reimbursement directly under CERCLA § 107(a)(4)(A)[for states] or (B)[for any other party] and/or § 113(f)[for PRP-plaintiffs seeking contribution].

Although virtually anyone may clean up a CERCLA site (*i.e.,* a site where there is an actual or threatened release of hazardous substances into the environment) and sue the PRPs for reimbursement, the existence of a CERCLA release imposes no automatic cleanup requirement on the PRPs. Only the issuance of an administrative or court order under § 106 triggers a PRP's obligation to conduct cleanup activities. In contrast, CERCLA § 103, 42 U.S.C. § 9603, creates an independent, automatic requirement for "any person in charge" of a facility to *report* (but not necessarily clean up) the release of a "reportable quantity" of any hazardous substance.

All CERCLA cleanups, regardless of who undertakes them, are governed by the National Contingency Plan, 40 C.F.R. Part 300, which specifies the steps to be taken to identify and investigate CERCLA sites, evaluate possible cleanup strategies, and decide upon and implement the actual cleanup (formally and generically known as a "response action," encompassing both removal and remedial actions). In order for the EPA or a state to recover response costs, it must prove that the costs were incurred in a manner "not inconsistent" with the NCP; all other parties must prove that their costs were incurred in a manner "consistent" with the NCP. CERCLA § 107(a)(4)(A) and (B). Judicial review of the EPA's cleanup actions and decisions is limited to the administrative record, and Congress has directed the courts to uphold the EPA's selection of a response action unless proven to be "arbitrary and capricious or otherwise not in accordance with law." § 113(j)(2).

During the early 1980s, few sites were actually cleaned up under CERCLA. Rather, the CERCLA program was characterized by a burgeoning bureaucracy, extensive and expensive litigation, and a morale-sapping management scandal. Momentum began developing for the amendment of CERCLA. In contrast to the initial enactment of CERCLA, which occurred speedily and without the usual legislative history, Congress worked for some two years considering, debating, and issuing committee reports regarding proposed Superfund amendments, culminating in the Superfund Amendments and Reauthorization Act of 1986 ("SARA").

SARA amended CERCLA in several significant respects. Among other things, it increased the size of the Superfund from $1.5 to $8.5 billion, and set a series of milestones for the EPA to meet in adding sites to the NPL, investigating them, and cleaning them up. It set cleanup standards, requiring that sites be remediated to the extent that would be required under all "applicable or relevant and appropriate requirements" of other federal and state environmental laws. It authorized the EPA to enter into various settlement agreements with PRPs, in order to streamline the cleanup process and expand the number of sites being cleaned up. It enhanced the role of the states in the CERCLA program and provided for public participation in the selection of cleanup remedies and in the approval of EPA-PRP settlement agreements.

Both before and after the SARA amendments, CERCLA has spawned a tremendous volume of litigation. Initially, the cases generally featured the EPA proceeding against PRPs for reimbursement of cleanup costs and for court orders requiring the PRPs to undertake cleanup activity. Gradually, there has also developed a sizeable body of cases involving suits by one PRP against another, or many others, seeking cost recovery or contribution. The tenor of the decisions has subtly shifted during CERCLA's second decade. Whereas initially the courts almost universally deferred to the EPA's interpretation of the law's broad provisions, since the early 1990s the appellate courts have listened more favorably to the PRPs' arguments concerning liability and defenses.

Criticism of CERCLA's liability scheme, decision making procedures, cleanup standards, and slow yet costly progress—among other aspects of the law—has become more widespread and more heated in recent years. A substantial overhaul of the statute came close to enactment in late 1994, but the 1994 elections, which replaced the Democrats with the Republicans as the majority party in Congress, halted that process. Among the issues addressed were more efficient procedures for allocating liability among potentially responsible parties, streamlined procedures for selecting cleanup plans, revised criteria for determining "how clean is clean," increased public involvement in cleanup decisionmaking, an experimental approach for resolving insurance coverage disputes, incorporating environmental justice concerns into the CERCLA program, and establishing special liability rules for lenders and liability limits for small contributors and municipalities. Congress continues to consider significant amendments, but the prospects for sufficient consensus on key issues, such as liability rules, seem remote as of mid-1997.

In the absence of—and perhaps designed to preempt—legislative changes to Superfund, the EPA has adopted a series of administrative reforms to "reinvent" Superfund. In 1993, the agency announced a package of administrative changes that it was planning for the Superfund program, with the goals to:

> (a) enhance enforcement fairness and reduce transaction costs; (b) enhance cleanup effectiveness and consistency; (c) enhance meaningful public involvement; and (d) enhance the State role in the Superfund program.

EPA, *Superfund Administrative Improvements: Final Report* (June 1993) at 2. To implement this initiative, the EPA has taken or intends to take the following steps: encourage greater use of binding allocation and alternative dispute resolution to facilitate allocation among PRPs; foster more settlements with small contributor PRPs; issue presumptive remedy guidance documents for certain categories of Superfund sites that are amenable to a generic cleanup approach and that represent a considerable percentage of Superfund sites; develop action levels and cleanup levels for various contaminants in soil; implement an environmental justice strategy within the Superfund program; and promote early and more effective community involvement in the Superfund program. In 1995, the EPA supplemented its reinvention effort with new enforcement policies to encourage the purchase (and cleanup) of contaminated properties, new cleanup decisionmaking guidance to take future uses of contaminated land into consideration in selecting cleanup remedies. And in 1996, the EPA announced additional administrative reforms designed to expedite cleanups, to be more responsive to local communities, to encourage settlements among PRPs, and to release very small parties from liability.

While both legislative and administrative efforts were underway to reform Superfund, one District Court decision nearly stopped the program in its tracks. After much discussion and controversy concerning the constitutional and policy issues raised, the decision was reversed on appeal. Because the issues remain the subject of policy debate, and because the case highlights the breadth of the Superfund statute, the appellate decision is presented here.

UNITED STATES V. OLIN CORP.
107 F.3d 1506 (11th Cir. 1997)

Before ANDERSON, Circuit Judge, and KRAVITCH and HENDERSON, Senior Circuit Judges.

KRAVITCH, Senior Circuit Judge.

Congress passed the Comprehensive Environmental Response, Compensation, and Liability Act ("CERCLA") to counteract the environmental threats associated with hazardous waste disposal. In this case, the district court dismissed the government's complaint brought under CERCLA against Olin Corporation ("Olin"). It ruled that: (1) the Constitution prohibits enforcement of CERCLA against a party if the environmental effects of that party's conduct remain limited to its own property; and (2) CERCLA's cleanup liability provisions apply prospectively only. The government appeals and we reverse.

I.

Olin has operated a chemical manufacturing facility in McIntosh, Alabama since 1951. Until 1982, the plant produced mercury- and chlorine-based commercial chemicals that contaminated significant segments of Olin's property. This appeal involves one such portion of the site, called Operable Unit # 1 ("OU- 1"). Groundwater and soil pollution at OU-1 make it unfit for future residential use. Nevertheless, contamination from OU-1 presently remains localized to Olin's site because the company regulates groundwater flow beneath its property.[1]

II.

The government brought a civil action in the district court, seeking a cleanup order against Olin and reimbursement for response costs, pursuant to sections 106(a) and 107 of CERCLA. After negotiations, the parties agreed to a consent decree that called for Olin to pay all costs associated with remediation of OU-1. The proposal resolved Olin's liability for contamination at OU-1 caused by disposal activities before and after CERCLA's effective date of December 11, 1980.

When the parties presented the consent decree to the district court, it *sua sponte* ordered them to address the impact of the Supreme Court's decision in *United States v. Lopez*, 115 S.Ct. 1624, (1995) (invalidating Gun-Free School Zones Act under the Commerce Clause), on the legality of their proposal. Olin complied with that order by answering the original complaint. It asserted that the *Lopez* Court's construction of the Commerce Clause precluded constitutional application of CERCLA in this case. In addition, Olin contended that CERCLA was not intended to impose liability for conduct predating the statute's enactment. The district court agreed with Olin on both counts, denied the motion to enter the consent decree and dismissed the government's complaint.

III.

We review *de novo* the constitutional challenge to CERCLA and the purely legal question of whether the statute's cleanup liability provisions apply retroactively.

---

[1]The district court found that contaminants may migrate off-site, if a well in OU-1 should leak. *United States v. Olin Corp.*, 927 F.Supp. 1502, 1506 (S.D.Ala.1996). The government also notes that pollutants from Olin's operations have appeared off-site, albeit within federally-allowed concentration levels.

A.

The district court found that the enforcement of CERCLA against Olin violated the Commerce Clause as interpreted by the Supreme Court in *Lopez*. The *Lopez* Court held that the Commerce Clause empowers Congress to regulate: (1) channels of interstate commerce; (2) instrumentalities of and persons or things in interstate commerce; and (3) intrastate activities that substantially affect interstate commerce. This case, like *Lopez*, concerns the third category.

Lopez did not alter the constitutional standard for federal statutes regulating intrastate activities. *** Simply stated, "the proper test requires an analysis of whether the regulated activity 'substantially affects' interstate commerce." *Id.* 115 S.Ct. At 1631. Congress can maintain the constitutionality of its statutes under this standard by including in each a "jurisdictional element which would ensure, through case-by-case inquiry, that the [regulated activity] in question affects interstate commerce." *Id.* 115 S.Ct. at 1631. In addition, Congress, or a committee thereof, can make legislative findings indicating that a statute regulates activities with a substantial effect on interstate commerce.***

When Congress fails to ensure a statute's compliance with the Commerce Clause, however, courts must determine independently whether the statute regulates "activities that arise out of or are connected with a commercial transaction, which viewed in the aggregate, substantially affect [ ] interstate commerce." *Lopez*, 115 S.Ct. at 1631. This determination turns on whether the statute constitutes "an essential part of a larger regulation of economic activity, in which the regulatory scheme could be undercut unless the intrastate activity were regulated." *Id.* A court's focus, thus, cannot be excessively narrow; if the statute regulates a *"class of activities* ... and that *class* is within the reach of the federal power, the courts have no power 'to excise, as trivial, individual instances' of the class." *Perez v. United States*, 402 U.S. 146, 154 (1971) ***

The district court's Commerce Clause analysis conflicts with the foregoing standard in two main respects. First, the district court indicated that under *Lopez* a statute must regulate *economic* activity directly to satisfy the Commerce Clause. Actually, as noted above, *Lopez* reiterates that a statute will pass constitutional muster if it regulates an activity, whatever its nature, "that arise[s] out of or [is] connected with a commercial transaction, which viewed in the aggregate, substantially affects interstate commerce." *See Lopez*, 115 S.Ct. at 1631. The district court also concluded that *Lopez* requires every statute enacted pursuant to Congress's Commerce Clause authority to contain a jurisdictional element. In fact, the *Lopez* Court recognized that a statute without a jurisdictional element still would stand under the Commerce Clause, if the law satisfied the substantial effects test.

Our evaluation of CERCLA under the foregoing framework leads us to reject Olin's constitutional challenge. Specifically, we conclude that although Congress did not include in CERCLA either legislative findings or a jurisdictional element, the statute remains valid as applied in this case because it regulates a class of activities that substantially affects interstate commerce.   The proper analysis first requires identification of the "class of activities" involved in the case. *** The government contends this suit involves regulation of releases of hazardous substances generally; Olin objects to this broad classification. In our view, the disposal of hazardous waste at the site of production, or "on-site," constitutes the narrowest, possible class.[8]

In light of this understanding, we must assess whether on-site waste disposal substantially affects interstate commerce. Because the legislative history of CERCLA documents how the unregulated management of hazardous substances, even strictly within individual states, significantly impacts interstate commerce, we conclude the statute can be applied constitutionally under the circumstances of this case.

When the Senate considered S. 1480, a bill containing cleanup liability provisions later substantially incorporated into CERCLA, its Committee on Environment and Public Works ("the Committee") took notice of many facts that show a nexus between all forms of improper waste disposal and interstate commerce. First, the Committee noted the growth of the chemical industry and the concomitant costs of handling its waste. It also cited a 1980 report by the Office of Technology Assessment which gauged agricultural losses from chemical contamination in six states at $283 million.[10] The Committee reported that the commercial damages resulting from unregulated waste management were not attributable solely to interstate trafficking in hazardous materials for disposal, but also arose from accidents associated with purely intrastate, on-site disposal activities, such as improper waste storage in tanks, lagoons and chemical plants. Thus, CERCLA reflects Congress's recognition that both on-site and off-site disposal of hazardous waste threaten interstate commerce.

Olin notes that the record contains no evidence that its on-site disposal has caused off-site damage, much less harmed interstate commerce. *** Olin's claim fails because, as the foregoing discussion documents, the regulation of intrastate, on-site waste disposal constitutes an appropriate element of Congress's broader scheme to protect interstate commerce and industries thereof from pollution.

Olin also objects to enforcement of CERCLA in this case because it contends its disposal activities are not economic in nature. As stated above, the Commerce Clause conditions congressional authority not upon the qualities of the regulated activity, but rather the degree to which that activity affects interstate commerce. Further, to the extent a chemical plant can dispose of its waste on-site free of regulation, it would have a market advantage over chemical companies that lack on-site disposal options; Olin's actions, therefore, have an economic character.

For these reasons, we hold that, as applied in this case, CERCLA constitutes a permissible exercise of Congress's authority under the Commerce Clause.

---

[8]Because the statute passes constitutional muster even when the class of activities is parsed as narrowly as possible, we need not determine definitively what class of activities actually ought to control.

[10]In addition, Congress had substantial information that improper disposal of hazardous waste threatened natural resource-dependent, interstate industries, such as commercial fishing. *See, e.g., Legislative History* at 739 (statement of Sen. Culver) (noting that "half of the potential fishing in the Great Lakes [was] lost annually due to contamination-related curtailments"); 756 (statement of Sen. Leahy) (observing that contamination from releases in Virginia resulted in "[c]ountless numbers of commercial fishing ventures be[ing] forced out of business").

B.

The district court also based its dismissal order on its conclusion that CERCLA's response cost liability scheme applies only to disposals after the statute's enactment. This ruling not only conflicts with this court's recent description of CERCLA, but also runs contrary to all other decisions on point. *** The district court, however, held that *Landgraf v. USI Film Products*, 511 U.S. 244 (1994), "demolishes the interpretive premises on which prior cases had concluded that CERCLA is retroactive." ***

This court has recognized that *Landgraf* "provides the analytical framework for determining whether newly enacted statutory provisions are applicable to pending cases." *Hunter v. United States*, 101 F.3d 1565, 1569 (11th Cir.1996) (en banc).[14] In *Hunter*, we observed that "[a] court's first, and sometimes last, task under *Landgraf* analysis is 'to determine whether Congress has expressly prescribed the statute's proper reach.' If Congress has done so, that is the end of the *Landgraf* analysis, and the court simply follows the evident intent of Congress." *Id.* (quoting *Landgraf*, 511 U.S. at 280-81). *Hunter*, however, left open the question of whether "evidence of legislative intent, other than in an express statutory command" would satisfy *Landgraf*'s first prong. *Id.*

Because CERCLA contains no explicit statutory command regarding retroactive application of its cleanup liability regime, this court must decide what, if any, further inquiry should occur. Although the *Landgraf* Court reaffirmed the presumption against retroactive application of statutes, it emphasized that courts must effectuate congressional intent regarding retroactivity. The Court ruled that its approach simply was designed to "assure [ ] that Congress itself has affirmatively considered the potential unfairness of retroactive application and determined that it is an acceptable price to pay for the countervailing benefits." *Id.* As a result, we conclude that even absent explicit statutory language mandating retroactivity, laws may be applied retroactively if courts are able to discern "*clear* congressional *intent* favoring such a result." *Id.* at 280 (emphasis added). Accordingly, we must review the language, structure and purpose of the statute, as well as its legislative history, to determine whether Congress made clear its intent to apply CERCLA's remediation liability scheme to conduct pre-dating the statute's enactment.

We examine first CERCLA's language. As noted above, the statute contains no explicit statement regarding retroactive application of its cleanup liability provisions. Olin mistakenly contends that CERCLA's text therefore offers no insight into Congress's intent on this subject. CERCLA imposes liability for response costs upon

---

[14] This passage from *Hunter* states only that *Landgraf* guides review of "newly enacted" laws. The *Landgraf* Court did not indicate whether courts should apply the decision to older statutes, such as CERCLA. To the extent *Landgraf* constitutes a dramatically new rule of statutory construction, as Olin and the district court suggest, a strong argument can be made that courts ought not to employ it to upset years of reliance on prior interpretations of existing laws. Because this complex issue was not raised by the parties, however, and because we view *Landgraf*, not as charting a radical new course, but as reaffirming a "traditional presumption," *Landgraf*, 511 U.S. at 280-81, we assume it governs our review of CERCLA today.

"owners and operators" of "any site or area where a hazardous substance has been deposited...." 42 U.S.C. §§ 9601(9)(B), 9607(a)(1). Its reach also extends to "any person who *at the time of disposal* of any hazardous substance *owned or operated*" such a facility. 42 U.S.C. § 9607(a)(2) (emphasis added). Congress thus targeted both current and former owners and operators of contaminated sites. By imposing liability upon former owners and operators, Congress manifested a clear intent to reach conduct preceding CERCLA's enactment.

Olin contends that by including this language Congress sought to reach *only* "future former owners and operators," i.e. persons who would become former owners and operators after December 11, 1980, CERCLA's effective date. It has pointed to nothing in the statute or its legislative history which supports this strained view. In fact, language elsewhere in CERCLA confirms that Congress intended that persons who were former owners and operators as of December 11, 1980, would bear the costs of cleaning up sites they formerly controlled. For example, section 103 provides that:

> *Within one hundred and eighty days after December 11, 1980, any person* who owns or operates or *who at the time of disposal owned or operated ...* a facility at which hazardous substances ... are or *have been* stored, treated, or disposed of shall ... notify the Administrator of the Environmental Protection Agency of the existence of such facility, specifying the amount and type of any hazardous substance to be found there, and any known, suspected, or likely releases of such substances from such facility.

42 U.S.C. § 9603(c)(emphasis added).

Read reasonably, the foregoing subsection addresses conduct that occurred *before CERCLA's effective date.* It expressly mandates that persons who were former owners and operators *as of December 11, 1980,* make the required notification regarding their pre-enactment conduct within six months, or forfeit "any defenses to liability set out in section [107] of this title...." *Id.* If, as Olin asserts, these former owners and operators faced no liability under section 107, section 103 makes virtually no sense. We conclude the language of section 103 confirms that Congress believed its imposition of liability for cleanup upon former owners and operators in section 107(a) covered persons who were former owners and operators on December 11, 1980, as well as owners and operators who sold their interests after that date.

An analysis of CERCLA's purpose, as evinced by the statute's structure and legislative history, also supports the view that Congress intended the statute to impose retroactive liability for cleanup. Olin acknowledges that CERCLA was designed to deal with contamination that preceded the statute's effective date of December 11, 1980. See *Legislative History* at 308-19 (Committee Report) (discussing concern for pre-enactment contamination, including inactive sites). It insists, however, that Congress intended for taxpayers in both industry and the general public to bear the response costs associated with these earlier disposal problems. This argument ignores the fact that "[a]n essential purpose of CERCLA is to place the ultimate responsibility for the clean up of hazardous waste on 'those responsible for problems caused by the disposal of chemical poison.'" *Redwing Carriers, Inc. v. Saraland Apts.*, 94 F.3d 1489,

1501 (11th Cir.1996). Congress's twin goals of cleaning up pollution that occurred prior to December 11, 1980, and of assigning responsibility to culpable parties can be achieved only through retroactive application of CERCLA's response cost liability provisions; this fact provides additional evidence of clear congressional intent favoring retroactivity.

Further review of CERCLA's legislative history confirms that Congress intended to impose retroactive liability for cleanup. The chief predecessor bill to CERCLA, S. 1480, contained no express statement regarding retroactivity. "Nonetheless, all those commenting on [it and the parallel House bill] expressed the belief that the bills would apply retroactively to those responsible for the releases in existing waste sites." *Ninth Avenue*, 946 F.Supp. at 662. ***

Olin insists we should disregard this extensive legislative history because Congress passed a compromise bill. This argument fails because the cleanup liability provisions from S. 1480 were incorporated into CERCLA. Moreover, careful scrutiny of the legislative record leading up to CERCLA's passage reveals that the compromise never turned upon the statute's imposition of retroactive liability for cleanup, but rather upon the redaction of the prior bill's provisions on joint and several liability and personal injury.

For all these reasons, we find clear congressional intent favoring retroactive application of CERCLA's cleanup liability provisions.

* * *

8   KEY TERMS TRIGGERING CERCLA JURISDICTION

The EPA may use Superfund monies to conduct response activities when there is an actual or threatened "release" of a "hazardous substance" into the environment. CERCLA § 104(a)(1). The EPA may issue, or ask the court to issue, an order requiring PRPs to conduct response activities when there may be an imminent and substantial endangerment to public health or the environment due to an "actual or threatened release of a hazardous substance from a facility." § 106(a).

The key terms triggering CERCLA jurisdiction—"release," "hazardous substance," and "facility"—are broadly defined in the statute. A "release" is

any spilling, leaking, pumping, pouring, emitting, emptying, discharging, injecting, escaping, leaching, dumping, or disposing into the environment.

§ 101(22), 42 U.S.C. § 9601(22).

A "hazardous substance" is any substance designated as toxic, hazardous, or such under any one of six specified provisions of various environmental laws. § 101(14). The term includes hazardous substances and toxic pollutants under the Clean Water Act, hazardous wastes under RCRA, hazardous air pollutants under the Clean Air Act, imminently hazardous chemical substances under the Toxic Substances Control Act, and any other substance specifically designated as hazardous under § 102 of CERCLA.

Notably, the term hazardous substance specifically excludes petroleum and natural gas. There has been considerable litigation testing the boundaries of this exclusion. It has been held to encompass petroleum products to which concentrations of hazardous substances, such as lead, have been added, where the additives occur naturally, in lesser concentrations, in petroleum. *Wilshire Westwood Associates v. Atlantic Richfield Corp.*, 881 F.2d 801 (9th Cir. 1989). It does not extend, however, to petroleum-based wastes (as opposed to products). *Cose v. Getty Oil Co.*, 4 F.3d 700 (9th Cir. 1993).

Finally, a "facility" is any sort of structure, natural or synthetic, as well as "any site or area where a hazardous substance has been deposited, stored, disposed of, or placed, or otherwise come to be located." § 101(9).

The cases in this chapter construe and apply these crucial CERCLA terms. They also provide a preview of the enormity and complexity of CERCLA litigation. With cleanup expenses extraordinarily high, and statutory language notably vague, CERCLA liability issues have been heavily litigated.

The cases focus initially on the definition of hazardous substance. The decision excerpted below is the second one issued by the Second Circuit in litigation stemming from the cleanup of two municipal landfills. In the first decision, *B.F. Goodrich v. Murtha*, 958 F.2d 1192 (2d Cir. 1992), *municipalities* that sent household waste to the landfills argued that because household waste is excluded from the definition of hazardous waste under RCRA, 40 C.F.R. § 261.4(b)(1), it is also excluded from the definition of hazardous substance under CERCLA. The Second Circuit rejected that argument:

*** This narrow RCRA exemption in no way limits the definition of hazardous substance under CERCLA. The EPA expressly recognized the exemption's limited scope when it stated that the exempted "[solid] wastes might otherwise be considered hazardous wastes." To construe this exemption to apply also to CERCLA would frustrate the Act's broad remedial purposes as well as unjustifiably expand the scope of the Resource and Recovery Act's regulations.

Congress and the EPA have carefully distinguished between *wastes*, to which the Resource and Recovery Act applies, and *substances*, to which CERCLA applies. It may be seen therefore that the exemption which appellants urge should be extended to CERCLA applies to household *waste*. CERCLA, though, applies to hazardous *substances*. ***

* * *

Nor does including wastes that are not subject to the stringent Subpart C regulations under the Resource and Recovery Act within the definition of hazardous substances under CERCLA create a conflict between the two statutes. Subpart C imposes tough standards for operating *active* toxic waste sites, but does not cover sites operated *prior* to its enactment, *not* sites where the owner is unknown or bankrupt, *nor* does it address spills, illegal dumping or releases generally. RCRA is preventative; CERCLA is curative. It does not follow that because the environmental risk posed by household waste is deemed insufficient to justify the most stringent regulations governing its day-to-day handling that the environmental harm caused when that risk is realized is insufficient to require holding liable those responsible for that harm. ***

*** Where a substance is not exempted from the definition of hazardous substance set forth in CERCLA, but merely is exempted from regulation under a separate statute, we decline to incorporate the exemption into § 9601(14). A regulatory exemption cannot take precedence over Congress' concerns spelled out in § 9601(14) of the Act.

Id. at 1202-03.

On remand, the district court dismissed nearly all of the remaining parties who had sent some form of municipal waste to the landfills. The Second Circuit reversed, summarizing the case law regarding the definition of hazardous substance.

B.F. GOODRICH V. BETKOSKI
99 F.3d 505 (2d Cir. 1996)

Before CARDAMONE, WALKER, and McLAUGHLIN, Circuit Judges.
CARDAMONE, Circuit Judge.

This appeal, arising originally from the disposal of hazardous substances at two Connecticut landfills, Beacon Heights and Laurel Park, requires us to determine whether defendants accused of generating and transporting hazardous substances deposited at the two landfill sites might be liable under the Comprehensive Environmental Response, Compensation, and Liability Act (CERCLA) to contribute to the costs of cleaning up the sites. Under CERCLA, several classes of responsible parties are liable for most costs incurred in responding to and remediating sites where hazardous substances are found. We must, in addition, decide if certain parties remain susceptible to suit by the United States and the State of Connecticut for response costs incurred by these governments.

Plaintiffs-appellants the United States, the State of Connecticut, the Beacon Heights Coalition, and the Laurel Park Coalition appeal from a judgment entered May 2, 1995 by the United States District Court for the District of Connecticut (Dorsey, C.J.). The court granted judgment on the pleadings against the United States and Connecticut and granted summary judgment against the Beacon Heights Coalition and the Laurel Park Coalition and in favor of nearly 100 defendants alleged in plaintiffs' complaints to be potentially responsible parties in an action under CERCLA.

The Beacon Heights and Laurel Park Coalitions are groups of industrial waste generators that sought contribution from third parties after having settled their liability with the United States, the State of Connecticut, and the Murthas and affiliated entities—the owners/operators of the two landfill sites. The Laurel Park Coalition sought initially to add 1151 other potentially responsible parties to the litigation. The district court ground away at this number slowly, yet it "ground exceeding small." Insisting that these plaintiffs only implead those parties against whom they had a claim that was both legally and factually substantiated, the district court reduced to 41 the 1151 third party defendants that these plaintiffs moved to add, thus eliminating over 1000 potential parties from the suit.

Later, with motions for summary judgment before it, the district court construed some of CERCLA's basic provisions in a manner inconsistent with our precedents and, ruling that the coalitions had failed to advance sufficient proof, thereby was able to grant summary judgment to nearly all of the roughly 100 defendants, dismissing plaintiffs' complaints against them. ***

BACKGROUND

* * *

A. *Initial Litigation*

The Beacon Heights and Laurel Park landfills have both been designated as Superfund sites by the Environmental Protection Agency (EPA). Terrance and Harold Murtha, and several corporations controlled by them (collectively, Murtha), owned and operated Laurel Park from 1961 until 1987, and owned and operated Beacon Heights from 1970 to 1987. In 1987 Murtha was sued in separate actions by the EPA, the State of Connecticut's Department of Environmental Protection (DEP), Uniroyal Chemical Company, Inc., and a coalition of corporations led by B.F. Goodrich Company. Murtha filed third party actions for contribution or indemnification against some 200 third party defendants. These parties were accused either of generating or of transporting hazardous substances to the landfills. Most of the defendants named in the Murtha third party suits were not named by the EPA as potentially responsible parties.

In September 1987, when the Murtha litigation began, the EPA entered into a consent decree concerning the remediation of Beacon Heights with 33 potentially responsible parties who may have generated hazardous substances that were later deposited in that landfill. These parties, later known as the Beacon Heights Coalition, agreed to undertake the remediation of that site and to reimburse the government for its future oversight costs in excess of $500,000. Since this coalition did not provide for past costs or for those future response costs unrelated to oversight, the EPA sued several non-settling potentially responsible parties in a separate action to recover its past and future remediation costs.

The EPA also filed two lawsuits concerning the costs of remediating the Laurel Park landfill. One led to a settlement with another industrial coalition of various potentially responsible parties, now known as the Laurel Park Coalition. In an August 1992 consent decree, the Laurel Park Coalition agreed to perform remediation at the site, pay for the government's future oversight costs in excess of $200,000, and pay the EPA $500,000 for its past response costs. The EPA then sued, as it did in the Beacon Heights case, the non-settling potentially responsible parties to recover past costs and future response costs not addressed by the consent decree. The State of Connecticut, which is also involved in the Laurel Park cleanup, received over $1 million from the coalition for response costs and sued the same non-settling parties for unreimbursed costs.

Murtha also settled its litigation with the United States, with Connecticut, and with the two coalitions (coalitions, plaintiffs, or appellants). The parties embodied their agreement in a consent decree (Murtha consent decree) which also was entered by the district court in August 1992. Murtha resolved its liability at both landfill sites for $5,375,000; this amount was apportioned among several parties. The Beacon Heights Coalition received $1,875,000 and $322,500 was given to the EPA for unreimbursed costs relating to Beacon Heights. Murtha assigned its third party claims to the Beacon Heights Coalition. The EPA also received $625,000 for unreimbursed costs at Laurel Park, as did the State of Connecticut, with the remaining $1,975,000 set aside for remediation at that site. Although the Laurel Park Coalition had not been formed when the Murtha consent decree was negotiated, the parties agreed that should an industrial coalition form within 18 months of the entry of Murtha's consent decree, the coalition would receive the funds. Because this condition was met, the Laurel Park Coalition received the $1.975 million set aside by Murtha.

Many of the third party defendants were municipalities and municipal corporations that generated and collected municipal solid waste. They claimed that CERCLA exempted municipal waste from its coverage and that an exemption for household waste in the Resource Conservation and Recovery Act (RCRA), was incorporated into CERCLA. The district court rejected these arguments, and we affirmed. The municipal generators therefore remained in the case as named defendants and potentially responsible parties.

B. *Summary Judgment Decisions*

The Beacon Heights Coalition was already armed with Murtha's assignment of its third party claims against generators and transporters of hazardous substances. The Laurel Park Coalition then moved to add to the action as third party defendants 1151 potentially responsible parties. The district court granted the motion to the extent of allowing 41 parties to be joined, but denied it as to the 1110 other potential parties.

In April 1992, approximately six weeks after we rejected the municipal defendants' claim of CERCLA exemption, the district court decided *sua sponte* to permit parties to file motions for summary judgment. Nearly all of the original third party defendants filed such motions. Both coalitions opposed the motions and in turn cross-moved for the same relief.

* * *

Summary judgment was eventually granted to every third party defendant-appellee that had moved for such relief, and the district court subsequently dismissed *sua sponte* nearly all the remaining third party defendants, including many that did not move for that relief. Of the 88 defendants sued by the coalitions who had not entered into settlement agreements, all but four were dismissed.

Judgment on the pleadings was entered against the United States and the State of Connecticut in their suits against non-settling potentially responsible parties. The district court reasoned that the EPA and DEP had presented no figures for incurred response costs that were not covered by the $3,500,000 net *Murtha* settlement, and therefore dismissed both governments' claims for additional reimbursement. It also granted summary judgment in favor of the remaining three of the eight defendants at Beacon Heights sued by the EPA.

From an amended judgment entered May 2, 1995, the United States, the State of Connecticut, and both coalitions appeal. We affirm in part, reverse in part, and remand for further proceedings.

DISCUSSION

The coalitions point to a number of reasons calling for reversal. They contend the district court granted summary judgment to many of the defendants based on a misapplication of substantive CERCLA law, and that instead their cross-motions for summary judgment should have been granted. They also maintain that procedural errors were committed that require reversal.

* * *

I THE LAW OF CERCLA

A. *Basic Principles*

Our construction of CERCLA does not begin with this case. Rather, we are guided by previous writings on this subject in this and other Circuits. CERCLA is a "broad remedial statute," *Murtha I*, 958 F.2d at 1197, and was enacted with the purpose of "[f]irst, assuring that those responsible for any damage, environmental harm, or injury from chemical poisons bear the costs of their actions." S.Rep. 848, 96th Cong., 2d Sess. 13 (1980) (Senate Report). As a remedial statute, CERCLA should be construed liberally to give effect to its purposes. These include facilitating efficient responses to environmental harm, holding responsible parties liable for the costs of the cleanup, and encouraging settlements that reduce the inefficient expenditure of public funds on lengthy litigation.

CERCLA makes four classes of persons liable—(1) present owners and operators of facilities that accepted hazardous substances, (2) past owners and operators of such facilities, (3) generators of hazardous substances, and (4) certain transporters of hazardous substances. 42 U.S.C. § 9607(a). *** Responsible parties are liable for a broad range of remediation expenses, including all costs of removal of the substances not inconsistent with the national contingency plan, other necessary response costs, damages for injury to natural resources, and the cost of health assessments. *See* 42 U.S.C. § 9607(a)(4).

The Act imposes strict liability. Strict liability is intended to make sure that those who "benefit financially from a commercial activity" internalize the environmental costs of the activity as a cost of doing business. Senate Report at 13.***

A CERCLA plaintiff establishes a *prima facie* case by proving that (1) the defendant is within one of the four categories of responsible parties enumerated in § 9607(a); (2) the landfill site is a facility as defined in § 9601(9); (3) there is a release or threatened release of hazardous substances at the facility; (4) the plaintiff incurred costs responding to the release or threatened release; and (5) the costs and response actions conform to the national contingency plan.

Once a plaintiff makes a *prima facie* showing, a defendant may avoid liability only if it establishes by a preponderance of the evidence that the release or threatened release was caused by an act of God, an act of war, certain acts or omissions of third parties other than those with whom the defendant has a contractual relationship, or a combination of these reasons. 42 U.S.C. § 9607(b).*** Significantly, it is "not required

that the [plaintiff] show that a specific defendant's waste caused incurrence of clean-up costs." Because CERCLA imposes strict liability, there is no causation requirement.
 "Hazardous substance" is expansively defined to include

(A) any substance designated pursuant to section 1321(b)(2)(A) of Title 33, (B) any element, compound, mixture, solution, or substance designated pursuant to section 9602 of this title, (C) any hazardous waste having the characteristics identified under or listed pursuant to section 3001 of the Solid Waste Disposal Act ..., (D) any toxic pollutant listed under section 1317(a) of Title 33, (E) any hazardous air pollutant listed under section 112 of the Clean Air Act ..., and (F) any imminently hazardous chemical substance or mixture with respect to which the [EPA] Administrator has taken action pursuant to section 2606 of Title 15.

42 U.S.C. § 9601(14). Pursuant to subsection (B), the EPA has listed more than 700 hazardous substances in Table 302.4 of 40 C.F.R. § 302.4 (1995). We have noted that "[t]he breadth of § 9601(14) cannot be easily escaped, and we have expressly held that '[q]uantity or concentration is not a factor.'" *Alcan*, 990 F.2d at 720 (quoting *Murtha I*, 958 F.2d at 1200). In other words, the Act's definition includes "even minimal amounts of pollution." *Alcan*, 990 F.2d at 720.

*   *   *

B. *Analysis of District Court's CERCLA Interpretation*

The coalitions aver that many third party defendants-appellees were granted summary judgment based on an erroneous application of CERCLA and the case law interpreting the statute. We address each claim of error.

1. *Component Parts*

The district court held, that "[a]bsent a finding by EPA that a particular product warrants classification as a [hazardous substance] ..., it cannot be found that the product, notwithstanding its constituent elements, is an [hazardous substance] or [hazardous waste]." It later clarified that holding, by explaining that "mere presence of an element, a named [hazardous substance], as a constituent of a product does not render the product a [hazardous substance]." *Murtha III*, 840 F.Supp. at 184.

In *Murtha I* we rejected the contention that a specific mixture or waste solution must be listed within § 9601(14) or incorporated by reference in order to fall within CERCLA's coverage. We explained that "[w]hen a mixture or waste solution contains hazardous substances, that mixture is itself hazardous for purposes of determining CERCLA liability. Liability under CERCLA depends only on the presence in any form of listed hazardous substances." *Murtha I*, 958 F.2d at 1201.

It is enough that a mixture or waste solution contain a hazardous substance for that mixture to be deemed hazardous under CERCLA. The waste product itself "need not be listed by name—instead of its constituent components—to fall within the Act." *Murtha I*, 958 F.2d at 1201.***

Our understanding is also consistent with Congress' plan. Legislative history reveals that "the release of any [listed hazardous or toxic substance] *or any constituent of them* invokes the notice requirements and response provisions and any costs of removal or remedial action or any damages are subject to the liability provisions of the bill." Senate Report at 24-27, (emphasis added). In short, it makes no difference that the specific wastes disposed of by the appellees were not themselves listed as hazardous substances, because so long as their component parts were listed as hazardous substances there may be CERCLA liability.

Appellees declare this approach will lead to CERCLA liability if a discarded object had any EPA listed hazardous substance in its chemical genealogy, whether or not the chemical component's characteristics had been unalterably changed in the manufacturing process. Even if this objection is sound in theory, it is not relevant. The instant case involves not only discarded objects like pens or plastic containers that might include a hazardous substance in their chemical make-up. Appellees are accused of dumping waste that contained hazardous substances in separable, identifiable forms. According to an affidavit submitted by the coalitions, the cumulative waste stream discarded in the Murtha's landfills included municipal sludge, incinerator ash, varnishes, paints, tar remover, caulking compounds, pesticides, glues, degreasers, and automotive lubricants. Obviously, disposal of this sort of waste poses a greater threat of releasing hazardous substances than is presented by—to use an example offered by the appellees at oral argument—the disposal of a single plastic pen.

In an attempt to avoid this conclusion, appellees invoke *Massachusetts v. Blackstone Valley Elec. Co.*, 67 F.3d 981, 992-93 (1st Cir.1995). Blackstone held that the EPA should make an initial determination of whether ferric ferrocyanide (FFC)—in this case a blue-colored substance on wood chips—is a cyanide and therefore a hazardous substance. The First Circuit ruled that even if FFC contained cyanide as a chemical component, the cyanide might not exist in a form convertible to free cyanide and therefore might not be a CERCLA hazardous substance. *Id.* at 990-91. However, in this case, the First Circuit focused on whether FFC was a hazardous substance. It did not suggest that were FFC found to be a hazardous substance, liability might be avoided because "wood chips"—the product allegedly discarded by the polluter—were not in themselves hazardous substances within the Act's definition. In short, the appellees' reliance on *Blackstone* is misplaced.

Thus, those dismissals in the present case that were predicated on the notion that a waste product is not covered by CERCLA unless specifically listed as a hazardous substance—even when its component parts are hazardous substances—misconstrued CERCLA and must be reversed.

2. *Releasability*

The trial court ruled further that "[t]he absence of evidence of breakdown of products that contain [hazardous substances] ... precludes a finding that disposal of that product constitutes a disposal of [hazardous substances]." *Murtha II*, 815 F.Supp. at 545. Later, it explained that statement by saying that "[l]iability does not lie if the material disposed of would release a [hazardous substance] only on the intervention of another force." *Murtha III*, 840 F.Supp. at 188. The coalitions believe that these pronouncements were wrong.

As noted, to make out a *prima facie* CERCLA case, a plaintiff must show a "release, or a threatened release ... of a hazardous substance." § 9607(a)(4). Accordingly, if a hazardous substance is only used in a non-releasable form in the manufacturing of a product, it may scientifically be impossible for the plaintiff to show a "threatened release." Hence, the district court properly required plaintiffs to show a release or threatened release. But, when it required them to show an actual breakdown of products containing hazardous substances, and determined there was no liability if the hazardous substances would only be released by an intervening force, it acted in a manner contrary to precedent.

In *Alcan*, we held that proof that a defendant's waste did not release listed hazardous substances is only relevant to the issue of apportionment of damages, not to the issue of liability. Independent releasability is not required to establish liability; a defendant otherwise liable may show "nonreleasability" in order to mitigate its share of damages. It follows logically that a defendant who disposes of hazardous substances that are not independently releasable may still be held liable, even though that defendant may not be required to pay damages when the cost apportionment phase of the litigation is reached.

In addition, the trial court's reading of CERCLA is inconsistent with the Act's language, which provides only the four already recited causation-related defenses. 42 U.S.C. § 9607(b). ***

Moreover, if we required a plaintiff to show more than a release or threatened release, we essentially would be asking the plaintiffs to prove that a specific defendant's hazardous substances caused the release of a hazardous substance. No causation is needed, however, to establish liability under CERCLA, because it is, as stated, a strict liability statute. ***

*** Although appellants must show a release or threatened release in order to make out a *prima facie* case, the additional releasability requirement of product breakdown finds no support in CERCLA.

3. *Negligible Amounts*

The coalitions further contend that the district court impermissibly required a showing that appellees disposed of hazardous substances above a threshold amount. It granted summary judgment to an appellee where the amounts of hazardous substances it disposed of were "minuscule," *Murtha III*, 840 F.Supp. at 184, or "[n]ominal," *Murtha II*, 815 F.Supp. at 545. Twice we have said that quantity "is not a factor" when determining CERCLA liability because had Congress wanted to distinguish liability on the basis of quantity, it would have so provided. *Murtha I*, 958 F.2d at 1200; *see also Alcan*, 990 F.2d at 720 ("The statute on its face applies to 'any' hazardous substance, and it does not impose quantitative requirements."). The absence of threshold quantity requirements in CERCLA leads logically to the conclusion that the Act's "hazardous substance" definition includes even minimal amounts. The dismissals on these grounds constitute legal error.

4. *EPA Designation*

The trial judge implied, in a few cases, that the EPA's decision not to designate a party as a potentially responsible party is relevant in determining CERCLA liability. ***In *Murtha I*, 958 F.2d at 1205, we concluded that EPA policy "merely indicates that the EPA presently does not intend to pursue enforcement actions against" unnamed parties. However, here the district court weighed the plaintiffs' evidence of liability "against the backdrop of the EPA Municipal Policy that a [party] would not be charged as a PRP absent evidence that its waste deposited at the site in question contained specific [hazardous substances]." *Murtha III*, 840 F.Supp. at 188.

EPA enforcement decisions are not helpful in deciding whether a party is properly joined as a defendant in a given action. *See Murtha* I, 958 F.2d at 1205 (explaining that EPA prosecutes only largest contributors or those with the means to pay, leaving those defendants to seek contribution from other potentially liable polluters). *** Congress has explicitly authorized private rights of action independent of EPA enforcement decisions. For these reasons, the agency's decision not to initiate its own enforcement action is irrelevant in determining whether a defendant might be liable under CERCLA.

* * *

NOTES

1. The issue labeled here as "negligible amounts" has been raised—always unsuccessfully—by many parties in many CERCLA contexts. The District Court in South Carolina set the tone in *United States v. Carolawn Co.*, 14 Envtl. L. Rep. (Envtl. L. Inst.) 20696 (D.S.C. 1984), where Mobil Chemical Company argued that the water-based paint wastes which it admittedly sent to the site in question were not hazardous substances.

> Mobil admits that its wastes contained trace amounts of copper, lead, zinc, chromium, cadmium, mercury, nickel, silver, arsenic, and selenium, all substances designated as toxic under 33 U.S.C. §1317(a) (Section 307(a) of the Clean Water Act), but maintains that because "water-based paint waste" is not specifically listed as a hazardous substance under any of the statutory provisions referenced in CERCLA Section 101(14), it is not a hazardous substance under CERCLA. Mobil further argues that, in any event, the hazardous constituents of its water-based paint waste were not present in sufficient concentrations or quantities to make the waste a hazardous substance under CERCLA. Mobil's arguments not only run

counter to the express language of CERCLA, but are also at odds with the statute's legislative history and recent caselaw on this issue.[1]

With respect to Mobil's first contention, this court concludes that the fact that "water-based paint waste" is not specifically listed under any of statutory provisions referenced in CERCLA Section 101(14) is not dispositive—whether a material is hazardous under CERCLA depends on the character of its constituents. If a waste material contains hazardous substances, then the waste material is itself a hazardous substance for purposes of CERCLA. To distinguish a waste solution or mixture from its hazardous constituents defies reason. Clearly, if taken out of solution, the constituents would be "hazardous substances." Thus, to the extent that Mobil's wastes contain substances which are hazardous under CERCLA, those wastes are hazardous substances for purposes of imposing CERCLA liability.

Mobil's argument that the hazardous constituents of its wastes were not present in sufficient amounts to make those wastes hazardous substances under CERCLA also must fail. The definition of "hazardous substance" in CERCLA Section 101(14) simply does not distinguish hazardous substances on the basis of quantity of concentration.[3] Instead, the provision refers only to lists, such as the list of toxic pollutants promulgated pursuant to Section 307 of the Clean Water Act, 33 U.S.C. § 1317, which are also non-specific with respect to quantity or concentration. *Id.* at 20697.

---

[1] Apparently, Mobil's water-based paint wastes are not presently regulated under either the Resource Conservation and Recovery Act, 42 U.S.C. § 6901, *et seq*, or the Clean Water Act, 33 U.S.C. § 1251, *et seq.*, notwithstanding the fact that constituents of Mobil's wastes are listed as toxic pollutants under the Clean Water Act. Significantly, however, Congress enacted both of these laws and can be presumed to understand their operation, including the fact that the listing of a substance as hazardous or toxic does not necessarily subject that substance to regulation. This court can only conclude that Congress intended to cast an especially broad remedial net with CERCLA, designed to address the special concerns presented by hazardous wastes [sic] dumps. In enacting CERCLA, the congressional focal point was not so much the degree of existing regulation, but rather that certain substances have been identified as having hazardous propensities, and that these substances, if allowed to accumulate and commingle at poorly managed hazardous waste dumps, might threaten or destroy natural resources and ground water supplies. ***

---

[3] As evidenced by CERCLA Sections 102 and 103, which, in tandem, require facility operators to notify the government of the release of a "reportable quantity" of hazardous substance—usually one pound—Congress was well aware when enacting CERCLA how to make provisions specific with respect to quantity or concentration of a hazardous substance. Presumably, if Congress had intended the definition of hazardous substances to be contingent upon the presence of a certain amount or concentration of a hazardous substance, it would have so provided.

2. Alcan Aluminum Corp. ("Alcan") later launched an aggressive attack on the principle, articulated in *Carolawn*, that the presence of any concentration of a hazardous substance, even if only a trace amount, is sufficient to trigger CERCLA liability.

In at least three different cases, Alcan argued that a waste emulsion that it produced and sent to various disposal sites is not a CERCLA hazardous substance. The emulsion contains trace concentrations of metals (cadmium, copper, and lead) on the list of toxic pollutants under the Clean Water Act and the list of hazardous substances referenced in § 101(14)(B) ("any element, compound, mixture, solution, or substance designated pursuant to section 102 of this Act").

Each of the courts to have passed on Alcan's arguments has held that the presence of a hazardous substance in the emulsion, regardless of concentration, is sufficient to bring the emulsion within the CERCLA definition of hazardous substance, notwithstanding Alcan's claims that the concentrations of the hazardous substances in its emulsion are no greater than those in the brief filed by the government in the case, *City of New York v. Exxon Corp.*, 744 F.Supp. 474 (S.D.N.Y.1991), adhered to on reconsideration, 766 F.Supp. 177 (S.D.N.Y.1991), or than the concentrations in nature, breakfast cereal, and milk, *United States v. Alcan Aluminum Corp.*, 755 F.Supp. 531 (N.D.N.Y.1991). *See also United States v. Alcan Aluminum Corp.*, 964 F.2d 252 (3d Cir.1992). Collectively, these Alcan cases stand for the rule that a substance need not be hazardous, in fact, in order to be a hazardous substance under CERCLA.

3. Another aspect of *B.F. Goodrich Co. v. Betkoski* and its forerunner, *B.F. Goodrich Co. v. Murtha*, is the scope of municipal liability under CERCLA. Municipalities may face liability as owners and/or operators of municipal landfills, as well as arrangers who disposed of municipal waste at solid waste landfills, per *Murtha*.

The EPA estimates that approximately 23 percent of all sites on the NPL are landfills that received municipal and other (such as industrial) waste. 62 Fed. Reg. 37231 (1997). Moreover, some one-third of the total NPL sites involve local governments as PRPs, whether current or past site owners, arrangers, or transporters. *Superfund: Local Governments Involved in Over 400 Sites on National Priorities List, Clean Sites Reports*, 22 Env't Rep. (BNA) 9999 (Feb. 7, 1992).

The EPA has treaded lightly on the politically sensitive issue of municipal liability for CERCLA cleanup costs. In December 1989, the EPA issued an Interim Municipal Settlement Policy, stating that the EPA would not pursue generators and transporters regarding municipal solid waste at CERCLA sites unless site-specific evidence suggested that the waste contained hazardous substances derived from commercial, institutional, or industrial—as opposed to residential—sources.

Since then, the EPA has attempted to set criteria to govern settlements with municipal PRPs. In 1992, the EPA proposed a highly controversial guidance document indicating that municipalities should be liable for approximately four percent of the cost of cleaning up municipal landfill sites. The four percent benchmark was based on the EPA's estimate of the average cost per acre to remediate municipal solid waste compared to industrial waste. *Superfund: Proposal on Municipal Liability Issue Draws Industry Fire, White House Intervention*, 22 Env't Rep. (BNA) 2869 (Apr. 24, 1992). In July 1997, the EPA published a new proposal to guide settlements with municipal PRPs, with one formula addressing municipals who arranged for the transport, or who transported, municipal solid wastes to what are now NPL sites, and another formula for municipalities that owned or operated landfills that are now NPL sites. 62 Fed. Reg. 37231 (1997).

4. The following case addresses the scope of a statutory, rather than regulatory, exemption from the definition of hazardous substance. It also highlights the fact that CERCLA's jurisdiction extends to substances that need not be wastes.

LOUISIANA-PACIFIC CORP. V. ASARCO INC.
24 F.3d 1565 (9th Cir. 1994), *cert. denied*, 513 U.S. 1103 (1995)

Before WRIGHT, THOMPSON and KLEINFELD, Circuit Judges.
THOMPSON, Circuit Judge.

OVERVIEW

This suit arises from the pollution of several sites near the Port of Tacoma ("the Port") by heavy metal contaminants leached from a slag and woodwaste mixture. ASARCO, Inc. ("ASARCO") produced the slag as a by-product of its smelting operations. ASARCO was found liable to the site owners and operators under the Comprehensive Environmental Response, Compensation and Liability Act of 1980, (1988) ("CERCLA"); the Washington Hazardous Waste Management Act.

On appeal, ASARCO contends slag is excluded from CERCLA's definition of hazardous substances under the Bevill Amendment, and the jury's finding that slag was a product for WPLA purposes precluded a finding that it was a hazardous substance under the HWMA and CERCLA. *******

* * *

FACTS

ASARCO has been smelting copper from copper ore at its smelter near Tacoma since 1905. Smelting separates copper out of copper ore and produces large amounts of a by-product called slag. For many years ASARCO dumped most of its slag into Commencement Bay. It had an agreement with the Metropolitan Park District of Tacoma to maintain a breakwater at that site.

In about 1973, ASARCO embarked on a plan to develop a market for its slag. It contracted with Black Knight, Inc. ("Black Knight") to take all of ASARCO's slag and resell what it could. Black Knight decided to market the slag for use as "ballast" in logyards. The logyards used the slag essentially like gravel, to provide firmer ground. This made the storage of logs and the operation of heavy equipment easier. The logyards would use a load of slag until it became too mixed together with woodwaste and other debris. They would then have it hauled away and put down a new load.

Beginning in 1978, the six logyards involved in this suit hauled their slag/woodwaste to the B & L Landfill.

In 1980, the Environmental Protection Agency ("the EPA") found high concentrations of heavy metals in water runoff from one of the Murray-Pacific logyards. The EPA turned its findings over to the Washington Department of Ecology ("the WDOE"). The WDOE determined that slag was the likely cause of the contamination. Over the course of the next several years the WDOE sent letters, made phone calls, and held meetings with representatives of the affected sites, but it took no formal action. In 1986, WDOE began formally requiring cleanups. This case concerns who will bear the cost of these cleanups.

The first party to file suit was Louisiana-Pacific Corp. ("Louisiana-Pacific"). It sued ASARCO for response costs for the cleanup of its logyard and for contribution or indemnity for its liability for the cost of cleanup of the B & L Landfill. It brought the suit under CERCLA. ASARCO counterclaimed against Louisiana-Pacific under CERCLA and state law.

ASARCO also brought third-party claims against several other logyards that had disposed of slag/woodwaste mix at the B & L Landfill. It also sued William Fjetland, the owner and operator of B & L Landfill and B & L Trucking (which had transported the mix), and L-Bar Products, Inc. ("L-Bar"), which had bought assets of Industrial Mineral Products ("IMP"), the parent company of Black Knight. Some of these third-party defendants then counter-claimed against ASARCO. ***

The Port, which owned some of the logyard sites, then sued ASARCO for response costs under CERCLA and state law, and for indemnity and contribution for cleaning up the B & L Landfill. ASARCO filed counter-claims and cross-claims. Later ASARCO amended its third-party complaint in the Louisiana-Pacific action to include claims against another Fjetland company and IMP.

* * *

I

CERCLA LIABILITY

ASARCO argues its liability to all plaintiffs under CERCLA should be reversed because slag contamination is excluded from CERCLA liability under the Bevill Amendment, and the jury's finding that slag is a product under the WPLA precluded a finding by the court that it was a waste under CERCLA. ASARCO further argues that the liability imposed on it for the cleanup of the Portac site should be reversed because the cleanup did not comply with the NCP. Finally, ASARCO argues that even if it is liable under CERCLA, the district court erred in awarding the plaintiffs attorney fees and costs.

A.   Is slag a hazardous substance under CERCLA despite the Bevill Amendment reference in section 9601(14)(C)?

ASARCO contends that slag is excepted from the definition of "hazardous substance" under CERCLA, 42 U.S.C. § 9601(14). This section of the statute provides:

> The term "hazardous substance" means (A) any substance designated pursuant to section 1321(b)(2)(A) of Title 33, (B) any element, compound, mixture, solution, or substance designated pursuant to section 9602 of this title, (C) any hazardous waste having the characteristics identified under or listed pursuant to section 3001 of the Solid Waste Disposal Act [42 U.S.C.A. § 6921] (*but not including any waste the regulation of which under the Solid Waste Disposal Act [42 U.S.C.A. § 6901 et seq.] has been suspended by Act of Congress*), (D) any toxic pollutant listed under section 1317(a) of Title 33, (E) any hazardous air pollutant listed under section 112 of the Clean Air Act [42 U.S.C.A. § 7412], and (F) any imminently hazardous chemical substance or mixture with respect to which the Administrator has taken action pursuant to section 2606 of Title 15. The term does not include petroleum, including crude oil or any fraction thereof which is not otherwise specifically listed or designated as a hazardous substance under subparagraphs (A) through (F) of this paragraph, and the term does not include natural gas, natural gas liquids, liquefied natural gas, or synthetic gas usable for fuel (or mixtures of natural gas and such synthetic gas).

42 U.S.C. § 9601(14) (1988) (emphasis added). It is the underlined exception, which is a reference to the "Bevill Amendment" to the Resource Conservation and Recovery Act of 1976, 42 U.S.C. § 6901 et seq. (1988) ("the RCRA"), on which ASARCO relies.[5]

It is undisputed that slag is a material exempted from RCRA regulation under the Bevill Amendment. ASARCO contends the incorporation of this exemption into section 9601(14)(C) of CERCLA operates to except slag from CERCLA regulation as well. The EPA and the plaintiffs contend the exception in CERCLA § 9601(14)(C) merely prevents slag from being characterized as a hazardous substance under that particular subsection. They argue that if slag releases substances characterized as hazardous under subsections 9601(14)(A), (B), (D), (E) or (F), slag is subject to CERCLA regulation.

---

[5]The Bevill Amendment provides, in relevant part that

> [n]otwithstanding the provisions of paragraph (1) of this subsection, each waste listed below shall, except as provided in subparagraph (B) of this paragraph, be subject only to regulation under other applicable provisions of Federal or State law in lieu of this subchapter until at least six months after the date of submission of the applicable study required to be conducted ... and after promulgation of regulations in accordance with subparagraph (C) of this paragraph:
>
> (i) Fly ash waste, bottom ash waste, *slag waste*,....

42 U.S.C. § 6921(b)(3)(A) (1988) (emphasis added).

This is a question of first impression in this circuit. The D.C. Circuit in *Eagle-Picher Indus., Inc. v. United States EPA*, 759 F.2d 922 (D.C.Cir.1985), concluded that the specific exception in subsection C applied only to that subsection and that mining wastes and fly ash were subject to CERCLA liability as hazardous substances under other subsections of section 9601(14). We agree with this approach.

The district court found that slag's components include copper, lead, arsenic and zinc. These are hazardous substances under subsections (A), (B) and (D) of section 9601(14). *See* 40 C.F.R. § 302.4 (listing copper, arsenic, lead and zinc under CERCLA § 102); 40 C.F.R. § 401.15 (listing copper, arsenic, lead and zinc under Clean Water Act § 307); 40 C.F.R. § 116.4 (listing arsenic trioxide under Clean Water Act § 311).

It is sufficient for CERCLA regulation that a substance is covered by any of the subsections of section 9601(14). The fact that slag is excepted from subsection (C) by the Bevill Amendment has no bearing on whether slag in its component forms is excepted from the other subsections. If it were to be so excepted, logically a more general exception applicable to all of the subsections, or at least to those that would encompass slag by including its components, would have been used. This is what Congress did when it excepted petroleum products from all of the subsections by the general exception at the end of section 9601(14) which provides:

> The term ["hazardous substance"] does not include petroleum, including crude oil or any fraction thereof which is not otherwise specifically listed or designated as a hazardous substance under subparagraphs (A) through (F) of this paragraph, and the term does not include natural gas, natural gas liquids, liquefied natural gas, or synthetic gas usable for fuel (or mixtures of natural gas and such synthetic gas).

42 U.S.C. § 9601(14) (1988).

Had Congress intended to except slag from CERCLA regulation as it did petroleum products, it easily could have done so. It did not. It is clear from the plain language and structure of section 9601 that the specific exception for slag in subsection (C) applies only to that subsection and that slag is regulated by CERCLA to the extent that it falls under any other subsection of section 9601(14).

* * *

Assuming *arguendo* that section 9601(14) is ambiguous as ASARCO contends, any ambiguity has been laid to rest by the interpretation of the statute by the EPA, the agency charged with administering CERCLA.

* * *

The EPA has interpreted section 9601(14) to mean that the Bevill Amendment exception in subsection (C) refers only to that subsection. 48 Fed.Reg. 40663 (1983). The reasonableness of this interpretation is demonstrated by our analysis of what we have concluded to be the plain meaning of the statute.

ASARCO nonetheless argues we should hold that the EPA's interpretation of the statute is unreasonable because it would result in the complete nullification of the Bevill Amendment exception in subsection (C), an exception which specifically applies to slag. It points to the uncontradicted trial testimony of Dr. Twidwell, a doctor of metallurgical engineering with extensive experience. Dr. Twidwell testified that the components of all or virtually all Bevill Amendment wastes would fall under one of the other five categories of hazardous substances in section 9601(14). ASARCO argues Congress would not have enacted a meaningless provision of the statute. According to ASARCO, unless slag is entirely exempted from CERCLA by the Bevill Amendment exception in subsection (C), that exception is meaningless, because what the Bevill Amendment excepts from the statute in subsection (C) would be cancelled out by the inclusion of slag components in other subsections of section 9601.

ASARCO's argument is based on a false premise. It assumes that Congress meant for the statute to say something other than what it plainly says. What is clear is that Congress thought about an exemption for petroleum products and about hazardous wastes, including slag which is covered by the Bevill Amendment. Congress expressly provided a general exemption for petroleum products. It provided an exemption for slag only in subsection (C).

We hold that the specific exception for slag in subsection (C) of section 9601(14) of CERCLA applies only to that subsection and that slag and its components are regulated to the extent they fall within any of the other subsections of section 9601(14). Because the components slag leaches into the soil fall within at least one of the other subsections of section 9601(14), slag is regulated as a hazardous substance by CERCLA.

B.   If slag is a "product" under the WPLA, may it also be a "waste" under CERCLA?

ASARCO contends that the jury's special verdict finding that slag was a "product" for purposes of the Washington Products Liability Act precludes the district court from finding that slag is a "waste" under CERCLA.

Washington law defines a product as "any object possessing intrinsic value, capable of delivery either as an assembled whole or as a component part or parts, and produced for introduction into trade or commerce." Wash.Rev.Code Ann. § 7.72.010(3) (West 1992). The jury, by its special verdict, determined that slag fit this definition. CERCLA, on the other hand, imposes liability on "any person who ... arranged for disposal or treatment ... of hazardous substances owned or possessed by such person...." 42 U.S.C. § 9607(a)(3) (1988). The issue raised by ASARCO is whether the sale of slag to the logyards can simultaneously be both the sale of a product with intrinsic value in trade or commerce under Washington law, and the disposal of a hazardous substance under CERCLA. We conclude that it can.

The WPLA and CERCLA address different concerns. The WPLA is a codification of the common law of products liability, with such changes as the Washington legislature thought appropriate. CERCLA is a federal law designed to facilitate the cleanup of waste that threatens the environment. A by-product of a metallurgical process, if sold, can be a product for purposes of one and waste for purposes of the other. This is especially so given that CERCLA is to be broadly interpreted to achieve its remedial goals.

District courts have concluded that CERCLA liability is possible for the disposal of wastes that are also products. *See, e.g., United States v. Conservation Chem. Co.,* 619 F.Supp. 162, 240-41 (W.D.Mo.1985) (sale of lime slurry and fly ash for cleanup of environmental site); *State of New York v. General Elec. Co.,* 592 F.Supp. 291, 297 (N.D.N.Y.1984) (sale of used transformer oil to dragstrip for use in controlling dust); *United States v. A & F Materials Co., Inc.,* 582 F.Supp. 842, 844-45 (S.D.Ill.1984) (sale of caustic solution to neutralize acidic oil).

In *A & F Materials,* the district court was faced with the question whether the sale of spent "caustic solution," a by-product of the manufacture of jet aircraft, could subject McDonnell Douglas to CERCLA liability. McDonnell Douglas was able to sell the solution for 7.2 cents per gallon to A & F Materials which used it to neutralize acidic oil. *Id.* at 844. In deciding whether this was a waste disposal for CERCLA purposes, the court said "the definition of waste was intended to cover those hazardous materials which are of nominal commercial value and which were sometimes sold or reused and sometimes discarded." *Id.* The court concluded that the question whether the solution was a waste was a disputed issue of fact and that summary judgment was inappropriate. *Id.* at 845.

Slag, like the caustic solution in *A & F Materials,* is at best a by-product. ASARCO's principal business is the smelting of copper. McDonnell Douglas's principal business is the manufacture of aircraft. Both slag and the caustic solution are by-products with a nominal commercial value. The logging companies paid $3.50 per ton for slag, and preferred it to gravel as a "ballast." Similarly, A & F paid 7.2 cents per gallon for the caustic solution and used it to neutralize acidic oils. Both by-products were materials their producers wanted to get rid of whether they could sell them or not. ASARCO had dumped slag in Commencement Bay for years before that means of disposal became infeasible. McDonnell Douglas paid to have the caustic solution hauled away after A & F stopped buying it. We conclude that the jury's finding that slag was a product under the WPLA did not preclude the court from finding it was a waste under CERCLA.[6]

* * *

---

[6] ASARCO points to a number of cases in which courts have held that products were not waste for purposes of CERCLA or that sales were not disposal. *See, e.g., 3550 Stevens Creek Assoc. v. Barclays Bank,* 915 F.2d 1355 (9th Cir.1990), *cert. denied,* 500 U.S. 917, 111 S.Ct. 2014, 114 L.Ed.2d 101 (1991); *Dayton Indep. School Dist. v. U.S. Mineral Products Co.,* 906 F.2d 1059 (5th Cir.1990); *Florida Power & Light Co. v. Allis Chalmers Corp.,* 893 F.2d 1313 (11th Cir.1990). These cases, however, involved products that were produced as the producers' principal business products, not by-products that the producers had to get rid of. Here, ASARCO's accounting manager responsible for devising a solution to the problem of slag accumulation described the dilemma facing ASARCO as follows: "Our life was hanging by a thread. There was a limited area for disposing of the slag. If you can't get rid of the slag, you are out of business."

NOTES

1. Do you agree with the Ninth Circuit's response to the argument that limiting the Bevill Amendment exception to § 101(14)(C) nullifies the exception entirely? The Ninth Circuit rejected the argument as inconsistent with the plain meaning of the statute. Is it?

2. In light of the courts' consistent application of CERCLA's exceptionally-broad definition of hazardous substance, potentially responsible parties have sought other legal bases on which to pin the underlying argument that their substance is not harmful. Sometimes the argument focuses on whether there is an actual or threatened "release" of the hazardous substance in question.

3. In *Stewman v. Mid-South Wood Products of Mena, Inc.*, 993 F.2d 646 (8th Cir. 1993), the plaintiffs owned property neighboring a wood treatment facility, part of which was cleaned up by its current and former owners pursuant to a CERCLA consent decree. After the EPA certified that the cleanup had been completed, plaintiffs sued the current and former owners and operators, as well as the EPA and others involved with the cleanup, alleging that the cleanup had not been successful and that their properties were contaminated with hazardous substances from the Superfund site. Finding that the concentrations of hazardous substances on plaintiffs' properties were so low as to be naturally occurring (according to defendants' experts), the district court held that there was no release or threatened release of hazardous substances from the site. The Eighth Circuit affirmed:

> *** Appellants argue it is undisputed that the Mid-South site has been and is the repository for waste products from wood processing, specifically, creosote compounds, PCP, and CCA. They further argue that all of these substances have been "released" into the environment from the Mid-South site and have migrated off the site by means of ground water, surface water and air-borne dust. Appellants contend that water samples taken from the Mid-South site contain PCP, arsenic, and chromium and that the district court erred in finding there had been no release or threat of release because the test levels were lower than the test levels in the Safe Drinking Water Act. Appellants admit the test levels are low, but they argue that under CERCLA there is no minimum quantitative requirement for a release of a hazardous substance, that is, any release of a substance on the List of Hazardous Substances (or other federal or state environmental standard) violates CERCLA as a matter of law.
>
> Ehlco and Mid-South agree that there is no minimum quantitative requirement for a release of hazardous substances, but argue a "factual inquiry" is required in order to determine whether the particular hazard justified any response action and therefore "caused" the incurrence of response costs. *See, e.g., Amoco Oil Co. v. Borden, Inc.*, 889 F.2d 664, 669-70 (5th Cir. 1989); *see also United States v. Alcan Aluminum Corp.*, 964 F.2d 252, 259 (3d Cir. 1992). Mid-South argues that *** there can be

no CERCLA liability unless some quantitative level has been reached, posing a threat to the public or the environment. Mid-South argues appellants failed to prove that the substances came from the Mid-South site as opposed to nature because chromium, copper, and arsenic occur naturally. Ehlco argues there is no CERCLA liability for cleaning up naturally occurring substances or for discharges pursuant to state or federal permits, which, it argues, is what occurred here.

*** The district court credited the testimony of expert witness Dr. Harbison and found the methodology of appellants' expert to be suspect. The district court adopted Dr. Harbison's view that no release of hazardous substances from the Mid-South site had occurred and that there was no threat of such a release. After a careful review of the record, we hold the district court's finding of no release or threat of release is not clearly erroneous.

We agree with the holding in *Amoco* that there is no minimum quantitative requirement to establish a release or threat of a release of a hazardous substance under CERCLA. In *Amoco*, the court found that there had been a release because defendant had disposed of hazardous substances on the property and gas was emanating from the hazardous substances. In *Alcan*, the parties stipulated that there had been a release. In the present case, unlike *Amoco* and *Alcan*, the issue was whether or not there had been a release at all.

Id. at 649.

4. Applying its own precedent in *Amoco*, the Fifth Circuit recently suggested that the concept of a de minimis, non-actionable release may be gaining some favor.

LICCIARDI V. MURPHY
111 F.3d 396 (5th Cir. 1997)

Before HIGGINBOTHAM, SMITH and BARKSDALE, Circuit Judges.
PER CURIAM.

I

From 1991 through 1993, the Licciardis hired a number of environmental testing and consulting firms to take and test environmental samples from their property located adjacent to Murphy Oil's Meraux refinery in Louisiana. Armed with results of these tests, the Licciardis filed suit under § 107 of the Comprehensive Environmental Response, Compensation, and Liability Act, 42 U.S.C. § 9607, alleging that the samples demonstrate that Murphy contaminated their property with leaded tank bottoms and refinery sludge in violation of environmental law.

The bench trial was bifurcated into liability and damages phases. Following the liability phase, the district court entered its findings. The court found that a certain "black tarry substance" from a sample taken from the Licciardis' property came from Murphy's refinery, finding that the level of lead concentration in the soil at the testing site exceeded background levels. The court held that defendant's release of the substance caused plaintiffs' response costs. The district court observed that the "presence of any hazardous substances [above background levels] on plaintiffs' property is sufficient to justify their incurring response costs." After ordering briefs from the parties on damages, the trial court awarded the Licciardis $12,337, the amount which Murphy stipulated to as the Licciardis' expense for testing for substances defined as "hazardous" under CERCLA. Both sides appeal. Murphy contests any finding of liability while the Licciardis assert that all of their expenses on sampling and testing should have been awarded as damages.

II

There are four elements to a CERCLA cost-recovery action, such as the one here: (1) the site must be a "facility" under § 9601(9); (2) the defendant must be a "responsible person" under § 9607(a); (3) a release or threatened release of a hazardous substance must have occurred; and (4) the release or threatened release must have caused the plaintiff to incur response costs. *Amoco Oil Co. v. Borden, Inc.*, 889 F.2d 664, 668 (5th Cir.1989). The first and second of these elements are not in issue here. Murphy is a "responsible person" and its refinery is a "facility." The district court correctly noted that lead is a "hazardous substance" under 40 C.F.R. § 302.4.

In *Amoco*, we rejected the proposition that CERCLA "liability attaches upon release of *any* quantity of a hazardous substance." 889 F.2d at 670 (emphasis original). We explained that the question of whether a release has "caused" or justified response costs is tempered by the purpose of the Act. *Id.* Although we acknowledged that it is "not the exclusive means of justifying response costs, [ ] a plaintiff who has incurred response costs meets the liability requirement as a matter of law if it is shown that *any* release violates ... *any* applicable state or federal standard, including the most stringent." *Id.* at 671 (emphasis original). However, the district court's reliance upon a violation of a standard and *Amoco* was misplaced, as we will explain.

The district court concluded that any lead found in the sample "exceeding background levels" constituted a release that caused the Licciardis' response costs under CERCLA if the lead came from Murphy's refinery. Although the district court did not specify, the record reflects that its reference to "background levels" refers to the 1984 U.S. Geological Survey.

The U.S. Geological Survey measures empirical evidence relating certain topological and geological facts for a point on the globe. It is not a legal standard. We are aware of no environmental law, state or federal, that establishes the U.S. Geological Survey "background level" as a standard, requirement, or criterion. Relatedly, it is not clear that the Survey figure used by the district court was relevant; according to an expert who testified at trial, the "background level" relied upon by the district court was established "30 to 50 miles away from the Meraux refinery."

The trial court also considered the drinking water standard and the toxic concentration leaching procedure (or "TCLP") standard. According to plaintiffs' expert, the drinking water standard establishes a legally acceptable limit for lead "at the tap," but none of the experts at trial attempted to link the standard to groundwater tests. Moreover, plaintiffs' expert admitted at trial that she had not carried out any groundwater testing, and that there was insufficient data to form any opinion that the Licciardis' property had been affected by groundwater migration from the refinery. As for the TCLP standard, plaintiffs' expert explained that even if a material contains lead, EPA does not consider it "hazardous" unless the lead is capable of "leaching" out of the material. The TCLP standard, she explained, is an extraction procedure under which a scientist simulates a landfill environment with rainfall and acidity controls, then tests for lead in the resulting leachate. Plaintiffs admitted in their Supplemental Post-Trial Memorandum that the "TCLP analysis was below regulatory levels." Thus, even though they have expended significant effort and resources testing their property and hiring experts, plaintiffs have been unable to offer any evidence that any regulatory standard has been breached.

Without the Geological Survey, the drinking water standard, or the TCLP standard as possible bases for finding that Murphy's release caused response costs, we ask whether, in the absence of any other evidence, a finding of hazardous substance "above background levels" is sufficient to support a finding that the release caused response costs. As we explained in *Amoco*, responsible parties are not liable unless there is evidence that they "posed [a] threat to the public or the environment." While *Amoco* allows a CERCLA plaintiff to prove that response costs were caused by a release without resort to an applicable legal standard of justification, bare proof that there was a release is not enough; as we have explained, liability does not attach to the release of "*any* quantity of a hazardous substance." *Id.* at 670-71. "[T]he question of whether a release has caused the incurrence of response costs should rest upon a factual inquiry into the circumstances of a case and the relevant factual inquiry should focus on whether the particular hazard justified any response actions." Id. at 670. We have been pointed to no evidence that the found "release" justified the response costs. We cannot sustain the district court's finding of liability.

NOTES

1. Is this decision consistent with Second Circuit's construction of CERCLA jurisdiction in *B.F. Goodrich v. Betkoski*? Is it compatible with the Ninth Circuit's approach in *Louisiana-Pacific Corp. v. ASARCO, Inc.*?

2. How does CERCLA apply to a substance that biodegrades over time, so that when the site where it has been deposited is eventually remediated, the hazardous components are no longer present? One court has responded as follows:

> In essence, Celanese is arguing that any hazardous substances in its waste were released at the site a long time ago, have long since

biodegraded, and therefore, those hazardous substances have not caused the contamination that required remediation. Celanese's arguments on these points are persuasive, but those arguments go to damages, not liability precisely because CERCLA imposes strict liability on any party whose waste is contained at the site.

Textron, Inc. v. Barber-Coleman Co., 903 F.Supp. 1570, 1581 (E.D.N.C. 1995).

9   THE EPA'S POWERS UNDER CERCLA SECTIONS 104, 106, AND 107

CERCLA provides the EPA with an impressive arsenal of legal weaponry. The principal components of this arsenal are CERCLA § 104, which authorizes the EPA to use Superfund monies to conduct response activities, § 107, which enables the EPA to sue PRPs to recover such response costs, and § 106, which empowers the EPA to issue administrative orders or seek court orders requiring PRPs to conduct response activities. Complementing these provisions granting various powers to the EPA are several noteworthy provisions that restrict the PRPs' maneuverability in contesting the EPA's decisions and actions. For example, the recipient of an administrative order issued by the EPA under § 106 may not challenge its issuance or content unless and until an enforcement action is brought, at which time the recipient PRP may be subject to civil penalties of up to $25,000 per day and treble damages for the EPA's cleanup costs if the PRP cannot prove that it had "sufficient cause" for not complying with the order when issued.§§ 106(b)(1)(civil penalty), 107(c)(3)(treble damages), and 113(h)(no pre-enforcement review of § 106 order). And, as addressed in the following chapters, liability is strict and presumptively joint and several, with few and narrow defenses.

The statutory bar on pre-enforcement review, §113(h), was added to CERCLA by the 1986 amendments. Before then, however, courts had implied such a bar from the statutory scheme. For example, the Second Circuit explained as follows:

> Other courts—concluding that Congress did not provide for pre-enforcement judicial review under CERCLA—have held that subject matter jurisdiction is lacking in federal district court. These courts believe that Congress envisioned a procedure that permits the EPA to move expeditiously in the face of a potential environmental disaster. To introduce the delay of court proceedings at the outset of a cleanup would conflict with the strong congressional policy that directs cleanups to occur prior to a final determination of the partys' rights and liabilities under CERCLA. These policy concerns extend across the spectrum of possible EPA responses including the response taken here—ordering a private party to remedy a chemical spill. Hence, we agree "unequivocally that pre-enforcement review of EPA's remedial actions ... (is) contrary to the policies underlying CERCLA." *Wheaton Industries*, 781 F.2d at 356. The district court lacks jurisdiction to consider the appropriateness of appellant's act of God defense.

Wagner Seed Co. v. Daggett, 800 F.2d 310, 314-15 (2d Cir. 1986).

Of the numerous and varied constitutional attacks launched against CERCLA by the PRP community when the statute was initially enacted, the only one which gave the courts some pause was the claim that the unavailability of pre-enforcement review of an administrative order, combined with severe penalties for noncompliance, violated the order recipients' constitutional rights to due process. The following case, which was filed before the 1986 amendments but decided by the Eighth Circuit after their enactment, addresses the constitutional issue.

SOLID STATE CIRCUITS, INC. v. UNITED STATES ENVIRONMENTAL PROTECTION AGENCY
812 F.2d 383 (8th Cir. 1987)

Before HEANEY and BOWMAN, Circuit Judges, and MORRIS S. ARNOLD, District Judge for the Western District of Arkansas.
HEANEY, Circuit Judge.

In this appeal, appellants challenge the district court's finding that the punitive damages provision of the Comprehensive Environmental Response, Compensation, and Liability Act (CERCLA), 42 U.S.C. § 9607(c)(3), does not violate their due process rights. We affirm.

I. FACTUAL BACKGROUND

On March 6, 1985, after two months of negotiations, the United States Environmental Protection Agency (EPA) issued a clean-up order to Solid State Circuits, Inc. (Solid State) and Paradyne Corporation (Paradyne) pursuant to section 106(a) of CERCLA, 42 U.S.C. § 9606(a). The order contained factual findings including: (1) from April, 1968, to October, 1973, Solid State conducted manufacturing operations in a leased building in Republic, Missouri; (2) Solid State used trichloroethylene (TCE) and a copper based plating solution in its operation, and stored the used chemicals in an unlined pit in the basement of a building at the site; (3) TCE and copper are harmful to humans; (4) in 1982, corporate ownership of Solid State was transferred to Paradyne; (5) recent soil and groundwater samples from the vicinity of the site show TCE and copper contamination; (6) the contamination poses a threat to the drinking water of Republic, Missouri, the aquifers underlying the site, and the health of humans and animals in the vicinity. The order concluded that Solid State's handling of the TCE and copper was the cause of the contamination and the chemicals posed an "imminent and substantial endangerment to the public health, welfare, or the environment." The order directed Solid State and Paradyne, as responsible parties, to obtain access to contaminated areas, to provide security at the facility, to submit a detailed clean-up plan to the EPA, and to notify the EPA within two days of their intent to comply with the order. No party contends that either applicable EPA regulations or CERCLA provided for an administrative hearing at which the findings of fact or conclusions of law in the order could have been challenged.

On March 14, 1985, Solid State and Paradyne filed suit in federal district court to enjoin the EPA from enforcing the order, from assessing daily penalties for failure to comply with the order, and from assessing treble damages for failing to comply with the order. As part of the suit, Paradyne attempted to raise, as defenses to the EPA's order, that it was not a responsible party under CERCLA and that even if it were, it could not gain access to the contaminated site under reasonable terms to perform required clean-up operations because it has no property interest whatsoever in the site. Paradyne and Solid State also challenged the constitutionality of the treble damage and fine provisions of CERCLA, 42 U.S.C. § 9606(b) and § 9607(c)(3), on the ground that the provisions deprived them of their due process rights to challenge the validity and applicability of the EPA's order without facing ruinous fines and penalties.

On April 18, 1985, the EPA, pursuant to section 104 of CERCLA, 42 U.S.C. § 9604, began the clean-up it had ordered Paradyne and Solid State to perform. The clean-up was completed by November of 1985.

On May 20, 1985, the EPA moved to dismiss the suit by Paradyne and Solid State. The EPA argued that the court had no jurisdiction to review the merits of an order issued pursuant to section 106 of CERCLA because the statute does not provide for pre-enforcement review of such orders. In addition, the EPA argued that since it had begun its own clean-up of the site, it would not seek to enforce its order or to collect daily penalties for noncompliance. Thus, the EPA argued that the court should dismiss the case because the issues whether to enjoin enforcement of the order or collection of daily penalties were moot, and because the issue whether to enjoin assessment of treble damages was not yet ripe inasmuch as the EPA can only assess such damages as part of a separate action in federal district court under CERCLA § 107, and no such action had yet been brought.

The district court agreed it lacked subject matter jurisdiction to engage in pre-enforcement review of the merits of an order issued by the EPA pursuant to section 106 of CERCLA. Thus, the court refused to address the merits of Paradyne's and Solid State's defenses to the order. The court also agreed that the EPA's commencement of the clean-up rendered Paradyne's and Solid State's request for an injunction prohibiting the EPA from seeking to enforce its order or to collect penalties for non-compliance moot. The court, however, found it had jurisdiction to consider the claim by Paradyne and Solid State relating to the constitutionality of that portion of CERCLA's statutory scheme subjecting them to treble damages for failing to comply with the EPA's order.

*** Proceeding to the merits of the constitutional claim, the court held that there is no violation of due process in the application of the CERCLA statutory scheme ***. Thus, the court refused to enjoin the EPA from seeking to assess treble damages against Paradyne and Solid State pursuant to section 107(c)(3) of CERCLA. Paradyne and Solid State appeal the district court's ruling only with respect to the due process issue.

II. THE STATUTORY SCHEME OF CERCLA

Recognizing the grave consequences arising from delays in cleaning up hazardous waste sites, Congress gave the EPA authority to direct clean-up operations prior to a final judicial determination of the rights and liabilities of the parties affected. Thus, if the EPA has determined that a hazardous substance has been or is likely to be released at a facility, and has issued an order to the responsible party directing clean-up operations, it has several enforcement options available.

First, the EPA may bring an action in federal district court seeking an order directing compliance with its order using the contempt powers of the court as a sanction for non-compliance. *See* CERCLA § 106(a), 42 U.S.C. § 9606(a). Second, it may bring an action in federal district court seeking to impose fines of up to $5,000 a day for non-compliance. *See* CERCLA § 106(b), 42 U.S.C. § 9606(b).[4] Finally, if the EPA determines that a release of a hazardous substance may pose an imminent and substantial danger to the public health or welfare and that the responsible parties will not properly respond, it may arrange for the required clean-up itself and pay for it using funds from the Hazardous Substance Response Trust Fund (Superfund) created as part of CERCLA. *See* CERCLA § 104(a), 42 U.S.C. § 9604(a) (authorizing the EPA to conduct clean-up); CERCLA § 221, 42 U.S.C. § 9631 (creating Superfund); CERCLA § 111(a), 42 U.S.C. § 9611(a) (authorizing the EPA to pay clean-up costs from the Superfund).

Since Superfund money is limited, Congress clearly intended private parties to assume clean-up responsibility. In addition, it sought to ensure that responsible parties would not delay clean-up activities until the EPA felt it necessary to perform the required work itself. Thus, in addition to allowing the EPA to bring an action for actual costs incurred by the Superfund in conducting the clean-up, *see* CERCLA § 107(a), Congress established a cause of action allowing the EPA, in its discretion, to bring a claim in federal district court to recover up to three times the amount of any costs incurred by the Superfund from any person who is liable for a release or threatened release of a hazardous substance and who fails without sufficient cause to properly comply with the EPA's order. *See* CERCLA § 107(c)(3).

---

[4] At the time the EPA issued its orders, CERCLA § 106(b) provided:

> Any person who willfully violates, or fails or refuses to comply with, any order of the President under subsection (a) of this section may, in an action brought in the appropriate United States district court to enforce such order, be fined not more than $5,000 for each day in which such violation occurs or such failure to comply continues.

The section has since been amended to include a "sufficient cause" defense. The provision now reads: "(1) Any person who, without sufficient cause, willfully violates * * *." Superfund Amendments and Reauthorization Act of 1986 (to be codified at 42 U.S.C. § 9606(a)(1)).

III. ANALYSIS

Because neither CERCLA nor applicable EPA regulations or practice provides for a pre-enforcement hearing at which the merits of the EPA's order could be tested, *** Paradyne and Solid State argue that the statutory scheme of CERCLA violates their right to due process by depriving them of any meaningful opportunity to test the validity of the EPA's order "without incurring the prospect of debilitating or confiscatory penalties." *Brown & Williamson Tobacco Corp. v. Engman*, 527 F.2d 1115, 1119 (2d Cir.1975), *cert. denied*, 426 U.S. 911 (1976).

In essence, Paradyne and Solid State argue that upon receiving the EPA order they found themselves stuck between a rock and a hard place. They assert that, under the statutory scheme, if they had chosen to comply with the EPA's order and were later found to have a valid defense to liability, they would have been forced to bring an action against the responsible party in order to obtain reimbursement for the clean-up. If the responsible party could not have been located or determined or had turned out to be judgment proof, they would have been forced to bear the cost of a clean-up for which they were not liable. On the other hand, if Paradyne and Solid State had refused to comply, they would have been exposed to the possibility of treble liability under CERCLA § 107(c)(3).[9] In addition, Paradyne and Solid State contend that even if the

---

[9] Although coming too late to do them any good, the hardship posed by the dilemma Paradyne and Solid State supposedly faced upon being served with the clean-up order has been ameliorated significantly by the recent amendments to CERCLA. Section 106(b) of CERCLA has been amended to allow a person who receives and complies with a clean-up order a right of action against the Superfund for costs incurred in performing the required clean-up provided certain conditions are met. The amendment states:

(2)(A) Any person who receives and complies with the terms of any order issued under subsection (a) may, within 60 days after completion of the required action, petition the President for reimbursement from the Fund for the reasonable costs of such action, plus interest. ***

(B) If the President refuses to grant all or part of a petition made under this paragraph, the petitioner may within 30 days of receipt of such refusal file an action against the President in the appropriate United States district court seeking reimbursement from the Fund.

(C) Except as provided in subparagraph (D), to obtain reimbursement, the petitioner shall establish by a preponderance of the evidence that it is not liable for response costs under section 107(a) and that costs for which it seeks reimbursement are reasonable in light of the action required by the relevant order.

(D) A petitioner who is liable for response costs under section 107(a) may also recover its reasonable costs of response to the extent that it can demonstrate, on the administrative record, that the President's decision in selecting the response action ordered was arbitrary and capricious or was otherwise not in accordance with law. Reimbursement awarded under this subparagraph shall include all reasonable response costs incurred by the petitioner pursuant to the portions of the order found to be arbitrary and capricious or otherwise not in accordance with law.

* * *

Superfund Amendments and Reauthorization Act of 1986 (to be codified at 42 U.S.C. § 9606(a)(2)).

EPA did not bring an action for treble damages, they would still have had to carry the potential treble liability on all public financing disclosures for an indefinite period because, at the time the EPA issued its order, there was no statute of limitations on EPA cost recovery actions. Paradyne and Solid State contend this "Hobson's choice" between compliance and potential treble liability effectively prevents a challenge to an EPA order.

The due process argument has its origins in *Ex Parte Young*, 209 U.S. 123 (1908). That case establishes that a statutory scheme violates due process if "the penalties for disobedience are by fines so enormous and imprisonment so severe as to intimidate [an affected party] from resorting to the courts to test the validity of the legislation." *Id.* at 209 U.S. 147. It concludes that in such a situation "the result is the same as if the law in terms prohibited the [affected party] from seeking judicial construction of laws which deeply affect its rights." *Id.*

Paradyne and Solid State, however, acknowledge that the constitutional requirements of *Ex Parte Young* are met if the challenged statutory scheme may be interpreted so that no penalty is imposed if the challenging party has reasonable grounds to contest the validity or applicability of an administrative order. ***

Expansion of the *Ex Parte Young* doctrine to preclude imposition of statutory penalties if the plaintiff has reasonable grounds to contest the validity or applicability of an administrative order is important in this case because the challenged treble damage provision of CERCLA provides:

> If any person who is liable for a release or threat of release of a hazardous substance fails *without sufficient cause* to properly provide removal or remedial action upon order of the President pursuant to section 9604 or 9606 of this title, such person may be liable to the United States for punitive damages in an amount at least equal to, and not more than three times, the amount of any costs incurred by the Fund as a result of such failure to take proper action.

CERCLA § 107(c)(3)(emphasis added). Thus, this case presents the question whether the sufficient cause defense provided in CERCLA § 107(c)(3) affords adequate protection against imposition of the treble damage penalty to allow a challenge to an EPA clean-up order as required by *Ex Parte Young* and its progeny.

Paradyne and Solid State argue that the sufficient cause defense provides adequate protection only if it is interpreted to encompass a subjective good faith belief in the invalidity or inapplicability of an EPA clean-up order. In support of their position, they point to *Aminoil, Inc. v. United States*, 646 F.Supp. 294 (C.D. Cal.1986) (*Aminoil II*). In that case, the court stated:

Thus, we note that, in the future, parties wishing to avoid treble liability may apparently perform any required clean-up, with the assurances that if recovery is unavailable from a third party and they are not a responsible party, recovery may be had from the Superfund.

[T]he phrase "sufficient cause" should be interpreted to mean a "good faith" defense. Under such an interpretation, plaintiffs are sufficiently protected against the threat of punitive damages under § 9607(c)(3). Punitive damages may only be assessed where the Government proves that plaintiffs have refused to comply with the order in bad faith. For example, if the Government can prove that plaintiffs have challenged the merits of the order simply for the purpose of delay, punitive damages should be assessed. Consequently, the risk that plaintiffs would forego a valid challenge to the order would not offend Due Process principles.

Id. at 299.   Thus, Paradyne and Solid State contend that only by adopting an interpretation similar to that enunciated in *Aminoil II* can this Court find the treble damage provision constitutional.

The EPA, on the other hand, urges us to interpret sufficient cause as encompassing an objective standard arguing that:

As a federal agency, EPA must be presumed to act correctly, and ultimately review of the administrative order must be on an arbitrary and capricious standard. Thus, only a reasonable belief that the agency acted arbitrarily and capriciously in issuing the order would be sufficient cause for non-compliance.

Brief of Appellee at 31 n.15. ***

As a matter of constitutional law, we believe that the label "objective" or "subjective" is not as important as the functional significance of the standard. To put it another way, to pass constitutional requirements, the standard must provide parties served with EPA clean-up orders a real and meaningful opportunity to test the validity of the order. At the same time, the standard must protect the government's interest in encouraging parties to conduct clean-ups promptly and in promoting settlements once the EPA has performed clean-ups itself so as to avoid using resources necessary to respond to threats posed by hazardous waste on litigation to replenish the Superfund. We are, therefore, convinced that "sufficient cause" as used in CERCLA § 107(c)(3) may be constitutionally interpreted to mean that treble damages may not be assessed if the party opposing such damages had an objectively reasonable basis for believing that the EPA's order was either invalid or inapplicable to it.[11]

---

[11] We emphasize that the only issue properly before this Court is the constitutionality of CERCLA's treble damage provision. The question of the proper interpretation of that section as a matter of statutory construction is only before this Court insofar as it may be necessary to determine its constitutionality. ***

We note, however, without deciding the issue, that the legislative history of the recent CERCLA Amendments states:

The phrase "without sufficient cause" is currently set forth as a defense to liability for treble damages in section 107(c)(3) of CERCLA. The government has argued and the courts have interpreted this phrase to mean that a party will not be liable for treble damages for failing to comply with an EPA order when the party has a reasonable good faith belief that it has a valid defense to that order. ***

To avoid potential unfairness that might arise from the limitation on the timing of review of section 106 orders, this amendment expressly extends the "sufficient cause" defense to the penalty provision in section 106. The amendment contemplates that the phrase "sufficient cause"

Under this standard, a court assessing the objective reasonableness of a party's challenge to a clean-up order must keep in mind that the EPA is presumed to have acted correctly, and its decision to issue such an order may be found erroneous only if it acted arbitrarily or capriciously. Thus, in order to establish the objective reasonableness of a challenge to an EPA clean-up order, a party must show that the applicable provisions of CERCLA, EPA regulations and policy statements, and any formal or informal hearings or guidance the EPA may provide, give rise to an objectively reasonable belief in the invalidity or inapplicability of the clean-up order. We note, however, that in some instances, CERCLA itself is silent or ambiguous, and the EPA has failed to promulgate regulations or to issue position statements that could allow a party to weigh in advance the probability that the clean-up order is valid or applicable. Absent such guidance, it will also be difficult for a court to determine the reasonableness of a challenge to the order notwithstanding the presumption of validity an agency order enjoys.

In such instances, therefore, it would be patently unreasonable and inequitable for a court to require a challenging party to prove the reasonableness of its challenge to avoid imposition of treble damages. Thus, we hold that if neither CERCLA nor applicable EPA regulations or policy statements provides the challenging party with meaningful guidance as to the validity or applicability of the EPA order, *Ex Parte Young* and its progeny require that the burden rest with the EPA to show that the challenging party lacked an objectionably [sic] reasonable belief in the validity or applicability of a clean-up order.

Although shifting the burden may seem onerous, we agree with the *Wagner Electric* court that the EPA could greatly limit sufficient cause defenses by issuing regulations and policy statements and by providing for informal hearings that would enable a party to better determine the validity and applicability of an EPA order prior to the time it must decide whether to comply with a clean-up order or risk treble damages. By providing such guidance at an early stage, the EPA will best protect the interests of all concerned and promote faster more efficient clean-ups while making

---

will continue to be interpreted to preclude the assessment of penalties or treble damages when a party can establish that it had a reasonable belief that it was not liable under CERCLA or that the required response action was inconsistent with the national contingency plan. The court must base its evaluation of the defendant's belief on the objective evidence of the reasonableness and good faith of that belief. Given the importance of EPA orders to the success of the CERCLA program, courts should carefully scrutinize assertions of "sufficient cause" and accept such a defense only where a party can demonstrate by objective evidence the reasonableness and good faith of a challenge to an EPA order.

The amendment also contemplates that courts will continue to interpret "sufficient cause" to encompass other situations where the equities require that no penalties or treble damages be assessed.

H.R.Rep. No. 253(I) 99th Cong., 2d Sess. 82, *reprinted in* 1986 U.S. Code Cong. & Admin.News 2835, 2864. Thus, it appears from the last sentence of the quoted passage that Congress intended courts to remain flexible and to refuse to award the EPA punitive damages if to do so would be patently unjust in light of the public and governmental interests at stake. We fully expect that as the EPA and the courts face concrete cost recovery and treble damage cases, section 107(c)(3) of CERCLA will develop accordingly.

certain liability for clean-ups remains with those responsible. Accordingly, we affirm.

NOTES

1. During CERCLA's first decade, the EPA used sparingly its authority to issue administrative orders under § 106. Although virtually all settlement agreements requiring PRPs to undertake investigatory or cleanup activities recited § 106 as authority therefor, the EPA rarely invoked § 106 to issue unilateral administrative orders. Since the late 1980s, however, the EPA has relied more heavily on § 106 orders to attempt to compel slow-moving or uncooperative PRPs to participate more actively in response activities. *See, e.g.,* Michael P. Healy, *The Effectiveness and Fairness of Superfund's Judicial Review Preclusion Provision,* 15 VA. ENVTL. L.J. 271 (1995-1996).

2. The civil penalty for violating an administrative order issued under § 106 was increased from $5,000 (as stated in *Solid State Circuits*) to $25,000 when CERCLA was amended in 1986.

3. The crucial issue of what circumstances might successfully trigger the "sufficient cause" defense has been the subject of *dicta,* as in *Solid State Circuits,* and commentary, *see, e.g.,* Richard H. Mays, *Who's Afraid of CERCLA §106 Administrative Orders?* 3 Toxics L. Rep. (BNA) 1305 (March 15, 1989), but little precedential case law.

a. In *United States v. LeCarreaux,* 1991 WL 341191 (D.N.J. July 39, 1991), the EPA issued administrative orders to numerous PRPs to undertake cleanup actions at the Duane Marine Salvage Corporation site in Perth Amboy, New Jersey. Most of the PRPs complied with the orders, conducted the cleanup activities that the EPA had specified (at a cost of more than $1.8 million), and sued the site owner (who was also president of the hazardous substance treatment and storage company that operated the site) for contribution. Subsequently, the EPA sued both the site owner and a transporter, apparently the two principal PRPs that had not complied with the administrative orders, to recover approximately $216,000 in response costs that the EPA had incurred, as well as daily civil penalties and treble damages for not complying with the administrative orders.

The court held the recalcitrant PRPs liable not only for the EPA's response costs, but also for civil penalties and treble damages. The court rejected the PRPs' arguments that they were protected from civil penalties and treble damages for not complying with the administrative order because they believed that they were exempt from CERCLA liability under the act of God and act of third party defenses in § 107(b), and because they lacked the financial ability to comply with the orders.

*** [G]iven LeCarreaux's clear liability and his refusal to comply with the Administrative Order, the Court concludes that LeCarreaux's good faith defense is not objectively reasonable. First, despite LeCarreaux's contention that the fire was the sole cause of the releases, there is no evidence linking the fire to the post-fire releases, nor is there any evidence that defendant took precautions to prevent those subsequent releases.

Additionally, this Court is reluctant to find that financial status is a "sufficient cause" for failure to comply with the Administrative Order. Public policy demands that businesses be required to take into account their financial risks before dealing in hazardous materials. Further, LeCarreaux provides no evidence concerning his financial status beyond his lawyer's and his own claims of economic distress. His affidavit vaguely asserts that he is "on the brink of insolvency."

Id. at 26.

b. In *United States v. DWC Trust Holding Co.*, 1996 WL 250011 (D.Md. Jan. 22, 1996), David Chertkof created the DWC Trust, which was the owner—for investment purposes—of what later became known as the Snow Hill Lane Site. After his death, his children and grandchildren served as trustees of the trust. After the EPA discovered hazardous substances in the soil and found the site to pose an imminent threat to public health and the environment, it issued §106 administrative orders to the children and grandchildren, directing them to cleanup the site.

*** Taylor [defendants' attorney, who specialized in environmental and administrative law] advised Defendants that generally a defendant could avoid the imposition of punitive damages by asserting an objectively reasonable good faith defense. Taylor also informed Defendants that they would be reasonable in asserting two possible defenses: an inheritance defense and a third party defense. ***

*** Taylor told Defendants they had three options: compliance; expending the money for the cleanup and then suing to recover it; and defending against the order. Taylor recommended the third option, after advising Defendants again of their strong defenses to the order.

Id. at *4. Although the defendants discussed with the EPA the possibility of paying for part of the cleanup, no such agreement was actually reached. The EPA conducted the cleanup and then sued the children and grandchildren to recover the agency's cleanup costs, as well as penalties and treble damages for noncompliance with the § 106 orders.

On the parties' cross-motions for summary judgment regarding the defendants' liability for penalties and treble damages, the court ruled for the defendants.

*** Defendants claim that they had sufficient cause for their failure to comply because they were told by their attorney, Taylor, that they could reasonably assert both an inheritance defense and a third party defense. In addition, Defendants maintain that their own knowledge corroborated this advice because they knew that (1) they had inherited the Site after the dumping occurred, (2) they had never dumped hazardous materials at the Site, and (3) they had never allowed any else to do so either. ***

* * *

The present case is distinguishable from *LeCarreaux* because there is objective evidence which supports the reasonableness and good faith of

Defendants' defenses. As to the inheritance defense, the record before the Court establishes that the dumping most likely occurred between 1938 and 1966, and not later than 1976. Defendants did not inherit their shares of the property until 1982. As to the third party defense, the record supports Defendants' claim that they neither dumped hazardous substances at the Site nor allowed any one else to do so. ***

Plaintiff has not submitted any evidence to dispute these claims but has argued instead that Defendants failed to exercise due care or take precautions against the foreseeable acts and omissions of third parties. While these are elements of both defenses, it is not reasonable to require Defendants to prove they had knowledge of every element of their potential defenses at the time they received their attorney's advice. The Court finds that in this case, Defendants' personal knowledge corroborated their attorney's advice and provided them with a sufficiently objective and reasonable basis for believing that they had good faith defenses.

The Court does agree with the EPA's argument that the mere fact that an attorney has advised a potentially responsible party that he or she may have defenses to CERCLA liability should not, in and of itself, constitute "sufficient cause" for purposes of §§ 106 and 107 of CERCLA. *** The party must fully disclose all relevant facts to the attorney and must seek the attorney's advice in order to determine the lawfulness of future conduct. The actual advice the attorney provides the party must itself be objectively reasonable and must be corroborated by the party's independent factual knowledge. The Court finds that these requirements were satisfied in the present case.

The Court does not hold today that Defendants' innocent landowner and third party defenses are valid or that they may not be liable for the costs of the cleanup of the Site. *** The EPA may be able to establish that none of those defenses are available to Defendants. For the purposes of the present motion, however, the EPA has failed to convince the Court that Defendants' belief that they had good faith defenses was not objectively reasonable.

Id. at *6-*8.

4. Because CERCLA cleanup costs frequently run tens of millions of dollars, parties have some incentive to litigate the nuances of the treble damages provision. In *United States v. Parsons*, 936 F.2d 526 (11th Cir. 1991) the Eleventh Circuit held that the EPA may recover up to *four times* its actual response costs, calculated by adding the actual response costs, recoverable under § 107(a), plus an additional three times actual response costs, recoverable under § 107(c)(3) for noncompliance, without sufficient cause, with a § 106 administrative order.

5. Although the primary justification for barring pre-enforcement review is to enable the cleanup to proceed unimpeded, the rule applies even after the cleanup is accomplished.

In *Voluntary Purchasing Groups, Inc. v. EPA*, 889 F.2d 1380 (5th Cir. 1989), the EPA had conducted a removal action at a former pesticide and herbicide processing facility and sent letters to ten PRPs, including Voluntary Purchasing Groups (a farmers' co-op making lawn, garden, and farm chemicals), demanding reimbursement of response costs already incurred (some $2 million) and stating that they would be liable for future response costs. The letter warned the PRPs that, if they did not respond with a commitment to pay the incurred response costs, then the EPA "may pursue civil litigation against you."

VPG filed suit seeking a declaratory judgment that it was not properly named as a PRP for the site. VPG asserted that it had not generated or disposed of any hazardous waste at the site, had not participated in the operation of the site, had simply leased equipment to the company that had operated the site, and had already removed the equipment, under the EPA's supervision.

Shortly after VPG filed its suit, the EPA sued VPG and six of the other PRPs to recover past and future response costs. The EPA moved to dismiss VPG's declaratory judgment action. Although the District Court denied the motion, the Fifth Circuit reversed and ordered VPG's suit dismissed. The court noted that the principal purpose of § 113(h) was to ensure that judicial review not delay the commencement and performance of cleanup activities. And although cleanup activities had already been completed at the site in question (the potential for future actions existed, but none was evidently planned as of yet), the court construed CERCLA to deprive PRPs of the ability to initiate litigation challenging the EPA's cleanup actions:

> Although review in the case at hand would not delay actual cleanup of hazardous wastes, it would force the EPA—against the wishes of Congress—to engage in "piecemeal" litigation and use its resources to protect its rights to recover from any PRP filing such a declaratory judgment action. The potential magnitude of this problem becomes apparent when one considers the vast number of PRP letters "outstanding" and the fact that cost recovery suits often involve many parties residing in a variety of locales. *See, e.g., In re United States*, 816 F.2d 1083, 1089 and n.5 (6th Cir.1987) (suit involved more than 250 parties and over 600 parties were impleaded as third party defendants). If PRPs were allowed to file suits for declaratory judgment prior to cost recovery suits being filed by the EPA, much of the EPA's time and resources could end up being allocated to litigation in this area.

> Declaratory judgment actions by PRPs (even if such suits were limited to cases where, as here, suit would not delay actual cleanup of hazardous substances) could also lead to a waste of resources as the EPA will not necessarily try to hold all recipients of a PRP letter legally liable. Moreover, the crazy quilt litigation that could result from allowing PRPs to file suits for declaratory judgments of non-liability prior to the initiation of government cost-recovery actions could force the EPA to confront inconsistent results. Hence, we believe that sanctioning VPG's declaratory

judgment actions could lead to inefficient uses of EPA resources and would certainly detract from the EPA's ability to apportion its enforcement resources as it deems most appropriate. These results would be incompatible with the design of CERCLA and the discretion granted to the EPA in carrying out the statute.

Id. at 1390.

6. The paucity of guidance as to acceptable excuses for not complying with a § 106 administrative order, the costly penalties for noncompliance without sufficient cause, and the unavailability of pre-enforcement judicial review of such orders lead many PRPs who receive an order they find objectionable either to attempt to negotiate with the EPA to modify the order, or to comply with it and seek cost recovery and/or contribution from other PRPs or from the Superfund. The following case addresses the last option. The facts and procedural history highlight the difficult choices PRPs frequently face.

EMPLOYERS INSURANCE OF WAUSAU V. BROWNER
52 F.3d 656 (7th Cir. 1995), *cert. denied,* 116 S.Ct. 699 (1996)

Before POSNER, Chief Judge, CUDAHY, Circuit Judge, and GRANT, District Judge of the Northern District of Indiana.

POSNER, Chief Judge.

We have consolidated the appeals in two intimately related cases that arise under the Comprehensive Environmental Response, Compensation, and Liability Act of 1980. *** In one of the cases, Employers Insurance of Wausau, an insurance company that the EPA had ordered to clean up a contaminated site, sued the President of the United States, invoking a 1986 amendment to the Superfund law that provides that "any person who receives and complies with the terms of any order" issued by the EPA to clean up a contaminated site may "after completion of the required action" petition the President for reimbursement of "the reasonable costs of such action"—"response costs," as they are called—and if the petition is turned down may, within sixty days, sue the President in federal district court. §§ 9606(b)(2)(A), (B). The petitioner can obtain judicial relief either by proving by a preponderance of the evidence that it is not liable for response costs (and that the costs it incurred for which it seeks reimbursement were not excessive), § 9606(b)(2)(C), or that the particular response action ordered was arbitrary and capricious, or otherwise unlawful. § 9606(b)(2)(D). The district judge dismissed the suit on the ground that Employers Insurance had failed to complete the clean-up ordered by the EPA.

In the other suit, Employers Insurance sued the Administrator of the EPA, to whom the President has delegated the task of responding to petitions for reimbursement, contending primarily that the statutory procedures for challenging clean-up orders are constitutionally inadequate. This suit was filed under 28 U.S.C. § 1331 as a "nonstatutory" review proceeding (of which more later), an accepted method of challenging the procedures used by an agency. The district judge thought the statutory procedures adequate, rejected the plaintiff's other contentions, and dismissed the suit. The constitutional challenge is baseless; as we shall see, the remedies that the Superfund law creates against invalid clean-up orders fully satisfy the requirements of due process. Between them, the two suits (and a third, whose dismissal we affirmed in *Employers Ins. of Wausau v. United States*, 27 F.3d 245 (7th Cir.1994)) fire what we are constrained to describe as a noisy and largely incomprehensible broadside of charges the majority of which lack, at least so far as we are able to understand them, sufficient merit to warrant discussion.

How did it come about that an *insurance* company was ordered to clean up contaminated land? Employers Insurance had issued a fire insurance policy to the occupant of a building in Michigan. The building caught fire and several electrical transformers were damaged. In a settlement with its insured, Employers Insurance agreed to have certain oils and other fluids drained from the transformers and removed from the insured's premises. According to the EPA—Employers Insurance denies this—the insurance company arranged for the transportation of some seven hundred gallons of these fluids to an oil recycling facility elsewhere in Michigan. Shortly afterward, the facility was found to be contaminated with PCBs (polychlorinated biphenyls) and VOCs (volatile organic compounds), and the PCB contamination was traced to the fluids that had come from the transformers. The EPA designated Employers Insurance as a potentially responsible party within the meaning of the Act—responsible, that is, for the contamination and hence for cleaning it up—and it ordered the insurance company, along with several other alleged contributors to the contamination of the recycling facility, to participate in the clean-up. After initial resistance, Employers Insurance agreed to participate, and it submitted a plan, which the EPA approved, detailing its participation. Neither the order that the EPA issued, nor the plan of compliance that Employers Insurance submitted, is limited in so many words to the elimination of the PCB contamination. But after Employers Insurance finished that part of the clean-up, it stopped work, claiming that it was not responsible for, and therefore would not clean up, any contamination not caused by PCBs. It petitioned the EPA (nominally the President) for reimbursement of the costs that it had incurred in the clean-up—an amount in excess of $2 million. The EPA turned the insurance company down (precipitating these two suits) on the ground that the company had not completed the job.

Employers Insurance claims that it is not responsible for *any* of the contamination at the recycling facility, not even the PCB contamination, because it had not, as the EPA thought it had, arranged for the transportation of the noxious fluids, which would have made it a responsible party. § 9607(a)(3). It also denies that its petition for reimbursement was premature; it *had*, it contends, completed the clean-up that it was ordered to do; and it argues that it is entitled to the independent judgment of the district court on whether or not this is so. The EPA concedes that if the insurance company did not arrange for the transportation of the fluids, the company is entitled to full reimbursement—but not until it complies fully with the clean-up order. And, the agency argues further, its determination that the company did not comply fully with the order may be set aside by a court only if that determination is found to be unreasonable ("arbitrary and capricious") in a separate judicial proceeding—not in a reimbursement proceeding, which the agency insists is premature.

After Employers Insurance abandoned the clean-up, the EPA stepped in and arranged for the completion of the job at a cost of several hundred thousand dollars. The agency has not yet tried to recover this expense or any part of it from Employers Insurance. Indeed, there is no reason to think the company *was* responsible for any of the contamination that it refused to clean up. And it is only responsible parties who are required by the Superfund law to pay the costs of cleaning up contaminated sites. The concern of Employers Insurance is not with the money that the EPA spent to complete the clean-up and might conceivably though improbably seek to recover from the company, but with the $2 million that the company spent and is unable to get reimbursed because it did not complete the job.

Without the provision authorizing suits for reimbursement of response costs, a person potentially responsible for toxic-waste pollution who was served with a clean-up order would have just two choices: comply with the order, or refuse to comply, in which event the EPA could either seek a mandatory injunction against the refuser, § 9606(a), or hire someone to clean up the polluted site at the EPA's expense and then seek to recover that expense by a suit against the person it had ordered to do the clean-up. § 9613(h)(1). The defendant would have an opportunity in that suit to put the EPA to its proof that the Superfund law really did require the defendant to clean up the site. But it could not challenge the order in advance of having to comply; that route is, as we shall see, closed. Its choice would be to comply or to run the risk of being found to have violated a valid order. This would be a hard choice because there are heavy sanctions for disobeying a valid clean-up order, including large civil fines and treble damages. §§ 9606(b)(1), 9607(c)(3). We stress "valid"; it is of course a good defense to a suit to collect these amercements that the order is invalid. Even if it is valid, the district court in which sanctions are sought can abate them in whole or in part if persuaded that the party had a reasonable though erroneous basis for believing that the clean-up order was invalid. *** Still, there is a risk that the court will not find that the party acted reasonably, and this risk places pressure on the party to comply even if it has serious doubts whether the order is valid. For if it loses it may end up bearing much more than just the response costs for which the EPA sued.

The provision for reimbursement trims the horns of this dilemma by offering a party served with a clean-up order a third way. It need not disobey the order and risk heavy sanctions. It need not obey and swallow the heavy costs of compliance. It can obey and then when it has completed the clean-up required by the order sue for the return of its expenses on the ground that it was not a responsible party within the meaning of the statute after all.

But what happens when, as in the present case, a party takes what we are calling the third way but does not complete the clean-up? Completion of the action required by the EPA is an express statutory condition for seeking reimbursement. Does this mean that if for reasons utterly beyond a party's control it fails to complete the clean-up ordered by the agency it forfeits all right to seek reimbursement for expenses that it incurred, even if it turns out that it was never liable under the Superfund law? And even if it turns out, as here, that the clean-up *has* been completed, albeit by someone else? That is the EPA's position. Its lawyer told us at argument that, should the agency unreasonably refuse to acknowledge the completion of the clean-up, this would be final agency action which, because it harms the party by (in the EPA's view) blocking the party's right to seek reimbursement yet is not subject to a special statutory procedure prescribing the method of judicial review, is judicially reviewable by means of a suit for declaratory judgment brought in federal district court. Reviewable, that is, by the so-called "nonstatutory review" route, the catch-all remedy for persons aggrieved by final agency action for which no statute specifies a path of judicial review. But it would not be reviewable, in the EPA's view, by means of a suit for reimbursement.

We may assume without having to decide that the agency's refusal to acknowledge the completion of the clean-up is reviewable by the nonstatutory-review route; for while the Superfund law prescribes and explicitly makes exclusive the routes for obtaining judicial review of clean-up orders, § 9613(h), the agency action that we are discussing—a refusal to acknowledge compliance with such an order — is not itself a clean-up order, not quite anyway. Even so, we do not see why such an action could not also be reviewed in a suit for reimbursement. If the party ordered to clean up a contaminated site claims to have completed the work, he has a claim for reimbursement, the reimbursement provision being available to "any person who receives and complies with the terms of any" Superfund clean-up order. § 9606(b)(2)(A). If the EPA turns down the claim on the ground that the clean-up has not been completed (or if completed, not completed by the party ordered to complete it, and therefore the agency's order was not complied with), the party has a right to sue and the agency can defend by showing that the clean-up has not been completed and thus that a condition of maintaining such a suit has not been fulfilled. The district court will adjudicate this ground for dismissal exactly as it would do in a separate proceeding to challenge the agency's refusal to acknowledge the completion of the clean-up. *** Ordinarily the refusal to acknowledge completion of the clean-up and the denial of the petition for reimbursement *** will be contained in the same order; they were here.

A more troublesome case is where the agency takes steps to postpone completion, making it impossible for the party to argue that it has completed the action required of it by the agency. Employers Insurance argues that it complied fully with the clean-up order, which it interprets as being limited to PCB contamination, but that when it finished the EPA told it to do more. Like the miller's daughter in "Rumpelstiltskin," the company worries that if it did the more the EPA would find something else for it to do, thus postponing indefinitely the time when it could obtain reimbursement. The EPA's response (at oral argument, so possibly ill-considered) is that the party can challenge each of the successive orders in a nonstatutory review proceeding. We are surprised by this response. The successive orders would be clean-up orders, and, with exceptions not material to this case, the Superfund law allows these to be challenged only in proceedings by the agency to enforce the order (either by injunction or by a suit to recover the expense of the clean-up or to impose penalties for noncompliance with the clean-up order) or proceedings by the allegedly responsible person to seek reimbursement of the costs incurred in complying with the order. §§ 9613(h)(1)-(3).

Even if a nonstatutory review proceeding were possible, the party's right to reimbursement could (in principle anyway) still be delayed indefinitely, each successfully challenged order being succeeded by another order. That cannot have been the intention of the statute's draftsmen, as we can show by attending carefully to the statutory language. The right of reimbursement extends to "any person who receives and complies with the terms of [any order]," and ripens into a right to petition and to sue "after completion of the required action." § 9606(b)(2)(A). Obviously "required" means "required by the order." Once a party completes whatever action is required by the terms of any order, it can seek reimbursement for the costs of *that* action. The fact that the agency issues another order (which the party is free to ignore if it is willing to run the risk of being made the defendant in an enforcement action) does not diminish the party's rights to challenge the previous order.

The EPA does not acknowledge having issued a second order, an order that Employers Insurance clean up contamination unrelated to PCBs. It claims that the broader scope was implicit in the original order. The dispute is thus over the interpretation of the order rather than over the agency's right to issue successive orders and deny reimbursement until the last one (if there is a last one) is complied with fully. If the EPA is wrong about the meaning of the original order, this means that the order has been complied with fully—the action required by it completed—and Employers Insurance is entitled to proceed with its suit for reimbursement. The interpretive question, like the question whether a party has completed whatever action the agency wanted him to take, is one that the district court can decide in the reimbursement suit ***.

The most difficult case is where the party cannot complete the required action for reasons beyond its control. ***

Employers Insurance does not argue, however, that it would have been infeasible or unduly burdensome for it to shell out another couple of hundred thousand dollars to complete the clean-up project on which it had already spent in excess of $2 million. It is a large company with thousands of employees, and its annual revenues from premiums exceed $1 billion. It does argue, absurdly as it seems to us, that if it spent $1, or indeed 1 cent, on cleaning up the contaminated site, it would be entitled to sue for reimbursement of that expense and use the suit as a vehicle for obtaining an adjudication of its claim not to be a responsible party. The terms "compliance" and "completed" in the statute cannot be tortured long or hard enough to yield authorization for such a procedure, which is inspired not by anything in the Superfund law but by the provision for refund suits in the Internal Revenue Code—which anyway requires (with immaterial exceptions) payment in full before the suit is filed. If a party ordered to clean up doesn't want to spend any money, it can refuse to obey the order, wait to be sued, and use that suit as the vehicle for obtaining a determination of its liability. The risk of losing and being made to pay heavy sanctions, a risk mitigated by the defense of sufficient cause as glossed in *Solid State Circuits*, would not violate the Constitution even if there were no reimbursement provision; it certainly does not violate it given the additional if imperfect remedy which that provision grants. The energy that Employers Insurance devoted in its briefs to attempting to create constitutional qualms about the remedial structure of the Superfund law was misdirected.

The most difficult question presented by *this* case is whether the EPA is authorized to gut the provision for reimbursement by issuing unreasonably, oppressively broad orders. Suppose the order had required Employers Insurance to clean up the recycling facility and, while it was at it, also to clean up the residual contamination in Chernobyl from the nuclear disaster there in 1986. If the insurance company cleaned up just the recycling facility it would not be complying with the order and if the EPA is right it would never be able to seek reimbursement. Our actual case is less extreme. But according to Employers Insurance, the EPA was completely unreasonable in ordering it *** to clean up not only PCB contamination for which it would be responsible if it did arrange for the transportation of the fluids from its insured's transformers, but also unrelated contamination at the site, for which it could not possibly bear any responsibility.

We imagine that in a case, illustrated by our Chernobyl hypothetical, in which the clean-up order is so grotesquely broad as plainly to exceed the agency's powers, the party against whom it is directed can comply with the valid part of the order and disregard the rest as void, a nullity, and having complied with the valid part seek reimbursement for the costs of that compliance. ***

But that is not our case. The agency takes the position, which may or may not be correct but is not irrational, that a polluter who wants to take advantage of the reimbursement provision may be required to clean up not only his own mess, as it were, but other messes at the same site. The agency's position is at least consistent with the design of the reimbursement provision, which is to defer liability issues until after the clean-up is completed—that is, until the reimbursement proceeding. The requirement that the reimbursement-seeker clean up the entire site could rationally be believed to contribute to the Act's central objective of promoting the clean-up of contaminated land. And the burden on the party targeted by the order will in most cases be bearable, since he can certainly get reimbursement for the costs that he is asked to incur *not* as a responsible party. The alternative—each polluter at a site just removing the contaminants for which *he* is responsible—may be inefficient, for the polluters may stumble over each other trying to remove separate pollutants. The pollutants may have been deposited in the same spot by successive waves of polluters, in which case multiple removals would greatly increase total costs. *** [T]he EPA's desire to have one polluter clean up the entire site is not so flagrantly unreasonable as to entitle the polluter to disregard an order embodying that desire on the ground that the order is so plainly beyond the agency's power that it should be treated as a nullity.

This is not to deny that there would be a problem of the tail wagging the dog if the polluter responsible for only a tiny fraction of the contamination of the site were ordered to clean up the whole thing, perhaps because he had the deepest pocket of all the responsible parties. *** It is not the situation here. Employers Insurance was being asked to spend only about 10 percent more to clean up the non-PCB contamination than it had spent to clean up the PCB contamination for which (if it was the arranger) it was indeed a responsible party.

In the suit that names the Administrator of the EPA as the defendant rather than the President, the insurance company argued in the district court that the agency lacks statutory authority to condition reimbursement on the cleaning up of pollution for which the party ordered is not responsible. Insofar as the company sought merely to vacate or narrow the order as inconsistent with the authorizing statute, it ran afoul of section 9613(h), the provision that provides the exclusive methods of challenging clean-up orders—and they do not include a suit for injunctive or declaratory relief by the person ordered to perform a clean-up. In any event, the company abandoned its attempt to invalidate the order as overbroad in its opening brief in this court. Its attempt to revive the attempt in its reply brief came too late; the argument had been waived.

In any event, the main thrust of the suit against the Administrator was not that the order was overbroad; it was that the Superfund law does not give a party ordered to clean up a toxic-waste site an adequate opportunity to challenge the order. The relief sought was to invalidate the limitations that section 9613(h) places on the possible routes for challenging such orders. Such relief could be obtained only in a suit against the Administrator and therefore the suit is not precluded by those limitations; it is, as we suggested at the outset of this opinion, a proper invocation of nonstatutory review. As such it merely had no merit, while insofar as it sought a declaration that the clean-up order was too broad it strayed outside the permissible bounds of such a suit and was barred by the exclusive-remedies provision.

The company is left to argue that it *did* comply with the order and that the agency is mistaken to think otherwise—the agency has misinterpreted its own order. We must consider first what our standard of review is. The relevant section, § 9606(b)(2)(A) ***, does not say. The two other provisions potentially involved in this case, (C) and (D), imply different standards of review—plenary in (C) (the "preponderance of evidence" provision), deferential in (D) (the "arbitrary and capricious" provision). Ordinarily the interpretation of a document (the clean-up order) is considered a question of law, and appellate review is plenary. But when the document is an order, the court or agency that issued it is, sensibly enough, considered to have special insight into its meaning, so review is deferential. An additional consideration in this case is that the question of compliance with the EPA's order depends not only on what the order says and means but also on what the target of the order, the insurance company, did. The agency's opinion turning down the petition for reimbursement is based not only on a purely interpretive determination that the clean-up order was not limited to PCBs but also on a factual determination that the measures which Employers Insurance took to comply with the order did not succeed in eliminating the other contaminants. This raises issues of a purely technical nature on which the agency's determination is entitled to the usual deference that is given to administrative determinations. And the order itself is full of technical terms, and we think the EPA is entitled to some scope in interpreting their meaning as well. ***

*** [T]he agency does have statutory authority to issue clean-up orders, and that authority carries with it, we should think, the authority to interpret those orders, and specifically to determine in this case whether its order required the cleaning up of contaminants for which the party ordered had no responsibility.

Employers Insurance points out that the procedure by which the EPA made this determination was not hedged about with the usual safeguards of the adjudicative process, and it argues that the absence of those safeguards justifies a more searching judicial review. The petition for reimbursement was indeed handled informally, by officials who have none of the trappings or protections of judicial officers, and the petitioner, while given ample opportunity (which it took) to submit documents in support of its position, did not have most of the rights of parties to an adjudication, such as the right of cross-examination. The company argues that findings made in so maimed a proceeding should not receive any deference from a court.

But the principles that require judicial deference to administrative findings are not limited to findings made in adjudications. Indeed the broadest deference is given to the findings made in rulemaking proceedings, most of them "informal" in the same sense as the proceeding in this case. The degree of deference is tied not to the formality or elaborateness of the procedures used by the agency but to the character of the issue in relation to whatever procedures were employed to resolve it. The issue of compliance with the EPA's clean-up order in this case was technical in character and was addressed in a proceeding that provided for a full exchange of evidence and argument before the agency made its final decision, which it set forth at length in a reasoned, and as it seems to us reasonable (though not necessarily correct), opinion. There is no indication that it is the kind of issue that would have been illuminated by cross-examination.

We conclude that the EPA's finding that Employers Insurance failed to comply with the clean-up order must be upheld unless it is arbitrary or capricious, or in the equivalent terminology of civil suits unless it is clearly erroneous. And it is not. The order by its terms embraces all hazardous substances at the recycling facility, regardless of the particular type of hazardous substance. No doubt the EPA could have given the order a narrower reading, interpolating a limitation to hazardous substances for whose presence at the site Employers Insurance was responsible. But it chose not to do so and we cannot say that it acted unreasonably in refusing. We have already pointed to the reasons why the EPA might want to impose on a source of one pollutant the responsibility for cleaning up the entire site that had been contaminated by that pollutant, even if the site had been contaminated by other pollutants as well. So broad an order might or might not be proper, but, Employers Insurance having waived *that* issue, the only issue left is what the EPA *meant*. We think it meant, or more precisely could reasonably be understood to have meant, that Employers Insurance could not stop its clean-up efforts when the last of the PCBs was removed. Employers Insurance is therefore entitled to no judicial relief.

NOTES

1. With the hindsight of this opinion, what would you advise Employers Insurance to do (a) upon the initial receipt of the § 106 order? (b) at this point?

2. The frustration experienced by Employers Insurance in the foregoing case is not unrepresentative of petitioners' experience in seeking reimbursement from the Superfund.

Recall the *Wagner Seed* case summarized at the opening of this chapter. After unsuccessfully attempting to challenge the EPA's §106 order, Wagner Seed complied with the order and cleaned up the site, expending $2.3 million in the process. After it completed the cleanup to the EPA's satisfaction, the company petitioned the Superfund for reimbursement under § 106(b)(2). The EPA denied Wagner's petition, and the federal district court for the District of Columbia upheld the agency's decision that reimbursement was not available because Wagner had already commenced the cleanup when the new provision was enacted. *Wagner Seed Co. v. United States*, 709 F.Supp. 249 (D.D.C. 1989), *aff'd,* 946 F.2d 918 (D.C.Cir. 1991), *cert. denied,* 503 U.S. 970 (1992).

3. As *Employers Insurance* suggests, CERCLA grants to the EPA exceptionally wide latitude not only in issuing § 106 orders, but also in virtually every step in the process of deciding how a site should be remediated and whom should be held responsible for the cleanup costs. This authority is further enhanced by § 113(j)(1), which limits the scope of judicial review to the administrative record. Moreover, § 113(j)(2) directs the reviewing court to "uphold the President's [*i.e.,* the EPA's] decision in selecting the response action unless the objecting party can demonstrate, on the administrative record, that the decision was arbitrary and capricious or otherwise not in accordance with law."

4. Faced with this statutory scheme, PRPs have devised numerous and varied creative, yet generally fruitless, arguments to attempt to circumvent the bar against pre-enforcement review.

In *Cooper Industries, Inc. v. EPA*, 775 F.Supp 1027 (W.D.Mich.1991), the EPA and the Michigan Department of Natural Resources ("MDNR") were nearing the conclusion of, but had not yet concluded, the process of selecting a cleanup plan for a contaminated groundwater well field. Cooper Industries, a PRP for the site, had participated in the administrative proceedings regarding remedy selection, but the EPA denied the company's request for a meeting to discuss the remedy. Cooper Industries then filed suit, seeking to compel the EPA and MDNR to allow Cooper to participate more actively in the remedy selection process.

The gist of Cooper's complaint is that it will suffer irreparable harm if the EPA selects a remedial action and issues a Record of Decision without complying with the statutory provisions regarding public participation. This assertion rests, in part, upon section 9613(j) of CERCLA, which limits judicial review of agency action to the administrative record. According to Cooper, because meaningful public participation is necessary in order to compile a fair and adequate administrative record, the lack of meaningful public participation prior to the closing of the administrative record, the selection of a remedy, and the issuance of the ROD, will prejudice Cooper's later attempts to challenge the remedy selected. Cooper argues that under the enforcement provisions of sections 9606 and 9607 of CERCLA, it may be liable for, or forced to implement, remedial actions that may not be the most cost efficient solutions or that may not fully remediate the problem. Cooper asserts that, due to its inability to conduct and place in the record further studies and analyses that could suggest a remedial action different and less expensive than the remedy proposed by the EPA, the administrative record will be devoid of the information necessary to avoid prospective liability for the response action.

* * *

In an attempt to avoid CERCLA's jurisdictional bar, Cooper argues that section 9613(h) does not apply because it applies only to challenges to response actions. Cooper maintains that it does not challenge a response action, as no response action has yet been selected. In Cooper's view, it merely seeks the aid of this Court in requiring the EPA and MDNR to comply with their statutory duties requiring them to provide meaningful participation in the remedy selection process and to identify potentially responsible parties as early as possible before selecting a response action. In essence, Cooper attempts to avoid the statutory bar to judicial review by characterizing its claim as a challenge to the process of remedy selection and asserting that such procedural challenges are distinct, for jurisdictional purposes, from claims that attack the EPA's choice of remedy.

The Court is not persuaded, however, that the distinctions asserted by Cooper are relevant to the question of subject matter jurisdiction, as "challenges to the procedure employed in selecting a remedy nevertheless impact the implementation of the remedy and result in the same delays Congress sought to avoid by passage of the statute." *Schalk v. Reilly*, 900 F.2d 1091, 1097 (7th Cir.), *cert. denied*, 111 S. Ct. 509 (1990). Moreover, Courts faced with suits alleging procedural errors in remedy selection have uniformly rejected claims that seek injunctive relief directing the EPA to supplement the administrative record and to rescind the Record of Decision.

* * *

Moreover, as evidenced by CERCLA's expansive definitions of removal and remedial actions, the ban on preimplementation review extends not only to parties' contentions that the remedy selected does not meet the substantive requirements of CERCLA, but also to procedural claims regarding the EPA's remedy selection process. *** The RI/FS [Remedial Investigation/Feasibility Study] process challenged by Cooper includes action taken "consistent with permanent remedy" of the contamination of Sturgis' municipal well field, and, therefore, falls within the statute's broad definition of remedial action.

In a variation of the argument presented here, the plaintiff in *Neighborhood Toxic Cleanup Emergency v. Reilly*, 716 F. Supp. 828 (D.N.J. 1989), sought an order requiring the EPA to reopen the Record of Decision and to reconsider the selected remedy in light of new information. The plaintiff alleged that the EPA failed to obtain proper data before finalizing the remedial plan and that, therefore, the safety measures to be taken at the site could prove inadequate. The court, after an extensive analysis of CERCLA's statutory language and legislative history, held that section 9613 deprived it of jurisdiction to review the Record of Decision selecting a remedy until "either a distinct phase of that remedy is complete or until a specific remedial measure is taken in violation of some CERCLA/SARA requirement." *Id*. at 837. The court specifically based its holding on "the congressional purpose of removing litigation as an obstacle to rapid cleanup." *Id*.

This Court finds the same principle controlling in the instant case. Cooper attempts to distinguish *Neighborhood Toxic Cleanup* and *Cordova* by arguing that the plaintiffs in those cases sought relief after the EPA had already selected a remedy and issued a ROD, whereas Cooper seeks relief before the issuance of a ROD. However, where the underlying principle of the bar to pre-enforcement review is the need to prevent litigation that may delay rapid cleanup, the principle is no less applicable where a party seeks injunctive relief on the eve of the EPA's remedy selection and Record of Decision. Pre-enforcement judicial review, whether before or after the selection of a remedy, thwarts the purpose of prompt response intended by CERCLA.

Id. at 1035-36, 1037-39.

Claims that the ongoing or prospective implementation of a CERCLA cleanup plan will violate other environmental statutes have typically been dismissed under § 113(h). *See, e.g., Arkansas Peace Center v. Arkansas Department of Pollution Control and Ecology*, 999 F.2d 1212 (8th Cir. 1993), *cert. denied*, 511 U.S. 1017 (1994) (unsuccessful attempt to allege that the construction and operation of an incinerator for a CERCLA cleanup would violate RCRA).

5. In sum, CERCLA § 113(h) generally enables the EPA (and, to some extent, private parties invoking the citizen suit provisions) to control the timing whereby cleanup orders, decisions, and actions become subject to judicial review.

6. In recent years, however, courts have allowed to proceed—notwithstanding § 113(h)—some actions regarding CERCLA cleanup decisions or orders.

a. *Compare United States v. State of Colorado*, 990 F.2d 1565 (10th Cir. 1993), *cert. denied*, 510 U.S. 1092 (1994) (in chapter 17), where a state environmental agency was allowed to proceed with its enforcement action to ensure that the CERCLA cleanup being undertaken by the Army conformed with the state's version of RCRA, *with McClellan Ecological Seepage Situation v. Perry*, 47 F.3d 325 (9th Cir. 1995), *cert. denied*, (1995), where a citizens group was precluded from proceeding with its RCRA and Clean Water Act claims regarding the inactive waste sites at an Air Force base undergoing a CERCLA cleanup (but was allowed to proceed with RCRA claims regarding the base's active waste disposal sites that were not subject to the CERCLA cleanup).

b. *Compare Durfey v. DuPont*, 59 F.3d 121 (9th Cir. 1995), where tort claims for medical monitoring costs by persons allegedly exposed to hazardous substances from a CERCLA site were held not to be response costs and therefore not barred by § 113(h), *with Hanford Downwinders Coalition, Inc. v. Dowdle*, 71 F.3d 1469 (9th Cir. 1995), where claims by persons allegedly exposed to the same substances from the same site were barred because they were seeking to force the Agency for Toxic Substances and Disease Registry to conduct medical monitoring under § 104, and such activities were held to be "response" activities subject to the § 113(h) bar on pre-enforcement review. The Ninth Circuit distinguished these rulings as follows:

> A plain reading of the statute supports the conclusion that the ATSDR health assessment and surveillance activities at issue in this case fall within the statutory definition of removal actions. ***
>
> We have held, however, that the definition of "removal" does not encompass all activity related to protecting the public health from hazardous releases. In *Durfey v. E.I. DuPont De Nemours Co.*, 59 F.3d 121 (9th Cir. 1995), and *Price v. United States Navy*, 39 F.3d 1011 (9th Cir. 1994), we held that private party medical monitoring activities, initiated and coordinated independently of ongoing CERCLA cleanup efforts, were not § 9601 removal or remedial actions. In each case, we held that excluding private medical monitoring programs from CERCLA's definition of removal actions was appropriate for two reasons. First, we distinguished private medical monitoring programs from the five examples of removal actions provided by Congress in § 9601(23), noting that those examples principally concern the threats posed by the physical removal of hazardous waste rather than medical monitoring of the long-term health effects of past hazardous releases. Second, we determined that the relevant legislative history evinced a clear congressional intent to exclude private medical monitoring activity from CERCLA.

The reasoning in *Durfey* and *Price* does not apply to health assessment and surveillance actions engaged in by a governmental agency pursuant to explicit CERCLA provisions. A careful examination of the specific examples of removal actions provided by Congress convinces us that ATSDR health assessment and surveillance activities are within the scope of § 9601(23). ***

Id. at 1477-78.

c. The Ninth Circuit also allowed to proceed, notwithstanding § 113(h), state law claims for damages due arising from the diversion of water under a CERCLA cleanup.

Plaintiffs' damage claim does not "challenge" the CERCLA cleanup plan and is thus unaffected by CERCLA's provision limiting such challenges. 42 U.S.C. § 9613(h). Although determination of whether ARCO's diversions were "wrongful" may require examination of the EPA's orders, resolution of the damage claim would not involve altering the terms of the cleanup order. If the plaintiffs prevail, the remedy would be financial compensation for lost crops and profits. Such a remedy would not interfere with ARCO's implementation of the cleanup.

Beck v. Atlantic Richfield Co., 62 F.3d 1240, 1243 (9th Cir. 1995), *cert. denied,* 116 U.S. 1568 (1996).

The Ninth Circuit distinguished the plaintiffs' claim for damages from their claim for injunctive relief:

*** We conclude that the district court does not have jurisdiction over West Side's claim for injunctive relief because that claim constitutes a "challenge" to the CERCLA cleanup effort over which the district would not have jurisdiction until the cleanup was completed.

Ibid.

7. In the following case, a Third Circuit panel allowed a claim for injunctive relief to proceed, notwithstanding § 113(h).

UNITED STATES V. PRINCETON GAMMA-TECH, INC.
31 F.3d 138 (3d Cir. 1994)

Before MANSMANN, NYGAARD, and WEIS, Circuit Judges.
WEIS, Circuit Judge.

The Comprehensive Environmental Response, Compensation, and Liability Act of 1980 (CERCLA), as amended, limits judicial review of Environmental Protection Agency (EPA) cleanup programs. However, we conclude that when the EPA sues to recover initial expenditures incurred in curing a polluted site, a district court may review a property owner's bona fide allegations that continuance of the project will cause irreparable harm to public health or the environment and, in appropriate circumstances, grant equitable relief. Because the district court in this case believed that it lacked jurisdiction under these circumstances, we will reverse its order denying injunctive relief.

Defendant Gamma-Tech owns real property above the Passaic Formation aquifer in Rocky Hill, New Jersey. After trichloroethylene (TCE) contamination was discovered in the groundwater at two sites on Gamma-Tech property, they were placed on the National Priorities List, a list of hazardous waste sites that require the use of Superfund money under CERCLA. ***

* * *

After further investigation and monitoring of the contamination, the EPA issued a second Record of Decision in 1988 outlining its plan for a remedy. In brief, the EPA proposed to extract contaminated water from the primary contamination plume in the shallow aquifer, to treat it, and then to reinject it into the aquifer. In addition, the plan provided for the installation of "open-hole" wells that penetrate through the shallow source to the deep aquifer to allow for monitoring and sampling. After the decision was announced, the public and potentially responsible parties were given the opportunity to comment on the plan.

At least some of the proposed wells have already been installed on the property, but the pump treatment system has not yet been fully implemented. The final design was expected to be completed in the fall of 1993 and the remedial process begun in the spring of 1994. It is anticipated that the cleanup will be completed in five to seven years.

In 1991, the EPA brought suit against Gamma-Tech pursuant to CERCLA, 42 U.S.C. § 9607(a), seeking reimbursement of "response costs" already incurred at the two sites. The agency also sought a declaratory judgment on Gamma-Tech's liability for future response costs.

Gamma-Tech filed a cross-motion for a preliminary injunction directing the EPA to cease the installation of open-hole wells into the deep layer of the aquifer, to encase existing open-hole wells, and to cease construction of the remedial system provided for in the 1988 decision (the water extraction and treatment plan). In support of its motion, Gamma-Tech asserted that the EPA's selected remedy will exacerbate the existing environmental damage and cause further irreparable harm to the environment. According to Gamma-Tech, the system devised by the EPA will cause contaminated water from the shallow strata of the aquifer to be drawn down into the deep zone where contamination has not been established conclusively, thus increasing, rather than remedying, the pollution of the water supply.

The district court concluded that it lacked subject matter jurisdiction to grant Gamma-Tech's request for injunctive relief. The court based its conclusion on the general principle, garnered from statutory and decisional law, that district courts have no jurisdiction over claims challenging the EPA's choice of remedies until after completion of a distinct phase of the cleanup.

Appealing under 28 U.S.C. § 1292(a)(1), Gamma-Tech asserts that once the EPA brought its cost-recovery suit under CERCLA, the general jurisdictional bar to the review of challenges was lifted pursuant to the cost-recovery action exception under 42

U.S.C. § 9613(h)(1). The district court thus had authority to grant an injunction even though the remedial work has not yet been completed. ***

I.

By enacting CERCLA, Congress intended to combat the hazards that toxic waste sites pose to public health or the environment. The EPA was granted broad powers to eliminate or reduce toxic contamination in the environment by either requiring responsible parties to clean up the sites, 42 U.S.C. § 9606, or by undertaking the task itself, 42 U.S.C. § 9604.

Because of the menace to public health and the environment, Congress was anxious to safeguard EPA remedial efforts from delay resulting from litigation brought by potentially responsible parties. In the Superfund Amendments and Reauthorization Act of 1986 (SARA), Congress adopted a "clean up first, litigate later" philosophy. ***

SARA generally bars preliminary judicial review of challenges to the EPA's response actions.   42 U.S.C. § 9613(h), entitled "Timing of review," provides in pertinent part:

> No Federal court shall have jurisdiction under Federal law ... to review any challenges to removal or remedial action selected under section 9604 ... in any action except one of the following:
>
> "(1) An action under section 9607 of this title to recover response costs or damages or for contribution.
>
> * * * * * *
>
> (4) An action under section 9659 of this title (relating to citizens suits) alleging that the removal or remedial action taken under section 9604 of this title or secured under 9606 of this title was in violation of any requirement of this chapter...."

The language in section 9613(h) demonstrates Congress' intent that the EPA be free to conduct prompt and expeditious cleanups without obstructive legal entanglements.   By providing several exceptions to the timeliness bar, however, Congress recognized that the limitation on court challenges should not be absolute.

We now examine the exceptions listed in subsections 9613(h)(1) and (h)(4) in greater detail to determine when those exceptions would serve to lift the jurisdictional bar to challenges to response actions. ***

A.   *Cost-Recovery Action Exception Under Subsection 9613(h)(1).*

The exclusion under subsection 9613(h)(1) retains jurisdiction in the federal courts after a cost-recovery or contribution action has been brought by the government under 42 U.S.C. § 9607 of CERCLA. Section 9607 permits the EPA to sue a potentially responsible party for reimbursement of response costs.

It is the cost-recovery suit that opens the door for alleged responsible parties to contest their liability as well as to challenge the EPA's response action as being unnecessarily expensive or otherwise not in accordance with applicable law. *** The language in subsection 9613(h)(1), the corresponding legislative history, and relevant caselaw establish that once the EPA brings an enforcement action under section 9607, the agency is subject to challenges to its response action.

Courts have held that liability and cost-effectiveness suits filed by potentially responsible parties to challenge a selected response plan were premature when the EPA had not yet sought enforcement through a cost-recovery action. Those opinions describe the suit for reimbursement of response costs as the opportunity for challenging the EPA's remedial or removal decisions. ***

Legislative history similarly indicates that review of challenges is available once a cost-recovery action is brought. "Therefore, the [section 9613(h)] amendment reaffirms that, in the absence of a government enforcement action, judicial review of the selection of a response action should generally be postponed until after the response action is taken." H.R.Rep. No. 99- 253(III), 99th Cong., 2d Sess. 22. ***

The pattern of precluding review of challenges until a cost-recovery action is brought is clear enough where the EPA does not file suit until after all of its work has been completed. Congress, however, authorized the EPA to seek reimbursement for costs even before the conclusion of the cleanup process. 42 U.S.C. § 9613(g)(2) permits a cost-recovery action to be brought as soon as "costs have been incurred."

The question thus becomes whether the exception under subsection 9613(h)(1) would lift the bar to challenges against response actions even where the EPA brings a cost-recovery suit before cleanup is complete, as is permitted under subsection 9613(g)(2). Because an interim decision on costs may affect the completion of the project, such suits introduce an additional factor into the jurisdictional question.

Nothing in the timeliness language of either subsections 9613(g)(2) or 9613(h)(1) indicates any differentiation between the scope of an action where all the remedial work has been completed and one filed while the project is still in progress. Section 9607(a)(4)(A) does limit a party's liability in a cost-recovery action, however, to costs "incurred." Thus, in an action brought before a project has been completely carried out, reimbursement is limited to expenses "incurred" before the date of judgment, leaving to future litigation costs that come due thereafter.

Once it has been established that subsection 9613(h)(1) applies and that review under that exception is available, a court must then resolve the question of what types of challenges may be considered and what remedies are available. Although the statute makes no distinction between cost-recovery suits brought after completion of a project and those brought while work is continuing, the remedies may differ because of the possibility of affecting future work at a site.

42 U.S.C. § 9607(b) sets out defenses to liability *vel non* as contrasted with disputes over the amount of the claim due or the legality of the remedy selected. In *United States v. Hardage*, 982 F.2d 1436, 1446 (10th Cir.1992), the Court held that a responsible party may contest EPA expenditures as well as its liability in a response action. ***

Pursuant to 42 U.S.C. § 9605, the EPA has published a National Contingency Plan for the effective removal of hazardous substances in 40 C.F.R. pt. 300, regulations that set out procedures for the selection of response actions. These regulations direct the EPA to evaluate alternative remedies, weighing such factors as the overall protection of human health and the environment, long-term effectiveness, reduction of toxicity through treatment, potential environmental impacts of the remedial action, cost feasibility, and availability of services and materials, among others. Remedial actions inconsistent with the policy objectives of the National Contingency Plan may be challenged in defending a cost-recovery action.

Potentially responsible parties may also defend cost-recovery actions on the ground that the EPA's decision in the selection of a response action was "arbitrary and capricious or otherwise not in accordance with law." 42 U.S.C. § 9613(j)(2).

* * *

B.   *Citizens' Suit Exception Under Subsection 9613(h)(4)*

*** 42 U.S.C. § 9659 authorizes any person, including a potentially responsible party, to sue the government on allegations that the EPA violated a regulation or requirement of the Act or failed to perform non-discretionary acts or duties. *** The district court is given authority to enforce CERCLA standards or regulations, to direct action necessary to correct the violation, and to impose civil penalties.

Subsection 9613(h)(4) grants a district court jurisdiction to review challenges raised by a citizens' suit, but some doubt exists about when such a suit may be entertained. The legislative history on that point is confusing, and the issue is a troublesome one that has been the subject of several appellate opinions.

In *Schalk v. Reilly*, 900 F.2d 1091, 1095 (7th Cir.1990) and *Alabama v. EPA*, 871 F.2d 1548, 1557 (11th Cir.1989), the Courts of Appeals decided that even if a remedy or a discrete phase of a remedy has been selected by the EPA, no citizens' suit challenge may be recognized before the remedy has been completed. The opinions in those two cases noted that the language of the citizens' suit exception of section 9613(h)(4) applies only to those "removal or remedial action[s] *taken* under section 9604 [response actions by EPA] ... or *secured* under section 9606 [abatement order]...." *Schalk*, 900 F.2d at 1095 (emphasis in original); *see Alabama v. EPA*, 871 F.2d at 1557. Noting the statute's use of the past tense, the Courts of Appeals stated that absent clear legislative intent to the contrary, the statutory language establishes that the remedial action must already have been implemented and completed before challenges can be made against it.

In the *Schalk* case, incineration had been selected as the form of remedy, but had not yet been put into operation. In those circumstances, the Court concluded that it lacked jurisdiction to consider a citizens' suit in which it was alleged that the EPA had violated the National Contingency Plan by failing to prepare an environmental impact statement. *Schalk*, 900 F.2d at 1095; *see also Alabama v. EPA*, 871 F.2d at 1556 (citizens' suit alleged EPA failed to comply with notice and comment provision); *Arkansas Peace Ctr. v. Arkansas Dep't of Pollution Control & Ecology*, 999 F.2d 1212, 1216-19 (8th Cir.1993) (citizens' suit alleged incineration remedy failed to meet EPA regulations), *cert. denied*, 114 S.Ct. 1397 (1994).

Although these interpretations of the timing of the review of citizens' suits have superficial pertinency, none of the Courts of Appeals were confronted with bona fide assertions of irreparable environmental damage resulting from violations of CERCLA's policies. In circumstances where irreparable environmental damage will result from a planned response action, forcing parties to wait until the project has been fully completed before hearing objections to the action would violate the purposes of CERCLA. This concern was articulated in congressional deliberations and elicited conflicting statements by members of the conference committee that was convened to resolve differences between the Senate and House versions of SARA.

* * *

From these conflicting views of the members of Congress who directly participated in the drafting of the statute, one might be tempted to resort to the wag's statement that, when the legislative history is unclear, one should refer to the language of the statute. However, in this instance it must be conceded that the term "action taken" in subsection 9613(h)(4) does not speak in clear terms either. ***

Senator Stafford's comments supply a pragmatic guideline to interpretation. He said that

> "the courts must draw appropriate distinctions between dilatory or other unauthorized lawsuits by potentially responsible parties involving only monetary damages and legitimate citizens' suits complaining of irreparable injury that can be only addressed only [sic] if a claim is heard during or prior to response action."

132 Cong.Rec. 28,409 (1986) ***.

The problem may be illustrated by an extreme scenario that has the EPA deciding to take leaking drums containing a highly toxic substance from a dump site and to empty them into a nearby lake, thus causing permanent damage to public health and the environment. If citizens cannot prevent such dumping from taking place, no effective remedy exists.

The citizens' suit provision is effectively nullified if litigation must be delayed until after irreparable harm or damage has been done. In such circumstances, a statutory interpretation that calls for the full completion of the plan before review is permitted makes the citizens' suit provision an absurdity. That conclusion is further supported by the language of 42 U.S.C. § 9659(c) authorizing equitable relief, in that a court may "enforce" a regulation or "order" an officer to perform a specific duty. Invoking those powers would affect future actions by the agency. ***

Several district courts have grappled with the timing of review under the citizens' suit exception and have reached inconsistent results in cases where irreparable harm to public health or the environment was alleged. *Cabot Corp.*, 677 F.Supp. at 829, for example, concluded that "[h]ealth and environmental hazards must be addressed as promptly as possible rather than awaiting the completion of an inadequately protective response action." In *Neighborhood Toxic*, 716 F.Supp. at 834, the court commented that even where there are allegations that a remedial plan is unsafe to public health, review of a citizens' suit is only allowed after the first phase of the cleanup is complete. In that case, however, plaintiffs did not assert that they could prove environmental harm, but merely demanded that the EPA perform a public health study to support its choice of remedy.

In the Courts of Appeals cases previously cited, where the citizens' suits were held to be premature, allegations of genuine irreparable damage were not discussed and presumably were not present. The issue presented here appears to be a case of first impression in the appellate courts. With this general background on the law, we review the parties' contentions.

II.

Gamma-Tech asserts that when the EPA filed the suit for response costs, the district court obtained jurisdiction, including its inherent injunctive powers, over all challenges to the government's selection of a remedy for the polluted site. Although it relies on subsection 9613(h)(1), Gamma-Tech asserts that the citizens' suit exception in subsection 9613(h)(4) supports justiciability of contentions that the EPA's action violates CERCLA by being inconsistent with the National Contingency Plan. ***

The EPA argues that its cost-recovery action seeks only reimbursement for the actual expenditures incurred as of the time of the suit, and that subsection 9613(h)(1) does not permit challenges to portions of a response action not yet completed and for which costs have not yet been incurred. Moreover, the EPA contends that courts do not have the power to grant equitable relief in a section 9607 cost-recovery action.

The EPA does concede that Gamma-Tech may contest its liability for actual costs claimed by the government that are inconsistent with the National Contingency Plan. However, relying on this Court's opinion in *Boarhead Corp. v. Erickson*, 923 F.2d 1011 (3d Cir.1991), the EPA maintains that because the remedy has not yet been fully implemented, the citizens' suit provision does not permit judicial review despite allegations of irreparable harm.

In *Boarhead*, a property owner sought to enjoin the EPA's cleanup activities until the agency conducted appropriate reviews under the National Historic Preservation Act. We held that CERCLA's jurisdictional provisions prevailed over the Preservation Act.

Boarhead is clearly distinguishable and does not control the matter before us for two crucial reasons. First, *Boarhead* was brought by a property owner and was not, as here, a suit brought by the government where the exception in subsection 9613(h)(1) comes into play. Second, the case before us is based on allegations that the EPA has violated and will continue to violate CERCLA itself, not another unrelated statute—a point that the Court noted and did not decide. Consequently, *Boarhead* and the other previously cited cases where the property owners brought suit prematurely do not govern a court's power to grant injunctive relief in the circumstances where there are allegations that the EPA's action will cause irreparable harm inconsistent with the National Contingency Plan.

In assessing the scope of review and the availability of remedies in this cost-recovery action, it is important to clarify just what it is that the EPA seeks in this suit. The complaint alleges that, as of September 28, 1990 (approximately five months before the complaint was filed), disbursements by the government amounted to at least $1,816,151. The EPA seeks this sum and, in addition, all response costs incurred "as of the date of judgment."

The EPA, therefore, seeks reimbursement for part of the expense of implementing the pumping and treating remedy that is scheduled to be in operation before this case returns to the district court. When the case reaches trial, some costs will have been incurred for every phase of the remedial plan, although only a portion of the anticipated expenses for the pump treatment processing will have been incurred by then.

That being so, Gamma-Tech is free to challenge those phases that have been completed and also that portion of the remedial plan that has not yet been fully completed as of the date of judgment, but for which some expenses have been incurred. The timeliness requirement of section 9613(h) has been met as to everything claimed as of the date of judgment. We thus have no need to consider here whether under different circumstances, the commencement of a cost-recovery action under section 9607 would allow challenges to *all* aspects of the remedial plan even if no expenses have been incurred for a specific phase to come into effect in the future.

The next issue is the scope of the relief that Gamma-Tech may obtain. Compliance with the National Contingency Plan criteria previously mentioned (e.g., protection of public health and the environment, including the overall feasibility of the plan) is a substantial factor in determining what costs the EPA may recover from Gamma-Tech. *** [S]ection 9613(j)(3) outlines the scope of the remedy that the district court may grant. If the response the EPA has selected is determined to be arbitrary and capricious, or "otherwise not in accordance with law," the court is only permitted to award the response costs that are consistent with the National Contingency Plan. The court may also grant "*such other relief* as is consistent with the National Contingency Plan." 42 U.S.C. § 9613(j)(3) (emphasis added).

Notably, section 9613(j)(3) does not exclude injunctive relief as a remedy. The broad language "such other relief" implies the contrary. *See Weinberger v. Romero-Barcelo*, 456 U.S. 305, 320 (1982) ("[A] major departure from the long tradition of equity practice should not be lightly implied."); *Califano v. Yamasaki*, 442 U.S. 682, 705 (1979) ("Absent the clearest command to the contrary from Congress, federal courts retain their equitable power to issue injunctions in suits over which they have jurisdiction."); *Mitchell v. Robert DeMario Jewelry, Inc.*, 361 U.S. 288, 291-92 (1960) ("When Congress entrusts to an equity court the enforcement of prohibitions contained in a regulatory enactment, it must be taken to have acted cognizant of the historic power of equity to provide complete relief in light of the statutory purposes.").

Therefore, if the response selected by the EPA is inconsistent with the National Contingency Plan—for example, the remedial plan is harmful to public health—nothing in the statute prohibits a court from utilizing its inherent power to direct the agency to cease the harmful practice and, in addition, to deny claims for expenses incurred to that point in carrying out that phase of the remedy.

Permitting the EPA to continue with actions that have been found to be inconsistent with the National Contingency Plan would be contrary to the spirit and intent of CERCLA. The Act is designed to facilitate the cleanup of hazardous waste sites, but that process must be conducted by methods that meet specified criteria. Thus, in some circumstances, granting injunctive relief would be consistent with the National Contingency Plan pursuant to the provisions of section 9613(j)(3) and, in fact, injunctions may be required to insure compliance with the Plan. We therefore reject the EPA's contention that injunctions, per se, are barred in a suit for response provisions costs.

*   *   *

Both parties have cited to the citizens' suit provision in subsection 9613(h)(4) as support for their respective positions. Even though it is a potentially responsible party, Gamma-Tech could qualify as a plaintiff in a citizens' suit alleging irreparable harm to the environment. Hence, Gamma-Tech argues that as a defendant in the EPA's cost-recovery suit, it should be permitted to allege matters that would normally be considered in a separate citizens' suit.

The EPA, on the other hand, takes the position that a citizens' suit will not lie in the circumstances presented here because the remedial action at the pollution site has not yet been completed. The EPA relies on such cases as *Schalk, Alabama v. EPA*, and *Arkansas Peace Ctr.* As we noted earlier, however, we find the holdings in those cases to be inapposite to the facts presented here, where bona fide assertions of irreparable environmental damage were made.

We are persuaded that when irreparable harm to public health or the environment is threatened, an injunction may be issued under the citizens' suit exception of subsection 9613(h)(4) even though the cleanup may not yet be completed. As discussed earlier, delay in preventing such injury is contrary to the objectives of CERCLA and results in the evisceration of the right to the remedy envisioned by the citizens' suit provision. We are convinced that Congress did not intend such a result. It follows that if the section 9613(h)(4) exception allows an injunction to be issued in a separate citizens' suit that is filed simultaneously in the same court with an answer to a cost-recovery action for which review is available under section 9613(h)(1), there is no logical basis to deny similar relief in the cost-recovery litigation when irreparable harm has been established.

The EPA's objection to an injunction appears to be based, to a large extent, on the potential for interference with future work at a polluted site. But that possibility exists in every case in which the agency brings its cost-recovery action before conclusion of the work to be performed at the site.

It is clear that if a court finds that an aspect of the response action already completed was contrary to the National Contingency Plan, the judgment could not include the expenses attributable to that particular activity. It would be highly unlikely that the EPA would continue to spend money on that same remedial activity in the future if it knew that the recovery of costs for that work from the responsible party would not be permitted in later suits. Nor is it likely that the EPA would continue its course of action in the face of a court decree that its remedial processes have failed to comply with the law. Thus, future work is affected to the extent that a denial of reimbursement for a particular item is, for all intents and purposes, a finding that a particular aspect of a project violates applicable law.

* * *

Based on our review of the statute, its legislative history, and the procedural posture of this suit, we hold that where a bona fide allegation of irreparable injury to public health or the environment is made, injunctive relief is available in a cost-recovery action under subsection 9613(h)(1).

Our holding does not mean that frivolous litigation will be permitted to delay critical cleanup efforts. Courts must be wary of dilatory tactics by potentially responsible parties who might raise specious allegations of irreparable harm to public health or the environment merely to obtain immediate review. The mere possibility of such abuse, however, does not justify an abdication by the courts of their responsibility to adjudicate legitimate claims of irreparable harm.

Our holding on jurisdiction does not imply that relief must be granted here. We note first that the parties' versions of the facts are in dispute, and perhaps more important, Congress' intention that cleanup not be delayed or diverted by dilatory litigation must be honored. To overcome that admonition, Gamma-Tech, as the alleged responsible party, has the burden to establish that the EPA's choice of remedy was indeed arbitrary and capricious or otherwise contrary to law.

In cases like the one at hand, a reviewing court should give deference to the scientific expertise of the agency. ***

* * *

III.

* * *

Accordingly, the order of the district court will be reversed insofar as the court held that it had no jurisdiction to review the contentions of irreparable harm and the request for an injunction. The case will be remanded for further proceedings consistent with this opinion.

NOTES

1. Is the panel's reliance on the phrase "such other relief as may be necessary" in CERCLA § 113(j) to support injunctive relief in this case consistent with the Supreme Court's construction of similar language in *Meghrig v. KFC Western, Inc.*, 116 S.Ct. 1251 (1996) (in chapter 17)?

2. The most extraordinary aspect of *Princeton Gamma-Tech* is the panel's holding that an injunction halting an ongoing CERCLA cleanup is not barred by § 113(h) in the face of allegations of irreparable harm. Three years later, the Third Circuit, sitting en banc, expressly overruled this aspect of *Princeton Gamma-Tech*.

*** Section 9613(h)(4) expressly states that the citizen suit exception to the preclusion of federal court jurisdiction over challenges to EPA removal or remedial actions applies only to review of actions that have been "taken." Given that the subsection specifically deals with the "timing of review," we find Congress's use of the past tense significant, and a clear indication of its intention that citizen-initiated review of EPA removal or remedial actions take place only after such actions are complete.

* * *

We also find the last sentence of § 9613(h)(4) supportive of our interpretation of the statute. According to that sentence, "an action may not be brought with regard to a removal where a remedial action is to be undertaken at the site." 42 U.S.C. § 9613(h)(4). A "removal" action is an action taken in the short term to "prevent, minimize, or mitigate damage" to public health or the environment from the release or threatened release of a hazardous substance, 42 U.S.C. § 9601(23), while a "remedial" action involves a "permanent remedy taken instead of or in addition to removal actions" to contain a hazardous substance and minimize harm to public health and the environment. 42 U.S.C. § 9601(24). Thus, EPA may take both "removal" and "remedial" actions at the same site with respect to the same "release" of hazardous materials. The concluding sentence of § 9613(h)(4) provides that in such situations a citizens' suit challenging a "removal" action may not be brought even after completion of that removal action, so long as "remedial" action remains "to be undertaken." This provision demonstrates beyond peradventure, we believe, that Congress intended to preclude any judicial involvement in EPA removal and remedial actions until after such actions are complete.

* * *

Were we to adopt the plaintiffs' interpretation of § 9613(h)(4) and permit judicial review of EPA remedial actions before completion whenever a challenge includes bona fide allegations of irreparable harm to public health or the environment, we would undermine Congress's clearly expressed intent because we would create a situation in which response actions could be seriously delayed while EPA refutes allegations of irreparable harm which, while "bona fide," may simply reflect a legitimate difference of opinion about the preferred remedy for a particular site. Congress clearly intended that such differences of opinion be communicated directly to EPA during the pre-remediation public notice and comment period, not expressed in court on the eve of the commencement of a selected remedy.

The courts of appeals of the Seventh, Eighth, Ninth and Eleventh Circuits have read §§ 9613(h)(4) and 9659(a)(2) in the same way as we today read it. Each of these courts of appeals has held that these sections do not permit district courts to exercise jurisdiction over citizens suits challenging incomplete EPA remedial actions even where impending irreparable harm is alleged.

The majority in *Princeton Gamma-Tech* rejected this "absolute" reading of § 9613(h)(4) because it found that a complete prohibition of judicial review of citizens' suits that allege irreparable harm to public health and the environment was "contrary to the objectives of CERCLA," and "ma[de] the citizens' suit provision an absurdity." We are less convinced than was the *Princeton Gamma-Tech* majority, however, that the absolute limitation on judicial review established by § 9614(h)(4) is either absurd or "contrary to the objectives of CERCLA." First, EPA removal and remedial actions are designed to deal with situations involving grave and immediate danger to the public welfare. As we have noted, Congress apparently concluded that delays caused by citizen suit challenges posed a greater risk to the public welfare than the risk of EPA error in the selection of methods of remediation. Second, while Congress limited judicial review through § 9613(h), it did not thereby exclude the public from playing a role in ensuring that EPA actions under CERCLA are consistent with the objectives of the stature. Instead, Congress made the policy choice to substitute elaborate pre-remediation public review and comment procedures for judicial review. In addition, it gave the states, as representatives of the public, a significant role in the enforcement, in federal court, of the substantive standards established for remedial actions. See 42 U.S.C. § 9621(e)(2). Finally, Congress apparently left citizens the option of obtaining relief in state court nuisance actions. See H.R. Conf. Rep. No. 99-962, at 224 (1986) ("New section [9613(h)] is not intended to affect in any way the rights of persons to bring nuisance actions under State law with respect to releases or threatened releases of hazardous substances, pollutants, or contaminants."). Finally, even if we perceived an arguable tension between our reading and the objectives of CERCLA, our conclusion would not be altered. When statutory language is as clear as it is here, "it is simply not [the] function [of] a reviewing court to act as a super-legislature and second-guess the policy choices that Congress made." *Princeton Gamma-Tech*, 31 F.3d at 153 (Nygaard, J., concurring).

Because we find that the plain language and legislative history of § 9613(h)(4) compel the conclusion that Congress intended to prohibit federal courts from exercising subject matter jurisdiction over all citizens' suits challenging incomplete EPA remedial actions under CERCLA, we will overrule that portion of *Princeton Gamma-Tech* which held that a district court has jurisdiction under § 9613(h)(4) during the pendency of an EPA remedial action when plaintiffs make bona fide allegations of irreparable harm. ***

Clinton County Commissioners v. USEPA, 116 F.3d 1018, 1022-25 (3d Cir. 1997) (en banc).

If you live next door to and downwind from a Superfund site where the EPA has, over your protest, selected a cleanup remedy involving incineration of contaminated soils, and you believe that the incinerator will emit hazardous air pollutants, what if any provisions of RCRA and/or CERCLA could you invoke to ensure that your health would be adequately protected? What other options might you exercise?

3. The only other appellate court to have entertained the notion of an injunction against the U.S. government addressing an ongoing CERCLA remedy is the Tenth Circuit in *U.S. v. State of Colorado*, 990 F.2d 1565 (10th Cir. 1993), *cert. denied*, 510 U.S. 1092 (1994) (in chapter 17). In that case, the State of Colorado sought an injunction to ensure that the Army's ongoing CERCLA cleanup complied with the state's version of RCRA. It does not appear to be the type of frontal attack on a remedy that the Third Circuit panel had sanctioned in *Princeton Gamma-Tech*.

4. In two other cases, appellate courts have imposed constitutionally-based limitations on the EPA's discretion in conducting cleanup activities.

a. In *Reardon v. United States*, 947 F.2d 1509 (1st Cir.1991), the First Circuit held that the provision in CERCLA § 107(l) that enables the EPA to file a notice of lien on property it cleans up, without providing the property owner prior notice and an opportunity for hearing, unconstitutionally deprives persons of their property without due process.

Although the First Circuit entertained (and upheld) the PRPs' constitutional claims before the EPA had commenced enforcement proceedings, it went to some length to distinguish that case from the general rule against pre-enforcement review of the EPA's cleanup actions and orders.

> The Reardons' due process claim is not a challenge to the way in which EPA is administering the statute; it does not concern the merits of any particular removal or remedial action. Rather, it is a challenge to the CERCLA statute itself—to a statutory scheme under which the government is authorized to file lien notices without any hearing on the validity of the lien.
>
> *** We do not believe that the statute expresses a clear congressional intent to preclude the type of constitutional claim the Reardons are making—challenge to several statutory provisions which form part of CERCLA. However, it is important to make clear that not *all* constitutional challenges involving CERCLA fall outside the scope of § 9613(h). A constitutional challenge to EPA administration of the statute may be subject to § 9613(h)'s strictures. Such a claim may well be a "challenge to removal or remedial action selected under section 9604 of this title, and may thus fall within § 9613(h)'s bar. We find only that a constitutional challenge to the CERCLA *statute* is not covered by § 9613(h).

Id. at 1514-15.

b. In *Hendler v. United States*, 952 F.2d 1364 (Fed.Cir.1991), the Federal Circuit held the EPA's use of property adjacent to a superfund site for groundwater monitoring and extraction wells to be a compensable taking. As part of its effort to monitor groundwater conditions at the Stringfellow Acid Pits superfund site in California, the EPA determined that it was necessary to place groundwater monitoring (and possible extraction) wells on neighboring properties, and issued an order granting itself access to the neighboring properties to install and operate the wells. The Hendlers owned one such property, and they filed suit seeking compensation for the EPA's use of their property. In holding that the EPA's installation and operation of the wells was a compensable taking, the court differentiated between the EPA's conceded authority to have acted as it did, and the EPA's duty to compensate the neighboring property owners for the taking of their property.

10 POTENTIALLY RESPONSIBLE PARTIES

CERCLA specifies four categories of parties that may be held liable for performing response actions and/or reimbursing others for response costs. These parties are referred to as potentially responsible parties, or PRPs. CERCLA describes them as follows:

(1) the owner and operator of a vessel or a facility;

(2) any person who at the time of disposal of any hazardous substance owned or operated any facility at which such hazardous substances were disposed of;

(3) any person who by contract, agreement, or otherwise arranged for disposal or treatment, or arranged with a transporter for transport for disposal or treatment, of hazardous substances owned or possessed by such person, by any other party or entity, at any facility or incineration vessel owned or operated by another party or entity and containing such hazardous substances; and

(4) any person who accepts or accepted any hazardous substances for transport to disposal or treatment facilities, incineration vessels or sites selected by such person, from which there is a release, or a threatened release which causes the incurrence of response costs *** .

CERCLA § 107(a)(1)-(4), 42 U.S.C. § 9607(a)(1)-(4).

Although the listing of PRP categories appears in § 107 as an identification of parties liable for response costs (as well as natural resource damages and certain health assessment costs), the courts have construed it as also identifying the parties subject to EPA or court-issued cleanup orders under § 106. *See, e.g., United States v. Hardage,* 663 F.Supp. 1280 (W.D.Okla.1987); *United States v. Conservation Chemical Co.,* 589 F.Supp. 59 (W.D.Mo.1984).

The statute's relatively few words describing the categories of liable parties have given rise to an extensive body of case law construing the scope of each category and the nature of liability imposed. This chapter focuses first on the nature of CERCLA liability, and then on the basic categories of "owners," "operators," and "generators/arrangers" subject to CERCLA liability. The next chapter examines the manner in which these terms have been expanded to encompass related parties such as corporate executives and employees, parent or successor corporations, and lenders.

As the following cases make clear, CERCLA imposes strict liability, making issues of fault or negligence essentially irrelevant to a finding of liability. CERCLA also provides three statutory defenses—if an otherwise-liable PRP can prove that the release in question was caused solely by an act of God, act of war, or act of an independent third party, then the PRP may avoid liability. CERCLA § 107(b)(1)-(3). In addition, a fourth defense is at least theoretically available to current landowners who meet the rigorous requirements of the "innocent landowner" defense. These statutory defenses are narrowly drawn; they are addressed in chapter 12.

A. *Nature of CERCLA Liability*

Although it is a district court decision in what is now an ocean of appellate decisions construing CERCLA, the following case has had a singularly profound impact on the development of CERCLA case law.

UNITED STATES V. CHEM-DYNE CORP.
572 F.Supp. 802 (S.D.Ohio 1983)

CARL B. RUBIN, Chief Judge.

This matter is before the Court on the Motion of the defendants for Partial Summary Judgment under the Comprehensive Environmental Response, Compensation and Liability Act, 42 U.S.C. § 9607 ("CERCLA"). Plaintiff United States has sued 24 defendants, who allegedly generated or transported the hazardous substances located at the Chem-Dyne treatment facility, for reimbursement of the Superfund money expended to institute remedial action at the site. In order to expedite discovery and trial preparation, the defendants have moved for an early determination that they are not jointly and severally liable for the clean-up costs at Chem-Dyne.

A. Statutory Construction

The defendants have moved for a determination of the scope of liability under CERCLA, 42 U.S.C. § 9607 which is a matter of first impression to this Court. At present, there is no case authority specifically addressing this point.

The analysis begins with an examination of the germane statutory language. The statutory definition of liability is the standard of liability which obtains under 33 U.S.C. § 1321. 42 U.S.C. § 9601(32). The pertinent language provides that when the owner or operator of a vessel from which oil or hazardous substances is discharged in violation of § 1321(b)(3), he shall be liable to the United States Government for the actual costs ... 33 U.S.C. § 1321(f)(1). At the time of CERCLA's enactment, this section had been interpreted to impose a strict liability standard. It is proper to assume Congress was aware of the judicial interpretation of section 1321 as a strict liability standard. In fact, the legislative history of the statute directly supports this finding.

The liability section lists the classes of persons potentially liable under the Act for the costs incurred by government removal or remedial action. In contrast to plaintiff's assertion that joint and several liability is clear from the express statutory language, the Court finds the language ambiguous with regard to the scope of liability. Consequently, in an attempt to discern the Congressional intent, the Court will review and weigh the legislative history of the Act.

* * *

As background, two different superfund bills proceeded simultaneously through the House and Senate. On November 24, 1980, the Senate made its final amendment to its bill, thereby eliminating the term strict, joint and several liability from its provisions. Subsequently, on December 3, 1980, the House struck the language in its bill and substituted the language of the Senate bill, which was later enacted.

The defendants quote at length from Senator Helms' speech:

> Retention of joint and several liability in S. 1480 received intense and well-deserved criticism from a number of sources, since it could impose financial responsibility for massive costs and damages awards on persons who contributed only minimally (if at all) to a release or injury. Joint and several liability for costs and damages was especially pernicious in S. 1480, not only because of the exceedingly broad categories of persons subject to liability and the wide array of damages available, but also because it was coupled with an industry-based fund. Those contributing to the fund will frequently be paying for conditions they had no responsibility in creating or even contributing to. To adopt a joint and several liability scheme on top of this would have been grossly unfair.
>
> The drafters of the Stafford-Randolph substitute have recognized this unfairness, and the lack of wisdom in eliminating any meaningful link between culpable conduct and financial responsibility. Consequently, all references to joint and several liability in the bill have been deleted...
>
> It is very clear from the language of the Stafford-Randolph substitute itself, from the legislative history, and from the liability provisions of section 311 of the Federal Water Pollution Control Act, that now the Stafford-Randolph bill does not in and of itself create joint and several liability.

126 Cong. Rec. S15004 (Nov. 24, 1980). This view of statutory construction is at odds with the guidelines provided by the Supreme Court. Senator Helms was an opponent of the bill. *Id.* at S14988. Accordingly, his statements are entitled to little weight in construing the statute.

Senator Stafford, sponsor of the bill, succinctly noted that there was an elementation of the term joint and several liability as well as an elimination of the scope of liability. Senator Randolph, sponsor, explained the significance of these modifications:

> We have kept strict liability in the compromise, specifying the standard of liability under section 311 of the Clean Water Act, but we have deleted any reference to joint and several liability, relying on common law

principles to determine when parties should be severally liable... The changes were made in recognition of the difficulty in prescribing in statutory terms liability standards which will be applicable in individual cases. The changes do not reflect a rejection of the standards in the earlier bill.

Unless otherwise provided in this act, the standard of liability is intended to be the same as that provided in section 311 of the Federal Water Pollution Control Act (33 U.S.C. 1321). I understand this to be a standard of strict liability.

It is intended that issues of liability not resolved by this act, if any, shall be governed by traditional and evolving principles of common law. An example is joint and several liability. Any reference to these terms has been deleted, and the liability of joint tortfeasors will be determined under common or previous statutory law.

Id. at S14964.

* * *

Statements of the legislation's sponsors are properly accorded substantial weight in interpreting the statute, although the remarks of a single legislator are not controlling. The fact that the term joint and several liability was deleted from a prior draft of the bill or that the term liability refers to the standard under 33 U.S.C. § 1321, in and of itself, is not dispositive of the scope of liability under CERCLA. Perhaps in other contexts, when Congress deletes certain language it "strongly militates against a judgment that Congress intended a result that it expressly declined to enact." *Gulf Oil Corp. v. Coop Paving Co.*, 419 U.S. 186, 200 (1974). This case, however, presents an exceptional situation. A reading of the entire legislative history in context reveals that the scope of liability and term joint and several liability were deleted to avoid a mandatory legislative standard applicable in all situations which might produce inequitable results in some cases. The deletion was not intended as a rejection of joint and several liability. Rather, the term was omitted in order to have the scope of liability determined under common law principles, where a court performing a case by case evaluation of the complex factual scenarios associated with multiple-generator waste sites will assess the propriety of applying joint and several liability on an individual basis.

B. Scope of Liability

Because the legislative history evinces the intent that the scope of liability under CERCLA, 42 U.S.C. § 9607, be determined from traditional and evolving principles of common law, the next issue becomes whether state or federal common law should be applied. In situations where, as here, there is a lack of an express statutory provision selecting state or federal law, the inevitable incompleteness presented by all legislation means that interstitial federal lawmaking is a basic responsibility of the federal courts.

***

* * *

The improper disposal or release of hazardous substances is an enormous and complex problem of national magnitude involving uniquely federal interests. Typically, an abandoned waste site will consist of waste produced by companies in several states within the area or region. The pollution of land, groundwater, surface water and air as a consequence of this dumping presents potentially interstate problems. A driving force toward the development of CERCLA was the recognition that a response to this pervasive condition at the state level was generally inadequate. The subject mater dealt with in CERCLA is easily distinguished from areas of primarily state concern, such as domestic relations or real property rights, where state law was applied and there was no overriding interest in nationwide uniformity. Additionally, the Superfund monies expended, for which the United States seeks reimbursement, are funded by general revenues and excise taxes. The degree to which the United States will be able to protect its financial interest in the trust fund is directly related to the scope of liability under CERCLA and is in no way dependent upon the laws of any state. When the United States derives its authority for reimbursement from the specific Act of Congress passed in the exercise of a constitutional function or power, its rights should also derive from federal common law. In conclusion, the rights, liabilities and responsibilities of the United States under 42 U.S.C. § 9607 are governed by a federal rule of decision.

* * *

Finding, then, that the delineation of a uniform federal rule of decision is consistent with the legislative history and policies of CERCLA and finding further that no compelling local interests mandate the incorporation of state law, a determination of the content of the federal rule is the final step in the analysis. ***

* * *

Typically, as in this case, there will be numerous hazardous substance generators or transporters who have disposed of wastes at a particular site. The term joint and several liability was deleted from the express language of the statute in order to avoid its universal application to inappropriate circumstances. An examination of the common law reveals that when two or more persons acting independently caused a distinct or single harm for which there is a reasonable basis for division according to the contribution of each, each is subject to liability only for the portion of the total harm that he has himself caused. But where two or more persons cause a single and indivisible harm, each is subject to liability for the entire harm. Furthermore, where the conduct of two or more persons liable under § 9607 has combined to violate the statute, and one or more of the defendants seeks to limit his liability on the ground that the entire harm is capable of apportionment, the burden of proof as to apportionment is upon each defendant. These rules clearly enumerate the analysis to be undertaken when applying 42 U.S.C. § 9607 and are most likely to advance the legislative policies and objectives of the Act.

C. Summary Judgment

The defendants *** have moved for an early determination that they are not jointly and severally liable for the reimbursement of cleanup costs at Chem-Dyne. The proposition of the defendants is that because joint and several liability is not expressly provided for in CERCLA, there is no basis for its imposition. We find this to be an incorrect interpretation of the Act, and will apply the law under 42 U.S.C. § 9607 as delineated in the prior discussion. ***

* * *

The question of whether the defendants are jointly or severally liable for the clean-up costs turns on a fairly complex factual determination. Read in the light most favorable to the plaintiff, the following facts illustrate the nature of the problem. The Chem-Dyne facility contains a variety of hazardous waste from 289 generators or transporters, consisting of about 608,000 pounds of material. Some of the wastes have commingled but the identities of the sources of these wastes remain unascertained. The fact of the mixing of the wastes raises an issue as to the divisibility of the harm. Further, a dispute exists over which of the wastes have contaminated the ground water, the degree of their migration and concomitant health hazard. Finally, the volume of waste of a particular generator is not an accurate predictor of the risk associated with the waste because the toxicity or migratory potential of a particular hazardous substance generally varies independently with the volume of the waste.

This case, as do most pollution cases, turns on the issue of whether the harm caused at Chem-Dyne is "divisible" or "indivisible." If the harm is divisible and if there is a reasonable basis for apportionment of damages, each defendant is liable only for the portion of harm he himself caused. In this situation, the burden of proof as to apportionment is upon each defendant. On the other hand, if the defendants caused an indivisible harm, each is subject to liability for the entire harm. The defendants have not carried their burden of demonstrating the divisibility of the harm and the degrees to which each defendant is responsible.

* * *

NOTES

1. Following *Chem-Dyne*, PRPs—particularly in cases where many different parties sent different substances to a common site for treatment or disposal—attempted to avoid joint and several liability by contending that harm was divisible on the basis of the relative volumes of waste sent by different parties to the site. As typified by *United States v. Monsanto Co.*, 858 F.2d 160 (4th Cir. 1988), *cert. denied*, 490 U.S. 1106 (1989), courts routinely reject such efforts.

Placing their argument into the Restatement framework, the generator defendants concede that the environmental damage at Bluff Road constituted a "single harm," but contend that there was a reasonable basis for apportioning the harm. They observe that each of the off-site generators with whom SCRDI contracted sent a potentially identifiable volume of waste to the Bluff Road site, and they maintain that liability should have been apportioned according to the volume they deposited as compared to the total volume disposed of there by all parties. In light of the conditions at Bluff Road, we cannot accept this method as a basis for apportionment.

The generator defendants bore the burden of establishing a reasonable basis for apportioning liability among responsible parties. To meet this burden, the generator defendants had to establish that the environmental harm at Bluff Road was divisible among responsible parties. They presented no evidence, however, showing a relationship between waste volume, the release of hazardous substances, and the harm at the site.[25] Further, in light of the commingling of hazardous substances, the district court could not have reasonably apportioned liability without some evidence disclosing the individual and interactive qualities of the substances deposited there. Common sense counsels that a million gallons of certain substances could be mixed together without significant consequences, whereas a few pints of others improperly mixed could result in disastrous consequences.[26] Under other circumstances proportionate volumes of hazardous substances may well be probative of contributory harm. In this case, however, volume could not establish the effective contribution of each waste generator to the harm at the Bluff Road site.

Although we find no error in the trial court's imposition of joint and several liability, we share the appellants' concern that they not be ultimately responsible for reimbursing more than their just portion of the governments' response costs. In its refusal to apportion liability, the district court likewise recognized the validity of their demand that they not be required to shoulder a disproportionate amount of the costs. It ruled, however, that making the governments whole for response costs was the primary consideration and that cost allocation was a matter "more appropriately considered in an action for contribution between responsible parties after plaintiff has been made whole." *SCRDI*, 653 F.Supp. at 995 & n.8. Had we sat in place of the district court, we would have ruled as it did on the apportionment issue, but may well have retained the action to dispose of the contribution questions. See 42 U.S.C.A. § 9613(f) (West

---

[25] At minimum, such evidence was crucial to demonstrate that a volumetric apportionment scheme was reasonable.   The governments presented considerable evidence identifying numerous hazardous substances found at Bluff Road. An EPA investigator reported, for example, that in the first cleanup phase RAD Services encountered substances "in every hazard class, including explosives such as crystallized dynamite and nitroglycerine. Numerous examples were found of oxidizers, flammable and nonflammable liquids, poisons, corrosives, containerized gases, and even a small amount of radioactive material." Under these circumstances, volumetric apportionment based on the overall quantity of waste, as opposed to the quantity and quality of hazardous substances contained in the waste would have made little sense.

[26] We agree with the district court that evidence disclosing the relative toxicity, migratory potential, and synergistic capacity of the hazardous substances at the site would be relevant to establishing divisibility of harm.

Supp.1987). That procedural course, however, was committed to the trial court's discretion and we find no abuse of it. As we have stated, the defendants still have the right to sue responsible parties for contribution, and in that action they may assert both legal and equitable theories of cost allocation.

Id. at 172-73.

As the Fourth Circuit notes, even under a joint and several liability scheme, the liable parties may still allocate the costs among themselves by means of contribution claims, which are expressly authorized in CERCLA § 113(f). But in a scheme where it could take up to a decade between the initial identification of the site and responsible parties, and the *commencement* of remedial activities, and where the total investigation and response costs are typically in seven figures, to defer allocating the damages among the jointly and severally liable parties could pose hardship for some of the "less"—but still jointly and severally—liable PRPs. In fact, Judge Widener dissented from panel's decision in *U.S. v. Monsanto* solely on this issue:

> *** While it may be true that a subsequent suit for contribution may adequately apportion the damages among the defendants, I am of opinion [sic] that the district court, as a court of equity, is required to retain jurisdiction and answer that question now.

Id. at 176.

2. After years of PRPs and courts treating joint and several liability as virtually a non-issue, particularly where different parties' wastes were commingled and the courts summarily concluded that the harm was therefore indivisible, the Third Circuit in 1992 put a new gloss on the matter. *U.S. v. Alcan Aluminum Corp.*, 964 F.2d 252 (3d Cir. 1992), was an EPA cost recovery action against 20 PRPs, 19 of whom entered into a settlement with the EPA. The EPA then sought, and obtained, summary judgment against Alcan, the only non-settling defendant, and Alcan appealed to the Third Circuit.

The Third Circuit followed well-settled CERCLA precedent (including *Chem-Dyne* and *Monsanto*) in holding that "CERCLA contains no quantitative requirement in its definition of 'hazardous substance'" and that CERCLA liability does not require proof that the hazardous substance deposited by Alcan at the site in question "caused the release or caused the Government to incur response costs. Rather, the Government must simply prove that the defendant's hazardous substances were deposited at the site from which there was a release and that the release caused the incurrence of response costs." *Id.* at 259, 266.

The court then departed from past practice in CERCLA cases by holding that the district court erroneously failed to hold an evidentiary hearing on Alcan's claim that the harm at that site was divisible.

> *** [I]n our view, the common law principles of joint and several liability provide the only means to achieve the proper balance between Alcan's and the Government's conflicting interests and to infuse fairness into the statutory scheme without distorting its plain meaning or disregarding congressional intent.

* * *

These provisions [from the Restatement (Second) of Torts, regarding joint and several liability] underscore the intensely factual nature of the "divisibility" issue and thus highlight the district court's error in granting summary judgment for the full claim in favor of EPA without conducting a hearing. For this reason, we will remand this case for the court to determine whether there is a reasonable basis for limiting Alcan's liability based on its personal contribution to the harm to the Susquehanna River.

Our conclusions on this point are completely consistent with our previous discussion on causation, as there we were concerned with the Government's burden in demonstrating liability in the first instance. Here we are dealing with Alcan's effort to avoid liability otherwise established. We observe in this regard that Alcan's burden in attempting to prove the divisibility of harm to the Susquehanna River is substantial, and the analysis will be factually complex as it will require an assessment of the relative toxicity, migratory potential and synergistic capacity of the hazardous waste at issue. But Alcan should be permitted this opportunity to limit or avoid liability. If Alcan succeeds in this endeavor, it should only be liable for that portion of the harm fairly attributable to it. ***

* * *

In sum, on remand, the district court must permit Alcan to attempt to prove that the harm is divisible and that the damages are capable of some reasonable apportionment. We note that the Government need not prove that Alcan's emulsion caused the release or the response costs. On the other hand, if Alcan proves that the emulsion did not or could not, when mixed with other hazardous wastes, contribute to the release and the resultant response costs, then Alcan should not be responsible for any response costs. In this sense, our result thus injects causation into the equation but, as we have already pointed out, places the burden of proof on the defendant instead of the plaintiff. We think that this result is consistent with the statutory scheme and yet recognizes that there must be some reason for the imposition of CERCLA liability. Our result seems particularly appropriate in light of the expansive meaning of "hazardous substance." Of course, if Alcan cannot prove that it should not be liable for any response costs or cannot prove that the harm is divisible and that the damages are capable of some reasonable apportionment, it will be liable for the full claim of $473,790.18.

Id. at 268-71. Perhaps the most significant language in the Third Circuit's opinion is footnote 29, addressing the concept of divisibility:

*** [W]e also reject the Government's argument that a hearing is unnecessary because Alcan has admitted that its emulsion was "commingled" with the other generators' waste: "commingled" waste is not synonymous with "indivisible" harm. We observe that some courts have held that a generator may present evidence that it has paid more than its "fair share" in a contribution proceeding, expressly permitted under 42

U.S.C. § 9613(f)(2). *See, e.g., *** United States v. Monsanto*, 858 F.2d at 173. In a sense, the "contribution" inquiry involves an analysis similar to the "divisibility" inquiry, as both focus on what harm the defendant caused. However, we believe that this inquiry *** is best resolved at the initial liability phase and not at the contribution phase since it involves precisely relative degrees of liability. Thus, if the defendant can prove that the harm is divisible and that it only caused some portion of the injury, it should only be held liable for that amount. In our view, the logical consequence of delaying the apportionment determination may well be drastic, for it seems clear that a defendant could easily be strong-armed into settling where other defendants have settled in order to avoid being held liable for the remainder of the response costs. Indeed, in this case the court determined that Alcan, one of 20 defendants, was liable for $473,790.18 in response costs, although the total response costs amounted to $1,302,290.18. Thus, although Alcan comprised only 5% of the defendant pool, it was required by the court to absorb over 36% of the costs. Furthermore, Alcan's share of the liability seems to be disproportionate on a volume basis as well. We also point out that contribution will probably not be available from a settling defendant in an action by the United States. 42 U.S.C. § 9613(f)(2). We note, of course, that a determination in a given case that harm is indivisible will not negate a defendant's right to seek contribution from other non-settling defendants, as the contribution proceeding is an equitable one in which a court is permitted to allocate response costs based on factors it deems appropriate, whereas the court is not vested with such discretion in the divisibility determination.

Id. at 270, n.29.

3. Under *Alcan*, what are (a) the concept and (b) the role of causation: (i) in the government's case against PRPs? (ii) in the PRPs' attempts to prove that harm, although presumptively joint and several, is divisible in a particular case? and (iii) in a contribution case, where liability is held to be joint and several and the PRPs then bring contribution claims against each other to apportion equitably their collective liability to the government?

4. On remand, Alcan eschewed an evidentiary hearing, claiming that it was entitled as a matter of law to a determination that it was not subject to joint and several liability for the site cleanup.

The crux of the parties' dispute pertains to whether Alcan's potential contribution to the environmental harm to the Susquehanna River is limited to an assessment of the impact of the trace-level metals found in its used emulsion or should encompass the environmental significance of the used emulsion as a whole. Alcan insists that its potential liability can only be determined in the context of those constituents of its used emulsion that are defined to be "hazardous substances" and which render inapplicable CERCLA's petroleum exclusion—the heavy metals added in trace levels to its emulsion as a consequence of the manufacturing process. According to Alcan, the below background levels of the metal constituents of its used emulsion could not have caused an environmental problem relating to metals at the Site. Alcan also asserts that the Government's response actions were unrelated to the presence of metals. Thus, argues Alcan, it cannot be held liable for any of the Government's response costs.

The Government responds by contending that the absence of environmental problems and response actions related to metals at the Site are immaterial. According to the Government, "it was the emulsion as a whole, not just the individual constituents in the emulsion, which contributed to the harm at the Site."

Essentially, Alcan is arguing that even if its used emulsion, as a whole, is environmentally harmful, it should not be subject to any liability because the constituents that remove the used emulsion from CERCLA's petroleum exclusion could not be the cause for that environmental harm. This effort to dissect its waste material into components regulated by CERCLA and those not regulated by CERCLA is not consistent with the remedial purposes sought to be advanced by this legislation. ***

*** [T]he environmental harm posed by the medium that contains CERCLA-defined "hazardous substances" cannot be ignored. If the medium, with its "hazardous substance" constituents at ambient or below ambient levels, is environmentally benign, even when mixed with other hazardous wastes, then liability should not be imposed. Thus, for example, if Alcan had generated federally-approved drinking water that was dumped into the borehole it would not be subject to liability because that drinking water, even though it contains naturally-occurring levels of chromium and other metals, could not have caused any environmental harm.

In this case, Alcan has presented neither evidence nor argument that its used emulsion is environmentally benign. While the constituents of the used emulsion which bring it within CERCLA's ambit may not have contributed to the harm, Alcan has not contended that its used emulsion itself was harmless.

* * *

Another way to consider the issue is to determine whether the discharge of only the used emulsion into the Susquehanna River would have caused environmental harm warranting some cleanup response. Alcan has not argued that it could dump thousands of gallons of its used emulsion into a river without posing a threat to the environment. Because Alcan's used emulsion falls within CERCLA's purview, the complete absence of evidence that the used emulsion itself is environmentally benign compels denial of Alcan's summary judgment motion.

United States v. Alcan Aluminum Corp., 892 F.Supp. 648, 653-55. The court not only denied Alcan's motion regarding divisibility, it went further and granted summary judgment in favor of the government, subjecting Alcan to joint and several liability. *Id.*

at 656-57. The Third Circuit affirmed without opinion, 96 F.3d 1434 (3d Cir. 1996), and the Supreme Court denied *certiorari*, 1997 WL 134429 (June 23, 1997).

5. In another Alcan case, the Second Circuit "essentially adopt[ed] the Third Circuit's reasoning in *United States v. Alcan Aluminum Corp.*, 964 F.2d 252, 267-71 (3d Cir. 1992)." *U.S. v. Alcan Aluminum Corp.*, 990 F.2d 711 (2d Cir. 1993).

The Second Circuit case involved a waste treatment and disposal facility that had been operated by Pollution Abatement Services ("PAS") in Oswego County, New York, had received wastes from numerous generators, became contaminated, and was cleaned up by the EPA and New York State. The governments brought a cost recovery action against 83 of the PRPs, 82 of which settled with a combined payment of 74 percent of the governments' cleanup costs. Alcan refused to settle, brought Cornell University into the suit—although the governments had not—for its one-time disposal at PAS of neutralized run-off water (generated when a fire at a coal pile at the University was extinguished), and challenged the governments' assumption that all PRPs were jointly and severally liable.

The following excerpts summarize the Second Circuit's analysis of the joint and several liability issue:

Having rejected Alcan's proffered defenses to liability, one would suppose there is no limit to the scope of CERCLA liability. To avoid such a harsh result courts have added a common law gloss onto the statutory framework. They have at once adopted a scheme of joint and several liability but at the same time have limited somewhat the availability of such liability against multiple defendants charged with adding hazardous substances to a Superfund site. The Restatement (Second) of Torts § 433A (1965) has been relied upon in determining whether a party should be held jointly and severally liable, for the entire cost of remediating environmental harm at the site. *****

Based on these common law principles, Alcan may escape any liability for response costs if it either succeeds in proving that its oil emulsion, when mixed with other hazardous wastes, did not contribute to the release and the clean-up costs that followed, or contributed at most to only a divisible portion of the harm. Alcan as the polluter bears the ultimate burden of establishing a reasonable basis for apportioning liability. The government has no burden of proof with respect to what caused the release of hazardous waste and triggered response costs. It is the defendant that bears that burden. To defeat the government's motion for summary judgment on the issue of divisibility, Alcan need only show that there are genuine issues of material fact regarding a reasonable basis for apportionment of liability. As other courts have noted, apportionment itself is an intensely factual determination.

In so ruling we candidly admit that causation is being brought back into the case—through the back door, after being denied entry at the front door—at the apportionment stage. We hasten to add nonetheless that causation—with the burden on defendant—is reintroduced only to permit a defendant to escape payment where its pollutants did not contribute more than background contamination and also cannot concentrate. To state this standard in other words, we adopt a special exception to the usual absence of a causation requirement, but the exception is applicable only to claims, like Alcan's, where background levels are not exceeded. And, we recognize this limited exception only in the absence of any EPA thresholds.

Contrary to the government's position, commingling is not synonymous with indivisible harm, and Alcan should have the opportunity to show that the harm caused at PAS was capable of reasonable apportionment. It may present evidence relevant to establishing divisibility of harm, such as, proof disclosing the relative toxicity, migratory potential, degree of migration, and synergistic capacities of the hazardous substances at the site.

Id. at 721-22. Ultimately, the Second Circuit ruled that factual disputes precluded the granting of summary judgment for either side on the divisibility issue.

6. When this book went to press, the remand of this case was pending. *See* 1996 WL 637559 (N.D.N.Y. Oct. 28, 1996) (on Alcan's motion for summary judgment on the issue of divisibility, the court requested rebriefing on five issues).

7. The Third and Second Circuit decisions attracted considerable attention, not because they held joint and several liability inapplicable to those cases (which they did not), but because they enabled Alcan fully to present its case on divisibility at the liability portion of the case, without having to wait for a subsequent contribution proceeding.

The Fifth Circuit then became the first appellate court affirmatively to find divisibility sufficient to overcome the presumption in favor of joint and several liability. Set forth below are the facts and the portions of the opinion regarding joint and several liability; a significant holding regarding the EPA's cleanup decisionmaking is excerpted in chapter 14.

IN RE BELL PETROLEUM SERVICES, INC.
3 F.3d 889 (5th Cir. 1993)

Before JOLLY and DUHE, Circuit Judges, and PARKER, Chief Judge of the Eastern District of Texas.

JOLLY, Circuit Judge.

The Environmental Protection Agency (EPA) seeks to recover its response costs under the Comprehensive Environmental Response, Compensation and Liability Act (CERCLA) because of a discharge of chromium waste that contaminated a local water supply. Sequa Corporation appeals from the imposition of joint and several liability, challenges the EPA's decision to provide an alternate water supply system to the area in which the groundwater was contaminated by the chromium discharge, and contests the calculation of prejudgment interest and the application of the proceeds of the EPA's settlement with its co-defendants. We REVERSE the portion of the judgment imposing joint and several liability, and REMAND for further proceedings. Our review of the administrative record has convinced us that the EPA's decision to provide an alternate water supply was arbitrary and capricious; accordingly, we REVERSE the portion of the district court's judgment allowing the EPA to recover the costs of designing and constructing that system, and REMAND for deletion of those amounts and recalculating prejudgment interest.

I

In 1978, a citizen in the Odessa, Texas area complained about discolored drinking water. The Texas Water Commission conducted an investigation. It ultimately focused on a chrome-plating shop that was operated successively from 1971 through 1977 by John Leigh, Western Pollution Control Corporation (hereinafter referred to as Bell), and Woolley Tool Division of Chromalloy American Corporation (which later merged with Sequa), at 4318 Brazos Street, just outside the city limits of Odessa. The investigation showed that during the chrome-plating process, finished parts were rinsed, and the rinse water was pumped out of the building onto the ground.

In 1984, the EPA designated a 24-block area north of the Brazos Street facility as a Superfund site—"Odessa Chromium I." It authorized a response action pursuant to its authority under CERCLA § 104, and entered into a cooperative agreement with the State of Texas. The State was to perform a remedial investigation, feasibility study, and remedial design work for the site, with the EPA reimbursing the State for ninety percent of the costs. The remedial investigation revealed that the Trinity Aquifer, the only source of groundwater in the area, contained elevated concentrations of chromium.

A "focused" feasibility study (FFS) was undertaken to evaluate the need to provide an alternative water supply pending completion of the remaining portion of the feasibility study and implementation of final remedial action.[3] The FFS concluded that the City of Odessa's water system should be extended to provide service in the Odessa Chromium I area. On September 8, 1986, the EPA Regional Administrator issued a Record of Decision (ROD), finding that city water service should be extended to the site. Pursuant to the cooperative agreement, the State, through its contractor, designed and constructed the system, which was completed in 1988.

---

[3] The EPA estimated that a final remedy would be in place in 10-15 years. A "remaining portion" feasibility study was conducted, and the EPA selected a final remedial action in March 1988. Those activities are not at issue in this appeal.

II

In December 1988, the EPA filed a CERCLA cost-recovery action against Bell, Sequa, and John Leigh, which was consolidated with an adversary proceeding the EPA had filed against Bell in Bell's bankruptcy case. The EPA sought to recover direct and indirect costs it incurred in studying, designing, and constructing the alternate water supply system.

In July 1989, the district court entered a case management order providing that the case would be decided in three phases: Phase I—liability, Phase II—recoverability of the EPA's response costs, and Phase III—"responsibility." In September 1989, the district court granted in part, and denied in part, the EPA's motion for summary judgment as to liability. In its memorandum opinion, it stated that the relative culpability of the parties and the "divisibility of liability" issues would be decided during Phase III. Although the district court ruled that CERCLA did not require the EPA to prove causation, it held an evidentiary hearing and made alternative findings and conclusions addressing causation, holding that "Leigh, Bell and Sequa caused the contamination."[4] In March 1990, the district court granted the EPA's motion for clarification of the September 1989 summary judgment, holding that its previous opinion had provided that the defendants were jointly and severally liable. It also entered a declaratory judgment as to the defendants' liability for future response costs.

The Phase II proceeding on recoverability of response costs was handled through cross-motions for summary judgment. The district court held that the defendants had not met their burden of proving that the EPA's decision to implement an alternate water supply was arbitrary and capricious, and held that they were liable for the EPA's direct and indirect response costs, plus prejudgment interest from the date such costs were incurred. On March 2, 1990, the EPA sought approval of a proposed consent decree, in which it settled its claims against Bell for all costs, past and future, for $1,000,000. Sequa objected to the settlement, contending that Bell was not being required to pay its fair share. The district court granted Sequa's request for a hearing on the fairness of the proposed consent decree, and entered an order providing that a Phase III hearing regarding apportionment of liability was to be conducted before it ruled on the motion for entry of the consent decree. *** After the Phase III hearing in June 1990, *** the

---

[4] Approximately a month after the district court entered its findings of fact and conclusions of law on causation, our court decided *Amoco Oil Co. v. Borden, Inc.*, 889 F.2d 664 (5th Cir.1989). In *Amoco*, we noted that, "in cases involving multiple sources of contamination, a plaintiff need not prove a specific causal link between costs incurred and an individual generator's waste." Other courts have likewise concluded that proof of causation is not required in CERCLA cases. *E.g., United States v. Alcan Aluminum Corp. (Alcan-PAS)*, 990 F.2d 711, 721 (2d Cir.1993) (the government is not required to "show that a specific defendant's waste caused incurrence of clean-up costs"); *United States v. Alcan Aluminum Corp. (Alcan-Butler)*, 964 F.2d 252, 266 (3d Cir.1992) ("the Government must simply prove that the defendant's hazardous substances were deposited at the site from which there was a release and that the release caused the incurrence of response costs"); *United States v. Monsanto Co.*, 858 F.2d 160, 170 (4th Cir.1988) (liability is subject only to the causation-based affirmative defenses set forth in CERCLA § 107(b); "Congress has, therefore, allocated the burden of disproving causation to the defendant who profited from the generation and inexpensive disposal of hazardous waste.").

district court *** approved the consent decree. It held that the evidence at the Phase I and Phase III hearings demonstrated that there was no method of dividing the liability among the defendants which would rise to any level above mere speculation, because each of the proposed apportionment methods involved a significant assumption factor, inasmuch as records had been lost, and because each of the apportionment methods differed significantly. In the alternative, it concluded that, based on equitable factors, responsibility should be divided as follows: Bell—35%; Sequa—35%; and Leigh—30%.

In December 1990, the district court entered an order approving another consent decree, pursuant to which the EPA settled its claims against Leigh for past and future costs—for $100,000.

In sum, the district court held that Sequa is jointly and severally liable for $1,866,904.19, including the costs of studying, designing, and constructing the alternate water supply system. In addition, Sequa is jointly and severally liable for all future costs incurred by the EPA in studying, designing, and implementing a permanent remedy.

* * *

IV

Joint and Several Liability

Since CERCLA's enactment, the federal courts have struggled to resolve the complicated, often confusing, questions posed by the concept of joint and several liability, and its application under a statute whose provisions are silent with respect to the scope of liability, but whose legislative history is clear that common law principles of joint and several liability may affect liability. The issue is one of first impression in this Circuit.

A

Common Law: The *Restatement of Torts*

Although joint and several liability is commonly imposed in CERCLA cases,[7] it is not mandatory in all such cases. Instead, Congress intended that the federal courts determine the scope of liability in CERCLA cases under traditional and evolving common law principles, guided by the *Restatement (Second) of Torts*.

Section 433 of the *Restatement* provides that:

(1) Damages for harm are to be apportioned among two or more causes where

(a) there are distinct harms, or

---

[7] Many of the cases in which joint and several liability has been imposed involve hazardous waste sites at which numerous substances have been commingled. In such cases, determining the contribution of each cause to a single harm will often require a very complex assessment of the relative toxicity, migratory potential, and synergistic capacity of the hazardous wastes at issue. Under such circumstances, it is hardly surprising that defendants have had difficulty in meeting their burden of proving that apportionment is feasible. ***

(b) there is a reasonable basis for determining the contribution of each cause to a single harm.

(2) Damages for any other harm cannot be apportioned among two or more causes.

Restatement (Second) of Torts, § 433A.

The nature of the harm is the key factor in determining whether apportionment is appropriate. Distinct harms—e.g., where two defendants independently shoot the plaintiff at the same time, one wounding him in the arm and the other wounding him in the leg— are regarded as separate injuries. Although some of the elements of damages (such as lost wages or pain and suffering) may be difficult to apportion, "it is still possible, as a logical, reasonable, and practical matter, ... to make a rough estimate which will fairly apportion such subsidiary elements of damages." *Id.*, *comment* b on subsection (1).

The *Restatement* also discusses "successive" harms, such as when "two defendants, independently operating the same plant, pollute a stream over successive periods of time." Apportionment is appropriate, because "it is clear that each has caused a separate amount of harm, limited in time, and that neither has any responsibility for the harm caused by the other."

The final situation discussed by the *Restatement* in which apportionment is available involves a single harm that is "divisible"—perhaps the most difficult type of harm to conceptualize. Such harm, "while not so clearly marked out as severable into distinct parts, [is] still capable of division upon a reasonable and rational basis, and of fair apportionment among the causes responsible.... Where such apportionment can be made without injustice to any of the parties, the court may require it to be made." Two examples of such harm are described in the comment. The first is where cattle owned by two or more persons trespass upon the plaintiff's land and destroy his crops. Although "the aggregate harm is a lost crop, ... it may nevertheless be apportioned among the owners of the cattle, on the basis of the number owned by each, and the reasonable assumption that the respective harm done is proportionate to that number." The second example involves pollution of a stream by two or more factories. There, "the interference with the plaintiff's use of the water may be treated as divisible in terms of degree, and may be apportioned among the owners of the factories, on the basis of evidence of the respective quantities of pollution discharged into the stream."

* * *

CERCLA is a strict liability statute, one of the purposes of which is to shift the cost of cleaning up environmental harm from the taxpayers to the parties who benefited from the disposal of the wastes that caused the harm. *** Often, liability is imposed upon entities for conduct predating the enactment of CERCLA, and even for conduct that was not illegal, unethical, or immoral at the time it occurred. We recognize the importance of keeping these facts in mind when attempting to develop a uniform federal common law for CERCLA cases. We also recognize, however, that CERCLA, as a strict liability statute that will not listen to pleas of "no fault," can be terribly unfair in certain instances in which parties may be required to pay huge amounts for damages to which their acts did not contribute. Congress recognized such possibilities and left it to the courts to fashion some rules that will, in appropriate instances, ameliorate this harshness. Accordingly, Congress has suggested, and we agree, that common-law principles of tort liability set forth in the *Restatement* provide sound guidance. In applying those principles to this CERCLA case, we think that it will be helpful to examine briefly some of the relevant CERCLA jurisprudence.

B

The Jurisprudence

The first published case to address the scope of liability under CERCLA is *United States v. Chem-Dyne Corp.*, 572 F.Supp. 802 (S.D.Ohio 1983), which was cited approvingly in the legislative history of the SARA amendments to CERCLA. In that case, 24 defendants, who allegedly generated or transported hazardous substances located at Chem-Dyne's treatment facility, sought "an early determination" that they were not jointly and severally liable for the EPA's response costs. ***

The court described the nature of the "fairly complex factual determination" involved in deciding whether the defendants were jointly and severally liable ***. The court concluded that the defendants had not met their burden of demonstrating the divisibility of the harm and the degree to which each was responsible, and denied their motion for summary judgment.

United States v. Ottati & Goss, Inc., 630 F.Supp. 1361 (D.N.H.1988), was a cost recovery action against operators and former operators of drum reconditioning businesses, property owners, and generators of wastes contained in the drums that were sent to the site for reconditioning. The evidence showed that chemical substances leaked or spilled from drums and were mixed together. Although the generators satisfied their burden of proving approximately how many drums each brought to the site, the court nevertheless imposed joint and several liability, because "the exact amount or quantity of deleterious chemicals or other noxious matter [could not] be pinpointed as to each defendant[, and] [t]he resulting proportionate harm to surface and groundwater [could not] be proportioned with any degree of accuracy as to each individual defendant."

A similar situation existed in *O'Neil v. Picillo*, 883 F.2d 176 (1st Cir.1989). The site at issue there was a Rhode Island pig farm that had been used as a waste disposal site. The site was described as having "massive trenches and pits 'filled with free-flowing, multi-colored, pungent liquid wastes' and thousands of 'dented and corroded drums containing a veritable potpourri of toxic fluids.'" The defendants argued that it was possible to apportion the removal costs, because there was evidence of the total number of barrels excavated during each phase of the clean-up, the number of barrels in each phase attributable to them, and the cost of each phase. There was testimony that, of the approximately 10,000 barrels excavated, only 300-400 could be attributable to a particular defendant. The court concluded that because most of the waste could not be identified, and the defendants had the burden of accounting for the uncertainty, the imposition of joint and several liability was appropriate.[9]

On the other hand, the Third Circuit reversed a summary judgment in favor of the EPA, and remanded the case for further factual development on the scope of liability, in *United States v. Alcan Aluminum Corp. (Alcan-Butler)*, 964 F.2d 252, 255 (3d Cir.1992). This case involved the Butler Tunnel Site, a network of approximately five square miles of underground mines, tunnels, caverns, pools, and waterways, drained by the Butler Tunnel into the Susquehanna River in Pennsylvania. During the 1970s, millions of gallons of liquid wastes containing hazardous substances were disposed of through a borehole that led directly into the mine workings. In 1985, 100,000 gallons of contaminated water were released from the site into the river.

The government filed a cost-recovery action against 20 defendants; all but Alcan settled. The district court granted summary judgment for the government, holding that Alcan was jointly and severally liable for the response costs. The Third Circuit held that the "intensely factual nature of the 'divisibility' issue" highlighted the district court's error in granting summary judgment without conducting a hearing. It remanded the case in order to give Alcan the opportunity to limit or avoid liability by attempting to prove its personal contribution to the harm to the Susquehanna River. Thus, under the Third Circuit's approach, Alcan could escape liability altogether if it could prove that its "emulsion did not or could not, *when mixed with other hazardous wastes*, contribute to the release and the resultant response costs."

* * *

The Second Circuit essentially adopted the Third Circuit's approach to joint and several liability in another case involving Alcan, *United States v. Alcan Aluminum Corp. (Alcan-PAS)*, 990 F.2d 711 (2d Cir.1993). That case involved a waste disposal and treatment center operated during the 1970s by Pollution Abatement Services (PAS). Alcan used PAS for the disposal or treatment of 4.6 million gallons of oil emulsion. The government brought a cost-recovery action against 83 defendants. As in *Alcan-Butler*, all of the defendants except Alcan settled. The Second Circuit reversed a summary judgment in favor of the government, stating that "Alcan should have the opportunity to show that the harm caused at PAS was capable of reasonable apportionment." It held that Alcan was entitled to "present evidence relevant to establishing divisibility of harm, such as, proof disclosing the relative toxicity, migratory potential, degree of migration, and synergistic capacities of the hazardous substances at the site."

The court stated that Alcan could escape liability if it could prove that its oil emulsion, when mixed with other hazardous wastes, did not contribute to the release and resulting clean-up costs. It acknowledged that "causation is being brought back into the case—through the backdoor, after being denied entry at the frontdoor—at the

---

[9] The court noted that, even if there had been evidence of the number of barrels attributable to each defendant, more would be required to demonstrate that the removal costs were capable of apportionment, because the cost of removing barrels varied depending upon their contents. Furthermore, the costs of removing contaminated soil, in which the wastes had commingled, "would necessarily be arbitrary."

apportionment stage." However, it pointed out that causation was "reintroduced only to permit a defendant to escape payment where its pollutants did not contribute more than background contamination and also cannot concentrate."

* * *

A "moderate" approach to joint and several liability was adopted in *United States v. A & F Materials Co., Inc.*, 578 F.Supp. 1249 (S.D.Ill.1984). That case involved a disposal site at which over 7,000,000 gallons of waste were deposited. The court concluded that a rigid application of the *Restatement* approach to joint and several liability was inappropriate. Under the *Restatement* approach, a defendant who could not prove its contribution to the harm would be jointly and severally liable. The court thought that such a result would be inconsistent with congressional intent, because Congress was "concerned about the issue of fairness, and joint and several liability is extremely harsh and unfair if it is imposed on a defendant who contributed only a small amount of waste to a site."

The court concluded that six factors delineated in an unsuccessful amendment to CERCLA proposed by Representative (now Vice President) Gore could be used to "soften" the modern common law approach to joint and several liability in appropriate circumstances. Under this "moderate" approach, a court has the power to impose joint and several liability upon a defendant who cannot prove its contribution to an injury, but it also has the discretion to apportion damages in such a situation according to the "Gore factors":

(i) the ability of the parties to demonstrate that their contribution to a discharge[,] release or disposal of a hazardous waste can be distinguished;

(ii) the amount of the hazardous waste involved;

(iii) the degree of toxicity of the hazardous waste involved;

(iv) the degree of involvement by the parties in the generation, transportation, treatment, storage, or disposal of the hazardous waste;

(v) the degree of care exercised by the parties with respect to the hazardous waste concerned, taking into account the characteristics of such hazardous waste; and

(vi) the degree of cooperation by the parties with Federal, State, or local officials to prevent any harm to the public health or the environment.

* * *

To summarize, our review of the jurisprudence leads us to conclude that there are three distinct, although closely-related, approaches to the issue of joint and several liability. The first is the "*Chem-Dyne* approach," which relies almost exclusively on the principles of the *Restatement (Second) of Torts*. Under that approach, a defendant who seeks to avoid the imposition of joint and several liability is required to prove the amount of harm it caused.

The second approach, the "*Alcan* approach," is adopted by the Second and Third Circuits. Although that approach also relies on the *Restatement*, it recognizes that, under the unique statutory liability scheme of CERCLA, the plaintiff's common law burden of proving causation has been eliminated. *** [T]he *Alcan* approach suggests that a defendant may escape liability altogether if it can prove that its waste, even when mixed with other wastes at the site, did not cause the incurrence of response costs.

The third approach is the "moderate" approach taken in *A & F*. Under that approach, the court applies the principles of the *Restatement* in determining whether there is a reasonable basis for apportionment. If there is not, the court may impose joint and several liability; the court, however, retains the discretion to refuse to impose joint and several liability where such a result would be inequitable.

Although these approaches are not entirely uniform, certain basic principles emerge. First, joint and several liability is not mandated under CERCLA; Congress intended that the federal courts impose joint and several liability only in appropriate cases, applying common-law principles. Second, all of the cases rely on the *Restatement* in resolving the issues of joint and several liability. The major differences among the cases concern the timing of the resolution of the divisibility question, whether equitable factors should be considered, and whether a defendant can avoid liability for all, or only some portion, of the damages. Third, even where commingled wastes of unknown toxicity, migratory potential, and synergistic effect are present, defendants are allowed an opportunity to attempt to prove that there is a reasonable basis for apportionment (although they rarely succeed); where such factors are not present, volume may be a reasonable means of apportioning liability.

With respect to the timing of the "divisibility" inquiry, we believe that an early resolution is preferable. We agree with the Second Circuit, however, that this is a matter best left to the sound discretion of the district court. We also agree with the majority view that equitable factors, such as those listed in the Gore amendment, are more appropriately considered in actions for contribution among jointly and severally liable parties, than in making the initial determination of whether to impose joint and several liability.[13] We therefore conclude that the *Chem-Dyne* approach is an appropriate

---

[13] In adopting the majority view, we do not intend to imply that concerns for fairness and avoiding injustice should never be considered in deciding whether joint and several liability is appropriate. In this respect, we note that the legislative history of the SARA amendments to CERCLA, which created an express statutory right of contribution, cites the *A & F* decision for the proposition that the Gore factors may be considered in determining whether to grant apportionment in an action for contribution; the legislative history also cites *Chem-Dyne* for the proposition that the party seeking apportionment has the burden of establishing that it should be granted. Both of those decisions, however, deal with apportionment in terms of whether joint and several liability should be imposed, rather than in terms of contribution among jointly and severally liable parties. Considering CERCLA's "well-deserved notoriety for vaguely-drafted provisions and an indefinite, if not contradictory, legislative history," we do not view these citations as a basis for courts to determine joint and several liability based on those factors.

As discussed in the *Restatement* comments, there may be exceptional cases in which it would be unjust to impose several liability, such as when one of the defendants is so hopelessly insolvent that the plaintiff will be unable to recover any damages from it. We believe, however, that consideration of such factors will rarely be appropriate or necessary in CERCLA cases, especially when the plaintiff is the government. Under CERCLA's strict liability scheme, the deck of legal cards is heavily stacked in favor of the government. The legislative history shows that because Congress was concerned about the potential harshness or unfairness to defendants, it refused to adopt mandatory joint and several liability in order to give courts the ability to ameliorate such results in appropriate cases. We do not consider the financial condition of Leigh or Bell to be relevant to the decision in this case. The EPA entered into its

framework for resolving issues of joint and several liability in CERCLA cases. Although we express no opinion with respect to the *Alcan* approach, because it is not necessary with respect to the issues we are faced with in this case, we nevertheless recognize that the *Restatement* principles must be adapted, where necessary, to implement congressional intent with respect to liability under the unique statutory scheme of CERCLA.

C
Application of Joint & Several Liability
* * *

In the district court, the EPA contended that there was no reasonable basis for apportionment, because the harm to the Trinity Aquifer was a single harm, and a that single harm is the equivalent of an indivisible harm, thus mandating the imposition of joint and several liability. Apparently now recognizing the lack of support for that position,[15] the EPA on appeal acknowledges that apportionment is available, at least theoretically, when there is a reasonable basis for determining the contribution of each cause to a single harm. It asserts, however, that Sequa failed to meet its burden of proof on that issue. Sequa responds that the district court was misled by the EPA's incorrect view of the law, and erroneously required it to prove a certain—as opposed to reasonable—basis for apportionment.

Essentially, the question whether there is a reasonable basis for apportionment depends on whether there is sufficient evidence from which the court can determine the amount of harm caused by each defendant. If the expert testimony and other evidence establishes a factual basis for making a reasonable estimate that will fairly apportion liability, joint and several liability should not be imposed in the absence of exceptional circumstances. The fact that apportionment may be difficult, because each defendant's exact contribution to the harm cannot be proved to an absolute certainty, or the fact that it will require weighing the evidence and making credibility determinations, are inadequate grounds upon which to impose joint and several liability.

Our review of the record convinces us that Sequa met its burden of proving that, as a matter of law, there is a reasonable basis for apportionment. This case is closely analogous to the *Restatement*'s illustrations in which apportionment of liability is appropriate. For example, where cattle owned by two or more defendants destroy the plaintiff's crops, the damages are apportioned according to the number of cattle owned by each defendant, based on the reasonable assumption that the respective harm done is proportionate to that number. Thus, the *Restatement* suggests that apportionment is

---

settlements with those defendants with full awareness of Sequa's opposition to the settlements, as well as to the imposition of joint and several liability.

[15] The Second and Third Circuits have rejected similar arguments by the EPA. *See, e.g., Alcan-PAS,* 990 F.2d at 722 (rejecting the EPA's contention that "commingled" waste is synonymous with "indivisible" harm); *Alcan-Butler,* 964 F.2d at 270 n. 29 (same).

appropriate even though the evidence does not establish with certainty the specific amount of harm caused by each defendant's cattle, and even though there is a possibility that only one of the defendant's cattle caused all of the harm, while the other defendant's cattle idly stood by. Likewise, pollution of a stream by two or more factories may be treated as divisible in terms of degree, and apportioned among the defendants on the basis of evidence of the respective quantities of pollution discharged by each.

As is evident from our previous discussion of the jurisprudence, most CERCLA cost-recovery actions involve numerous, commingled hazardous substances with synergistic effects and unknown toxicity. In contrast, this case involves only one hazardous substance—chromium—and no synergistic effects. The chromium entered the groundwater as the result of similar operations by three parties who operated at mutually exclusive times. Here, it is reasonable to assume that the respective harm done by each of the defendants is proportionate to the volume of chromium-contaminated water each discharged into the environment.

Even though it is not possible to determine with absolute certainty the exact amount of chromium each defendant introduced into the groundwater, there is sufficient evidence from which a reasonable and rational approximation of each defendant's individual contribution to the contamination can be made. The evidence demonstrates that Leigh owned the real property at the site from 1967 through 1981, and conducted chrome-plating activities there in 1971 and 1972. In 1972, Bell purchased the assets of the shop and leased the property from Leigh. It continued to conduct similar, but more extensive, chrome-plating activities there until mid-1976. In August 1976, Sequa purchased the assets from Bell, leased the property from Leigh, and conducted similar chrome-plating activities at the site until late 1977. In response to the EPA's motion for summary judgment, Sequa introduced evidence regarding chrome flake purchases during each operator's tenure. It also introduced evidence with respect to the value of the chrome-plating done by each, as well as summaries of sales. Given the number of years that had passed since the activities were conducted, the records of these activities were not complete. However, there was testimony from various witnesses regarding the rinsing and wastewater disposal practices of each defendant, and the amount of chrome-plating activity conducted by each.

During the Phase III hearing, Sequa introduced expert testimony regarding a volumetric approach to apportionment. The first expert, Henderson, calculated the total amount of chromium that had been introduced into the environment by Leigh, Bell, and Sequa, collectively and individually. The second expert, Mooney, calculated the amount of chromium that would have been introduced into the environment by each operator on the basis of electrical usage records.

In addition to rejecting apportionment because of competing theories, the district court also rejected volume as a basis for apportionment, because there was no method of dividing the liability among the defendants which would rise to any level of fairness above mere speculation. It stated that each of the proposed apportionment methods involved significant assumption factors, because records had been lost, and because the theories differed significantly.

The existence of competing theories of apportionment is an insufficient reason to reject all of those theories. It is true, as the district court noted, that the records of chrome-plating activity were incomplete. However, under the facts and circumstances of this case, and in the light of the other evidence that is available, that factor may be taken into account in apportioning Sequa's share of the liability. Finally, the fact that Sequa's experts relied on certain assumptions in forming their opinions is not fatal to Sequa's ability to prove that there is a reasonable basis for apportionment. Expert opinions frequently include assumptions. If those assumptions are well-founded and reasonable, and not inconsistent with the facts as established by other competent evidence, they may be sufficiently reliable to support a conclusion that a reasonable basis for apportionment exists.

In sum, we conclude that the district court erred in imposing joint and several liability, because Sequa met its burden of proving that there is a reasonable basis for apportioning liability among the defendants on a volumetric basis. We therefore remand the case to the district court for apportionment.

* * *

NOTES

1. On remand, the district court reportedly found that Sequa was liable for only four percent of the cleanup costs, *U.S. v. Bell Petroleum Services, Inc.*, No. MO-88-CA-005 (W.D. Tex., Mar. 11, 1994); *see Court Limits Liability of Company Cited for Chromium Contamination of Ground Water*, 24 Env't Rep. (BNA) 2002 (Mar. 25, 1994), but the court's decision not to consider additional evidence on this issue was reversed on appeal, and the matter was again remanded to the district court. *United. States v. Bell Petroleum Services, Inc.*, 64 F.3d 202 (5th Cir. 1995).

2. In the wake of these cases, particularly the two *Alcan* cases because they apply more generally to multi-party CERCLA sites, issues of joint and several liability or, alternatively, divisibility of harm, have assumed a new-found prominence. Although there is little additional appellate authority on these issues, many district courts have addressed these matters.

3. The most successful attempts to avoid joint and several liability have involved sites with geographically distinct areas of contamination.

a. At a former wood treatment plant, hazardous substances had contaminated the soil and groundwater. Burlington Northern Railroad was the successor to another railroad company that owned a portion of the site from 1908 to 1969, during which time hazardous substances were disposed of at the site, giving rise to prior owner liability under CERCLA § 107(a)(2). However, Burlington Northern was able to avoid joint and several liability for some of the groundwater and soil contamination (while still facing joint and several liability for other areas).

*** [T]he Court finds that the environmental harm at the Site is divisible geographically. BN presented numerous exhibits, taken from the Environmental Protection Agency's (EPA) own data and figures from the

Remedial Investigation (RI) and Feasibility Study (FS), which show two separate areas of groundwater contamination. Based on the convincing testimony of Dr. Robert Sterrett, and the reliable and impressive work by ReTec, the Court determines that pentachlorophenol drives the groundwater remedy selection by the EPA. Furthermore, the Court is convinced that there are two pentachlorophenol plumes at the Site: one emanating from the pond impoundment area located primarily on the Parcel, and one emanating from the processing plant area to the east of the Parcel. The soil contamination at the Site is similarly divisible geographically.

Since neither BN nor its predecessor ever had an ownership interest in the land on which the processing plant stood, and that plume has neither merged with the pond plume nor migrated onto the Parcel, BN is not responsible or liable for the plume emanating from the processing plant area. ***

C. Conclusion

Therefore, the Court holds that BN is jointly and severally liable for response costs incurred in connection with (1) sludges in the pond impoundments; (2) contaminated groundwater in the pond plume, including the portion of the plume beyond the boundary of the Parcel; (3) contaminated soils within the Parcel; and (4) contaminated soils outside the Parcel but in the area affected by the pond plume and sludges on the Parcel. BN is not liable for response costs incurred in connection with the processing plant plume or contaminated soils not included in the above categories. ***

United States v. Broderick Investment Co., 862 F.Supp. 272, 277 (D.Colo. 1994).

b. Regarding a site contaminated with lead from various sources, the District Court for the Eastern District of Virginia was at a loss "to separate the harms or the costs of cleanup," and found the harm indivisible. However, the court held that the defendants could nonetheless avoid joint and several liability because there existed a reasonable basis for apportionment. *Pneumo Abex Corp. v. Bessemer and Lake Erie Railroad Co.*, 936 F.Supp. 1250 (E.D. Va. 1996).

c. See also *Kamb v. United States Coast Guard*, 869 F.Supp. 793, 799 (N.D. Cal. 1994)(liability for cleaning up former gun range not joint and several because there was a reasonable basis for apportioning CERCLA liability based on the volume of lead each contributed to the Site and based on the divisibility of the Site into two discrete sections: a trap/skeet range, not used by the defendants; and a firing range).

4. The foregoing cases limit, but do not eliminate, PRP liability based on divisibility of harm. In at least one case, in a ruling that may be limited to the private party context (in contrast to cost recovery claims by the U.S. or a state), a party that would otherwise be liable under CERCLA § 107(a)(3) for sending hazardous substances to a site, was dismissed from the private party action after proving that the hazardous

substances it sent to the site did not contribute pollutants at levels above background. *Acushnet Co. v. Coaters Inc.*, 937 F.Supp. 988 (D.Mass. 1996).

5. These cases represent a significant trend away from virtually a blanket rule of joint and several liability, and toward a more careful analysis, in the liability phase of an action, to issues of divisibility and apportionment. By no means is it suggested that joint and several liability has become the exceptional case; it remains the norm. *See, e.g., Akzo Coatings Inc. v. Aigner Corp.*, 960 F.Supp. 1354 (N.D. Inc. 1996) (although CERCLA site consisted of several geographically distinct areas of contamination, all were within CERCLA "facility" and therefore harm not divisible). *See also BancAmerica Commercial Corp. v. Trinity Industries, Inc.*, 900 F.Supp. 1427 (D.Kan. 1995).

6. The remainder of this chapter will focus on the categories of liable parties set forth in CERCLA § 107(a)(1)-(4).

B. Liability of Past and Present Facility Owners

STATE OF NEW YORK V. SHORE REALTY CORP.
759 F.2d 1032 (2d Cir. 1985)

Before FEINBERG, Chief Judge, OAKES, and NEWMAN, Circuit Judges.
OAKES, Circuit Judge.

This case involves several novel questions about the scope of the Comprehensive Environmental Response, Compensation, and Liability Act of 1980 and the interplay between that statute and New York public nuisance law. ***

On February 29, 1984, the State of New York brought suit against Shore Realty Corp. ("Shore") and Donald LeoGrande, its officer and stockholder, to clean up a hazardous waste disposal site at One Shore Road, Glenwood Landing, New York, which Shore had acquired for land development purposes. At the time of the acquisition, LeoGrande knew that hazardous waste was stored on the site and that cleanup would be expensive, though neither Shore nor LeoGrande had participated in the generation or transportation of the nearly 700,000 gallons of hazardous waste now on the premises.*** On October 15, 1984, the district court granted the State's motion for partial summary judgment. Apparently relying at least in part on CERCLA, it directed by permanent injunction that Shore and LeoGrande remove the hazardous waste stored on the property, subject to monitoring by the State, and held them liable for the State's "response costs," *see* 42 U.S.C. § 9607(a)(4)(A). In the alternative the court based the injunction on a finding that the Shore Road site was a public nuisance. Following a remand by this court on December 14, 1984, the district court on January 11, 1985, stated with more particularity the undisputed material facts underlying its decision finding defendants liable for the State's response costs and clarifying its earlier decision by basing the injunction solely on state public nuisance law. The court also modified its earlier decision by suggesting that CERCLA does not authorize injunctive relief in this case.

We affirm, concluding that Shore is liable under CERCLA for the State's response costs. We hold that Shore properly was found to be a covered person under 42 U.S.C. § 9607(a); that the nonlisting by the Environmental Protection Agency ("EPA") of the site on the National Priorities List ("NPL"), 42 U.S.C. § 9605(8)(B), is irrelevant to Shore's liability; that Shore cannot rely on any of CERCLA's affirmative defenses; but that, as suggested in the amicus brief filed for the United States and the district court's supplemental memorandum, injunctive relief under CERCLA is not available to the State. We nevertheless hold that the district court, exercising its pendent jurisdiction, properly granted the permanent injunction based on New York public nuisance law. Moreover, we hold LeoGrande jointly and severally liable under both CERCLA and New York law.

FACTS
* * *

LeoGrande incorporated Shore solely for the purpose of purchasing the Shore Road property. All corporate decisions and actions were made, directed, and controlled by him. By contract dated July 14, 1983, Shore agreed to purchase the 3.2 acre site, a small peninsula surrounded on three sides by the waters of Hempstead Harbor and Mott Cove, for condominium development. Five large tanks in a field in the center of the site hold most of some 700,000 gallons of hazardous chemicals located there, though there are six smaller tanks both above and below ground containing hazardous waste, as well as some empty tanks, on the property. The tanks are connected by pipe to a tank truck loading rack and dockage facilities for loading by barge. Four roll-on/roll-off containers and one tank truck trailer hold additional waste. And before June 15, 1984, one of the two dilapidated masonry warehouses on the site contained over 400 drums of chemicals and contaminated solids, many of which were corroded and leaking.[3]

It is beyond dispute that the tanks and drums contain "hazardous substances" within the meaning to CERCLA. 42 U.S.C. § 9601(14). The substances involved—including benzene, dichlorobenzenes, ethyl benzene, tetrachlorethylene, trichloroethylene, 1,1,1,-trichloroethene, chlordane, polychlorinated biphenyls (commonly know as PCBs), and bis (2-ethylhexyl) phthalate—are toxic, in some cases carcinogenic, and dangerous by way of contact, inhalation, or ingestion. These substances are present at the site in various combinations, some of which may cause the toxic effect to be synergistic.

The purchase agreement provided that it could be voided by Shore without penalty if after conducting an environmental study Shore had decided not to proceed.

---

[3] When these drums concededly were "bursting and leaking," Shore employees asked the State to enter the site, inspect it, and take steps to mitigate the "life-threatening crisis situation." Pursuant to stipulation and order entered on June 15, 1984, Shore began removing the drums. Some may still remain at the site.

LeoGrande was fully aware that the tenants, Applied Environmental Services, Inc., and Hazardous Waste Disposal, Inc., were then operating—illegally, it may be noted—a hazardous waste storage facility on the site. Shore's environmental consultant, WTM Management Corporation ("WTM"), prepared a detailed report in July, 1983, incorporated in the record and relied on by the district court for its findings. The report concluded that over the past several decades "the facility ha[d] received little if any preventive maintenance, the tanks (above ground and below ground), pipeline, loading rack, fire extinguishing system, and warehouse have deteriorated." WTM found that there had been several spills of hazardous waste at the site, including at least one large spill in 1978. Though there had been some attempts at cleanup, the WTM testing revealed that hazardous substances, such as benzene, were still leaching into the groundwater and the waters of the bay immediately adjacent to the bulkhead abutting Hempstead Harbor. After a site visit on July 18, 1983, WTM reported firsthand on the sorry state of the facility, observing, among other things, "seepage from the bulkhead," "corrosion" on all the tanks, deterioration of the pipeline and loading rack, and fifty to one hundred fifty-five gallon drums containing contaminated earth in one of the warehouses. The report concluded that if the current tenants "close up the operation and leave the material at the site," the owners would be left with a "potential time bomb." WTM estimated that the cost of environmental cleanup and monitoring would range from $650,000 to over $1 million before development could begin. After receiving this report Shore sought a waiver from the State Department of Environmental Conservation ("DEC") of liability as landowners for the disposal of the hazardous waste stored at the site. Although the DEC denied the waiver, Shore took title on October 13, 1983, and obtained certain rights against the tenants, whom it subsequently evicted on January 5, 1984.

Nevertheless, between October 13, 1983, and January 5, 1984, nearly 90,000 gallons of hazardous chemicals were added to the tanks. And during a state inspection on January 3, 1984, it became evident that the deteriorating and leaking drums of chemicals referred to above had also been brought onto the site. Needless to say, the tenants did not clean up the site before they left. Thus, conditions when Shore employees first entered the site were as bad as or worse than those described in the WTM report. As LeoGrande admitted by affidavit, "the various storage tanks, pipe lines and connections between these storage facilities were in a bad state of repair." While Shore claims to have made some improvements, such as sealing all the pipes and valves and continuing the cleanup of the damage from earlier spills, Shore did nothing about the hundreds of thousands of gallons of hazardous waste standing in deteriorating tanks. In addition, although a growing number of drums were leaking hazardous substances, Shore essentially ignored the problem until June, 1984.

On September 19, 1984, a DEC inspector observed one of the large tanks, which held over 300,000 gallons of hazardous materials, with rusting floor plates and tank walls, a pinhole leak, and a four-foot line of corrosion along one of the weld lines. On three other tanks, flakes of corroded metal "up to the size and thickness of a dime" were visible at the floorplate level.*** In addition, defendants do not contest that Shore employees lack the knowledge to maintain safely the quantity of hazardous chemicals on the site. And, because LeoGrande has no intention of operating a hazardous waste storage facility, Shore has not and will not apply for a permit to do so. Nor do defendants contest that the State incurred certain costs in assessing the conditions at the site and supervising the removal of the drums of hazardous waste.

CERCLA

CERCLA's history reveals as much about the nature of the legislative process as about the nature of the legislation. In 1980, while the Senate considered one early version of CERCLA, the House considered and passed another. The version passed by both Houses, however, was an eleventh hour compromise put together primarily by Senate leaders and sponsors of the earlier Senate version. Unfortunately, we are without the benefit of committee reports concerning this compromise. Nevertheless, the evolution of the legislation provides useful guidance to Congress's intentions. The compromise contains many provisions closely resembling those from earlier versions of the legislation, and the House and Senate sponsors sought to articulate the differences between the compromise and earlier versions. One of the sponsors claimed that the version passed "embodie[d] those features of the Senate and House bills where there has been positive consensus" while "eliminat[ing] those provisions which were controversial." 126 Cong. Rec. 30,932 (statement of Sen. Randolph).

* * *

CERCLA authorizes the federal government to respond in several ways. EPA can use Superfund resources to clean up hazardous waste sites and spills. 42 U.S.C. § 9611. The National Contingency Plan ("NCP"), prepared by EPA pursuant to CERCLA, *id.* § 9605, governs cleanup efforts by "establish[ing] procedures and standards for responding to releases of hazardous substances." At the same time, EPA can sue for reimbursement of cleanup costs from any responsible parties it can locate, *id.* § 9607, allowing the federal government to respond immediately while later trying to shift financial responsibility to others. Thus, Superfund covers cleanup costs if the site has been abandoned, if the responsible parties elude detection, or if private resources are inadequate. In addition, CERCLA authorizes EPA to seek an injunction in federal district court to force a responsible party to clean up any site or spill that presents an imminent and substantial danger to public health or welfare or the environment. 42 U.S.C. § 9606(a).***

Congress clearly did not intend, however, to leave cleanup under CERCLA solely in the hands of the federal government. A state or political subdivision may enter into a contract or cooperative agreement with EPA, whereby both may take action on a cost-sharing basis. 42 U.S.C. § 9604(c), (d). And states, like EPA, can sue responsible parties for remedial and removal costs if such efforts are "not inconsistent with" the NCP. *Id.* § 9607 (a)(4)(A). While CERCLA expressly does not preempt state law, *id.* § 9614(a), it precludes "recovering compensation for the same removal costs or damages or claims" under both CERCLA and state or other federal laws, *id.* § 9614(b), and prohibits states from requiring contributions to any fund "the purpose of which is to pay compensation for claims ... which may be compensated under" CERCLA, *id.* § 9614(c). Moreover, "any ... person" who is acting consistently with the requirements of the NCP may recover necessary costs of response." *Id.* § 9607(a)(4)(B). Finally, responsible parties are liable for "damages for injury to, destruction of, or loss of natural resources, including the reasonable costs of assessing such injury, destruction, or loss resulting from such a release." 42 U.S.C. § 9607(a)(4)(C).

Congress intended that responsible parties be held strictly liable, even though an explicit provision for strict liability was not included in the compromise. Section 9601(32) provides that "liability" under CERCLA "shall be construed to be the standard of liability" under section 311 of the Clean Water Act, 33 U.S.C. § 1321, which courts have held to be strict liability, and which Congress understood to impose such liability. Moreover, the sponsors of the compromise expressly stated that section 9607 provides for strict liability. Strict liability under CERCLA, however, is not absolute; there are defenses for causation solely by an act of God, an act of war, or acts or omissions of a third party other than an employee or agent of the defendant or one whose act or omission occurs in connection with a contractual relationship with the defendant. 42 U.S.C. § 9607(b).

DISCUSSION

A.   Liability for Response Costs Under CERCLA

We hold that the district court properly awarded the State response costs under section 9607(a)(4)(A). The State's costs in assessing the conditions of the site and supervising the removal of the drums of hazardous waste squarely fall within CERCLA's definition of response costs, even though the State is not undertaking to do the removal. ***

1. *Covered Persons.* CERCLA holds liable four classes of persons:

(1) the owner and operator of a vessel (otherwise subject to the jurisdiction of the United States) or a facility,

(2) any person who at the time of disposal of any hazardous substance owned or operated any facility at which such hazardous substances were disposed of,

(3) any person who by contract, agreement, or otherwise arranged for disposal or treatment, or arranged with a transporter for transport for disposal or treatment, of hazardous substances owned or possessed by such person, by any other party or entity, at any facility owned or operated by another party or entity and containing such hazardous substances, and

(4) any person who accepts or accepted any hazardous substances for transport to disposal or treatment facilities or sites selected by such person.

42 U.S.C. § 9607(a). As noted above, section 9607 makes these persons liable, if "there is a release, or a threatened release which cause the incurrence of response costs, of a hazardous substance" from the facility, for, among other things, "all costs of removal or

remedial action incurred by the United States Government or a State not inconsistent with the national contingency plan."

Shore argues that it is not covered by section 9607(a)(1) because it neither owned the site at the time of disposal nor caused the presence or the release of the hazardous waste at the facility. While section 9607(a)(1) appears to cover Shore, Shore attempts to infuse ambiguity into the statutory scheme, claiming that section 9607(a)(1) could not have been intended to include all owners, because the word "owned" in section 9607(a)(2) would be unnecessary since an owner "at the time of disposal" would necessarily be included in section 9607(a)(1). Shore claims that Congress intended that the scope of section 9607(a)(1) be no greater than that of section 9607(a)(2) and that both should be limited by the "at the time of disposal" language. By extension, Shore argues that both provisions should be interpreted as requiring a showing of causation. We agree with the State, however, that section 9607(a)(1) unequivocally imposes strict liability on the current owner of a facility from which there is a release or threat of release, without regard to causation.

Shore's claims of ambiguity are illusory; section 9607(a)'s structure is clear. Congress intended to cover different classes of persons differently. Section 9607(a)(1) applies to all current owners and operators, while section 9607(a)(2) primarily covers prior owners and operators. Moreover, section 9607(a)(2)'s scope is more limited than that of section 9607(a)(1). Prior owners and operators are liable only if they owned or operated the facility "at the time of disposal of any hazardous substance"; this limitation does not apply to current owners, like Shore.***

Shore's causation argument is also at odds with the structure of the statute. Interpreting section 9607(a)(1) as including a causation requirement makes superfluous the affirmative defenses provided in section 9607(b), each of which carves out from liability an exception based on causation. ***

Our interpretation draws further support from the legislative history. Congress specifically rejected including a causation requirement in section 9607(a). The early House version imposed liability only upon "any person who caused or contributed to the release or threatened release." H.R. 7020, 96th Cong., 2d Sess. § 3071(a), 126 Cong. Rec. 26,779. The compromise version, to which the House later agreed, imposed liability on classes of persons without reference to whether they caused or contributed to the release or threat of release. ***

Furthermore, as the State points out, accepting Shore's arguments would open a huge loophole in CERCLA's coverage. It is quite clear that if the current owner of a site could avoid liability merely by having purchased the site after chemical dumping had ceased, waste sites certainly would be sold, following the cessation of dumping, to new owners who could avoid the liability otherwise required by CERCLA. Congress had well in mind that persons who dump or store hazardous waste sometimes cannot be located or may be deceased or judgment-proof. ***

* * *

2. *Release or Threat of Release.* We reject Shore's repeated claims that it has put in dispute whether there has been a release or threat of release at the Shore Road site. The State has established that it was responding to "a release, or a threatened

release" when it incurred its response costs. We hold that the leaking tanks and pipelines, the continuing leaching and seepage from the earlier spills, and the leaking drums all constitute "releases." 42 U.S.C. § 9601(22). Moreover, the corroding and deteriorating tanks, Shore's lack of expertise in handling hazardous waste, and even the failure to license the facility, amount to a threat of release.

In addition, Shore's suggestion that CERCLA does not impose liability for threatened releases is simply frivolous. Section 9607(a)(4)(A) imposes liability for "all costs of removal or remedial action." The definitions of "removal" and "remedial" explicitly refer to actions "taken in the event of the threat of release of hazardous substances."

3. *The NPL and Consistency with the NCP.* Shore also argues that, because the Shore Road site is not on the NPL [National Priorities List], the State's action is inconsistent with the NCP [National Contingency Plan] and thus Shore cannot be found liable under section 9607(a). This argument is not frivolous. Section 9607(a)(4)(A) states that polluters are liable for response costs "not inconsistent with the national contingency plan." And section 9605, which directs EPA to outline the NCP, includes a provision that requires EPA to publish the NPL. Nevertheless, we hold that inclusion on the NPL is not a requirement for the State to recover its response costs.

The State claims that, while NPL listing may be a requirement for the use of Superfund money, it is not a requisite to liability under section 9607. The State relies on the reasoning of several district courts that have held that liability under section 9607 is independent of the scope of section 9611, which governs the expenditure of Superfund monies, and by extension, section 9604, which governs federal cleanup efforts. *See, e.g., id.; United States v. Northeastern Pharmaceutical & Chemical Co.,* 579 F. Supp. 823, 850-51 (W.D.Mo.1984) *("NEPACCO"); United States v. Wade,* 577 F. Supp. 1326, 1334-36 (E.D.Pa.1983). These courts have reasoned that CERCLA authorizes a bifurcated approach to the problem of hazardous waste cleanup, by distinguishing between the scope of direct federal action with Superfund resources and the liability of polluters under section 9607. While implicitly accepting that Superfund monies can be spent only on sites included on the NPL, they conclude that this limitation does not apply to section 9607. And it is true that the relevant limitation on Superfund spending is that it be "consistent with" the NCP, 42 U.S.C. § 9604(a), while under section 9607(a)(4)(A), liability is limited to response costs "not inconsistent with" the NCP. ***

*** Instead of distinguishing between the scope of section 9607 and the scope of section 9604, we hold that NPL listing is not a general requirement under the NCP. We see the NPL as a limitation on remedial, or long-term, actions—as opposed to removal, or short-term actions—particularly federally funded remedial actions. ***

CERCLA's legislative history also supports our conclusion. Congress did not intend listing on the NPL to be a requisite to all response actions. ***

Moreover, limiting the scope of NPL listing as a requirement for response action is consistent with the purpose of CERCLA. The NPL is a relatively short list when compared with the huge number of hazardous waste facilities Congress sought to clean up. And it makes sense for the federal government to limit only those long-term—

remedial—efforts that are federally funded. We hold that Congress intended that, while federally funded remedial efforts be focused solely on those sited on the NPL, states have more flexibility when acting on their own.

Finally, we reject Shore's argument that the State's response costs are not recoverable because the State has failed to comply with the NCP by not obtaining EPA authorization, nor making a firm commitment to provide further funding for remedial implementation nor submitting an estimate of costs. *** Shore apparently is arguing that EPA has ruled that the State cannot act on its own and seek liability under CERCLA. We disagree. Congress envisioned states' using their own resources for cleanup and recovering those costs from polluters under section 9607(a)(4)(A). We read section 9607(a)(4)(A)'s requirement of consistency with the NCP to mean that states cannot recover costs inconsistent with the response methods outlined in the NCP. *** Thus, the NCP's requirements concerning collaboration in a joint federal-state cleanup effort are inapplicable where the State is acting on its own. *** Indeed, the kind of action taken here is precisely that envisioned by the regulations.

4. *Affirmative defense.* Shore also claims that it can assert an affirmative defense under CERCLA, which provides a limited exception to liability for a release or threat of release caused solely by

> an act or omission of a third party other than an employee or agent of the defendant, or than one whose act or omission occurs in connection with a contractual relationship, existing directly or indirectly, with the defendant (except where the sole contractual arrangement arises from published tariff and acceptance for carriage by a common carrier by rail), if the defendant establishes by a preponderance of the evidence that (a) he exercised due care with respect to the hazardous substance concerned, taking into consideration the characteristics of such hazardous substance, in light of all relevant facts and circumstances, and (b) he took precautions against foreseeable acts or omissions of any such third party and the consequences that could foreseeably result from such acts or omissions.

42 U.S.C. § 9607(b)(3). We disagree. Shore argues that it had nothing to do with the transportation of the hazardous substances and that it has exercised due care since taking control of the site. Who the "third part(ies)" Shore claims were responsible is difficult to fathom. It is doubtful that a prior owner could be such, especially the prior owner here, since the acts or omissions referred to in the statute are doubtless those occurring during the ownership or operation of the defendant.[23] Similarly, many of the acts and omissions of the prior tenants/operators fall outside the scope of section 9607(b)(3), because they occurred before Shore owned the property. In addition, we find that Shore cannot rely on the affirmative defense even with respect to the tenants' conduct during

---

[23] While we need not reach the issue, Shore appears to have a contractual relationship with the previous owners that also blocks the defense. The purchase agreement includes a provision by which Shore assumed at least some of the environmental liability of the previous owners.

the period after Shore closed on the property and when Shore evicted the tenants. Shore was aware of the nature of the tenants' activities before the closing and could readily have foreseen that they would continue to dump hazardous waste at the site. In light of this knowledge, we cannot say that the releases and threats of release resulting of these activities were "caused solely" by the tenants or that Shore "took precautions against" these "foreseeable acts or omissions."

B. *Injunctive Relief Under CERCLA*

Having held Shore liable under CERCLA for the State's response costs, we nevertheless are required to hold that injunctive relief under CERCLA is not available to the State. Essentially, the State urges us to interpret the right of action under section 9607 broadly, claiming that "limiting district court relief [under section 9607] to reimbursement could have a drastic effect upon the implementation of Congress's desire that waste sites be cleaned." Conceding that section 9607 does not explicitly provide for injunctive relief, the State suggests that the court has the inherent power to grant such equitable relief.

The statutory scheme, however, shows that Congress did not intend to authorize such relief. Section 9606 expressly authorizes EPA to seek injunctive relief to abate "an actual or threatened release of a hazardous substance from a facility." Implying the authority to seek injunctions under section 9607 would make the express injunctive authority granted in section 9607 surplusage. *** In addition, the scope of injunctive relief under section 9607 would conflict with the express scope of section 9606. The standard for seeking abatement under section 9606 is more narrow than the standard of liability under section 9607. Section 9606 authorizes injunctive relief only where EPA "determines that there may be an imminent and substantial endangerment to the public health or welfare or the environment." Section 9607 contains no such limitation. ***

If there were any doubt about the statutory language, the legislative history would compel us to reject the State's argument. Congress specifically declined to provide states with a right to injunctive relief. ***

C. *Common Law of Public Nuisance*

* * *

In challenging the decision below, Shore fails to distinguish between a public nuisance and a private nuisance. The former "is an offense against the State and is subject to abatement or prosecution on application of the proper governmental agency" and "consists of conduct or omissions which offend, interfere with or cause damage to the public in the exercise of rights common to all ... in a manner such as to ... endanger or injure the property, health, safety or comfort of a considerable number of persons." *Copart Industries, Inc. v. Consolidated Edison Co.*, 362 N.E.2d 968, 971 (1977). The latter, however, "threatens one person or a relatively few ..., an essential feature being an interference with the use or enjoyment of land .... It is actionable by the individual person or persons whose rights have been disturbed." *Copart Industries*, 362 N.E.2d at

971. Public and private nuisance bear little relationship to each other. Although some rules apply to both, other rules apply to one but not the other.

Under New York law, Shore, as a landowner, is subject to liability for either a public or private nuisance on its property upon learning of the nuisance and having a reasonable opportunity to abate it. *** It is immaterial therefore that other parties placed the chemicals on this site; Shore purchased it with knowledge of its condition—indeed of the approximate cost of cleaning it up—and with an opportunity to clean up the site. LeoGrande knew that the hazardous waste was present without the consent of the State or its DEC, but failed to take reasonable steps to abate the condition. Moreover, Shore is liable for maintenance of a *public* nuisance irrespective of negligence or fault. Nor is there any requirement that the State prove actual, as opposed to threatened, harm from the nuisance in order to obtain abatement. Finally, the State has standing to bring suit to abate such a nuisance "in its role as guardian of the environment."

* * *

NOTES

1. *Shore Realty* was one of the first appellate court decisions construing CERCLA's liability provisions, and it was widely read and discussed when it was handed down. With nearly two decades of CERCLA history, it is now somewhat difficult to determine what was so remarkable about the court's holdings regarding Shore's and LeoGrande's liability as the current owner and operator. Does not § 107(a)(1) impose liability on the current owner and operator regardless of when or how the hazardous substances were placed on the site? Compare § 107(a)(1), imposing liability on current owners and operators, with § 107(a)(2), which imposes liability on past owners and operators only if hazardous substances were disposed of at the site during their ownership or operation.

2. Although the liability regime of § 107 has been held to apply to § 106, the state's authority to pursue cost recovery under § 107 has not been similarly extended to the issuance of cleanup orders under § 106. Some, but not all, states now have state law authority to issue cleanup orders.

Virtually every state has some version of a superfund law, if for no other reason, to provide for the 10 percent cost share that the state is required to contribute to a Superfund-financed cleanup within that state. As long as the state's cleanup costs were incurred in a manner "not inconsistent with the [CERCLA] national contingency plan," a state's authority to pursue cost recovery under § 107(a)(4)(A) is co-extensive with that of the EPA, regardless of whether the monies used by the state (for which it seeks reimbursement) originated from the federal Superfund or from a state law source.

State superfund laws vary considerably in scope and content. Some track CERCLA very closely, whereas others differ substantially from the federal law. In contrast to RCRA, there is no procedure for the EPA to delegate its CERCLA authority, in whole or in part, to the states. Section 104(c)(3) specifies the funding and other obligations that a state must assume when the federal Superfund is used to conduct remedial actions at a site within that state.

3. Another significant case emphasizing that CERCLA imposes liability on current site owners and operators solely by virtue of their status as owners and operators, regardless of their involvement or lack of involvement in the activities that caused the site to be contaminated, is *United States v. Monsanto,* excerpted below. The portion presented immediately below addresses the liability of "innocent absent" site owners. Another portion of the opinion, concerning the liability of generators that sent waste to the site, is mentioned in the notes in section D of this chapter.

UNITED STATES V. MONSANTO CO.
858 F.2d 160 (4th Cir. 1988)
cert. denied, 490 U.S. 1106 (1989)

Before WIDENER, SPROUSE and ERVIN, Circuit Judges.
SPROUSE, Circuit Judge.

Oscar Seidenberg and Harvey Hutchinson (the site-owners) and Allied Corporation, Monsanto Company, and EM Industries, Inc. (the generator defendants), appeal from the district court's entry of summary judgment holding them liable to the United States and the State of South Carolina (the governments) under section 107(a) of the Comprehensive Environmental Response, Compensation, and Liability Act of 1980 (CERCLA). 42 U.S.C.A. § 9607(a) (West Supp.1987). The court determined that the defendants were liable jointly and severally for $1,813,624 in response costs accrued from the partial removal of hazardous waste from a disposal facility located near Columbia, South Carolina. ***

I.

In 1972, Seidenberg and Hutchinson leased a four-acre tract of land they owned to the Columbia Organic Chemical Company (COCC), a South Carolina chemical manufacturing corporation. The property, located along Bluff Road near Columbia, South Carolina, consisted of a small warehouse and surrounding areas. The lease was verbal, on a month-to-month basis, and according to the site-owners' deposition testimony, was executed for the sole purpose of allowing COCC to store raw materials and finished products in the warehouse. Seidenberg and Hutchinson received monthly lease payments of $200, which increased to $350 by 1980.

In the mid-1970s, COCC expanded its business to include the brokering and recycling of chemical waste generated by third parties. It used the Bluff Road site as a waste storage and disposal facility for its new operations. In 1976, COCC's principals incorporated South Carolina Recycling and Disposal Inc. (SCRDI), for the purpose of assuming COCC's waste-handling business, and the site-owners began accepting lease payments from SCRDI.

SCRDI contracted with numerous off-site waste producers for the transport, recycling, and disposal of chemical and other waste. Among these producers were agencies of the federal government and South Carolina,[2] and various private entities including the three generator defendants in this litigation. Although SCRDI operated other disposal sites, it deposited much of the waste it received at the Bluff Road facility. The waste stored at Bluff Road contained many chemical substances that federal law defines as "hazardous."

Between 1976 and 1980, SCRDI haphazardly deposited more than 7,000 fifty-five gallon drums of chemical waste on the four-acre Bluff Road site. It placed waste laden drums and containers wherever there was space, often without pallets to protect them from the damp ground. It stacked drums on top of one another without regard to the chemical compatibility of their contents. It maintained no documented safety procedures and kept no inventory of the stored chemicals. Over time many of the drums rusted, rotted, and otherwise deteriorated. Hazardous substances leaked from the decaying drums and oozed into the ground. The substances commingled with incompatible chemicals that had escaped from other containers, generating noxious fumes, fires, and explosions.

On October 26, 1977, a toxic cloud formed when chemicals leaking from rusted drums reacted with rainwater. Twelve responding firemen were hospitalized. Again, on July 24, 1979, an explosion and fire resulted when chemicals stored in glass jars leaked onto drums containing incompatible substances. SCRDI's site manager could not identify the substances that caused the explosion, making the fire difficult to extinguish.

In 1980, the Environmental Protection Agency (EPA) inspected the Bluff Road site. Its investigation revealed that the facility was filled well beyond its capacity with chemical waste. The number of drums and the reckless manner in which they were stacked precluded access to various areas in the site. Many of the drums observed were unlabeled, or their labels had become unreadable from exposure, rendering it impossible to identify their contents. The EPA concluded that the site posed "a major fire hazard."

Later that year, the United States filed suit under section 7003 of the Resource Conservation and Recovery Act, 42 U.S.C. § 6973, against SCRDI, COCC, and Oscar Seidenberg. The complaint was filed before the December 11, 1980, effective date of CERCLA, and it sought only injunctive relief. Thereafter, the State of South Carolina intervened as a plaintiff in the pending action.

In the course of discovery, the governments identified a number of waste generators, including the generator defendants in this appeal, that had contracted with SCRDI for waste disposal. The governments notified the generators that they were potentially responsible for the costs of cleanup at Bluff Road under section 107(a) of the

---

[2] The federal instrumentalities that contracted with SCRDI included the Environmental Protection Agency, the Army, the Air Force, and the Center for Disease Control. The South Carolina Department of Health and Environmental Control also contracted with SCRDI for waste disposal.

newly-enacted CERCLA. As a result of these contacts, the governments executed individual settlement agreements with twelve of the identified off-site producers.***

Using funds received from the settlements, the governments contracted with Triangle Resource Industries (TRI) to conduct a partial surface cleanup at the site. ***

* * *

Thereafter, South Carolina completed the remaining 25% of the surface cleanup. It used federal funds from the Hazardous Substances Response Trust Fund (Superfund), 42 U.S.C. § 9631, as well as state money from the South Carolina Hazardous Waste Contingency Fund, and in-kind contribution of other state funds to match the federal contribution.

In 1982, the governments filed an amended complaint, adding the three generator defendants and site-owner Harvey Hutchinson, and including claims under section 107(a) of CERCLA against all of the nonsettling defendants. The governments alleged that the generator defendants and site-owners were jointly and severally liable under section 107(a) for the costs expended completing the surface cleanup at Bluff Road.

In response, the site-owners contended that they were innocent absentee landlords unaware of and unconnected to the waste disposal activities that took place on their land. They maintained that their lease with COCC did not allow COCC (or SCRDI) to store chemical waste on the premises, but they admitted that they became aware of waste storage in 1977 and accepted lease payments until 1980.

* * *

After an evidentiary hearing, the district court granted the governments' summary judgment motion on CERCLA liability. The court found that all of the defendants were responsible parties under section 107(a), and that none of them had presented sufficient evidence to support an affirmative defense under section 107(b). The court further concluded that the environmental harm at Bluff Road was "indivisible," and it held all of the defendants jointly and severally liable for the governments' response costs.

* * *

II.

* * *

In our view, the plain language of section 107(a) clearly defines the scope of intended liability under the statute and the elements of proof necessary to establish it. We agree with the overwhelming body of precedent that has interpreted section 107(a) as establishing a strict liability scheme. Further, in light of the evidence presented here, we are persuaded that the district court correctly held that the governments satisfied all the elements of section 107(a) liability as to both the site-owners and the generator defendants.

A. *Site-Owners' Liability*

In light of the strict liability imposed by section 107(a), we cannot agree with the site-owners contention that they are not within the class of owners Congress intended to hold liable. The traditional elements of tort culpability on which the site-owners rely simply are absent from the statute. The plain language of section 107(a)(2) extends liability to owners of waste facilities regardless of their degree of participation in the subsequent disposal of hazardous waste.

Under section 107(a)(2), any person who owned a facility at a time when hazardous substances were deposited there may be held liable for all costs of removal or remedial action if a release or threatened release of a hazardous substance occurs. The site-owners do not dispute their ownership of the Bluff Road facility, or the fact that releases occurred there during their period of ownership. Under these circumstances, all the prerequisites to section 107(a) liability have been satisfied.[13] *See Shore Realty*, 759 F.2d at 1043-44 (site-owner held liable under CERCLA section 107(a)(1) even though he did not contribute to the presence or cause the release of hazardous substances at the facility).[14]

The site-owners nonetheless contend that the district court's grant of summary judgment improperly denied them the opportunity to present an affirmative defense under section 107(b)(3). Section 107(b)(3) sets forth a limited affirmative defense based on the complete absence of causation. *See Shore Realty*, 759 F.2d at 1044. It requires proof that the release or threatened release of hazardous substances and resulting damages were caused solely by "a third party other than ... one whose act or omission occurs in connection with a contractual relationship, existing directly or indirectly, with the defendant...." 42 U.S.C. § 9607(b)(3). A second element of the defense requires proof that the defendant "took precautions against foreseeable acts or omissions of any such third party and the consequences that could foreseeably result from such acts or omissions." *Id.* We agree with the district court that under no view of the evidence could the site-owners satisfy either of these proof requirements.

First, the site-owners could not establish the absence of a direct or indirect contractual relationship necessary to maintain the affirmative defense. They concede they entered into a lease agreement with COCC. They accepted rent from COCC, and after SCRDI was incorporated, they accepted rent from SCRDI. *See United States v. Northernaire Plating Co.*, 670 F.Supp. 742, 747-48 (W.D.Mich.1987) (owner who leased facility to disposing party could not assert affirmative defense). Second, the site-owners presented no evidence that they took precautionary action against the foreseeable

---

[13] The site-owners' relative degree of fault would, of course, be relevant in any subsequent action for contribution brought pursuant to 42 U.S.C.A. § 9613(f) (West Supp.1987). Congress, in the Superfund Amendments and Reauthorization Act of 1986, established a right of contribution in favor of defendants sued under CERCLA section 107(a). *** The legislative history of this amendment suggests that in arriving at an equitable allocation of costs, a court may consider, among other things, the degree of involvement by parties in the generation, transportation, treatment, storage, or disposal of hazardous substances.

[14] Congress, in section 101(35) of SARA, acknowledged that landowners may affirmatively avoid liability if they can prove they did not know and had no reason to know that hazardous substances were disposed of on their land at the time they acquired title or possession. 42 U.S.C.A. § 9601(35) (West Supp.1987). This explicitly drafted exception further signals Congress' intent to impose liability on landowners who cannot satisfy its express requirements.

aware COCC was a chemical manufacturing company, they were completely ignorant of all waste disposal activities at Bluff Road before 1977. They maintained that they never inspected the site prior to that time. In our view, the statute does not sanction such willful or negligent blindness on the part of absentee owners. The district court committed no error in entering summary judgment against the site-owners.

* * *

NOTES

1. *Shore Realty* and *Monsanto* represent the black-letter law on current landowner liability—until quite recently. It still remains a legal "slam-dunk" for the EPA (or any other party) to establish the prima facie liability of a current landowner. In few cases, however, current landowners have met with some success in asserting the third-party defense. *See* chapter 12.

2. In contrast, proving a prima facie case against a prior owner or operator is not as straightforward. Prior owners and operators are not subject to CERCLA liability unless they owned or operated the site "at the time of disposal of any hazardous substance" there. § 107(a)(2).

When the Second Edition of this casebook was published (1992), and even as recently as the 1994-1995 Supplement, the only appellate authority construing this language held that a prior owner could be liable if the only "disposal" that occurred during her ownership was the ongoing leakage of hazardous substances that had been deposited on the site before she acquired it. *Nurad, Inc. v. William E. Hooper & Sons Co.*, 966 F.2d 837 (4th Cir. 1992), *cert. denied sub nom. Mumaw v. Nurad, Inc.*, 506 U.S. 940 (1992).

In *Nurad*, William E. Hooper & Sons stored mineral spirits in underground storage tanks on the site in question for use in its textile finishing plant. Hooper then closed the plant, ceased using the tanks, but did not remove any mineral spirits remaining in them. The property changed hands, but no subsequent owners or lessees used the tanks. When the State of Maryland required the then-current owner (Nurad) to close the tanks properly, it did so and then sued prior owners and operators for reimbursement of its tank removal and soil clean-up costs. Hooper and an intervening owner (Mumaw) claimed that they were not owners at the time of disposal of hazardous substances. The Fourth Circuit disagreed.

*** The statute defines "disposal" in 42 U.S.C. § 9601(29) by incorporating by reference the definition found in the Resource Conservation and Recovery Act (RCRA). That definition states:

> The term "disposal" means the discharge, deposit, injection, dumping, spilling, leaking, or placing of any solid waste or hazardous waste into or on any land or water so that such solid waste or hazardous waste or any constituent thereof may enter the environment or be emitted into the air or discharged into any waters, including ground waters.

42 U.S.C. § 6903(3). Some of the words in this definition appear to be primarily of an active voice. This is true of "deposit," "injection," "dumping," and "placing." Others of the words, however, readily admit to a passive component: hazardous waste may leak or spill without any active human participation. The district court arbitrarily deprived these words of their passive element by imposing a requirement of active participation as a prerequisite to liability.

Indeed, this circuit has already rejected the "strained reading" of disposal which would limit its meaning to "active human conduct." *United States v. Waste Ind., Inc.*, 734 F.2d 159, 164-65 (4th Cir.1984). In *Waste Industries*, the court held that Congress intended the 42 U.S.C. § 6903(3) definition of disposal "to have a range of meanings," including not only active conduct, but also the reposing of hazardous waste and its subsequent movement through the environment. *Id.* at 164. ***

We think the district court was bound to follow *Waste Industries* in interpreting the term "disposal." It is true that *Waste Industries* interpreted the definition in the context of RCRA, but Congress expressly provided that under CERCLA the term "shall have the meaning provided in section 1004" of RCRA (42 U.S.C. § 6903(3)). 42 U.S.C. § 9601(29). Moreover, the aim of both RCRA and CERCLA is to encourage the cleanup of hazardous waste conditions. Whether the context is one of prospective enforcement of hazardous waste removal under RCRA or an action for reimbursement of response costs under CERCLA, a requirement conditioning liability upon affirmative human participation in contamination equally frustrates the statutory purpose.

*** Under the district court's view, an owner could avoid liability simply by standing idle while an environmental hazard festers on his property. Such an owner could insulate himself from liability by virtue of his passivity, so long as he transfers the property before any response costs are incurred. A more conscientious owner who undertakes the task of cleaning up the environmental hazard would, on the other hand, be liable as the current owner of the facility, since "disposal" is not a part of the current owner liability scheme under 42 U.S.C. § 9607(a)(1). The district court's view thus introduces the anomalous situation where a current owner, such as Nurad, who never used the storage tanks could bear a substantial share of the cleanup costs, while a former owner who was similarly situated would face no liability at all. A CERCLA regime which rewards indifference to environmental hazards and discourages voluntary efforts at waste cleanup cannot be what Congress had in mind.

The district court's view of the CERCLA definition of disposal is also at odds with CERCLA's strict liability emphasis. The trigger to liability under § 9607(a)(2) is ownership or operation of a facility at the time of disposal, not culpability or responsibility for the contamination. We must decline therefore to engraft onto the statute additional prerequisites to the reimbursement of response costs which Congress did not place there.

Thus, we hold that § 9607(a)(2) imposes liability not only for active involvement in the "dumping" or "placing" of hazardous waste at the facility, but for ownership of the facility at a time that hazardous waste was "spilling" or "leaking." The only remaining question is whether a statutory disposal of hazardous waste occurred during the period of Hooper's and Mumaw's ownership.

We think for the following reasons that it did. Initially, the record supports the conclusion that both the Hooper Co. and Mumaw owned the facility at a time when the mineral spirits were "leaking" from the tanks. Nurad has established that the Hooper Co. began to install the USTs some time before 1935 and that mineral spirits reposed in the tanks until they were removed by Nurad in 1988-89. Nurad has further presented uncontroverted evidence that at the time the tanks were removed the soil around several of the tanks was contaminated with mineral spirits. Indeed, the district court found that the "mineral spirits in the excavated soil show an exact chromatographic match" with those in one tank, and that another of the tanks had "corrosion holes in the bottom and was underlain by discolored soils that emanated solvent odors." Neither the Hooper Co. nor Mumaw has pointed to anything to overcome the presumption that the leaking that has occurred was not a sudden event, but the result of a gradual and progressive course of environmental contamination that included these defendants' period of ownership. We do not think in such circumstances that Congress intended to impose upon a CERCLA plaintiff the onerous burden of pinpointing at what precise point a leakage may have begun. This circuit has been careful not to vitiate what was intended as remedial legislation by erecting barrier upon barrier on the road to reimbursement of response costs. ***

Id. at 844-46.

3. Recently, two other circuits have addressed this issue, creating a new "majority" view that a more active form of disposal is necessary before a prior owner or operator is liable under § 107(a)(2).

UNITED STATES V. CDMG REALTY CO.
96 F.3d 706 (3d Cir. 1996)

Before BECKER, McKEE, and McKAY, Circuit Judges.
BECKER, Circuit Judge.

This appeal requires us to determine the meaning of the word "disposal" in the Comprehensive Environmental Response, Compensation, and Liability Act (CERCLA). Plaintiff HMAT Associates, the current owner of contaminated property, was sued by the United States under CERCLA for the costs of cleaning up the site. HMAT sought contribution from Defendant Dowel Associates, the company that sold the land to HMAT, on the ground that Dowel was a prior owner "at the time of disposal," see 42 U.S.C. § 9607(a)(2). HMAT concedes that no one dumped waste at the property during Dowel's ownership, but offers two reasons why "disposal" took place during Dowel's tenure. HMAT first advances a "passive" disposal theory: that "disposal" occurred because contamination dumped in the land prior to Dowel's purchase of the property spread during Dowel's ownership. HMAT also offers an "active" disposal theory: that a soil investigation conducted by Dowel to determine whether the land could support construction caused the dispersal of contaminants, and that this constitutes "disposal."

On cross-motions for summary judgment, the district court ruled in favor of Dowel. The court rejected HMAT's argument that the spread of contamination unaided by human conduct can confer CERCLA liability and held that any disturbance of contaminants caused by Dowel's soil testing was too insignificant to amount to "disposal." HMAT appeals the court's grant of Dowel's summary judgment motion and the denial of its own motion.

We hold that the passive migration of contamination dumped in the land prior to Dowel's ownership does not constitute disposal. Finding it unnecessary to reach the question whether the movement of contaminants unaided by human conduct can ever constitute "disposal," we conclude that the language of CERCLA's "disposal" definition cannot encompass the spreading of waste at issue here. This conclusion is based on an examination of CERCLA's text, is supported by the structure of the statute, and is consistent with CERCLA's purposes.

Regarding Dowel's soil testing, we hold that there is no threshold level of disturbance required to constitute "disposal," and that HMAT has identified evidence that would justify a factfinder's conclusion that contaminants were spread in the testing. We also hold, however, that because CERCLA clearly contemplates that prospective purchasers be allowed to conduct soil investigations to determine whether property is contaminated, a plaintiff must show not only that a soil investigation has caused the spread of contaminants, but also that the investigation was conducted negligently.

Thus, although we agree with the district court that HMAT's passive theory is not viable, HMAT may be able to proceed on its active theory. Accordingly, we will vacate the district court's grant of summary judgment to Dowel and remand for further proceedings consistent with this opinion.

I. Facts and Procedural History

The property at issue in this case, a ten-acre parcel of land in Morris County, New Jersey, was once part of the Sharkey's Farm Landfill (Sharkey's Landfill). Sharkey's Landfill operated as a municipal landfill from 1945 until 1972. During its operation, the landfill received waste from several counties in northern New Jersey. In addition to accepting municipal solid waste, the landfill received approximately 750,000 pounds of hazardous chemical waste from Ciba-Geigy Company, a large pharmaceutical concern. Additional chemical waste from other sources may also have been deposited there. For example, Koppers Chemical Company allegedly disposed of about 3,000,000 gallons of wastewater of unknown composition in the landfill. Between 1966 and 1972, county and state agencies received steady complaints about odors, smoke from fires, lack of proper cover, and the presence of dead animals in the landfill. The landfill was closed to further disposal in 1972.

The Environmental Protection Agency (EPA) and the New Jersey Department of Environmental Protection and Energy (NJDEPE) began investigating Sharkey's Landfill in the mid to late 1970s. In 1982, the EPA placed Sharkey's Landfill on the National Priorities List of Hazardous Waste Sites.

In December 1981, Dowel purchased the property. The land was vacant at the time of purchase, and it remained vacant during Dowel's ownership. Neither Dowel nor any other person deposited waste at the site during Dowel's term of ownership. Dowel's only activity on the land was a soil investigation, conducted in September 1981 (three months prior to finalizing its purchase) to determine the land's ability to support construction. The soil investigation, which was performed by Thor Engineering, involved nine drill borings, each twelve to eighteen feet into the ground. Thor's logs show that its equipment bored through various waste materials and groundwater and that several of the boreholes "caved" during the testing.

In November 1983, the NJDEPE notified Dowel that it was investigating the property and that Dowel should cease any planned activities at the site. In 1984, the EPA notified Dowel that Dowel was potentially liable for the cleanup costs of the site and invited it to undertake voluntary cleanup.

In 1987, Dowel sold the property to HMAT. In the contract of sale, Dowel fully disclosed that the property was part of the Sharkey Landfill, that the landfill was under investigation by state and federal environmental authorities, and that the property was part of a possible Superfund site.

In October 1989, EPA and NJDEPE commenced actions against parties potentially liable for the costs of cleaning up the Sharkey Landfill and seeking a declaration of future liability. HMAT, as the current owner of the property, was named as a defendant under CERCLA § 107(a)(1). Dowel was not sued. However, HMAT filed a third-party suit against Dowel, seeking contribution from Dowel as a former owner of the property "at the time of disposal" pursuant to CERCLA §§ 107(a)(2) and 113(f). ***

* * *

II. Passive Spreading in a Landfill as Disposal

A. Introduction

CERCLA is a broad and complex statute aimed at the dangers posed by hazardous waste sites. Among other things, CERCLA provides a cause of action to recover "response costs" incurred in remedying an environmental hazard, and allows those liable for response costs to seek contribution from other liable parties. A plaintiff must meet four elements to establish CERCLA liability: (1) that hazardous substances were disposed of at a "facility"; (2) that there has been a "release" or "threatened release" of hazardous substances from the facility into the environment; (3) that the release or threatened release has required or will require the expenditure of "response costs"; and (4) that the defendant falls within one of four categories of responsible parties. If these requirements are met, responsible parties are liable for response costs regardless of their intent.***

The parties agree that the first three requirements are met. Their dispute concerns whether Dowel is a responsible party. HMAT contends that Dowel is liable as a person who owned or operated the facility "at the time of disposal" of a hazardous substance. [42 U.S.C. § 9607(a)(2).]

CERCLA defines "disposal" by incorporating the definition used by the Resource Conservation and Recovery Act (RCRA). See 42 U.S.C. § 9601(29) ("The terms 'disposal', 'hazardous waste', and 'treatment' shall have the meaning provided in section 1004 of the Solid Waste Disposal Act."). Under RCRA,

> The term "disposal" means the discharge, deposit, injection, dumping, spilling, leaking, or placing of any solid waste or hazardous waste into or on any land or water so that such solid waste or hazardous waste or any constituent thereof may enter the environment or be emitted into the air or discharged into any waters, including ground waters.

42 U.S.C. § 6903(3). Focusing on the breadth of this definition, HMAT reads "disposal" to encompass the passive migration of contaminants. HMAT offers no evidence that any passive migration has occurred here but asks us to take judicial notice that waste tends to spread once it is put in the ground, See Office of Remedial Response, United States Environmental Protection Agency, Superfund Exposure Assessment Manual 8 (1988) [Hereinafter Superfund Manual] (waste in landfills tends to migrate due to, inter alia, rain, groundwater movement, and wind) and waste therefore must have spread during the six years Dowel owned the property. Several courts have been sympathetic to this argument. ***

We are unpersuaded. A thorough examination of the text and structure of CERCLA convinces us that the passive migration of contaminants alleged here does not constitute disposal. Our conclusion is based on the plain meaning of the words used in the disposal definition and is supported by the structure of CERCLA's liability scheme. We also believe that our interpretation is consistent with CERCLA's purposes.

B. The Language

1. The Definition of "Disposal"

The definition of disposal begins with "the discharge, deposit, injection, dumping, spilling, leaking, or placing of any solid waste or hazardous waste into or on any land or water." 42 U.S.C. § 6903(3). Courts holding that passive migration can constitute disposal have focused on the words "leaking" and "spilling," terms that generally do not denote active conduct.

We think there is a strong argument, however, that in the context of this definition, "leaking" and "spilling" should be read to require affirmative human action. Both "leaking" and "spilling" also have meanings that require some active human conduct. "Leak" can be defined as "to permit to enter or escape through a leak." *Webster's Third New International Dictionary, Unabridged* 1285 (Philip Babcock Gove & the Mirriam-Webster Editorial Staff eds., 1986) [hereinafter *Webster's*]. Similarly, "spill" can mean "to cause or allow to pour, splash, or fall out." *Id.* at 2195. Meaning derives from context, hence the constructional canon *noscitur a sociis*, which states that one may infer meaning by examining the surrounding words. The words surrounding "leaking" and "spilling"—"discharge," "deposit," "injection," "dumping," and "placing"—all envision a human actor. In the context of these other words, then, Congress may have intended active meanings of "leaking" and "spilling."

But we need not address this question in the broad terms of whether disposal always requires active human conduct. Even if it does not, we conclude that the passive migration at issue in this case cannot constitute disposal. While "leaking" and "spilling" may not require affirmative human conduct, neither word denotes the gradual spreading of contamination alleged here. A common definition of "leak"—and the one most favorable to HMAT—is "to enter or escape through a hole, crevice, or other opening." *Webster's, supra* at 1285. This definition requires that a substance "leak" from some *opening*. For example, the definition would encompass the escape of waste through a hole in a drum. But HMAT has offered no evidence of leaking drums. *Compare, e.g., Nurad, Inc. v. William E. Hooper & Sons Co.*, 966 F.2d 837, 846 (4th Cir.) (the plaintiff presented evidence showing that tanks had leaked), *cert. denied*, 506 U.S. 940 (1992). And there is no other evidence that waste escaped from any opening during Dowel's ownership.

The definition of "spilling" is also unavailing. Although "spilling" too sometimes denotes the movement of liquid in the absence of human action, such a definition does not cover the spreading of waste at issue here. Passive definitions of "spill" suggest a rapid torrent, not gradual passive migration over the course of several years. *See Webster's, supra* at 2195 (defining "spill" as, inter alia, "to flow, run, or fall out, over, or off with waste, loss, or scattering as the result" and as "to come, go, or pass with a turbulent rush[; to] pour in an unrestrained, profuse, or disorderly manner"). Consider, for example, an "oil spill."

2. A Comparison With "Release"

It is especially unjustified to stretch the meanings of "leaking" and "spilling" to encompass the passive migration that generally occurs in landfills in view of the fact that another word used in CERCLA, "release," shows that Congress knew precisely how to refer to this spreading of waste. A prior owner who owned a waste site at the time of "disposal" is only liable in the event of a "release" or "threatened release." 42 U.S.C. § 9607. CERCLA defines release in relevant part as follows:

> The term "release" means any spilling, leaking, pumping, pouring, emitting, emptying, discharging, injecting, escaping, leaching, dumping, or disposing into the environment (including the abandonment or discarding of barrels, containers, and other closed receptacles containing any hazardous substance or pollutant or contaminant)....

42 U.S.C. § 9601(22). The definition of "release" is thus broader than that of "disposal": "release" encompasses "disposing" and some elements of the "disposal" definition and also includes some additional terms.

Most importantly, the definition of "release" includes the term "leaching," which is not mentioned in the definition of "disposal." "Leaching" is "the process or an instance of separating the soluble components from some material by percolation." *Webster's, supra* at 1282. Leaching of contaminants from rain and groundwater movement is a principal cause of contaminant movement in landfills, and is the most predominant cause of groundwater contamination from landfills. *** The word "leaching" is commonly used in the environmental context to describe this migration of contaminants. Congress's use of the term "leaching" in the definition of "release" demonstrates that it was aware of the concept of passive migration in landfills and that it knew how to explicitly refer to that concept.

Yet Congress made prior owners liable only if they owned land at the time of "disposal," not at the time of "release."

3. "At the *Time* of Disposal"

Our conclusion that the meaning of the words in the "disposal" definition cannot cover the passive migration alleged in this case is buttressed by the language of CERCLA's liability provision. If the spreading of contaminants is constant, as HMAT would have us assume, characterizing liable parties as "any person who at the time of disposal ... owned or operated any facility," 42 U.S.C. § 9607(a)(2), would be a rather complicated way of making liable all people who owned or operated a facility after the introduction of waste into the facility. Furthermore, there would be no need for the separate responsible party category of current owner or operator, § 9607(a)(1). Although CERCLA is not written with great clarity, we will not impute to Congress an intent to set up a simple liability scheme through a convoluted methodology.

C. Structure: The Innocent Owner Defense

Our conclusion that the language of CERCLA's definition of "disposal" does not include the passive migration alleged here is also supported by a significant aspect of CERCLA's liability scheme, the innocent owner defense. Since the 1986 Superfund Amendments and Reauthorization Act (SARA), CERCLA has exempted certain "innocent owners" from liability.

CERCLA provides a defense to liability if the defendant can prove that the release or threatened release was caused solely by an act or omission of a third party. 42 U.S.C. § 9607(b)(3). The defense is generally not available if the third party causing the release is in the chain of title with the defendant. *See* 42 U.S.C. § 9601(35)(A). However, the defense is available in such circumstances if the person claiming the defense is an "innocent owner." To establish the innocent owner defense the defendant must show that "the real property on which the facility is located was acquired by the defendant after the disposal or placement of the hazardous substance on, in, or at the facility" and that "[a]t the time the defendant acquired the facility the defendant did not know and had no reason to know that any hazardous substance which is the subject of the release or threatened release was disposed of on, in, or at the facility."

Because CERCLA conditions the innocent owner defense on the defendant's having purchased the property "after the disposal" of hazardous waste at the property, "disposal" cannot constitute the allegedly constant spreading of contaminants. Otherwise, the defense would almost never apply, as there would generally be no point "after disposal." We think it unlikely that Congress would create a basically useless defense.

The innocent owner defense's apparent limitation to current owners also supports the conclusion that "disposal" does not encompass the passive spreading alleged here. The provision establishing the innocent owner defense states: "Nothing in this paragraph or in section 9607(b)(3) of this title [, which provides the causation defenses including the third party defense,] shall diminish the liability of any previous owner or operator who would be otherwise liable under this chapter." 42 U.S.C. § 9601(35)(C). This language certainly suggests that the innocent owner defense is unavailable to prior owners or operators.

While the question whether the innocent owner defense is available only to present owners is not before us—and we do not decide the issue—we note that such a limitation makes sense only if passive spreading of waste in a landfill is not included in disposal. If passive migration is excluded from "disposal," past owners will generally only be liable as owners "at the time of disposal" when they have committed or allowed affirmative acts of disposal on their property. They would thus have little need for the innocent owner defense, which requires, inter alia, that a defendant did not "cause[ ] or contribute [ ] to the release or threatened release," 42 U.S.C. § 9601(35)(D); "exercised due care with respect to the hazardous substance concerned," § 9607(b)(3)(a); and "took precautions against foreseeable acts or omissions of any such third party [causing the release] and the consequences that could foreseeably result from such acts or omissions," § 9607(b)(3)(b). On the other hand, if prior owners were liable because waste spread during their tenure and the innocent owner defense is available only to current owners, prior owners would be in a significantly worse position than current owners: they would be liable for passive migration of waste even if they had no reason to know of the waste's presence. We do not believe that this was Congress's intent.

D. CERCLA's Purposes

We have explained our confidence that the meaning of the words defining "disposal" does not encompass the gradual spreading of waste in a landfill and that this conclusion is supported by the structure of the innocent owner defense. We also conclude that this reading of "disposal" is consistent with CERCLA's purposes.

Congress enacted CERCLA with two principal goals in minds—to facilitate the cleanup of potentially dangerous hazardous waste sites, and to force polluters to pay the costs associated with their pollution. Our holding is clearly consistent with the latter purpose. Those who owned previously contaminated property where waste spread without their aid cannot reasonably be characterized as "polluters"; excluding them from liability will not let those who cause the pollution off the hook. And, many of these owners *will* pay for the pollution: if they disclose the fact that the land contains waste, their selling price will reflect the cost of CERCLA liability. If they have knowledge of contamination and do not disclose it to a transferee, they are liable for response costs even after the transfer. 42 U.S.C. § 9601(35)(C). The only prior owners who will not pay any cleanup costs are those who bought and sold the land with no knowledge that the land is contaminated.

And our holding will not undermine the goal of facilitating the cleanup of potentially dangerous hazardous waste sites. Even if owners of previously contaminated land can evade liability by transferring the land, ample incentives remain to promote cleanup. Present owners and operators remain strictly liable for the costs of cleanup, as do some prior owners, people who arranged for disposal, and transporters of hazardous substances. Moreover, a number of provisions ensure that contamination will be discovered and the fact of contamination disclosed if the land is transferred. CERCLA imposes criminal liability (including prison sentences) for failure to report a "release" of hazardous substances above a certain threshold. *See* 42 U.S.C. § 9603. As mentioned, if an owner transfers land that it knows to be contaminated without disclosing the contamination, it remains liable even after the transfer. In addition, the innocent owner defense encourages potential buyers to investigate the possibility of contamination before a purchase. *See* 42 U.S.C. § 9601(35)(B) (in order to claim the innocent owner defense, a defendant must have undertaken all appropriate inquiry).

Thus, for the reasons we have stated, we agree with the district court that HMAT cannot proceed on its "passive" theory of disposal: the movement of contaminants alleged here does not constitute "disposal." However, because we conclude that HMAT may proceed on its "active" theory of disposal, the issue to which we now turn, we will vacate the court's order granting summary judgment to Dowel on HMAT's CERCLA claim.

III. Soil Investigation as Disposal

Having concluded that passive migration does not constitute disposal, we now consider HMAT's other asserted basis of liability. HMAT argues that Dowel's soil investigation, which was meant to determine the land's ability to support construction, caused the mixing, shifting, and spreading of contaminants and that this constitutes disposal. Although the district court suggested that HMAT's evidence of spreading was "speculative," it did not resolve whether the evidence was sufficient to allow a factfinder to conclude that the drilling caused any subsurface mixing. Instead, the court concluded that even accepting HMAT's version of events, Dowel's drilling "fell short of that conduct accepted as being enough of a disturbance to constitute disposal." According to the district court, only "significant disturbance of already contaminated soil constitutes disposal."

A. No Threshold to Disposal

We disagree with the district court's reading of "disposal." Under 42 U.S.C. § 6903(3), "disposal" is defined in part as the "discharge" or "placing" of waste "into or on any land or water." "Disposal" thus includes not only the initial introduction of contaminants onto a property but also the spreading of contaminants due to subsequent activity. ***

**[T]he dispersal of contaminants need not reach a particular threshold level in order to constitute "disposal." "Disposal" consists of "the discharge ... or placing of *any* solid waste or hazardous waste into or on *any* land or water." 42 U.S.C. § 6903(3) (emphasis added). There is no exception for de minimis disturbances. The fact that a defendant's dispersal of contaminants is trivial may provide a ground to allocate less liability to that defendant, but it is not a defense to liability.

B. The Evidence

The evidence presented by both parties shows that a genuine issue of material fact remains as to whether Dowel's drilling caused the dispersal of contaminants.***

* * *

*** HMAT's evidence that Thor's equipment went through waste, soil, and groundwater and that several boreholes "caved", in combination with its expert's opinion, is sufficient to support a finding that a dispersal of contaminants occurred. Dowel's evidence, that despite the contact between its equipment, waste, soil, and groundwater, its boring method caused no mixing, is sufficient to support the opposite finding. Thus summary judgment in favor of either party is inappropriate.

C. Soil Investigation

As we have explained, HMAT has identified evidence from which a factfinder could conclude that Dowel has caused a dispersal of contaminants. Ordinarily, that would be sufficient to submit the question of whether a "disposal" occurred to a factfinder. However, this is not an ordinary case: the alleged act of disposal consists of a soil investigation, and CERCLA clearly contemplates that some soil investigation be allowed to examine contaminated property. Thus, it is not enough for a plaintiff to show that a soil investigation has caused the spread of contaminants. Rather, we conclude that in order to establish that "disposal" has occurred based on a soil investigation, a plaintiff must also show that the investigation was conducted negligently.

CERCLA's innocent owner defense encourages prospective property buyers to conduct soil investigations. The innocent owner defense requires, inter alia, that "[a]t the time the defendant acquired the facility the defendant did not know *and had no reason to know* that any hazardous substance which is the subject of the release or threatened release was disposed of on, in, or at the facility." 42 U.S.C. § 9601(35)(A)(i) (emphasis added). CERCLA provides explicit guidance on how a defendant is to establish that it had "no reason to know" of a prior disposal:

> To establish that the defendant had no reason to know ... the defendant must have undertaken, at the time of acquisition, all appropriate inquiry into the previous ownership and uses of the property consistent with good commercial or customary practice in an effort to minimize liability. For purposes of the preceding sentence the court shall take into account any specialized knowledge or experience on the part of the defendant, the relationship of the purchase price to the value of the property if uncontaminated, commonly known or reasonably ascertainable information about the property, the obviousness of the presence or likely presence of contamination at the property, and the ability to detect such contamination by appropriate inspection.

§ 9601(35)(b). CERCLA thus contemplates that prospective purchasers "undertake[] ... all appropriate inquiry" and will engage in "appropriate inspection."

In order to give effect to the innocent owner defense and its requirement that prospective purchasers engage in appropriate inquiry and inspection, an "appropriate" soil investigation cannot itself trigger CERCLA liability. Otherwise, prospective purchasers who by diligently inspecting for contamination cause the dispersal of any contaminants will find themselves liable for causing a "disposal." And the innocent owner defense would offer such prospective purchasers no protection: if they buy the property after discovering contamination, they will be ineligible for the defense because they will not be "innocent" (i.e., they will "know and ha[ve] reason to know" of a prior disposal, § 9601(35)); if they do not buy the property, they will be ineligible for the defense because they will not be "owners" (i.e., they will not have "acquired the facility" as required by 42 U.S.C. § 9601(35)(A)). ***

But a party cannot escape liability for performing a soil investigation negligently and thereby unnecessarily spreading pollution. Several CERCLA provisions suggest that persons otherwise insulated from CERCLA liability may nonetheless become liable if they act negligently. In order to take advantage of a third-party defense (i.e., that a release was caused solely by a third party), a defendant must show that "he exercised due care with respect to the hazardous substance concerned, taking into consideration the characteristics of such hazardous substance, in light of all relevant facts and circumstances." 42 U.S.C. § 9607(b)(3)(a). And another provision, 42 U.S.C. § 9607(d)(1), insulates from liability actions consistent with the National Contingency Plan unless they are negligently performed ***. These provisions are themselves inapplicable to the issue at hand. However, they express a useful principle for determining when an action that is exempted from liability becomes so inconsistent with CERCLA's purposes that it is no longer so insulated, and this informs our judgment. We conclude that only "appropriate" soil investigations—i.e., those that do not negligently spread contamination—fall outside the definition of "disposal." Such a rule best harmonizes CERCLA's clear intention to allow soil investigations and its goal of remedying hazardous waste sites.

We recognize that the soil investigation at issue here was not meant to discover the presence of contamination but was aimed at assessing the land's ability to support construction. However, we conclude that the purpose of the investigation is irrelevant. Determining the motive of the investigating party seems a costly and difficult inquiry. Moreover, we do not wish to deter the productive use of property by discouraging soil investigations aimed at assessing development possibilities.

In addition to applying the wrong test of "disposal," the district court did not focus on whether Dowel's soil testing was negligently performed, and we believe that the parties should have a chance to add to the record on this issue. Therefore, we will vacate the district court's order dismissing HMAT's CERCLA claim and remand for further proceedings.

IV. Conclusion

For the foregoing reasons, the passive spreading of contamination in a landfill does not constitute "disposal" under CERCLA. Soil testing that disperses contaminants, however, may constitute "disposal" and HMAT has identified evidence that would justify a factfinder's conclusion that contaminants were dispersed in Dowel's testing. Nevertheless, because CERCLA contemplates that some soil investigation be allowed, HMAT must show not only that the soil investigation caused the spread of contaminants but also that the investigation was conducted negligently. The judgment of the district court will therefore be vacated and the case remanded for further proceedings consistent with this opinion.

NOTES

1. The Third Circuit suggests, but does not decide, that the statutory definition of disposal requires active human conduct. Instead, the Third Circuit holds that even if passive disposal is sufficient to trigger prior owner liability, gradual spreading of contamination—as contrasted with leakage from a tank or drum—is not the type of passive disposal within the statutory definition. If the Third Circuit were addressing the facts from *Nurad*, involving leakage from underground tanks, would it have held the

intervening prior owner liable? Should a prior owner's CERCLA liability turn on whether the leakage that occurred during its ownership (but typically without its knowledge or participation) came from a defined object such as a drum or, instead, involved the spreading of preexisting soil or groundwater contamination?

2. The Fifth Circuit has also distanced itself from *Nurad.*

Joslyn cites *Nurad* for the proposition that Koppers is a responsible party under CERCLA simply by virtue of being a past owner of the contaminated property. Joslyn would have us read *Nurad* to require a finding of liability regardless whether Koppers introduced hazardous substances to the site or whether a disposal occurred during Koppers ownership of the site. We do not believe that *Nurad*'s definition of disposal can be read so broadly, and we decline to expand the Fourth Circuit's reasoning to eliminate the disposal element of CERCLA liability.

* * *

While we decline to decide whether this circuit should adopt the Fourth Circuit's definition of disposal, Joslyn has failed to show that any hazardous waste "leaked" or "spilled" during Koppers' ownership of the property. The district court specifically found that "There is no evidence that leaking or spilling of hazardous substances occurred during Koppers' brief period of ownership." Joslyn has provided no evidence which would lead us to believe that this determination was clearly erroneous.

Joslyn's final attempt at bootstrapping its claims under the *Nurad* holding arises from the Fourth Circuit's exposition of the policy behind CERCLA.

> It is easy to see how the district court's requirement of active participation would frustrate the statutory policy of encouraging "voluntary private action to remedy environmental hazards." Under the district court's view, an owner could avoid liability simply by standing idle while an environmental hazard festers on his property. *** The district court's view thus introduces the anomalous situation where a current owner, such as Nurad, who never used the storage tanks could bear a substantial share of the cleanup costs, while a former owner who was similarly situated would face no liability at all. A CERCLA regime which rewards indifference to environmental hazards and discourages efforts at waste cleanup cannot be what Congress had in mind.

Id. at 845-46. Joslyn claims that to allow Koppers—a sophisticated purchaser who knew of the contamination—to escape liability in this situation would frustrate the purposes of CERCLA as set out by the Fourth Circuit.

We decline to follow Joslyn's reasoning for two reasons. First, as stated previously, to be found liable under the CERCLA statutory scheme, a former owner must have owned the property during a period when a disposal occurred. We have already affirmed the district court's finding that a disposal did not occur during Koppers ownership, and we decline to read the disposal requirement out of the statutory scheme.

Second, an even larger policy consideration overshadows the policy elucidated by the Fourth Circuit. In this instance, unlike *Nurad* and the majority of cases on the subject, suit is being brought by a former owner who is the primary contaminator of the property. In *Nurad*, suit was brought by the current owner who was not responsible for the contamination. To allow Joslyn to recover under *Nurad*'s policy—no avoidance of liability through inaction—flies in the face of the polluter pays principle.

Joslyn—a nineteen year polluter of the site—is proposing a scheme under which it could defray part of its clean-up cost by passing the contaminated property through a series of innocent landowners and then, when the contamination is discovered, demanding contribution from each. Not only does this violate the very policy that Joslyn purports to champion, but it would allow a polluter to escape a portion of its liability by conveying the property while ignoring the contamination which it caused. While Congress determined to encourage clean-up by holding the current landowner liable for the pollution regardless of fault and then permitting contribution from past polluters, § 9607(a)'s disposal requirement for prior landowners eliminates the legal legerdemain that Joslyn is attempting.

Joslyn Manufacturing Co. v. Koppers Co., 40 F.3d 750, 761-62 (5th Cir. 1994).

3. In *CDMG*, the Third Circuit's analysis of the prior owner provision in the context of other CERCLA provisions placed considerable weight on the innocent landowner defense. That defense will be addressed in greater detail in chapter 12.

4. Consider CERCLA § 101(35)(C), 42 U.S.C. §9601(35)(C), which imposes current owner liability on, and precludes the use of the statutory defenses by, a prior owner who has actual knowledge of site contamination and sells the property without so disclosing. Does that address the Fifth Circuit's policy concerns?

NOTE REGARDING BROWNFIELDS

One side effect of imposing CERCLA liability on current owners solely by virtue of their ownership status is to ward off potential buyers of urban properties with a history of industrial and/or commercial use—and, therefore, the likelihood of some hazardous substance contamination. Many of these "brownfield" sites are abandoned or idled, and their redevelopment would likely bring jobs and economic opportunity to the area. And although many of these sites have some contamination, they are, by definition, not the heavily contaminated sites eligible for or listed on the National Priorities List. But with current owner liability, and with lenders wary of financing the acquisition of contaminated property for fear—until statutory changes in late 1996 (see chapter 11.D)—of incurring CERCLA liability as well, thousands of brownfield sites around the country have been virtually paralyzed by CERCLA-itis.

This phenomenon has attracted the concerned interest of the EPA, many states, numerous cities (many of which hold title to significant numbers of brownfield sites, due to tax forfeitures), legislators in Congress, and environmental justice constituencies, among others. During the past few years, various initiatives have been undertaken to mitigate the brownfield dilemma.

The EPA has used its Superfund spending authority under CERCLA § 104(d)(1) to fund pilot projects by states, municipalities, and Indian Tribes to assess the nature and extent of contamination and to plan and design cleanup efforts at brownfield sites. In addition, the agency removed some 27,000 of the nearly 40,000 sites on the Comprehensive Environmental Response, Compensation, and Liability Information System ("CERCLIS"), the EPA's inventory of potential Superfund sites, with the designation No Further Remedial Action Planned. Furthermore, the EPA has adopted a more expansive view of its authority under CERCLA § 122(g) to enter into settlement agreements with prospective purchasers who agree to undertake some cleanup activities in exchange for the EPA's covenant not to sue. Guidance on Agreements with Prospective Purchasers of Contaminated Property, 60 Fed. Reg. 34792 (1995). On a less formal level, the EPA has also indicated a willingness to issue "comfort/status letters" to inform potential purchasers of the EPA's potential interest, or lack thereof, in the environmental conditions at a particular site. Policy on the Issuance of Comfort/Status Letters, 62 Fed. Reg. 4624 (1997).

Also on the federal level, Congress has substantially alleviated lenders' fears of CERCLA liability by specifying the nature of participation in management that would vitiate the secured creditors' exemption from CERCLA liability. Asset Conservation, Lender Liability, and Deposit Insurance Protection Act, Pub. L. No. 104-208 (1996).

More than 30 states have enacted laws or adopted regulatory programs to encourage the voluntary cleanup of contaminated sites, including brownfields. The EPA has begun offering funding to states that utilize their voluntary cleanup programs for brownfield revitalization. To be eligible for funding, the EPA expects state programs to provide opportunities for meaningful community involvement in the cleanup decisionmaking process, to ensure that voluntary cleanup actions protect human health and the environment, and, among other things, to possess sufficient enforcement authority to ensure completion of voluntary cleanup activities. EPA, Interim Approaches for Regional Relations with State Voluntary Cleanup Programs (Nov. 14, 1996).

One of the more sensitive aspects of brownfield redevelopment is the extent of cleanup required. While developers press for cleanup plans to reflect land use patterns—*i.e.*, to employ less stringent cleanup standards for industrial than for residential property—local residents and environmental justice constituencies "do not want to achieve urban renewal and job creation at the expense of becoming environmental 'second class' citizens." E. Lynn Grayson and Stephen A.K. Palmer, *The Brownfields Phenomenon: An Analysis of Environmental, Economic, and Community Concerns*, 25 Envtl. L. Rep. 10337 (1995). "Early, ongoing, and meaningful public participation" in brownfield redevelopment is seen as a mechanism for integrating environmental justice concerns into brownfield projects. National Environmental Justice

Advisory Council, Report on Public Dialogues on Urban Revitalization and Brownfields (Dec. 1996).

C. Liability of Past and Present Facility Operators

The same two provisions imposing liability on present and past facility owners also impose liability on present and past facility "operators." CERCLA §§ 107(a)(1) and (2). The EPA has pursued a wide variety of parties under the operator rubric, ranging from tenants who conduct activities at a site, to consultants and contractors, to corporate officers, parent corporations, and lenders. The operator category is probably the most potentially-expansive category of PRP.

One explanation for the ill-defined scope of this broad category is the absence of statutory guidance. As the Seventh Circuit explained:

*** § 9601(20)(A)(ii) informs us that "(t)he term ... 'owner or operator' means ... in the case of an onshore facility or an offshore facility, any person owning or operating such facility". This is circular, although it does imply that if Mena is neither "onshore" nor "offshore"—perhaps because in outer space?—then an owner or operator is not a statutory "owner or operator". The definition of "owner or operator" for purposes of earthbound sites must come from a source other than the text. The circularity strongly implies, however, that the statutory terms have their ordinary meanings rather than unusual or technical meanings.

Edward Hines Lumber Co. v. Vulcan Materials Co., 861 F.2d 155, 156 (7th Cir. 1988).

In general, the courts focus on the nature and extent of a person or entity's control over a site to determine whether operator status should attach. The following case illustrates one of the circumstances where contractors have faced operator liability.

KAISER ALUMINUM & CHEMICAL CORP. V. CATELLUS DEVELOPMENT CORP.
976 F.2d 1338 (9th Cir. 1992)

Before KOZINSKI and THOMPSON, Circuit Judges, and REA, District Judge for the Central District of California.

THOMPSON, Circuit Judge.

Catellus Development Corporation ("Catellus") appeals the dismissal of its third-party complaint against James L. Ferry & Son ("Ferry"). In that complaint, Catellus sought contribution under the Comprehensive Environmental Response, Compensation, and Liability Act of 1980 ("CERCLA"), for costs incurred in cleaning up a contaminated construction site. We have jurisdiction under 28 U.S.C. § 1291, and we reverse.

FACTS

Catellus's predecessor, Santa Fe Land Improvement Company, sold 346 acres of land to the City of Richmond, California ("Richmond"). Richmond hired Ferry to excavate and grade a portion of the land for a proposed housing development. While excavating the development site, Ferry spread some of the displaced soil over other parts of the property. This soil contained hazardous chemical compounds, including paint thinner, lead, asbestos, and petroleum hydrocarbons.[15]

Richmond sued Catellus to recover part of the cost of removing the contaminated soil from the property. Catellus filed a third-party complaint against Ferry for contribution under 42 U.S.C. § 9613(f)(1), alleging that Ferry exacerbated the extent of the contamination by extracting the contaminated soil from the excavation site and spreading it over uncontaminated areas of the property. The district court concluded that Ferry was not a person who could be held liable under CERCLA section 9607(a) and thus dismissed Catellus's complaint for failure to state a claim on which relief could be granted. This appeal followed.

* * *

DISCUSSION
* * *

We agree with the district court that Catellus has failed to state a claim for contribution against Ferry under sections 9607(a)(1) and (3). Catellus has not alleged that Ferry currently owns or operates the development site. *** Nor has it alleged that Ferry arranged for the contaminated soil to be disposed of "by any other party or entity" under 9607(a)(3). Ferry disposed of the soil itself by spreading it over the uncontaminated areas of the property. We conclude, however, that Catellus's allegations are sufficient to state a claim against Ferry under sections 9607(a)(2) and (4).

A. Liability Under Section 9607(a)(2)

A defendant may be liable under 9607(a)(2) for the cost of cleaning up a contaminated facility if, "at the time of disposal of any hazardous substance [he] owned or operated [the] facility at which [the] hazardous substances were disposed of."

Ferry was not an owner of the facility. The question is whether the allegations of Catellus's complaint are sufficient to show that Ferry was an operator of the facility and that it disposed of a hazardous substance.

---

[15] These chemicals were apparently deposited on the property during the 1940s when the site was used as a shipbuilding plant by the Richmond Shipbuilding Corporation, the predecessor of Kaiser Aluminum and Chemical Corporation.

1. Operator

CERCLA defines an owner or operator as "any person owning or operating such facility...." 42 U.S.C. § 9601(20)(A). *** The circularity of this definition renders it useless. ***

Relying on the Seventh Circuit's decision in *Hines* [*Edward Hines Lumber Co. v. Vulcan Materials, supra*], Ferry argues that it cannot be considered an "operator" under section 9607(a)(2). In *Hines*, a contractor designed and built a wood treatment plant. After the plant was completed, the owner began processing wood for resale. During this process, hazardous materials were released on the site where the plant was located. The owner was forced to clean up the site, and then sued the contractor for contribution as an "operator" of the plant under section 9607(a)(2).

Although the Seventh Circuit affirmed a grant of summary judgment in favor of the contractor, *Hines* does not stand for the proposition that a contractor can never be liable as an operator under section 9607(a)(2). On the contrary, it is clear from the court's analysis in Hines that the contractor was not liable as an "operator" because, although he designed and built the wood treatment plant, he had no authority to control the day-to-day operation of the plant after it was built; and it was during the operation of the plant that the hazardous materials were released.

We read *Hines* as reiterating the well-settled rule that "operator" liability under section 9607(a)(2) only attaches if the defendant had authority to control the cause of the contamination at the time the hazardous substances were released into the environment. ***

Unlike *Hines*, the activity which produced the contamination in the present case— the excavation and grading of the development site—occurred during, not after, the construction process. We conclude that Catellus's allegations of Ferry's operations on the property tend to show that Ferry had sufficient control over this phase of the development to be an "operator" under section 9607(a)(2).[6]

2. Disposal of Hazardous Materials

Catellus alleges that Ferry excavated the tainted soil, moved it away from the excavation site, and spread it over uncontaminated portions of the property. These

---

[6] In its pleadings, Catellus alleged that:

> *** On information and belief, in or about 1982 Ferry performed excavation, dredging, filling, grading and other construction and demolition (collectively, "excavation") operations on the Property. In the course of these operations, Ferry mixed substances— which, if plaintiffs' allegations are true, were contaminants—with soil and other fill materials, and then dispersed the resulting mixture throughout portions of the Property.

Consequently, if plaintiffs' allegations are true, then, on information and belief, Ferry negligently and carelessly (1) released contaminants on the Property and (2) arranged for transportation, treatment and disposal of said contaminants.

allegations are sufficient to support its claim that Ferry disposed of a hazardous substance as the term "disposed of" is used in 42 U.S.C. § 9607(a)(2).

CERCLA defines "disposal" as:

the discharge, deposit, injection, dumping, spilling, leaking, or placing of any ... hazardous waste into or on any land ... so that such ... waste ... may enter the environment ... or be discharged into any ground waters.

See 42 U.S.C. § 9601(29) (adopting the definition set forth in section 1004 of the Solid Waste Disposal Act, 42 U.S.C. § 6903(3)). This definition has been interpreted to include the dispersal of contaminated soil during the excavation and grading of a development site. *Tanglewood East Homeowners v. Charles-Thomas, Inc.*, 849 F.2d 1568 (5th Cir.1988).

In *Tanglewood*, developers built a housing subdivision on the site of a former wood treatment plant. During construction, they filled several creosote pools with soil and then graded the subdivision—spreading the creosote-tainted soil over the entire site. The Fifth Circuit held that by dispersing the contaminated soil throughout the subdivision the developers had disposed of it for purposes of section 9607(a).

In reaching this conclusion, the Fifth Circuit reasoned that the term "disposal" should not be limited solely to the initial introduction of hazardous substances onto property. Rather, consistent with the overall remedial purpose of CERCLA, "disposal" should be read broadly to include the subsequent "move[ment], dispers[al], or release[] [of such substances] during landfill excavations and fillings."

We agree with the Fifth Circuit's analysis. CERCLA's definition of "disposal" expressly encompasses the "placing of any ... hazardous waste ... on any land." 42 U.S.C. § 6903(3). Congress did not limit the term to the initial introduction of hazardous material onto property. Indeed, such a crabbed interpretation would subvert Congress's goal that parties who are responsible for contaminating property be held accountable for the cost of cleaning it up.

* * *

CONCLUSION

Catellus alleged facts sufficient to state a claim against Ferry under 42 U.S.C. § 9607(a)(2), on the ground that Ferry was the operator of a facility at which it disposed of hazardous substances. The complaint also states a claim against Ferry under 42 U.S.C. § 9607(a)(4), on the ground that Ferry accepted hazardous substances for transport to sites selected by it.

* * *

NOTES

1. A substantial number of "operator" claims have been filed against federal and state agencies, asserting that the agencies' involvement with the site—whether before or during its operation, or in the context of remedial activities—qualifies for operator status under CERCLA's liability scheme.

2. Following is the most prominent case holding the federal government liable as an operator of a plant supporting the government's role in the World War II.

FMC CORP. V. UNITED STATES DEPARTMENT OF COMMERCE
29 F.3d 833 (3d Cir. 1994) (en banc)

Before SLOVITER, Chief Judge, and BECKER, STAPLETON, MANSMANN, GREENBERG, HUTCHINSON, SCIRICA, COWEN, NYGAARD, ALITO, ROTH, and LEWIS, Circuit Judges.
GREENBERG, Circuit Judge.

I. *FACTUAL AND PROCEDURAL BACKGROUND*

The United States and the United States Department of Commerce appeal from a final judgment entered on September 17, 1992, by the United States District Court for the Eastern District of Pennsylvania. The court held the United States jointly and severally liable, as an "owner," "operator" and "arranger," for response costs for which the plaintiff FMC Corporation is or will be responsible under the Comprehensive Environmental Response, Compensation, and Liability Act ("CERCLA") to clean up hazardous waste created at an industrial facility during World War II. FMC acquired this facility many years after the war. *** FMC brought this action because the Environmental Protection Agency ("EPA") sought to recover the response costs from it. FMC seeks contribution, claiming that the United States also is liable because the War Production Board ("WPB"), which later was subsumed within the Department of Commerce, owned parts of the facility, operated the facility during World War II, and arranged for the disposal of the wastes created. FMC and the United States have settled the claim against the United States as an "owner," but the government contends that its conduct other than as an owner was regulatory activity from which the United States is protected from liability by its sovereign immunity. It further argues that, in any event, it was neither an "operator" nor an "arranger" within CERCLA. Accordingly, it contends that it cannot be liable other than as an owner. We reject the government's contentions and thus will affirm.

* * *

B. *Factual Background*

The facility at issue in this case is located in Front Royal, Virginia, and was owned by American Viscose Corporation from 1937 until 1963, when FMC purchased it. In 1940, American Viscose constructed a plant on the Front Royal site and began manufacturing textile rayon. Before World War II, the machines at the facility were not set up to produce high tenacity rayon. However, after Pearl Harbor, the government determined that the country needed increased production of high tenacity rayon for the manufacturing of war-related products, including airplane and truck tires. Inasmuch as the demand anticipated for high tenacity rayon greatly exceeded the projected supply, the WPB commissioned American Viscose to convert its plant to make high tenacity rayon and American Viscose did so.

Unquestionably, at least by current standards, environmental controls were lax at the facility. Thus, it is not surprising that inspections in 1982 revealed carbon bisulfide, a chemical used in manufacturing high tenacity rayon, in the ground water in the vicinity of the plant. Consequently, the EPA began cleanup operations and notified FMC of its potential liability under CERCLA. In 1990, FMC filed this suit against the Department of Commerce under section 113(f) of CERCLA, and the Declaratory Judgment Act. FMC alleged that, as a result of the government's activities during World War II, the United States was jointly liable with FMC as an "owner" and "operator" of the facility, and as an "arranger for disposal" of hazardous wastes there. In particular, FMC claimed that the government became involved so pervasively in the facility that it effectively operated the plant along with American Viscose and, accordingly, should share in the response costs.

* * *

The facility is a 440-acre site and includes a manufacturing plant and 23 waste disposal basins and landfill areas. The plant was owned and operated by American Viscose from 1940 to 1963, FMC from 1963 to 1976, and Avtex Fibers- Front Royal, Inc. from 1976 to 1989. American Viscose is now out of business, and Avtex is in bankruptcy reorganization.

In January 1942, an executive order established the WPB. The WPB was empowered to issue directives to industry regarding war procurement and production, including directives concerning purchasing, contracting, specifications, construction, requisitioning, plant expansion, conversion, and financing. Moreover, in 1942, the WPB's powers were expanded to include the seizure and operation of non-complying industries.

At the outset of the war, the United States lost 90% of its crude rubber supply because the Japanese occupied parts of Asia from which this country previously had obtained rubber. Consequently, we turned to synthetic substitutes, like high tenacity rayon, to strengthen and lengthen the life of heavy duty truck and aircraft tires, thus reducing natural rubber consumption. The WPB designated high tenacity rayon as "one of the most critical [products] in the entire production program." The WPB required American Viscose to convert the Front Royal facility to enable it to produce high tenacity rayon, and the facility became one of the few plants in the country manufacturing that product. The WPB's requirement that American Viscose convert the facility and expand its capacity to produce high tenacity rayon diverted the facility's resources from the production of regular textile rayon.

The government considered facilities producing high tenacity rayon to be "war plants" subject to its maximum control. The director of the WPB's Textile, Clothing and Leather Division, the division directly responsible for high tenacity rayon, regarded the American Viscose facility to a considerable extent to be a government project directly related to the war effort. Inasmuch as the facility was used for a program critical to the success of the war effort, if American Viscose did not comply with the

government's production requirements, the government would have seized the facility.
***

To implement the required plant conversion and expansion, the government through the Defense Plant Corporation ("DPC") leased government-owned equipment and machinery for use at the facility, including 50 spinning machines, an acid spin bath system, piping for the spinning machines and spin bath system, slashing equipment, and waste trucks. But the government did not allow American Viscose to install the leased equipment. Instead, the government contracted with Rust Engineering Company to design and install the DPC-owned equipment at the facility. Under its contract with Rust, the government had substantial control over and participation in the work related to the DPC equipment. For example, all plans, specifications, and drawings were submitted to the DPC for approval; Rust had to obtain prior DPC approval for the purchase of supplies; DPC could promulgate rules governing all operations at the work site and require the removal from work of any Rust employee; and DPC was represented on-site by a government representative, who had the right to direct Rust. The government collected rent from American Viscose on the machinery through 1947, and owned the machinery until March 1948.

The five principal components of high tenacity rayon, sulfuric acid, carbon bisulfide, wood pulp, chemical cotton liners, and zinc, were quite scarce during the war. To assure American Viscose an adequate supply of sulfuric acid, the government built and retained ownership of a sulfuric acid plant adjacent to the facility. The plant was connected to the facility through a pipeline, and virtually its entire output was delivered through the pipeline. To satisfy the facility's need for carbon bisulfide, the government commissioned Stauffer Chemical Company to build a plant in the Front Royal area to produce 26.4 million pounds of carbon bisulfide per year. The government required American Viscose to use the raw materials that it obtained from the government or through the use of a government priority rating system for the specific purpose authorized. As a result of the government's involvement in the production of the basic raw materials necessary for manufacturing high tenacity rayon, and its control over the distribution of these raw materials, it determined the operating level of each rayon manufacturer.

In October 1942, the WPB ascertained that the labor force in the Front Royal area would be inadequate to meet future needs at the facility. Consequently, the government obtained draft deferments for personnel at the facility, directed workers in other industries to come to the plant, and provided housing for the additional workers. The government also participated in managing and supervising the workers, by sending personnel to investigate and resolve problems involving worker productivity, to cut down on absenteeism, and to resolve labor disputes. In May 1944, the WPB appointed a full-time representative to reside at Front Royal to address problems at the facility concerning manpower, housing, community services, and other related matters. Moreover, although the government did not hire the employees, it was obligated to reimburse American Viscose for the salaries of certain employees under a lease between the DPC and American Viscose.

After production began, the government placed a representative on-site with the authority to promulgate rules governing all operations at the site and to remove workers who were incompetent or guilty of misconduct. Through continuous informal contacts and communications, the government was involved directly and substantially with the facility's production activities and management decisions. The government controlled the supply and price of American Viscose's raw materials as well as the production level and the price of its product. Therefore, inasmuch as the facility was doing only government mandated work, the government significantly influenced the profit that American Viscose could make at the facility. Of course, the government was the end-user of almost all of the product manufactured at the facility, either because it purchased the product directly or because the product was sold to other industries for use in war materials.

The government knew that generation of hazardous waste inhered in the production process because its personnel present at the facility witnessed a large amount of highly visible waste disposal activity. Wastes were placed in large unlined basins located on site and, as basins were filled, new ones were dug. Portions of the sulfuric acid utilized in the production process that could not be reclaimed or treated at the facility were deposited in the on-site waste basins, as were carbon bisulfide and zinc contaminated wastes. From 1942 through 1945, at least 65,500 cubic yards of viscose waste were placed in the on-site basins. The disposal basins were visible to any person visiting the facility.

Inasmuch as the generation of waste was inherent in the production of high tenacity rayon, an increase in production automatically increased waste. This fact is significant because governmental pressure to maximize production overtaxed the machinery and equipment at the facility, thereby increasing the amount of material scrapped for disposal in the waste basins. Moreover, the government rejected material not adhering strictly to the production specifications, thereby further increasing the amount of waste. In addition, wastes were generated and disposed of by the government-owned equipment that was installed at the facility.

The district court concluded that the government was an owner and operator of the facility and an arranger of waste disposal. ***

After making its factual findings and conclusions of law, the district court ordered the case to trial to determine the allocation of liability between FMC and the government. However, FMC and the government settled the allocation issues, subject to the government's right to appeal the ruling holding it liable as an operator and arranger. Under the settlement, the government conceded its liability as an owner with respect to its property at the facility and accepted an allocation of 8% of the cleanup costs as owner. But if we uphold the government's liability as an operator and arranger, its total liability under the settlement agreement will be increased to 26% of the cleanup costs. ***

* * *

III. *DISCUSSION*

A. *Sovereign Immunity*

The government's first argument is that the United States did not waive its sovereign immunity under CERCLA for claims arising from its wartime regulatory activities even though CERCLA section 120(a)(1) provides that "[e]ach department, agency, and instrumentality of the United States ... shall be subject to, and comply with, this chapter in the same manner and to the same extent ... as any nongovernmental entity including liability under section." This argument starts from the well-settled principle that the federal government is immune from suit "save as it consents to be sued." *United States v. Testan*, 424 U.S. 392, 399 (1976). Furthermore, such consent "cannot be implied but must be unequivocally expressed," *id.*, 424 U.S. at 399, and waivers of sovereign immunity must be construed narrowly in favor of the government. Accordingly, the government contends that CERCLA's waiver, although express, is not unlimited and that we must construe it narrowly. Based on a series of cases involving suits brought by the owners of waste sites against the EPA for its activities in taking over these sites for cleaning, the government argues that the CERCLA waiver does not apply to federal regulatory actions that a non-governmental entity cannot undertake. Thus, it argues that because most of the WPB's activities impacting on the facility were regulatory we must discount them in our analysis of the government's possible liability. In its view, its remaining non-regulatory activities did not involve the government sufficiently with American Viscose to justify the imposition of CERCLA liability on the government.

In re Paoli R. Yard PCB Litig., 790 F.Supp. 94, 95-96 (E.D.Pa.), *aff'd*, 980 F.2d 724 (3d Cir.1992) (table), is an example of the type of case on which the government relies. There, the EPA took over a hazardous waste site in order to clean it up. In so doing, the EPA allegedly caused the further release of hazardous waste. Based on this release, the site's owner sued the EPA for contribution and indemnification for response costs. The owner argued that the EPA became an operator under CERCLA when it conducted the cleanup activities at the site. The district court dismissed the complaint, holding that the United States does not subject itself to liability as an operator when it is engaged in cleanup activities at a hazardous waste site. Rather, the United States "would be liable under section 107(a) of CERCLA if it was acting in a manner other than in its regulatory capacity."

Similarly, in another case where an owner alleged that the EPA became an "owner" or "operator" by taking over a waste site to initiate a cleanup, a district court held that the waiver of sovereign immunity under CERCLA is limited. *United States v. Atlas Minerals and Chems., Inc.*, 797 F.Supp. 411, 420 (E.D.Pa.1992). "[T]he waiver contained in [CERCLA section 120(a)(1)] only applies to situations in which the government has acted as a business," and "does not extend to situations in which the EPA has undertaken response or remedial actions at a hazardous waste site." The court reached this conclusion because:

when the EPA undertakes such actions, it is not acting like a private party;
it is acting to ameliorate a dangerous situation that, but for the prior actions
of the generators and transporters of the hazardous waste, would not exist.
797 F.Supp. at 421. ***

The government contends that these cases establish a *per se* rule that regulatory
activities cannot constitute the basis for CERCLA liability, because only a government
can regulate.   However, we think the distinction the government is trying to draw
between regulatory and non-regulatory activities misreads CERCLA and the case law.
In the first place, section 120(a)(1) does not state that regulatory activities cannot form
the basis of liability.   Rather, it states that the government is liable in the same manner
and to the same extent as any non-governmental entity.   Thus, when the government
engages in activities that *would* make a private party liable *if* the private party engaged
in those types of activities, then the government is also liable.   This is true even if no
private party could in fact engage in those specific activities.   For example, although no
private party could own a military base, the government is liable for clean up of
hazardous wastes at military bases because a private party would be liable if it did own
a military base.   *** Just as the government can be liable for hazardous wastes created
at a military base it owns, the government can be liable when it engages in regulatory
activities extensive enough to make it an operator of a facility or an arranger of the
disposal of hazardous wastes even though no private party could engage in the
regulatory activities at issue.

* * *

Our reading of section 120(a)(1) comports with the rest of CERCLA.   First of all,
the government's contention is inconsistent with our previous recognition that
"CERCLA is a remedial statute which should be construed liberally to effectuate its
goals." *Alcan Aluminum*, 964 F.2d at 258.   In practice, the "regulatory" exception
suggested by the government would be inconsistent "with CERCLA's broad remedial
purposes, most importantly its essential purpose of making those responsible for
problems caused by the disposal of chemical poisons bear the costs and responsibility
for remedying the harmful conditions they created." *Lansford-Coaldale Joint Water
Auth. v. Tonolli Corp.*, 4 F.3d 1209, 1221 (3d Cir.1993). *** Accordingly, if the United
States, even as a regulator, operates a hazardous waste facility or arranges for the
treatment or disposal of hazardous wastes, it should be held responsible for cleanup
costs, just as any private business would be, so that it will "'internalize' the full costs ...
[that hazardous] substances impose on society and on the environment." *United States
v. Atlas Minerals and Chems., Inc.*, 797 F.Supp. at 413 n. 1.

Second, our reading comports with the rest of CERCLA because section 107(b),
lists the only three defenses to section 107 liability available to any person, including the
government.   These enumerated defenses do not include the "regulatory" exception
which the government seeks to create and on which it relies. ***

Section 107(d)(2) provides further evidence that our reading of section 120(a)(1)
comports with the rest of CERCLA.   Although CERCLA permits the imposition of
liability on states and local governments for cleanup costs, section 107(d)(2) expressly
immunizes them from liability for actions "taken in response to an emergency created

by the release or threatened release of a hazardous substance generated by or from a facility owned by another person." Congress's creation of an exception for cleanup activities by state and local governments plainly shows that it intended to treat these activities differently from other government activities. Accordingly, CERCLA does not protect a government from liability simply because it acts in a regulatory capacity. Rather, a government is protected under section 107(d)(2) because it is responding to an environmental emergency.

* * *

Because the government's involvement with the American Viscose plant was not in response to a threatened release of hazardous materials, we hold that the relevant sovereign immunity question under CERCLA is not whether the government was acting in a regulatory capacity, but whether its activities, however characterized, are sufficient to impose liability on the government as an owner, operator, or arranger. Hence, we consider both the government's regulatory and non-regulatory activities with respect to the facility during the war and determine whether these activities taken in *toto* were of the type commonly associated with being an operator or arranger under CERCLA and are the type of activities in which private parties could engage. ***

* * *

B. *Operator Liability*

The definition of "operator" in CERCLA gives little guidance to the courts in determining if a particular person or entity is liable as an operator because the statute circularly defines "operator" as "any person ... operating such facility." 42 U.S.C. § 9601(20)(A)(ii). Fortunately, however, the case law provides us with criteria for identifying those who qualify as "operators" under CERCLA.

We start our discussion of whether the government was an operator by considering our opinion in *Lansford-Coaldale Joint Water Auth. v. Tonolli Corp.*, 4 F.3d 1209. In that case, we adopted the "actual control" test in determining whether operator liability should be imposed on one corporation for the acts of a related corporation. The actual control test imposes liability which would not be consistent with "traditional rules of limited liability for corporations" but nevertheless is consistent "with CERCLA's broad remedial purposes, most importantly its essential purpose of making those responsible for problems caused by the disposal of chemical poisons bear the costs and responsibility for remedying the harmful conditions they created." *Id.* at 1221 (internal quotation marks omitted). Under this test, a corporation will be liable for the environmental violations of another corporation if there is evidence that it exercised "substantial control" over the other corporation. At a minimum, substantial control requires "active involvement in the activities" of the other corporation. *Id.* at 1222. While *Lansford-Coaldale* arose in the context of related corporations, it is nevertheless instructive here.

In our view, it is clear that the government had "substantial control" over the facility and had "active involvement in the activities" there. The government determined what product the facility would manufacture, controlled the supply and price of the facility's raw materials, in part by building or causing plants to be built near the facility for their production, supplied equipment for use in the manufacturing process, acted to ensure that the facility retained an adequate labor force, participated in the management and supervision of the labor force, had the authority to remove workers who were incompetent or guilty of misconduct, controlled the price of the facility's product, and controlled who could purchase the product. *** [T]he government reasonably cannot quarrel with the conclusion that the leading indicia of control were present, as the government determined what product the facility would produce, the level of production, the price of the product, and to whom the product would be sold.

In these circumstances, we must conclude that the government was an operator of the facility unless we overrule or narrowly limit the unanimous panel decision in *Lansford-Coaldale*, a step we will not take. Instead, we look to other cases which construe "operator" insofar as they inform the overarching *Lansford-Coaldale* test of actual and substantial control over "the corporation's day-to-day operations and its policy making decisions." *Lansford-Coaldale*, 4 F.3d at 1222. *** None of these factors is dispositive, and each is important only to the extent it is evidence of substantial, actual control.

For example, in *United States v. New Castle County*, 727 F.Supp. 854, 869 (D.Del.1989), the district court listed the following factors as being relevant: whether the person or entity controlled the finances of the facility; managed the employees of the facility; managed the daily business operations of the facility; was responsible for the maintenance of environmental control at the facility; and conferred or received any commercial or economic benefit from the facility, other than the payment or receipt of taxes. Another court in deciding whether a parent could be liable as an operator along with the subsidiary, stated that courts should consider: whether the parent has the power to direct the activities of persons who control mechanisms causing the pollution; whether and to what extent the parent controls the subsidiary's marketing; whether the parent can execute contracts on behalf of the subsidiary; and whether the parent controls hiring, supervision, transfer and similar aspects of employment at the subsidiary. *Colorado v. Idarado Mining Co.*, 1987 WL 56460 (D.Colo. Apr. 29, 1987).

Courts have applied the *Lansford-Coaldale* standard and factors such as those considered in *New Castle County* and *Idarado Mining* in considering a state or local government's liability as an operator under CERCLA. For example, in *United States v. Stringfellow*, 1990 WL 488730 (C.D.Cal. Jan. 9, 1990), a special master concluded that California was liable under CERCLA as an operator and owner of a landfill. The special master noted that the state chose the location for the landfill, designed and constructed the site, hired, directed and supervised the employees with day-to-day operational responsibility for the site, and set the responsibilities for these employees.

In contrast, the Court of Appeals for the Fourth Circuit affirmed a district court finding that the South Carolina Department of Health and Environmental Control ("DHEC") was not an owner or operator of the abandoned Fort Lawn waste site. *United States v. Dart Indus., Inc.*, 847 F.2d 144 (4th Cir.1988). In *Dart*, the generators of the hazardous wastes alleged, in their third-party complaint, that DHEC was liable under CERCLA because it controlled the activities at the site pursuant to a South Carolina statute that gave it regulatory powers such as the power to approve and disapprove applications to store wastes at the site, to inspect the site, and to regulate the transportation of the wastes delivered to Fort Lawn. The court of appeals found that DHEC did not have operator status because there was no evidence that it directly managed the waste site's employees or finances or ran the day-to-day activities of the facility. Thus, DHEC did not engage in "hands on" activities contributing to the release of hazardous wastes. Similarly, in *New Castle County*, the district court declined to find the state liable as an operator of a landfill where it only periodically inspected the site and mandated the details of refuse soil compaction and construction, but did not manage the day-to-day operations of the landfill. But *Dart* and *New Castle County* are distinguishable because in neither case did the governmental entity implicated have the control that the federal government exercised at Front Royal, and in neither case was the governmental entity involved in the facility for the purpose of obtaining a product for its own use.

The government exerted considerable day-to-day control over American Viscose, and at the risk of being repetitious, we will explain why. In the first place, American Viscose would not have been making high tenacity rayon if not at the government's direction. To obtain the commercial product it needed, the government diverted American Viscose from its previous commercial endeavors. Thus, every day American Viscose did what the government ordered it to do. Second, although the government officials and employees personally did not take over the plant, the government maintained a significant degree of control over the production process through regulations, on-site inspectors, and the possibility of seizure. Third, the government built or had built plants supplying raw materials to American Viscose, controlled these plants, arranged for an increased labor force, and supervised employee conduct, at least to the extent of helping American Viscose deal with labor disputes and worker absenteeism. Fourth, the government supplied machinery and equipment for use in the manufacturing process. Fifth, the government controlled product marketing and price. Given this degree of control, and given the fact that the wastes would not have been created if not for the government's activities, the government is liable as an operator. Indeed, on the record before us, if we rejected the district court's conclusion that the government was an operator, we would create a precedent completely out of harmony with the case law on what makes a person an operator under CERCLA.

* * *

NOTES

1. The federal government has avoided both operator and arranger liability for its activities in connection with the manufacture of Agent Orange for the Vietnam War. *See United States v. Vertac Chemical Corp.,* 46 F.3d 803 (8th Cir. 1995), *cert. denied*, 115 U.S. 2609 (1995, and *Maxus Energy Corp. v. U.S.*, 898 F.Supp. 399 (N.D. Tex. 1995), *aff'd*, 95 F.3d 1148 (5th Cir. 1996) (table). In the Agent Orange cases, the courts applied substantially the same control test as employed by the Third Circuit in *FMC*, but reached different conclusions based on the facts. Although the federal government had

significant involvement in Agent Orange production, it did not own the plants or equipment and did not have a day-to-day presence directing operations.

2. The *FMC* decision cites *United States v. Stringfellow* as an example of a case where a state government was held liable for a CERCLA cleanup. In *Stringfellow*, the State of California was held liable for 65 percent of the CERCLA cleanup costs at a landfill where the state had selected the site, negligently supervised its construction, and delayed the cleanup. *United States v. Stringfellow*, 1995 WL 450856 (C.D. Cal. Jan. 24, 1995) (order adopting master's report).

Claims by private parties against states for CERCLA response costs were premised on *Pennsylvania v. Union Gas Co.*, 491 U.S. 1 (1989), which held that Congress validly waived state governments' sovereign immunity from claims for CERCLA cleanup costs. In 1996, a divided Supreme Court overruled *Pennsylvania v. Union Gas,* and held that the Eleventh Amendment protection of states' sovereign immunity cannot be trumped by congressional lawmaking authority under, for example, the Commerce Clause. *Seminole Tribe of Florida v. Florida*, 116 S.Ct. 1114, 1118 (1996).

3. Inasmuch as sovereign immunity does not extend to political subdivisions, CERCLA actions against municipalities and municipal entities, such as public sewer systems, continue apace. In *Westfarm Associates Limited Partnership v. Washington Suburban Sanitary Commission*, 66 F.3d 669 (4th Cir. 1995), *cert. denied*, 116 S.Ct. 1318 (1997), for example, the Sanitary Commission was held liable as an operator of the sewer system, from which leaked hazardous substances dumped by private parties.

4. One of the limits to operator liability was highlighted in *Long Beach Unified School District v. Dorothy B. Godwin California Trust*, 32 F.3d 1364 (9th Cir. 1994), which held that oil companies holding an easement to run pipeline across property contaminated by unrelated parties did not have sufficient authority over the site to be CERCLA operators.

> *** The holder of an easement can clearly be an operator under CERCLA. *** [W]hen a party uses the easement to operate a pipeline that releases hazardous materials, it is liable as an operator provided the other statutory elements are satisfied. In this respect, an easement holder is no different from anyone else.
>
> But the district doesn't allege that M&P's pipelines are leaking toxic waste, nor is there anything on the record to suggest this is the case. Rather, the district merely points to the fact that defendants' pipelines crossed Schafer's waste pit and claims this put defendants "in a position to prevent" the contamination.
>
> This allegation is not sufficient to render the defendants operators under the statute. To be an operator of a hazardous waste facility, a party must do more than stand by and fail to prevent the contamination. It must play an active role in running the facility, typically involving hands-on, day-to-day participation in the facility's management. *** Exercising the right to pass a pipeline over someone's property is as far removed from active management of the property as one could get, short of having no

connection to the property at all. This is much less than the active control we require before someone will be held liable as an "operator" under CERCLA.

Id. at 1367-68.

D. Liability of Generators or "Arrangers"

The CERCLA language designating the category of PRPs known as generators, or arrangers, § 107(a)(3), is set forth at the outset of this chapter. It has been held to encompass what can be viewed as two types of parties.

The first is similar to the RCRA generator, a party whose industrial or commercial activities have produced waste materials, which that party has given to a third party for treatment, storage, transportation, and/or disposal. Whereas the identification of such parties for CERCLA purposes is relatively straightforward, numerous issues have arisen concerning, among other matters, the nature of such parties' liability, particularly with respect to one another, and the extent of the connection that must be established between such parties and the CERCLA facility from which the release has occurred. The issues addressed in the first part of this chapter arise most frequently in multi-generator CERCLA cases.

In *United States v. Monsanto, supra,* the Fourth Circuit articulated additional principles that have prevailed in multi-generator litigation.

> The generator defendants first contend that the district court misinterpreted section 107(a)(3) because it failed to read into the statute a requirement that the governments prove a nexus between the waste they sent to the site and the resulting environmental harm. They maintain that the statutory phrase "containing such hazardous substances" requires proof that the specific substances they generated and sent to the site were present at the facility at the time of release. ***
>
> Reduced of surplus language, sections 107(a)(3) and (4) impose liability on off-site waste generators who:
>
> "arranged for disposal ... of hazardous substances ... at any facility
> ... *containing such hazardous substances* ... from which there is
> a release ... of a hazardous substance."
>
> 42 U.S.C.A. §§ 9607(a)(3), (4) (emphasis supplied). *** As used in the statute, the phrase "such hazardous substances" denotes hazardous substances alike, similar, or of a like kind to those that were present in a generator defendant's waste or that could have been produced by the mixture of the defendant's waste with other waste present at the site. It does not mean that the plaintiff must trace the ownership of each generic chemical compound found at a site. Absent proof that a generator defendant's specific waste remained at a facility at the time of release, a showing of chemical similarity between hazardous substances is sufficient.

* * *

Finally, the purpose underlying CERCLA's liability provisions counsels against the generator defendants' argument. Throughout the statute's legislative history, there appears the recurring theme of facilitating prompt action to remedy the environmental blight of unscrupulous waste disposal. In deleting causation language from section 107(a), we assume as have many other courts, that Congress knew of the synergistic and migratory capacities of leaking chemical waste, and the technological infeasibility of tracing improperly disposed waste to its source. *** *See United States v. Wade*, 577 F.Supp. 1326, 1332 (E.D.Pa.1983) ("To require a plaintiff under CERCLA to 'fingerprint' wastes is to eviscerate the statute.").

United States v. Monsanto, 858 F.2d at 169-70. *Compare* this language with the Fifth Circuit's analysis in *Licciardi v. Murphy Oil U.S.A., Inc.* (chapter 8). Are both courts using the term "causation" similarly?

In the ongoing mission to spread CERCLA liability as widely as possible, PRPs have themselves done much to extend the generator category to include not only entities sending wastes off-site for treatment or disposal, but also those who sell materials containing hazardous substances—in some circumstances. The *Cello-Foil Products* case, set forth below, exemplifies one, somewhat controversial, approach to this situation.

The second type of generator is more precisely described as an arranger, a party who may not physically generate the hazardous substances sent to the CERCLA facility, but whose actions are deemed to constitute arranging for disposal within the meaning of § 107(a)(3). The *Aceto Agricultural* case, set forth at the end of this chapter, surveys the case law pertaining to this second type of CERCLA generator.

UNITED STATES V. CELLO-FOIL PRODUCTS, INC.
100 F.3d 1227 (6th Cir. 1996)

Before JONES and NORRIS, Circuit Judges; DOWD, District Judge for the Northern District of Ohio.
JONES, Circuit Judge.

Plaintiffs, the United States, the Michigan Attorney General and the State of Michigan, appeal the district court's grant of summary judgment to Defendants Cello-Foil Products, Inc., Clark Equipment Company, General Foods Corporation, and Hoover Universal, Inc., in this action for environmental response costs brought pursuant to the Comprehensive Environmental Response, Compensation, and Liability Act (CERCLA). We conclude the district court erred in its application of the arranger liability portion of CERCLA and genuine issues of material fact exist that preclude summary judgment. Therefore, we reverse and remand this case for further proceedings.

I.

This case involves a major hazardous waste cleanup involving the Verona Well Field, which is the primary public water supply to over 35,000 residents of Battle Creek, Michigan. In 1981, Michigan authorities determined volatile organic chemicals were contaminating the well field. With the assistance of the United States Environmental Protection Agency, the State determined that two of Thomas Solvent Company's ("Thomas Solvent") facilities, known as the Raymond Road Facility and the Annex, were two of the sources of the contamination.

Thomas Solvent, a producer and seller of solvents, operated in Battle Creek from the time of its incorporation in 1963 until 1984, the year it filed for voluntary bankruptcy. During these years, Thomas Solvent sold virgin solvents to numerous customers, including Defendants. Thomas Solvent usually delivered the solvents in fifty-five gallon drums.

Thomas Solvent used the Raymond Road Facility for the storage, transfer, and packaging of solvents and for the cleaning of tanker trucks. Through a drum-deposit arrangement, Thomas Solvent shipped the solvents in its re-usable drums and charged its customers a deposit. Most often, the Thomas Solvent delivery person retrieved the used drums when delivering new, full drums. The returned drums were usually taken to the Raymond Road Facility. The customers were credited for the amount of the drum deposit, when they returned the old drums to Thomas Solvent.

The contents of the returned drums varied. Some of the drums' contents had been emptied as much as possible, some had been refilled with water, and some contained unused solvents of up to fifteen gallons. Thomas Solvent employees inspected the drums when the drums reached either the Raymond Road Facility or the Annex. Drums in need of reconditioning were sent to a reconditioner, often without being rinsed or cleaned. Drums not in need of reconditioning were emptied of any remaining contents, often, onto the ground. The emptied drums were either immediately refilled with solvent or cleaned with a rinseate solution. Prior to 1978, the used rinseate was usually dumped onto the ground. In later years, Thomas Solvent began to recycle the rinseate at off-site locations.

In 1992, the United States and the State each filed complaints against Defendants. The Defendants are four longstanding customers of Thomas Solvent, which returned drums to Thomas Solvent during the period when Thomas Solvent employees were rinsing drums and disposing of the rinseate on the ground. The complaints, brought pursuant to CERCLA § 107, collectively sought over $5 million in past response costs for cleanup activities at the Raymond Road Facility plus a declaratory judgment for future response costs. Plaintiffs alleged that Defendants had arranged for disposal of hazardous substances when they returned the drums to Thomas Solvent. ***

*** [T]he district court granted Defendants' motions for summary judgment on the issue of arranger liability. *** The Plaintiffs filed this timely appeal.

II.

In this case we are called upon to interpret the scope of CERCLA arranger liability. The relevant provision of CERCLA states that:

Notwithstanding any other provision or rule of law, and subject only to the defenses set forth in subsection (b) of this section—

* * * * * *

(3) any person who by contract, agreement, or otherwise arranged for disposal or treatment, or arranged with a transporter for transport for disposal or treatment, of hazardous substances owned or possessed by such person, by any other party or entity, at any facility or incineration vessel owned or operated by another party or entity and containing such hazardous substances, ... shall be liable....

42 U.S.C. § 9607(a). The Plaintiffs do not contend that the Defendants arranged for disposal by contract or agreement; rather, they assert that the Defendants "otherwise arranged for disposal" of their unused hazardous solvents through the drum-deposit arrangement. The Plaintiffs claim that the Defendants entered into an arrangement, whereby Thomas Solvent would pick up the residue-containing drums, take them to its Raymond Road Facility, dispose of the residue, and then credit the Defendants with their drum deposit. The district court found that the Defendants could not be held liable because they lacked "intent" to dispose of the residual hazardous substances.

CERCLA does not define the phrase "arrange for." *Amcast Indus. Corp. v. Detrex Corp.*, 2 F.3d 746, 751 (7th Cir.1993). We conclude that the requisite inquiry is whether the party intended to enter into a transaction that included an "arrangement for" the disposal of hazardous substances. The intent need not be proven by direct evidence, but can be inferred from the totality of the circumstances.

At first blush, discussing state of mind in a CERCLA case appears inappropriate. After all, if the tortured history of CERCLA litigation has taught us one lesson, it is that CERCLA is a strict liability statute. Notwithstanding the strict liability nature of CERCLA, it would be error for us not to recognize the indispensable role that state of mind must play in determining whether a party has "otherwise arranged for disposal ... of hazardous substances." 42 U.S.C. § 9607(a).

We derive the intent element from the canons of statutory construction. "Otherwise arranged" is a general term following in a series two specific terms and embraces the concepts similar to those of "contract" and "agreement." All of these terms indicate that the court must inquire into what transpired between the parties and what the parties had in mind with regard to disposition of the hazardous substance. Therefore, including an intent requirement into the "otherwise arranged" concept logically follows the structure of the arranger liability provision.

The theory that intent is relevant in this context is no stranger to us. The district court correctly noted that this circuit has read an intent or state of mind requirement into the "otherwise arranged for disposal" concept. In *AM Int'l, Inc. v. International Forging Equip. Corp.*, 982 F.2d 989 (6th Cir.1993), this circuit was called upon to decide the applicability of arranger liability to AM International (AMI), which entered into an agreement to sell a manufacturing facility to a realty company. The facility contained several types of machinery and fixtures necessary for the manufacture of component parts for offset duplicating machines. After ceasing their manufacturing process, AMI cleaned up the facility and cleared it of industrial wastes. Nevertheless, because the facility was sold on an "as is, where is" basis, certain manufacturing features, including electroplating baths, salt pots for heat-treating, and the waste water treatment plant, were left by AMI containing the appropriate solutions, so that the lines would be prepared for an immediate start-up of the facility by a new owner.

Following a long line of cases distinguishing the sale of a useful asset from an arrangement for disposal, the court held that AMI had not arranged for disposal of the hazardous substances that it left in the building. The court stated: "Liability only attaches to parties that have 'taken an affirmative act to dispose of a hazardous substance ... as opposed to convey a useful substance for a useful purpose.'" *Id.* at 999. Therefore, in the absence of a contract or agreement, a court must look to the totality of the circumstances, including any "affirmative acts to dispose," to determine whether the Defendants intended to enter into an arrangement for disposal. We believe that this principle is in line with the Seventh Circuit's "intentional action" requirement for arranger liability announced in *Amcast Indus. Corp. v. Detrex Corp.*, wherein the court concluded that the term "arranged for" "impl[ies] intentional action." 2 F.3d 746, 751 (7th Cir.1993), *cert. denied*, 510 U.S. 1044 (1994).

As mentioned above, examining state of mind or ascertaining intent at the contract, agreement, or other type of arrangement stage does not undermine the strict liability nature of CERCLA. The intent inquiry is geared only towards determining whether the party in question is a potentially liable party. Once a party is determined to have the requisite intent to be an arranger, then strict liability takes effect. If an arrangement has been made, that party is liable for damages caused by the disposal regardless of the party's intent that the damages not occur. Moreover, a party can be responsible for "arranging for" disposal, even when it has no control over the process leading to the release of substances. Therefore, once it has been demonstrated that a party possessed the requisite intent to be an arranger, the party cannot escape liability by claiming that it had no intent to have the waste disposed in a particular manner or at a particular site.

III.

In reviewing this summary judgment, we must determine whether the district court overlooked any genuine and material issues concerning the Defendants intent to arrange or not to arrange for the disposal of any solvents returned with the drums. The district court "[found] compelling Defendants' argument that, because they lacked intent to dispose of hazardous substances, they may not be held liable as arrangers." Employing the dictionary definition of "arrange" the district court concluded that, in order to arrange, the parties must "make preparations" or "plan." The district court also relied heavily on the Seventh Circuit's decision in *Amcast Indus. Corp. v. Detrex Corp.*, in which the court concluded that the term "arranged for" "impl[ies] intentional action." 2 F.3d at 751. The district court ultimately concluded that "[w]hatever else 'otherwise arranged for disposal means' ... it does not apply to situations where there was no intent to dispose of a hazardous substance."

Although the district court correctly incorporated a state of mind requirement into the otherwise arranged for disposal concept, the court erred by applying the standard to the facts of this case. The following language from the district court's opinion illustrates the court's error:

> [T]he court concludes, therefore, that Defendants are not liable under section 107(a)(3) absent a showing that they intended to dispose of the residual amounts of the hazardous substances remaining in their returned drums. It is immediately clear that the Government's claim against Defendants fails to establish liability. The *purpose* of Defendants' returning of the drums was to recover the deposits that Defendants had paid; *the Government has absolutely no proof that Defendants' purpose was to dispose of residual amounts of hazardous substances remaining in those drums.* That Defendants incidentally got rid of these residues does not mean that it was Defendants' purposeful intent to dispose of the residues; rather, this was merely incidental to the drum return.

J.A. at 128 (Memorandum Opinion at 9) (second emphasis added). The primary purpose of the drum return arrangement was to regain the deposit; however, we conclude the district court erred when it concluded the Government offered *absolutely no proof* that Defendants' further purpose was to dispose of the residual wastes returned with the drums.

The district court employed an overly restrictive view on what is necessary to prove intent, state of mind, or purpose, by assuming that intent could not be inferred from the indirect action of the parties. In doing so, the district court overlooked genuine issues of material fact. ***

Whether a party possesses the requisite intent is a question of fact. ***

In this case, summary judgment would have been appropriate only if no genuine issues regarding intent existed. Our review of the record, however, reveals genuine issues of material fact regarding whether the parties returned solvents to Thomas Solvent with the additional purpose of disposal of unused solvents. The volumes of deposition testimony create scenarios, some conflicting, from which a trier of fact could conclude that Defendants, without a contract or agreement, otherwise arranged for disposal of their hazardous substances by Thomas Solvent. Such a finding would preclude the district court's conclusion that any disposal was incidental to the primary drum return transaction. For example, deposition testimony elicited from employees of Thomas Solvent and Defendants creates an issue as to whether the Defendants ever took "affirmative acts to dispose" of unused solvent, as required by *AM Int'l*, 982 F.2d at 999. By leaving amounts of solvents in drums ranging from one-half to ten gallons, which Defendants knew Thomas Solvent would carry away, a trier of fact could infer that Defendants were taking affirmative acts to dispose. By the same token, the finder of fact could conclude that Defendants did not leave solvents in the drums or that their acts in leaving residual amounts of solvents in the drums does not support an inference of purposeful or intentional disposal, or find that the drums were filled with waste water and other debris. A finder of fact must resolve this issue, and thus, the district court acted too hastily in finding no showing of intent. The district court overlooked genuine issues of material fact that make the resolution of this issue inappropriate at the summary judgment stage.[6] ***

* * *

NOTES

1. What is the basis for the intent requirement articulated by the Sixth Circuit? Do you agree that it is not inconsistent with CERCLA's strict liability scheme?

2. Not all of the circuits that have addressed the issue have agreed that arranger liability includes an intent requirement. The Sixth Circuit relied in part on the Seventh Circuit's decision in *Amcast Industrial Corp. v. Detrex Corp.*, 2 F.3d 746 (9th Cir. 1993), *cert. denied*, 510 U.S. 1044 (1994), which involved the accidental spillage of chemicals being transported by a third party.

> *** [T]he same word can mean different things in different sentences *** even in the same statute, especially when the statute does not attempt to impose a single meaning by defining the word. In the context of the operator of a hazardous-waste dump, "disposal" includes accidental spillage; in the context of the shipper who is arranging for the transportation of a product, "disposal" excludes accidental spillage because you do not arrange for an accident ***.

> The words "arranged with a transporter for transport for disposal or treatment" appear to contemplate a case in which a person or institution that wants to get rid of its hazardous wastes hires a transportation company to carry them to a disposal site. If the wastes spill en route, then since spillage is disposal and the shipper had arranged for disposal—though not in that form—the shipper is a responsible person and is therefore liable for the clean-up costs. But when the shipper is not trying to arrange for the disposal of hazardous wastes, but is arranging for the delivery of a useful product, he is not a responsible person within the meaning of the statute and if a mishap occurs en route his liability is governed by other legal doctrines.

Id. at 751.

---

[6] One of the difficult issues this case presents is how much must be left in a returned drum before CERCLA liability attaches. As the evidence in this case indicates, typical commercially employed methods for emptying solvent barrels leaves some residue, approximately a tea cup's worth, in the barrel. If every party who left this amount of residue in a drum were liable, every drum return agreement or arrangement would be considered an arrangement for disposal. In light of the demonstrated physical problems in completely emptying these drums, we are not convinced that CERCLA is intended to reach all such transactions. Rather, whether a drum return arrangement is an arrangement for disposal should be determined on a case-by-case basis. Furthermore, there appear to be benefits of these agreements, such as the reuse and recycling of drums, which we do not wish our interpretation of the statute to discourage. Thus, at this point it is important to reiterate that whether an arrangement has been made is an issue to be determined viewing the totality of the circumstances.

The Eleventh Circuit treats intent as relevant, but not necessarily dispositive, in determining whether an entity arranged for disposal of hazardous substances. *South Florida Management District v. Montalvo*, 84 F.3d 402, 407 (11th Cir. Cir. 1996). And the Eighth Circuit has rejected the need to prove "specific intent" to arrange for the disposal. *United States v. TIC Investment Corp.*, 68 F.3d 1082, 1088-89 (8th Cir. 1995), *cert. denied*, 117 S.Ct. 50 (1996) (in chapter 11.B).

3. The following case exemplifies the second variant of generator/arranger liability. The federal and state governments sued eight pesticide manufacturers, but could only assert CERCLA claims against six of the eight because the pesticide wastes of two companies were not hazardous substances. Although the governments successfully sued the remaining two (in fact, all eight) under RCRA § 7003, because the pesticide wastes were nonetheless solid wastes under the RCRA statutory definition, the RCRA portions of the decision are not included here. The Eighth Circuit's decision allowing claims for reimbursement of already-incurred cleanup costs under RCRA § 7003 was subsequently cast in doubt by the Supreme Court's determination that private parties may not recover cleanup costs under virtually identical language in RCRA § 7002(a)(1)(B). *Meghrig v. K.F.C. Western, Inc.*, 116 S.Ct. 1251 (1996) (in chapter 17).

UNITED STATES V. ACETO AGRICULTURAL CHEMICALS CORP.
872 F.2d 1373 (8th Cir. 1989)

Before HEANEY and BEAM, Circuit Judges, and LARSON, Senior District Judge for the District of Minnesota.
LARSON, Senior District Judge.

This case arises from efforts by the Environmental Protection Agency (EPA) and the State of Iowa to recover over $10 million dollars in response costs incurred in the clean up of a pesticide formulation facility operated by the Aidex Corporation in Mills County, Iowa. Aidex operated the facility from 1974 through 1981, when it was declared bankrupt. Investigations by the EPA in the early 1980s revealed a highly contaminated site. Hazardous substances were found in deteriorating containers, in the surface soil, in fauna samples, and in the shallow zone of the groundwater, threatening the source of irrigation and drinking water for area residents. Using funds from the "Hazardous Substance Superfund," the EPA, in cooperation with the State of Iowa, undertook various remedial actions to clean up the site.

The EPA now seeks to recover its response costs from eight pesticide manufacturers who did business with Aidex, in particular, who hired Aidex to formulate their technical grade pesticides into commercial grade pesticides. The complaint alleges it is a common practice in the pesticide industry for manufacturers of active pesticide ingredients to contract with formulators such as Aidex to produce a commercial grade product which may then be sold to farmers and other consumers. Formulators mix the manufacturer's active ingredients with inert materials using the specifications provided by the manufacturer. The resulting commercial grade product is then packaged by the formulator and either shipped back to the manufacturer or shipped directly to customers of the manufacturer.

The complaint alleges that although Aidex performed the actual mixing or formulation process, the defendants owned the technical grade pesticide, the work in process, and the commercial grade pesticide while the pesticide was in Aidex's possession. The complaint also alleges the generation of pesticide-containing wastes through spills, cleaning of equipment, mixing and grinding operations, and production of batches which do not meet specifications is an "inherent" part of the formulation process. The United States and the State of Iowa allege *** that six of the eight companies are liable under section 9607(a)(3) of the Comprehensive Environmental Response, Compensation, and Liability Act (CERCLA), because by virtue of their relationships with Aidex they "arranged for" the disposal of hazardous substances.

The defendants have moved to dismiss the action under Fed.R.Civ.P. 12(b)(6), arguing that they contracted with Aidex for the processing of a valuable product, not the disposal of a waste, and that Aidex alone controlled the processes used in formulating their technical grade pesticides into commercial grade pesticides, as well as any waste disposal that resulted therefrom. The district court granted defendants' motion under RCRA, holding the absence of an allegation that defendants had authority to control how Aidex handled or disposed of the wastes precluded recovery under section 7003. The court denied the motion under CERCLA, however, holding that principles of common law in conjunction with the liberal construction required under CERCLA could support liability under section 9607(a)(3).

We granted all parties leave to file interlocutory appeals, and the case is now before us for decision. ***

* * *

IV. LIABILITY UNDER CERCLA

To establish a prima facie case of liability under CERCLA, plaintiffs must establish

> (1) the Aidex site is a "facility;"
> (2) a "release" or "threatened release" of a "hazardous substance" from the Aidex site has occurred;
> (3) the release or threatened release has caused the United States to incur response costs; and
> (4) the defendants fall within at least one of the four classes of responsible persons described in section 9607(a).

Bliss, 667 F.Supp. at 1304; *Conservation Chemical Co.*, 619 F.Supp. at 184.

The complaint adequately alleges facts which would establish the first three elements, and defendants do not challenge these allegations for purposes of this appeal. At issue in this appeal is whether the defendants "arranged for" the disposal of hazardous substances under the Act, and thus fall within the class of responsible persons described in section 9607(a)(3). In finding plaintiffs' allegations sufficient to hold defendants liable as responsible persons, the district court relied on the principle that CERCLA should be broadly interpreted and took guidance from common law rules regarding vicarious liability. In particular, the district court found that defendants could be liable under common law for the abnormally dangerous activities of Aidex acting as an independent contractor, *see Restatement (Second) of Torts* § 427A (1965), holding that the common law was an appropriate source of guidance when the statutory language and legislative history of CERCLA prove inconclusive.

The six CERCLA defendants challenge the district court's decision on appeal, arguing the court's "hazardous activity" analogy is inapplicable to the facts of this case, and that Aidex, not they, "owned the hazardous waste and made the crucial decision how it would be disposed of or treated, and by whom." *United States v. A & F Materials Co.*, 582 F.Supp. 842, 845 (S.D.Ill.1984). They argue Aidex was hired "to formulate, not to dispose," and that imposition of liability under CERCLA on these facts would lead to "limitless" liability. Finally, defendants assert the plain meaning of the statute requires an intent to dispose of some waste, or, at the very least, the authority to control the disposal process, and that neither are alleged by plaintiffs here.

The plaintiffs counter that defendants' ownership of the technical grade pesticide, the work in process, and the commercial grade product establishes the requisite authority to control Aidex's operations. Plaintiffs argue that because the generation of pesticide-containing wastes is *inherent* in the pesticide formulation process, Aidex could not formulate defendants' pesticides without wasting and disposing of some portion of them. Thus, plaintiffs argue, defendants could not have hired Aidex to formulate their pesticides without also "arranging for" the disposal of the waste.

* * *

We begin our analysis with the language of the CERCLA statute. ***

"Arrange for" is not defined by the statute, but "disposal" is. "Disposal" includes "the discharge, deposit, injection, dumping, spilling, leaking, or placing" of any hazardous substance such that the substance "may enter the environment." 42 U.S.C. § 6903(3). *See* 42 U.S.C. § 9601(29).

* * *

Congress used broad language in providing for liability for persons who "by contract, agreement, *or otherwise arranged for*" the disposal of hazardous substances. *See A & F Materials*, 582 F.Supp. at 845. While the legislative history of CERCLA sheds little light on the intended meaning of this phrase, courts have concluded that a liberal judicial interpretation is consistent with CERCLA's "overwhelmingly remedial" statutory scheme. *NEPACCO,* 810 F.2d at 733.

*** We thus interpret the phrase "otherwise arranged for" in view of the two essential purposes of CERCLA:

First, Congress intended that the federal government be immediately given the tools necessary for a prompt and effective response to the problems of national magnitude resulting from hazardous waste disposal. Second, Congress intended that those responsible for problems caused by the disposal of chemical poisons bear the costs and responsibility for remedying the harmful conditions they created.

Dedham Water Co., 805 F.2d at 1081 (citing *United States v. Reilly Tar & Chemical Corp.*, 546 F.Supp. 1100, 1112 (D.Minn.1982)).

The second goal—that those responsible should pay for clean up—would be thwarted by acceptance of defendants' argument that the allegations in plaintiffs' complaint do not sufficiently allege they "arranged for" disposal of their hazardous substances. While defendants characterize their relationship with Aidex as pertaining solely to formulation of a useful product, courts have not hesitated to look beyond defendants' characterizations to determine whether a transaction in fact involves an arrangement for the disposal of a hazardous substance. In *Conservation Chemical*, for example, the court found defendants' sale of lime slurry and fly ash byproducts to neutralize and treat other hazardous substances at a hazardous waste site could constitute "arranging for disposal" of the lime slurry and fly ash. 619 F.Supp. at 237-41. Denying defendants' motions for summary judgment, the court reasoned that defendants contracted with the owner of the site "for deposit or placement" of their hazardous substances on the site, and thus could be found liable under the statute. *Id.* at 241.

Other courts have imposed CERCLA liability where defendants sought to characterize their arrangement with another party who disposed of their hazardous substances as a "sale" rather than a "disposal." *See New York v. General Electric Co.*, 592 F.Supp. 291, 297 (N.D.N.Y.1984); *A & F Materials*, 582 F.Supp. at 845. ***

Courts have also held defendants "arranged for" disposal of wastes at a particular site even when defendants did not know the substances would be deposited at that site or in fact believed they would be deposited elsewhere. *See Ward*, 618 F.Supp. at 895; *State of Missouri v. Independent Petrochemical Corp.*, 610 F.Supp. 4, 5 (E.D.Mo.1985); *United States v. Wade*, 577 F.Supp. 1326, 1333 n. 3 (E.D.Pa.1983).

Courts have, however, refused to impose liability where a "useful" substance is sold to another party, who then incorporates it into a product, which is later disposed of. *E.g., Florida Power & Light Co. v. Allis Chalmers Corp.*, 27 Env't Rep.Cas. (BNA) 1558 (S.D.Fla.1988); *United States v. Westinghouse Electric Corp.*, 22 Env't Rep.Cas. 1230 (BNA) (S.D.Ind.1983). *See also Edward Hines Lumber Co. v. Vulcan Materials Co.*, 685 F.Supp. 651, 654-57 (N.D.Ill.), *aff'd on other grounds*, 861 F.2d 155 (7th Cir.1988). Defendants attempt to analogize the present case to those cited above, but the analogy fails. Not only is there no transfer of ownership of the hazardous substances in this case (defendants retain ownership throughout), but the activity undertaken by Aidex is significantly different from the activity undertaken by, for example, Florida Power & Light. Aidex is performing a process on products owned by defendants for defendants' benefit and at their direction; waste is generated and disposed of contemporaneously with the process. Florida Power & Light, on the other hand, purchased electrical transformers containing mineral oil with PCBs from defendant Allis Chalmers, used the transformers for approximately 40 years, and then made the decision to dispose of them at the site in question. *Florida Power & Light*, 27 Env't Rep.Cas. (BNA) at 1558-60. Allis Chalmers was thus far more removed from the disposal than the defendants are in this case.

Defendants nonetheless contend they should escape liability because they had no authority to control Aidex's operations, and our *NEPACCO* decision states "(i)t is the authority to control the handling and disposal of hazardous substances that is critical under the statutory scheme." *NEPACCO*, 810 F.2d at 743. In *NEPACCO*, we were confronted with the argument that only individuals who *owned* or *possessed* hazardous substances could be liable under CERCLA. We rejected that notion and imposed liability, in addition, on those who had the authority to control the disposal, even without ownership or possession. *Id.* at 743-44. Defendants in this case, of course, actually owned the hazardous substances, as well as the work in process. *NEPACCO* does not mandate dismissal of plaintiffs' complaint under these circumstances.

Finally, defendants' contention that the district court erred in looking to the common law must also be rejected. As the Seventh Circuit has recently held, the sponsors of CERCLA anticipated that the common law would provide guidance in interpreting CERCLA. While the *Edward Hines* Court refused to find a company was an "operator" of a facility when the common law did not provide for liability, 861 F.2d at 157-58, in this case, the common law supports the imposition of liability on defendants. *See Restatement (Second) of Torts* §§ 413, 416, 427 and 427A (1965).

For all of the reasons discussed above, accepting plaintiffs' allegations in this case as true and giving them the benefit of all reasonable inferences therefrom, we agree with the district court that the complaint states a claim upon which relief can be granted under CERCLA. Any other decision, under the circumstances of this case, would allow defendants to simply "close their eyes" to the method of disposal of their hazardous substances, a result contrary to the policies underlying CERCLA. Accordingly, we affirm the court's judgment denying defendants' motion to dismiss for failure to state a claim upon which relief can be granted.

* * *

NOTES

1. In *Aceto*, the Eighth Circuit cited several district court cases where parties who had not directly produced hazardous substances were alleged to be liable as arrangers under CERCLA § 107(a)(3) for the cleanup of sites contaminated by those substances. Review carefully the *Aceto* court's discussion of the facts and holdings of the other arranger cases, and consider whether the different results reflect different legal standards for imposing arranger liability, or different facts assessed under a common standard.

2. Test your theory by evaluating the following factual scenarios, drawn from other arranger liability cases decided by other appellate courts:

a. Oil companies Shell, ARCO, and Gulf leased service station facilities and sold petroleum products to service station owners, who sent waste oil to a storage site where leakage caused soil, surface water, and groundwater contamination. The State of New York had initially proceeded against General Electric, which fell into the first type of generator category because wastes were sent from its facility to the storage/leakage site. GE agreed to clean up the site, and then sought contribution from 30 service stations that had allegedly sent waste oil to the site, as well as the three major oil companies. GE claimed that the oil companies were "arrangers" because they had the authority (admittedly not exercised) to direct the dealers to dispose of their wastes in a particular manner. *See General Electric Co. v. Aamco Transmissions*, 962 F.2d 281 (2d

Cir.1992). The Second Circuit held that the oil companies were not subject to arranger liability based solely on their economic bargaining power, without actual involvement in the dealers' waste disposal decisions. "[I]t is the obligation to exercise control over hazardous waste disposal, and not the mere ability or opportunity to control the disposal of hazardous substances that makes an entity an arranger under CERCLA's liability provision."

      b. Beazer supplied raw materials to Jones-Hamilton ("J-H") for use in formulating wood preservation compounds. Beazer retained ownership of the raw materials. In addition, the written agreement governing this relationship recognized "a tolerance of up to two percent by volume *** for spillage or shrinkage in any calendar month," and required Jones-Hamilton to comply with all applicable federal, state and local laws and to indemnify Beazer against all losses it might suffer due to Jones-Hamilton's failure so to comply. After the agreement terminated, the state required Jones-Hamilton to clean up contamination at the site. After spending more than $2 million, Jones-Hamilton sued Beazer for contribution under CERCLA § 113(f), claiming that, even if the indemnity agreement required J-H to indemnify Beazer for J-H's violation of environmental laws, it did not extend to Beazer's violations as an "arranger". The Ninth Circuit agreed. *See Jones-Hamilton Co. v. Beazer Materials & Services, Inc.*, 959 F.2d 126 (9th Cir.1992).

      3. In *Prudential Insurance Co. v. United States Gypsum Co.*, 711 F.Supp. 1244 (D.N.J.1989), the court rejected the claim, by companies that own office buildings containing asbestos, that asbestos manufacturers and distributors "arranged for its disposal" when they sold the asbestos for installation in the buildings for fireproofing and insulation. Other attempts to invoke CERCLA's cost recovery provisions for asbestos removal expenses have also been rebuffed. *See, e.g., 3550 Stevens Creek Associates v. Barclays Bank of California*, 915 F.2d 1355 (9th Cir.1990), *cert. denied*, 500 U.S. 917 (1991); *G.J. Leasing Co. v. Union Electric Co.*, 54 F.3d 379 (7th Cir. 1995).

      4. Would you find arranger liability where a company sells an old, unneeded manufacturing plant, with an appraised value of $200,000, to a manufacturing facility refurbisher for $25,000 on the ground that the seller was thereby arranging for the disposal of PCB-containing oils in transformers at the facility? The United States District Court for the Western District of Michigan held that arranger liability could be established in such circumstances, and denied the seller's motion for summary judgment. *Sanford Street Local Development Corp. v. Textron, Inc.*, 768 F.Supp. 1218 (W.D.Mich.1991), *order vacated per stipulation*, 805 F.Supp. 29 (W.D. Mich. 1991).

      5. The limits of arranger liability continue to be tested. Among the many cases addressing this issue, the following merit note:

      a. Cases finding arranger liability: *Catellus Development Corp. v. United States*, 34 F.3d 748 (9th Cir. 1994) (auto parts company that sold used batteries for lead reclamation liable for reclaimer's ultimate disposal of battery casings on property contaminated by lead from the casings); *Emergency Technical Services Corp. v. Morton International*, 1993 WL 210531 (N.D. Ill. June 11, 1993) (consultant that was solely responsible for the timing, manner, and location of disposal of the generator's waste held liable as arranger); *California v. Summer del Caribe*, 821 F.Supp. 574 (N.D. Cal. 1993) (can manufacturer potentially liable for contamination from by-product (solder dross) sold to metal reclamation facility); and *California v. Verticare*, 1993 WL 245544 (N.D. Cal. 1993) (pesticide distributors who agreed to retrieve leftover chemicals from pesticide applicator could be liable as arrangers).

      b. Cases not finding arranger liability: *AM International v. International Forging Equipment*, 982 F.2d 989 (6th Cir. 1993) (former lessee who left useful chemicals in building after leasehold expired); *Amcast Industrial v. Detrex*, 2 F.3d 746 (7th Cir. 1993) (chemical manufacturer that shipped products to customers via transporter not liable for accidental spills caused by transporter); and *CP Systems v. Recovery Corp*, 1994 WL 174162 (N.D. Ill. 1994) (company that gave disposal advice to customers, but had no authority to control waste disposal, not liable as arranger regarding materials disposed of by customers).

NOTE REGARDING TRANSPORTER LIABILITY

      The one PRP category that the statute defines in limiting terms is transporter liability. Transporters are liable only when they select the disposal or treatment site to which they transport a third party's hazardous substances. CERCLA § 107(a)(4). Even this category, however, has received some expansive construction.

      *** We also reject Petroclean's assertion that it cannot be liable unless the court finds that it made the ultimate selection of the facility as the disposal location regardless of whether it contributed to the selection of the facility ultimately utilized. We basically agree with Tippins that § 107(a)(4) applies if the transporter's advice was a substantial contributing factor in the decisions to dispose of the hazardous waste at a particular facility. As we interpret that section, a transporter selects the disposal facility when it actively and substantially participates in the decision-making process which ultimately identifies a facility for disposal. Since there is no dispute that Petroclean did so—Petroclean had considerable input into the selection process and, importantly, Tippins relied upon Petroclean's expertise in hazardous waste management when making its disposal decision—Petroclean is liable as a transporter.

Tippins Inc. v. USX Corp., 37 F.3d 87, 90 (3d Cir. 1994).

11 Expanding Scope of Liable Parties

CERCLA is an extremely costly environmental program. It involves lengthy and expensive studies to identify, evaluate, and decide how to clean up contaminated sites. It requires substantial engineering design expenditures to develop and modify appropriate technologies to address widely-varying site conditions. Many millions of dollars are frequently spent before the actual cleanup even begins. Once cleanup activities commence, many millions more are committed to constructing and implementing the cleanup plan, to governmental oversight where PRPs are conducting the remedy, and to operation and maintenance of cleanup activities, such as groundwater treatment, for years if not decades. A more detailed discussion of cleanup procedures will follow in chapter 14. The relevance of CERCLA's high costs to this chapter is that they have lead the EPA, states, and even PRPs to search for "deep pockets" to help pay these costs. This chapter addresses the potential CERCLA liability of corporate officers and employees, parent corporations, successor corporations, and lenders. Although these cases typically arise under the owner and operator categories of § 107(a)(1) and (2), they also invoke the arranger provisions of 107(a)(3) and, on at least one occasion, the transporter category under 107(a)(4).

The expansion of the PRP categories to encompass these entities was not entirely a matter of happenstance. In June 1984, the EPA's Assistant Administrator for Enforcement and Compliance Monitoring issued a memorandum entitled "Liability of Corporate Shareholders and Successor Corporations For Abandoned Sites Under the Comprehensive Environmental Response, Compensation, and Liability Act" ("the EPA Memorandum"). It was directed to virtually all EPA personnel with authority concerning CERCLA enforcement, in the EPA's Washington, D.C. headquarters as well as all regional offices. The EPA Memorandum outlined a two-tiered approach to extending CERCLA liability to corporate shareholders (individuals and parent corporations) and successor corporations. First, the EPA should attempt to establish the liability of such entities directly under the broad PRP designations in CERCLA § 107(a). Second, the EPA should use traditional doctrines of corporate law that, although generally disfavoring the extension of corporate liability to a corporation's shareholders and successors, do allow certain exceptions, and the EPA enforcement personnel should focus on the potential use of those exceptions.

The EPA Memorandum explained as follows the reasons for seeking to impose CERCLA liability on corporate shareholders:

> Normally, it is the corporate entity that will be held accountable for cleanup costs under CERCLA. In certain instances, however, EPA may want to extend liability to include corporate shareholders. This may arise,

for example, where a corporation, which had owned or operated a waste disposal site at the time of the contamination, is no longer in business. The situation may also occur if a corporation is still in existence, but does not have sufficient assets to reimburse the fund for cleanup costs. There are two additional policy reasons for extending liability to corporate shareholders. First, this type of action would promote corporate responsibility for those shareholders who in fact control the corporate decisionmaking process; it would also deter other shareholders in similar situations from acting irresponsibly. Second, the establishment of shareholder liability would aid the negotiation process and motivate responsible parties toward settlement.

* * *

*** [A] court may find the statutory language itself is sufficient to impose shareholder liability notwithstanding corporation law. Alternatively, to establish shareholder liability, a court may find that the general principles of corporation law apply but, nonetheless, set aside the limited liability principle through the application of the equitable doctrine of "piercing the corporate veil."

C.M. Price, Liability of Corporate Shareholders and Successor Corporations... (June 13, 1984) at. 1-2 and 4.

A. Corporate Officers and Employees

Under common law, corporate shareholders are not personally liable for the corporation's liabilities unless the rigorous test for "piercing the corporate veil" is satisfied. The EPA Memorandum summarized the state common law approach:

> In order to determine whether to disregard corporate form and thereby pierce the corporate veil, courts generally have sought to establish two primary elements. First, that the corporation and the shareholder share such a unity of interest and ownership between them that the two no longer exist as distinct entities. Second, that a failure to disregard the corporate form would create an inequitable result.

Id. at 5. The EPA also noted that federal courts, in cases involving the enforcement of some federal statutes, have employed a less rigorous test: whether it is "in the interests of public convenience, fairness and equity" to disregard the corporate form in light of the statutory purposes.

To date, the EPA has focused its efforts, with considerable success, on holding corporate shareholders, as well as officers and employees, liable directly under CERCLA, without regard to the common law tests for piercing the corporate veil, by proving that they personally operated the facility, or that they personally arranged for the disposal of hazardous substances. As the Seventh Circuit said, upon surveying the case law and joining the majority view:

> *** Of course, it is generally settled that the shareholders, directors and officers of a corporation are not liable for the obligations or delicts of the corporation. But several courts have held that, despite the apparent clash between CERCLA "owner" and "operator" responsibility and the shield protecting corporate officers and directors from responsibility for corporate violations, corporate officers and directors may well be liable as "operators" within the meaning of CERCLA. 42 U.S.C. §§ 9601(20(A), 9607(a); *see also, e.g., Riverside Mkt. Dev. Corp. v. International Bldg. Prods., Inc.,* 931 F.2d 327, 330 (5th Cir. 1991) ("CERCLA prevents individuals from hiding behind the corporate shield when, as 'operators,' they themselves actually participate in the wrongful conduct prohibited by the Act."); *United States v. Kayser-Roth Corp.,* 910 F.2d 24, 26-27 (1st Cir. 1990) (noting cases in which shareholders were held liable as "operators" under CERCLA); *United States v. Northeastern Pharmaceutical & Chemical Co.,* 810 F.2d 726, 743-44 (8th Cir. 1986) (holding that Congress intended CERCLA liability to attach to corporate officers). We agree that the direct, personal liability provided by CERCLA "is distinct from the derivative liability that results from 'piercing the corporate veil ...'" *Riverside,* 931 F.2d at 330 (citing *Northeastern Pharmaceutical,* 810 F.2d at 744). ***

Sidney S. Arst Co. v, Pipefitters Welfare Education Fund, 25 F.3d 417, 420 (7th Cir. 1994).

Following are two Eighth Circuit decisions involving corporate officer and employee liability under CERCLA. The first addresses two different approaches that courts have taken to determine when corporate officers or employees are subject to direct liability as CERCLA operators. The second distinguishes the test for individual liability as an operator under § 107(a)(2) from that for individual liability as an arranger under § 107(a)(3).

UNITED STATES V. GURLEY
43 F.3d 1188 (8th Cir. 1994), *cert. denied,* 116 S.Ct. 73 (1995)

Before HANSEN, Circuit Judge, GIBSON, Senior Circuit Judge, and KOPF, District Judge for the District of Nebraska.

HANSEN, Circuit Judge.

The Environmental Protection Agency (EPA), on behalf of the United States, brought this action to recover the costs of cleaning up a hazardous waste site near Edmondson, Arkansas. The district court entered judgment for the EPA, imposing liability for past costs ($1,786,502.92) and future costs (estimated at $6,000,000) on defendants Gurley Refining Company, Inc.; its principal shareholder and president, William Gurley; and an employee, Larry Gurley. These defendants appeal, raising several issues, the most significant of which are the argument that the present action is precluded by a prior action brought against the Gurley Refining Company, Inc., in 1983 and the argument that Larry Gurley's role in the company's disposal of hazardous waste was too tenuous to make him liable as an "operator" of a hazardous waste facility. We affirm in part and reverse in part.

I.

*** From 1970 to 1975, the Gurley Refining Company (GRC) rerefined used motor oil. GRC treated the used motor oil with sulfuric acid, mixed it with clay to absorb impurities, filtered out the clay, and sold the resulting rerefined oil. GRC then disposed of an acidic sludge and the spent clay in a borrow pit it had leased from R.A. Caldwell pursuant to a permit issued for that purpose by the Arkansas Department of Pollution Control and Ecology (ADPCE). The wastes of the rerefining process contained hazardous materials such as barium, lead, zinc, PCBs, and sulfuric acid.

In October 1975, GRC discontinued its rerefining processes and stopped disposing of wastes at the pit. In 1978, the United States Fish and Wildlife Service discovered that contaminated water from the pit had spilled over and damaged nearby fish and waterfowl habitats. The Service reported this to the EPA, which performed some work on the pit to prevent future spillovers.

But in the spring of 1979, after heavy rains, the pit overflowed again, releasing about a half million gallons of oily water into the surrounding area. The EPA could not persuade Caldwell or GRC to clean up the pit, so later that year it again performed work on the site to contain and treat wastes. In 1983, the EPA brought an action against Caldwell and GRC under the Federal Water Pollution Control Act, also known as the Clean Water Act (CWA), to recover the costs it had incurred in 1979. In 1985, the district court entered judgment in favor of the EPA and against Caldwell and GRC in the amount of $76,758.60. GRC did not appeal.

Meanwhile, in 1983, the pit was listed on the EPA's National Priorities List. In 1985, an investigation conducted on behalf of the EPA revealed that the site was still contaminated. In 1986, a feasibility study proposed four alternative courses of remedial action. The EPA chose the third alternative, which called for stabilization of the soil and contaminates, disposal of the soil and contaminates in an on-site landfill, backfilling of the excavated area, construction of flood protection, on-site treatment of contaminated water, and annual groundwater monitoring.

Then in 1987, the EPA brought this action to recover the costs, both past and future, of the remedial action it had adopted after the 1986 study. *** The district court entered judgment for the EPA on March 27, 1992, concluding that GRC, William Gurley, and Larry Gurley should be jointly and severally liable for cleanup costs. *** The district court also entered a declaratory judgment that those three defendants shall be liable for the costs of all remedial action taken by the EPA in the future. The three defendants appeal.

II.

* * *

A.

Larry Gurley argues that he should not be held liable because, in short, he was merely an employee of GRC. ***

1.

Liability for the release of hazardous substances may be imposed on "any person who at the time of disposal of any hazardous substance *owned* or *operated* any facility at which such hazardous substances were disposed of." 42 U.S.C. § 9607(a)(2) (emphasis added). The EPA does not contend that Larry Gurley had an ownership interest in either GRC or the site of the facility. Thus, he can be held liable only if he is an "operator." Larry Gurley argues specifically that the term "operator" should be limited to those individuals who had the "authority, responsibility, and capacity to control the corporate conduct in question." He contends that he did not have the authority to determine whether or how to dispose of hazardous wastes because he was not an officer, director, or shareholder in GRC and because his father, William Gurley, possessed nearly exclusive authority over GRC's operations.

CERCLA defines "owner or operator" simply as, "in the case of an onshore facility or an offshore facility, any person owning or operating such facility." § 9601(20)(A)(ii). It is clear that the term "person" may include individuals, *see* § 9601(21), but it is not clear when an individual should be deemed to have "operated" a hazardous waste disposal facility. In *United States v. Northeastern Pharm. & Chem. Co.*, 810 F.2d 726 (8th Cir.1986) (NEPACCO), *cert. denied*, 484 U.S. 848 (1987), we held that an individual could be held liable for the release of hazardous substances under a different subsection, which imposes liability on a person who "arranged for disposal or treatment ... of hazardous substances owned or possessed by such person," *see* 42 U.S.C. § 9607(a)(3). We found that the individual defendant "possessed" the hazardous substances because he "had actual 'control' over the NEPACCO plant's hazardous substances." *NEPACCO*, 810 F.2d at 743. We also stated, "It is the authority to control the handling and disposal of hazardous substances that is critical under the statutory scheme." *Id.* Thus, we affirmed a finding that the individual had "possessed" hazardous substances on two closely related but distinct grounds: that the individual had "actual control" of the hazardous substances and that he had "authority to control" their disposal.

Federal courts have struggled with these two concepts when addressing the question of whether an individual may be found liable as an "operator" under § 9607(a)(2). In some circuits, a plaintiff must prove that an individual defendant had actual responsibility for, involvement in, or control over the disposal of hazardous waste at a facility. See *Sidney S. Arst Co. v. Pipefitters Welfare Educ. Fund*, 25 F.3d 417, 421 (7th Cir.1994) (holding that plaintiff must allege that individual defendant "*directly* and *personally* engaged in conduct that led to the specific environmental damage at issue"); *Riverside Market Devel. Corp. v. International Bldg. Prods., Inc.*, 931 F.2d 327, 330 (5th Cir.) (holding that proper focus is "the extent of [individual] defendant's personal participation in the alleged wrongful conduct"), *cert. denied*, 502 U.S. 1004 (1991); *New York v. Shore Realty Corp.*, 759 F.2d 1032, 1052 (2nd Cir.1985) (holding that individual defendant was "operator" because he was "in charge of the operation of the facility"). ***

On the other hand, in one circuit, a plaintiff can succeed by proving less than that; an individual defendant "'need not have exercised actual control in order to qualify as [an] operator[s] under § 9607(a)(2), so long as the *authority* to control the facility was present.'" *United States v. Carolina Transformer Co.*, 978 F.2d 832, 836-37 (4th Cir.1992) (emphasis added) (quoting *Nurad, Inc. v. Hooper & Sons Co.*, 966 F.2d 837, 842 (4th Cir.), *cert. denied*, 506 U.S. 940 (1992)). ***

An individual defendant who has actual control over the operation of a facility presumably also has authority to control the operation of the facility, with the possible exception of an individual acting *ultra vires*, a situation not present in this case or in the cases cited above. Thus, in reality, the two approaches differ in that one requires a plaintiff to prove that the defendant both had the authority to control the operation of the facility *and* actually exercised that authority, while the other requires a plaintiff to prove only that a defendant had the authority to control the operation of the facility.

We believe that the latter approach is inconsistent with the term "operator," whose common meaning is "one that produces a physical effect or engages himself in the mechanical aspect of any process or activity." *Webster's Third New Int'l Dictionary* 1581 (1986). Likewise, the verb "to operate" means "to perform a work or labor," to "exert power or influence," to "produce an effect," "to cause to occur," or to "bring about by or as if by the exertion of positive effort or influence." *Id.* at 1580-81. These definitions connote some type of action or affirmative conduct, an element not required by those courts that ask only whether a defendant had the authority to control the operation of the facility. We prefer not to interpret the statute in a manner that would produce the anomalous result of imposing CERCLA liability on an "operator" who in fact never "operated" a facility. Thus, we hold that an individual may not be held liable as an "operator" under § 9607(a)(2) unless he or she (1) had authority to determine whether hazardous wastes would be disposed of and to determine the method of disposal and (2) actually exercised that authority, either by personally performing the tasks necessary to dispose of the hazardous wastes or by directing others to perform those tasks. We believe that this rule is the wiser of the two choices reflected in the existing case law and is faithful to our closely analogous decision in *NEPACCO*.

The district court made oral findings that Larry Gurley "personally participated in the disposal of the hazardous substances in question in the pit that is involved in this litigation" and that he "had extensive authority in an effort to implement the policies and practices of the corporate entity, which included the disposal of these hazardous substances." In fact, the district court found those facts to be "crystal clear." These findings address both prongs of the standard we have set out above. ***

The record reveals that GRC had approximately six employees from 1970 to 1975 and that William Gurley, who was the principal shareholder, had ultimate responsibility for the business and took an active role in its management. In particular, William

Gurley negotiated the lease with R.A. Caldwell for the property that later contained the pit, oversaw construction of the disposal facility, and directed employees to dispose of rerefining wastes there. The record also reveals that Larry Gurley began working in the rerefining plant in 1969 after his graduation from college. In that role, he helped load the trucks that hauled hazardous wastes to the pit. In 1972, he moved into the administrative offices, where he served as GRC's purchasing agent.

But several parts of the record also reveal that Larry Gurley's duties were broader than just purchasing. First, Larry Gurley testified in 1983 in *Caldwell v. Gurley Refining Co.*, 533 F.Supp. 252 (E.D.Ark.1982), *aff'd*, 755 F.2d 645 (8th Cir.1985), that he eventually became "director of operations," a job which "basically put me in control of the day to day operations of the plant and anything that pertains to that." He testified that his father tended to other businesses while he took care of GRC. Second, when the ADPCE contacted GRC in 1973 to express its concern about the pit, Larry Gurley personally responded in a letter that said, "I received your letter concerning the pit where we dump our waste material. I made a visual inspection of the pit area today." Third, Larry Gurley testified in 1983 that he "would have to take responsibility for" installing a pump and hose in the pit in 1974 that caused ADPCE to complain. Fourth, in 1974, Larry Gurley personally responded to a letter from the West Memphis, Arkansas, City Attorney concerning the discharge of oil from the pit into the surrounding area. Fifth and finally, Larry Gurley's responsibility for waste disposal is evidenced by the role he played in closing down the pit and filing reports with the ADPCE. He personally sent at least one letter to the ADPCE, and he wrote and signed a report concerning the closure of the pit. He testified that the report reflected an engineer's recommendations and GRC's agreement with the ADPCE, which he apparently had negotiated.

Although Larry Gurley argues that he acted as a mere "wordsmith" for his father, we are not convinced. The letters were sent under Larry Gurley's name. In fact, William Gurley testified in 1983 that Larry Gurley bore responsibility for the report filed with the ADPCE because "[h]e was operational manager; he had the latitude to make decisions of this kind." Although Larry Gurley testified at the trial of this case that he simply followed William Gurley's directions on these matters, it is apparent that he had substantial responsibilities of his own between 1972 and 1975. The district court, which read the transcripts of the 1983 trial and heard the testimony of Larry Gurley and William Gurley at the trial of this action, reasonably concluded that Larry Gurley "personally participated in the disposal of the hazardous substances" and "had extensive authority" over GRC's disposal of hazardous wastes.

We think Larry Gurley's argument places too much emphasis on his status within GRC and not enough emphasis on his actual activities. Although he was not an officer, director, or shareholder, he nonetheless had substantial responsibilities for GRC's waste disposal. Perhaps persons who are officers, directors, or shareholders are more likely to cause a company to dispose of hazardous wastes, but we decline to confer immunity on all persons who do not hold such positions. An individual defendant's responsibility for the disposal of hazardous waste should be judged on a case-by-case basis. In this case, the evidence clearly and strongly supports the district court's findings that Larry Gurley had authority to determine GRC's hazardous waste disposal activities and that he actually exercised that authority.

For these reasons, the district court did not err when it found that Larry Gurley was liable as an "operator." See 42 U.S.C. § 9607(a)(2).

UNITED STATES V. TIC INVESTMENT CORP.
68 F.3d 1082 (8th Cir. 1995), *cert. denied*, 117 S.Ct. 50 (1996)

Before McMILLIAN and LOKEN, Circuit Judges, and VAN SICKLE, District Judge for the District of North Dakota.
McMILLIAN, Circuit Judge.

TIC Investment Corp. (TICI), TIC United Corp. (TICU), and Stratton Georgoulis (collectively defendants) appeal from two interlocutory orders entered in the United States District Court for the Northern District of Iowa, granting partial summary judgment in favor of Allied Products Corp. (Allied), and the United States of America, on the issue of defendants' potential liability as "arrangers" under § 107(a)(3) of the Comprehensive Environmental Response, Compensation, and Liability Act (CERCLA). The district court held that defendants were directly liable as arrangers under CERCLA in connection with the disposal of wastes containing hazardous substances produced by the White Farm Equipment Co. (WFE) during the years 1980 to 1985. Upon granting partial summary judgment on the issue of defendants' liability, the district court certified its orders for interlocutory appeal pursuant to 28 U.S.C. § 1292(b). *******

I. Background

*** From 1971 through 1985, WFE owned and operated a farm implement manufacturing plant in Charles City, Iowa. The WFE plant produced wastes containing hazardous substances, which were disposed of at a nearby location (the dumpsite) which was owned by H.E. Construction Co. (HEC). During a period including the years 1980 to 1985, HEC transported WFE's wastes to the dumpsite, charging WFE on a per load basis. In 1979, WFE entered into a lease agreement with HEC whereby WFE leased the dumpsite from HEC for a two-year period in exchange for $1.00. After the lease expired, it was not renewed, but WFE continued to use the dumpsite for disposal of its wastes.

In November 1980, TICI purchased WFE out of the bankruptcy reorganization of WFE's then-parent corporation, White Motors Corp. At that time, and at all relevant times thereafter, Georgoulis was the sole shareholder, president, and chairman of the board of TICI. During the period from December 1980 through October 1985, the corporate structure was as follows. WFE was wholly owned by an investment holding company, White Farm U.S.A., Inc. (WF USA), which in turn was wholly owned by a holding company, White Farm Industries, Inc. (WFI). During approximately the first year of the relevant time period, WFI was wholly owned by TICI, a holding company. For the remaining four years, WFI was wholly owned by TICU, also a holding company. Georgoulis was, at all relevant times, the sole shareholder of TICI and TICU. TIC Services Co. (TIC Services), a subsidiary of TICI, provided various corporate services to TICI and TICU and their subsidiaries. These services included insurance, accounting, legal and tax work, and payment of employee salaries. During the years from 1980 to 1985, Georgoulis was, as previously noted, president and chairman of the board of TICI, president and chairman of the board of TICU, and president and chairman of the board of TIC Services. (Hereinafter, TICI, TICU, and TIC Services are collectively referred to as the TIC entities.) Georgoulis was also chairman of the board of WFE, chairman of the board of WF USA, and chairman of the board of WFI. He was president of WFE for part of the five-year period in question. On two separate occasions, Georgoulis hired another person as WFE president; each served nominally for about one year before being fired by Georgoulis.

We assume, for purposes of this appeal, that neither Georgoulis nor any employee of the TIC entities had personal knowledge of the contract between WFE and HEC for the disposal of WFE's wastes at the dumpsite. Nor did Georgoulis or any employee of the TIC entities have any personal knowledge of the disposal practices at the dumpsite, or was in any way directly involved in waste disposal matters. However, it is beyond genuine dispute that, at all relevant times, Georgoulis had authority to control, and did in fact exert direct control over many significant aspects of the ongoing operations and management of WFE. Georgoulis, whose TICI and TICU offices were located in Dallas, Texas, was often present in WFE's corporate offices in Oakbrook, Illinois; at other times, Georgoulis talked daily, if not several times a day, with the WFE officers at the Oakbrook office. Georgoulis was directly involved in personnel matters including union contract negotiations, manpower reductions, pension benefits for nonunion WFE employees, and insurance benefits for WFE retirees. He had final authority over the areas of manpower and staffing at WFE. He also made the decision to close and consolidate some of WFE's operations in other parts of the country. From 1980 to 1983, Georgoulis was not only the chairman of the board of WFE, he was also one of only two WFE board members, which ensured that no action of the board could take place without his approval.

It is also not genuinely disputed that an active working relationship existed between the parent corporations, TICI and TICU, and their subsidiary, WFE. For example, TICI and TICU management took part in lowering labor and personnel costs at WFE. One of the TIC holding companies guaranteed a $15 million working capital loan for WFE and arranged for WFE's lines of credit. TIC Services charged WFE a corporate fee for corporate services; for a portion of the relevant time period, TIC Services charged (but did not collect) a fee containing a 40% increase over WFE's proportional share. Also, for the years 1982 and 1983, TIC Services paid the salaries of the chief executive officer of WFE and billed WFE for reimbursement.

In 1983, the major lender for WFE, Borg-Warner Acceptance Corp. (BWAC), entered into a capital and revolving loan agreement for the refinancing of WFE and, at that time, required WFE to expand its Board of Directors to five members. However, even after that time, Georgoulis continued to serve on the board of directors and remained chairman of the board. WFE defaulted on its loan from BWAC in May 1985. Consequently, BWAC became owner of all of WFE's assets, which BWAC sold to Allied in October 1985.

In 1988, the United States Environmental Protection Agency placed the dumpsite on the National Priorities List and began remediation at the site. The United States and Allied have each incurred response costs in connection with the remediation effort and each has brought a separate cost recovery action against defendants, pursuant to CERCLA. On cross-motions for summary judgment, the district court entered partial summary judgment holding that defendants were directly liable as arrangers of disposal at the dumpsite, within the meaning of § 9607(a)(3). Following the district court's certification under 28 U.S.C. § 1292(b), defendants appealed.

II. Discussion
* * *

B. *Arranger liability under CERCLA*

On this appeal, there is no dispute that the dumpsite is a facility within the meaning of CERCLA, that a release or threatened release of a hazardous substance from the dumpsite has occurred, and that the release or threatened release has caused the United States and Allied to incur response costs. The only disputed question on appeal is whether, as a matter of law, defendants fall within one of the four classes of responsible persons under 42 U.S.C. § 9607(a). *** Our focus is on whether defendants fall within the third category of responsible persons described as "arrangers." Given the undisputed facts that WFE at all relevant times was wholly owned by either TICI or TICU, and that at all relevant times Georgoulis was the sole shareholder of TICI and TICU, there is no dispute that the hazardous substances disposed of at the dumpsite were owned by defendants. We need only decide whether or not defendants "arranged for" disposal of hazardous substances at the dumpsite during the years 1980 to 1985, within the meaning of CERCLA, 42 U.S.C. § 9607(a)(3).

There are several cases from our circuit in which arranger liability under 42 U.S.C. § 9607(a)(3) has been litigated. *See, e.g., United States v. Vertac Chem. Corp.*, 46 F.3d 803 (8th Cir.) (*Vertac*), *cert. denied*, 115 S.Ct. 2609 (1995); *United States v. Aceto Agric. Chems. Corp.*, 872 F.2d 1373 (8th Cir.1989) (*Aceto*); and *United States v. Northeastern Pharmaceutical & Chem. Co.*, 810 F.2d 726 (8th Cir.1986) (*NEPACCO*), *cert. denied*, 484 U.S. 848 (1987). Nevertheless, the precise issues before us, involving individual and corporate liability, have never been addressed. ***

C. *Arranger liability of Georgoulis as a corporate officer*

"CERCLA § 107(a)(3), 42 U.S.C. § 9607(a)(3), imposes strict liability upon 'any person' who arranged for the disposal or transportation for disposal of hazardous substances. As defined by the statute, the term 'person' includes both individuals and corporations and does not exclude corporate officers or employees." *NEPACCO*, 810 F.2d at 743. Relying on *NEPACCO* and cases from other circuits, the district court held that the proper standard to be applied in assessing a corporate officer's potential liability as an arranger is the same as that which is used to determine operator liability under § 9607(a)(2), and that standard is an "authority to control" test. The district court added, however, that there must also be some "showing that the defendant actually exercised his or her authority" over the operations of the corporation; this additional requirement, the district court explained, "is to establish that the defendant was not a mere figurehead, and that he or she played more than a passive role in the corporation." The district court thus concluded in the present case that "[d]ue to Georgoulis' authority to control WFE and his actual exercise of control over WFE, he is directly liable as an arranger under CERCLA." The district court reached this conclusion notwithstanding the fact that there was no evidence that Georgoulis had any personal knowledge of WFE's waste disposal practices.

Defendants argue that the case law makes an important distinction between, on the one hand, the strict liability that attaches once a person is found to be within one of the four categories of responsible persons under CERCLA and, on the other hand, the intent requirement that necessarily underlies a finding that a person is within one of those categories. For a person to be classified as an arranger, defendants argue, the law requires that the person "take[ ] some intentional action to arrange for disposal of a hazardous substance." *** Defendants maintain that they did not engage in intentional action in the present case because neither Georgoulis nor any employees of the TIC entities had any personal knowledge of the HEC disposal contract or the disposal practices at the dumpsite, nor did they actively participate in any waste disposal decisions.

* * *

We agree with defendants' argument that, in the wake of *Gurley* and *Vertac*, a finding of arranger liability requires some level of actual participation in, or exercise of control over, activities that are causally connected to, or have some nexus with,[4] the arrangement for disposal of hazardous substances or the off-site disposal itself.

---

[4]Based upon this notion of a "nexus," some courts have recognized that arranger liability can be established, absent any active involvement related to the disposal or arrangement for disposal of hazardous substances, where the defendant had the *obligation* to exercise control over the disposal or arrangement for disposal of hazardous substances. *Cf. General Elec. Co. v. AAMCO Transmissions, Inc.*, 962 F.2d 281, 286-87 (2d Cir.1992) (affirming summary judgment in favor of defendant oil companies on issue of their potential arranger liability where "the undisputed facts demonstrate[d] that the oil companies had no obligation to exercise control over the manner in which their dealers disposed of waste motor oil").

Defendants have taken this proposition one step further, however, by arguing that, as a matter of law, arranger liability requires proof that the person had the specific intent to arrange for the disposal of hazardous substances. ***

As noted by the district court, Congress's goals in enacting CERCLA were "(1) to ensure that those responsible for the problems caused by hazardous wastes are required to pay for the clean-up costs ... and (2) to ensure that responsible persons are not allowed to avoid liability by remaining idle." Consistent with these goals, this court in *Aceto* rejected the notion that generators of hazardous substances could simply "close their eyes" to the method of disposal of their hazardous substances to avoid any liability for response costs. Contrary to defendants' assertions, *Aceto* undermines their legal argument. The defendants in *Aceto* argued that the allegations in the complaint were insufficient to state a claim under § 9607(a)(3), where the defendants had allegedly contracted to have another party "formulate," rather than "dispose of," technical grade pesticides containing hazardous substances. This court was persuaded by the argument that the defendants knew or should have known that "because the generation of pesticide-containing wastes is inherent in the pesticide formulation process, Aidex [the party with which the defendants contracted] could not formulate defendants' pesticides without wasting and disposing of some portion of them." *Id.* at 1379. Thus, this court implicitly rejected a specific intent requirement and held that the complaint adequately alleged that the defendants had arranged for disposal of hazardous substances.

Similarly, upon a careful reading of *Gurley*, we find that this court's decision in that case supports the district court's finding of Georgoulis's liability as an arranger in the present case. As noted above, this court held, in *Gurley*, that a particular individual employee was liable as an operator under CERCLA, 42 U.S.C. § 9607(a)(2), because that individual (1) had the authority to determine whether hazardous wastes would be disposed of and the method of disposal and (2) actually exercised that authority, either by personally performing the tasks necessary to dispose of the hazardous wastes or by directing others to perform those tasks. Notably, that individual in *Gurley* was a non-officer, non-director, non-shareholder employee. The holding in *Gurley* must be viewed in this context.[5] Indeed, in attempting to define the outer limits of individual

---

[5]We also note that the finding of individual liability in *United States v. Gurley*, 43 F.3d 1188 (8th Cir.1994) (*Gurley*), *cert. denied*, 116 S.Ct. 73 (1995), was based upon the fact that the appellant had himself personally participated in the disposal activities at the facility in question, which was a borrow pit used for disposal of wastes containing hazardous substances. The court therefore was not faced with the issue of whether, or under what circumstances, an individual could be found personally liable in the absence of any personal participation in the disposal activities. Clearly, the standard mentioned in *Gurley* would not apply generally in all individual operator liability cases. For example, it might not apply where the primary function of the facility at the time of disposal was manufacturing, rather than disposal. ***

This provision in CERCLA merely requires that the person in question own or operate the facility at which hazardous substances are disposed of, at the time of disposal; nowhere does this subsection require that the person be involved in the disposal activities themselves. Likewise, as the case parentheticals in *Gurley* indicate, *see* 43 F.3d at 1193, the courts which have held that the actual exercise of authority is a requirement of operator liability have recognized that it is sufficient for the person to have exercised authority or control over the *operations* of the facility. Consistent with the plain meaning of the

operator liability for mere employees, this court specifically recognized that "[p]erhaps persons who are officers, directors, or shareholders are more likely to cause a company to dispose of hazardous wastes." *Id.* Nevertheless, defendants now urge us to take language from *Gurley* out of context to conclude that Georgoulis cannot be personally liable as an arranger absent proof of his personal involvement in the arrangement for disposal, notwithstanding the facts that he was an officer, director, and shareholder and that he had the authority to control—and did in fact control—practically every major aspect of WFE's operations. From a policy standpoint, such a holding would violate the goals underlying CERCLA by creating a loophole for powerful individuals like Georgoulis. A corporate officer, who has virtually unlimited control over a company and in fact exercises that control but knows well enough to close his or her eyes to the specific details of the company's hazardous waste disposal practices, could avoid CERCLA liability; meanwhile, the employee charged with the job of actually carrying out the disposal activities or making the disposal arrangements—even if he or she has no meaningful decisionmaking authority—could *not* avoid personal liability. ***

Therefore, based upon our understanding of CERCLA, and our interpretation of the case law from our circuit, we hold that arranger liability under § 9607(a)(3) does not impose the specific intent requirement urged by defendants. We agree with the United States' argument that defendants' proposed specific intent standard would

> insulate[ ] from liability those who own and intrusively run organizations, those who effectively dictate their hazardous waste decisions through day-to-day strict control of budgets, production, and capital investment, those who strip the company of its cash and its independent decision-making, but who do not trouble themselves with the cost-cutting disposal practices of their company.

Brief for Appellee United States at 36.

We now hold that the proper standard to be applied in this case imposes direct arranger liability on a corporate officer or director if he or she had the authority to control and did in fact exercise actual or substantial control, directly or indirectly, over the arrangement for disposal, or the off- site disposal, of hazardous substances. *** Our holding today recognizes that, for purposes of determining arranger liability under § 9607(a)(3), whether an individual exercises his or her authority over a corporation which generates and arranges for the disposal, treatment, or transportation of hazardous substances, *is* relevant under the statutory scheme. For arranger liability to attach to a corporate officer or director, there must be some actual exercise of control, *and* it must include the exercise of some control, directly or indirectly, over the arrangement for disposal, or the off-site disposal, of hazardous substances.[7]***

---

§ 9607(a)(2), none have *required* the person to have exercised authority or control over the disposal activities, although such conduct would, in most instances, satisfy the "actual control" requirement.

[7]This standard differs from the standard for finding operator liability arising out of the exercise of control by one entity over another. To establish arranger liability, the exercise of control must be causally related to the arrangement for disposal, or the off-site disposal, rather than merely the operations or

In the present case the undisputed facts reveal that Georgoulis did not simply delegate authority and rely on the judgment of others; as a practical matter, his mandates left no room for others to exercise any decisionmaking authority or judgment in any area of the business, including hazardous waste disposal. Had Georgoulis truly delegated authority to others and allowed those individuals to exercise their judgment with respect to WFE's waste disposal practices without his interference, he would not be liable as an arranger under the standard we have adopted today. In the present case, however, the undisputed facts show that Georgoulis had the authority to control virtually every aspect of WFE's operations and did in fact directly control many aspects of WFE's operations and indirectly control others. We find it beyond dispute that Georgoulis, in his capacity as board chairman and chief executive officer of WFE, so usurped the power of those who were only nominally running WFE that he undertook responsibility for all of WFE's decisionmaking; he so tightly controlled WFE, particularly its budgetary aspects, that he left WFE employees no other choice but to continue with the relatively inexpensive arrangement that had historically existed between WFE and HEC. In other words, Georgoulis's actions inexorably led to the continuation of the disposal of WFE's wastes at the dumpsite. It is therefore beyond genuine dispute that he exercised substantial indirect control over the disposal arrangement. We base this conclusion upon a fact-intensive examination of the totality of the circumstances. *** The lack of evidence showing that Georgoulis was personally involved in, or aware of, the details of the disposal arrangement does not bar his liability.

NOTES

1. In *Gurley*, the Eighth Circuit indicated that the majority of circuits to have ruled on the issue have required actual control, rather than authority to control, as the test for operator liability. In addition to the Seventh, Fifth, and Second Circuits cited by the Eighth, joining this view are the First, *United States v. Kayser-Roth Corp.*, 910 F.2d 24 (1st Cir. 1990), *cert. denied*, 498 U.S. 1084 (1991), the Third, *Lansford-Coaldale Joint Water Authority v. Tonolli Corp.*, 4 F.3d 1209 (3d Cir. 1993), and the Eleventh Circuits, *Jacksonville Electric Authority v. Bernuth Corp.*, 996 F.2d 1107 (11th Cir. 1993). Some of these cases involve individual liability; others address parent company liability. The analyses typically do not differentiate between the two situations, however.

---

activities of the ostensible arranger. The language of CERCLA's arranger subsection specifically requires that one arrange for disposal or treatment, or arrange for transportation for disposal or treatment. 42 U.S.C. § 9607(a)(3). The language related to operator liability, by contrast, merely requires that one operate the facility at which hazardous substances are disposed of, at the time of the disposal; it does not require any involvement in the disposal activities themselves. 42 U.S.C. § 9607(a)(2).

2. Whether the test is actual control or authority to control, the next question is, control over what? Quoting *Gurley*, the Eleventh Circuit outlined at least two different approaches.

> The Eighth Circuit has rejected the "authority to control" test articulated by the Fourth Circuit in *Nurad* in favor of the following standard:
>
>> [A]n individual may not be held liable as an "operator" under § 9607(a)(2) unless he or she (1) had authority to determine whether hazardous wastes would be disposed of and to determine the method of disposal and (2) actually exercised that authority, either by personally performing the tasks necessary to dispose of the hazardous wastes or by directing others to perform those tasks.
>
> *United States v. Gurley*, 43 F.3d 1188, 1193 (8th Cir. 1994), *cert. denied*, 116 S.Ct. 73 (1995).
>
> The Eighth Circuit's rule in *Gurley* goes beyond our reasoning in *Jacksonville Elec.* in protecting officers, shareholders and employees from operator liability. Under *Gurley*, an officer or shareholder of a corporation can only be found liable as an operator when they actually controlled the disposal of hazardous substances at a facility. In contrast, we stated in *Jacksonville Elec.* that "[a]ctual involvement in decisions regarding the disposal of hazardous substances is a sufficient, but not a necessary, condition to the imposition of operator liability." *Jacksonville Elec.*, 996 F.2d at 1110. Under this Circuit's standard, an individual need not have actually controlled the specific decision to dispose of hazardous substances. Rather, it is enough if the individual "actually participated in the operations of the facility ... [or] actually exercised control over, or was otherwise intimately involved in the operations of, the corporation immediately responsible for the operation of the facility." *Id.*

Redwing Carriers, Inc. v. Saraland Apartments, 94 F.3d 1489, 1505 n.19 (11th Cir. 1996).

If operator liability attaches to any corporate officer, shareholder, or employee by virtue of "participating in the operations of the facility," what employees are not exposed to individual CERCLA liability? Is the Eleventh Circuit's formulation potentially more expansive than an authority-to-control test?

Consider the Seventh Circuit's guidance:

> ***To survive a motion to dismiss a plaintiff must allege that persons associated with the corporation *directly* and *personally* engaged in conduct that led to the specific environmental damage at issue in the case. Without such direct, personal involvement, the corporation and not the associated individuals must be regarded as owning or operating the hazardous waste site in question. It would

certainly be unreasonable to infer simply from general allegations of corporate ownership or operation of a waste site that individuals acting on the corporation's behalf are themselves liable. Thus, a plaintiff does not state a claim for owner or operator liability if she merely alleges that certain individuals had general corporate authority or served generally in a supervisory capacity. Active participation in, or exercise of specific control of, the activities in question must be shown.

Sidney S. Arst Co. v. Pipefitters Welfare Educational Fund, 25 F.3d 417, 421-422 (7th Cir. 1994).

3. Is the Eighth Circuit's test for individual liability consistent with CERCLA's strict liability standard? Was not the principle of strict liability the one aspect of CERCLA's liability standard, borrowed from § 311 of the Clean Water Act, that was clearly established at the time of CERCLA's enactment?

4. In at least one case, individual shareholders of a hazardous substance transporter were sued under the transporter liability provisions of CERCLA § 107(a)(4).

Although it may be preferable to have the same liability standard apply to individual officers, shareholders and directors under each subsection of § 107(a), CERCLA's language fails to indicate that traditional concepts of limited liability are to be disregarded under § 107(a)(4). ***

Congress could have specified that majority shareholders or officers of corporations engaged in the waste hauling business are personally responsible for releases of hazardous substances from disposal facilities selected by their companies. Congress could have utilized the phrase "owner or operator" of a transporter, just as it used the phrase "owner or operator" of a facility. It did neither. On the contrary, the sparse legislative history indicates that Congress anticipated that "issues of liability not resolved by this Act ... shall be governed by traditional and evolving principles of common law." Under these circumstances, it is appropriate to limit liability to those persons who are clearly made liable by the language Congress used—those who actively participate in the process of accepting hazardous substances for transport and have a substantial role in the selection of the disposal facility.

* * *

*** [H]owever, liability under § 107(a)(4) is not limited to those who "personally participated in the transportation of hazardous wastes." It is not necessary that the officer personally accept the waste for transport ***. Nor is it necessary that the officer participate in the selection of the disposal facility. Liability may be imposed where the officer is aware of the acceptance of materials for transport and of his company's substantial participation in the selection of the disposal facility. An officer who has authority to control disposal decisions should not escape liability under § 107(a)(4) when he or she has actual knowledge that a subordinate has selected a disposal site and, effectively, acquiesces in the subordinate's actions.

United States v. USX Corp., 68 F.3d 811, 824-825 (3d Cir. 1995).

5. How would you advise the Vice President for Environmental Compliance of a chemical or other manufacturing company that generates wastes containing hazardous substances? What sort of plan should he adopt to ensure that he avoids personal liability for CERCLA cleanup activities involving the company's wastes? Would your advice for avoiding operator liability differ from your advice for avoiding arranger liability? To what extent, if at all, is the Vice President's individual interest in avoiding personal liability at odds with the company's interest in minimizing its CERCLA liability?

B. Parent Corporations

The principles governing parent corporation liability under state and federal common law, and under CERCLA directly, are essentially the same as those governing individual shareholder (and corporate officer and employee) liability, addressed above. Do you think that the courts should apply those principles differently in the individual context than in the parent corporation context? If so, what factors might affect the courts' application of the somewhat amorphous tests governing individual and parent corporation liability?

Following are two cases that take conflicting approaches to the issue of parent corporation liability under CERCLA. The first case represents the majority view, sanctioning the imposition of direct CERCLA liability upon parent companies when the operator/control test is satisfied. Under this approach, a piercing the corporate veil analysis applies when determining whether a parent corporation is liable as a CERCLA owner of a facility nominally owned by its subsidiary, but the more lenient control test applies to determine whether a parent is liable as a facility operator. *See, e.g., United States v. Kayser-Roth Corp.*, 910 F.2d 24 (1st Cir. 1990), *cert. denied*, 498 U.S. 1084 (1991). The second case is an en banc decision of the Sixth Circuit that eschews that approach in favor of the traditional, more restrictive test of piercing the corporate veil before subjecting a parent corporation to CERCLA liability, whether as owner or operator, for contamination at its subsidiary's facility.

SCHIAVONE V. PEARCE
79 F.3d 248 (2nd Cir. 1996)

Before NEWMAN, Chief Judge, MAHONEY, Circuit Judge, and SAND, District Judge of the District of Southern District of New York.
SAND, District Judge.

Defendant-third-party plaintiff-appellant Kerr-McGee Chemical Corporation ("Kerr-McGee") appeals from an order entered June 1, 1995, pursuant to an opinion dated August 25, 1994, in the United States District Court for the District of Connecticut, Peter C. Dorsey, *Chief Judge*, granting third-party-defendant-appellee Union Camp Corporation's ("Union Camp") motion for summary judgment. ***

Background

Union Bag & Paper, the predecessor of Union Camp, formed American Creosoting Corporation ("AmCre Corp.") in 1956 to facilitate Union Camp's acquisition of certain assets from American Creosoting Company. With funds supplied by Union Camp, AmCre Corp., a wholly owned subsidiary of Union Camp, purchased these assets, which included a business on certain leased real property in North Haven, Connecticut. American Creosoting Company had operated a creosoting facility on this property since 1922. On July 24, 1964, Union Camp entered into a stock purchase agreement with Kerr-McGee Oil, the predecessor of Kerr-McGee Corporation, whereby Kerr-McGee acquired AmCre Corp. In Section 4 of this stock purchase agreement ("the indemnification agreement"), which the parties accepted in New York and contemplated closing in New York, Union Camp agreed to indemnify and hold harmless AmCre Corp. and Kerr-McGee for legal claims and suits filed against them prior to August 1, 1965. *** Subsequent to its purchase of AmCre Corp., Kerr-McGee changed the name of AmCre Corp. to Moss American, Inc. ("Moss American"). In 1974 Kerr-McGee Chemical Corporation, a subsidiary of Kerr-McGee Corporation, merged with Moss American, assuming all Moss American's liabilities.

A contract between AmCre Corp. and the New York, New Haven and Hartford Railroad Company ("the Railroad"), concerning the operations of the creosoting plant in North Haven, Connecticut ("the plant"), forms the basis of the underlying action. From approximately 1921 through 1966, the Railroad owned the property on which the plant is located and leased it to American Creosoting Company. The property, which changed ownership several times over subsequent years, suffered creosote contamination as a result of the plant's storage, handling, and disposal activities. Prior to September 25, 1984, at the behest of the Connecticut Department of Environmental Protection, the then-owners of the property, defendants Herbert H. Pearce ("Pearce") and Donald B. Lippincott ("Lippincott"), implemented a remedial program to cleanse the land. Their curative efforts, however, were not without critics.

Plaintiff Michael Schiavone, who purchased the property from Pearce and Lippincott by warranty deed on or about October 23, 1984, commenced the underlying lawsuit, alleging that Pearce and Lippincott had inadequately remediated the creosote contamination, causing plaintiff to incur substantial clean-up costs. Plaintiff named Kerr-McGee as a defendant. Kerr-McGee impleaded Union Camp, seeking contribution based on Union Camp's management of the plant, through the activities of Union Camp's wholly-owned subsidiary and the title owner of the plant, AmCre Corp., from 1956 through 1964.

During that period, Union Camp and AmCre Corp. shared the same board of directors, and several of AmCre Corp.'s high-ranking officers, specifically its president, general counsel, assistant comptroller, and assistant treasurer, were also employed by Union Camp. During the years in question, Union Camp's legal department rendered services to AmCre Corp., including the review and approval of the 1958 renewal of the contract concerning the operations of the plant. Kerr-McGee states that several Union Camp employees participated, as officers and directors of AmCre Corp., in the negotiations surrounding the 1958 contract renewal. Kerr-McGee also maintains that during this period, the interlocking Union Camp-AmCre Corp. board of directors examined and approved capital expenditures, including pollution-control equipment, for AmCre Corp.'s creosoting plants. It is Kerr-McGee's contention that Union Camp's sustained involvement in the plant's operations reflects an exercise of control by Union Camp sufficient to render Union Camp directly liable for the environmental harm caused.

Union Camp moved for summary judgment on both the CERCLA and state statutory claims. On August 25, 1994, the district court granted the motion, finding that the indemnification agreement shifted all Union Camp's liabilities, including environmental liabilities, to Kerr-McGee. The district court did not address the factual question of the extent of Union Camp's direct liability, if any, as it deemed Kerr-McGee's CERCLA and state statutory claims to be barred, based on the indemnification agreement. ***

This appeal followed.

Discussion
* * *

B. CERCLA Liability

   1. Operator Liability
* * *

In light of the indemnification agreement, a perceived tension exists between any liabilities Union Camp may have independently, as an operator under CERCLA, and any liabilities that Union Camp may possess derivatively, as the parent of AmCre Corp. This seeming conflict turns on the characterization of Union Camp's liability: whether, although "arising out of or attributable to the operations or activities of [AmCre Corp.]," it nevertheless results from Union Camp's *own* actions related to management of the plant, or whether it instead results from AmCre Corp.'s actions only, with Union Camp's liability arising from traditional concepts of corporate veil piercing. ***

This perceived tension between direct liability and liability based on veil piercing can be reconciled, however, when examined against the overall goals of CERCLA and the uniqueness of its statutory scheme. Congress enacted CERCLA with the expansive, remedial purpose of ensuring "that those responsible for any damage, environmental harm, or injury from chemical poisons bear the costs of their actions." S.Rep. No. 848, 96th Cong., 2d Sess. 13 (1980). One of CERCLA's primary goals is to extend liability to all those involved in creating harmful environmental conditions. Courts should construe the statute liberally in order to effect these congressional concerns. An interpretation of CERCLA that imposes operator liability directly on parent corporations whose own acts violate the statute is consistent with the general thrust and purpose of the legislation.

Courts have held parent corporations independently liable, as operators, for the activities of their subsidiaries. *See, e.g., United States v. TIC Inv. Corp.*, 68 F.3d 1082, 1091 (8th Cir.1995); *Jacksonville Elec. Auth. v. Bernuth Corp.*, 996 F.2d 1107, 1110 (11th Cir.1993); *City of New York v. Exxon Corp.*, 112 B.R. 540, 547-48 (S.D.N.Y.1990). Recognizing that the resulting liability may not be consistent with traditional rules of corporate liability, *United States v. USX Corp.*, 68 F.3d 811, 822 (3d Cir.1995), courts have found such direct liability nonetheless to be compatible with CERCLA's expansive goals. *** Indeed, a parent and its subsidiary have both been held independently accountable, as operator and owner respectively, for environmental harms stemming from the same activities. Such a departure from common law principles of corporate insulation can be explained by the uniqueness of CERCLA's legislative scheme, specifically by the recognition that "CERCLA liability is often broader than these traditional purposes would justify." Richard B. Stewart & Bradley M. Campbell, Lessons From Parent Liability Under CERCLA, 6 Nat.Resources & Env't 7, 9 (Winter 1992).

Courts imposing operator liability directly on a parent corporation have drawn support not only from legislative intent, but also from related statutory language. The most compelling argument points to the distinction between "owner" and "operator," as evidenced by Congress' inclusion of both terms. Observing that " 'owner' liability and 'operator' liability denote two separate concepts," courts stress the disjunctive character of CERCLA liability.

This distinction has particular relevance in the context of parent and subsidiary corporations where the theory of liability selected mandates different bases of proof. A finding of *owner* liability invokes the parent-subsidiary relationship and can be made only in circumstances that permit corporate veil piercing. *USX Corp.*, 68 F.3d at 823 ("[T]raditional principles of corporate law would not permit 'owner' liability to be extended to a corporate parent unless piercing the corporate veil were warranted."). Such *owner* liability is entirely distinct from parent *operator* liability, proof of which looks to the independent actions of the parent corporation, evidenced through its control over the polluting site.[5] As the Third Circuit has explained,

> Under CERCLA, a corporation may be held liable as an owner for the actions of its subsidiary corporation in situations in which it is determined that piercing the corporate veil is warranted.... Operator liability, in contrast, is generally reserved for those situations in which a parent or sister corporation is deemed, due to the specifics of its relationship with its affiliated corporation, to have had substantial control over the facility in question.

Lansford-Coaldale, 4 F.3d at 1220 (citations omitted). Any liabilities Union Camp may have as an *operator*, then, stem directly from its control over the plant. Unlike *owner* liability, the basis for such operator liability is wholly independent of any liability on the part of AmCre Corp.

* * *

While many courts thus find in the legislative intent, evidenced both generally and textually, a willingness to extend CERCLA liability beyond the established bounds of corporate common law, there is an alternative approach that strictly adheres to traditional veil-piercing concepts. *See Joslyn Mfg. Co. v. T.L. James & Co.*, 893 F.2d 80, 82-83 (5th Cir.1990), *cert. denied*, 498 U.S. 1108 (1991). In the absence of a more specific legislative direction, this school refuses to treat CERCLA as authorizing a departure from longstanding principles of corporate law. As the Fifth Circuit has emphasized, "Significantly, CERCLA does not define 'owners' or 'operators' as including the parent company of offending wholly-owned subsidiaries. Nor does the legislative history indicate that Congress intended to alter so substantially a basic tenet of corporate law." *Joslyn Mfg.*, 893 F.2d at 82.

Although we are not unmindful of the weighty concerns expressed by the Fifth and Sixth Circuits, we subscribe instead to the views adopted by the First, Third, Fourth, *** Seventh, *** Eighth, and Eleventh Circuits, and of several district courts within this circuit. A recognition of direct operator liability for parent corporations is both compatible with the statutory language and consistent with CERCLA's broad remedial scheme. Any operator liability that Union Camp may have, then, even though related to the activities of its subsidiary AmCre Corp.—the legal owner of the offending plant—is specific to Union Camp alone. Separate and distinct from "any obligation or liability of [AmCre Corp.]," Union Camp's potential operator liability thus falls outside the scope of the indemnification agreement.

* * *

Conclusion

---

[5]The question of what control must be exercised by the parent corporation has received differing judicial responses. Some courts require *actual control* to sustain a finding of operator liability. Other courts deem merely the *authority to control* sufficient. The Second Circuit has yet to endorse any approach to this question, and we decline to do so now, as such a ruling lies beyond the scope of the present appeal. The district court, having dealt only with issues relating to the indemnification agreement, never addressed the question whether Union Camp's own acts would subject it to CERCLA liability.

The order of the district court *** is vacated. The case is remanded for a determination of Union Camp's liability under CERCLA § 9607(a)(2) and Conn.Gen.Stat. § 22a-452.

UNITED STATES V. CORDOVA CHEMICAL CO. OF MICHIGAN
113 F.3d 572 (6th Cir. 1997) (en banc)

Before MARTIN, Chief Judge,   MERRITT, KENNEDY, MILBURN, NELSON, RYAN, BOGGS, NORRIS, SILER, BATCHELDER, DAUGHTREY, and MOORE, Circuit Judges.
NORRIS, Circuit Judge.

This appeal highlights the difficulty that often attends the apportionment of liability for the clean-up costs of sites that have been subjected to long-term environmental degradation. In the present case, brought pursuant to the Comprehensive Environmental Response, Compensation, and Liability Act ("CERCLA"), the environmental damage occurred over a period of decades and during the watch of several owners.

A central concern on appeal is the criteria required under CERCLA before a parent corporation can be held financially liable for pollution that occurred on a site owned by a subsidiary. Because we adopt a stricter standard than did the district court for imposition of such liability, we reverse certain of its determinations and remand for further proceedings.

I. PROCEEDINGS BELOW
* * *

Beginning in 1957, a series of owners used the Dalton Township site to manufacture chemicals. The initial owner, the Ott Chemical Company ("Ott I"), controlled the site from 1957 until 1965. During this time, the groundwater flowing underneath the site became contaminated, a development confirmed by tests conducted in 1964.

Pollution of soil, surface water, and groundwater continued after the Ott Chemical Company ("Ott II"), a wholly owned subsidiary of CPC International, Inc. ("CPC"), took over ownership of the site in 1965. The use of unlined lagoons as a means of chemical waste disposal was the principal cause of the contamination. According to the district court, this practice spanned the period from 1959 until at least 1968.

Seepage from these lagoons did not, however, constitute the sole source of pollution that occurred during the ownership of Ott I and Ott II. Further contamination emanated from chemical spills from train cars, from chemical drums, from overflows of chemicals contained in a cement-lined equalization basin, and from other sources.

Groundwater pollution did not go completely untreated during this time; from 1965 until 1974, purge wells were operated intermittently in an attempt to alleviate the problem.

In 1972, the Story Chemical Company ("Story") acquired the site from Ott II and continued to operate it until 1977, when bankruptcy ended operations. At that point, the trustee in bankruptcy assumed title to the site and attempted to find a buyer.

Active governmental response to the pollution problems at the site began in 1977, after Story's bankruptcy, when the Michigan Department of Natural Resources ("MDNR") visited the site to assess the situation. In view of the severity of the environmental problems and the lack of resources to pay for a cleanup, the MDNR became active in an effort to attract a purchaser who would participate financially in clean-up efforts. This search led to the signing of a document on October 13, 1977, by the Cordova Chemical Company ("Cordova/California"), a wholly owned subsidiary of Aerojet-General Corporation ("Aerojet"), and the MDNR. The district court described the agreement and its aftermath:

> It addressed the problem of environmental contamination at the property and set forth obligations with respect to cleanup activities....
>
> ....
>
> ... MDNR agreed to remedy the waste container and sludge problems, and Cordova/California agreed to eliminate the phosgene gas and give MDNR $600,000 to defray the costs of the agency's cleanup of the waste containers, sludge and residential wells.
>
> ....
>
> With respect to Cordova/California's $600,000 payment and the company's responsibility or liability for the contamination at the site it was acquiring, the [agreement] stated:
>
> ....
>
> Cordova Chemical Company shall not have any responsibility or liability in connection with any other corrective actions which the Department of Natural Resources or any other governmental agency may hereafter deem necessary....
>
> ....
>
> However, the agreement did not provide for a total cleanup of the site's severe environmental problems....
>
> In particular, MDNR and Cordova/California did not reach an agreement regarding a remedy for the groundwater contamination problem. Instead, the fate of the groundwater problems was not resolved, with MDNR left to tackle the problem as part of its overall regulatory responsibility for the site.
>
> ....
>
> ... Cordova/California and MDNR fulfilled their cleanup obligations under the [agreement].

Having executed this document, Cordova/California purchased the site the following day from the Story bankruptcy trustee. Cordova Chemical Company of

Michigan ("Cordova/Michigan"), a wholly owned subsidiary of Cordova/California, acquired ownership of the site in 1978. Cordova/Michigan retains ownership, although manufacturing operations at the site ceased in 1986.

The district court made the following observations regarding conditions at the site during the ownership of the Cordova companies:

> During their period of operations, [the companies] neither buried waste nor dumped it onto the ground. No chemical waste was disposed into the unlined lagoons that had been used during the Ott I and Ott II eras. Before beginning chemical manufacturing, Cordova/Michigan repaired the equalization basin and chemical sewer system. When operating, Cordova/Michigan discharged chemical waste through off-site disposal or to a sewer that flowed to the Muskegon County treatment facility.

In short, although the preexisting groundwater contamination problem was not remedied during their ownership, the trial court concluded that neither Cordova/California nor Cordova/Michigan exacerbated the condition.

The federal Environmental Protection Agency became involved in cleanup of the site in 1981. Since then, the EPA has formulated a long-term response to the environmental damage that has occurred at the site; the cost of this effort will run into the millions of dollars.

II. CERCLA LIABILITY

*** The parties stipulated that the site is a "facility" as defined by CERCLA, that it contains "hazardous substances," that "releases" of hazardous substances have occurred and threaten to continue, and that CPC, the MDNR, Aerojet, Cordova/California, and Cordova/Michigan are "persons" as defined by the statute.

Because courts that have been asked to render liability decisions in CERCLA actions frequently invoke the remedial purpose of the act, we will review that subject before considering the liability of those parties now before us.

Congress enacted CERCLA as a "remedial statute designed to protect and preserve public health and the environment." *Kayser-Roth*, 910 F.2d at 26. *** Accordingly, courts generally will not interpret § 9607(a) in a way that apparently frustrates the statute's goals in the absence of specific congressional intent to the contrary.

It must be recognized, however, that it is difficult to divine the specific, as opposed to the general, goals of Congress with respect to CERCLA liability since the statute represents an eleventh hour compromise. ***

Courts would not be warranted, therefore, in pointing to the "remedial legislation" litany *** as a reason for filling in the blanks left by this sketchy legislative history to impose liability under nearly every conceivable scenario. Thus, while the liability provisions concerning facility operators should be construed so that financial responsibility for clean-up operations falls upon those entities that contributed to the environmental problem, the widest net possible ought not be cast in order to snare those who are either innocently or tangentially tied to the facility at issue. In fact, this court has pointed out that, "Congress intended that those responsible for disposal of chemical poisons bear the cost and responsibility for remedying the harmful conditions they created." *Anspec*, 922 F.2d at 1247 (emphasis added).

In turning to the specific facts now before us, we adhere to the tenet that liability attaches only to those parties who are culpable in the sense that they, by some realistic measure, helped to create the harmful conditions.

* * *

III. DISCUSSION

A. CPC

The district court reasoned that liability potentially could attach to CPC as a parent corporation in two ways: direct liability under CERCLA's "operator" language or by common law veil-piercing. Clearly, since the facility was titled in the subsidiary's name, CPC could be found liable as an owner only through veil piercing. The court determined that CPC was liable as an operator of the site for environmental damage that occurred during the ownership of Ott II; this liability was grounded in section 107(a)(2) of CERCLA, which renders "any person [liable] who at the time of disposal of any hazardous substance owned or operated any facility at which such hazardous substances were disposed of." 42 U.S.C. § 9607(a)(2). To reach this conclusion, the court necessarily had to hold CPC, as a parent corporation, accountable for the environmental conduct of its wholly owned subsidiary corporation, Ott II. And, because the court held CPC directly liable as an operator, it did not reach the question of whether CPC was liable as an owner pursuant to the traditional common law doctrine of veil-piercing.

It is not at all clear from the district court's opinion whether the basis for finding parental liability as an operator *** is the actual operation of the subsidiary's business or, on the other hand, the exertion of power or influence through active participation in the subsidiary's business. Although they are used interchangeably in the district court's opinion, the two concepts are not interchangeable. If anything, the facts recited by the district court support liability under the latter standard but not under the former. This confusion underscores the inevitable difficulty that arises when courts attempt to erect new concepts of corporate liability within the framework of CERCLA in the absence of direction from Congress. We are not persuaded that, in enacting CERCLA, Congress contemplated the abandonment of traditional concepts of limited liability associated with the corporate form in favor of an undefined "new, middle ground."

Actually, another scenario occurs to us under which one could argue that a parent corporation should be deemed to have directly operated a facility owned by its subsidiary. At least conceivably, a parent might independently operate the facility in the stead of its subsidiary; or, as a sort of joint venturer, actually operate the facility alongside its subsidiary. However, this is not a theory of operator liability relied upon by the district court, or alluded to in its opinion.

CERCLA defines the "owner or operator" of an onshore facility as "any person owning or operating such facility." 42 U.S.C. § 9601(20)(A)(ii). When the facility has been conveyed to a unit of state or local government, the definition differs. It then includes "any person who owned, operated or otherwise controlled activities at such facility immediately [before the transfer to the governmental authority]." 42 U.S.C. § 9601(20)(A)(iii). It thus appears that the drafters of the statute distinguished an operator from a person who "otherwise controlled" a facility. When the owner of a facility contracts out the daily running of the operation to a third party, that party presumably attains operator status (and its attendant liability). However, when a parent corporation actively participates in the affairs of its subsidiary consistent with the restrictions imposed by traditional corporations law, nothing in the definition just cited or in the rest of the statute indicates that the parent has assumed the role of operator.

Despite the definition of "owner or operator," several circuits, like the district court below, have determined that parent corporations can attain operator status by exerting significant control over the operations of their subsidiaries.

While some may wish to extend the reach of CERCLA to maximize the impact of its remedies, nothing in the statute or its legislative history warrants the invocation by courts of vague, expansive concepts *** which threaten the efficacy of time-honored limited liability protections afforded by the corporate form. As the Court of Appeals for the Fifth Circuit has noted in this context, "[i]f Congress wanted to extend liability to parent corporations it could have done so, and it remains free to do so." *Joslyn Mfg. Co. v. T.L. James & Co., Inc.*, 893 F.2d 80, 83 (5th Cir. 1990).

The district court's approach presents a number of problems. First, it replaces the relatively bright line provided by the traditional doctrine of piercing the corporate veil with a nebulous "control" test. When, precisely, is a parent acting in a manner consistent with its investment relationship as opposed to a manner that triggers operator liability? The indicia enumerated by the district court, such as participation in the subsidiary's board of directors and involvement in specific policy decisions, offer little guidance. Certainly, these activities are not grounds traditionally relied upon as warranting the disregard of separate corporate existences.

Second, the threat of unlimited liability will likely deter private sector participation in the cleanup of existing sites. The case before us illustrates this point. There is no dispute that the MDNR actively sought a private sector partner to take over and assist in the remediation of the site. Aerojet indicated an interest on the condition that it could cap its potential liability for environmental cleanup, which it sought to accomplish through the negotiation of the agreement with the MDNR and the use of subsidiaries. To scuttle such sensible and legitimate precautions in favor of an unpredictable "control" test would actually contravene the public interest by discouraging businesses from being involved in such projects.

Accordingly, we *** hold that where a parent corporation is sought to be held liable as an operator pursuant to 42 U.S.C. § 9607(a)(2) based upon the extent of its control of its subsidiary which owns the facility, the parent will be liable only when the requirements necessary to pierce the corporate veil are met. In other words, under the circumstances of this case, whether the parent will be liable as an operator depends upon whether the degree to which it controls its subsidiary and the extent and manner of its involvement with the facility, amount to the abuse of the corporate form that will warrant piercing the corporate veil and disregarding the separate corporate entities of the parent and subsidiary.

Whether the circumstances in this case warrant a piercing of the corporate veil will be determined by state law. Michigan appears to follow the general rule that requires demonstration of patent abuse of the corporate form in order to pierce the corporate veil. There must be such a unity of interest and ownership that the separate personalities of the corporation and its owner cease to exist, and the circumstances must be such that adherence to the fiction of separate corporate existence would sanction a fraud or promote injustice. *** Organization of a corporation for the avowed purpose of avoiding personal responsibility does not in itself constitute fraud or reprehensible conduct justifying a disregard of the corporate form.

The district court relied upon a number of factors in determining that CPC "actively participated in and exerted significant control over Ott II's business and decision-making" and was therefore directly liable under 42 U.S.C. § 9607(a)(2) as an operator: 100% ownership of Ott II; participation on Ott II's board of directors; a cross-pollination of officers who were involved in decision-making and daily operations; active participation by CPC officials in environmental matters; and financial control of Ott II through approval of budgets and capital expenditures. While these factors reveal a parent that took an active interest in the affairs of its subsidiary, they do not indicate such a degree of control that the separate personalities of the two corporations ceased to exist and that CPC utilized the corporate form to perpetrate the kind of fraud or other culpable conduct required before a court can pierce the veil. While CERCLA contemplates allocating financial responsibility to those corporations that cause environmental degradation, it does not authorize assignment of liability to parent corporations that abide by the proper use of the corporate form.

In summary, then, it seems to us that under the "owned or operated" language of 42 U.S.C. § 9607(a)(2), there are three scenarios under which a parent corporation could be held liable for the disposal of hazardous substances at a facility whose owner of record was the parent's subsidiary corporation. First, as an owner, by piercing the corporate veil. Second, as an operator, where the parent directly operates the facility itself, either independently of its subsidiary, or as an actual co-operator alongside the subsidiary. Although a parent conceivably could be held liable under this theory, it is not the one relied upon by the district court, and, in any event, is not supported by the facts in the record before us.

Finally, operator liability may be based upon the conduct of the parent in the course of its affiliation with its subsidiary, including the degree of control exerted by the parent over its subsidiary. This is the scenario utilized by the district court, relying upon its "new, middle ground" standard to define the circumstances under which the parent will be liable. As pointed out above, we conclude that this "new, middle ground" is unworkable, and that traditional veil piercing is the only standard under which this scenario for liability can be assessed reliably.

*　*　*

NOTES

1. How significant is the distinction between "owner" and "operator" status to the determination of parent corporation liability under CERCLA? The approach typified by the Second Circuit relies on a distinction between the two in upholding a different, less rigorous, test for operator liability. In contrast, the Sixth Circuit's analysis employs the veil-piercing test in assessing parental liability under both the owner and operator rubrics. (See the first and third scenarios mentioned at the end of the *Cordova Chemical* excerpt above.) The Sixth Circuit's second scenario at least theoretically allows an alternative test for determining whether a parent corporation is a CERCLA operator: "where the parent directly operates the facility itself, either independently of its subsidiary, or as an actual co-operator alongside the subsidiary." In light of the circular definition of the term operator under CERCLA, can you specify allegations for asserting operator liability against a parent corporation under this second scenario?

2. Of factual interest is *Jacksonville Electric Authority v. Bernuth Corp.*, 996 F.2d 1107 (11th Cir. 1993), where the Eleventh Circuit addressed the potential CERCLA liability of Tufts University as the parent of a wood treatment company whose operations had resulted in creosote and arsenic contamination. An alumnus had given Tufts 96 percent of the company's stock as a testamentary gift; 14 years later, Tufts acquired the remaining shares and owned 100 percent of the stock for an additional three years. Applying a control test, the court held that Tufts was not subject to operator liability in its capacity as corporate parent.

> When reviewing the record to evaluate the sufficiency of the evidence of Tufts' operation of the Eppinger facility, we seek more than just indicia of a parent-subsidiary relationship. We look for evidence that Tufts was actively involved in Eppinger's occupational business affairs, or that Tufts itself actually participated in the contamination. It is particularly important that the record contain such evidence in a case such as this, where the parent company—the trustees of a university—is in an entirely different business than that of the subsidiary.
>
> *** [T]he evidence before the district court is not enough to satisfy JEA's burden of proving the necessary involvement in Eppinger's affairs to take Tufts beyond its roles of majority shareholder and parent corporation to transform it into an operator liable under CERCLA.

Id. at 1111.

3. Given the split of authority on this issue, how would you advise a parent company in one of the circuits that has not yet addressed the test for parent corporation liability under CERCLA? How much stock would you place in the distinction between owner and operator liability?

C. Successor Corporations

The EPA Memorandum summarized as follows the common law approach to successor corporation liability:

> The liability of a successor corporation, according to traditional corporate law, is dependent on the structure of the corporate acquisition. Corporate ownership may be transferred in one of three ways: 1) through the sale of stock to another corporation; 2) by a merger or consolidation with another corporation; or 3) by the sale of its assets to another corporation. Where a corporation is acquired through the "purchase of all of its outstanding stock, the corporate entity remains intact and retains its liabilities, despite the change of ownership." By the same token, a purchasing corporation retains liability for claims against the predecessor company if the transaction is in the form of a merger or consolidation. Where, however, the acquisition is in the form of a sale or other transference of all of a corporation's assets to a successor corporation, the latter is not liable for the debts and liabilities of the predecessor corporation.
>
> There are four exceptions to this general rule of nonliability in asset acquisitions. A successor corporation is liable for the actions of its predecessor corporation if one of the following is shown:
>
> (a) The purchaser expressly or impliedly agrees to assume such obligations;
>
> (b) The transaction amounts to a "de facto" consolidation or merger;
>
> (c) The purchasing corporation is merely a continuation of the selling corporation; or
>
> (d) The transaction was fraudulently entered into in order to escape liability.

EPA Memorandum at 11-12. *See also* 15 W. Fletcher, *Cyclopedia of the Law of Private Corporations* § 7122 at 231 (perm. ed. 1990)(Cum. Supp. 1996). The EPA further explained that, in the product liability context, some courts have expanded the circumstances under which successor liability is imposed. In that context, some courts used the existing framework, "either modifying or recasting the 'de facto' and 'mere continuation' exemptions to include an element of public policy," while other courts adopted a new basis for imposing successor liability, based upon the "continuity of business operations." The EPA Memorandum advised its enforcement personnel to urge the courts to adopt the continuity of business approach to successor liability under CERCLA.

At this point in time, several circuits have embraced the concept of successor corporation liability under CERCLA. Some have found liability based on one or more of the four traditional exceptions to the general rule that a company may purchase the assets of another without also absorbing its liabilities. Others have gone beyond the traditional exceptions, whether by expanding the "mere continuation" exception or by recognizing a new exception, along the lines of the continuity of enterprise exception originally recognized in product liability cases. Some courts have employed federal law, others have relied on state law to address issues of successor corporation liability. The bottom line is that, regardless of approach, successor corporations are not infrequently facing CERCLA liability for actions of their predecessors.

The Third Circuit foreshadowed this trend in its 1988 holding that CERCLA imposes liability on successor corporations when (as under the traditional test) the successor entity results from a merger or consolidation.

> It is not surprising that, as a hastily conceived and briefly debated piece of legislation, CERCLA failed to address many important issues, including corporate successor liability. The meager legislative history available indicates that Congress expected the courts to develop a federal common law to supplement the statute.
>
> The concerns that have led to a corporation's common law liability *** for the torts of its predecessor are equally applicable to the assessment of responsibility for clean-up costs under CERCLA. The Act views response liability as a remedial, rather than a punitive, measure whose primary aim is to correct the hazardous condition. Just as there is liability for ordinary torts or contractual claims, the obligation to take necessary steps to protect the public should be imposed on a successor corporation.
>
> The costs associated with clean-up must be absorbed somewhere. Congress has emphasized funding by responsible parties, but if they cannot be ascertained or cannot pay the sums necessary, federal monies may be used.
>
> Expenses can be borne by two sources: the entities which had a specific role in the production or continuation of the hazardous condition, or the taxpayers through federal funds. CERCLA leaves no doubt that Congress intended the burden to fall on the latter only when the responsible parties lacked the wherewithal to meet their obligations.
>
> Congressional intent supports the conclusion that, when choosing between the taxpayers or a successor corporation, the successor should bear the cost. Benefits from use of the pollutant as well as savings resulting from the failure to use non-hazardous disposal methods inured to the original corporation, its successors, and their respective stockholders and accrued only indirectly, if at all, to the general public. We believe it in line with the thrust of the legislation to permit—if not require—successor liability under traditional concepts.

Smith Land & Improvement Corp. v. Celotex Corp., 851 F.2d 86, 91-92 (3d Cir. 1988), *cert. denied*, 488 U.S. 1029 (1989).

Since *Smith Land*, several cases have not only applied the traditional test for successor liability under CERCLA, but have expanded the exceptions to embrace the "substantial continuity" or "continuity of enterprise" exception. One such case is set forth below; the Eighth Circuit views the substantial continuity exception as an outgrowth of the traditionally-recognized exception where the successor is a "mere continuation" of the corporation whose assets it acquired. *See also B.F. Goodrich v. Betkoski*, 99 F.3d 505, 518-519 (2d Cir. 1996), *clarified*, 112 F.3d 88 (2d Cir. 1997).

UNITED STATES V. MEXICO FEED AND SEED CO.
980 F.2d 478 (8th Cir. 1992)

Before JOHN R. GIBSON, Circuit Judge, HEANEY, Senior Circuit Judge, and BEAM, Circuit Judge.
BEAM, Circuit Judge.

This is an appeal from a district court judgment finding Moreco Energy, Inc. (Moreco), Pierce Waste Oil Service, Inc. (PWOS), and Jack Pierce (Pierce) jointly and severally liable under 42 U.S.C. § 9607 for clean-up costs of $1,024,321.79 plus prejudgment interest. Moreco, PWOS, and Pierce also appeal the court's judgment for James Covington and Mexico Feed and Seed Company (Mexico) on their 42 U.S.C. § 9613(f) cross-claim for a contribution of $36,500 to their response costs.

* * *

I. BACKGROUND

James Covington owned a 53-acre tract in Audrain County, Missouri. He used three acres of the tract as the business offices of Mexico, of which he is president. During the mid-1960s, Jack Pierce, the president and owner of PWOS, a waste oil hauling company, approached Covington about putting some tanks on Mexico's premises. PWOS intended to store waste oil in these tanks, until enough was collected to haul to its Springfield, Illinois, processing plant. Pierce and Covington entered into an oral lease, allowing PWOS to place four tanks on a 40' by 40' parcel for $150 a year. That parcel is the focus of this litigation.

PWOS actively used the tanks until 1976. After that time PWOS stopped using them and allowed them to fall into disrepair. Rent was paid only through May, 1975. At least once after 1976, PWOS pumped one of the tanks out after Covington complained it was leaking. Neither Mexico nor Covington ever used the tanks for their own purposes nor did they accept ownership of the tanks in lieu of rent. No third party ever used the tanks, although once several people were arrested for trying to remove oil from the tanks.

During the time PWOS used the tanks, it hauled oil to the tanks from numerous clients who were later found to have PCBs at their sites. PWOS never tested the oil for PCBs. Oil was spilled around the tanks while PWOS trucks loaded and unloaded material. After PWOS stopped using the tanks, they developed holes which allowed rain and snow to accumulate in the tanks and oil residue to ooze out. PWOS never cleaned the sludge out of the tanks.

In the summer of 1983 Pierce sold the assets of PWOS to Moreco, a pre-existing corporation in the re-refining business with operations in several states, including one at McCook, Illinois. Moreco had sales volumes approximately five times those of PWOS. Moreco purchased PWOS's assets to strengthen its ability to collect waste oil for processing at its McCook facility. It was primarily interested in the trucks, routes, drivers, and collecting expertise PWOS had accumulated. There is no allegation that the sale was not an arm's length transaction, that the terms of the sale were unfair, or that the sale price was in any way less than the fair value of the PWOS assets Moreco received. Pierce has not yet received the full purchase price. At the time of the sale, Jack Pierce owned 90 percent of PWOS's stock. He retired from the presidency of PWOS a few months before the sale and never worked for Moreco. In February of 1984, Pierce dissolved PWOS and distributed the proceeds.

Moreco had Pierce list PWOS's assets in order to avoid acquiring hidden liabilities. PWOS's assets included oil hauling trucks and hundreds of storage tanks. The four offending tanks were not included in either the list of hard assets purchased or that of hard assets not purchased. In an inartful attempt to make sure PWOS's customer base, customer list, and goodwill were not interpreted to be excluded from the sale by the list, the list of hard assets purchased ended with a statement that the list was not exclusive. Moreco never used the tanks at issue in this case, or even knew of their existence until the EPA brought it to their attention.

Moreco ran PWOS's collection network in essentially the same manner as PWOS had run it, with many of the same employees, collection routes and trucks except it redirected the end point of the network to its McCook facility. The PWOS name was not immediately removed from the collection trucks, and it remained on receipts, insurance policies, and in state regulatory agency paperwork for a few years. Martin Pierce, Jack's son, was hired by Moreco to run the daily operations of a portion of the PWOS network. He was supervised through weekly meetings with Moreco's president. Martin Pierce was elected to Moreco's board of directors several years after the sale. There was no continuity of shareholders or directors between PWOS and Moreco at the time of the purchase.

In 1984 the EPA inspected the tanks and discovered that they contained high concentrations of PCBs. The contamination radiated out about 100 feet into the soil around the tanks, due to a process of "weathering." That degree of "weathering" indicated the initial contamination had occurred as much as 20 years earlier.

The EPA cleaned up the site, incurring response costs. The government brought suit under 42 U.S.C. § 9607 to recover its costs. It sued the Covingtons and Mexico, as owners of the site (the land); Pierce and PWOS, as owners and operators of the site (the tanks); and finally Moreco, as the corporate successor to PWOS.

The Covingtons and Mexico settled with the government during the pendency of this litigation and filed a cross-claim against Pierce, PWOS, and Moreco for the amount they personally paid the government ($20,000) and for the legal fees they had incurred due to the placement of PCBs on their property.

II. DISCUSSION

* * *

B. Moreco

* * *

2. *Successor Liability*

Moreco's ultimate liability depends on the resolution of a series of legal issues. The first is whether corporate successors are covered persons for the purposes of 42 U.S.C. § 9607. The second is whether the mere continuation or the broader "substantial continuity" theory will suffice to establish corporate successorship for CERCLA purposes. If so, the third issue is whether the facts, as the district court found them, are legally sufficient to find that Moreco was a corporate successor of Pierce's PWOS.

i) CERCLA and Corporate Successors

First we will consider whether corporate successors are within the plain meaning of "corporation" as used in CERCLA. In case of ambiguity, or to double check our plain meaning interpretation, we will look to CERCLA's purpose to ensure we are giving the language of the statute the meaning its drafters most likely intended to convey.

CERCLA extends liability for clean-ups to the "covered persons" listed in 42 U.S.C. § 9607. Section 9607 details which "persons" are "covered" and which "persons" are not. Section 9601(21) defines "person." " '[P]erson' means an individual, firm, corporation, association, partnership, consortium, joint venture, commercial entity...." 42 U.S.C. § 9601(21). Section 5 of 1 U.S.C. informs us that when "company" or "association" are used in reference to a corporation, they shall be deemed to include successors and assigns. By implication, then, Congress must have considered the word "corporation" to inherently include corporate successors.

This interpretation of the word corporation is further supported by the doctrine of corporate successor liability, which was settled law even in the time of Blackstone. *Anspec Co. v. Johnson Controls, Inc.*, 922 F.2d 1240, 1246 (6th Cir.1991) (citing 1 W. Blackstone, *Commentaries*, 467-69). In fact, corporate successor liability is so much part and parcel of corporate doctrine, it could be argued that Congress would have to explicitly exclude successor corporations if it intended its use of a legal term of art, "corporation," not to include established conceptions of the extent, life span, and path of corporate liabilities.

An examination of the context in which Congress used the word "corporation" confirms our determination that corporate successors are plainly within the meaning of "person" in 42 U.S.C. § 9607. CERCLA is a remedial environmental statute with two essential purposes: 1) to provide swift and effective response to hazardous waste sites; and 2) to place the cost of that response on those responsible for creating or maintaining the hazardous condition. When including corporations within that set of entities which must bear the cost of cleaning up the hazardous conditions they have created, Congress could not have intended that those corporations be enabled to evade their responsibility by dying paper deaths, only to rise phoenix-like from the ashes, transformed, but free of their former liabilities. It would serve little purpose to include corporations responsible for hazardous waste sites, but not their corporate successors, within the class of "covered persons." Even in cases of good faith, a bona-fide successor reaps the economic benefits of its predecessor's use of hazardous disposal methods, and, as the recipient of the benefits, is also responsible for the costs of those benefits. Thus, a review of the purpose of CERCLA further reinforces our initial determination that successor corporations are subsumed within the plain meaning of the term "corporation."

We are therefore disposed to find that our colleagues in the Third, Sixth, and Ninth Circuits correctly held that successor corporations are within the meaning of "persons" for the purposes of CERCLA liability. *Anspec*, 922 F.2d at 1240; *Louisiana-Pacific Corp. v. Asarco, Inc.*, 909 F.2d 1260 (9th Cir.1990); *Smith Land*, 851 F.2d at 86.

ii) Mere Continuations as Corporate Successors

The purpose of corporate successor liability, as indicated, is to prevent corporations from evading their liabilities through changes of ownership when there is a buy out or merger. Likewise, exceptions to the traditional rule that mere asset purchasers are not liable as successors developed to prevent corporate evasions of debt through transactional technicalities. An asset purchaser will be considered as a corporate successor when one of the following applies:

(1) The purchasing corporation expressly or impliedly agrees to assume the liability;

(2) The transaction amounts to a "de facto" consolidation or merger;

(3) The purchasing corporation is merely a continuation of the selling corporation; or

(4) The transaction was fraudulently entered into in order to escape liability.

Asarco, 909 F.2d at 1263.[9] Because corporate successors are within CERCLA's ambit of liability, CERCLA must also incorporate the traditional doctrines developed to prevent corporate successors from adroitly slipping off the hook. Any other result would thwart CERCLA's essential purpose of holding responsible parties liable for clean up costs.

Moreco, however, was not found to be a successor to PWOS under the traditional "mere continuation" theory, which emphasizes an "identity of officers, directors, and stock between the selling and purchasing corporations." *Tucker v. Paxson Machine Co.*, 645 F.2d 620, 626 (8th Cir.1981). The district court applied a broadened test of successorship, "substantial continuity," which has evolved from the "mere continuation" test in contexts where the public policy vindicated by recovery from the

---

[9]The issue of whether federal or state law should be used in analyzing successor liability was not raised by the parties and we do not decide it. However, considering the national application of CERCLA and fairness to similarly situated parties, the district court was probably correct in applying federal law.

implicated assets is paramount to that supported by the traditional rules delimiting successor liability. The test has been used in the context of labor relations, product liability, and federal environmental regulation.

The "substantial continuity" test originated with a line of Supreme Court labor relations cases, the germinal case being *Golden State Bottling Co. v. NLRB*, 414 U.S. 168 (1973). The Court extended traditional doctrines to further the public policy behind the labor act, while maintaining the public policy of fairness to all parties. It held that a "bona fide purchaser, acquiring, *with knowledge that the wrong remains unremedied*, the employing enterprise which was the locus of the unfair labor practice, may be considered in privity with its predecessor for purposes of [unfair labor practices]." *Id.* at 180 (emphasis added). The Court then briefly outlined what has come to be known as the "substantial continuation" or "continuity of enterprise" test, noting that the "substantial continuation" purchaser's knowledge of pending wrongs unremedied made broadening the net of liability fair.[10] *Id.* at 182-85. The factor of knowledge or notice ensured that "substantial continuation" corporations not only would be able to protect themselves through purchase price adjustments or satisfactory indemnity provisions, but would be in some way responsible for the unfair labor practice remedied.

Likewise, in the context of product liability, the factors of knowledge and responsibility have been present when "substantial continuation" liability has been imposed on an asset purchaser. In *Mozingo v. Correct Mfg. Corp.*, 752 F.2d 168 (5th Cir.1985), to which the government refers, the asset purchaser was not a completely independent corporation, but a corporation formed by the selling corporation and Way, the seller's director and recent controlling stockholder. Way also became the purchaser's president and outright owner. Therefore, the purchaser was well aware of and closely tied to the seller's defective products; no liability was imposed without responsibility. The strong nexus between the seller's defective product and the purchasing corporation justified imposing the wider net of "substantial continuation" liability on the asset purchaser, and, but for the "substantial continuation" test, responsible parties would have evaded liability.

As we again point out, CERCLA is aimed at imposing clean up costs on the parties responsible for the creation or maintenance of hazardous waste sites. Therefore, in the CERCLA context, the imposition of successor liability under the "substantial continuation" test is justified by a showing that in substance, if not in form, the successor is a responsible party. The cases imposing "substantial continuation" successorship have correctly focused on preventing those responsible for the wastes from evading liability through the structure of subsequent transactions.

For example, in [*United States v.*] *Distler*, 741 F.Supp. at 637 [(W.D.Ky. 1990)], three top employees incorporated to buy out their corporate employer. Although

---

[10]The test considers an identity of stock, stockholders, and officers, but not determinatively. It also considers whether the purchaser retained the same facilities, same employees, same name, same production facilities in the same location, same supervisory personnel; and produced the same product; maintained a continuity in assets; continued the same general business operations; and held itself out to the public as a continuation of the previous enterprise.

none of them had previously held their employer's stock, they, as general manager, general sales manager, and plant manager, essentially ran the business. They had no other business or employment either before or after the transaction. They were well aware of their former employer's practices. Although the corporation remained unchanged in everything but ownership, the traditional test would not have considered it a corporate successor. Thus, had the court not found a "substantial continuation," those responsible for hazardous waste would have escaped liability, and the purposes of CERCLA would have been thwarted.

In *United States v. Carolina Transformer Co.*, 739 F.Supp. 1030 (E.D.N.C. 1989), *aff'd*, 978 F.2d 832, 838 (4th Cir.1992), CERCLA successor liability was likewise imposed under the "substantial continuation" theory. There, the children of the owner of the selling corporation owned the purchasing corporation. The father also controlled the purchasing corporation, and could write checks on the purchaser's corporate account. There was no colorable question of the purchaser's knowledge of and benefit from the seller's conduct for which CERCLA liability attached, or of the seller's and purchaser's practical identity. Under the traditional tests, since these two corporations were technically owned by different parties, the purchaser could have evaded CERCLA liability and again the purpose of the statute would have been thwarted.

In *Asarco*, the Ninth Circuit refused to apply the "substantial continuity" test for successorship to a corporate asset purchaser for purposes of CERCLA liability. It found the test inapplicable because the purchaser had no actual notice of the seller's potential CERCLA liability, as the seller had not yet been identified as a potentially responsible party, and because the seller's offending installation had ceased operating nine months before the asset sale.

* * *

The issue is, whether, under these facts and in view of the development of the case law after *Golden State Bottling*, we can hold Moreco a responsible party, liable as a "substantial continuation" successor to PWOS, for the purposes of CERCLA.

In contrast to the facts discussed in *Distler* and *Carolina Transformer*, Moreco does not consist merely of PWOS's former assets. It is a larger, pre-existing corporation, which bought PWOS's assets in an arm's-length transaction in order to service one of its several re-refineries. It had been a competitor of PWOS. The PWOS network was of interest to Moreco because the network could funnel oil to an under-supplied Moreco installation. Moreco used PWOS's trucks and tanks to supply that installation. Thus, the trucking network could not render Moreco itself a mere continuation of PWOS.

In addition, as in *Asarco*, Moreco had no actual notice. It had no knowledge of the offending tanks nor had PWOS been identified as a potentially responsible party for CERCLA purposes in regard to the tanks. Unlike *Distler* and *Carolina Transformer*, the asset purchase transaction was between two competitors, not a cozy deal where responsible parties merely changed the form of ownership yet in substance remained the same, nor one where the actual managers of a corporation took over its ownership with full knowledge of its past practices. Nor is this a case where a purchasing corporation either in collusion with the seller, or independently, bought only "clean" assets, and knowingly left "dirty" assets behind with an insufficient asset pool to cover any potential liability. Nor is this a case of willful blindness. This is a case where a seller's "dirty" assets were not disclosed, where no amount of inspection could alert the purchaser to the "dirty" assets and thus enable it to adjust its price. Here, like in *Asarco*, the seller stopped using the "dirty" assets well before the sale. The government itself has previously admitted that Moreco did not buy or know of the dirty tanks, and thus could not have known that its asset purchase might affect the government's ability to have the responsible parties pay the clean-up costs.

There is no allegation that Moreco did not give Pierce and PWOS adequate consideration for the assets it did buy. Moreco still owes Pierce $300,000, which, of course, the government may collect under its judgment against Pierce. The PWOS corporate veil was effectively, if not technically, pierced when Pierce, PWOS's owner, was held jointly and severally liable for both his own and PWOS's actions. Therefore, the very concern animating the doctrine of corporate successor liability—that the corporate veil thwart plaintiffs in actions against corporations which have sold their assets and distributed the proceeds—is not present.

The only evidence that the government presented against Moreco was that the PWOS network suited its needs, Moreco was slow in getting PWOS's name off the assets it purchased, and that because it had shopped well, Moreco was not obligated to change much of the PWOS network in order to supply its re-refinery. This does not amount to a "substantial continuation" for the purpose of holding Moreco responsible and liable under CERCLA.

* * *

NOTES

1. In footnote 9, the Eighth Circuit suggested that it was applying federal rather than state law to define the circumstances under which successor corporations face CERCLA liability. A minority view, the Sixth Circuit applies state law. In *City Management Corp. v. U.S. Chemical Co.*, 43 F.3d 244 (6th Cir. 1994), the Sixth Circuit, applying Michigan law, held that the continuity of enterprise expansion of the mere continuation exception applies only in product liability cases, and did not extend to CERCLA cases.

2. Pretty Paint Co., a paint manufacturer whose waste by-products include hazardous substances which are sent off-site for treatment and disposal, seeks to acquire the assets, but not the liabilities, of Fancy Paint Co., a competitor. Pretty Paint asks your advice as to whether the acquisition will subject it to CERCLA liability for releases (a) at sites to which Fancy Paint sent hazardous substances prior to the acquisition or (b) at the Fancy Paint manufacturing facility, which is among the assets to be sold to Pretty Paint and which was contaminated during Fancy Paint's ownership. What is your advice? How might Pretty Paint structure the acquisition to minimize its potential successor liability under CERCLA?

D. Lenders

When Congress enacted CERCLA in 1980, one of the few exemptions from the Act's sweeping designation of PRPs appeared specifically to protect lenders from liability. The definition of "owner or operator" excluded from its scope "a person, who, without participating in the management of a vessel or facility, holds indicia of ownership primarily to protect his security interest in the vessel or facility." CERCLA § 101(20)(A). During the next 16 years, this apparent exemption proved to be considerably less protective than the lending community had expected. Ironically, the existence of the exemption actually spawned, in part, the filing of a number of CERCLA cases seeking to hold lenders liable for CERCLA response costs.

The development of lender liability under CERCLA has, in retrospect, proceeded in three phases, with each phase featuring a different branch of government playing the preeminent role.

1. The Courts

The first phase was triggered by two district court decisions, in 1985 and 1986, and culminated in an unrelated circuit court decision in 1990. Cumulatively, these three cases sent shock waves through the lending community across the country.

In *United States v. Mirabile*, 1985 WL 97 (E.D. Pa. 1985), the borrower/site operator brought its three lenders into a CERCLA cost recovery action. The court granted summary judgment to two of the lenders, both of whom had liens on the contaminated property, on the ground that they had not "participated in the management" of the facility, notwithstanding that one of the lenders had held title to the property for a short time in connection with a foreclosure, and the other lender had the ability (which it had not exercised) under its loan agreement to participate fairly extensively in the company's decisionmaking. The court denied summary judgment to the third lender, however, because although the lender did not have a security interest in the contaminated property, a bank officer was allegedly involved in the day-to-day operations of the borrower during the borrower's bankruptcy proceedings. In *United States v. Maryland Bank & Trust Co.*, 632 F.Supp. 573 (D.Md.1986), the bank had foreclosed and taken title to contaminated property, and still held title when the EPA conducted a cleanup and sought cost recovery. The bank was held liable not by means of the lender exemption/participation in management analysis, as in *Mirabile*, but directly as the site owner.

The net effect of these two district court decisions was to redefine the lender's worst-case scenario. Not only might CERCLA liability render the borrower insolvent and unable to repay an outstanding loan, and not only might CERCLA render the lender's collateral worthless, but CERCLA might require the lender to pay out additional money, perhaps many times the amount of the loan, to clean up the borrower's site. Lenders responded by requiring environmental audits in commercial loan deals, by becoming more sensitive to their borrowers' potential environmental problems, and by becoming more wary of acquiring powers or taking actions that might be deemed participation in their borrowers' management.

These concerns were measurably intensified by *United States v. Fleet Factors Corp.*, 901 F.2d 1550 (11th Cir. 1990), *cert. denied*, 498 U.S. 1046 (1991). The Eleventh Circuit stated that it viewed the lender exemption, particularly the provision precluding participation in the management of the facility, as an independent basis for finding liability.

> The government correctly formulates this issue as being comprised of two distinct, but related, means of finding Fleet liable under § 9607(a)(2). First, Fleet is liable under the statute if it operated the facility within the meaning of the statute. Alternatively, Fleet can be held liable if it had an indicia of ownership in SPW and managed the facility to the extent necessary to remove it from the secured creditor liability exemption. Although we can conceive of some instances where the facts showing participation in management are different from those indicating operation, this is not such a case. The sum of the facts alleged by the government is sufficient to hold Fleet liable under either analysis. In order to avoid repetition, and because this case fits more snugly under a secured creditor analysis, we will forgo an analysis of Fleet's liability as an operator.

Id. at 1556 n6. Do you agree that the exemption language in the owner or operator definition, §101(20)(A), for those who do not participate in management provides a basis for affirmatively holding a lender liable even if it does not satisfy the "operator" test? Is the lender in such circumstances liable as an owner? As a secured creditor who participates in management? If the latter, was the Eleventh Circuit recognizing five, rather than four, categories of PRPs: past and present owners; past and present operators; generators or arrangers; transporters; and holders of indicia of ownership who participate in management?

The most controversial aspect of the *Fleet Factors* decision was the court's discussion of the type of participation in management that would deprive a lender of the secured creditors' exemption.:

> Although similar, the phrase "participating in the management" and the term "operator" are not congruent. Under the standard we adopt today, a secured creditor may incur section 9607(a)(2) liability, without being an operator, by participating in the financial management of a facility to a degree indicating a capacity to influence the corporation's treatment of hazardous wastes. It is not necessary for the secured creditor actually to involve itself in the day-to-day operations of the facility in order to be liable—although such conduct will certainly lead to the loss of the protection of the statutory exemption. Nor is it necessary for the secured creditor to participate in management decisions relating to hazardous waste. Rather, a secured

creditor will be liable if its involvement with the management of the facility is sufficiently broad to support the inference that it could affect hazardous waste disposal decisions if it so chose. ***

Id. at 1557-58. Thus, a lender could incur liability without being deemed an operator, and without satisfying what is now the operator test in most circuits—actual control, rather than mere authority to control, the facility in question. After articulating that test, however, the court went to some length to catalog Fleet's alleged involvement in SPW's financial and operational management.

In the wake of *Fleet Factors,* lenders were uncertain whether the critical element triggering lender liability under CERCLA was the lender's potential authority over the borrower, or its exercise of such authority? Three months after the Eleventh Circuit handed down the *Fleet Factors* decision, the Ninth Circuit decided *In re Bergsoe Metals,* 910 F.2d 668 (9th Cir. 1990), construing *Fleet Factors* as follows:

We leave for another day the establishment of a Ninth Circuit rule on this difficult issue. It is clear from the statute that, whatever the precise parameters of "participation," there must be some actual management of the facility before a secured creditor will fall outside the exception. Here there was none, and we therefore need not engage in line drawing.

* * *

EAC next points to certain of the Port's rights under the leases, such as the right to inspect the premises and to reenter and take possession upon foreclosure. This argument suffers from the same flaw as the last; nearly all secured creditors have these rights. That a secured creditor reserves certain rights to protect its investment does not put it in a position of management. What is critical is not what rights the Port had, but what it did. The CERCLA security interest exception uses the active "participating in management." Regardless of what rights the Port may have had, it cannot have participated in management if it never exercised them. And there is no evidence that the Port exercised any control over Bergsoe once the two parties signed the leases.

Id. at 672-73. Most interesting is the Ninth Circuit's method of agreeing with, while recasting, the holding in *Fleet Factors*:

EAC also contends that the Port had the right "to direct that hazardous waste be stored properly." We find nothing in the leases granting the Port such a right. In any event, there is no evidence that the Port ever exercised this right. EAC generally errs in equating the power to manage with actual management. *As did the Eleventh Circuit in Fleet Factors, we hold that a creditor must, as a threshold matter, exercise actual management authority before it can be held liable for action or inaction which results in the discharge of hazardous wastes.*

Id. at 673, n.3 (emphasis supplied).

In *Fleet Factors*, the EPA urged the court to construe the lender exemption narrowly, exposing to CERCLA liability "any secured creditor that participates *in any manner* in the management of a facility." (emphasis supplied) The court rejected this construction because it would preclude lenders from pursuing their normal business activities without subjecting themselves to CERCLA liability.

2. EPA Rulemaking

Shortly after *Fleet Factors*, the EPA took a much broader view of the lender exemption. Spurred somewhat by the lending community's horrified reaction to the *Fleet Factors* test, and more significantly by the savings and loan industry failures, which had resulted in federal agencies holding large real estate portfolios, the EPA construed the lender exemption to enable a lender to conduct a wide range of activities without incurring CERCLA liability. Thus began the second phase in the history of lender liability under CERCLA, going from an expansion to a contraction of the scope of lender liability.

The EPA set forth its new, broader interpretation of the lender exemption in a 1992 rulemaking designed to amend the National Contingency Plan. 57 Fed. Reg. 18344 (1992). Compare the following excerpts from the EPA's preamble to its lender liability rule with the holdings in *Fleet Factors, Mirable*, and *Maryland Bank and Trust*.

Whether the holder has participated in management sufficiently to void the exemption is a fact-sensitive inquiry. *Participation in the management of a facility means actual participation in the management or operation of the facility by the holder, and does not include the mere capacity or unexercised right or ability to influence facility operations.* In all cases, the determination of whether a holder is participating in management depends on the holder's actions with respect to the facility, rather than the outcomes associated with such actions. This regulation contains a list of activities commonly undertaken by holders that the Agency considers to be consistent with holding ownership indicia primarily to protect a security interest. These activities, if undertaken by a holder, are not considered evidence of participation in the management of the facility. In addition, to address those other activities not specifically listed in this rule, a general test of management participation is provided. The general test specifies that a holder is considered to be participating in management within the meaning of section 101(20)(A) of CERCLA when it exercises decisionmaking control over the borrower's environmental compliance (such that the holder has undertaken responsibility for the borrower's hazardous substance handling or disposal practices), or where the holder assumes overall management responsibility encompassing the day-to-day decision making of the enterprise.

With respect to the specifically listed activities, a holder acts consistently with holding ownership indicia primarily to protect a security interest, for example, when policing the loan, undertaking financial workout with a borrower where the obligation is in default or in threat of default, or by foreclosing and preparing the facility for sale or liquidation. In addition, the holder is not considered to be acting outside the scope of the exemption by monitoring the borrower's business, or by requiring or conducting on-site inspections and audits of the environmental condition of the facility or the borrower's financial condition, or monitoring other aspects of the facility considered relevant or necessary by the holder, or requiring certification of financial information or compliance with applicable duties, laws or regulations, or requiring other similar actions, provided that the holder does not otherwise participate in the management of the facility, as provided in this regulation. Such oversight and obligations of compliance imposed by the holder are not considered part of the management and operation of a facility. (Note that although such requirements and oversight may inform and perhaps strongly influence the borrower's management of a facility, the holder is not considered to be participating in management where the borrower continues to make operational decisions at the facility.)

* * *

It is not possible to specifically cover in this final rule or any regulation every conceivable situation in which a holder might act, or to make specific provisions for every action that a holder might undertake without voiding the exemption. A general test or standard of participation in a facility's management has been formulated to provide a framework within which to assess the consistency of a holder's actions with the limitations of section 101(20)(A).

Although oversimplified here ***, the rule's two-prong test or standard of management participation provides that while the borrower is still in possession (i.e. pre-foreclosure) a holder participates in the management of a facility only if the holder either exercises decisionmaking control over a facility's environmental compliance obligations, or where the holder's actions manifest or assume responsibility for the overall management of the facility's day to day operations. The general test adopts a functional approach which focuses on the holder's actual decisionmaking involvement in the operational (as opposed to the financial or administrative) affairs of the secured facility. The first prong looks to where the holder has exercised decisionmaking control over the borrower's environmental compliance (i.e., the borrower's hazardous substance disposal or handling practices). If so, the holder is "participating in the management" of the facility within the meaning of section 101(20)(A). Similarly, the second prong looks to where the holder is functioning as the overall manager by exercising management at a level encompassing the borrower's environmental obligations, or over all or substantially all of the operational aspects of the borrower's enterprise, regardless of whether decisionmaking control over the enterprise's environmental compliance responsibilities has been explicitly assumed or not. This level of actual involvement in the management of the facility is sufficient to constitute "management participation" for purposes of section 101(20)(A).

The general test prohibits a holder from artificially "carving out" environmental matters from its purview as a means to otherwise participate in the facility's operational management yet maintain the exemption. Under the second prong of the general test, the ability to "carve out" environmental compliance responsibilities from other operational aspects of the borrower's business or enterprise demonstrates that the holder has manifested or assumed operational responsibility at a management level that includes such matters, and doing so is considered to be participation in the facility's management. However, management participation does not include the unexercised right to become involved in operational facility decisionmaking. Whether the exercise of rights that a holder might have—whether under the contract or other agreement (if any) or otherwise, including the enforcement of loan terms and covenants or other rights—rises to the level of participation in the facility's management is measured by reference to the general test.

57 Fed. Reg. at 18375, 18379-80 (emphasis added).

In a challenge brought by the State of Michigan and the Chemical Manufacturers Association, the D.C. Circuit struck down the EPA's lender liability rule. *Kelley v. Environmental Protection Agency*, 15 F.3d 1100 (D.C. Cir. 1994), *cert. denied*, 513 U.S. 1110 (1995). The court held that CERCLA did not authorize the EPA to issue rules construing liability provisions; that task belonged to courts.

*** Where Congress does not give an agency authority to determine (usually formally) the interpretation of a statute in the first instance and instead gives the agency authority only to bring the question to a federal court as the "prosecutor," deference to the agency's interpretation is inappropriate. As we have explained, that is all that EPA can do regarding liability issues. Moreover, even if an agency enjoys authority to determine such a legal issue administratively, deference is withheld if a private party can bring the issue independently to federal court under a private right of action. Petitioners are such private parties; they wish to preserve the right to sue lenders when, in petitioners' view, a lender's behavior transgresses the statutory test—whether or not EPA would regard the lender as liable. As we read the statute, Congress intended that petitioners' claim in such an event should be evaluated by the federal courts independent of EPA's institutional view.

Id. at 1108-1109.

The invalidation of the EPA rule did not cause as much disruption as might be expected. During the nearly four years between the Eleventh Circuit's decision in *Fleet Factors* and the D.C. Circuit's decision, lenders successfully avoided CERCLA liability in a significant number of district court and appellate court decisions. Whereas some courts relied on the since-invalidated EPA rule, other courts reached that result directly under the statutory language (construing it in a manner consistent with the EPA rule). The following case exemplifies the latter approach.

WATERVILLE INDUSTRIES, INC. V. FINANCE AUTHORITY OF MAINE
984 F.2d 549 (1st Cir. 1993)

Before BREYER, Chief Judge, BOWNES, Senior Circuit Judge, and BOUDIN, Circuit Judge.

BOUDIN, Circuit Judge.

Waterville Industries, Inc., brought suit against the Finance Authority of Maine ("FAME") seeking contribution to "response costs" assessed against Waterville Industries by the Environmental Protection Agency under the Comprehensive Environmental Response, Compensation and Liability Act ("CERCLA"), 42 U.S.C. § 9601 *et seq.* FAME, claiming the protection of statutory exceptions to CERCLA liability, appeals from the district court's decision that it is responsible for 60 percent of those costs. ***

I

This action arises out of efforts to clean up two waste water lagoons located at a defunct textile mill in Waterville, Maine. Although the genesis of the mill is neither clear from the record nor critical to the case, it appears that the First Hartford Corporation developed the mill in the early 1970's with state assistance. In or about 1972, First Hartford acquired the property, sold it to Waterville Textile Development Corporation—a quasi-public corporation unconnected with the appellee in this case—and then leased it back. Loans in connection with the project were made to First Hartford by Society for Savings, an out-of-state lender, and secured by mortgages on the property, which Society for Savings held. The loans were guaranteed by appellant FAME, an instrumentality of the state of Maine.

In 1980, First Hartford defaulted on the loans. As a result, FAME pursuant to its guarantee made substantial payments to Society for Savings to cure the defaults, assumed First Hartford's future obligations to Society for Savings, and received from the latter an assignment of the mortgages. On the same day that it received the mortgages, March 14, 1980, FAME accepted a deed in lieu of foreclosure from Waterville Textile Development Corporation and became the holder of title to the property.

On the same day, FAME leased the property back to First Hartford to allow First Hartford to continue to operate the mill. The new lease required First Hartford to make monthly payments directly to Society for Savings to cover obligations coming due on the original debt which FAME had assumed. The lease also required First Hartford to pay an additional $22,340 per month directly to FAME. During the period in which First Hartford operated the mill as a lessee of FAME, First Hartford released certain hazardous wastes into two lagoons associated with the mill.

First Hartford continued to experience financial trouble after the March 14, 1980, transactions, and filed for Chapter 11 bankruptcy protection on February 20, 1981. First Hartford ceased operations at the mill on October 6, 1981. Apparently a dispute then occurred between First Hartford and FAME as to whether First Hartford had a continuing interest in the property. This dispute was resolved in a "settlement stipulation" approved by the bankruptcy court on July 29, 1982, which provided that "title to the Real Property is vested solely in [FAME]," but which gave First Hartford until October 15, 1982, to find a buyer for the property.

First Hartford did not find a buyer by October 15, 1982, and on or about March 29, 1983, FAME contracted with an auctioneer to sell the property. An auction was held on August 19, 1983, and MKY Realty was the high bidder. On September 23, 1983, FAME and MKY Realty entered into a contract for the sale of the property, and on November 15, 1983, FAME conveyed the property to Gano Industries, the nominee of MKY Realty. Gano Industries later changed its name to Waterville Industries, the appellee in this case.

II.

In September 1988, the EPA filed an administrative complaint against Waterville Industries seeking penalties and response costs under CERCLA in connection with the clean-up of the lagoons. As the current owner of the property, Waterville Industries was liable for such costs under the statute. 42 U.S.C. § 9607(a)(1). Waterville Industries entered into a consent agreement with EPA to clean up the property. It has now incurred substantial engineering costs in connection with the clean-up, and further expenses are expected. Waterville Industries then brought this action pursuant to CERCLA contending that FAME, as a former owner of the property, is liable for contribution. ***

*** Waterville Industries argues that FAME is liable for contribution because it "owned" the property between March 14, 1980, and October 6, 1981, during which time hazardous substances were released into the lagoons by First Hartford. The statute, however, contains exceptions to the definition of an "owner," one of which excludes from that status "a person, who, without participating in the management of a vessel or facility, holds indicia of ownership primarily to protect his security interest in the vessel or facility." 42 U.S.C. § 9601(20)(A).

FAME has contended throughout the litigation that it falls within this security interest exception from CERCLA liability. Waterville Industries' main response is that when FAME accepted a deed in lieu of foreclosure on March 14, 1980, it "became the owner in fee simple of the land, and the mortgages merged into the deed and disappeared." At that point, Waterville Industries argues, FAME no longer had a "security interest" to protect because it was the outright owner of the property, and therefore the secured creditor exception by its terms became inapplicable. The district court accepted this reasoning. ***

Our own analysis begins with the construction of CERCLA's security interest exception, plainly an issue of law. The purpose of the exception, apparent from its language and the statutory context, is to shield from liability those "owners" who are in essence lenders holding title to the property as security for the debt. *** [L]egislative history and case law confirm that Congress had in mind not only the classic case of the bank mortgage but also equivalent devices serving the same function, such as lease financing arrangements.[4]

Our review of the record persuades us that what FAME received from Waterville Textile Development Corporation through the March 14, 1980, transactions was the nominal title typical of the lender in a lease financing transaction. Waterville Textile Development Corporation was a quasi-public development corporation used in connection with the 1972 loans in order to hold title to the property; it purchased the property from First Hartford for $1 and then leased it back to First Hartford. That lease in turn gave First Hartford an option to buy the property for $1 at the end of the lease (or, based on formula payments, even before the lease expired if it chose). This is an ordinary lease financing arrangement, commonly called a sale and lease back.

When FAME acquired title from Waterville Textile Development Corporation on March 14, 1980, it simultaneously re-leased the property to First Hartford ***. Thus, First Hartford's payment obligations were altered but its option to buy the property for $1 remained in force and the lease financing character of the transaction remained unchanged.

The payments required under the new March 14, 1980, lease reinforce our conclusion. First Hartford was committed to continue payments to Society for Savings just as before and also to make monthly payments of just over $22,000 directly to FAME. ***

We think that the able district judge may have been misled on the security interest issue by the failure of the parties to develop the precise rights of First Hartford under the March 14, 1980, lease, including (by incorporation of the original 1972 lease) the option to purchase for $1. *** If FAME had re-leased the property to Waterville Industries on March 14, 1980, without continuing the purchase option, our line of analysis would be different and FAME's current position could be weaker.

*** We note also that EPA has recently adopted regulations declaring that the security interest exception applies to "title held pursuant to lease financing transactions."

---

[4] See H.R.Rep. No. 172, pt. 1, 96th Cong., 1st Sess. 36 (1979) (an "owner" does not include a person who "hold[s] title ... in connection with a lease financing arrangement under the appropriate banking laws, rules or regulations"); *In re Bergsoe Metal Corp.*, 910 F.2d 668 (9th Cir.1991) (lease financing is a security interest under CERCLA).

40 C.F.R. § 300.1100(b)(1). These regulations do not govern for they were not in effect at the time of the events in this case. ***

The more difficult problem for FAME is its status under the exemption *after* October 6, 1981, when First Hartford ceased operation. Thereafter—precisely when is less certain—First Hartford presumably lost its rights under the lease and, as sometimes happens to security holders, FAME's titular ownership became real and no longer merely a security interest. However, we think such a maturation of ownership does not divest the owner of protection under CERCLA's security interest exception so long as the owner proceeds within a reasonable time to divest itself of ownership. Why this is so, and how FAME then fares under this reading of the statute, are separate questions which we address in that order.

Admittedly, CERCLA itself does not explicitly provide any period for divestiture after the collapse of a financing arrangement, but such a "safety zone" seems to us implicit in the statute. Were it otherwise, every sale and lease-back arrangement would subject the lender-lessor to the risk of sudden CERCLA liability whenever the lessee, by default or otherwise, lost its contractual rights to regain full ownership. So long as the lender-lessor makes a reasonably prompt effort to divest itself of its unwelcome ownership, we think continued coverage under the exception serves its basic policy: to protect bona fide lenders and to avoid imposing liability on "owners" who are not in fact seeking to profit from the investment opportunity normally presented by prolonged ownership. ***

EPA has followed the same path in its new regulations. *** Again, we have reached our own conclusion independently of the regulations, which technically do not apply to pre-adoption events. Certainly EPA's choice of 12 months for its safe harbor cannot govern this case, for such bright-line rules make sense only when known to affected parties in advance. Instead, we think the question is whether, under all the circumstances, FAME acted reasonably promptly to divest itself of ownership once the lease arrangement ended.

The earliest time that one would expect a security holder to start to divest itself of unwelcome ownership would ordinarily be when the security holder obtained full title free of serious encumbrances. So long as First Hartford held a lease with an option to buy for $1, FAME was still only a security holder protected by the exception. *** Not until July 15, 1982, did First Hartford and FAME enter into a stipulation that "affirmed that title to the real property was vested solely in [FAME's predecessor] and terminated the rights of First Hartford and First Hartford Realty in the various leases." Even then First Hartford was given until October 15, 1982, to seek a buyer for the property.

Thus, it was only after October 15, 1982, that FAME was finally in a position to give an unclouded and unencumbered title to a purchaser. Within six months of that date, FAME had contracted (in late March 1983) with an auctioneer to sell the property. After an auction, FAME agreed (in September 1983) to sell the property to MKY Realty, the successful auction bidder, and it conveyed title not long afterwards (in November 1983). Based on this sequence of events, we think it is apparent that FAME made diligent efforts to dispose of the property in a timely fashion: until October 1981, FAME had only a security interest; a quarrel over First Hartford's interest delayed matters until October 1982; and within six months thereafter, FAME had placed the property on the market leading to its sale within the year.

III.

In conclusion, we are satisfied based on the record that FAME is fully protected by the security interest exception. Waterville Industries complains bitterly in its brief that FAME sold it the property through MKY Realty without making full disclosure of the hazardous wastes or of notices of violation sent to FAME, and there is separate litigation between the parties on this subject. But the right of contribution under CERCLA is a statutory one that here turns solely on FAME's status as an "owner," a status defeated by the security interest exception. Waterville Industries' other claims against FAME, whatever their nature or merits, are a matter for another forum.

* * *

NOTES

1. The First Circuit again held a lender exempt from CERCLA liability in *Northeast Doran v. Key Bank Of Maine,* 15 F.3d 1 (1st Cir. 1994), a factually amusing case. In *Northeast Doran,* Key Bank foreclosed on its mortgagor's property, made plans to auction it off, and commissioned a site assessment, which indicated potential groundwater contamination. Although Key Bank received the assessment results three days before the auction, it signed a purchase and sale agreement with Doran—a company that had been leasing and occupying the property for the past year and one-half—without disclosing the site assessment results. Only when Doran applied to Key Bank for financing to purchase the property did the bank reveal the site assessment results. Doran made other financing arrangements, purchased the site, and then notified the Maine Department of Environmental Protection of the potential contamination at the site. DEP sued Doran as the "owner," and Doran in turn sued Key Bank.

Relying substantially on its *Waterville Industries* decision, the First Circuit held:
> Doran does not allege, nor could it on the record, that Key's effort to divest itself of title to the property was anything less than "reasonably prompt." More importantly, in support of its allegation that Key held the property for a purpose *other than* as security for its mortgage on the property, Doran cites only the existence of the assessment, and Key's withholding of its results. Standing alone, however, the existence of a site assessment, even one which reveals the existence of possible environmental contamination and which is concealed from the eventual purchaser, is insufficient to remove a holder from the "security interest holder" exception in section 9601(20)(A). ***

Id. at 3. As in *Waterville Industries,* the court noted that the EPA's lender liability rule—"though prospective and not dispositive in the instance case"—was consistent with the court's ruling. *Id.* n.1. *See also United States v. McLamb*, 5 F.3d 69 (4th Cir. 1993).

3. Congress Amends the Act

Congress initiated the third—and current—phase in the convoluted history of lender liability under CERCLA by amending the statute to conform to the views articulated in the invalidated EPA rule. Asset Conservation, Lender Liability, and Deposit Insurance Protection Act of 1996, Pub. L. No. 104-208 (1996). The Act amends the definition of owner and operator to clarify the circumstances under which "participation in management" exceeds the scope of the secured creditors' exemption. The amended definition indicates that most routine lending activities would not constitute such participation in management, and that a lender becomes subject to CERCLA liability only when it "actually participates in the management or operational affairs of a vessel or facility." It effectively nullifies *Fleet Factors* insofar as it states that the capacity to influence or the unexercised right to control operations do not constitute participation in management, absent actual participation in management or operational affairs. Finally, the new provisions protect not only secured creditors, but also, for the first time, fiduciaries. See new § 107(n).

In the first reported decision addressing the amended lender liability language, the Sixth Circuit stated: "A comparison of the amendments to CERCLA relevant here and the EPA 'lender liability rule' *** makes it clear that these amendments effectively codify the EPA rule." *Kelley v. Tiscornia*, 104 F.3d 361 (Table), 1996 WL 732323 (6th Cir. Dec. 19, 1996).

12 STATUTORY DEFENSES TO CERCLA LIABILITY

Notwithstanding the tremendous volume of litigation that has arisen under CERCLA, the central statutory provisions are relatively straightforward, particularly in comparison with the other principal environmental laws. This is especially notable in the liability provisions: § 107(a) lists the categories of parties liable for response costs and natural resource damages; and § 107(b) sets forth three defenses to such liability. The language of § 107(b) is as follows:

There shall be no liability under subsection (a) of this section for a person otherwise liable who can establish by a preponderance of the evidence that the release or threat of release of a hazardous substance and the damages resulting therefrom were caused solely by—

(1) an act of God;

(2) an act of war;

(3) an act or omission of a third party other than an employee or agent of the defendant, or than one whose act or omission occurs in connection with a contractual relationship, existing directly or indirectly, with the defendant ***, if the defendant establishes by a preponderance of the evidence that (a) he exercised due care with respect to the hazardous substance concerned, taking into consideration the characteristics of such hazardous substance, in light of all relevant facts and circumstances, and (b) he took precautions against foreseeable acts or omissions of any such third party and the consequences that could foreseeably result from such acts or omissions; or

(4) any combination of the foregoing paragraphs.

In addition, the 1986 amendments provided a fourth statutory defense, known as the innocent landowner defense, which is a variation of the third-party defense. This chapter addresses first the third-party defense set forth in § 107(b)(3), and then the innocent landowner defense created by a combination of §§ 101(35) and 107(b)(3).

A. The Third-Party Defense

In the first decade of CERCLA litigation, PRPs' attempts to invoke the third-party defense were summarily rejected. *See, e.g., State of New York v. Shore Realty Corp.*,

759 F.2d 1032 (2d Cir. 1985) (in chapter 10.B). In the following two cases, however, the Second Circuit breathed new life into the defense. Keep in mind as you read these cases that it remains extremely difficult for a PRP to avoid liability based on the third-party defense.

WESTWOOD PHARMACEUTICALS, INC. V. NATIONAL FUEL GAS DISTRIBUTION CORP.
964 F.2d 85 (2d Cir. 1992)

Before FEINBERG, TIMBERS, and MINER, Circuit Judges.
TIMBERS, Circuit Judge.

Appellant Westwood Pharmaceuticals, Inc. (Westwood) appeals from an order *** denying Westwood's motion for reconsideration of that portion of an order *** denying Westwood's motion for summary judgment on its claim that appellee National Fuel Gas Distribution Corporation (National Fuel) is liable in Westwood's action brought pursuant to §§ 107(a)(2), 113(f) and 113(g) of the Comprehensive Environmental Response, Compensation and Liability Act (CERCLA).

On October 14, 1988, Westwood commenced this action against National Fuel seeking to recover costs incurred in investigating and remedying chemical contamination at certain premises in Buffalo it had purchased from National Fuel's predecessor in interest, Iroquois Gas Corporation (Iroquois). Westwood moved for partial summary judgment on the liability issues presented by its CERCLA action. After the district court denied Westwood's motion for summary judgment, Westwood moved for reconsideration of its order. The district court on June 19, 1991 denied Westwood's motion for reconsideration. On August 6, 1991, at the request of Westwood, the district court amended its order to include certification for an interlocutory appeal pursuant to 28 U.S.C. § 1292(b). On November 6, 1991, a panel of our Court granted Westwood's petition for leave to appeal pursuant to § 1292(b).

On appeal, Westwood contends (1) that the mere existence of a contractual relationship, without more, between it and National Fuel precludes National Fuel from invoking the third-party defense of CERCLA §107(b)(3); and, alternatively, (2) that CERCLA § 101(35)(C) precludes National Fuel from raising the third-party defense provided for in § 107(b)(3). For the reasons that follow, we affirm the order of the district court denying Westwood's motion for reconsideration of the district court's earlier order that denied Westwood's motion for summary judgment on the issue of National Fuel's liability under CERCLA.

I.
* * *

The site which is the subject matter of this action was purchased in 1925 by Iroquois. Iroquois conducted gas manufacturing and storage operations on the land through 1951.   For several years thereafter it continued to use the site for gas compression and storage.   During these operations Iroquois placed or used various underground pipes and structures at the site.   In 1968, Iroquois demolished certain structures on the northeast portion of the site, but left other structures on the site standing.

Iroquois sold the site to Westwood in 1972 for $60,100.   Westwood demolished the remaining structures on the site and constructed a warehouse on the southern portion of the site.   During these construction activities and associated soil testing, Westwood discovered various subsurface contaminants.

In the instant action Westwood seeks to recover the response costs—the costs of cleaning up the contaminants—for which it claims National Fuel is liable.   Westwood's complaint alleged claims pursuant to CERCLA as stated above, and related common law claims of public nuisance, private nuisance, and restitution.   CERCLA § 107(a)(2) makes "any person who at the time of disposal of any hazardous substance owned or operated any facility at which hazardous substances were disposed of" liable for the response costs incurred by another.   "Facility" is defined in § 101(9) as "any site or area where a hazardous substance has been deposited, stored, disposed of, or placed, or otherwise come to be located."

In its answer to Westwood's complaint, National Fuel alleged various affirmative defenses.   *** [T]he district court, among other things, granted National Fuel's motion to dismiss Westwood's private nuisance and restitution claims; denied National Fuel's motion with respect to Westwood's CERCLA and public nuisance claims; and denied Westwood's motion for summary judgment which asserted that National Fuel was liable on its CERCLA claim.

The district court held that National Fuel had raised a triable issue of fact by contending that, under the "third-party defense" of CERCLA § 107(b)(3), it was not liable on Westwood's CERCLA claims.   Section 107(b)(3) provides in relevant part:

> "There shall be no liability under subsection (a) of this section for a person otherwise liable who can establish by a preponderance of the evidence that the release or threat of release of a hazardous substance and the damages resulting therefrom were caused solely by—
>
> .   .   .   .   .   .
>
> (3) an act or omission of a third party other than an employee or agent of the defendant, or than one whose act or omission occurs *in connection with a contractual relationship*, existing directly or indirectly, with the defendant ... if the defendant establishes by a preponderance of the evidence that (a) he exercised due care with respect to the hazardous substance concerned, taking into consideration the characteristics of such hazardous substance, in light of all relevant facts and circumstances, and (b) he took precautions against foreseeable acts or omissions of any such third party and the consequences that could foreseeably result from such acts or omissions...." (emphasis added).

National Fuel did not dispute the fact that its 1972 sales contract with Westwood was a "contractual relationship," since CERCLA § 101(35)(A) provides that "[t]he term 'contractual relationship', for the purpose of section 9607(b)(3) of this title includes, but is not limited to, land contracts, deeds or other instruments transferring title or possession...." National Fuel asserted, however, that Westwood's construction activities were not undertaken by Westwood "in connection with" the contractual relationship between National Fuel and Westwood. Furthermore, National Fuel asserted that, if in fact it placed hazardous substances at the site, it exercised due care with respect to such substances and took precautions against the foreseeable acts or omissions of third persons. Specifically, National Fuel asserted that any such substances that were not eventually removed from the premises for off-site use or disposal were left inside secure subsurface receptacles. Moreover, National Fuel asserted that the structural integrity of these subsurface receptacles left at the site would not have been breached and therefore hazardous substances would not have escaped but for the unforeseeable construction activities of Westwood.

The district court held that the phrase "in connection with" in § 107(b)(3) requires that there be some relationship between the disposal/releasing activity and the contract with the defendant for a defendant to be barred from raising the third-party defense. Since it held that National Fuel had raised a triable issue of fact by contending that Westwood was the sole cause of the release or threatened release of hazardous substances at the site, the court denied Westwood's motion for summary judgment which asserted that National Fuel was liable under CERCLA § 107(a)(2).

The district court *** reaffirmed its holding that the mere existence of a contractual relationship does not preclude a former owner from invoking the third-party defense, and rejected Westwood's contention that § 101(35)(C) forecloses a prior owner like National Fuel from asserting the third-party defense provided for in § 107(b)(3). ***

* * *

III.

The district court held that the phrase "in connection with" requires that there be some relationship between the disposal/releasing activity and the contract with the defendant for the defendant to be barred from raising the third-party defense of § 107(b)(3). The court stated that to hold otherwise would render the language "in connection with" superfluous, a result generally at odds with an accepted principle of statutory construction.

Other cases considering this or similar questions also have indicated that something more than a mere contractual relationship is required. In *United States v. Hooker Chemicals & Plastics Corp.*, 680 F.Supp. 546 (W.D.N.Y.1988), the court held that defendants' contractual relationship with the present landowner—defendants had deeded the land to the City—precluded defendant from raising the third-party defense of § 107(b)(3) since "[defendant] was able to control the acts of these subsequent purchasers because of the nature of its relationship with these defendants in this case." In *Shapiro v. Alexanderson*, 743 F.Supp. 268 (S.D.N.Y.1990), the court held that the contractual relationship clause of § 107(b)(3) does not embrace "all acts by a third party with any contractual relationship with a defendant. Such a construction would render the language 'in connection with' mere surplusage." "The act or omission must occur in a context so that there is a connection between the acts and the contractual relationship." In *Shapiro*, the court described the "classic scenario" in which a landowner would be precluded from asserting a § 107(b)(3) defense: when the third party is operating a landfill pursuant to a contract with the owner.

We agree with the district court that a landowner is precluded from raising the third-party defense only if the contract between the landowner and the third party somehow is connected with the handling of hazardous substances. The result would be the same if the contract allows the landowner to exert some control over the third party's actions so that the landowner fairly can be held liable for the release or threatened release of hazardous substances caused solely by the actions of the third party. The mere existence of a contractual relationship between the owner of land on which hazardous substances are or have been disposed and a third party whose act or omission was the *sole* cause of the release or threatened release of such hazardous substances into the environment does not foreclose the owner of the land from escaping liability, provided that the owner satisfies the additional requirements of § 107(b)(3)(a) and (b).

* * *

V.

To summarize:

We hold that the district court correctly held that the phrase "in connection with a contractual relationship" in CERCLA § 107(b)(3) requires more than the mere existence of a contractual relationship between the owner of land on which hazardous substances are or have been disposed of and a third party whose act or omission was the sole cause of the release or threatened release of such hazardous substances into the environment, for the landowner to be barred from raising the third-party defense provided for in that section. In order for the landowner to be barred from raising the third-party defense under such circumstances, the contract between the landowner and the third party must either relate to the hazardous substances or allow the landowner to exert some element of control over the third party's activities.

* * *

NOTES

1. Should the reasoning and holding of *Westwood Pharmaceuticals* extend to landowners who conduct no activities at the site, but lease it to others, and a release occurs as a result of the tenants' activities? Prior to the Second Circuit's decision, the Fourth Circuit held that the existence of the contractual relationship between landowner and tenant/lessee precludes the availability of the third-party defense. *See, e.g., United States v. Monsanto Co.,* 858 F.2d 160, 169(4th Cir. 1988), *cert. denied,* 490 U.S. 1106 (1989).

2. In addition to proving the absence of a contractual relationship, a defendant seeking to prevail on the third-party defense must also prove that the release was caused *solely* by the third party. Courts have rigorously applied the "caused solely" element of

the defense, requiring that the defendant prove "the complete absence of causation" on his part. *Id.*, 858 F.2d at 168.

3. In several cases, the fate of a PRP's asserted third-party defense has turned on whether or not it exercised the requisite "due care" with respect to the hazardous substances involved. The following case is as generous as any, from the perspective of parties asserting the third-party defense, in finding due care.

STATE OF NEW YORK V. LASHINS ARACDE CO.
91 F.3d 353 (2d Cir. 1996)

Before MAHONEY, WALKER, and CALABRESI, Circuit Judges.
MAHONEY, Circuit Judge.

Plaintiffs-appellants-cross-appellees the State of New York and Thomas C. Jorling, as trustee of the State of New York's natural resources (collectively "New York"), appeal from a final judgment entered June 20, 1995 in the United States District Court for the Southern District of New York, Charles L. Brieant, *Judge*, that granted summary judgment to defendants-appellees-cross-appellants Lashins Arcade Company and Lashins Arcade Corporation (collectively "Lashins") and denied New York's motion for summary judgment in this action brought under § 107(a) of the Comprehensive Environmental Response, Compensation and Liability Act of 1980, *** ("CERCLA"), *** [and state law claims]. The complaint sought, *inter alia*, damages for costs New York incurred investigating and cleaning up the release of tetrachloroethene, or perchloroethylene ("PCE"), and its breakdown compounds, trichloroethene ("TCE"), 1,2-dichloroethene ("DCE"), and vinyl chloride, into the groundwater in the vicinity of the Bedford Village Shopping Arcade (the "Arcade") in Westchester County, New York. PCE is a chemical used as a solvent in dry cleaning operations.

The district court awarded Lashins summary judgment based upon the third-party defense provided by § 107(b)(3) of CERCLA, and dismissed the action "as against the Lashins defendants." ***

* * *

We affirm the judgment of the district court.

Background

This appeal involves the release of hazardous substances at the Arcade, which resulted in groundwater contamination in the area. The Arcade, a 6,800 square foot one-story building housing six retail stores, was built in 1955, and was owned by Holbrook B. Cushman until his death in 1966. The property was then held in trust by Cushman's widow, Beatrice Cushman, and the Bank of New York until 1972. Cushman leased a store in the Arcade to Astrologo from about 1958 to 1963, where Astrologo operated a dry cleaning business. The store was next leased to defendant Rocco Tripodi (with whom defendant Bedford Village Cleaners, Inc. is affiliated) in 1963, who maintained the dry cleaning business at the Arcade until 1971. During this period, Tripodi dumped powdered wastes from his dry cleaning machines, which contained the volatile organic compound ("VOC") PCE, on the ground outside the Arcade behind his store. In December 1971, Tripodi moved his dry cleaning business out of the Arcade, and no other dry cleaning establishment has operated there since that time. In November 1972, the trust sold the Arcade to Miriam Baygell, who owned the property until her death in 1977, when it was inherited by her husband, Milton Baygell.

In 1978, the Westchester County Department of Health (the "WCDOH") conducted a countywide survey regarding possible groundwater contamination by VOCs. The survey found elevated VOC levels in the hamlets of Katonah, Armonk, and Bedford Village. Further sampling of private wells in Bedford Village conducted by the WCDOH in 1979 revealed groundwater contamination in an area southeast of the Arcade. These samples contained high concentrations of PCE and its breakdown compounds, TCE and DCE. The WCDOH issued "boil water" notices to affected homeowners.

In 1982, the New York State Department of Environmental Conservation (the "NYSDEC") authorized state funds for an investigation and remediation of the groundwater problem at the Arcade and the nearby Hunting Ridge Shopping Mall pursuant to *** the New York Environmental Conservation Law. The investigations conducted from 1982 to 1986 revealed fluctuating levels of VOC contamination in the wells adjacent to the Arcade. A "Phase I" investigation, completed in June 1983 by the Wehran Engineering Company ("Wehran"), reported that the highest level of contamination in the Arcade was found in the area formerly occupied by the dry cleaning establishment.

Following the Phase I investigation, the "Bedford Village Wells" site was listed on the New York State Registry of Inactive Hazardous Waste Disposal Sites (the "Registry"). *** This site was described as including the Arcade, the Hunting Ridge Shopping Mall, an Exxon gasoline station, the Bedford Theater Building, and an apartment building adjacent to the theater. In December 1987, the Arcade was separated from the Hunting Ridge Shopping Mall, and each was thereafter designated as a separate site in the Registry.

By letter dated October 12, 1983 and addressed to Miriam Baygell (who by that time was deceased), the NYSDEC advised that it intended to conduct a Phase II investigation of the Bedford Village Wells, and also stated that Ms. Baygell had the right to conduct such an investigation herself. Milton Baygell did not respond to this letter, which he may never have received. In any event, Wehran conducted the Phase II fieldwork for the NYSDEC commencing in 1984, and reported its final conclusions in June 1985. During this period, the WCDOH requested in a letter to Milton Baygell dated March 6, 1984 that he install a granular activated carbon ("GAC") filter in the well supplying the Arcade with water to remedy the VOC problem; Baygell installed the GAC filter in May 1985.

The final Phase II Report concluded that VOC contamination persisted at the Arcade site. ***

In 1986, the United States Environmental Protection Agency (the "EPA") joined with the WCDOH to investigate the Arcade. Their joint surveys confirmed that VOCs persisted in three private wells at the Bedford Village Wells site, and low VOC concentrations also appeared east and southeast of the Arcade in water supplies that had previously been uncontaminated. In view of this problem, the NYSDEC requested and obtained approval from the EPA for a Remedial Investigation/Feasibility Study ("RI/FS") of the entire Bedford Village Wells site. The NYSDEC retained Dvirka and Bartilucci Consulting Engineers ("Dvirka and Bartilucci") to perform the RI/FS in December 1986, and the firm began its field work the following summer.

Meanwhile, in January 1987, Milton Baygell entered into negotiations with Lashins for the sale of the Arcade after a real estate broker contacted Lashins about the property. In the course of these negotiations, Baygell's attorney, Donald Mazin, wrote Lashins' attorney, Henry Hocherman, on March 20, 1987 to inform him that "there are chemicals in the ground being treated by ultra violet and activated carbon machines situated in the rear of the building to clean the water. Chemicals have to be replaced approximately every 8-9 months." Prior to executing the contract of sale, Lashins contacted the Arcade's water service contractor, Environmental Recovery Co., who advised Lashins that the well on the premises had a water filter, but assured Lashins that the filter was "routine" and had been installed in response to an area-wide groundwater contamination problem, and that the suspected source of the contamination was a nearby Exxon gas station.

In addition, Lashins states that it contacted the Town of Bedford prior to purchasing the Shopping Arcade to determine whether there were any violations or other present or past problems with the property, and was assured that there were none. Lashins further asserts that it interviewed the Arcade's tenants, all of whom spoke enthusiastically about the property. New York contends, however, that Lashins made no inquiry concerning the groundwater contamination (other than the discussion with Environmental Recovery Co.) prior to purchasing the Arcade. In any event, Lashins executed a contract of sale with Baygell on April 6, 1987, and the transaction closed on June 26, 1987.

Lashins claims that at the time of the closing, it was unaware that the NYSDEC was conducting an administrative proceeding involving the Arcade, or that it had contracted with a firm to conduct the RI/FS concerning the Bedford Village Wells site. Baygell did not transmit any NYSDEC notices to Lashins, no public notice was issued, and the Arcade tenants, the Town of Bedford, and the local bank were allegedly unaware of the situation.

Lashins was first informed that the NYSDEC was conducting a formal investigation of the Arcade by letter dated August 13, 1987. That letter advised Lashins of the impending RI/FS requested by the NYSDEC, and stated that NYSDEC representatives intended to enter the Arcade property "for the purpose of drilling, installing and operating groundwater monitoring wells and taking samples of soil, septage, surface water, and groundwater."

New York also informed Milton Baygell of the RI/FS by letter dated September 18, 1987. ***

After purchasing the Arcade, Lashins maintained the existing GAC filter and took water samples which were analyzed by a laboratory for VOC contamination on a semi-annual basis. It also instructed all tenants to avoid discharging any hazardous substances into the waste and septic systems, subsequently incorporated this requirement into the tenant leases, and conducted periodic inspections of the tenants' premises to assure compliance with this obligation.

The RI/FS was completed in February 1990. It concluded, *inter alia*, that the contamination in the affected wells,

"although unconfirmed, most probably originated from a former dry cleaning establishment located in the Shopping Arcade.

... The extent of significant ground water contamination appeared to be limited to the area of and immediately contiguous to the Shopping Arcade....

....

... [A]lthough it appears that levels of ground water contamination have been generally declining, preliminary analysis of the data obtained from 1982 to 1986 does not indicate a clear trend of declining contamination for all wells. Based on this information, it was suspected that sources (including contaminated soils) may be continuing to release organic chemicals to the surrounding environment."

The NYSDEC issued a Record of Decision on March 30, 1990 setting forth its plan to abate and remedy the actual and threatened release of hazardous substances from the Arcade. Three remedial measures were suggested: (1) installation of GAC filters (which were already in place) for the affected homes and businesses; (2) a new source of water supply; and (3) re-charge of the contaminated ground water by a "pump and treat" system. Further studies were conducted to implement this Record of Decision. ***

* * *
Discussion
* * *

As an initial matter, there is no dispute that New York has established a *prima facie* case against Lashins under § 9607(a) for recovery of expenses incurred investigating and cleaning up the release of PCE at the Arcade. ***

Since Lashins is a current owner of the Shopping Arcade, it is a potentially responsible defendant under § 9607(a)(1), notwithstanding the fact that it did not own the Arcade at the time of disposal of the hazardous substances. Thus, Lashins may be held strictly liable for New York's response costs unless it can satisfy one of CERCLA's affirmative defenses. We now turn to Lashins' claim that it may avoid such liability under the third-party defense of § 9607(b)(3).

Section 9607(b)(3) provides an affirmative defense for a party who can establish that the offending "release ... of a hazardous substance and the damages resulting therefrom were caused solely by ... an act or omission of a third party," provided that: (1) the third party is not "one whose act or omission occurs in connection with a contractual relationship, existing directly or indirectly, with the defendant," (2) the defendant "took precautions against foreseeable acts or omissions of any such third party and the consequences that could foreseeably result from such acts or omissions," and (3) the defendant "exercised due care with respect to the hazardous substance concerned, taking into consideration the characteristics of such hazardous substance, in light of all relevant facts and circumstances."

The offending release here was clearly caused by third parties (Tripodi, Bedford Village Cleaners, Inc., Astrologo, and (New York contends) Milton Baygell). Although paragraphs (1)-(3) of § 9607(b) speak exclusively in the singular, referring to events and damages "caused solely by—(1) *an* act of God; (2) *an* act of war; [or] (3) *an* act or omission of a third party," § 9607(b) (emphasis added), paragraph (4) of § 9607(b) refers to "any combination of the foregoing paragraphs." We read paragraph (4) as allowing consideration of multiple causes within, as well as among, the several preceding paragraphs. Thus, in our view, damage that resulted from an earthquake and a subsequent flood would fall within paragraph (1) of § 9607(b), and damages caused by a number of acts by a single third party (as typically occurs when pollution is caused by a course of conduct), or a number of acts by several third parties (as in this case), would fall within paragraph (3). ***

In this case, the only one of the allegedly offending third parties with whom Lashins had a contractual relationship was Milton Baygell. Further, Baygell's allegedly offending conduct did not "occur in connection with a contractual relationship ... with [Lashins]" within the meaning of § 9607(b)(3), and therefore Lashins may not be disqualified from the protection afforded by § 9607(b)(3) because of its contractual relationship with Baygell.

This conclusion is mandated by *** *Westwood Pharmaceuticals, Inc. v. National Fuel Gas Distribution Corp.*, 964 F.2d 85 (2d Cir.1992).

In *Westwood*, the seller of the contaminated site sought exoneration from the buyer's conduct, whereas in this case the buyer seeks exoneration from the seller's activities, but this is surely an immaterial distinction in terms of the *Westwood* rationale. ("[A] landowner is precluded from raising the third-party defense only if the contract between the landowner and the third party somehow is connected with the handling of hazardous substances."). The straightforward sale of the Arcade by Baygell to Lashins clearly did not "relate to hazardous substances" or vest Lashins with authority "to exert some element of control over [Baygell's] activities" within the contemplation of our ruling in *Westwood*.

The second requirement for the successful assertion of a third-party defense demands that the defendant shall have taken adequate precautions against actions by the third party that would lead to a release of hazardous waste. Given that the last release in the instant case happened more than fifteen years before Lashins' purchase of the

Arcade, there was obviously nothing Lashins could have done to prevent actions leading to a release.

Thus, the resolution of this appeal turns upon the validity of the district court's ruling that Lashins was entitled to summary judgment on the question whether Lashins "exercised due care with respect to the hazardous substance concerned ... in the light of all relevant facts and circumstances" within the meaning of § 9607(b)(3). This requirement is not defined in the statute. CERCLA's legislative history, however, provides some guidance: "[T]he defendant must demonstrate that he took all precautions with respect to the particular waste that a similarly situated reasonable and prudent person would have taken in light of all relevant facts and circumstances." H.R.Rep. No. 1016, 96th Cong., 2d Sess., pt. 1, at 34 (1980). Further, "due care 'would include those steps necessary to protect the public from a health or environmental threat.' " *United States v. A & N Cleaners & Launderers, Inc.*, 854 F.Supp. 229, 238 (S.D.N.Y.1994) (quoting H.R.Rep. No. 253, 99th Cong., 2d Sess. 187 (1986) U.S.Code Cong. & Admin.News 1986, 2835); *see also Kerr-McGee Chem. Corp.*, 14 F.3d at 325 & n. 3 (due care not established when no affirmative measures taken to control site); *Lincoln Properties v. Higgins*, 823 F.Supp. 1528, 1543-44 (E.D.Cal.1992) (due care exercised where defendant removed contaminated wells).

Against this background, New York contends that Lashins inadequately investigated the contamination problem before buying the Arcade despite being notified about it, and after its purchase "did *nothing* to contain, control or clean up the pollution except to continue to maintain a filter on its own property."[1] New York points to cases such as *A & N Cleaners* and *Kerr-McGee Chemical Corp.* where § 9607(a) liability was imposed because the defendant did not take active measures to address a hazardous waste problem, and adds that *Kerr-McGee Chemical Corp.* and *United States v. DiBiase Salem Realty Trust*, Civ. A. No. 91-11028-MA, 1993 WL 729662 (D.Mass. Nov. 19, 1993), establish that the "due care" standard does not permit a landowner to remain passive simply because public environmental authorities are addressing a hazardous waste situation.

We are not persuaded by New York's arguments, nor by the authorities that New York cites to us. The pertinent language of § 9607(b)(3) focuses the "due care" inquiry upon "all relevant facts and circumstances" of the case at hand. In this case, the RI/FS by Dvirka and Bartilucci had been commissioned six months before Lashins purchased the Arcade, and before Lashins had even learned that the Arcade was for sale. It would have been pointless to require Lashins to commission a parallel investigation once it acquired the Arcade and became more fully aware of the environmental problem. Pressed at oral argument as to what Lashins might appropriately have been required to

---

[1]There appears to be no serious dispute that in addition, Lashins regularly took water samples and had them analyzed by a laboratory for VOC contamination, instructed all tenants to avoid discharging hazardous substances into the waste and septic systems, incorporated this requirement into the tenant leases, and conducted periodic inspections to assure compliance with this obligation.

do at that juncture, New York contended that Lashins was obligated to pay some or all of the cost of the RI/FS undertaken at the behest of the EPA and the NYSDEC.

This is surely an anomalous proposal. Response costs are assessed when there is liability under § 9607(a). It is counterintuitive to suppose that a defendant is required to pay some or all of those response costs in order to establish the affirmative defense provided by § 9607(b)(3) to liability under § 9607(a), thereby rendering the affirmative defense partly or entirely academic.

Nor do we discern any policy reasons for imposing such a rule. We agree with *HRW Systems, Inc. v. Washington Gas Light Co.*, 823 F.Supp. 318 (D.Md.1993), that the "due care" mandate of § 9607(b)(3) does not "impose a duty on a purchaser of land to investigate prior to purchase, in order to determine whether there is pollution on the land caused by someone with whom the purchaser is not in contractual privity." *Id.* at 349. No claim is made that Lashins' purchase of the Arcade deprived New York of any remedy available to it against any predecessor owners or operators under § 9607(a); consent decrees were in fact entered against Tripodi and Astrologo. It is surely the policy of CERCLA to impose liability upon parties responsible for pollution, rather than the general taxpaying public, but this policy does not mandate precluding a "due care" defense by imposing a rule that is tantamount to absolute liability for ownership of a site containing hazardous waste.

Finally, the cases cited by New York do not require the negation of Lashins' "due care" defense. None involved a defendant who played no role in the events that led to the hazardous waste problem and came on the scene after public authorities were well along in a program of investigation and remediation. *Kerr-McGee Chemical Corp.* involved a landowner who was aware of the environmental problem and made no attempt to address it after preliminary investigative efforts by federal and state authorities provided notice of the contamination. *See* 14 F.3d at 325 & n. 3. In *A & N Cleaners*, the defendant landowners' sublessee (who subsequently became a lessee) was operating the offending dry cleaning establishment throughout the entire period of the defendants' ownership. *See* 854 F.Supp. at 232. In *DiBiase Salem Realty Trust*, a portion of the pollution occurred after the landowner commenced ownership, *see* 1993 WL 729662 at *1, and the landowner did nothing to address the problem after becoming aware of the hazardous wastes as a result of preliminary investigations by state authorities, *see id.* at *7. ***

In sum, we perceive no basis for reversal of the district court's award of summary judgment to Lashins on the basis that Lashins satisfied its obligation to "exercise[ ] due care" with respect to the Arcade within the meaning of § 9607(b)(3). In so ruling, we proclaim no broad rule of exemption from the liability imposed by § 9607(a). Rather, mindful of the mandate of § 9607(b)(3) that the "due care" inquiry focus upon "all relevant facts and circumstances" of the case presented for decision, we conclude that Lashins' "due care" obligation did not require it to go beyond the measures that it took to address the contamination problem at the Arcade, and to supplant, duplicate, or underwrite the RI/FS previously commissioned by the EPA and NYDESC to address pollution that ensued from activities which occurred more than fifteen years before Lashins purchased the Arcade.

* * *

NOTES

1. Although the Second Circuit cited many cases, it made no reference to perhaps the most well-known Second Circuit CERCLA decision, *State of New York v. Shore Realty Corp.*, 759 F.2d 1032 (2d Cir. 1985) (in chapter 10.B). Are the decisions consistent with one another? After *Westwood Pharmaceuticals* and *Lashins Arcade*, how much precedential value does *Shore Realty* have today?

2. Does it seem "fair"—in the context of the CERCLA liability rules explored in the preceding chapters—that a party may acquire a Superfund site after it has been publicly so identified and, with minimal effort and expenditure, completely avoid liability for the preexisting contamination? If the market value of the shopping center was depressed when Lashins Arcade acquired it—in light of its prior listing on the New York State Registry of Inactive Hazardous Waste Disposal Sites, and the ongoing investigation by the State and, indirectly at least, the EPA—will Lashins Arcade realize any windfall in the increased value of its property due to the state's cleanup efforts (particularly the groundwater "pump and treat" program, which is typically expensive)?

3. The Second Circuit cited with approval the Seventh Circuit's decision in *Kerr-McGee Chemical Corp. v. Lefton Iron & Metal Co.*, 14 F.3d 321 (7th Cir. 1994), which also involved an attempt by the current owner of contaminated property to assert a third-party defense based on the activities of the prior owner. In *Kerr-McGee*, a predecessor of Kerr-McGee used the site from 1927 to 1969 to manufacture wood products, which involved wood treatment using creosote and other hazardous substances, "significant amounts" of which remained at the site when the site was then sold to Lefton Land in 1972—before CERCLA was enacted, and before the site was identified as requiring cleanup. In 1984, Lefton Land transferred title to Lefton Iron.

In 1988, the State of Illinois commenced proceedings to require Kerr-McGee and the Lefton companies to cleanup the site. Kerr-McGee settled, and commenced a cleanup effort expected to exceed $5 million in cost. When Kerr-McGee sued the Lefton companies, they raised the third-party defense. The Seventh Circuit held that the Lefton's could not take advantage of the defense, because they had not demonstrated the necessary due care.

> *** Section 107(b) requires that Lefton Land demonstrate, among other things, that it took precautions to prevent the "threat of release" or other foreseeable consequences arising from the pollution on the site. Lefton Land failed to make such a showing: the evidence at trial showed that although Lefton Land was aware of the wood preservatives on the site, it made no attempt to remove those substances or to take any other positive steps to reduce the threat posed by the creosote. Lefton Land is, therefore,

subject to CERCLA liability. Lefton Iron is also liable. Lefton Iron was also aware of the wood preservatives on the site and made no attempt to remove the polluting chemicals, and this is sufficient to impose CERCLA liability.

Id. at 325.

If a company is seeking to acquire land, and the land is contaminated, is the purchaser better off if the site is already under aggressive state or federal scrutiny than if it is not? If you were advising a client who has picked the "perfect" site for corporate expansion, and you learn that the site is within the boundaries of a National Priorities List site, does *Lashins Arcade* provide the "cover" necessary to acquire the site without incurring CERCLA liability under § 107(a)(1)?

4. Another appellate decision upholding the assertion of the third-party defense is *Redwing Carriers, Inc. v. Saraland Apartments*, 94 F.3d 1489 (11th Cir. 1996). Redwing Carriers operated a trucking terminal at the site in question from 1961 to 1972; its activities contaminated the site with hazardous substances that combined to form a black, tar-like substance. The property changed hands twice in 1971, and in 1973 it was acquired by Saraland Apartments, Ltd., which built an apartment complex on the site. Saraland Apartments, Ltd. first became aware of tar seepage at the site in 1977. In 1984, after tar seepage was also noted by HUD and by residents of the apartment complex, a group of investors bought out the original partners in Saraland Apartments, Ltd. Robert Coit and Roar Company became the limited partners. In 1985 and 1990, Redwing entered into two administrative orders by consent with the EPA requiring it to investigate and clean up the site. Redwing sued, among others, the general partners. The Eleventh Circuit upheld their third-party defense.

> Coit and Roar have satisfied all the elements of this defense. The general partners never had a direct or indirect contractual relationship with either Redwing or Meador Contracting Company—the only two parties whose conduct potentially caused the release or threat of release of hazardous substances at the Saraland Site. Redwing closed its trucking terminal on the property in 1972. Approximately two years later, Meador graded and filled the property while building the apartment complex. Coit and Roar had no contact with these parties when they purchased their partnership interest in Saraland Limited in 1984—12 years after Redwing last buried toxic substances on the site. It is plain that the environmental damage to this property was done long before Coit and Roar ever became partners in Saraland Limited.
>
> The record indicates that since 1984, the general partners have exercised due care towards hazardous substances contaminating the property. A HUD report identified tar seeps on the property in August 1984, and three months later Coit approved a maintenance plan to remove the seeps. In April and May of 1985, the EPA conducted its preliminary investigation of the Site. Two months later, the EPA entered into its first consent order with Redwing requiring Redwing to, among other things, periodically remove tar-like material from the surface of the property.

Thus, less than a year after Coit and Roar became general partners, a program was in place to remedy the tar seeps on the property.

Meanwhile, Coit and Roar have demonstrated they did nothing to exacerbate conditions at the Site. Redwing has identified only two events after 1984—the repaving of the parking lot and the maintenance work on the gas line—that allegedly increased the amount of contaminated soil on the property. As general partners, Coit and Roar approved these projects. Nothing suggests, however, that in repaving the parking lot and repairing the gas line, workers disturbed contaminated soil or otherwise disposed of hazardous substances on the Site. The record supports the general partners' position that they have taken all necessary precautions in addressing a toxic waste problem created almost entirely by Redwing.

Id. at 1508. The general partners might still face liability, however, if the partnership is found liable on remand for some portion of cleanup costs related to the construction work it undertook (building the apartment complex). *Id.* at 1508-09.

5. Already burdened by substantial duties under the Clean Water Act, sewer operators have been facing CERCLA liability for releases of hazardous substances that their users put into the sewer system. Attempts to invoke the third-party defense have met with mixed results.

In *Westfarm Associates v. Washington Suburban Sanitary Commission*, 66 F.3d 669 (4th Cir. 1995), *cert. denied*, 116 S.Ct. 1318 (1996), a trade association of dry cleaners (International Fabricare Institute, or IFI) discharged hazardous substances into the public sewer system operated by the Washington Suburban Sanitary Commission (WSSC) for two Maryland counties. Westfarm, which owned land adjacent to the sewer, discovered contamination that it traced to leaks in the sewer system. Westfarm sued WSSC and the trade association.

The court held that the sewer system was a "facility" under CERCLA § 101(9), and that CERCLA imposes liability for multiple releases: the release into the sewer system by the trade association; and the release out of the sewer system through its passive leaks, in accord with Fourth Circuit precedent under *Nurad, Inc. v. William E. Hooper & Sons Co.*, 966 F.2d 837 (4th Cir. 1992), *cert. denied*, 506 U.S. 940 (1992). The court then evaluated WSSC's third-party defense.

*** We find that WSSC failed to produce sufficient evidence of the "due care" element of the defense.

*** WSSC claims that it presented sufficient evidence from which a reasonable jury could find that it exercised due care and took precautions against foreseeable acts of IFI. WSSC claims that IFI's acts of dumping PCE [perchloroethylene] into the sewers were unforeseeable, and therefore due care did not require WSSC to take any precautions.

As we have previously explained in connection with a landowner's claim that a tenant's waste disposal was unforeseeable, CERCLA does not sanction "willful or negligent blindness." *Monsanto*, 858 F.2d at 169 ***. The undisputed evidence at summary judgment indicated that WSSC knew from inspecting IFI's facility that IFI used PCE and knew that IFI poured hazardous substances into the sewer. In fact, WSSC regulations permitted discharges of certain quantities of toxic organics and other hazardous substances. WSSC was also aware that cracks were present in its sewer. Yet WSSC took no precautions—such as mending the pipese or banning the discharge of toxic organics—against the foreseeable result that hazardous substances such as PCE would be discharged into the sewer. *** WSSC had the power to abate the foreseeable release of PCE, yet failed to exercise that power. In light of such failure, we cannot find that any genuine dispute was created that WSSC exercised due care or took precautions against the foreseeable acts of third parties such as would have entitled it to the "innocent landowner" defense. ***

Id. at 682-83.

In contrast, a different sewer system that also leaked PCE originating from dry cleaner-users satisfied the due care and precautions against foreseeable acts elements of the third-party defense with the following facts.

The County must show that it exercised due care with respect to PCE "in light of all relevant facts and circumstances" and that it took precautions against the "foreseeable acts or omissions" of third parties. In 1983, the California legislature enacted Assembly Bill ("AB") 1803, which required counties to test their wells for PCE and related solvents. The County promptly tested its wells, and upon discovering contamination, it performed videotaped inspections and sealed the casing of Well No. 1. The County subsequently took the contaminated wells out of service and is now destroying them "in a manner intended to prevent the possible flow of contamination through those wells." The County also tested, inspected and sealed joints in the sewer lines near Well No. 1 in an effort to protect the well.

The County has also apparently exercised due care and taken reasonable precautions with respect to its sewer system. The County's sewer lines were built and have been maintained in accordance with industry standards. A County ordinance prohibits the discharge of cleaning solvents into the sewer. None of the dry cleaners ever applied for permission to discharge hazardous substances. Violations of the law are not "foreseeable acts"; thus, the County did take reasonable precautions.

Lincoln Properties, Ltd. v. Higgins, 823 F.Supp. 1528, 1543-44 (E.D. Cal. 1992).

6. Will cases like *Lashins Arcade, Redwing Carriers,* and *Lincoln Properties* be helpful to prior owners or operators in jurisdictions subscribing to *Nurad*, where liability may arise solely from passive disposal occurring during their ownership or operation? Do these cases significantly mitigate the apparent harshness of § 107(a)(1), imposing strict liability on current owners by virtue of being site owners? Do these cases undermine the congressional intent to subject current owners to strict liability under § 107(a)(1)? Do they reduce the significance of the innocent landowner defense (addressed below)?

Consider the thoughts of one commentator:

The dilemma facing courts, as well as governments and property owners, is where to draw the line between what are and what are not a current owner's due care obligations in these Superfund cost recovery cases. Requiring the current owner to conduct or pay entirely for the investigation *and* for the remediation would render the defense worthless or, more accurately, too expensive. However, relieving the current owner of any obligation to investigate and/or take some affirmative steps to control the contamination would obliterate the liability Congress attached to current owners.

Robert Emmet Hernan, *Due and Don't Care Under CERCLA: An Emerging Standard for Current Owners*, 27 Envtl. L. Rep. (Envtl. L. Inst.) 10064 (Feb. 1997).

B. The Innocent Landowner Defense

Before SARA (and before *Westwood Pharmaceuticals* and some of the cases cited therein), it was understood that property purchasers could not utilize the third-party defense where hazardous substances had been placed on the site by previous owners, because the purchase and sale agreement constituted a direct or indirect contractual relationship between the purchaser and the third party. Congress acted to protect such purchasers by enacting the innocent landowner defense as part of the 1986 SARA amendments to CERCLA. The defense appears in the definitions portion of the statute, § 101(35). Congress created the defense by defining the term "contractual relationship," for purposes of the third-party defense, to include "land contracts, deeds or other instruments transferring title or possession," *except* where the requirements of § 101(35)(A)-(C) are satisfied.

The innocent landowner defense potentially applies to three types of current property owners (and probably lessees): non-governmental entities which intentionally acquired the site; non-government entities which acquired it by inheritance or bequest; and governmental entities which acquired the site by escheat or other involuntary transfer, or by means of eminent domain. All such entities must establish that the hazardous substances were placed at the site before they acquired it, § 101(35)(A), and that they satisfy the generally-applicable requirements of the third-party defense, that is, that they exercised due care regarding the hazardous substance concerned, and that they took precautions against foreseeable acts or omissions of third parties. § 107(b)(3)(a) and (b).

In addition, non-governmental entities which intentionally acquired the site must establish that, at they time they acquired the property, they neither knew nor had reason to know of the disposal of hazardous substances at the property. § 101(35)(a)(i). The Act further specifies that, in order to prove such lack of knowledge or reason to know:

*** [T]he defendant must have undertaken, at the time of acquisition, all appropriate inquiry into the previous ownership and uses of the property consistent with good commercial or customary practice in an effort to minimize liability. For purposes of the preceding sentence the court shall take into account any specialized knowledge or experience on the part of the defendant, the relationship of the purchase price to the value of the property if contaminated, commonly known or reasonably ascertainable information about the property, the obviousness of the presence or likely presence of contamination at the property, and the ability to detect such contamination by appropriate inspection.

§ 101(35)(B).

Initially, those seeking to invoke the innocent landowner defense were current property owners who acquired their CERCLA sites in the past, without knowing of the contamination, and now seek to invoke the defense to avoid CERCLA liability.

In at least one, vigorously-litigated case where an already-contaminated site was purchased in 1969 without a site inspection, the court rejected the notion that the absence of an inspection automatically precludes proof of due diligence for purposes of the innocent landowner defense. *United States v. Serafini*, 706 F.Supp. 354 (M.D. Pa. 1988). Ultimately, however, the government persuaded the court that it was not customary practice in Scranton, Pennsylvania in 1969 to purchase property without viewing it, and the government defeated the attempt to invoke the defense. *United States v. Serafini*, 711 F.Supp. 197 (M.D. Pa. 1988), and *United States v. Serafini*, 791 F.Supp. 107 (M.D. Pa. 1990).

A 1991 survey of case law found only two cases in which the innocent landowner defense was upheld. Aaron Gershonowitz and Miguel Padilla, *Superfund's Innocent Landowner Defense: Elusive or Illusory?*, 6 Toxics L. Rep. (BNA) 626 (Oct. 16, 1991). One, *U.S. v. Pacific Hide and Fur Depot, Inc.*, 716 F.Supp. 1341 (D.Idaho 1989), involved children and widows of the owners of a family company, who acquired their ownership interests through inheritance without any knowledge of the potential or actual presence of contamination at the company's site. The other, *International Clinical Laboratories, Inc. v. Stevens,* 1990 WL 43971 (E.D.N.Y.1990), was a cost recovery case by the present owner, who had neither owned nor conducted operations at the site when the contamination occurred but who had nonetheless incurred substantial expenditures for cleanup activities required by the state, against the prior owner and operators who had owned and operated the site when the contamination occurred. The current owner (ICL) had not known of the preexisting contamination when it acquired the site, the purchase price did not suggest the presence of contamination, and the contamination was not visible. And although the site was listed on New York's Inactive Hazardous Waste Disposal Sites list, ICL was unaware of that listing. In holding that ICL was entitled to full reimbursement from the prior owner and operators of the response costs it had incurred, the court stated the ICL satisfied the innocent landowner defense, but that even if it did not, its equitable share of the response costs would be zero.

In light of the due diligence requirement, and the relatively advanced techniques for detecting contamination, the innocent landowner defense is not likely to protect many current purchasers from future CERCLA liability. In fact, the existence of such knowledge focuses "innocent" owners more frequently on the third-party defense than the innocent landowner defense. *See, e.g., Lashins Arcade* and *Kerr-McGee*, excerpted above.

The innocent landowner defense has encouraged many current purchasers to conduct pre-acquisition environmental audits of the property to be acquired. The audits are often performed in the hope of finding no contamination and therefore building a record for future invocation of the innocent landowner defense, should CERCLA problems develop. In practice, the principal effect of these audits has been to detect existing contamination, and enable the buyer and seller to negotiate revised terms and conditions of the acquisition (e.g., reduced purchase price, placement into escrow of portion of purchase price to cover cleanup by buyer, delayed closing with seller conducting cleanup, and additional representations, warranties, and indemnities).

Offering some guidance regarding the elements of an appropriate inquiry by a potential buyer into the environmental conditions of a site are two standards issued by the American Society for Testing and Materials (ASTM) in May 1993. One standard, TRANSACTION SCREEN PROCESS, Standard E.50.02.01 (ASTM 1993), recommends steps to take to determine whether an environmental site assessment is warranted. The function of the transaction screen is to identify the existence of potentially contaminating circumstances, such that further inquiry would be appropriate. The second standard, PHASE I ENVIRONMENTAL SITE ASSESSMENT PROCESS, Standard E.50.02.02 (ASTM 1993), calls for a review of records concerning the site, a physical inspection, interviews with current owners, occupants, and governmental officials, and a report by an environmental professional opining as to the existence of "recognized environmental conditions." Whether courts will deem the preparation of a Phase I Environmental Site Assessment in accordance with the ASTM standard to constitute "all appropriate inquiry" for purposes of the innocent landowner defense (assuming that no contamination is discovered in the assessment) remains to be seen. Will less suffice? Will more be required? Will the nature of the site and the sophistication of the purchaser affect the answer to those questions? *See* CERCLA § 101(35)(B).

Consider *LaSalle National Trust, N.A. v. Schaffner*, 1993 WL 499742 (N.D. Ill. 1993). Chicagoland Laundry and Cleaners ran a dry cleaning operation at a site in Chicago, Illinois from 1969 until 1989. The dry cleaning activity used perchloroethylene, which caused environmental contamination at the site. In 1989, William Levy purchased the site, and then placed it in the LaSalle National Trust. In 1990, Levy commissioned soil tests around known underground storage tanks, which tests revealed the existence of perchloroethylene in the soil and groundwater. Levy then dropped his plans to develop the site, and began the cleanup process. After LaSalle sued Chicagoland for cost recovery, Chicagoland filed third-party claims against Levy, as beneficial owner of LaSalle Trust. Levy asserted the innocent landowner defense, and the court ruled as follows:

> Chicagoland argues that Levy has failed to show, as is his burden, that he made "all appropriate inquiry" prior to purchasing the property. Although it is alleged that Levy hired a consultant for an environmental audit prior to the purchase, there is no evidence that this audit was "consistent with good commercial and customary practices." In fact,

Chicagoland notes, Levy has brought a separate action against that consultant, Versar, Inc., alleging that the audit did not satisfy this standard. More importantly, Chicagoland argues that the report prepared by Versar should have alerted Levy to the potentiality of PCE contamination because it revealed that Chicagoland used PCE and noted staining on the concrete floor where the dry cleaning machines had been.

Versar's pre-purchase Phase I study for Levy indicated that the inspection of the facility "focused on identification of hazardous materials usage and storage practices." According to the report, "[t]he building contains one 1,500 gallon perchloroethylene tank." "The perchloroethylene tank is not diked for spell (sic) containment and a floor drain is located with (sic) 10 feet of the tank. This drain is connected to city sewers. If an uncontrolled release should occur, the drain would be a direct path to the environment." Additionally, "[prior] to using Safety-Kleen [to pick-up PCE sludge and spent PCE filters], the [PCE] waste was disposed of [in] a common refuse dumpster and landfill. The disposal [m]ethod for perchloroethylene used previous to the Safety-Kleen system raises a concern as to the possibility of the Chicagoland Laundry service becoming a potentially responsible party in environmental litigation." Versar also performed a Phase II study for Levy to study known underground gas and oil storage tanks. The Versar Phase II report indicates "[w]hile completing the Phase II work, Versar noted that floors beneath removed dry cleaning machines were stained. These stains probably result from dry cleaning fluid leakáge." Genuine issues of material fact exist with respect to whether or not Levy made "all appropriate inquiry" sufficient to escape liability and whether he should be charged with knowledge of the contamination, precluding the innocent owner exception. Therefore summary judgment will be denied as to Chicagoland's CERCLA claims.

Id. at *7.

Problem #6: PRPs AND DEFENSES

MEMORANDUM

TO: Junior Associate
        Dewey Beatem & Howe

FROM: Senior Partner

RE: Hazmat Airport Site
        Our client: Local Express, Inc.

The personnel committee informs me that you, our newest, youngest, greenest associate, are deeply devoted to environmental law. Here is your earliest (and perhaps only) opportunity to demonstrate your excellence in the area.

Our client, Local Express, Inc. ("Local") was just served with a document purporting to be a Unilateral Administrative Order, issued by the EPA under CERCLA § 106, demanding that Local conduct extensive studies and then undertake what could undoubtedly be a multimillion dollar cleanup at the Hazmat International Airport. After summarizing the salient facts, as told to me by Local's president, I will pose the challenging questions for you to answer, in a concise yet complete memorandum.

Facts

The Hazmat Airport occupies a 500-acre area, all of which is presently owned by the City of Hazmat. Last year, the City added 100 of the 500 acres to the Airport by acquiring several smaller parcels that had been adjoining the Airport. The purpose of that acquisition was to enable more of the companies that service the Airport's operations to be located in closer proximity to the Airport.

One such company is our client Local, an overnight air courier service that is wholly-owned by National Express, Inc. ("National"). National was planning to establish a presence at the Hazmat Airport, and incorporated Local as a new subsidiary corporation specifically for that purpose.

National entered into a lease agreement with the City of Hazmat that enables Local to build a new facility on some presently-undeveloped property (within the Airport's recently-acquired 100 acres) and conduct its overnight air courier activities on that property for the next 10 years. The construction of the Local facility is being funded 50% by an interest-free loan from National, and 50% by a commercial loan from Money Bank, which took a security interest in the future facility. Before National entered into the lease, and before National and the Bank agreed to fund the loans, both entities wanted an environmental assessment of the property in question.

Facts

The Hazmat Airport occupies a 500-acre area, all of which is presently owned by the City of Hazmat. Last year, the City added 100 of the 500 acres to the Airport by acquiring several smaller parcels that had been adjoining the Airport. The purpose of that acquisition was to enable more of the companies that service the Airport's operations to be located in closer proximity to the Airport.

One such company is our client Local, an overnight air courier service that is wholly-owned by National Express, Inc. ("National"). National was planning to establish a presence at the Hazmat Airport, and incorporated Local as a new subsidiary corporation specifically for that purpose.

National entered into a lease agreement with the City of Hazmat that enables Local to build a new facility on some presently-undeveloped property (within the Airport's recently-acquired 100 acres) and conduct its overnight air courier activities on that property for the next 10 years. The construction of the Local facility is being funded 50% by an interest-free loan from National, and 50% by a commercial loan from Money Bank, which took a security interest in the future facility. Before National entered into the lease, and before National and the Bank agreed to fund the loans, both entities wanted an environmental assessment of the property in question. They accepted the lowest bid for an environmental assessment, which involved a review of public records regarding the prior ownership of the property and telephone calls to state and local environmental agencies, but did not involve a site visit or sampling. The environmental assessment raised no "red flags" concerning any contamination of the property. In addition, Airport personnel assured National and the Bank that the environmental assessment conducted by the City prior to its acquisition of the property last year gave the property "a clean bill of health," although the Airport refused, citing confidentiality concerns, to provide a copy of the City's assessment to National and the Bank. National then signed the lease, National and the Bank advanced the funds, and Local entered into a construction contract.

Shortly after construction commenced, the contractor unearthed a large pit containing numerous drums, several of which were crushed and/or leaking, and visibly-contaminated soil. Unfortunately, the contractor's equipment pierced and crushed a number of drums when first encountering the buried pit, and those drums immediately began leaking as well. Strong fumes emanated from the pit, and the contractor refused to proceed with the new construction until the waste pit was cleaned up. The brand-new personnel at Local had no experience with environmental problems and did not know how to respond.

They left increasingly-desperate and lengthy messages at the National offices, but no one from National returned their calls. Concerned by the Express companies' inaction, and mindful of the fact that construction costs were mounting even while no work was being performed, the Bank obtained Local's permission to enter the property and retained an environmental consulting firm to sample the contaminated soil and leaking drums. The analyses indicated the presence of a number of hazardous substances, as well as hazardous constituents but not hazardous wastes under RCRA. At the Bank's instruction, Local reported these findings to the Airport and to the EPA's National Response Center. That was two months ago and, for reasons unknown to us, nothing seems to have occurred since then at the site.

After receiving notice of the burial pit, the EPA sent an investigator to obtain more information about the site. The investigator learned that, from 1965-1979, Dirty Drum, Inc. ("DDI") operated a drum reconditioning facility at the property presently leased to Local. DDI received used drums that contained chemical waste residues, some of which would have been characteristic hazardous wastes had RCRA been in effect. DDI cleaned out the residues, reclaimed and resold all reclaimable materials, disposed of the nonreclaimable materials off-site, and restored and resold the drums. When the initial RCRA regulations were proposed in 1978, DDI determined that it would not be able to operate profitably under RCRA, and ceased active operations in 1979. DDI then "closed" the facility by digging a large pit and dumping into it all of the dirty drums and waste materials that remained on-site. The process of burying the drums and wastes caused several of the drums to become crushed or cut, and their contents began (and still continue) seeping into the surrounding soil and, ultimately, the underlying groundwater.

DDI sold its assets to Clean Drum, Inc. ("CDI"), a drum reconditioner that never conducted operations at the site and, in 1982, moved all of DDI's tangible assets from the DDI location to other CDI locations. In 1985, CDI sold the real estate on which DDI had operated to Sam Speculator, who bought the now-vacant property, sight unseen, purely for resale purposes. Sam neither conducted activities on the property nor leased it to others. Frustrated by six years of unsuccessful attempts to sell the property, Sam finally sold it in 1991, at a very low price, to the City of Hazmat as part of the 100-acre Airport acquisition described above. In 1992, the City leased it to National.

Questions

1. Does CERCLA authorize the EPA to pursue Local for the cleanup of this mess? Why or why not? Does Local have any basis for avoiding liability under CERCLA for this site?

2. It may seem unfair to require Local to jump into action fulfilling the EPA's order, when the EPA has ignored the real culprits. What are Local's options in response to the EPA order?

3. If Local cannot avoid liability and ignore the order, whom else might Local pursue—or urge the EPA to pursue—to help clean up or pay for the cleanup of this site? Please evaluate any defenses that each of these other parties might reasonably assert.

13 PRIVATE ACTIONS AND ALLOCATION

A. Claims and Defenses

Once PRPs accepted as a new reality the severity of CERCLA's liability scheme, with broad categories of PRPs and narrow defenses, and the enormity of CERCLA's cleanup and transaction costs, many turned to private cost recovery and contribution actions to attempt to minimize their own CERCLA exposure. Even as governmental activity under CERCLA waxes and wanes with budgetary and political fortunes, private party CERCLA litigation continues to mushroom.

A party may proceed under CERCLA for reimbursement of some or all of its cleanup costs regardless of whether the site in question is subject to any government enforcement or cleanup activity.   As long as a party has incurred response costs—whether voluntarily or pursuant to a governmental or court order—it may recoup some or all of those past costs by means of a cost recovery and/or contribution claim under CERCLA. Moreover, a party need not complete a cleanup before suing others for cost recovery. As long as a discrete portion of the cleanup activity has been completed, a party may seek reimbursement of costs already expended, as well as a declaratory judgment that the defendants are liable for future response costs. Thus, the cost recovery and/or contribution provisions enable PRPs to spread their past, present, and future response costs without having to incur all such costs up-front and assume the risk of seeking reimbursement in the future.

Two provisions of CERCLA appear to authorize private parties that incur response costs to shift those costs to, or share them with, (other) PRPs. Under § 107, the four categories of PRPs are liable not only for federal and state governments' cleanup costs, § 107(a)(4)(A), but also for "any other necessary costs of response incurred by *any other person* consistent with the national contingency plan" (emphasis supplied). § 107(a)(4)(B). And under § 113(f)(1), "any person may seek contribution from any other person who is liable or potentially liable under section 107(a) ***."

For several years, it remained unclear whether a PRP could take full advantage of both provisions. The resolution of this issue is of considerable significance to PRPs. Whereas cost recovery actions under § 107(a) presumptively utilize joint and several liability, contribution actions under § 113(f) require the plaintiff to prove each defendant's equitable share of the cleanup costs. Different statutes of limitations apply to claims asserted under the different provisions. And the contribution protection offered under § 122 to parties that settle with the EPA may not protect settlors against cost recovery claims under § 107(a). Although some district courts continue to allow PRPs to invoke § 107(a)(4)(A), virtually every circuit court to have addressed the issue has held that a liable party may proceed solely under the contribution provisions of § 113(f). The Seventh Circuit subscribes to the general rule, but it has recognized an exception for PRP landowners who played no role in the presence of hazardous substances on their property. *See Rumpke of Indiana, Inc. v. Cummins Engine Co.*, 107 F.3d 1235 (7th Cir. 1997) (set forth later in this chapter).

The following case traces the development of this issue and articulates the majority view.

NEW CASTLE COUNTY V. HALLIBURTON NUS CORP.
111 F.3d 1116 (3rd Cir. 1997)

Before MANSMANN and LEWIS, Circuit Judges, and DUPLANTIER, District Judge.

MANSMANN, Circuit Judge.

We must decide whether a person who is potentially responsible for the clean-up of a hazardous waste site under the Comprehensive Environmental Response, Compensation, and Liability Act (CERCLA) may bring a cost recovery claim against other potentially responsible persons under CERCLA section 107(a)(4)(B) separate from a contribution claim under section 113(f) of the Superfund Amendments and Reauthorization Act (SARA). We conclude that a potentially responsible person may not bring a section 107 cost recovery claim against another potentially responsible person, and we will therefore affirm the judgment of the district court.

I.

This appeal arises from efforts to clean up the Tybouts Corner Landfill, a hazardous substance site located in Delaware. In 1980, the United States filed suit against New Castle County, the owner and operator of the landfill, and against the predecessor of Rhone-Poulenc, Inc., who arranged for the disposal of hazardous substances at the landfill. The case was originally brought under the Resource Conservation and Recovery Act, but the complaint was amended in 1984 to add counts under CERCLA. The CERCLA counts sought to have the defendants conduct remedial action and reimburse the EPA for its response costs. The amended complaint also added as a defendant the predecessor of Zeneca, Inc., an arranger for disposal at the landfill.

On April 19, 1989, the EPA entered into a series of consent decrees with New Castle County, Rhone-Poulenc and Zeneca (collectively "New Castle") and others, requiring them to finance and implement remedial action at the landfill. Prior to entry of the consent decrees, the EPA contracted with Halliburton NUS Corporation ("NUS") to perform a Remedial Investigation/Feasibility Study to determine appropriate response actions. As part of that determination, NUS installed several monitoring wells in areas where refuse had been placed during the landfill's operation. One of the wells, TY-311, was installed to assess the "Merchantville Formation," a clay strata separating a shallow formation containing groundwater impacted by landfill material and a formation containing groundwater used by New Castle County as drinking water. NUS reported that the Merchantville Formation was missing in the vicinity of TY-311.

According to New Castle, NUS improperly constructed well TY-311 such that (1) NUS' conclusion about the missing formation was incorrect and (2) NUS' construction of the well improperly opened a "window" between the two groundwater formations. New Castle learned of these alleged mistakes on the part of NUS in a report dated October 28, 1991. On October 26, 1993, New Castle filed this lawsuit against NUS. In Count II, New Castle asserted that NUS was liable under CERCLA section 107(a)(4)(B) for all or part of the response costs incurred by New Castle in connection with the landfill. ***

NUS moved for summary judgment as to Count II on the ground that it actually constituted a claim for *contribution* under CERCLA section 113(f)(1), and that the claim was therefore time-barred under section 113's three-year statute of limitations (unlike a section 107 *cost recovery* action, which is generally governed by a six-year statute of limitations).

The district court held that Count II constituted a claim for contribution under section 113. The court also determined that New Castle's cause of action accrued on the date of the consent decrees.

The district court further concluded that the limitations period on New Castle's contribution action was not equitably tolled and thus expired three years after the consent decrees were entered. The court dismissed Count II with prejudice. ***

II.

CERCLA and SARA together create two different kinds of legal actions by which parties can recoup some or all of the costs associated with clean-ups: section 107 cost recovery actions and section 113 contribution actions.

***Cost recovery actions are generally subject to a six- year statute of limitations. § 9613(g)(2).

Section 113 of SARA provides that "[a]ny person may seek contribution from any other person who is liable or potentially liable under [section 107], during or following any civil action under [section 107]." "No action for contribution for any response costs or damages may be commenced more than 3 years after ... the date of ... entry of a judicially approved settlement with respect to such costs or damages." § 9613(g)(3).

The primary question in this appeal is whether New Castle's action against NUS is a cost recovery action or a contribution action. If it is a cost recovery action, it is timely; if it is a contribution action and we do not apply the discovery rule or equitable tolling, the action is not timely. ***

Every court of appeals that has examined this issue has come to the same conclusion: a section 107 action brought for recovery of costs may be brought only by *innocent* parties that have undertaken clean-ups. An action brought by a potentially responsible person is by necessity a section 113 action for contribution. See *Redwing*

Carriers, Inc. v. Saraland Apartments, 94 F.3d 1489, 1496 (11th Cir.1996); *United States v. Colorado & Eastern R.R. Co.*, 50 F.3d 1530, 1536 (10th Cir.1995); *United Technologies Corp. v. Browning-Ferris Indus., Inc.*, 33 F.3d 96, 99 (1st Cir.1994); *Akzo Coatings, Inc. v. Aigner Corp.*, 30 F.3d 761, 764 (7th Cir.1994); *see also Amoco Oil Co. v. Borden, Inc.*, 889 F.2d 664, 672 (5th Cir.1989). We agree with the conclusion reached by our sister courts.

A section 107 cost recovery action imposes strict liability on potentially responsible persons for costs associated with hazardous waste clean-up and site remediation. ***

In general, a section 107 cost recovery action also imposes joint and several liability on potentially responsible persons. ***

If New Castle is correct, a potentially responsible person found liable under section 107 could bring a section 107 action against another potentially responsible person and could recoup all of its expenditures regardless of fault. This strains logic. "[I]t is sensible to assume that Congress intended only innocent parties—not parties who were themselves liable—to be permitted to recoup the whole of their expenditures." *United Technologies*, 33 F.3d at 100.

In contrast, the term "contribution" is a standard legal term that refers to a claim "by and between jointly and severally liable parties for an appropriate division of the payment one of them has been compelled to make." *Id.* at 99 (quoting *Akzo Coatings*, 30 F.3d at 764). To resolve contribution claims, section 113 provides that "the court may allocate response costs among liable parties using such equitable factors as the court determines are appropriate." 42 U.S.C. § 9613(f)(1).[6]

In other words, while a potentially responsible person should not be permitted to recover all of its costs from another potentially responsible person, the person should be able to recoup that portion of its expenditures which exceeds its fair share of the overall liability. Section 113 provides potentially responsible persons with the appropriate vehicle for such recovery. ***

Thus, section 113 does not in itself create any new liabilities; rather, it confirms the right of a potentially responsible person under section 107 to obtain contribution from other potentially responsible persons.

Our analysis finds support in the background and legislative history of SARA. Prior to the passage of SARA (and before the existence of section 113), it was not clear whether a potentially responsible person under section 107 could recover from other potentially responsible persons that portion of its clean-up costs that exceeded its fair share. Courts responded to this uncertainty by recognizing an implicit cause of action for contribution where persons have been subject to joint and several liability and have incurred costs in excess of their fair share.

---

[6]Thus, while a defendant in a section 107 action can only avoid joint and several liability by demonstrating that the harm at a given site is divisible, parties to a section 113 action may allocate liability among potentially responsible persons based on equitable considerations.

Congress codified this right when it created section 113. A principal goal of section 113 was to "clarif[y] and confirm[ ] the right of a person held jointly and severally liable under CERCLA to seek contribution from other potentially liable parties, when the person believes that it has assumed a share of the cleanup or cost that may be greater than its equitable share under the circumstances." H.R.Rep. No. 99-253(I), at 79 (1985); H.R. Conf. Rep. No. 99-962, at 221 (1986).

Thus, prior to the passage of SARA and section 113, section 107 potentially responsible persons were required to rely upon an uncertain common law right of contribution. It was only upon passage of section 113 that these persons had a clear, statutory right to seek an equitable division of clean-up costs. The history and language of section 113 lend support to our conclusion that it, and not section 107, is the appropriate mechanism for obtaining a fair allocation of responsibility between two or more potentially responsible persons.

New Castle observes that section 107 provides that a potentially responsible person shall be liable for costs incurred by "any ... person," 42 U.S.C., § 9607(a)(4)(B), and that the section is not expressly limited to innocent parties. In *Akzo Coatings*, the Court of Appeals for the Seventh Circuit recognized that while section 107 permits recovery by any person, the "person" must experience an injury of the type giving rise to a claim under section 107 to obtain relief under that section. 30 F.3d at 764. Since section 107 was designed to enable innocent persons who incur expenses cleaning up a site to recover their costs from potentially responsible persons, a potentially responsible person does not experience section 107 injury and cannot obtain section 107 relief. Instead, a claim by a potentially responsible person is "a quintessential claim for contribution." *Id.* Section 113(f)(1) confirms this fact, permitting a party to seek contribution from "any other" party potentially liable under section 107.

Likewise, the appellants in *United Technologies* observed that section 107 states that responsible parties shall be liable to "any other person." 33 F.3d at 101. The appellants contended that the court should not limit section 107 "person[s]" to innocent parties. The Court of Appeals for the First Circuit rejected this argument, finding that such a reading would enable section 107 to swallow section 113, thus nullifying the three-year statute of limitations associated with actions for contribution. ***

New Castle argues that potentially responsible persons should have the choice to proceed under either section 107 or section 113. We disagree. Allowing a potentially responsible person to choose between section 107 (with a six-year statute of limitations and joint and several liability) and section 113 (with a three-year statute of limitations and apportioned liability based upon equitable considerations) would render section 113 a nullity. Potentially responsible persons would quickly abandon section 113 in favor of the substantially more generous provisions of section 107. We will not read section 107 so broadly that section 113 ceases to have any meaningful application. ***

* * *

We do not decide under what circumstances a private individual may rely on section 107, or whether we endorse any of the exceptions for "innocent" landowners suggested by our sister courts. It is sufficient that we decide that a potentially responsible person under section 107(a), who is not entitled to any of the defenses enumerated under section 107(b), may not bring a section 107 action against another potentially responsible person.

Where both parties are "non-innocent" responsible persons, our sister courts have unanimously held that any action to reapportion costs between the parties is an action for contribution. ***

While it is possible that a private person may, under certain circumstances, bring a section 107 action, New Castle is not that person. At oral argument, New Castle conceded that it is a potentially responsible person under section 107(a). New Castle is therefore not permitted, under any scenario, to pursue a section 107 cost recovery action against other potentially responsible persons.

* * *

NOTES

1. The general rule that a PRP may not invoke § 107(a)(4)(A) to seek cost recovery from other PRPs renders moot the questions whether joint and several liability applies among PRPs, and whether PRPs may assert defenses against fellow PRPs beyond the defenses specified in CERCLA § 107(b). *See, e.g., General Electric Co. v. Litton Industrial Automation Systems, Inc.*, 920 F.2d 1415, 1418 (8th Cir. 1990), *cert. denied*, 499 U.S. 937 (1991) (unclean hands defense is not available in private party cost recovery action under § 107(a)(4)(B), because "CERCLA is a strict liability statute, with only a limited number of statutorily-defined defenses available").

2. Even in contribution actions, courts have not been receptive to equitable defenses that would relieve a party entirely of liability. Rather, the facts that would otherwise support a defense such as unclean hands or caveat emptor are more likely to be considered in the mix of factors affecting an equitable distribution of cleanup costs among the PRPs in a contribution action.

> The defenses enumerated in section 9607(b) are not exclusive in suits for contribution. Other sections suggest additional defenses in a broad sense; for example, the Act limits to three years the period in which an action may be brought, 42 U.S.C.A. § 9613(g). A party which has resolved its liability to the government is not liable for contribution; the settlement may reduce the claim pro tanto. § 9613(f)(2). In addition, agreements to indemnify or hold harmless are enforceable between the parties but not against the government. § 9607(e). Moreover, the defenses in section 9607(b) coexist with equitable considerations that may mitigate damages.

> Although not a defense to a government suit for clean-up costs, caveat emptor if applied between private parties arguably would not contradict the statutory text. Several considerations, however, lead us to conclude that this venerable doctrine is not in keeping with the policies underlying CERCLA. First, caveat emptor completely bars recovery by a purchaser

regardless of other equities affecting the parties. That result frustrates Congress' desire to encourage clean-up by any responsible party. If fair apportionment of the expense is not assured, it is unlikely that one party will undertake remedial actions promptly when it could simply delay, awaiting a legal ruling on the contribution liability of other responsible parties.

Second, CERCLA authorizes the government to seek reimbursement of response costs from any of the responsible parties, leaving them to share the expense equitably. As the House report recognizes, choosing one defendant from among several can cause ill will between the government and the unlucky party selected.

*   *   *

CERCLA expressly conditions the amount of contribution on the application of equitable considerations. *** [I]f the tract's price is reduced to allow for future environmental clean-up claims, the purchaser should not be entitled to double compensation. Nonetheless, the amount of the discount, if any, the cost of response, and other considerations may enter into the allocation of contribution by the district court in its exercise of discretion.

We conclude, therefore, that under CERCLA the doctrine of caveat emptor is not a defense to liability for contribution but may only be considered in mitigation of amount due.

Smith Land & Improvement Corp. v. Celotex Corp., 851 F.2d 86 (3d Cir. 1988), *cert. denied*, 488 U.S. 1029 (1989).

3. As noted in *Smith Land,* indemnity agreements are recognized in contribution actions. CERCLA contemplates that the parties to a property transaction may negotiate an allocation of potential future cleanup liability. Employing perhaps the most obtuse language to be found in CERCLA, section 107(e)(1) states that "[n]o indemnification, hold harmless, or similar agreement or conveyance shall be effective to transfer from [one person to another] *** the liability imposed under this section." The next sentence provides that nothing in the foregoing language "shall bar any agreement to insure, hold harmless, or indemnify a party to such agreement for any liability under this section." Finally, § 107(e)(2) states that nothing in CERCLA, specifically including § 107(e)(1), shall bar any cause of action that any PRP may have against any other person.

In other words, if a purchase and sale transaction includes an agreement by the seller to indemnify and hold harmless the buyer regarding any CERCLA liability that may arise as a result of pre-closing conditions at the property, and the EPA sues the buyer, the current owner, under § 107(a)(1) for cleanup costs covered by the indemnity, the buyer may not avoid liability to the EPA on the basis of the indemnity agreement. Any liability incurred by the buyer, however, may be transferred back to the seller by means of the indemnity agreement. The net effect of these provisions is to ensure that the EPA has maximum access to the widest range of assets to accomplish Superfund cleanups, leaving the private parties subject to the risks that the indemnity agreement will turn out not to be enforceable, or that the seller lacks sufficient assets to satisfy its indemnity obligations. *See, e.g., Mardan Corp. v. C.G.C. Music Ltd.*, 804 F.2d 1454 (9th Cir. 1986).

In *Mardan,* a broadly-worded settlement agreement between the past and present site owners was held to bar the present owner from asserting a claim against the otherwise-liable past owner under section 107, where both knew when the agreement was signed that cleanup activity might be required at the site. With the stakes so high, it is not surprising that numerous parties have litigated the scope and application of their indemnity provisions, which are typically construed according to state law. *See, e.g., Lion Oil Co. v. Tosco Corp.*, 90 F.3d 268 (8th Cir. 1996)(purchaser could not enforce indemnity provided by seller because parties had subsequently executed release); *SmithKline Beecham Corp. v. Rohm and Haas Co.*, 89 F.3d 154 (3d Cir. 1996)(broadly-worded pre-CERCLA indemnity agreement held to cover CERCLA cleanup costs); *Taracorp, Inc. v. NL Industries, Inc.*, 73 F.3d 738 (7th Cir. 1996)(environmental indemnity held to encompass off-site, arranger-triggered CERCLA liability; not limited to on-site contamination); *Olin Corp. v. Consolidated Aluminum Corp.*, 5 F.3d 10 (2d Cir. 1993) (indemnity agreement held to have passed CERCLA liability from seller to buyer); and *John S. Boyd Co. v. Boston Gas Co.*, 992 F.2d 401 (1st Cir. 1993) (1959 corporate agreement held not to transfer unforeseen environmental cleanup liabilities).

4. Notwithstanding the harsh, strict liability regime of CERCLA, parties frequently raise defenses related to causation. In *Dedham Water Co. v. Cumberland Farms Dairy, Inc.*, 889 F.2d 1146 (1st Cir. 1989), the defendant argued that "since actual contamination of the plaintiff's property by the defendant's releases of hazardous substances did not occur, the liability requirement has not been met, and therefore the defendant is not liable under CERCLA." *Id.* at 1152. The First Circuit held CERCLA was not so exacting in terms of causation:

> To our knowledge, every court that has addressed this issue, with the exception of the district court in the instant case, has held that it is not necessary to prove actual contamination of plaintiff's property by defendant's waste in order to establish liability under CERCLA. There is nothing in the statute, its legislative history, or the case law, which requires proof that the defendant's hazardous waste actually have migrated to plaintiff's property, causing contamination of plaintiff's property, before CERCLA liability is triggered. Nor is there anything in the statute suggesting that a "two-site" case be treated differently than a one-site case, where the issue is whether a release or threat of release caused "response costs." And we have found no cases making the distinction the district court did.

> Since the district court failed to properly consider Dedham's claim that even if Cumberland's releases did not cause the contamination of Dedham's wells, Cumberland's releases and threatened releases caused it to incur response costs, there must be a new trial.

Id. at 1154.

Ultimately, Cumberland Farms prevailed. On remand, the district court found that Dedham Water did not undertake its response action in response to the threat of a release from the Cumberland Farms site. *Dedham Water Co. v. Cumberland Farms Dairy, Inc.,* 770 F.Supp. 41 (D.Mass. 1991). The court reiterated the finding from the prior trial, which had not been challenged on appeal, that the pollution of the Dedham Water wells was not caused by the release of contaminants from the Cumberland Farms facility. The issue that was now before the court was "whether the treatment plant was built in response to a threat of release of contaminants from the defendant's facility to the plaintiffs' well field." After carefully examining the chronology of events, the court determined that, although there was "a rather remote possibility" that the hazardous substances released at Cumberland Farms "might migrate to the plaintiffs' well field at some time in the future," Dedham Water had decided to undertake its response action (*i.e.,* to build a water treatment plant) before learning that Cumberland Farms was a possible source of its contamination.

> The defendant, according to the testimony in this case, is a blatant polluter, and the plaintiffs operate a public water supply system. It would be gratifying to exact reimbursement from the defendant for the benefit of the plaintiffs. As long as causation is a necessary element of liability, however, I cannot do so on this record.

Id. at 43. This time, the First Circuit affirmed. 972 F.2d 453 (1st Cir. 1992).

For another variation on the two-site theme, see *Control Data Corp. v. S.C.S.C. Corp.,* 53 F.3d 930 (8th Cir. 1995) (in subchapter 13.C).

5. Compare the concept of causation in *Dedham Water* (defendant's release need not cause plaintiff's contamination, but must cause plaintiff to incur response costs to remedy such contamination) with the concept of causation in the generator/arranger liability cases, such as *United States v. Monsanto,* 858 F.2d 160 (4th Cir. 1988), *cert. denied,* 490 U.S. 1106 (1989) (noted in chapter 10.D). (The EPA need not prove that a particular generator's hazardous substances are in fact part of a release. It is sufficient to prove that the generator arranged for the disposal of hazardous substances at the site, and that hazardous substances similar to those of the generator are at the site.)

6. An extensive analysis of the causation defense is set forth in *Acushnet Co. v. Coaters Inc.,* 937 F.Supp. 988 (D.Mass. 1996). The site in question was an abandoned quarry to which numerous parties had sent hazardous and industrial waste for some 40 years. After the EPA entered into a settlement for site cleanup with several of the parties, the settlors sued non-settlors who had also sent materials to the site. The court focused not on whether the settlors' claim was grounded in § 107(a)(4)(B) or § 113(f), but on whether one of the non-settlor defendants, New England Telephone and Telegraph Company (NETT) was a liable party under § 107(a), which would be a necessary element of either claim.

It was undisputed that NETT sent to the site discarded utility poles, some of which had been treated with creosote, which contains hazardous substances known as polycyclic aromatic hydrdocarbons (PAHs). The plaintiffs' argument, which the court found persuasive, was as follows:

> NETT argues that the Plaintiffs must prove that NETT in some way caused the Plaintiffs to incur "response costs," if Plaintiffs are to prevail in their claims for compensation under CERCLA. Moreover, NETT has

proffered uncontradicted expert testimony asserting that NETT did not and, in fact, could not have caused the Plaintiffs to incur any "response costs," as those costs are defined under CERCLA.

NETT's expert testified that PAHs used in creosote-treated utility pole butts could not have leached into the surrounding soil to create a level of PAHs in the soil greater than the pre-existing background levels of PAHs already in the soil. Therefore, NETT asserts that the elevated levels of PAHs in the soil at the Site must have been caused by waste other than utility pole butts. NETT's expert testified that even if NETT disposed of creosote-treated utility pole butts at the Site, the butts could not have contributed to any response costs incurred by the Plaintiffs. The response costs that have been incurred *** have been (and will be) required, not because of PAH levels to which NETT contributed in any way, but because of contamination as to which there is no proffer of evidence that NETT contributed in any way.

Id. at 992-93. The court rejected the plaintiffs' legal challenge to NETT's argument, and granted NETT's motion for summary judgment absolving it of CERCLA liability for the site.

7. The next case considers another successful attempt by an apparent PRP to avoid CERCLA liability, not by being dismissed from a proceeding to which it was involuntarily added, but by initiating an action against other PRPs and potentially shifting all of its liability to them. The decision contains two parts; the first, set forth immediately below, amplifies the exceptional circumstances under which an apparent PRP may bring a cost recovery action under § 107(a)(4)(B). The second part, which addresses the effect of a prior settlement on the plaintiff's claims in this case, is included in subchapter 13.B.

RUMPKE OF INDIANA, INC. V. CUMMINS ENGINE CO.
107 F.3d 1235 (7th Cir. 1997)

Before BAUER, EASTERBROOK, and DIANE P. WOOD, Circuit Judges.
DIANE P. WOOD, Circuit Judge.

The net of potential liability under the Comprehensive Environmental Response, Compensation and Liability Act *** is wide indeed, reflecting the need both to clean up the nation's toxic waste sites and the practical imperative to find the necessary money for the job. The cleanup will be less likely to occur if potentially responsible parties do not come forward, yet the often astronomical sums needed to restore these sites can deter prompt remedial action. CERCLA protects parties who settle claims with the government from liability for contribution in suits relating to "matters addressed" in administratively or judicially settled consent decrees. In this interlocutory appeal *** we have been asked to decide several questions relating to the breadth of one of those settlements. The central issue is whether a 1982 consent decree approved in *United States v. Seymour Recycling Corp.*, 554 F.Supp. 1334 (S.D.Ind.1982), to which Cummins Engine Co. and its fellow appellants were parties (to which we refer as the "Cummins group"), stands in the way of the efforts of Rumpke of Indiana, Inc. ("Rumpke"), either to recover its costs of cleaning up a site arguably not covered by the *Seymour* decree under § 107(a) of the Act, or to obtain contribution from the Cummins group under § 113(f)(1) of the Act, 42 U.S.C. § 9613(f)(1). We agree with the district court that the *Seymour* decree did not encompass the matters Rumpke is now raising and we accordingly affirm its order.

I

The background facts are relatively straightforward. In 1984, Rumpke bought a 273-acre dump known as the Uniontown Landfill from George and Ethel Darlage. At that time, the Darlages informed Rumpke that the landfill had never accepted hazardous waste. For reasons undisclosed on this record, Rumpke did not conduct its own inspection of the land for environmental hazards prior to the sale. In light of where we are today, it is easy to predict what happened next. In 1990, to its professed surprise, Rumpke discovered that the Darlages' beliefs about the landfill had been quite wrong. In fact, a cocktail of hazardous wastes had been deposited at Uniontown for many years, and volatile organic compounds (VOCs) were migrating to surrounding areas. Looking into the matter, Rumpke determined that much of this material had come from the Seymour Recycling Corporation, which was located about ten miles away in Seymour, Indiana. For many years, Seymour had distilled for reuse acetones, alcohols, paint thinners, chlorinated solvents, and freon materials, all of which had been discarded by various manufacturers. The distilling process yielded both reusable solvents and a toxic sludge. Seymour disposed of the sludge by shoveling it into 55-gallon drums, or on other occasions, incinerating it and storing the resulting ash in similar drums. Rumpke believed that some of those 55-gallon drums made their way to the Uniontown landfill. Because Seymour Recycling was by this time out of the picture, Rumpke brought this action against the manufacturers that used to send materials to Seymour Recycling for processing.

Rumpke's lawsuit opened a Pandora's Box of its own. Whatever one might say about the Uniontown site, it had become clear in the 1980's that the Seymour site was an environmental disaster area. Seymour Recycling had left some 60,000 drums and 98 bulk storage tanks, in various stages of decay, strewn about the site. By 1980, the drums and tanks were leaking, exploding, and sending clouds of toxic chemicals into the air over nearby residential areas. The United States responded with a complaint in May 1980, alleging violations of section 7003 of the Resource Conservation and Recovery Act (RCRA) and section 311 of the Clean Water Act. In 1982, the United States filed an amended complaint adding allegations under CERCLA, §§ 106 and 107, which had been enacted in the meantime. The amended complaint added 24 new defendants who allegedly had transported hazardous wastes to the Seymour site for handling, storage, disposal, or treatment. At the same time, the State of Indiana and the County of Jackson moved to intervene in the action.

The amended complaint was accompanied by a proposed consent decree that was filed with the court, as required by § 122(d), which the court accepted in due course. The decree resolved all obligations and responsibilities of the settling companies with respect to "the Seymour site." The companies paid agreed amounts into the Seymour Site Trust Fund, which was then available to trustees to perform the work described in an exhibit to the decree. It provided for penalties in the event the work was not performed satisfactorily; it gave the United States and the State the right to access and inspect the site at all times until the work was completed; and it contained various administrative provisions. The decree also promised, in section XII, that the United States, the State, and the local governments would not bring any more civil actions against the settling companies:

> ... arising out of or related to the storage, treatment, handling, disposal, transportation or presence or actual or threatened release or discharge of any materials at, to, from or near the Seymour site, including any action with respect to surface cleanup and soil or groundwater cleanup at the Seymour site.

Our case arises because the defendants Rumpke wants to pursue—Cummins, Ford Motor Company, International Business Machines Corp., General Motors Corp., and Essex Group, Inc.—were among the *Seymour* settling parties.

II

After Rumpke filed its action with respect to the contaminated Uniontown site, the Cummins group moved for summary judgment against Rumpke's claims. They argued that Rumpke's suit was blocked by the language just quoted from the 1982 *Seymour* consent decree, by virtue of CERCLA § 113(f)(2), which reads as follows:

> A person who has resolved its liability to the United States or a State in an administrative or judicially approved settlement shall not be liable for claims for contribution regarding matters addressed in the settlement. Such settlement does not discharge any of the other potentially liable persons unless its terms so provide, but it reduces the potential liability of the others by the amount of the settlement.

The Cummins group reasoned that (1) the Rumpke suit presented "claims for contribution," and (2) the claims were "matters addressed in the settlement" by virtue of section XII of the decree. Specifically, with appropriate ellipses, they argued that section XII covered actions "arising out of ... the ... transportation ... of any materials ... from ... the Seymour site." Rumpke's claim against them alleged that materials from the named manufacturers had been transported from the Seymour site to the Uniontown site; thus, they asserted, it fell squarely within the language of section XII and the claim was barred by § 113(f)(2). *Q.E.D.*

In the order on interlocutory appeal, the district court did not dwell on the question whether the Rumpke suit presented claims for contribution, evidently for two reasons. First, it noted that Rumpke's suit was in part based on § 107(a) of the Act, which provides for private cost recovery, rather than contribution. It acknowledged that *Akzo Coatings, Inc. v. Aigner Corp.*, 30 F.3d 761 (7th Cir.1994), held that claims by one potentially responsible party (PRP) (here, Rumpke as present landowner) against another (here, the Cummins group) must normally be brought as contribution claims under § 113(f)(1), but it noted that *Akzo* also recognized an exception to that rule. Under the exception, a landowner may bring a § 107 action to recover for its direct injuries "if the party seeking relief is itself not responsible for having caused any of the hazardous materials to be spilled onto the property." The court found that it was factually uncertain whether Rumpke was entitled to invoke the *Akzo* exception, and it accordingly denied summary judgment for the Cummins group on that point. Second, the court knew that Rumpke's complaint also asserted, in Count II, an express claim for contribution under § 113(f)(1). Thus, recognizing that the case at least for Count II raised a contribution claim, the court's order proceeded immediately to the question whether the *Seymour* settlement resolved all potential liability of the Cummins group with respect to the Uniontown site.

Construing the language of the *Seymour* decree as a whole, the court found that it dealt only with the Seymour site. ***

* * *

III

A. Claims for Direct Cost Recovery and Contribution

Rumpke's suit against the Cummins group was based on both the cost recovery theory of § 107(a) and the contribution theory of § 113(f)(1). The district court, as noted above, did not find it necessary to decide definitively whether the § 107(a) theory was sustainable, because it believed that issues of fact needed to be resolved regarding the question whether Rumpke was the kind of innocent landowner entitled to bring a § 107(a) cost recovery action under our *Akzo* opinion. It did not discuss the differences between § 113(f)(1) and § 107(a) in the order we are reviewing. We believe, nonetheless, that we should reach the question whether this suit may proceed under § 107(a), or under § 113(f)(1), or both. If § 107(a) is unavailable as a matter of law to Rumpke, we have only the § 113(f)(1) arguments to consider, which in turn requires us to interpret the *Seymour* consent decree. On the other hand, if Rumpke is entitled to proceed under § 107(a), the contribution bar of § 113(f)(2) may not apply at all; if it does not, then the dispute about the scope of the *Seymour* decree might be beside the point. ***

1. *Rumpke's § 107(a) claim.* Rumpke pointed out in both its brief and at oral argument that it is not subject to any administrative cleanup order from the Indiana Department of Environmental Management (IDEM), the federal Environmental Protection Agency (EPA), or any other public authority. Thus, Rumpke is not a party that is now or ever has been subject to a civil action under CERCLA § 106 ***. It is also undisputed that no party has ever brought a cost recovery action against Rumpke under § 107. Instead, Rumpke has stated that it "intends to act, consistent with the National Contingency Plan, to assure that the VOCs it has discovered outside of the waste disposal area of the Uniontown Landfill, but within the property boundaries of the Landfill, do not become a threat to health or the environment." Furthermore, like the

district court, on this review from a grant of summary judgment, we assume that Rumpke did nothing to contribute to the presence of the hazardous substances. Its status as a PRP for CERCLA purposes is based solely on its ownership of the Uniontown site—ownership, we assume at this stage, it acquired without knowledge of the presence of environmental hazards and after all the deposits had been made.

The question is whether our *Akzo* exception applies to Rumpke: may a landowner PRP bring a direct liability suit for cost recovery under § 107(a) against other PRPs (in this case "arrangers"), if it contributed nothing to the hazardous conditions at the site, or is the *Akzo* exception available only to a narrower group of parties, such as the landowner who discovers someone surreptitiously dumping wastes on its land? In this connection, it is useful to review our decision in *Akzo* in somewhat more detail. In that case, Akzo sued Aigner Corporation and a number of other companies seeking contribution for initial cleanup work it had performed at the Fisher-Calo site and the costs it had incurred in studying the long term cleanup of the site with other PRPs. Akzo itself had sent hazardous wastes to the site. It argued nevertheless that it was entitled to bring a direct cost recovery action under § 107(a), because the language of § 107(a) broadly permits any "person" to seek recovery of appropriate cleanup costs. We rejected that argument, noting that:

> ... Akzo has experienced no injury of the kind that would typically give rise to a direct claim under section 107(a)—it is not, for example, a landowner forced to clean up hazardous materials that a third party spilled onto its property or that migrated there from adjacent lands. Instead, Akzo itself is a party liable in some measure for the contamination at the Fisher-Calo site, and the gist of Akzo's claim is that the costs it has incurred should be apportioned equitably amongst itself and the others responsible.... That is a quintessential claim for contribution.

30 F.3d at 764. Both the majority and the dissenting judges agreed, therefore, that Akzo's claim was governed solely by the contribution action § 113(f). In other words, when two parties who both injured the property have a dispute about who pays how much—a derivative liability, apportionment dispute—the statute directs them to § 113(f) and only to § 113(f).

Decisions in this area have not been notable for their clarity. The other courts of appeals that have considered the problem have agreed with our conclusion that claims properly characterized as those for contribution may normally be brought only under § 113(f). See, *e.g.*, *Redwing Carriers, Inc. v. Saraland Apartments*, 94 F.3d 1489, 1496 (11th Cir.1996); *United States v. Colorado & Eastern R.R. Co.*, 50 F.3d 1530, 1534-36 (10th Cir.1995); *United Technologies Corp. v. Browning-Ferris Industries*, 33 F.3d 96, 101-03 (1st Cir.1994), *cert. denied*, 115 S.Ct. 1176 (1995); *Amoco Oil Co. v. Borden, Inc.*, 889 F.2d 664, 672 (5th Cir.1989). These cases, like *Akzo*, all involved PRPs who themselves contributed to part of the problem. Also like *Akzo*, at least some of these courts have acknowledged that a class of cases might remain in which a PRP might sue under § 107(a).

As our *Akzo* decision implied, we see nothing in the language of § 107(a) that would make it unavailable to a party suing to recover for direct injury to its own land, under circumstances where it is not trying to apportion costs (*i.e.*, where it is seeking to recover on a direct liability theory, rather than trying to divide up its own liability for someone else's injuries among other potentially responsible parties). It is true that liability under § 107(a) is joint and several, and § 113(f) exists for the express purpose of allocating fault among PRPs. Nevertheless, one of two outcomes would follow from a landowner suit under § 107(a): either the facts would establish that the landowner was truly blameless, in which case the other PRPs would be entitled to bring a suit under § 113(f) within three years of the judgment to establish their liability among themselves, or the facts would show that the landowner was also partially responsible, in which case it would not be entitled to recover under its § 107(a) theory and only the § 113(f) claim would go forward. Neither one of those outcomes is inconsistent with the statutory scheme promoting allocation of liability.

The statutes of limitations available for § 107(a) and § 113(f) actions also provide no reason for concern. Superficially, it is true that a cost recovery suit under § 107(a) must be brought within six years (roughly speaking—in some circumstances a shorter 3-year period applies), see 42 U.S.C. § 9613(g)(2), while a seemingly shorter 3-year period applies to contribution actions, see 42 U.S.C. § 9613(g)(3). The question is, however, three years from when? Contribution actions may be brought within three years of either the date of judgment in any cost recovery action or within three years of the date of an administrative order under §§ 9622(g) or (h), or a judicially approved settlement order. In cases like Rumpke's, where no prior cost recovery action or applicable order has been entered, it would therefore be impossible to use § 107(a) as a tool for obtaining an advantage for limitations purposes. The contribution claim would not accrue until one of the events specified in § 9613(g)(2) occurred, at which time three years would be available in which to file an appropriate suit.

The language of § 113(f) also suggests that Rumpke's § 107(a) suit is consistent with the statute as a whole. Section 113(f)(1) begins with the following sentence:

> Any person may seek contribution from any other person who is liable or potentially liable under section 9607(a) of this title, during or following any civil action under section 9606 of this title or under section 9607(a) of this title.

Because neither a § 106 nor a § 107(a) proceeding has been concluded, Rumpke's action obviously does not "follow" such an action. Rumpke has brought its own § 107(a) action, in Count I of its complaint. If it turns out that Rumpke is not the innocent party it portrays itself to be, then Rumpke will not qualify for the *Akzo* exception. It would still be entitled to seek contribution for its expenses from the other PRPs, assuming it met the requirements of § 113(f)(1). (We acknowledge, as other courts have, that this seems to provide a disincentive for parties voluntarily to undertake cleanup operations, because a § 106 or § 107(a) action apparently must either be ongoing or already completed before § 113(f)(1) is available. This appears to be what the statute requires, however.)

If one were to read § 107(a) as implicitly denying standing to sue even to landowners like Rumpke who did not create the hazardous conditions, this would come perilously close to reading § 107(a) itself out of the statute. As one district court in New

Jersey recognized, this position would "mean that Section 107(a) private party plaintiffs will be few and far between. Truly innocent private party plaintiffs would be limited to, for example, a neighbor of a contaminated site who has acted to stem threatened releases for which he is not responsible, or a party who can claim one of the complete defenses set forth in 42 U.S.C. § 9607(b)." *Stearns & Foster Bedding Co. v. Franklin Holding Corp.*, 947 F.Supp. 790, 801 (D.N.J. 1996). Notwithstanding that observation, the New Jersey district court adopted the narrower approach to § 107(a), relying in part on a rather narrow reading of our *Akzo* opinion. *** We conclude instead that landowners who allege that they did not pollute the site in any way may sue for their direct response costs under § 107(a). To the extent this looks like an implied claim for contribution, where the landowner is alleging that its share should be zero, we note that dicta in the Supreme Court's decision in *Key Tronic Corp. v. United States*, 511 U.S. 809 (1994), suggests that the Court was not disturbed by that possibility.

Rumpke, as a landowner seeking to recover for direct injury to its property inflicted by the Cummins group, was therefore entitled to sue under § 107(a). Unlike the plaintiff in *Akzo*, Rumpke alleges that it was not responsible for any of the waste at the Uniontown site. On the basis of the present record, we must regard it as a landowner on whose property others dumped hazardous materials, before Rumpke even owned the property. We see no distinction between this situation and a case where a landowner discovers that someone has been surreptitiously dumping hazardous materials on property it already owns, apart from the potentially more difficult question of fact about the landowner's own responsibility in the latter case.

Last, we must consider whether the contribution bar of § 113(f)(2) has any role to play in a direct cost recovery action under § 107(a). We conclude that it does not. The theory of a direct cost recovery action is that other parties must pay Rumpke for the cost of restoring the property. Contribution among the defendants could be of no possible benefit to a party entitled to recover its full direct costs, nor could the settlement carve-out feature of § 113(f)(2) be of any possible benefit to Rumpke as a Uniontown PRP. Cummins conceded at oral argument that its *Seymour* settlement will not and cannot reduce Rumpke's liability as a landowner of Uniontown by as much as a penny. This means that § 113(f)(2) has no role to play insofar as this is a direct liability action under § 107(a)(1).

[balance of case in subchapter 13.B, below]

NOTES

1. If you were the district court judge to whom *Rumpke* was remanded, how would you proceed? What must Rumpke prove in order to be able to proceed under § 107(a)? What does the Seventh Circuit mean by the phrase "truly blameless" PRP? Is it requiring Rumpke to establish that although subject to prima facie liability under § 107(a)(1), it is entitled to a defense from liability either under the third-party or innocent landowner defenses? Based on the facts recited in the opinion, is Rumpke likely to fall

within either of those statutory defenses? Might Rumpke proceed under § 107(a) if it proves facts constituting equitable considerations justifying zero percent allocation of costs to it, even without proving non-liability by virtue of the statutory defenses?

2. An altogether different, but not mutually exclusive, tactic for avoiding or, more likely, limiting one's liability in a private action (as well as in a governmental cost recovery action) is to challenge the consistency of the costs incurred with the National Contingency Plan ("NCP"), 40 C.F.R. Part 300. In a private action, the plaintiff must demonstrate that its costs were incurred in a manner consistent with the NCP; the EPA or a state can prevail so long as their costs were incurred in a manner not inconsistent with the NCP. *Compare* CERCLA § 107(a)(4)(B) *with* § 107(a)(4)(A).

Since being revised in 1990, the NCP includes a separate subpart devoted specifically to private party cleanup and cost recovery actions. 40 C.F.R. Part 300, Subpart H. The NCP specifies that private party response actions need not be perfectly consistent with the NCP's guidelines; substantial compliance is sufficient. As the EPA explained in the preamble concerning new 40 C.F.R. § 300.700(c):

> The EPA believes that "consistency with the NCP" should be measured by whether the private party cleanup has, when evaluated as a whole, achieved "substantial compliance" with potentially applicable requirements, and resulted in a CERCLA-quality cleanup.

55 Fed. Reg. 8666, 8793 (1990).

Nonetheless, several private plaintiffs have been denied cost recovery on the grounds of lack of NCP consistency for failure to provide the requisite opportunity for public comment or to consider alternative cleanup options. *See, e.g., Pierson Sand & Gravel, Inc. v. Pierson Township,* 89 F.3d 835 (Table), 1996 WL 338624 (6th Cir., June 18, 1996).   This topic is further addressed in chapter 14.

Is lack of NCP consistency as useful a defense in a contribution action under § 113(f) as in a private cost recovery action under § 107(a)?

3. One "defense" equally applicable in both types of private actions is that a plaintiff's attempt to recoup attorney's fees under CERCLA is unauthorized. The Supreme Court resolved what had been a conflict among the circuits on this point. Note the Court's incidental references to the question whether a PRP may proceed under § 107(a)(4)(B) or solely under § 113(f).

KEY TRONIC CORP. V. UNITED STATES
511 U.S. 809 (1994)

JUSTICE STEVENS delivered the opinion of the Court.

Petitioner Key Tronic Corporation, one of several parties responsible for contaminating a landfill, brought this action to recover a share of its cleanup costs from other responsible parties. The question presented is whether attorney's fees are "necessary costs of response" within the meaning of § 107(a)(4)(B) of the

Comprehensive Environmental Response, Compensation, and Liability Act of 1980 (CERCLA) *** and therefore recoverable in such an action.

I

During the 1970's Key Tronic and other parties, including the United States Air Force, disposed of liquid chemicals at the Colbert Landfill in eastern Washington State. In 1980 the Washington Department of Ecology (WDOE) determined that the water supply in the surrounding area had been contaminated by these chemicals. Various lawsuits ensued, including formal proceedings against Key Tronic, the Air Force, and other parties.

Two of those proceedings were settled. In one settlement with WDOE and the Environmental Protection Agency (EPA), Key Tronic agreed to contribute $4.2 million to an EPA cleanup fund. In the other, the Air Force agreed to pay the EPA $1.45 million. The EPA subsequently released the Air Force from further liability pursuant to CERCLA § 122(g)(5), which provides that a party that has resolved its liability to the United States shall not be liable for contribution claims regarding matters addressed in the settlement.

Key Tronic thereafter brought this action against the United States and other parties seeking to recover part of its $4.2 million commitment to the EPA in a contribution claim under CERCLA § 113(f), and seeking an additional $1.2 million for response costs that it incurred before the settlements in a cost recovery claim under CERCLA § 107(a)(4)(B). The $1.2 million included attorney's fees for three types of legal services: (1) the identification of other potentially responsible parties (PRP's), including the Air Force, that were liable for the cleanup; (2) preparation and negotiation of its agreement with the EPA; and (3) the prosecution of this litigation.

The District Court dismissed Key Tronic's $4.2 million contribution claim against the Air Force when Key Tronic conceded that § 122(g)(5) precluded it from recovering any part of the consent decree obligation. Key Tronic's claim for $1.2 million of additional response costs could be pursued under CERCLA § 107(a)(4)(B), the court held, because it related to matters not covered by the Air Force's settlement with the EPA. *** Construing § 107 and § 101(25) "liberally to achieve the overall objectives of the statute," the District Court concluded that a private party may incur enforcement costs and that such costs include attorney's fees for bringing a cost recovery action under § 107. ***

The Court of Appeals reversed. Relying on its decision in *Stanton Road Associates v. Lohrey Enterprises*, 984 F. 2d 1015 (CA9 1993), which prohibited a litigant in a private response cost recovery action from obtaining attorney's fees from a party responsible for the pollution, the court held that the District Court lacked authority to award attorney's fees in this case. ***

Other courts addressing this question have differed over the extent to which attorney's fees are a necessary cost of response under CERCLA.

II

As its name implies, CERCLA is a comprehensive statute that grants the President broad power to command government agencies and private parties to clean up hazardous waste sites. Sections 104 and 106 provide the framework for federal abatement and enforcement actions that the President, the EPA as his delegated agent, or the Attorney General initiates. These actions typically require private parties to incur substantial costs in removing hazardous wastes and responding to hazardous conditions. Section 107 sets forth the scope of the liabilities that may be imposed on private parties and the defenses that they may assert.

Our cases establish that attorney's fees generally are not a recoverable cost of litigation "absent explicit congressional authorization." *Runyon v. McCrary*, 427 U.S. 160, 185 (1976). Recognition of the availability of attorney's fees therefore requires a determination that "Congress intended to set aside this longstanding American rule of law." *Runyon*, 427 U.S., at 185-186. Neither CERCLA § 107, the liabilities and defenses provision, nor § 113, which authorizes contribution claims, expressly mentions the recovery of attorney's fees. The absence of specific reference to attorney's fees is not dispositive if the statute otherwise evinces an intent to provide for such fees. *** Mere "generalized commands," however, will not suffice to authorize such fees.

The three components of Key Tronic's claim for attorney's fees raise somewhat different issues. We first consider whether the fees for prosecuting this action against the Air Force are recoverable under CERCLA. That depends, again, upon whether the "enforcement activities" included in § 101(25)'s definition of "response" encompass a private party's action to recover cleanup costs from other potentially responsible parties such that the attorney's fees associated with that action are then "necessary costs of response" within § 107(a)(4)(B).

III

The 1986 SARA amendments to CERCLA are the genesis of the term "enforcement activities"; we begin, therefore, by considering the statutory basis for the claim in the original CERCLA enactment and the SARA amendments' effect on it. In its original form CERCLA contained no express provision authorizing a private party that had incurred cleanup costs to seek contribution from other potentially responsible parties. In numerous cases, however, district courts interpreted the statute—particularly the § 107 provisions outlining the liabilities and defenses of persons against whom the Government may assert claims—to impliedly authorize such a cause of action.

The 1986 SARA amendments included a provision—CERCLA § 113(f)—that expressly created a cause of action for contribution. Other SARA provisions, moreover, appeared to endorse the judicial decisions recognizing a cause of action under § 107 by presupposing that such an action existed. *** Thus the statute now expressly authorizes a cause of action for contribution in § 113 and impliedly authorizes a similar and somewhat overlapping remedy in § 107.

As we have said, neither § 107 nor § 113 expressly calls for the recovery of attorney's fees by the prevailing party. In contrast, two SARA amendments contain explicit authority for the award of attorney's fees. A new provision authorizing private citizens to bring suit to enforce the statute, expressly authorizes the award of "reasonable attorney and expert witness fees" to the prevailing party. 42 U. S. C. § 9659(f). And an amendment to the section authorizing the Attorney General to bring abatement actions provides that a person erroneously ordered to pay response costs may in some circumstances recover counsel fees from the Government. *See* 42 U.S.C. § 9606(b)(2)(E). Since its enactment CERCLA also has expressly authorized the recovery of fees in actions brought by employees claiming discriminatory treatment based on their disclosure of statutory violations. *See* 42 U.S.C. § 9610(c) ***.

Judicial decisions, rather than explicit statutory text, also resolved an issue that arose frequently under the original version of CERCLA—that is, whether the award in a government enforcement action seeking to recover cleanup costs could encompass its litigation expenses, including attorney's fees. Here, too, District Courts generally agreed that such fees were recoverable. Congress arguably endorsed these holdings, as well, in the SARA amendment redefining the term "response" to include related "enforcement activities." Key Tronic contends that a private action under § 107 is one of the enforcement activities covered by that definition and that fees should therefore be available in private litigation as well as in government actions.

For three reasons, we are unpersuaded. First, although § 107 unquestionably provides a cause of action for private parties to seek recovery of cleanup costs, that cause of action is not explicitly set out in the text of the statute. To conclude that a provision that only impliedly authorizes suit nonetheless provides for attorney's fees with the clarity required by *Alyeska Pipeline Service Co. v. Wilderness Society*, 421 U.S. 240 (1975) would be unusual if not unprecedented. Indeed, none of our cases has authorized fee awards to prevailing parties in such circumstances.

Second, Congress included two express provisions for fee awards in the SARA amendments without including a similar provision in either § 113, which expressly authorizes contribution claims, or in § 107, which impliedly authorizes private parties to recover cleanup costs from other PRP's. These omissions strongly suggest a deliberate decision not to authorize such awards.

Third, we believe it would stretch the plain terms of the phrase "enforcement activities" too far to construe it as encompassing the kind of private cost recovery action at issue in this case. Though we offer no comment on the extent to which that phrase forms the basis for the Government's recovery of attorney's fees through § 107, the term "enforcement activity" is not sufficiently explicit to embody a private action under § 107 to recover cleanup costs. Given our adherence to a general practice of not awarding fees to a prevailing party absent explicit statutory authority, *Alyeska*, 421 U.S. at 262, we conclude that CERCLA § 107 does not provide for the award of private litigants' attorney's fees associated with bringing a cost recovery action.

IV

The conclusion we reach with respect to litigation-related fees does not signify that all payments that happen to be made to a lawyer are unrecoverable expenses under CERCLA. On the contrary, some lawyers' work that is closely tied to the actual cleanup may constitute a necessary cost of response in and of itself under the terms of §

107(a)(4)(B). The component of Key Tronic's claim that covers the work performed in identifying other potentially responsible parties falls in this category. Unlike the litigation services at issue in *Alyeska*, these efforts might well be performed by engineers, chemists, private investigators or other professionals who are not lawyers.
***

The District Court in this case recognized the role Key Tronic's search for other responsible parties played in uncovering the Air Force's disposal of wastes at the site and in prompting the EPA to initiate its enforcement action against the Air Force. Tracking down other responsible solvent polluters increases the probability that a cleanup will be effective and get paid for. Key Tronic is therefore quite right to claim that such efforts significantly benefited the entire cleanup effort and served a statutory purpose apart from the reallocation of costs. These kinds of activities are recoverable costs of response clearly distinguishable from litigation expenses.

This reasoning does not extend, however, to the legal services performed in connection with the negotiations between Key Tronic and the EPA that culminated in the consent decree. Studies that Key Tronic's counsel prepared or supervised during those negotiations may indeed have aided the EPA and may also have affected the ultimate scope and form of the cleanup. We nevertheless view such work as primarily protecting Key Tronic's interests as a defendant in the proceedings that established the extent of its liability. As such, these services do not constitute "necessary costs of response" and are not recoverable under CERCLA.

* * *

B. Settlements and Contribution Protection

Although there is a tremendous volume of case law construing CERCLA, most cases address preliminary legal issues and very few reflect the ultimate outcome of the case. Most CERCLA proceedings actually end in settlement, rather than judicially-imposed resolutions. In recognition of the significant role of settlements, the 1986 CERCLA amendments added a section devoted specifically to settlements, confirming the EPA's authority to enter into settlements and imposing substantive and procedural limitations on the settlement process. § 122, 42 U.S.C. § 9622.

CERCLA's settlement provisions can have a substantial impact on allocation issues. First, they authorize the EPA to prepare "nonbinding preliminary allocations of responsibility," presenting the EPA's assessment of the percentage contribution of each PRP. § 122(e)(3). Second, the provisions authorize the EPA to enter into "de minimis" settlements with low-volume/low-toxicity generator PRPs or innocent landowner PRPs. § 122(g). Such settlements may involve a final resolution more promptly than can or will be achieved for other PRPs, thus shifting the additional transaction costs to the remaining PRPs. They may also involve a broader release, or covenant not to sue, than may be obtainable by the non-de minimis PRPs. Third, the settlement provisions authorize the EPA to enter into "mixed funding" settlements, where the Superfund absorbs the costs of the "orphan shares" (*i.e.*, would-be PRPs who cannot be found or have no resources to contribute) and the payment required of the other PRPs is thereby reduced. § 122(b)(1). Fourth, and probably of greatest significance, the settlement provisions authorize the EPA to provide "contribution protection" to settling parties, whereby they "shall not be liable for claims for contribution regarding matters addressed in the settlement." §§ 122(g)(5) and (h)(4). The settlement provisions also prescribe procedural requirements, such as notice to and opportunity for comment by the public, and the requirement of court approval (except for administrative settlements with de minimis parties). They address the EPA's options for issuing covenants not to sue, for preexisting and future liability, and settlements regarding natural resource damage claims.

The following case sets forth the basic principles governing judicial review and approval of CERCLA settlements, and addresses the impact of settlements on the allocation of liability among PRPs. (The reader may wish to have a thesaurus on hand.)

UNITED STATES V. CANNONS ENGINEERING CORP.
899 F.2d 79 (1st Cir. 1990)

Before TORRUELLA and SELYA, Circuit Judges, and BOWNES, Senior Circuit Judge.

SELYA, Circuit Judge.

"Superfund" sites are those which require priority remedial attention because of the presence, or suspected presence, of a dangerous accumulation of hazardous wastes. Expenditures to clean up such sites are specially authorized pursuant to 42 U.S.C. § 9611 (1987). After the federal government, through the United States Environmental Protection Agency (EPA), identified four such sites in Bridgewater, Massachusetts, Plymouth, Massachusetts, Londonderry, New Hampshire, and Nashua, New Hampshire (collectively, the Sites), the EPA undertook an intensive investigation to locate potentially responsible parties (PRPs). In the course of this investigation, the agency created a de minimis classification (DMC), putting in this category persons or firms whose discerned contribution to pollution of the Sites was minimal both in the amount and toxicity of the hazardous wastes involved. *See* 42 U.S.C. § 9622(g) (1987). The agency staked out the DMC on the basis of volumetric shares, grouping within it entities identifiable as generators of less than one percent of the waste sent to the Sites. To arrive at a PRP's volumetric share, the agency, using estimates, constituted a ratio between the volume of wastes that the PRP sent to the Sites and the total amount of wastes sent there.

The EPA sent notices of possible liability to some 671 PRPs, including generators and nongenerators. Administrative settlements were thereafter achieved with 300 generators (all de minimis PRPs). In short order, the United States and the two host states, Massachusetts and New Hampshire, brought suits in the United States District Court for the District of Massachusetts against 84 of the PRPs who had rejected, or were ineligible for, the administrative settlement. The suits sought recovery of previously incurred cleanup costs and declarations of liability for future remediation under the Comprehensive Environmental Response, Compensation and Liability Act (CERCLA). The actions were consolidated.

With its complaint, the United States filed two proposed consent decrees. The first (the MP decree) embodied a contemplated settlement with 47 major PRPs, that is, responsible parties who were ineligible for membership in the DMC. This assemblage included certain generators whose volumetric shares exceeded the 1% cutoff point and certain nongenerators (like the owners of the Sites and hazardous waste transporters). The second consent decree (the DMC decree) embodied a contemplated settlement with 12 de minimis PRPs who had eschewed participation in the administrative settlement. As required by statute, notice of the decrees' proposed entry was published in the Federal Register. 53 Fed.Reg. 29,959 (Aug. 9, 1988). No comments were received.

The government thereupon moved to enter the decrees. Seven non-settling defendants objected. After considering written submissions and hearing arguments of counsel, the district court approved both consent decrees and dismissed all cross-claims against the settling defendants. The court proceeded to certify the decrees as final under Fed.R.Civ.P. 54(b). These appeals followed.

I

We approach our task mindful that, on appeal, a district court's approval of a consent decree in CERCLA litigation is encased in a double layer of swaddling. In the first place, it is the policy of the law to encourage settlements. That policy has particular force where, as here, a government actor committed to the protection of the public interest has pulled the laboring oar in constructing the proposed settlement. While "the true measure of the deference due depends on the persuasive power of the agency's proposal and rationale, given whatever practical considerations may impinge and the full panoply of the attendant circumstances," *Standard Financial*, 830 F.2d at 408, the district court must refrain from second-guessing the Executive Branch.

Respect for the agency's role is heightened in a situation where the cards have been dealt face up and a crew of sophisticated players, with sharply conflicting interests, sit at the table. That so many affected parties, themselves knowledgeable and represented by experienced lawyers, have hammered out an agreement at arm's length and advocate its embodiment in a judicial decree, itself deserves weight in the ensuing balance. The relevant standard, after all, is not whether the settlement is one which the court itself might have fashioned, or considers as ideal, but whether the proposed decree is fair, reasonable, and faithful to the objectives of the governing statute. Thus, the first layer of insulation implicates the trial court's deference to the agency's expertise and to the parties' agreement. While the district court should not mechanistically rubberstamp the agency's suggestions, neither should it approach the merits of the contemplated settlement *de novo*.

The second layer of swaddling derives from the nature of appellate review. Because approval of a consent decree is committed to the trial court's informed discretion, the court of appeals should be reluctant to disturb a reasoned exercise of that discretion. In this context, the test for abuse of discretion is itself a fairly deferential one. *** The doubly required deference—district court to agency and appellate court to district court—places a heavy burden on those who purpose to upset a trial judge's approval of a consent decree.

II

With this introduction, we turn to our twice-swaddled assessment of the decrees here at issue. In beginning, we abjure an exegetic description of the decrees themselves or of the factual/legal background upon which they are superimposed, instead referring the motivated reader to the district court's comprehensive description of the governments' claims, the administrative settlement, the MP decree, and the DMC decree. We note only a few of the decrees' historical antecedents.

Originally, the EPA extended an open offer to all de minimis PRPs, including five of the six appellants, proposing an administrative settlement based on 160% of each PRP's volumetric share of the total projected response cost, that is, the price of remedial actions, past and anticipated. The settlement figure included a 60% premium to cover unexpected costs and/or unforeseen conditions. Settling PRPs paid their shares in cash and were released outright from all liability. They were also exempted from suits for contribution, *see* 42 U.S.C. § 9622(g)(5) (1987).

Following consummation of the administrative settlement, plaintiffs entered into negotiations with the remaining PRPs. These negotiations resulted in the proposed MP decree (accepted by 47 "major" defendants) and the DMC decree. The terms of the former have been memorialized in the opinion below, 720 F.Supp. at 1034, and do not bear repeating. The latter was modelled upon the administrative settlement, but featured an increased premium: rather than allowing de minimis PRPs to cash out at a 160% level, an eligible generator could resolve its liability only by agreeing to pay 260% of its volumetric share of the total projected response cost. The EPA justified the incremental 100% premium as being in the nature of delay damages.

With this admittedly sketchy background, we proceed with our consideration of the instant appeals ***.

III
* * *

Our starting point is well defined. The Superfund Amendments and Reauthorization Act of 1986 (SARA) authorized a variety of types of settlements which the EPA may utilize in CERCLA actions, including consent decrees providing for PRPs to contribute to cleanup costs and/or to undertake response activities themselves. *See* 42 U.S.C. § 9622. SARA's legislative history makes pellucid that, when such consent decrees are forged, the trial court's review function is only to "satisfy itself that the settlement is reasonable, fair, and consistent with the purposes that CERCLA is intended to serve." H.R.Rep. No. 253, Pt. 3, 99th Cong., 1st Sess. 19 (1985). Reasonableness, fairness, and fidelity to the statute are, therefore, the horses which district judges must ride.

* * *

A. *Procedural Fairness.*

We agree with the district court that fairness in the CERCLA settlement context has both procedural and substantive components. To measure procedural fairness, a court should ordinarily look to the negotiation process and attempt to gauge its candor, openness, and bargaining balance.

In this instance, the district court found the proposed decrees to possess the requisite procedural integrity, and appellants have produced no persuasive reason to alter this finding. It is clear the district court believed that the government conducted negotiations forthrightly and in good faith, and the record is replete with indications to that effect. Most of appellants' contrary intimations are vapid and merit summary rejection. But their flagship argument—that the procedural integrity of the settlement was ruptured because appellants were neither allowed to join the MP decree nor informed in advance that they would be excluded—requires comment.

Appellants claim that they were relatively close to the 1% cutoff point, and were thus arbitrarily excluded from the major party settlement, avails them naught. Congress intended to give the EPA broad discretion to structure classes of PRPs for settlement purposes. We cannot say that the government acted beyond the scope of that discretion in separating minor and major players in this instance, that is, in determining that generators who had sent less than 1% of the volume of hazardous waste to the Sites would comprise the DMC and those generators who were responsible for a greater percentage would be treated as major PRPs. While the dividing line was only one of many which the agency could have selected, it was well within the universe of plausibility. *** Moreover, having established separate categories for different PRPs, the agency had no obligation to let defendants flit from class to class, thus undermining the rationale and purpose for drawing lines in the first place.

* * *

B. *Substantive Fairness.*

Substantive fairness introduces into the equation concepts of corrective justice and accountability: a party should bear the cost of the harm for which it is legally responsible. The logic behind these concepts dictates that settlement terms must be based upon, and roughly correlated with, some acceptable measure of comparative fault, apportioning liability among the settling parties according to rational (if necessarily imprecise) estimates of how much harm each PRP has done. ***

Even accepting substantive fairness as linked to comparative fault, an important issue still remains as to how comparative fault is to be measured. There is no universally correct approach. It appears very clear to us that what constitutes the best measure of comparative fault at a particular Superfund site under particular factual circumstances should be left largely to the EPA's expertise. Whatever formula or scheme EPA advances for measuring comparative fault and allocating liability should be upheld so long as the agency supplies a plausible explanation for it, welding some reasonable linkage between the factors it includes in its formula or scheme and the proportionate shares of the settling PRPs. Put in slightly different terms, the chosen measure of comparative fault should be upheld unless it is arbitrary, capricious, and devoid of a rational basis. *See* 42 U.S.C.§9613(j) (1987).

Not only must the EPA be given leeway to construct the barometer of comparative fault, but the agency must also be accorded flexibility to diverge from an apportionment formula in order to address special factors not conducive to regimented treatment. While the list of possible variables is virtually limitless, two frequently encountered reasons warranting departure from strict formulaic comparability are the uncertainty of future events and the timing of particular settlement decisions. ***

* * *

In this instance, we agree with the court below that the consent decrees pass muster from a standpoint of substantive fairness. They adhere generally to principles of comparative fault according to a volumetric standard, determining the liability of each PRP according to volumetric contribution. And, to the extent they deviate from this formulaic approach, they do so on the basis of adequate justification. In particular, the premiums charged to de minimis PRPs in the administrative settlement, and the increased premium charged in the DMC decree, seem well warranted.

The argument that the EPA should have used relative toxicity as a determinant of proportionate liability for response costs, instead of a strictly volumetric ranking, is a stalking horse. Having selected a reasonable method of weighing comparative fault, the agency need not show that it is the best, or even the fairest, of all conceivable methods. The choice of the yardstick to be used for allocating liability must be left primarily to the expert discretion of the EPA, particularly when the PRPs involved are numerous and the situation is complex. ***

Appellants' next asseveration—that the decrees favor major party PRPs over their less culpable counterparts—is a gross distortion. While the DMC and MP decrees differ to some extent in application of the volumetric share formula, requiring lower initial contributions under the latter, the good-faith justification for this divergence is readily apparent. In return for the premium paid, de minimis PRPs can cash out, thus obtaining two important benefits: reduced transaction costs and absolute finality with respect to the monetization of their overall liability. The major PRPs, on the other hand, retain an open-ended risk anent their liability at three of the Sites, making any comparison of proportionate contributions a dubious proposition. At the very least, assumption of this unquantifiable future liability under the MP decree warranted some discount—and the tradeoff crafted by the government's negotiators seems reasonable. Indeed, the acceptance of the first and second DMC settlement offers by so many of the de minimis PRPs is itself an indication of substantive fairness toward the class to which appellants belong. On this record, the district court did not misuse its discretion in ruling that the decrees sufficiently tracked the parties' comparative fault.

The last point which merits discussion under this rubric involves the fact that the agency upped the ante as the game continued, that is, the premium assessed as part of the administrative settlement was increased substantially for purposes of the later DMC decree. Like the district court, we see no unfairness in this approach. For one thing, litigation is expensive—and having called the tune by their refusal to subscribe to the administrative settlement, we think it not unfair that appellants, thereafter, would have to pay the piper. For another thing, rewarding PRPs who settle sooner rather than later is completely consonant with CERCLA's makeup.

Although appellants berate escalating settlement offers as discriminating among similarly situated PRPs, we think that the government's use of such a technique is fair and serves to promote the explicit statutory goal of expediting remedial measures for hazardous waste sites. *** That the cost of purchasing peace may rise for a laglast is consistent with the method of the statute; indeed, if the government cannot offer such routine incentives, there will be little inducement on the part of any PRP to enter an administrative settlement. *** We believe that the EPA is entitled to make use of a series of escalating settlement proposals in a CERCLA case and that, as the district court ruled, the serial settlements employed in this instance were substantively fair.

C. Reasonableness.

In the usual environmental litigation, the evaluation of a consent decree's reasonableness will be a multifaceted exercise. We comment briefly upon three such facets. The first is obvious: the decree's likely efficaciousness as a vehicle for cleansing the environment is of cardinal importance. Except in cases which involve only recoupment of cleanup costs already spent, the reasonableness of the consent decree, for this purpose, will be basically a question of technical adequacy, primarily concerned with the probable effectiveness of proposed remedial responses.

A second important facet of reasonableness will depend upon whether the settlement satisfactorily compensates the public for the actual (and anticipated) costs of remedial and response measures. Like the question of technical adequacy, this aspect of the problem can be enormously complex. The actual cost of remedial measures is frequently uncertain at the time a consent decree is proposed. Thus, although the settlement's bottom line may be definite, the proportion of settlement dollars to total needed dollars is often debatable. Once again, the agency cannot realistically be held to a standard of mathematical precision. If the figures relied upon derive in a sensible way from a plausible interpretation of the record, the court should normally defer to the agency's expertise.

A third integer in the reasonableness equation relates to the relative strength of the parties' litigating positions. If the government's case is strong and solid, it should typically be expected to drive a harder bargain. On the other hand, if the case is less than robust, or the outcome problematic, a reasonable settlement will ordinarily mirror such factors. *** The same variable, we suggest, has a further dimension: even if the government's case is sturdy, it may take time and money to collect damages or to implement private remedial measures through litigatory success. To the extent that time is of essence or that transaction costs loom large, a settlement which nets less than full recovery of cleanup costs is nonetheless reasonable. ***

In this case, the district court found the consent decrees to be reasonable. We agree. Appellants have not seriously questioned the technological efficacy of the cleanup measures to be implemented at the Sites. ***

D. *Fidelity to the Statute.*
*   *   *

It is crystal clear that the broad settlement authority conferred upon the EPA must be exercised with deference to the statute's overarching principles: accountability, the desirability of an unsullied environment, and promptness of response activities. The bases appear to have been touched in this instance. Appellants concede that the government made a due and diligent search to uncover the identity of PRPs; the classification of perpetrators and the use of a modified volumetric share formula appear reasonably related to assuring accountability; the settlements will unarguably promote early completion of cleanup activities; and the technical efficacy of the selected remedial measures is not in issue. On this basis, the consent decrees seem fully consistent with CERCLA.

One can, of course, conjure up ways in which particular consent decrees, while seemingly fair and reasonable, might nevertheless contravene the aims of the statute. Rather than attempting to catalogue a virtually endless list of possibilities, we address, in terms of what we discern to be the congressional will, certain points raised by the appellants.

1. *De Minimis Settlements.* In the SARA Amendments, Congress gave the EPA authority to settle with a de minimis PRP so long as (i) the agreement involved only a "minor portion" of the total response costs, and (ii) the toxicity and amount of substances contributed by the PRP were "minimal in comparison to the other hazardous substances at the facility." 42 U.S.C. § 9622(g)(1). The two determinative criteria are not further defined. Appellants, for a variety of reasons, question the boundaries fixed for the DMC class in this instance, contending that drawing lines so sharply, and adhering to those lines so blindly, thwarts CERCLA's legitimate goals.

*** [H]ad Congress meant the agency to employ a purely mechanical taxonomy, it would have so provided. We believe that Congress intended quite the opposite; the EPA was to have substantial discretion to interpret the statutory terms in light of both its expertise and its negotiating strategy in a given case. Therefore, in attempting to gauge a consent decree's consistency with the statute, courts must give a wide berth to the agency's choice of eligibility criteria. In this case, the criteria selected fell well within the ambit of Executive discretion.

2. *Disproportionate Liability.* In the SARA Amendments, Congress explicitly created a statutory framework that left nonsettlors at risk of bearing a disproportionate amount of liability. The statute immunizes settling parties from liability for contribution and provides that only the amount of the settlement—not the pro rata share attributable to the settling party—shall be subtracted from the liability of the nonsettlors. This can

prove to be a substantial benefit to settling PRPs—and a corresponding detriment to their more recalcitrant counterparts.

Although such immunity creates a palpable risk of disproportionate liability, that is not to say that the device is forbidden. To the exact contrary, Congress has made its will explicit and the courts must defer. *** Disproportionate liability, a technique which promotes early settlements and deters litigation for litigation's sake, is an integral part of the statutory plan.

In a related vein, appellants assail the district court's dismissal of their cross-claims for contribution as against all settling PRPs. They contend, in essence, that the district court failed to appreciate that they would potentially bear a greater proportional liability than will be shouldered by any of the settling parties. ***

As originally enacted, CERCLA did not expressly provide for a right of contribution among parties found jointly and severally liable for response costs. When CERCLA was amended by SARA in 1986, Congress created an express right of contribution among parties found liable for response costs. *See* 42 U.S.C. § 9613(f)(1). Congress specifically provided that contribution actions could not be maintained against settlors. *See* 42 U.S.C. § 9613(f)(2) (1987). This provision was designed to encourage settlements and provide PRPs a measure of finality in return for their willingness to settle. Congress plainly intended non-settlors to have no contribution rights against settlors regarding matters addressed in settlement. Thus, the cross-claims were properly dismissed; Congress purposed that all who choose not to settle confront the same sticky wicket of which appellants complain.

The statute, of course, not only bars contribution claims against settling parties, but also provides that, while a settlement will not discharge other PRPs, "it reduces the potential liability of the others by the amount of settlement." 42 U.S.C. § 9613(f)(2). The law's plain language admits of no construction other than a dollar-for-dollar reduction of the aggregate liability. The weight of considered authority so holds. *** This clear and unequivocal statutory mandate overrides appellants' quixotic imprecation that their liability should be reduced not by the amount of settlement but by the equitable shares of the settling parties. In a very real sense, the appellants' arguments are with Congress, not with the district court.

3. *Indemnity.* On a similar note, appellants bemoan the dismissal of their cross-claims for indemnity against the settling PRPs. We are unmoved. Although CERCLA is silent regarding indemnification, we refuse to read into the statute a right to indemnification that would eviscerate § 9613(f)(2) and allow non-settlors to make an end run around the statutory scheme.

*** Clearly, if appellants' claims for partial contribution can validly be barred in the course of implementing a CERCLA settlement, their claims for total contribution, i.e., indemnity, can likewise be foreclosed.

* * *

5. *Exclusions from Settlements.* The CERCLA statutes do not require the agency to open all settlement offers to all PRPs; and we refuse to insert such a requirement into the law by judicial fiat. Under the SARA Amendments, the right to draw fine lines, and

to structure the order and pace of settlement negotiations to suit, is an agency prerogative. *** So long as it operates in good faith, the EPA is at liberty to negotiate and settle with whomever it chooses.

* * *

V

Although the appellants have posited a host of other arguments, we deem discussion of them unnecessary. A district court, faced with consent decrees executed in good faith and at arm's length between the EPA and counselled polluters, must look at the big picture, leaving interstitial details largely to the agency's informed judgment. Once the district court has performed this tamisage, we must, absent mistake of law, be doubly deferential, respecting both the agency's expertise and the trial court's sound discretion. We may still intervene if an abuse of discretion looms—but we will not lightly disturb the lower court's approval of such a decree.

In this instance, the district court proceeded with evident care. Its conclusion that the decrees, as proposed, are fair, reasonable, and faithful to CERCLA's purposes is fully supportable. The district court considered the appropriate factors and appears to have weighed them in a completely acceptable manner.

We need go no further. Although appellants may suffer adverse effects from the consummation of the settlements embodied in the decrees, those effects stem not from any systemic unfairness but from the combination of Congress' plan and appellants' own conduct (including their negotiating strategy).

NOTES

1. Although *Cannons Engineering* typifies the courts' deferential approach to CERCLA settlements, some settlements have failed to garner judicial sanction. In *United States v. Montrose Chemical Corp.*, 50 F.3d 741 (9th Cir. 1995), the Ninth Circuit held that the district court abused its discretion in approving a consent decree that lacked an estimate of projected natural resource damages at issue.

We *** vacate the district court's approval of the consent decree and remand the matter for the district court to conduct an independent evaluation of the settlement with LACSD and the 150 local governmental agencies to determine whether it is "reasonable, fair, and consistent with the purposes that CERCLA is intended to serve." *See Cannons*, 899 F.2d at 85.

In conducting that evaluation, the court, in addition to considering any other relevant factors, should determine the proportional relationship between the $45.7 million to be paid by the settling defendants and the governments' current estimate of total potential damages. The court should evaluate the fairness of that proportional relationship in light of the degree of liability attributable to the settling defendants.

Moreover, we believe that the nature of the liability of the various defendants is of considerable relevance in determining whether the settlement is fair, reasonable and consistent with the public interest. For example, if joint and several liability does not apply to the natural resources damages, the governments' ability to collect the totality of remaining damages from the non-settling defendants certainly would have an impact on the settlement's merits.

* * *

We recognize that, in holding that the district court erred in approving the proposed consent decree, we treat relatively uncharted territory in the area of Superfund litigation. By so holding, however, we do not denigrate CERCLA's primary goal of encouraging early settlement. Nor do we vitiate the district courts' considerable discretion in approving such settlements. Deference, however, does not mean turning a blind eye to an empty record on a critical aspect of settlement evaluation. Where clear error occurs, we will reverse. Swaddling is not armor. Because we believe that the district court did not possess sufficient information to adequately determine whether the LACSD consent decree was fair, reasonable, and consistent with CERCLA's objectives, we vacate and remand

Id. at 747-48.

2. As the CERCLA cleanup process matures, with more sites subject to high-cost settlements providing for actual cleanup (rather than investigation and study), and as private party litigation—both derivative from and independent of governmental cleanups—escalates, the scope of CERCLA's contribution protection for settlors is being tested with increasing frequency.

In a significant number of cases, under varying circumstances, courts have allowed some contribution claims to proceed, upon finding that they do not encompass "matters addressed" in the settlement from which the contribution protection is derived.

In *Akzo Coatings, Inc. v. Aigner Corp.*, 30 F.3d 761 (7th Cir. 1994), the Seventh Circuit observed that CERCLA "does not specify how we are to determine what particular 'matters' a consent decree addresses." Because § 113(f)(1) directs the courts to employ equitable factors in resolving contribution claims, "rather than adopting any bright lines, Congress quite clearly envisioned a flexible approach to contribution issues." *Id.* at 765.

In that case, Akzo Coatings had complied with a § 106 order issued by the EPA in 1988 directing it (and some 20 other companies) to conduct emergency removal activities at one portion of a larger site that had been an industrial park. In 1992, the EPA entered into a settlement with some 200 PRPs regarding the cleanup of the rest of the site. Akzo did not participate in the settlement because it believed that its liability was limited to the portion of the site that it was addressing in response to the EPA's § 106 order. Akzo sued Aigner Corp., which had been named in the EPA's order and which had also entered into the subsequent settlement regarding the rest of the site. Aigner claimed contribution protection based on that settlement. The Seventh Circuit ruled that Aigner's contribution protection did not apply to Akzo's claims for contribution for compliance with the § 106 order.

Other courts have suggested that the "matters addressed" by a consent decree be determined with reference to the particular location, time frame, hazardous substances, and clean-up costs covered by the agreement. The United States correctly observes that this should not be treated as an exhaustive list of appropriate considerations, for the relevance of each factor will vary with the facts of the case. Ultimately, the "matters addressed" by a consent decree must be assessed in a manner consistent with both the reasonable expectations of the signatories and the equitable apportionment of costs that Congress envisioned.

Because Akzo's work stands apart in kind, context, and time from the work envisioned by the consent decree, we conclude that it is not a "matter addressed" by the decree. Akzo was required to engaged in "removal" work—that is, a short-term, limited effort to abate any immediate threat posed by the wastes present at the site. The consent decree, on the other hand, provides for the kind of long-term, "remedial" work necessary to accomplish a complete clean-up of the site. This distinction is reflected in the two different orders implementing the work. The 1988 order unilaterally directed Akzo to undertake certain "emergency removal activities," including the extraction and disposal of leaking drums and other hazards from the Two-Line Road facility. In contrast, the 1992 consent decree embodies a negotiated settlement designed to implement a long-range remedial plan for the entire site, as outlined in the EPA's 1990 Record of Decision ("ROD"). Neither the decree nor the ROD purports to incorporate the 1988 order; on the contrary, the ROD explicitly assumes that "all drums, tanks, and containers on the Two-Line Road property requiring remedial action are being addressed" by that order. Indeed, by the time Aigner entered into the consent decree, Akzo's removal work had already been completed. Consequently, it comes as no surprise that this work was not addressed in the consent decree ***. Because Akzo's preliminary clean-up work is thus so clearly distinct form the long-range remedial matters addressed by the decree, Akzo is entitled to seek contribution from the settling PRPs under section 113(f)(1).

Id. at 766-67.

United States v. Colorado & Eastern Railroad Co., 50 F.3d 1530 (10th Cir. 1995), involved two successive settlements pertaining to the same site. In the first settlement, two of the PRPs at a multi-PRP Superfund site agreed to pay $700,000 to the EPA for its already-incurred response costs, and to perform all remediation at the site (ultimately costing more than $15 million). In the second settlement, a different group of PRPs agreed to pay the EPA $100,000 for already-incurred response costs. One of the parties to the first settlement then sued the parties to the second settlement for $734,058, representing the additional cleanup costs that it had incurred due to the second settlors' alleged "excavation and soil removal activities, refusal to allow access and other actions." The Tenth Circuit carefully examined the scope of each of the two settlements, and allowed that claim to proceed. It determined that the claim for reimbursement of the first settlor's cleanup costs was not a matter addressed in the second settlors' agreement, which covered the EPA's past response costs. The second settlement did, however, bar the first settlor from seeking contribution for the $700,000 it had paid to the EPA for past response costs.

Set forth below is the balance of the *Rumpke* case excerpted in subchapter 13.A above. This evaluates a "matters addressed" issue arising in a two-site context.

RUMPKE OF INDIANA, INC. V. CUMMINS ENGINE CO.
107 F.3d 1235 (7th Cir. 1997)

Before BAUER, EASTERBROOK, and DIANE P. WOOD, Circuit Judges. DIANE P. WOOD, Circuit Judge.

* * *

2. *Rumpke's § 113(f)(1) claim.* If the facts show, contrary to Rumpke's protestations, that it was partially responsible for the mess at Uniontown, *Akzo* holds that it can proceed only under § 113(f)(1) in a suit for contribution. In that case, the scope of the settlement bar of § 113(f)(2) would become important. We therefore turn to the question whether the 1982 *Seymour* settlement addressed the Cummins defendants' liability for sites other than the Seymour site itself.

B.   *Matters Addressed in the Settlement*

The starting point for our analysis of this question is, as we noted in *Akzo*, the language of the consent decree itself. We said there that "the 'matters addressed' by a consent decree must be assessed in a manner consistent with both the reasonable expectations of the signatories and the equitable apportionment of costs that Congress has envisioned." 30 F.3d at 766 (citation omitted). This does not mean that the language of the decree is subject to an ill-defined equitable trump card; the congressional intent was viewed instead as something like a canon of construction for the language of the decree. The *Akzo* majority was especially concerned about the potential for negotiated consent decrees to affect third-party rights, through the contribution bar of § 113(f)(2). The statute itself addresses this problem directly, by making the contribution bar applicable only for administrative and judicially approved settlements, rather than to every private settlement that might be negotiated. In keeping with this extra care, *Akzo* held that terms in a decree that are especially likely to affect third-party rights must be more explicit. Using this approach, the court concluded that the consent decree before it did not bar Akzo's claim, largely because "Akzo's work [stood] apart in kind, context, and time from the work envisioned in the consent decree...." *Id.* at 767.

None of the factors found important in *Akzo* suggest that the 1982 *Seymour* decree addressed the settling parties' liability for waste from Seymour Recycling dumped at virtually any or every other spot on the globe, including the Uniontown landfill. Rumpke's Uniontown work is apart in "kind, context, and time" from the Seymour surface cleanup. The decree defined, very specifically, the parties' responsibilities for the Seymour Recycling site in Seymour, Indiana. For example, Exhibit B of the decree defined the decree's object as "The Removal and Disposal of Drummed Hazardous Chemicals and Waste Materials Located at: Seymour Recycling Center[,] Seymour, Indiana." Section VIII of the decree gave the United States, the State, and their authorized representatives "access to the Seymour site at all times until such time as the Work is completed." Section IX allowed the various governmental authorities "access to the site for the sampling of wastes at the site...." Section XII itself, on which the Cummins group has pinned its hopes, declared it to be the intention of the parties "[t]o avoid litigation ... in connection with the Seymour site...."

Read as a whole, we do not find the decree to be ambiguous. The Cummins defendants read far too much into their ellipsis-ridden phrase "arising out of ... the ... transportation ... of any materials ... from ... the Seymour site," when they claim that this covers all transshipments away from the site. If we are playing with ellipses, we could also say that the decree covers matters "arising out of the ... transportation ... of any materials ... near the Seymour site," but even Cummins' lawyer agreed that it would be absurd to conclude that the Cummins group was protected even if any of its wastes had ever been "near" Seymour, perhaps passing on their way to Uniontown or other locales.

We agree with the district court that section XII of the consent decree makes both internal sense and fits in with the entirety of the settlement quite comfortably if the word "from" is understood to relate to more modest phenomena such as leaching and other similar leakage from the Seymour site itself. *** The Cummins group is protected from liability for matters directly related to the Seymour site; the decree does not have the global reach they have urged here.

* * *

C. Allocation Issues

In cases brought by the EPA (or a state) against a group of PRPs, joint and several liability typically applies and, once the liability of the PRPs as a group is resolved (whether by judicial determination or settlement), the PRPs frequently settle among themselves as to each party's respective share. Among generator PRPs, each party's volumetric contribution to the hazardous substances at the site is generally used to determine relative shares.

As private CERCLA actions play an increasingly prominent role, courts are being called upon more frequently to allocate liability among two or more PRPs. Because the contribution provision directs courts to "allocate response costs among liable parties using such equitable factors as the court determines are appropriate," § 113(f)(1), it is difficult to generalize about allocation decisions. Following is a sampling of two appellate court decisions concerning the allocation of CERCLA liability among PRPs.

UNITED STATES V. R.W. MEYER, INC.
932 F.2d 568 (6th Cir. 1991)

Before GUY and BOGGS, Circuit Judges, and BERTELSMAN, District Judge of the Eastern District of Kentucky.
BERTELSMAN, District Judge.

This appeal involved the construction of the provisions of the Comprehensive Environmental Response, Compensation, and Liability Act (CERCLA) governing contribution actions among responsible parties following a cleanup of a hazardous waste site and an Immediate Removal Action by the Environmental Protection Agency (EPA).

BACKGROUND

The facts and background necessary to place this opinion in context were well stated by Chief Judge Hillman in his unpublished opinion awarding contribution, as follows:

"This matter stems from a suit brought by the United States against Northernaire Plating Company ("Northernaire") for recovery of its costs in conducting an 'Immediate Removal Action' pursuant to the Comprehensive Environmental Response, Compensation & Liability Act (hereinafter, "CERCLA"). Northernaire owned and operated a metal electroplating business in Cadillac, Michigan. Beginning in 1972, it operated under a 10-year lease on property owned by R.W. Meyer, Inc. ("Meyer"). Northernaire continued operations until mid-1981 when its assets were sold to Toplocker Enterprises, Inc. ("Toplocker"). From July of 1975 until this sale, Willard S. Garwood was the president and sole shareholder of Northernaire. He personally oversaw and managed the day-to-day operations of the company.

"Acting upon inspection reports from the Michigan Department of Natural Resources ("MDNR"), the United States Environmental Protection Agency ("EPA") conducted an Immediate Removal Action at the Northernaire site from July 5 until August 3, 1983. Cleanup of the site required neutralization of caustic acids, bulking and shipment of liquid acids, neutralization of caustic and acid sludges, excavation and removal of a contaminated sewer line, and decontamination of the inside of the building. All of the hazardous substances found at the site were chemicals and by-products of metal electro-plating operations.

"In an earlier opinion and order dated May 6, 1988, this court found the defendants Garwood, Northernaire, and Meyer jointly and severally liable to plaintiff for the costs of the Immediate Removal Action under Section 107(a) of CERCLA. The court awarded plaintiff $268,818.25 plus prejudgment interest. The court later determined the prejudgment interest due to be $74,004.97, making the total award to plaintiff $342,823.22.

"Each defendant, (Northernaire and Garwood moving together) has brought cross-claims for contribution against the other." ***

* * *

Apparently, the parties allowed the building to degenerate into a true environmental disaster area. As this court observed in the former appeal:

"In March 1983, officials from the EPA and the Michigan Department of Natural Resources (MDNR) examined the property. Their examination was prompted by earlier reports of MDNR officials indicating that the building had been locked and abandoned and that a child had received chemical burns from playing around discarded drums of electroplating waste that were left outside the building. State tests on samples of the soil, sludge, and drum contents disclosed the presence of significant amounts of caustic and corrosive materials. During their examination of the site, EPA and MDNR officials observed drums and tanks housing cyanide littered among disarray outside the facility. Based on their observations outside the building, the officials determined that Northernaire had discharged its electroplating waste into a "catch" basin and that the waste had seeped into the ground from the bottom of the basin. The waste then entered a pipe that drained into a sewer line that discharged into the sewage treatment plant for the city of Cadillac."

Meyer, 889 F.2d at 1498-99.

In the former appeal, this court affirmed the decision of the trial court finding that the damage to the site had been "indivisible" and imposing joint and several liability on the present parties to reimburse the EPA for the removal costs for the cleanup of the building.

The total cost of the cleanup plus prejudgment interest was $342,823.22. In this subsequent contribution action, the trial court held that two-thirds of the liability should be borne by Northernaire and its principal shareholder, each contributing one-third each. But the court held that the remaining one-third ($114,274.41) should be borne by the appellant property owner.

The appellant attacks this apportionment, arguing strenuously that its responsibility should be limited to an amount apportioned according to the degree that the sewer line mentioned in the above quote contributed to the cleanup costs. Applying this approach, the appellant generously offers to pay $1,709.03. Appellees accept the trial court's apportionment.

* * *

ANALYSIS

The trial court held that it was within its discretion to apply certain factors found in the legislative history of CERCLA in making its contribution apportionment. Although these factors were originally intended as criteria for deciding whether a party could establish a right to an apportionment of several liability in the EPA's initial removal action, the trial court found "these criteria useful in determining the proportionate share each party is entitled to in contribution from the other."

The criteria mentioned are:

"(1) the ability of the parties to demonstrate that their contribution to a discharge release or disposal of a hazardous waste can be distinguished;

"(2) the amount of the hazardous waste involved;

"(3) the degree of toxicity of the hazardous waste involved;

"(4) the degree of involvement by the parties in the generation, transportation, treatment, storage, or disposal of the hazardous waste;

"(5) the degree of care exercised by the parties with respect to the hazardous waste concerned, taking into account the characteristics of such hazardous waste; and

"(6) the degree of cooperation by the parties with Federal, State, or local officials to prevent any harm to the public health or the environment."

The trial court recognized that the lessee was the primary actor in allowing this site to become contaminated. (Appellant argues that the lessee was the only actor.) The trial court found, however, that in addition to constructing the defective sewer line which contributed to the contamination, appellant bore significant responsibility "simply by virtue of being the landowner." The trial court observed further that appellant "neither assisted nor cooperated with the EPA officials during their investigation and eventual cleanup of the ... site."

Chief Judge Hillman concluded, "As it is well within the province of this court, I have balanced each of the defendants' behavior with respect to the equitable guidelines discussed." As a result of the balancing, he made the apportionment described above.

The trial judge was well within the broad discretion afforded by the statute in making the apportionment he did.

Congress intended to invest the district courts with this discretion in making CERCLA contribution allocations when it provided, "the court may allocate response costs among the liable parties using such *equitable factors as the court determines are appropriate.*" 42 U.S.C. § 9613(f)(1) (emphasis added).

Essentially, appellant argues here that a narrow, technical construction must be given to the term "contribution," so that, as in common law contribution, contribution under the statute is limited to the percentage a party's improper conduct causally contributed to the toxicity of the site in a physical sense. This argument is without merit. On the contrary, by using the term "equitable factors" Congress intended to invoke the tradition of equity under which the court must construct a flexible decree balancing all the equities in the light of the totality of the circumstances.

* * *

Thus, under § 9613(f)(1) the court may consider any factor it deems in the interest of justice in allocating contribution recovery. Certainly, the several factors listed by the trial court are appropriate, but as it recognized, it was not limited to them. No exhaustive list of criteria need or should be formulated. However, in addition to the criteria listed above, the court may consider the state of mind of the parties, their economic status, any contracts between them bearing on the subject, any traditional equitable defenses as mitigating factors and any other factors deemed appropriate to balance the equities in the totality of the circumstances.

Therefore, the trial court quite properly considered here not only the appellant's contribution to the toxic slough described above in a technical causative sense, but also its moral contribution as the owner of the site. Review of the trial court's equitable balancing process is limited to a review for "abuse of discretion." This is in accord with the principle of equity that the chancellor has broad discretion to frame a decree.

This case, even though it involves over $300,000, is but a pimple on the elephantine carcass of the CERCLA litigation now making its way through the court system. Some of these cases involve millions or even billions of dollars in cleanup costs and hundreds or even thousands of potentially responsible parties.

I do not believe Congress intended to require meticulous findings of the precise causative contribution each of several hundred parties made to a hazardous site. In many cases, this would be literally impossible. Rather, by the expansive language used in § 9613(f)(1) Congress intended the court to deal with these situations by creative means, considering all the equities and balancing them in the interests of justice. ***

> "Courts are also following CERCLA Section 113(f) and taking 'equitable factors' into account in apportioning liability for response costs. The equitable factors which courts are examining in order to decide what kind of apportionment to make depend on the actual facts of each case. Nevertheless, many federal courts do consider common law equitable defenses such as unclean hands and *caveat emptor* as mitigating factors in deciding liability for response costs. This approach is in line with Congressional intent as long as courts do not consider these equitable defenses to be a total bar to a liability action, but merely mitigating factors in awarding damages. Courts are also using a modified comparative fault analysis that takes numerous factors such as culpability and cooperation into account in apportioning damages."

[Russo, *Contribution Under CERCLA*, 14 COLUM. J. ENVTL. L. 267, 286 (1989).]

Although such an approach cannot be applied with mathematical precision, it is the fairest and most workable approach for apportioning CERCLA liability. Such an approach furthers the legislative intent of encouraging the prompt cleanup of hazardous sites by those equitably responsible. The parties actually performing the cleanup can look for reimbursement from other potentially responsible parties without fear that their contribution actions will be bogged down by the impossibility of making meticulous factual determinations as to the causal contribution of each party. ***

CONTROL DATA CORP. V. S.C.S.C. CORP.
53 F.3d 930 (8th Cir. 1995)

Before RICHARD S. ARNOLD, Chief Judge, HEANEY, Senior Circuit Judge, and FAGG, Circuit Judge.
RICHARD S. ARNOLD, Chief Judge.

Control Data Corporation brought this suit under the Comprehensive Environmental Response, Compensation, and Liability Act of 1980 (CERCLA), and the Minnesota Environmental Response and Liability Act (MERLA). Following a bench trial, the District Court found the Schloff defendants—S.C.S.C. Corp., Schloff Chemical, and Irvin and Ruth Schloff—liable under CERCLA and allocated responsibility for 33 1/3 % of Control Data's response costs, as defined by CERCLA, to those defendants. ***

The Schloff defendants appeal. We affirm the judgment of the District Court finding the Schloff defendants liable under CERCLA and allocating 33 1/3 % of Control Data's response costs to them. ***

I. Factual Background

Control Data owns and operates a printed-circuit-board facility on Meadowbrook Road in St. Louis Park, Minnesota. Across Meadowbrook Road and Minnehaha Creek, the Schloff defendants owned and operated a dry-cleaning supply business, Schloff Chemical, from 1975 until 1989. Irvin Schloff was president of Schloff Chemical from 1963 to 1989, and exercised day-to-day control over its operations until 1985, when a General Manager was hired. Ruth Schloff has been the record owner of the real property where Schloff Chemical was located since 1974. S.C.S.C. Corp. is the current corporate incarnation of Schloff Chemical.

In 1987, Control Data discovered a leak in its sewer line. Fearing contamination, Control Data initiated an investigation, and, indeed, discovered the presence of volatile organic compounds in the groundwater underlying the Control Data site. Principal among these contaminants were 1,1,1 trichloroethane (TCA) and its degradation substances and tetrachloroethylene (PERC) and its degradation substances. A degradation substance is what a chemical becomes when it begins to break down. PERC and TCA degrade into many of the same substances.

After confirming that groundwater contamination existed, Control Data reported its findings to the Minnesota Pollution Control Agency (MPCA) and began cooperating with that agency in an effort to clean up the site. Control Data has admitted that it is the source of the TCA and its degradation substances. TCA has been spilled, or "released" in CERCLA terminology, many times by Control Data. But Control Data denied ever using, much less releasing, PERC, a circumstance which led the MPCA to search for other sources for the PERC contamination. It turns out that Schloff Chemical was that source.

Schloff Chemical released PERC several times between 1975 and 1989. The PERC released by Schloff Chemical formed a "plume," or discernible body of contaminants, that has migrated beneath Minnehaha Creek and joined with the TCA plume, created by Control Data's releases, on the Control Data site. It is now impossible to discern one plume from the other.

In April of 1988, Control Data entered into a consent decree with the MPCA that required it to investigate, monitor, and clean up the contamination. Pursuant to this agreement, Control Data has installed a remediation system which removes both the TCA and the PERC contaminants concurrently. This cleanup is ongoing and will proceed for an undetermined period of time.[3]

Control Data brought this lawsuit in order to recover a portion of the costs it incurred as a result of the PERC contamination on its site. The District Court found that the Schloff defendants were all liable under CERCLA because they were responsible for releasing hazardous substances into the environment, and that release had caused Control Data to incur response costs. Important to the District Court's reasoning was its finding that PERC is more toxic and more difficult to clean up than TCA. Since the remediation system was designed and constructed around the need to clean up PERC, the release of PERC created additional response costs.

This greater level of toxicity was also central in the District Court's allocation of liability. Though the Schloff defendants were responsible for only 10% of the contamination on the site, the District Court allocated 33 1/3 % of the cost of cleanup to them. It did so because PERC is more toxic, and thus more harmful and difficult to remove, than TCA.

* * *

II. CERCLA Framework

We begin our discussion, as we must, with the language of the statute. Recovery of response costs by a private party under CERCLA is a two-step process.[4] Initially, a plaintiff must prove that the defendant is liable under CERCLA. Once that is accomplished, the defendant's share of liability is apportioned in an equitable manner.

CERCLA liability is established under 42 U.S.C. § 9607(a). *** Thus, in order to prove liability, a plaintiff must show that a defendant is within one of the four classes of covered persons enumerated in subsections (1) through (4); that a release or

---

[3]The investigation led to the discovery of pollutants on the Schloff site as well. The MPCA required the Schloff defendants to clean up their own site. Since June of 1991, that effort has been directed by the MPCA because the Schloff defendants can no longer afford its cost.

[4]By contrast, an action by the federal government, a state, or an Indian tribe to recover response costs is a one-step process. Once liability is proved, all of the defendants are jointly and severally liable, unless a particular defendant can establish that his harm is divisible, a very difficult proposition. See *United States v. Alcan Aluminum Corp.*, 964 F.2d 252, 267-71 (3d Cir.1992); *Farmland Industries v. Morrison-Quirk Grain Corp.*, 987 F.2d 1335, 1340, 1342 n. 6 (8th Cir.1993).

threatened release from a facility has occurred; that the plaintiff incurred response costs as a result; and that the costs were necessary and consistent with the national contingency plan.

A problematic portion of this calculus is the causation element. At the outset, we note that CERCLA does not require the plaintiff to prove that the defendant caused actual harm to the environment at the liability stage. Harm to the environment is material only when allocating responsibility ***. Instead, CERCLA focuses on whether the defendant's release or threatened release caused harm to the plaintiff in the form of response costs. If so, and if the other elements are established, the defendant is liable under CERCLA.

Once liability is established, the focus shifts to allocation. Here, the question is what portion of the plaintiff's response costs will the defendant be responsible for? Allocation is a contribution claim controlled by 42 U.S.C. § 9613(f). ***

Courts have considered various factors in resolving contribution claims, see Nagle, *CERCLA, Causation, and Responsibility*, 78 Minn.L.Rev. 1493, 1522-23, n. 135 (1994), but the "Gore factors," so called after one of the sponsors of CERCLA, are the most widely used. The Gore factors are:

1. the ability of the parties to demonstrate that their contribution to a discharge, release, or disposal of a hazardous waste can be distinguished;

2. the amount of hazardous waste involved;

3. the degree of toxicity of the hazardous waste;

4. the degree of involvement by the parties in the generation, transportation, treatment, storage, or disposal of the hazardous waste;

5. the degree of care exercised by the parties with respect to the hazardous waste concerned, taking into account the characteristics of such hazardous waste; and

6. the degree of cooperation by the parties with Federal, State, or local officials to prevent any harm to the public health or the environment.

Id. at 1522 n. 133. A primary focus of these factors is the harm that each party causes the environment. Those parties who can show that their contribution to the harm is relatively small in terms of amount of waste, toxicity of the waste, involvement with the waste, and care, stand in a better position to be allocated a smaller portion of response costs.

One primary goal of this private cost-recovery framework is to "encourage timely cleanup of hazardous waste sites," *Litton Industrial*, 920 F.2d at 1418. Thus, this Court has consistently held that CERCLA is a strict-liability statute, imposing liability without regard to degree of care or motivation for the plaintiff's actions in initiating a cleanup. At the same time, CERCLA seeks "to place the cost of that response on those responsible for creating or maintaining the hazardous condition." *Mexico Feed & Seed*, 980 F.2d at 486. Therefore, in the allocation phase, harm to the environment and care on the part of the parties plays a more substantial role.

III. The Schloff Defendants' CERCLA Liability

The Schloff defendants argue that they should not be liable under CERCLA for that portion of the response costs which are attributable to the investigation of contamination on the Control Data site. They do not, however, challenge the District Court's determination that they are liable for a share of the cleanup costs. Simply put, the Schloff defendants argue that Control Data's release was the sole cause of the investigation. Thus, because the Schloff defendants' releases had nothing to do with initiating the investigation, they cannot be held liable. In order to accept the Schloff defendants' argument, we would have to hold that CERCLA imposes upon a plaintiff the requirement to prove that each type of response cost was separately caused by the defendant's release.

CERCLA simply cannot be read this strictly. First, the language of the statute precludes this holding. Under CERCLA, if a responsible party, as defined by subsections (1) through (4), releases hazardous materials into the environment, and that release "causes the incurrence of response costs," then the party is liable. 42 U.S.C. § 9607(a). The question then becomes, liable for what? CERCLA's answer is that the party is liable for "*any* other necessary cost of response incurred by any other person consistent with the national contingency plan."[9] 42 U.S.C. § 9607(a)(4)(B) (emphasis added). Thus, a plain reading of the statute leads us to the conclusion that once a party is liable, it is liable for its share, as determined by Section 9613(f), of "any" and all response costs, not just those costs "caused" by its release.

Second, the policy underlying CERCLA's private cost-recovery scheme precludes us from accepting the Schloff defendants' interpretation. As we noted previously, CERCLA's dual goals are to encourage quick response and to place the cost of that response on those responsible for the hazardous condition. Control Data quickly and efficiently responded to a perceived threat to the environment when it discovered its own release, thus fulfilling the first goal. In doing so, it discovered a second polluter, the Schloff defendants, who, in a perfect world according to CERCLA, should have reacted to their own releases much earlier. By not reacting and allowing the PERC plume to migrate, they became partially responsible for the hazardous condition of the Control Data site. Holding the Schloff defendants liable for a share of the costs of the investigation which uncovered their responsibility thus satisfies the second goal of CERCLA.

Under the Schloff defendants' interpretation, these goals would be frustrated. Control Data would have been better served simply to repair its own leak and do nothing about the contamination. Then, if another neighbor experienced a release which led to the discovery of the Control Data contamination, that third party would be liable for the entire cost of investigation. This result would offend CERCLA's goals. It would

---

[9]The "other ... costs" and "other person" in this sub-subsection distinguish private parties and their costs from costs of the United States Government, a State or an Indian tribe in subparagraph (A). That Control Data's costs were "necessary" and "consistent with the national contingency plan" is not disputed.

provide a disincentive for polluters to act quickly and aggressively to remedy the harm they have done in hopes that someone else will stumble upon their creation and be forced to bear the burden rightfully belonging to the original polluter.

Finally, the Supreme Court's most recent CERCLA decision convinces us that the Schloff defendants' argument must fail. In *Key Tronic Corp. v. United States*, 511 U.S. 809 (1994), Key Tronic and others, including the United States Air Force, dumped hazardous chemicals into a landfill in Spokane County, Washington. When the resulting contamination was found in the surrounding groundwater supply, Key Tronic, on its own initiative, responded. Part of this response was Key Tronic's effort to identify other responsible parties. This effort resulted in an Environmental Protection Agency enforcement action against the Air Force. The Supreme Court held that the costs attributable to this search, though paid to attorneys, were "recoverable costs of response clearly distinguishable from litigation expenses," which are not recoverable under CERCLA. 114 S.Ct. at 1967. (footnote omitted).

The reasoning of the Supreme Court is particularly applicable to the case before us. "Tracking down other responsible solvent polluters increases the probability that a cleanup will be effective and get paid for. Key Tronic is therefore quite right to claim that such efforts significantly benefited the entire cleanup effort apart ... from the reallocation of costs." *Key Tronic*, 114 S.Ct. at 1967. Likewise, Control Data's efforts to identify all of the contaminants on its property "significantly benefited" the entire effort. Without that effort, the full extent of the contamination, including contamination restricted to the Schloff site not at issue in this case, might not have been discovered and remedied. Perhaps it is fortuitous for Control Data that it happened on to the Schloff defendants' contamination, just as it was fortuitous for Key Tronic to happen on to the Air Force's. Both circumstances are more fortuitous, however, for the environment, which is the primary and decisive factor under CERCLA. We must affirm the judgment of the District Court imposing liability on the Schloff defendants for all response costs, including the costs of investigation.

* * *

IV. Allocating Liability

The Schloff defendants challenge the District Court's allocation of one third of the response costs to them when they contributed only 10% of the volume of pollution. Their challenge is two-fold, arguing first that insufficient evidence existed to find PERC more toxic than TCA, and second that even if PERC is more toxic, it is an insufficient basis to use to increase liability. We disagree on both points.

CERCLA's allocation scheme "is an equitable determination, in which the district court must make its own factual findings and legal conclusions. ***

In this case, the District Court based its finding that PERC is a more toxic chemical largely on the MPCA's requirement that it be cleaned up to a level of 7 parts per billion (ppb) existing in the groundwater supply, whereas TCA had to be cleaned up only to a level of 200ppb. Additionally, PERC is a carcinogen, whereas TCA is not. Finally, PERC is the more difficult substance to strip from the airstream in the remediation system. While the Schloff defendants correctly assert that no evidence was adduced from a licensed toxicologist, the evidence which was introduced was more than adequate to justify the District Court's finding that PERC is substantially more toxic than TCA.

The Schloff defendants also argue that toxicity should not be used to increase the allocation of liability without proof of additional costs associated with that toxicity. We first disagree with the assertion that the greater toxicity of PERC did not add to the cleanup costs. The District Court found that the presence of PERC influenced the design and construction of the remediation system, because it is harder to remove and must be removed to a lower level than TCA. The logical conclusion is that it will cost more to remove the pollution related to PERC than it will to remove an equal volume of TCA-related pollution.

In addition, the District Court justified its decision by noting that CERCLA seeks to remedy harm to the environment, and that the more toxic chemical causes the greater harm. We agree. Once again, CERCLA, in the allocation stage, places the costs of response on those responsible for creating the hazardous condition. Allocating responsibility based partially on toxicity does just that because those who release substances that are more toxic are more responsible for the hazardous condition. The District Court was fully justified in increasing the Schloff defendants' responsibility on the basis of toxicity.

* * *

NOTES

1. *R.W. Meyer* is not unusual in allocating a considerable share of the cleanup costs to a landowner who had no active role in causing the contamination. In *United States v. DiBiase*, 45 F.3d 541 (1st Cir. 1995), the EPA entered into a settlement with a sewerage district that had deposited sewage sludge at the site in question. The settlement required the sewerage district to pay 85 percent of the cleanup costs, implicitly leaving DiBiase, the current owner—who did not participate in the settlement and instead fought for judicial rejection thereof—with the remaining 15 percent. DiBiase acquired the site without knowing that the prior owner had given permission to the sewerage district to deposit its waste there. When DiBiase learned of the practice, he demanded that the sewerage authority cease the dumping, which it did. Thereafter, although DiBiase placed gates on the entrances to the property, he did not maintain them, and other, unknown parties intermittently dumped substances at the site. The EPA and the sewerage district obtained district court approval of their settlement for the cleanup of the site, and the First Circuit rejected DiBiase's arguments challenging the settlement on appeal.

> In the first place, appellant does not cite—and we have been unable to locate—any CERCLA case in which a demonstrably *liable* party has been held entitled to safe passage in a global settlement. ***

Second, *** we regard appellant's argument as a surreptitious attempt to relitigate his "innocent landowner" defense *** rejected by the district court ***.

In the third place, the allocation proposed by EPA and ratified by Judge Mazzone does not strike us as either substantially disproportionate or manifestly unfair. To be sure, SESD [the sewerage authority] played a leading role in the contamination of the Site and appellant, who came on the scene later, played an appreciably less prominent role. But, an actor cast in a bit part is not to be confused with a mere spectator, whose only involvement is to lounge in the audience and watch events unfold. *** Despite being warned of a potentially dangerous condition, he twiddled his thumbs; he failed to safeguard the Site, thus permitting third parties to dump at will and exacerbate an already parlous situation; fiddled while the earthen berms deteriorated; and turned a blind eye to evolving public health and safety concerns. Allocating 15% of the historic removal costs as appellant's share seems commensurate with these shortcomings and with the quantum of comparative fault fairly ascribable to him.

Fourth, appellant's concept—which seems to be that liable parties should go scot free in environmental cases if other parties are considerably more culpable—runs at cross-purposes with CERCLA's policy of encouraging settlements as opposed to endless court battles.

Id. at 545-46.

2. For an economic perspective on allocation issues, see Kenneth T. Wise, et al., *Allocating CERCLA Liabilities: The Applications and Limitations of Economics,* 11 Toxics L. Rep. (BNA) 830 (1997).

3. Like RCRA and virtually all other federal environmental laws, CERCLA does not authorize private "toxic tort" claims for personal injury or property damage. Congress considered, and ultimately decided against, including a "victims' compensation" provision in the SARA amendments to CERCLA. SARA did add § 309 to CERCLA, 42 U.S.C. § 9658, which mandates the use of a discovery rule in determining the statute of limitations in state law toxic tort claims arising from exposure to hazardous substances. In addition, some parties have asserted toxic tort claims as pendent claims along with CERCLA cost recovery claims.

4. Related to the allocation issues addressed in this chapter, as well as the overall issue of who bears liability for RCRA and CERCLA cleanup costs, is the matter of bankruptcy. The effects of the filing of a bankruptcy petition, the pendency of a bankruptcy proceeding, and the adjudication of bankruptcy on the debtor's CERCLA (and RCRA) liabilities have been heavily litigated. The cases teach far more about bankruptcy law than environmental law, but the environmental law student should at least be aware that there exists virtually an entire sub-specialty concerned with the effects of bankruptcy proceedings on the debtor's environmental liabilities. *See, e.g.,* Stanley M. Spracker and James D. Barnette, *The Treatment of Environmental Matters in Bankruptcy Cases,* 752 PLI/COMM 439 (1997).

14 CLEANUP PROCEDURES AND STANDARDS

Lawyers and law students can become so intrigued by the legal aspects of CERCLA—its retroactive application, its broadly-sweeping, strict liability scheme, its delegation of sweeping authority to the EPA—that they can lose sight of the statute's overriding objective: not to keep lawyers (and engineers) employed, but to clean up contaminated sites.   This chapter examines CERCLA's cleanup procedures and standards.

Whereas the great body of CERCLA law is comprised of the statutory language and cases construing that language, without administrative regulations—in stark contrast to RCRA—the area of cleanup procedures and standards is subject to important implementing regulations. At the heart of the CERCLA cleanup program is the National Oil and Hazardous Substances Pollution Contingency Plan, known generally as the National Contingency Plan ("NCP"), 40 C.F.R. Part 300. The NCP specifies the roles of the federal and state governments in responding to releases of oil and hazardous substances, and establishes procedures for making cleanup decisions.

The NCP was originally prepared under § 311 of the Clean Water Act, 33 U.S.C. § 1321, focusing on oil spills in navigable waters. It was amended following the 1980 enactment of CERCLA to address releases of hazardous substances in all media, and it was again amended in 1990 as required by the 1986 amendments to CERCLA. CERCLA § 105, 42 U.S.C. § 9605.

The D.C. Circuit upheld the 1990 revisions to the National Contingency Plan, rejecting numerous challenges except one concerning the EPA's blanket rule against delegating certain remedial authority to the states. *State of Ohio v. United States Environmental Protection Agency*, 997 F.2d 1520 (D.C.Cir. 1993).

Appended to the NCP is the National Priorities List ("NPL"), which lists the top-priority sites, determined by the EPA with input from the states, for response actions under CERCLA. 40 C.F.R. Part 300, App. B. The significance of a site being listed on the NPL is that the EPA may use Superfund monies to conduct removal and remedial actions at the site. Even if a site is not on the NPL, however, the EPA may still use Superfund monies for a removal, but not remedial, action. 40 C.F.R. § 300.425(b)(1). The EPA uses a mathematical model known as the Hazard Ranking System, 40 C.F.R. Part 300, App. A, to evaluate the relative hazards posed by a site being considered for inclusion on the NPL. The EPA conducts a rulemaking proceeding, with public notice and comment, prior to the addition of sites to (and, far less frequently, the deletion of sites from) the NPL. Although lawsuits challenging the EPA's decisions to include particular sites on the NPL are typically unsuccessful, the D.C. Circuit has remanded several NPL listing decisions, primarily because of inadequate sampling methods used by the EPA in assessing groundwater contamination or insufficient scientific explanations of its decision. *See, e.g., National Gypsum Co. v. EPA*, 968 F.2d 40 (D.C.Cir. 1992); *Kent County v. EPA*, 963 F.2d 391 (D.C.Cir. 1992); *Anne Arundel County v. EPA,* 963 F.2d 412 (D.C.Cir.1992); *Tex Tin Corp. v. EPA*, 935 F.2d 1321 (D.C.Cir.1991). The D.C. Circuit also struck down the EPA's "aggregation policy," which in some circumstances allowed the agency to consider noncontiguous parcels as a single NPL site for listing purposes, even where the component parcels would not individually meet the listing criteria.

*** The statute directs EPA to base the [NPL] listing criteria on "relative risk or danger to public health or welfare or the environment." [42 U.S.C.] § 9605(a)(8)(A).

In preparing the list, EPA is to apply the criteria thus established, and also to accommodate state preferences by including one facility designated by each state among its top 100 priorities. The EPA has duly promulgated risk-based criteria under which a listing is triggered by either a high score on its Hazard Ranking System or by a "health advisory." Here, relying on the latter, it has listed three areas as a single site. But one of the three areas—the "Coke Plant Site"—is over a mile away from the rest of the aggregate site. EPA makes no claim either that the Coke Plant Site qualifies for listing under the agency's risk-based criteria or that it has received state designation. Rather, EPA includes the Coke Plant Site only by virtue of its "Aggregation Policy," *** which sets forth various factors permitting aggregation of noncontiguous parcels as a single NPL site. The factors named in the Aggregation Policy bear only the dimmest relation to any idea of risk.***

* * *

*** Permitting the inclusion of low-risk sites on the NPL would thwart rather than advance Congress's purpose of creating a priority list based on evidence of high risk levels.

* * *

Because EPA lacks statutory authority to use its Aggregation Policy to list on the NPL a site that would not otherwise qualify, we vacate EPA's inclusion of the Coke Plant Site within its Tennessee Products Site listing. *The Mead Corp. v. Browner*, 100 F.3d 152, 153, 156-157 (D.C. Cir. 1996).

As of May 1997, the NPL included 1,206 sites, 1,055 in the General Superfund section and 151 in the Federal Facilities section. 62 Fed. Reg. 15572 (1997).

Subpart E of the NCP specifies procedures for identifying, evaluating, and cleaning up sites with an actual or threatened release of a hazardous substance. Such sites may be brought to the EPA's attention by any means, including required reports under CERCLA § 103 (*see* chapter 16) or any other law, EPA investigations, citizen complaints and petitions, and "inventory or survey efforts or random or incidental observation reported by government agencies or the public." 40 C.F.R. § 300.405, *quoting* § 300.304(a)(5). The EPA then determines whether a "removal" action (*i.e.,* a temporary, short-term action, defined at CERCLA § 101(23)) is warranted. 40 C.F.R.

§ 300.410-.415. Regardless of whether a removal action is undertaken, the site is also evaluated for purposes of a "remedial" action (*i.e.,* a permanent, more thoroughly-evaluated action, defined at CERCLA § 101(24)). 40 C.F.R. § 300.420. Whether a cleanup activity is characterized as removal or remedial is of considerable significance. It affects not only the availability of Superfund monies (non-NPL sites may qualify for removal but not remedial expenditures from the Superfund), but also the thoroughness—and cost—of the studies and reports that must be prepared, and the extent of the procedural requirements that must be satisfied, before actual cleanup activities may commence.

The first step in the more extensive remedial action process is the remedial site evaluation, which involves a "preliminary assessment" (primarily a review of existing documentary information about the site, and possibly including off-site and/or on-site "reconnaissance") and a "site inspection" (involving observation and, where appropriate, sampling). If the preliminary assessment/site inspection indicates that further action is warranted, then an intensive site investigation and analysis, known as a "remedial investigation/feasibility study" ("RI/FS") is undertaken. The RI involves fairly extensive sampling and data collection, treatability studies, and a baseline risk assessment. The FS entails the identification and screening of remedial alternatives. 40 C.F.R. § 300.430. Although the EPA frequently agrees to have PRPs (who so desire) conduct the RI/FS, the EPA has (at least temporarily) precluded PRPs from conducting the risk assessment portion of the RI/FS, and the EPA always reserves the authority to select its preferred remedial alternative for implementation.

The NCP specifies nine factors to be considered in remedy selection. First, there are two "threshold criteria": overall protection of human health; and compliance with "ARARs" (applicable or relevant and appropriate requirements of federal and state environmental laws). To be eligible for final selection, an alternative must satisfy the two threshold criteria (unless an ARAR waiver is obtained). Next, the EPA weighs five "balancing criteria": long-term effectiveness and permanence; reduction of toxicity, mobility, or volume through treatment; short-term effectiveness; implementability; and cost. Finally, the EPA considers two "modifying criteria": state acceptance; and community acceptance. The selected remedy is proposed, there follows a period of public and agency comment, and then the cleanup plan is finalized. The EPA's final remedy selection is documented in a "record of decision" ("ROD"). 40 C.F.R. § 300.430(f).

The next step is called "remedial design/remedial action" ("RD/RA"). 40 C.F.R. § 300.435. It is at this point, often years and millions of dollars later, that the most difficult and challenging decisions must be made. Because most CERCLA cleanups cannot be addressed by pre-existing design specifications waiting on the shelf, the efforts of a variety of engineers and scientists must be marshaled to develop a remedial design that implements that remedy selected in the ROD, and satisfies ARARs (unless waived). ARARs set the cleanup standard, the level of "how clean is clean (enough)." ARARs are triggered by virtually every aspect of a cleanup. For example, if the cleanup involves groundwater treatment, and the treatment process may generate air emissions and effluent discharges to surface water and/or groundwater, then the ARARs will specify the emission and effluent limits that must be attained. ARARs consist of federal environmental laws and regulations, and more stringent state environmental and facility siting laws and regulations. CERCLA § 121(d)(2).

An ARARs analysis entails three, or possibly four, stages. First, a potential ARAR must be evaluated to determine whether it is "applicable," whether it "specifically addresses a hazardous substance, pollutant, contaminant, remedial action, location, or other circumstance" at the site and would be legally binding even without any ARARs provision in CERCLA. 40 C.F.R. § 300.400(g)(1). Second, if a potential ARAR is not applicable, then eight factors must be weighed to determine whether the requirement is nonetheless "relevant and appropriate," *i.e.,* whether it "addresses problems or situations sufficiently similar to the circumstances of the release or remedial action contemplated, and whether the requirement is well-suited to the site." 40 C.F.R. § 300.400(g)(2). Third, although the statutory provisions regarding cleanup standards make no reference to such considerations, the EPA's NCP states that, as appropriate, "other advisories, criteria, or guidance" may be considered, in addition to applicable or relevant and appropriate requirements, in developing CERCLA remedies. 40 C.F.R. § 300.400(g)(3). Illustrative of the rampant overuse of acronyms in the world of CERCLA, the NCP designates this category of non-binding requirements as "TBC," for items "to be considered." Fourth, if a remedy that is otherwise appropriate for selection does not meet an ARAR, the EPA may invoke one of the narrowly-crafted ARAR waivers, the broadest of which is where "[c]ompliance with the requirement is technically impracticable from an engineering perspective." 40 C.F.R. § 300.430(f)(1)(ii)(C).

The following case represents one of the few judicial attempts thus far to grapple with ARARs. It also provides a good discussion of the decision-making processes regarding the evaluation of a site and the steps to be taken to clean it up.

UNITED STATES V. AKZO COATINGS OF AMERICA, INC.
949 F.2d 1409 (6th Cir. 1991)

Before JONES, Circuit Judge, ENGEL and WELLFORD, Senior Circuit Judges. ENGEL, Senior Circuit Judge.

This is an appeal by the State of Michigan from the entry of a consent decree between the United States Environmental Protection Agency ("EPA") and twelve defendants pursuant to the Comprehensive Environmental Response, Compensation, and Liability Act of 1980 ("CERCLA"), as amended by the Superfund Amendments and Reauthorization Act of 1986 ("SARA"). The consent decree would require the defendants, or potentially responsible parties ("PRPs"), to engage in remedial work to clean up a hazardous waste site in Rose Township, Oakland County, Michigan ("Rose Site"). The proposed remedial plan at the Rose Site calls for the excavation and incineration of surface soils contaminated with polychlorinated biphenyls ("PCBs"), lead, arsenic and other toxic materials and the flushing of the subsurface soils contaminated with a variety of volatile and semi-volatile organic compounds.

The state challenges the legality of the remedial action, and seeks to prevent entry of the consent decree. The Natural Resources Defense Council, the Environmental Defense Fund and the Sierra Club have filed a brief as amici curiae supportive of the state's position. The majority of the state's and amici's objections to the decree focus on the effectiveness of soil flushing at the Rose Site, where layers of clay are interspersed among beds of sand and silt. The PRPs cross appeal the district court's determination that the decree must comply with Michigan's groundwater anti-degradation law.

I. STATUTORY OVERVIEW
* * *

Throughout the 1980s, the Superfund hazardous waste cleanup program enjoyed centerstage prominence in environmental law. Nevertheless, the early years of CERCLA were difficult. CERCLA was a hastily-assembled bill which contained a number of technical flaws due to Congress' limited understanding of the hazardous waste problem and its effects on the environment. Both Congress and EPA, for example, believed in the late 1970s that a site could be adequately cleaned up by "scraping a few inches of soil off the ground." H.R. Rep. No. 253, 99th Cong., 2d Sess., pt. 1, at 54 (1986). Congress also grossly underestimated the number of sites requiring cleanup and the monies necessary to remedy the problem. EPA, as the delegatee of the President's authority under CERCLA, 42 U.S.C. § 9615, was criticized for the slow pace of cleanups, for failing to provide remedies that would protect public health and the environment, and for alleged "sweetheart" deals that reduced cleanup costs for industry at public expense. As a result, in 1986 Congress passed SARA, which reauthorized and amended CERCLA in several important ways. Congress sought to better define cleanup standards, to expand resources available to EPA for investigations and cleanups, to clarify EPA's authority under Superfund law, and to expand and clarify the states' role in any remedial action undertaken, or ordered, by EPA.
* * *

The federal legislative scheme and its history are persuasive that Congress did not intend to leave the cleanup under CERCLA solely in the hands of the federal government. CERCLA, as amended by SARA, provides a substantial and meaningful role for the individual states in the selection and development of remedial actions to be taken within their jurisdictions. In this case for example, pursuant to 42 U.S.C. § 9621(f) the State of Michigan had a reasonable opportunity to comment on the RI/FS [Remedial Investigation/Feasibility Study], the RAP [Remedial Action Plan] proposed in the amended ROD [Record of Decision], and other technical data related to the implementation of the proposed remedy. The state was also entitled to and did participate in the settlement negotiations that led to the decree at issue. Further, CERCLA is designed to accommodate more stringent "applicable or relevant and appropriate requirements" ("ARARs"), *i.e.* environmental standards of the state in which a site is located. Once a consent decree is proposed by EPA, the state can challenge it if EPA has proposed implementation of a remedy for which the federal agency has waived a valid and more stringent state requirement. The state may also enforce a decree to the extent the remedial action fails to comply with any state environmental requirements which have not been waived by EPA.

If no PRPs can be located, or if they are insolvent, a state or political subdivision may enter into a contract or cooperative agreement with EPA, whereby both may take action on a cost-sharing basis. A state may also sue PRPs for remedial and removal costs if such efforts are consistent with the National Contingency Plan (NCP). However, assuming it is not the "lead" agency, the state is limited in its ability to require alternative relief if and when a consent decree is entered into between PRPs and EPA.

Under CERCLA, Congress expressed its preference for thorough yet cost-effective remedies at hazardous waste sites. ***

II. FACTS

The Rose Site consists of about 110 acres on which liquid and solid industrial wastes were illegally dumped in the late 1960s. In 1979, the Michigan Toxic Substance and Control Commission declared a toxic substance emergency at the Site, and 5,000 drums of toxic waste were immediately removed. Investigation disclosed that the drums contained, among other chemical compounds, PCBs, phthalates, organic solvents, oil and grease, phenols and heavy metals. In 1983, the Rose Site was placed on the NPL [National Priorities List].

All sites placed on the NPL must undergo a Remedial Investigation and Feasibility Study ("RI/FS") to determine the extent of contamination and possible remedies. 42 U.S.C. § 9620(e)(1). Under a cooperative agreement with EPA, the Michigan Department of Natural Resources ("MDNR") began the RI/FS evaluation of the Rose Site in 1984. That study, completed in June of 1987, showed two primary areas of contamination: (1) an area which is less than one acre in size but contains groundwater contaminated by vinyl chloride and surface soils having elevated levels of arsenic; and (2) twelve acres in the southwest corner of the Site that contain surface soils contaminated with PCBs, lead, arsenic and other toxic metals; subsurface soils contaminated with a variety of volatile organic compounds ("VOCs") and semi-volatile organic compounds ("SVOCs"); and groundwater contaminated with PCBs, metals, VOCs and SVOCs.

A. The RI/FS and the Original ROD

After a detailed screening of possible remedies, the 1987 RI/FS recommended excavation and on-site thermal destruction to remedy the soil contamination,[6] plus ground water treatment to cleanse the water under the Rose Site. Soil flushing, a method

---

[6] This involves, almost literally, a baking of the soil using electrically-powered rods.

by which the contaminated soil is flushed with water and the resulting flushate is treated to designated cleanup levels and reinjected into the soil, was found to be ineffective at this Site due to the variable permeability of the Rose Site soils.

Pursuant to section 117(a) of CERCLA, 42 U.S.C. §9617(a), which requires that the public be given a reasonable opportunity to comment on a proposed cleanup, EPA published a notice of the remedy and held a public meeting near the Site. In September 1987, EPA issued a Record of Decision ("ROD"). ***

The 1987 ROD issued by EPA included a detailed explanation of the reasons for selecting the proposed remedy, and included specific findings that the remedy satisfied the requirements of CERCLA, complied with federal and state ARARs, and was cost effective. Soil flushing, though not adopted in the 1987 ROD, was not ruled out completely. The ROD listed eight criteria EPA would consider before substituting soil flushing for thermal incineration: economies of scale, community acceptance, cleanup time, land regulations, reliability of soil flushing, implementability, complete site remediation, and cost effectiveness.

B. The Proposed Consent Decree

In June of 1987, shortly before issuance of the original ROD, EPA began settlement negotiations with the PRPs. The State of Michigan participated in these discussions. In the course of the negotiations, EPA was persuaded that the soil flushing method might be a viable, less costly alternative to the incineration of the VOC/SVOC contaminated soil, and could still result in a cleanup that would comply with all federal and state ARARs.

In August of 1988, EPA and the twelve PRPs who are defendants in this action signed the consent decree which included a soil flushing remedy for the site. While under the original plan 50,000 cubic yards of contaminated soil were to be incinerated, the consent decree calls for incineration of only half that amount, augmented by soil flushing for the remaining 25,000 cubic yards. In economic terms this is represented as effecting savings of roughly $12 million. To offset the danger that this process might be insufficient, the decree requires the PRPs to prove, both in a laboratory and at the Rose Site, that soil flushing is capable of meeting Phase I water target cleanup levels ("TCLs") for the subsurface soils contaminated with VOCs and SVOCs within ten years after implementation of the system. Absent such proof, the PRPs would be required to fund and implement an alternate, permanent remedy designed to meet Phase I TCLs. Under the proposed consent decree, EPA is required to review the remedial action at the site at least every five years, and is permitted to seek further response action from the defendants if EPA determines that supplemental remedies are necessary. ***

* * *

In consideration of the work to be performed and the payments to be made by the settling defendants, the United States agrees in the proposed consent decree not to sue them, with some exceptions, for claims available under sections 106 and 107 of CERCLA and other federal and state environmental laws which are based on facts about the Site and its contamination known to EPA at the time of the entry of the decree. The covenant does contain reopening provisions which would allow EPA to seek further injunctive relief or cost recovery if conditions unknown until after entry of the decree reveal that the remedial action is not protective of human health and the environment.

C. Proceedings in the District Court and the Amended ROD

In September of 1988, EPA filed the proposed consent decree with the U.S. District Court for the Eastern District of Michigan pursuant to 42 U.S.C. § 9622(d)(1)(A). As required, notice of the proposed consent decree was published in the Federal Register on September 26, 1988. At the same time, EPA published a three page document entitled Proposed Settlement Plan—Explanation of Significant Differences ("ESD"). The ESD was published to comply with section 9617(c), which requires EPA to explain why a settlement or consent decree to which the agency agrees differs in any significant respect from the final plan or ROD previously issued for a particular site. In this case the ESD explained the basis for the decision to allow defendants to try soil flushing at the Rose Site in conjunction with incineration, when the 1987 ROD had called for soil incineration only.

* * *

On January 18, 1989, after considering the comments received, EPA issued an amended ROD for the Rose Site. The amended ROD formally adopts soil flushing as a remedy for VOC and SVOC-contaminated subsurface soils, but only if pilot testing proves that flushing is as protective as thermal destruction. In adopting the remedy it originally ruled out, EPA reasons that (1) the excavation of PCB contaminated soils will remove most of the unflushable contaminants; (2) the geology of the contaminated area may not be as complex as initially thought; and (3) pilot testing has not yet been performed to rule out soil flushing. EPA, in the amended ROD, further asserts that (1) if Phase II target cleanup levels are achieved, flushing will have done as well as incineration was required to do under the original ROD, and will have brought the Site into compliance with all federal and state ARARs; (2) flushing is more cost effective than incineration; (3) assuming the groundwater treatment system uses granular activated carbon to capture the contaminants, soil flushing will satisfy CERCLA's preference for remedies utilizing permanent and innovative treatments; and (4) soil flushing will reduce toxicity, mobility, and the volume of contaminants to the same extent as thermal destruction.

The State of Michigan filed a complaint with the district court and moved to intervene in the action between EPA and the settling defendants on February 14, 1989, pursuant to 42 U.S.C. § 9621(f)(2)(B). This provision allows a state to challenge a proposed consent decree which allegedly fails to meet the state's environmental protection standards. ***

On July 18, 1989, one day after oral argument, the district court granted EPA's motion for entry of the consent decree. ***

In its opinion, the district court held that Michigan's groundwater anti-degradation law does represent an ARAR for purposes of CERCLA, but found that the consent decree embodying a soil flushing remedy did not violate the state ARAR. The court found that Michigan's concerns about the complex geology of the Site had been adequately addressed by EPA, and observed that soil flushing had been used, with state approval, at other Michigan sites. The district court concluded that, on the administrative record, EPA's decision to enter into the consent decree was not arbitrary or capricious, and was reasonable, fair and not contrary to relevant federal and state laws. In addition, the district court held that CERCLA's provisions allowing EPA to settle claims for remedial action with the PRPs preempted the State of Michigan from imposing additional remedial action requirements on defendants under Michigan's Water Resources Commission Act, M.C.L.A. § 323.6; Michigan's Environmental Protection Act, M.C.L.A. § 691.1201 et seq.; and the common law of public nuisance.

III. ISSUES ON APPEAL

The State of Michigan now appeals the entry of the consent decree, and the district court's finding that CERCLA preempts some of the state's environmental remedies against these defendants. The PRPs cross-appeal the district court's finding that Michigan's anti-degradation law is an ARAR. ***

* * *

V. WHETHER THE CONSENT DECREE IS ARBITRARY AND CAPRICIOUS

The State of Michigan first argues, along with amici curiae, that EPA's decision to modify its ROD and consent decree to include soil flushing as a remedy for the Rose Site was arbitrary and capricious because the record does not support EPA's conclusion that the Site is conducive to soil flushing. Under the arbitrary and capricious standard, a lower court's discretionary action "cannot be set aside by a reviewing court unless it has a definite and firm conviction that the court below committed a clear error of judgment in the conclusion it reached upon the weighing of the relevant factors." *McBee v. Bomar*, 296 F.2d 235, 237 (6th Cir. 1961).

The 1987 RI/FS and ROD identified soil flushing as not applicable at the site for the following reasons:

    a. The soils are marginally suitable for this technology because of variable permeabilities;

    b. The soils contain both soluble and insoluble chemicals—flushing is only reliable for soluble chemicals and would have to be used with another technology to remove the entire source;

    c. Pilot testing would have to be performed before such a remedy is implemented; and

    d. Flushing is not well demonstrated, especially in cold weather environments like that of Michigan.

For the reasons that follow, we believe that the concerns noted in the RI/FS have all been adequately addressed by EPA in the ESD it published when it filed the decree with the district court.

As evidenced by its placement at the top of EPA's concerns in 1987, there is no question that EPA originally considered the soil conditions at the Rose Site to be the prime deterrent to the use of soil flushing. However, after the RI/FS was performed and after more soil samples were taken, EPA found that the soils to be flushed were not as complex as once thought. ***

* * *

*** It must be emphasized, however, that the Remedial Action Plan ("RAP") annexed to the consent decree expressly requires that the settling defendants demonstrate to EPA, both in a laboratory and on-site, that soil flushing will work before it is implemented. The required demonstration includes additional field tests to further define the permeability of the soils.

Based on our thorough review of the scientific evidence in the record, we do not find EPA's decision to experiment with soil flushing at the Rose Site to be arbitrary or without foundation. ***

* * *

VII. WHETHER THE PROPOSED DECREE COMPLIES WITH THE LAW
* * *

A.   Whether Michigan's Anti-degradation Law is an ARAR

The State of Michigan and amici curiae contend that the proposed remedy is not in accordance with the law because it does not meet the state's ARARs. Under CERCLA, the remedial action selected must comply with identified state ARARs that are more stringent than applicable federal standards unless the ARARs are waived. The relevant provision provides in part:

> With respect to any hazardous substance, pollutant or contaminant that will remain onsite, if (i) any standard, requirement, criteria, or limitation under any Federal environmental law, ... or (ii) any promulgated standard, requirement, criteria, or limitation under a State environmental ... law that is more stringent than any Federal standard, ... is legally applicable to the hazardous substance or pollutant or contaminant concerned or is relevant and appropriate under the circumstances, ... the remedial action selected ... shall require, at the completion of the remedial action, a level or standard of control for such hazardous substance or pollutant or contaminant which at least attains such legally applicable or relevant and appropriate standard, requirement, criteria, or limitation.

42 U.S.C. § 9621(d)(2)(A). Before deciding whether the decree must comply with such laws, we need to determine whether there are any state ARARs applicable to the Rose Site.

The district court found that the Michigan Water Resources Commission Act ("WRCA"), and its corresponding agency rules, Mich. Admin. Code R. 323.2201 et seq., ("Part 22 Rules") satisfy each of the criteria for ARARs to which a proposed remedy must comply under section 9621(d). Section 6(a) of the WRCA provides, in part:

> It shall be unlawful for any persons directly or indirectly to discharge into the waters of the state any substance *which is or may become injurious* to the public health, safety, or welfare; or which is or may become injurious

to domestic, commercial, industrial, agricultural, recreational or other uses which are being or may be made of such waters....

M.C.L.A. § 323.6(a) (emphasis added). The corresponding agency rules, the Part 22 Rules, provide for the nondegradation of groundwater in usable aquifers. Mich. Admin. Code R. 323.2205. Defendants challenge the district court's conclusion that said Michigan law and rules, collectively referred to as Michigan's anti-degradation law, qualify as a state ARAR.[30]

Under 42 U.S.C. § 9621(d), *supra*, a state environmental requirement or standard constitutes a state ARAR to which the remedy must comply if it is (1) properly promulgated, (2) more stringent than federal standards, (3) legally applicable or relevant and appropriate, and (4) timely identified.

1.   Whether Michigan's Anti-degradation Law is Properly Promulgated

To be considered an ARAR, the anti-degradation law must be "promulgated." According to EPA, "promulgated" as used in section 9621 refers to "laws imposed by state legislative bodies and regulations developed by state agencies that are of general applicability and are legally enforceable." EPA, *Superfund Program; Interim Guidance on Compliance with Applicable or Relevant and Appropriate Requirements; Notice of Guidance*, 52 Fed. Reg. 32495, 32498 (Aug. 27, 1987) [hereinafter *Interim Guidance*]. EPA evidently desired to differentiate "advisories, guidance, or other non-binding policies, as well as standards that are not of general application," *Interim Guidance*, 52 Fed. Reg. at 32498, from laws or rules promulgated by state legislatures or agencies that are imposed on all citizens of a particular state, which is the case with Michigan's anti-degradation law since it was enacted by the Michigan legislature, and the accompanying administrative rules were properly developed by the Michigan Water Resources Commission.

While defendants concede that Michigan's anti-degradation law has general applicability, they contend that it was not properly promulgated because its vagueness and lack of a quantifiable standard render it legally unenforceable. A standard is not constitutionally vague if it is drafted "with sufficient definiteness that ordinary people can understand what conduct is prohibited and in a manner that does not encourage arbitrary and discriminatory enforcement." *Kolender v. Lawson*, 461 U.S. 352, 357 (1983). As noted above, the WRCA does not permit anyone "directly or indirectly to discharge into the waters of the state any substance which is or may become injurious

---

[30] There are several kinds of applicable or relevant and appropriate environmental requirements (ARARs).

> ARARs may be chemical-specific (e.g., an established level for a specific chemical in groundwater), action-specific (e.g., a land disposal restriction for RCRA hazardous wastes), or location-specific (e.g., a restriction on actions that adversely affect wetlands).
> Thus the concept is much broader than that of a specific cleanup level for a site.

Starfield, *The 1990 Nat'l Contingency Plan—More Detail and More Structure, But Still a Balancing Act*, 20 ELR 10222 (June 1990).

to the public health, safety, or welfare; or ... to domestic, commercial, industrial, agricultural, recreational or other uses...." We believe such a standard is "sufficiently specific to provide a fair warning that certain kinds of conduct are prohibited." *Colten v. Kentucky*, 407 U.S. 104, 110 (1972).

* * *

Moreover, section 323.5 of the WRCA expressly requires the Water Resources Commission to "establish pollution standards for lakes, rivers, streams, and other waters of the state...." As we find is the case with section 323.6 of the WRCA, the Part 22 Rules which prohibit "degradations" of "groundwaters in any usable aquifer which would deteriorate the local background groundwater quality" are neither vague nor unenforceable. Likewise, the fact that a "degradation" of groundwaters may occur only when it is "determined by the commission to be a deterioration in terms of magnitude of the change and importance of the parameters describing groundwater quality," does not render Michigan's anti-degradation law constitutionally infirm. The "background water quality," measured by a hydrogeological study as required under the Part 22 Rules, provides a standard beyond which would-be polluters may not pollute. According to EPA, "[g]eneral State goals that are duly promulgated (such as a non-degradation law) *have the same weight as explicit numerical standards*, although the former have to be interpreted in terms of a site and therefore may allow more flexibility in approach." *Interim Guidance*, 52 Fed. Reg. at 32,498 (emphasis added).

Defendants emphasize that EPA, in its proposed rules, requires "general state goals" to be implemented by means of "specific requirements," which Michigan's current implementing regulations fail to do, as they only prohibit "degradations" of the "local background groundwater quality." However, as evidenced by its proposed rules *as a whole*, EPA is not limiting the validity of general state goals solely to those which are implemented via specific numerical standards promulgated in corresponding agency rules. Rather, the type of standard provided is one of several factors courts should consider in deciding whether a state goal is an ARAR. *** EPA's final revisions are even clearer: "Even if a state has not promulgated implementing regulations, a general goal can be an ARAR if it meets the eligibility criteria for state ARARs." *** *NCP, Final Rule*, 55 Fed. Reg. at 8746. Hence, EPA's own publications recognize that general requirements containing no specific numerical standards, or any implementing regulations at all for that matter, can be enforceable ARARs.

* * *

2. Whether Michigan's Anti-degradation Law is More Stringent than Federal Standards

Section 9621(d)(2)(A)(ii) also requires that for state standards to apply to a remedial action plan, they must be "more stringent than any Federal standard, requirement, criteria or limitation...." *** In its proposed revision of the NCP, EPA stated: "Where no Federal ARAR exists for a chemical, location, or action, but a State ARAR does exist, or where a state ARAR is broader in scope than the Federal ARAR, the State ARAR is considered more stringent." *Proposed Rule*, 53 Fed. Reg. at 51435.
***

We find that no comparable federal statute or rule identified by the parties broadly regulates direct or indirect discharges of any injurious or potentially injurious substance into groundwater resources as does section 6(a) of the WRCA. The WRCA is not directly comparable to the federal Safe Drinking Water Act ("SDWA") because it is broader in coverage and, depending on the site, as or more demanding in terms of cleanup requirements than the SDWA. We believe, therefore, that the WRCA is more stringent than the SDWA.

With regard to coverage, the provisions of the SDWA apply only to a limited number of substances while the WRCA applies to "any substance which is or may become injurious to the public health." Second, the SDWA applies only to public drinking water supply systems serving a certain minimum number of customers, while the WRCA applies to any waters of the state, whether private or public, including groundwaters.

Likewise, we find that the WRCA's cleanup requirements implemented by means of that Act's accompanying regulations are equally or in some cases more demanding, and thus not less stringent, than the federal maximum contaminant levels ("MCLs") under the SDWA. The Part 22 Rules prohibit degradation of groundwater "from local background groundwater quality." ***

In many instances, especially when dealing with synthetic compounds which do not naturally occur in groundwater, the Part 22 Rules will be more stringent than the SDWA. For example, the SDWA would limit the vinyl chloride concentration, which at the Rose Site is 140 parts per billion ("ppb") at several monitoring wells, to only 2 ppb. However, with no influence by discharges, the background concentration of vinyl chloride in the groundwaters of the Rose Site should be at or near zero. If the state commission determined the difference between the SDWA and the WRCA standards to be substantial enough, the level of cleanup required would therefore be higher under the Part 22 Rules as compared to the federal standard for vinyl chloride and other synthetic compounds. Moreover, the Part 22 Rules also prohibit materials at concentrations that exceed the MCLs for inorganic and organic chemicals, as specified in the federal drinking water regulations, from being discharged into groundwaters in usable aquifers *"even in those cases where the local background groundwater levels for these materials exceed the specified levels."* Mich.Admin.Code R. 323.2205(3) (emphasis added). With many contaminants in the groundwaters of the Rose Site, therefore, the Part 22 Rules will be at least as stringent as the SDWA, but with others, such as vinyl chloride, they will be more stringent. Accordingly, even if we focus on the Rose Site alone, as EPA seems to require with general state goals, *see Interim Guidance*, 52 Fed. Reg. at 32498, we find that the WRCA and the Part 22 Rules are more stringent than federal standards under the SDWA.

3.   Whether Michigan's Anti-degradation Law is Legally Applicable to the Rose Site or Relevant and Appropriate to the Remedial Action Selected

The third requirement under section 9621(d) is that the potential ARARs be "legally applicable to the hazardous substance or pollutant or contaminant concerned or

[] relevant and appropriate under the circumstances of the release or remedial action selected...."[38] To determine whether this requirement is satisfied, we must re-examine the scope of Michigan's anti-degradation law. Section 6(a) of the WRCA prohibits persons from discharging, "directly or indirectly," certain substances into the groundwaters. The Part 22 Rules define "discharges" to be "the addition of materials to ground waters from any facility or operation which acts as a discrete or diffuse source...."

The record in this case clearly establishes an ongoing, indirect discharge of injurious substances from the soil into the groundwater at the Site caused by the natural infiltration of water through contaminated soils, which in turn results in the leaching of contaminants. *** The record also establishes that the nature and distribution of these contaminants is such that they are or may become "injurious to the public health, safety or welfare...or [to] uses which are being made or may be made of such waters...." M.C.L.A. § 323.6(a).

We thus agree with the district court that "because soil flushing diffusely discharges toxicants from the soil into the ground water, the anti-degradation rules are legally applicable to the clean up of the Rose Township site" and to soil flushing in particular. ***

* * *

Even if Michigan's anti-degradation law were not applicable to this site, its consideration would certainly be "relevant and appropriate." Among possible factors to be considered, the environmental media ("groundwater"), the type of substance ("injurious") and the objective of the potential ARAR ("protecting aquifers from actual or potential degradation)," are all "relevant" in this case because they pertain to the conditions of the Rose Site. Moreover, considering the aforementioned factors, the use of Michigan's anti-degradation law is well-suited to the site at issue and therefore "appropriate" in this case.

Accordingly, we conclude that Michigan's anti-degradation law is properly promulgated, more stringent than the federal standard, legally applicable or relevant and appropriate, as well as timely identified (the latter factor not having been argued on appeal), and therefore constitutes an ARAR within the meaning of 42 U.S.C. § 9621(d)(2). The fact that Michigan's anti-degradation law is an ARAR, however, does not resolve the question of whether the decree must comply with that ARAR. A decree must comply with all federal and state ARARs *unless* EPA "waives" an ARAR and the

---

[38] "Applicable requirements" are those standards promulgated under federal or state law that specifically address a hazardous substance, pollutant, contaminant, remedial action, or other circumstance at a CERCLA site. In contrast, "relevant and appropriate requirements" are those standards which, while not applicable to a CERCLA remedial action, are promulgated under federal or state law and address problems or situations sufficiently similar to those encountered at a site that their use is well situated to that site. 300 C.F.R. § 300.6; *Interim Guidance*, 52 Fed.Reg. at 32497; *NCP Final Rule*, 55 Fed.Reg. at 8742.

state either does not challenge the waiver or the waiver is upheld in court against the state challenge.

B.   Whether the Decree's Remedial Action Will Attain the Cleanup Requirements of Michigan's Anti-Degradation Law

The briefs and district court opinion generate considerable confusion on the issues of whether the decree's remedial action will attain the cleanup requirements of Michigan's anti-degradation law and if not, whether EPA actually and properly "waived" that ARAR. *** In any event, the State of Michigan does not, and cannot at this point, allege that cleanup standards at the completion of the remedial action will fall below the ARARs. The state consented to the 1987 ROD and agreed that all ARARs would be met by the accompanying RAP. The 1987 ROD contains the same TCLs as the amended ROD, so the state has implicitly agreed that the amended ROD and consent decree's TCLs satisfy all ARARs, including Michigan's groundwater regulations. Instead, the state's argument that the consent decree does not attain ARARs only consists of criticisms of the selected methodology; i.e., soil flushing will fail to attain the decree's TCLs and thus the ARARs for the Rose Site.

The state argues that EPA has a duty to determine, prior to submitting the decree to the court, whether soil flushing would attain ARARs. ***

EPA's own regulations indicate that the agency has some obligation to evaluate proposed remedial actions in terms of whether they will attain ARARs *before* implementation. ***

Our review of the various CERCLA provisions dealing with ARARs also supports the state's argument that EPA must determine prior to implementation whether a remedy will meet designated ARARs for a particular site. ***

In this case it is clear EPA never conclusively determined during negotiations that soil flushing would attain the relevant ARAR at the completion of the remedy ***. Section 9621(d)(4) requires that EPA make specific findings and publish them when it invokes a waiver, the latter requirement clearly not having been complied with in this case. We nevertheless hold that EPA has waived the ARARs for soil flushing based on the finding that "the remedial action selected is only part of a *total* remedial action that will attain such level or standard of control when completed." 42 U.S.C. § 9621(d)(4)(A) (emphasis added). In other words, EPA recognized that if soil flushing did not in fact attain the ARARs the defendants would have to carry out an alternative remedy to comply with them. ***

Under section 9621, a state may intervene in an action before entry of the consent decree and challenge the waiver of an ARAR, and if the waiver is not supported by *substantial evidence*, the court is required to conform the remedial action to that ARAR. In this case, as we find that EPA implicitly waived all ARARs for soil flushing on the basis that the decree as a whole would attain them, the state must show by substantial evidence that EPA's waiver is unlawful.

* * *

*** [W]e find that there is substantial evidence in the record to support and justify EPA's conclusion that the remedial action *as a whole* will attain the ARARs for the Rose Site. Should soil flushing fail, defendants must propose an alternate remedy that will attain all TCL's embodied in the decree and be as protective to human health and the environment as excavation and incineration.

Again, we emphasize that EPA cannot and is under no legal obligation to determine with absolute certainty whether a proposed remedial action will attain ARARs. If the decree is binding on the parties, requires attainment of all ARARs, and provides sufficient safeguards for careful implementation of proposed remedies which include proven technologies that either have been or are being used at similar sites or which are subject to testing under specified performance conditions, then it will be difficult for a court which lacks scientific expertise to find that the state has proven by substantial evidence that the remedial action at a particular site will not attain ARARs. The record contains evidence indicating that both soil flushing and incineration have been successfully used to remedy hazardous sites to pre-determined cleanup levels. Moreover, the state in this case may always come back to court at the completion of the remedial action and persuade us that the Phase I and/or Phase II TCLs have not been achieved. See 42 U.S.C. § 9621(e). We agree with the district court that the state has failed to present enough evidence to persuade us that the remedial action as a whole will not attain ARARs at its completion.

* * *

IX. CONCLUSION

In summary, it is necessary to make some additional comments regarding the scope of our review. We have meticulously poured over the voluminous record and examined, in detail, all of the arguments made on appeal. *** We believe the consent decree adequately takes into account all of CERCLA's requirements.

In particular, we do not find that the adoption of soil flushing as a remedy for the Rose Site subsurface soils is an arbitrary and capricious choice. EPA's reversal of its original opinion on the effectiveness of soil flushing has been adequately explained. *** Allowing defendants to test soil flushing under EPA's supervision and pursuant to an established timetable is both fair and reasonable, especially given the fact that both EPA and the State of Michigan regard soil flushing as a cost-effective, proven technology.

We have found Michigan's anti-degradation law to be an ARAR. Nevertheless we conclude that EPA implicitly waived that ARAR, and that the state has not met its burden to show, by substantial evidence, that the waiver was unjustified. In essence, we agree with the district court that the remedial action as a whole can attain all federal and state ARARs. In addition, we point out that EPA has some flexibility in determining how to comply with Michigan's anti-degradation law. We cannot agree with amici that soil flushing, by definition, violates the state ARAR.

* * *

CERCLA and the revised NCP give EPA flexibility to pursue innovative, cost-effective remedies. Though the effectiveness of soil flushing at the Rose Site remains untested, EPA's inclusion of that remedy was not arbitrary or capricious and is fair and reasonable. We urge the settling defendants to start the testing phase promptly so that a thorough cleanup of the Rose Site may soon begin.

NOTES

1. *Akzo Coatings* underscores the point that although CERCLA expressly makes state laws eligible to serve as ARARs, certain conditions must be satisfied before they actually apply to a particular site. Local ordinances are not mentioned in CERCLA. The cases confirm that they are therefore not ARARs and, where they are inconsistent with the accomplishment of EPA-designated remedies, they are therefore preempted by CERCLA.

United States v. Denver, 100 F.3d 1509 (10th Cir. 1996), focused on a Denver zoning ordinance that prohibited the maintenance of hazardous waste in areas zoned for industrial use. After the EPA issued a CERCLA § 106 order and the recipient commenced the required cleanup, Denver issued a cease and desist order based on alleged violations of the zoning ordinance. The EPA obtained a declaratory judgment that the cease and desist order was unenforceable, and an injunction precluding its enforcement at this site.

> This is a case of conflict preemption. Denver concedes that it is impossible for Shattuck to comply with both Denver's zoning ordinance and the EPA's remedial order. This zoning ordinance also stands as an obstacle to the objectives of CERCLA, whose purpose is to effect the expeditious and permanent cleanup of hazardous waste sites, and to allow the EPA the flexibility needed to address site-specific problems.*** A zoning ordinance which bars the maintenance of hazardous waste dramatically restricts the range of options available to the EPA, and in this case the ordinance would prevent a permanent on-site remedy. We agree with the district court that Denver's zoning ordinance is in actual conflict with the EPA's remedial order.

> * * *

> For the same reasons, we reject Denver's argument that its zoning ordinances constitute "a state environmental or facility siting law" and thus fall within the definition of "applicable or relevant and appropriate requirements" of state law, with which the EPA must comply if the state requirements are more stringent than federal law. *** If congress had wished to include local zoning ordinances within the definition of "state law" it would surely have so stated.

Id. at 1512-13.

2. For different reasons, a local ordinance was also held inapplicable in *State of Missouri v. Independent Petrochemical Corp.,* 104 F.3d 159 (8th Cir. 1997), concerning the operation of an incinerator built specifically to clean up the dioxin-contaminated soil at the infamous Times Beach site in Missouri. Following the issuance of a draft EPA-

state air permit for the incinerator, St. Louis County enacted an ordinance setting emissions standards six times more stringent than those in the EPA-state permit for incinerators burning known concentrations of dioxin. The only such incinerator in the county was the Times Beach incinerator. Because the PRPs had agreed in a consent decree with the EPA and the State of Missouri to operate the incinerator in compliance with local air requirements, they then requested judicial clarification of their obligations under the CERCLA consent decree.

The County now argues that the parties to the Consent Decree agreed that Syntex would submit to the County's permitting authority, even though they were not required to do so by federal law. While the Thermal Treatment Workplan expressly acknowledges that under § 121(e)(1) of CERCLA, no local permit is required for any removal or remediation action conducted onsite, the Syntex defendants nevertheless agreed to apply for air, water and hazardous waste permits to construct and operate the thermal treatment unit, including a "St. Louis County Department of Health air construction/operating permit for the Thermal Treatment Unit." It is this clause in the workplan upon which the County maintains it has authority to enforce its 1995 ordinance.

The county overlooks the fact, however, that federal regulations provide that all ARARs are "frozen" as of the date of the ROD unless the EPA determines that new standards are "necessary to ensure that the remedy is protective of human health and the environment." 40 C.F.R. § 300.430(f)((1)(ii)(B)(1). *** The EPA's rationale for freezing the applicable standards as of the date of the ROD is to prevent "continually changing remedies to accommodate new or modified requirements," which would "adversely affect the operation of the CERCLA program, [and] would be inconsistent with Congress' mandate to expeditiously clean up site." 55 Fed. Reg. 8666, 8757 (1990).

*** The EPA was aware of the ordinance standards when it issued its Final Permit and declined to adopt the stricter standards. The EPA did not make the determination that a stricter dioxin emission standard was necessary to protect human health and the environment. In fact it implicitly rejected this standard by choosing not to adopt it in the Final Permit. Accordingly, federal law does not permit the modification of the dioxin emission standard as of this late date.

Id. at 162.

3. The rule that ARARs are frozen as of the date of the ROD may become controversial where there is a long delay between the issuance of the ROD and the commencement of remedial work. In the Times Beach case, St. Louis County enacted its air emissions ordinance some seven years after the EPA issued its ROD.

The time-consuming nature of the CERCLA process has always drawn criticism. A 1997 report by the General Accounting Office indicates that the process has grown even longer in recent years. The GAO compared the length of time from site discovery to NPL listing, and from NPL listing to cleanup completion, as of 1990 and as of 1996.

In 1990, it took an average of 5.8 years from site discovery to NPL listing; the average time grew to 9.4 years by 1996. In 1990, cleanup was completed an average of 3.9 years from NPL listing; by 1996, it took an average of 10.6 years for cleanup completion. (1997). *Peter F. Guerrero, Times to Assess and Clean Up Hazardous Waste Sites Exceed Program Goals* (1997) (testimony before the Subcommittee on National Economic Growth, Natural Resources, and Regulatory Affairs, House Committee on Government Reform and Oversight).

4. EPA has responded to this criticism of the Superfund program with a variety of administrative reforms.

a. The EPA has issued a series of guidance documents attempting to standardize, where possible, the decision-making process. For example, to fill the void created by the lack of environmental standards for contaminants in soil, requiring each site to be analyzed on a blank slate, the EPA issued two guidance documents for screening contaminated soil. 61 Fed. Reg. 27349 (1996). The EPA has also suggested presumptively-applicable remedies for certain categories of sites, such as municipal landfills, sites contaminated by PCBs, sites with contaminated groundwater, sites with volatile organic compounds in soil and groundwater, and former wood treatment sites.

b. In addition, the EPA has created a National Remedy Review Board to review higher-cost cleanup plans, showing the EPA's heightened sensitivity to cost-based criticism of the Superfund program. *See* Michael W. Steinberg and Joshua E. Swift, *EPA's New National Remedy Review Board Aims to Improve Superfund Decisions*, 26 ENV'T REP. (BNA) 2353 (1996).

c. The EPA has also agreed to review and, if appropriate, update remedial decisions not yet implemented where relevant technical, legal, and policy developments have occurred between the issuance of the ROD and the commencement of cleanup. *See* Timothy F. Malloy, *Second-Look Superfund Remedies: Strategies for Re-Evaluating Cleanup Decisions*, 10 Toxics L. Rep. (BNA) 1063 (1996).

5. *Akzo Coatings* illustrates the necessity for lawyers, engineers, and scientists to work closely together in the cleanup decision-making process. It also underscores the advantages that the EPA has in sustaining judicial challenges to its remedy decisions. In addition to the procedural advantages prescribed by CERCLA, which limits the scope of judicial review to the administrative record and requires the courts to uphold the EPA's remedy selection unless arbitrary and capricious, § 113(j), the highly technical nature of site evaluation, ARARs identification, and remedy selection all encourage courts to defer to the EPA's presumed technical expertise.

One well-known exception is *In re Bell Petroleum Services*, portions of which regarding joint and several liability are set forth in chapter 10.A. The following excerpt addresses the consistency of the EPA's cleanup actions with the NCP. (Please refer to the excerpt in chapter 10.A to review the facts.)

IN RE BELL PETROLEUM SERVICES, INC.
3 F.3d 889 (5th Cir. 1993)

Before JOLLY and DUHE, Circuit Judges, and PARKER, Chief Judge of the Eastern District of Texas.
JOLLY, Circuit Judge.

* * *

V

Alternate Water Supply System

Sequa also challenges the EPA's decision to provide an alternate water supply (AWS) as an interim measure pending the completion of final remedial action. The scope of our review of the EPA's selection of the AWS is governed by the 1986 amendments to CERCLA, which provide that such review is "limited to the administrative record." 42 U.S.C. § 9613(j)(1). We are to uphold the EPA's decision "unless the objecting party can demonstrate, on the administrative record, that the decision was arbitrary and capricious or otherwise not in accordance with law." 42 U.S.C. § 9613(j)(2). ***

Sequa challenges the EPA's decision to provide the AWS on a number of grounds, including that: (1) the administrative record demonstrates that the EPA failed to recognize that "substantial danger to public health or the environment," as specified in the National Contingency Plan, is the standard against which the decision to implement an alternative water supply system must be measured; (2) there is no analysis of why the EPA believed the public health was at risk and required protection at the subject site; (3) the Safe Drinking Water Act's maximum contaminant level for chromium is based on a lifetime (70-year) exposure, but the alternate water supply system was merely a short-term (10-15 year) response; further, the administrative record contains no discussion of whether chromium presents a danger to humans on the basis of short-term exposure; and (4) the EPA failed to analyze the likelihood that the contaminated water would be ingested.

The EPA's defense of its decision to implement the alternate water supply system is, we think, singularly weak. The EPA contends primarily that we should defer to its technical expertise. It argues that the existence of chromium at levels exceeding the maximum contaminant level allowed under the SDWA presumptively establishes that its response was appropriate. We cannot agree.

* * *

After thoroughly reviewing the administrative record, we conclude that the EPA's decision to furnish the AWS was arbitrary and capricious. In vain we have searched the over 5,000 pages of administrative record, and found not one shred of evidence that anyone in the area was actually drinking chromium-contaminated water. Amazingly, the EPA made no attempt to learn whether anyone was drinking the water, or whether anyone intended to utilize the AWS, until after it had made its decision to construct the AWS. One would think that surely such information was essential in order to reach an informed, rational decision as to whether an AWS was necessary, and whether it would reduce any significant threat to public health. The administrative record reveals that the chromium-contaminated wells in the area all served commercial establishments, which the EPA prohibited from connecting to the AWS. Moreover, the EPA did not require residents to connect to the system, and did not prohibit them from using contaminated water from their wells. *** No technical expertise is necessary to discern that the EPA's implementation of the AWS was arbitrary and capricious, as well as a waste of money.

* * *

We realize that, as a result of our decision disallowing the EPA's costs for the AWS, those costs will have to be borne by the Superfund. *** Without knowing, or even attempting to learn, whether the AWS would serve to protect the safety and health of anyone, the EPA officiously ignored the comments of Bell and Sequa, and the results of its own remedial investigation, and stubbornly proceeded to spend over $300,000 to furnish a water supply system that was not needed, was not allowed to be used by the commercial establishments whose wells *** were the only ones with chromium contamination in excess of the SDWA standards, and did very little—indeed, if anything—to reduce any perceived public health threat posed by the chromium-contaminated groundwater. We can only assume that the EPA was not concerned about the cost of the AWS, because it believed that it could recover whatever was spent from Sequa. Although the EPA's powers under CERCLA are indeed broad, Congress has not provided that private parties must pay for the consequences of arbitrary and capricious agency action.

* * *

NOTES

1. Although decisions finding governmental cleanup actions inconsistent with the NCP are unusual, *Bell Petroleum* is not a lark.

In *Washington Department of Transportation v. Washington Natural Gas Co.,* 59 F.3d 793 (9th Cir. 1995) a state agency's cleanup was also found to be inconsistent with the NCP. The agency involved was not the state's environmental agency, but the Washington Department of Transportation (WSDOT). It became involved with a cleanup when its work on an interstate highway project, the Tacoma Spur, was interrupted by the discovery of tarlike material in soil borings, which had been drilled to determine whether the soil would support planned highway structures. The geotechnical consulting company that was advising the WSDOT on the highway construction then became its environmental consultant. Although the state environmental agency advised the WSDOT to try to get the site listed on the NPL to obtain Superfund funding, "WSDOT did not want to pursue that option because it involved extra time and effort." *Id.* at 797. Although neither WSDOT nor the consultant used the National Contingency Plan to decide how to investigate and cleanup the site, they did consult with various state and federal agencies in the process. After completing the cleanup, the WSDOT invoked CERCLA § 107(a)(4)(A) to seek cost recovery from the PRPs.

At the outset, the Ninth Circuit held that the state transportation agency qualified as "the state" for purposes of CERCLA, and could therefore proceed under § 107(a)(4)(A), which entitles the EPA and states to the presumption that their response actions are consistent with the NCP. The court also held that the fact that WSDOT did not consult the NCP during the investigation and cleanup did not preclude it from proving that its actions were nonetheless consistent with it. After carefully assessing the cleanup effort, however, the Ninth Circuit found it to be inconsistent with the NCP.

*** WSDOT failed to assess accurately both the nature and the extent of the threat posed by the presence of PAHs in the soil, failed to evaluate alternatives in the matter prescribed in the NCP, and failed to provide opportunity for public comment. Given the high degree of inconsistency with the requirements set forth in the NCP, WSDOT's action is arbitrary and capricious. Therefore, WSDOT is not entitled to recover its response costs under 42 U.S.C. § 9607.

Id. at 805.

2. Consistency issues are becoming critical features of private CERCLA actions. Although government approval of a cleanup is not necessary to establish consistency, *Marriott Corp. v. Simkins Industries, Inc.*, 825 F.Supp. 1575 (S.D. Fla. 1993), it helps. *See, e.g., General Electric Co. v. Litton Industrial Automation Systems, Inc.*, 920 F.2d 1415 (8th Cir. 1990), *cert. denied*, 499 U.S. 937 (1991). Where a private cleanup is conducted pursuant to an EPA order under § 106, however, the private party is entitled to a presumption of consistency in seeking contribution or cost recovery. *BancAmerica Commercial Corp. v. Mosher Steel of Kansas, Inc.*, 103 F.3d 80 (10th Cir. 1996).

3. Private parties have encountered difficulty in proving consistency when they do not offer sufficient opportunity for public input in the cleanup decision-making process. *See, e.g., Pierson Sand & Gravel, Inc. v. Pierson Township*, 89 F.3d 835 (Table), 1996 WL 338624 (6th Cir. June 18, 1996); *VME Americas, Inc. v. Hein-Werner Corp.*, 946 F.Supp. 683 (E.D. Wis. 1996). *But see Louisiana-Pacific Corp. v. ASARCO*, 24 F.3d 1565 (9th Cir. 1994), *cert. denied*, 513 U.S. 1103 (1995)(public input in this case was held sufficient to establish substantial compliance, and therefore, consistency, with the NCP.

15 NATURAL RESOURCE DAMAGES

Although the lion's share of CERCLA activity has focused on site cleanup, the statute's natural resource damage provisions are also quite significant. Section 107(a) makes PRPs liable not only for response costs, but also for "damages for injury to, destruction of, or loss of natural resources, including the reasonable costs of assessing such injury, destruction, or loss resulting from *** a release" of a hazardous substance. CERCLA § 107(a)(4)(C). Unlike the cleanup provisions of CERCLA, which are administered by the EPA and accessible to virtually anyone through private cost recovery or contribution actions, the natural resource provisions are administered by the Department of the Interior ("DOI") and enforceable only by specifically-designated federal, state, and Indian tribe trustees. CERCLA § 107(f). The National Contingency Plan ("NCP") designates a variety of federal agencies as trustees for federal natural resources, with the Commerce Department's National Oceanic and Atmospheric Administration and the Interior Department playing the principal roles. In addition, the governor of each state has the authority to designate state officials to act as trustees for the state's natural resources.

A state's authority to delegate trustee powers to localities was upheld in *City of New York v. Exxon Corp.*, 766 F.Supp. 177 (S.D.N.Y.1991). There, the Governor of New York had designated the Commissioner of the New York State Department of Environmental Conservation as trustee for natural resources within, belonging to, managed or controlled by the state. The state trustee then delegated to a New York City official the authority to pursue the state's natural resource claims regarding New York City landfills that were contaminated and were the subject of cleanup/cost recovery actions as well as natural resource damage claims. The court recognized the validity of the delegation under CERCLA, and enabled the City to pursue the state's claims as state trustee with respect to those New York City-based natural resources.

In part, the natural resource provisions have not yet been widely invoked because of first the absence, and then the cloud surrounding, regulations governing the valuation of natural resource damages. The task of promulgating regulations governing damage assessments was conferred on the President, and then delegated to the Department of the Interior, and was to be completed by December 1982. CERCLA required the regulations to specify both Type A rules—"standard procedures for simplified assessments requiring minimal field observation," and Type B rules—"alternative protocols for conducting assessments in individual cases." CERCLA § 301(c)(2), 42 U.S.C. § 9651(c)(2). The Type B rules establish more complex procedures for assessing cases of more extensive damage, whereas the simplified procedures in the Type A rules are more suited to minor damage situations. DOI first published its Type B regulations in August 1986, 51 Fed. Reg. 27674 (1986), and Type A regulations in 1987, 52 Fed. Reg. 9042 (1987), and then revised both sets of regulations in 1988 in response to the 1986 amendments to CERCLA. 53 Fed. Reg. 5166 (1988).

The regulations initially specified that natural resource damages shall be "the lesser of restoration or replacement costs; or diminution of use values." 43 C.F.R. § 11.35(b)(2)(1987). In 1989, the D.C. Circuit invalidated this portion of the regulations, citing congressional preference for restoration costs to govern damage assessments.

> The fatal flaw of Interior's approach, however, is that it assumes that natural resources are fungible goods, just like any other, and that the value to society generated by a particular resource can be accurately measured in every case—assumptions that Congress apparently rejected. As the foregoing examination of CERCLA's text, structure and legislative history illustrates, Congress saw restoration as the presumptively correct remedy for injury to natural resources. To say that Congress placed a thumb on the scales in favor of restoration is not to say that it forswore the goal of efficiency. "Efficiency," standing alone, simply means that the chosen policy will dictate the result that achieves the greatest value to society. Whether a particular choice is efficient depends on *how the various alternatives are valued*. Our reading of CERCLA does not attribute to Congress an irrational dislike of "efficiency"; rather, it suggests that Congress was skeptical of the ability of human beings to measure the true "value" of a natural resource. Indeed, even the common law recognizes that restoration is the proper remedy for injury to property where measurement of damages by some other method will fail to compensate fully for the injury. Congress' refusal to view use value and restoration cost as having equal presumptive legitimacy merely recognizes that natural resources have value that is not readily measured by traditional means. Congress delegated to Interior the job of deciding at what point the presumption of restoration falls away, but its repeated emphasis on the primacy of restoration rejected the underlying premise of Interior's rule, which is that restoration is wasteful if its cost exceeds—by even the slightest amount—the diminution in use value of the injured resource.

State of Ohio v. United States Department of the Interior, 880 F.2d 432, 456 (D.C.Cir. 1989) (regarding Type B regulations). *See also State of Colorado v. Department of the Interior*, 880 F.2d 481 (D.C.Cir. 1989) (regarding Type A regulations).

In 1994, the Interior Department issued revised Type B regulations in response to the *Ohio* case. 59 Fed. Reg. 14262 (1994). Interior addressed all aspects of the *Ohio* remand except for the assessment of lost nonuse values. The revised final rule allows the natural resource trustee to recover the costs of restoration, rehabilitation, replacement, and/or acquisition of equivalent resources in all cases, replacing the "lesser of" rule invalidated in *Ohio*. The revised rule also gives trustees the discretion to add to the basic measure of damages the value of the resource services lost to the public from the date of the discharge or release until restoration, rehabilitation, replacement, and/or acquisition of equivalent resources is completed. The rule specifies a number of cost estimating methodologies for trustees to use in projecting the costs of restoration, rehabilitation, replacement, and/or acquisition of equivalent resources.

The revised Type B regulations were challenged on both procedural and substantive grounds. The following excerpt is but a small portion of a lengthy opinion addressing the challenges.

KENNECOTT UTAH COPPER CORP. V. UNITED STATES DEPARTMENT OF THE INTERIOR
88 F.3d 1191 (D.C. Cir. 1996)

Before GINSBURG, RANDOLPH and TATEL, Circuit Judges.
Opinion of the Court by GINSBURG, RANDOLPH, and TATEL, Circuit Judges.

In these consolidated cases we once again consider challenges to the Department of the Interior's "Type B" Natural Resource Damage Assessment regulations. Under both the federal Superfund statute and the Clean Water Act, federal and state officials, acting as trustees for the public, may recover money damages for the harm that the release of hazardous substances into the environment causes to certain natural resources. Type B NRDA regulations set forth a process that trustees may follow not only in calculating the monetary value of that injury to natural resources, but also in collecting and spending the funds they recover.

Interior first published final Type B NRDA regulations almost a decade ago. We invalidated portions of those regulations in *Ohio v. United States Department of the Interior*, 880 F.2d 432 (D.C.Cir.1989). In response to *Ohio*, Interior finally released revised regulations in March 1994.

* * *

I. BACKGROUND

The federal Superfund statute, more formally known as the Comprehensive Environmental Response, Compensation, and Liability Act of 1980 or "CERCLA," makes specified classes of parties *** potentially liable for the expenses that the federal and state governments, as well as Indian tribes, incur in responding to the release of hazardous substances into the environment. ***

In addition, and at the heart of this case, responsible parties are financially liable for "injury to, destruction of, or loss of natural resources, including the reasonable costs of assessing such injury, destruction, or loss," caused by the release of hazardous substances. 42 U.S.C. § 9607(a)(4)(C). *** Section 107 of CERCLA authorizes federal and state officials, acting as public trustees, to sue responsible parties to recover damages for the harm to natural resources caused by the release of hazardous substances. § 9607(f)(1). Trustees may use the funds they recover "to restore, replace, or acquire the equivalent of such natural resources." *Id.*

Section 311 of the Clean Water Act also authorizes federal and state officials to sue as public trustees to recover "any costs or expenses incurred by the Federal Government or any State government in the restoration or replacement of natural resources damaged or destroyed as a result of a discharge of oil or a hazardous substance" in navigable waters. 33 U.S.C. § 1321(f)(4). Trustees suing under § 311 of the Clean Water Act may use recovered funds "to restore, rehabilitate or acquire the equivalent of such natural resources." § 1321(f)(5).

Once a trustee suing under either § 107 of CERCLA or § 311 of the Clean Water Act determines the amount of damages in accordance with federal regulations promulgated under § 301(c) of CERCLA, the trustee's assessment enjoys a rebuttable presumption in administrative proceedings and in court. Section 301(c), in turn, requires the federal government to issue regulations that "specify[:] (A) standard procedures for simplified assessments" in situations requiring "minimal field observation" (Type A regulations); "and (B) alternative protocols for conducting assessments in individual cases" requiring more detailed evaluations (Type B regulations). § 9651(c)(2). The statute further provides that

> [s]uch regulations shall identify the best available procedures to determine such damages, including both direct and indirect injury, destruction, or loss and shall take into consideration factors including, but not limited to, replacement value, use value, and ability of the ecosystem or resource to recover.

Id. The government must review these regulations every two years, revising them as appropriate.

As in *Ohio v. United States Department of the Interior*, we are concerned here only with Type B regulations. In *Ohio*, we considered the Type B regulations that the Department of the Interior initially issued in August 1986, 51 Fed. Reg. 27,674 (1986), and later revised in February 1988, 53 Fed. Reg. 5,166 (1988). Addressing eleven issues, we granted the petition for review with respect to two and remanded a third to the agency, instructing Interior to proceed in issuing new regulations in conformity with our opinion "as expeditiously as possible." In response, in April 1991, Interior proposed new regulations, which left most of the prior rules in place, but changed specific sections to address the concerns we raised in *Ohio*. Although the public comment period on those proposed regulations ended in mid-July of 1991, Interior had still not approved or issued final rules by the time of the November 1992 Presidential election.

In mid-January 1993, shortly before President Clinton's inauguration, Interior's Assistant Secretary for Policy, Management and Budget approved a set of Type B regulations, which differed from those proposed in April 1991, and directed a subordinate to send the document to the Office of the Federal Register ("OFR") for publication as final regulations. The OFR received an original and two copies of these signed regulations—which we shall call the "1993 Document"—sometime after 2:00 p.m. on January 19, 1993, the final full day of the Bush Administration. On January 21—just two days after the OFR received the 1993 Document, and before the OFR filed the document for public inspection—an Interior employee, at the direction of the new acting Assistant Secretary for Policy, Management and Budget, telephoned the OFR to withdraw the document. The employee confirmed the request in writing later the same day. In accordance with its regulations and internal guidelines, the OFR stopped processing the 1993 Document and returned all three copies to Interior, recording the action in the "Kill Book," a handwritten ledger the OFR maintained to keep track of documents withdrawn by agencies.

* * *

Like their predecessors, the 1994 Regulations provide a four-stage framework for trustees to follow in assessing natural resource damages. In the first stage, trustees conduct a "pre-assessment screen," in which they review readily available information to determine whether there is a reasonable probability that a claim will be successful, thus justifying the expense and effort of conducting a full assessment. In the second stage, the trustee develops an "assessment plan," which describes in some detail how the trustee expects to determine the monetary value of injury suffered by the natural resources, including but not limited to stating whether the trustee intends to conduct a Type A or Type B assessment. During the third stage, the trustee conducts the assessment, which in the case of Type B assessments involve three phases: an "injury determination phase," when the trustee ascertains whether the release of a hazardous substance has, in fact, caused injury to natural resources, a "quantification phase," when the trustee determines the extent of the physical injury, as compared to the baseline conditions that would have existed if the hazardous substances had not been released into the environment; and the crucial "damage determination" phase, when the trustee determines the amount of money it will seek to compensate for the injuries to the natural resources. Having conducted the assessment, the trustee proceeds to the fourth stage, the "post-assessment" phase, during which the trustee prepares a report describing the assessment; presents a demand to potentially responsible parties for their share of the damages, filing suit if appropriate; and if successful in recovering funds, develops a plan to restore the injured natural resources.

* * *

*** Industry Petitioners raise eleven substantive challenges to the 1994 Regulations, claiming that the regulations not only exceed the agency's authority under CERCLA and the Clean Water Act, but also constitute arbitrary and capricious action. In its petition for review, the State of Montana argues that the 1994 Regulations do not go far enough in requiring trustees to restore natural resources to their untainted condition.

We consider each of the procedural and substantive issues in turn.

II. ANALYSIS
* * *

4. Cost effectiveness

The 1986 Regulations required trustees to choose the most cost-effective restoration option as the measure of damages. The 1994 Regulations eliminated this provision. The new rules require trustees to evaluate each option on the basis of its cost-effectiveness, but also to consider nine other listed factors and "all relevant considerations."

Industry Petitioners argue that Interior's decision not to require trustees to select the most cost-effective option violates CERCLA, ignores this court's decision in *Ohio*, and is arbitrary and capricious.

CERCLA contains no provision requiring, or even suggesting, that trustees select the most cost-effective restoration option. Both the legislative history, and this court's decision in *Ohio* indicate that cost-effectiveness is an important goal. Yet there is no reason to suppose that the only way to accomplish this objective is to make cost-effectiveness the determinative criterion for selecting a restoration option. ***

At any rate, Interior has not written this criterion out of the 1994 Regulations. Section 11.82(d)(1) requires trustees to evaluate each option based on its cost-effectiveness. The trustees must describe the options in the Restoration and Compensation Determination Plan and state the rationale for choosing the one selected. The Plan is subject to public review and comment.

Interior offered a good explanation for not treating cost-effectiveness as determinative. Cost-effectiveness compares options producing the same level of benefits. Since the level of benefits associated with different options is often unquantifiable, cost-effectiveness is not necessarily a useful method of evaluating those different options. Furthermore, there will often be tradeoffs between compensable use value and restoration costs. For example, a fast-paced recovery might cost more than a slower recovery, but would result in lower interim lost use values. Since the total damages are the sum of restoration costs and compensable value, requiring trustees to select the least expensive restoration option might result in higher total damages. We conclude that Interior's decision was reasonable, consistent with CERCLA, and with this court's decision in *Ohio*.

5. Gross disproportionality

The 1986 Regulations allowed trustees to recover "the lesser of" the cost of restoring the injured resource and the lost use value of the resource. The *Ohio* court invalidated the "lesser-of" rule, stating that "Congress established a distinct preference for restoration cost as the measure of recovery in natural resource damage cases." 880 F.2d at 459. The court recognized that CERCLA might permit Interior to create exceptions to the general rule in favor of restoration costs. For example, the court explained, when restoration is technically impossible, or when the costs of restoration are "grossly disproportionate" to the use value of the resource, Interior might establish use value as the measure of damages.

Industry Petitioners argue that *Ohio* required Interior to adopt a "gross disproportionality" standard to prevent trustees from selecting a restoration option if its costs were grossly disproportionate to the use value of the injured resource. The argument is based on a misreading of *Ohio*. The court there held that restoration costs were the preferred measure of damages. But the court also held that Interior had authority to apply a different measure of damages in certain cases. Rather than requiring

Interior to do so, however, the court stated that under CERCLA Interior had "some degree of latitude in deciding what measure shall apply." 880 F.2d at 443 n. 7.

Interior's decision not to adopt a gross disproportionality rule is a permissible response to the *Ohio* decision. The 1994 Regulations require trustees to develop a range of restoration options, from no action to intensive action. The trustees must evaluate each option based on factors such as cost-effectiveness and the relationship between expected costs and expected benefits. These evaluations and the trustee's rationale for choosing the selected option must be documented in the Restoration and Compensation Determination Plan, which is subject to public review and comment. Interior reasoned—and we see no reason to disagree—that these procedural safeguards would take the place of the gross disproportionality test and ensure that trustees do not select options that are excessively costly.

6. Consistency with response

In those instances in which a damaged resource requires both cleanup and restoration, § 11.82(d)(4) of the 1994 Regulations directs trustees to select a restoration alternative only after considering the cleanup ("response") remedy chosen by the EPA or other authorized agency for the same resource. The Industry Petitioners object because the rule does not mandate "consistency" between the restoration alternative and the response action. Interior points out, however, that the statute requires only "coordination," 42 U.S.C. § 9604(b)(2), not consistency, and asserts that the 1994 Regulations satisfy that standard.

* * *

Turning to the merits, we see that the CERCLA authorizes response actions by the EPA, the States, and private parties to remove hazardous substances and to remedy their release. According to the Industry Petitioners, the cleanup remedy that is selected for a site can have a significant impact upon the need for other measures to redress injuries to natural resources at the same site. For example, the removal of all contaminants may reduce the extent of any restoration needed thereafter. Because the two types of remedies may overlap or at least interact, the Industry Petitioners contend that not only coordination but also consistency is imperative. In support, they cite three different provisions of the CERCLA, providing first that the EPA must "promptly notify ... trustees of potential damages ... and ... coordinate the assessments, investigations and planning," 42 U.S.C. § 9604(b)(2); second, that trustees may not sue for damages before the EPA has selected a cleanup remedy; and third, that double recovery is prohibited.

The Industry Petitioners concede that the 1994 Regulations promote coordination and require that information be shared. Because the rule does not mandate consistency between the two regimes, however, the Industry Petitioners are concerned that trustees may ignore EPA response actions and adopt restoration procedures that are unduly costly. Interior's response is twofold: first, none of the statutory provisions cited by the Industry Petitioners demands consistency; second, the EPA and the trustees are charged with a different responsibility—to curb the release of hazardous substances and to restore natural resources, respectively.

While these two functions will assuredly benefit from coordination, there appears to be nothing in their nature that logically compels consistency. As Interior suggests, it seems eminently reasonable that trustees be granted the flexibility and discretion to accommodate their solutions to the unique circumstances of each case. Indeed, a certain degree of inconsistency might be necessary, particularly where short-term and long-term considerations dictate seemingly conflicting responses (*e.g.*, grass to prevent erosion, followed by reforestation, which kills the grass).

Therefore we conclude that the 1994 Regulations sensibly promote coordination, rather than requiring consistency, between restoration remedies and response actions. ***

* * *

13. Priority of remedies

In its petition, Montana claims that CERCLA requires trustees, when calculating the monetary value of the harm caused by release of hazardous substances into the environment during the "damage determination" phase of a Type B assessment, to prefer "restoration," "rehabilitation," and "replacement" of natural resources over the "acquisition of equivalent resources."

The 1994 Regulations require trustees, in the "damage determination" phase, to calculate the amount of monetary damages owed by responsible parties based on the cost of implementing the most appropriate remedial strategy. 43 C.F.R. § 11.81. To determine the most appropriate strategy, in turn, the regulations require trustees to develop a reasonable number of possible strategies involving the "restoration, rehabilitation, replacement and/or acquisition of the equivalent of the injured natural resources and the services those resources provide." §§ 11.81-11.82. Interior defines "restoration" and "rehabilitation" as synonyms, defining them as "actions undertaken to return injured resources to their baseline condition." § 11.82(b)(1)(i). It likewise defines "replacement" and "acquisition of the equivalent" as synonymous, meaning "the substitution for injured resources with resources that provide the same or substantially similar services." § 11.82(b)(1)(ii). Based on eleven factors, trustees must choose the appropriate strategy that would either return the resources to their previous condition (through restoration or rehabilitation), or substitute resources that provide substantially similar services (through replacement or acquisition of equivalent resources) or some combination of the two. Except when a strategy would require a federally authorized official to acquire land that the federal government would have to manage, the regulations do not establish a preference for one strategy over another.

In Montana's view, the statute requires Interior to favor restoration, rehabilitation, and replacement of natural resources, because they "result in a net benefit to the nation's natural resources," whereas "acquiring equivalent resources simply transfers into public ownership uninjured resources that are comparable to the injured resources." Montana's Br. at 2. While Montana's argument may have merit as a matter of policy, our task under *Chevron* is to determine if Interior's interpretation is permissible. Unlike Montana, we conclude that it is.

Beginning with *Chevron* step one, we think Congress has not clearly expressed a preference for physically restoring resources over acquiring comparable resources for the public's benefit. Montana relies on § 107(f) of CERCLA, which Congress amended in 1986 to read:

> Sums recovered by the United States Government as trustee under this subsection shall be retained by the trustee ... for use only to restore, replace, or acquire the equivalent of such natural resources. Sums recovered by a State as trustee under this subsection shall be available for use only to restore, replace, or acquire the equivalent of such natural resources by the State. The measure of damages in any action ... shall not be limited by the sums which can be used to restore or replace such resources.

As Montana concedes, this passage does not explicitly establish a preference for restoration and replacement. In discussing how federal and state governments can use the funds they recover, the first two sentences list three alternatives, expressing no preference among them. The third sentence merely states that damages recovered may exceed the cost of restoring or replacing resources, thus recognizing that a trustee may recover damages not only to restore an injured resource physically, but also to compensate the public for the lost use of resources during the interim period between the discharge of hazardous substances and the final implementation of a remedial plan.

Montana argues, nonetheless, that the third sentence implicitly establishes a hierarchy. In making this argument, it relies on *Ohio's* interpretation of the third sentence to mean that "*restoration* cost will serve as the basic measure of damages in many if not most CERCLA cases." 880 F.2d at 446 (emphasis added). According to Montana, because acquiring natural resources does not involve actual *restoration* of an injured resource, our interpretation of the statute precludes trustees from using acquisition as the "basic measure of damages" during the damage determination phase of an assessment.

Placed in its proper context, our statement in *Ohio* provides scant, if any, support for Montana's position. In *Ohio*, we reviewed challenges to Interior's 1986 Type B Regulations that had distinguished between "restoration or replacement costs" on the one hand, and the "use value" of injured resources on the other. The regulations required trustees to use the lesser of the two values in setting the amount of damages. Because "use value" was essentially the market value of the injured property, and because market value would almost always be less than the cost of restoring the natural resources, Interior's approach virtually assured that trustees could never recover enough money to restore, replace or acquire equivalent resources. We thus rejected those regulations as inconsistent with the statute's remedial structure and purpose. In arriving at that conclusion, we never considered, let alone established, a hierarchy among the statute's three remedial strategies—restoration, replacement, and acquisition of equivalent resources. To the contrary, we treated all of them as equivalent, generally using "restoration" as a shorthand way of referring to all three.

* * *

In light of the ambiguous statutory language and the absence of legislative history directly on point, we conclude that Congress has not clearly expressed a preference for restoration and replacement over the acquisition of equivalent resources. Proceeding to step two of *Chevron*, we find Interior's interpretation of § 107(f) reasonable. *** As Interior has explained, acquiring equivalent resources may do more to promote recovery of an injured resource than spending money directly to restore that resource. For example, acquiring land next to a damaged property may serve as a buffer to prevent nearby development from further harming the injured property, thereby increasing its chance of recovery. Moreover, although not establishing an automatic preference for restoration and replacement, Interior's regulations do not neglect the goal of restoring injured resources themselves. They require trustees, when choosing the most appropriate alternative, to consider the benefits and costs of each approach (and, in particular circumstances, a trustee may determine that restoration provides greater benefits than acquisition); consistency with federal, state and tribal policies (which may favor restoration); as well as the potential risk of additional injury to the particular injured resources under each alternative. We think it important to remember, as well, that fulfilling the "restorative purpose" of the statute is not entirely dependent on trustees' efforts to recover damages for harm to natural resources. Their efforts are in addition to the "response" actions, which clearly serve a restorative purpose in removing hazardous waste and "prevent[ing] or minimiz[ing] the release of hazardous substances" into the environment. 42 U.S.C. § 9601(23)-(25).

* * *

NOTES

1. Because the natural resource damage provisions apply only prospectively, and because the regulations have been under attack for so long, the statute of limitations has become an important issue. CERCLA § 113(g)(1) provides that the natural resource damages actions must be filed by three years after the later of either the discovery of the loss and its connection with the release, or the date on which the damage assessment regulations are promulgated. In the 1994 regulations, the DOI interpreted the term "promulgated" to mean when the regulations were finally revised. In an omitted portion of *Kennecott*, the court held that this was an unreasonable interpretation of CERCLA, and that the three year period began running, at the latest, when the Type A regulations were first made final in 1987. *Kennecott*, 88 F.3d at 1212. *See also State of California v. Montrose Chemical Corp. of California*, 104 F.3d 1507 (9th Cir. 1996).

2. In May 1996, the DOI revised its Type A regulations. 61 Fed. Reg. 20560 (1996). Since originally published in 1987, the Type A regulations have applied only to coastal and marine environments and the Great Lakes. Interior has stated that it would consider developing additional Type A procedures for other environments based on experience with these environments, but the 1996 revisions remain focused on the

coastal, marine, and Great Lakes environments. As revised, the Type A regulations authorize trustees to use a computer model, rather than an actual field evaluation, to assess Type A damages.

3. Although trustees are not required to use the regulations in calculating damages, their assessments enjoy a rebuttable presumption of validity if calculated in accordance with the regulations. The rebuttable presumption for assessments conducted under the Type A regulations is capped at $100,000. If a PRP submits a written request and justification to use the Type B regulations, and pays the reasonable cost of performing the field evaluation, the trustee must use Type B rather than Type A procedures.

4. Analyzing natural resource damage recoveries through April 1995, the General Accounting Office found that almost all natural resource claims have been settled without litigation, with 98 settlements covering natural resource damages of $106 million. Of these settlements, 48 did not require any payments beyond response costs. The total compensation for natural resource damages at Superfund sites has been less than one percent of the total cost to clean up the sites. U.S. GEN. ACCOUNTING OFFICE, SUPERFUND: OUTLOOK FOR AND EXPERIENCE WITH NATURAL RESOURCE DAMAGE SETTLEMENTS, RCED-96-71.

> Several factors limit the recoveries for natural resource injuries, according to Interior officials. First, injuries must be traced to particular releases of hazardous substances; second, a viable and solvent responsible party must be found; third, the claim must be filed within the statute of limitations; and fourth, a federal agency must have the financial resources available to assess the damage and develop the information necessary to support a claim. Furthermore, the Department of Justice officials state that the level of appropriations to fund federal natural resource damage programs is the single most important factor in determining how many sites can be assessed for damages.

Ibid.

The GAO found that because the Type B procedures are costly and time consuming to implement, trustees most often use an abbreviated procedure that combines readily available site-specific information with scientific literature to quantify damages. While such assessments do not carry the presumption of validity that a full-fledged Type B assessment would, they are generally sufficient for negotiating settlements in a cost-effective manner.

The GAO estimates that, among already-identified Superfund sites, 60 sites may eventually involve natural resource damages in excess of $5 million, and in 20 of those, damages could exceed $50 million.

5. Contingent valuation is a controversial method of assessing damages for use values, and non-use values where use values cannot be approximated. The contingent valuation method involves surveying potentially affected people to determine how much they would pay to keep their natural resources free from contamination, or how much they would demand if the resources were contaminated.

The Type B regulations have recognized contingent valuation as a method usable by trustees. In May 1994, Interior proposed to expand the use of the contingent valuation method for estimating lost non-use values in all cases. 59 Fed. Reg. 23098 (1994). Trustees have not shied away from this controversial method. One exception, under analogous provisions in the Oil Pollution Act of 1990, is the Exxon Valdez oil spill, where a contingent valuation survey lead to a $3 billion damage assessment. Before the survey was introduced into evidence, Exxon settled the case for $1.1 billion.

Proponents of contingent valuation believe that this method best reflects the true value of the resources to society, as conventional use value methods do not fully represent the loss society incurs when its natural resources are damaged. Critics argue, however, that the method is too subjective and unpredictable, and will lead to unfair and inconsistent damage assessments. *See generally* Brian R. Binger et al., *The Use of Contingent Valuation Methodology in Natural Resource Damage Assessments: Legal Fact and Economic Fiction*, 89 Nw. U. L. Rev. 1029 (1995).

16 RELEASE REPORTING

CERCLA has two reporting requirements. One is an ongoing requirement to report immediately the release of a hazardous substance in an amount equal to or greater than a "reportable quantity." CERCLA § 103(a), 42 U.S.C. § 9603(a); and 40 C.F.R. Part 302 (setting forth reportable quantities). The other is a one-time requirement, to notify the EPA—within 180 days of the initial enactment of CERCLA—of the existence of past or present facilities for the storage, treatment, or disposal of hazardous substances. CERCLA § 103(c); 42 U.S.C. § 103(c). This chapter will focus on the ongoing release reporting requirement.

Three salient features distinguish CERCLA's release reporting requirements from its release response and cleanup provisions. First, whereas CERCLA's response provisions do not require anyone voluntarily to clean up hazardous substances that have been released into the environment (absent an EPA or court order to do so), the Act's release reporting requirements apply automatically whenever there is a reportable release. Second, while the response provisions may entail extremely high costs (for cleaning up or reimbursing another party's cleanup costs) and civil penalties (for violating, without sufficient cause, a cleanup order), the release reporting requirements are punishable by criminal sanctions (fines in accordance with title 18 of the U.S. Code or three years imprisonment or both). CERCLA § 103(b). Third, while the response provisions are triggered by an actual or threatened release of hazardous substances, only an actual release activates the reporting requirement. In *Fertilizer Institute v. United States Environmental Protection Agency*, 935 F.2d 1303 (D.C. Cir. 1991), the court struck down the EPA's attempt to require release reporting for the storage of radionuclides in unenclosed containers.

*** CERCLA provides that the EPA must be notified when a hazardous substance is actually released into the environment. Nowhere in the statute is there any language requiring that the EPA be notified when there is a threatened release. This omission is especially significant given the sections of CERCLA that expressly distinguish between threats of releases and actual releases. *See, e.g.*, 42 U.S.C. §§ 9604, 9606. These sections give the EPA the authority to act with reference both to releases and to threatened releases. Under these circumstances, we must presume that Congress's failure to subject threatened releases to the reporting requirement was intentional. Accordingly we reject the EPA's claim that the threat of a release from an unenclosed containment structure is sufficient to allow the EPA to require reporting when a reportable quantity of a hazardous material is put in the structure. Under CERCLA's provisions, nothing less than the actual release of a hazardous material into the environment triggers its reporting requirement.

Id. at 1310.

Two cases follow, both involving criminal prosecutions for failure to report hazardous substance releases. The first case addresses the reportable quantity for a mixture, such as soil contaminated with a hazardous substance. The second underscores that the reporting requirement applies broadly to any "person in charge" of a facility.

UNITED STATES V. MACDONALD & WATSON WASTE OIL CO.
933 F.2d 35 (1st Cir. 1991)

Before CAMPBELL, Circuit Judge, TIMBERS, Senior Circuit Judge of the Second Circuit, and CYR, Circuit Judge.
LEVIN H. CAMPBELL, Circuit Judge.

[The facts are set forth in a different excerpt from this case, included in chapter 6.]

* * *

E. CERCLA § 103(b)(3)

CERCLA imposes criminal sanctions upon any person in charge of a facility from which a "reportable quantity" of a hazardous substance is released who fails to immediately notify the appropriate federal agency. CERCLA, § 103(b)(3). The default reportable quantity for a hazardous substance is one pound, CERCLA, § 102(b), unless superseded by regulations promulgated pursuant to CERCLA. Appellants MacDonald & Watson and NIC contend that the indictment and jury instructions improperly established the reportable quantity of soil contaminated with toluene as one pound. For this reason, they seek reversal of CERCLA convictions. The government responds that it properly charged, and the district court correctly instructed that the reportable quantity for soil contaminated with commercial chemical product toluene (hereinafter "toluene") is one pound. Alternatively, the government argues that, since the evidence was undisputed that ten large truckloads of the hazardous waste was released, any error in the charge and jury instructions was harmless. We hold that the one pound reportable quantity set out in the indictment and charged in the court's instructions was incorrect, but constituted harmless error.

We turn first to a determination of the reportable quantity proper for this hazardous substance. The term "hazardous substances," for purposes of CERCLA reporting, is defined in CERCLA to include all RCRA hazardous wastes as well as additional materials listed as hazardous wastes pursuant to CERCLA, § 102(a). EPA regulations promulgated under RCRA prior to the Master Chemical cleanup listed toluene as a hazardous waste. EPA also promulgated regulations pursuant to § 102(a) prior to the Master Chemical cleanup which establish a reportable quantity for toluene of 1,000 pounds. The RCRA regulations also provide that soil contaminated with toluene is a RCRA hazardous waste, which is, therefore, subject to CERCLA reporting requirements. It is necessary to resolve, first, whether toluene or toluene-contaminated soil is the relevant hazardous waste for release reporting purposes here, and second, the reportable quantity of that waste.

Appellants contend that reporting is required only where 1,000 pounds of *toluene* is released, because CERCLA's "no-mixing" rule provides that at the time of the release, "[r]eleases of mixtures and solutions are subject to these notification requirements only where a component hazardous substance of the mixture or solution is released in a quantity equal to or greater than its reportable quantity." 50 Fed. Reg. 13,474, 13,475 (April 4, 1985). This contention is incorrect. EPA clearly stated in the preamble to the "mixture rule" regulations that the rule does not apply where the concentration of the hazardous substance in the mixture is not known:

> [F]or CERCLA purposes, the [CERCLA] mixture rule applies to ... RCRA F and K waste streams (all of which tend to be mixtures) ... if the concentrations of all the hazardous substances in the waste are known. If the concentrations of the substances are unknown, the [reportable quantity] of the waste or unlisted waste applies.... [I]f the concentrations of the hazardous substances contained in the mixture are known, waste streams should be treated like any other mixture. If the releaser does not know the composition of the listed waste stream, EPA agrees that applying the [reportable quantity] of the entire waste stream is the only reasonably conservative alternative.

50 Fed. Reg. 13,463. In the present case, the concentration of toluene in the soil was unknown. The mixture rule is, therefore, inapplicable. A different result would, of course, undermine the CERCLA policy requiring reporting of dangerous releases of hazardous substances. If the concentration of the hazardous constituent in a mixture is unknown, it is impossible to prove the quantity of the constituent that is released, regardless of the magnitude of mixture released. Congress and the EPA could not have intended, and did not intend, that all releases of such mixtures may go unreported.

Having established that the amount of toluene-contaminated soil that was released (rather than toluene alone) is the relevant hazardous waste triggering the reporting obligation, the next question is the reportable quantity of toluene-contaminated soil. The government argues that, because soil contaminated with commercial chemical product toluene is an independent RCRA hazardous waste for which EPA has established no independent reportable quantity, the reportable quantity is one pound pursuant to CERCLA § 102(b). While there is some basis for this contention, it leads to the totally illogical result that one pound of toluene diluted by soil must be reported whereas only 1,000 pounds of pure toluene need be. We conclude that the reportable quantity for soil contaminated with toluene is the reportable quantity for toluene alone—1,000 pounds.

The fundamental concern underlying release reporting is the danger associated with the release of a listed hazardous waste. The reportable quantity for listed hazardous wastes is determined "based on chemical toxicity." The primary concern with the amount of the listed hazardous waste released is reflected in the "no-mixing" rule, which provides that released mixtures need be reported only when a reportable quantity of the component hazardous waste is released. Here, because the concentration of the toluene in the soil was unknown, the amount of toluene released could not be shown.

To resolve this problem, it makes no sense—given the EPA's determination that only 1,000 pounds or more of toluene need be reported—to require the reporting of one pound of toluene when mixed with soil. To the contrary, since soil itself is non-reportable, and since any amount of soil when mixed with toluene lowers the proportion of the latter in the total mix, the EPA's purpose is fully, and conservatively served simply by establishing the reportable quantity of the mixture at 1,000 pounds, the same as toluene. To be sure, as the concentration of toluene is not known, there is no principled way, based on toxicity, to determine a reportable quantity greater than 1,000 pounds. But anything less assures full compliance. The EPA appears to have recognized this in its regulations:

> Finally, the Agency wishes to clarify that, except as noted below, all hazardous wastes newly designated under RCRA will have a statutorily imposed [reportable quantity] of one pound until adjusted by regulation under CERCLA. See CERCLA section 102. *If a newly listed hazardous waste stream has only one constituent of concern, the waste will have the same (reportable quantity) as that of the constituent.* (The [reportable quantity] to be considered for this purpose would be the final [reportable quantity] of the constituent, whether statutorily imposed or by regulation.)

51 Fed. Reg. 6539 (Feb. 25, 1986). (Emphasis supplied).

Examination of the RCRA scheme establishing that a listed hazardous waste mixed with "soil, water or other debris" is itself a hazardous waste also reveals that the government's argument here is flawed. The government relies on a technical argument that § 261.33(d) designates independent hazardous wastes—for which EPA established no independent reportable quantity—and the reportable quantity must therefore be one pound under CERCLA § 102(b). EPA, however, could not have intended that 40 C.F.R. § 261.33 establish independent hazardous wastes for CERCLA reporting purposes. Under the RCRA regulatory scheme, wastes are deemed hazardous if they either (1) exhibit certain characteristics which are known to be correlated with a danger to human health or the environment; or (2) appear on a list of individual wastes found to pose certain dangers. EPA addressed in 40 C.F.R. § 261.33(d) a possible contention that a mixture of a listed hazardous waste and soil is an independent waste which, in its own right, is neither a "characteristic" hazardous waste nor a listed hazardous waste. Since listed hazardous wastes may not lose their dangerous nature through mixture with soil, water or other debris, EPA simply deemed such contaminated media to also be hazardous wastes. We think that EPA did not believe that, in closing this loophole, it would establish new and independent hazardous wastes consisting of each listed hazardous waste mixed with receiving media which would then require establishment of an independent reportable quantity under CERCLA § 102(b), else that reportable quantity of the mixture would remain one pound. To find that toluene-contaminated soil is an independent hazardous waste with a default reportable quantity of one pound would be to truly elevate linguistic form over substance.

We conclude that the reportable quantity for the toluene-contaminated soil was 1,000 pounds. The indictment charging that a reportable quantity of one pound of toluene-contaminated soil was not reported and the jury instructions to the same effect were, nevertheless, harmless error. It was never a subject of dispute that the toluene-contaminated soil was delivered to the Poe Street Lot in other than nine 25-yard dump trucks and one 20-yard dump truck. We see no basis on which it could be rationally concluded by any juror that less than 1,000 pounds of contaminated soil was released. Likewise, we find no substance in appellants' argument that the indictment was constitutionally flawed because it failed to allege an essential element of the offense. We see no basis on which the difference between 1,000 pounds and one pound would, in these circumstances, have affected defendants' ability to defend.

* * *

UNITED STATES V. CARR
880 F.2d 1550 (2d Cir. 1989)

Before KEARSE, CARDAMONE, and PIERCE, Circuit Judges.
PIERCE, Circuit Judge.

Appellant David James Carr appeals from a judgment *** convicting him under section 103 of the Comprehensive Environmental Response, Compensation and Liability Act of 1980 (CERCLA), 42 U.S.C. § 9603. Under section 103, it is a crime for any person "in charge of a facility" from which a prohibited amount of hazardous substance is released to fail to report such a release to the appropriate federal agency. Appellant, a supervisor of maintenance at Fort Drum, New York, directed a work crew to dispose of waste cans of paint in an improper manner, and failed to report the release of the hazardous substances—the paint—to the appropriate federal agency. At appellant's trial, the district court instructed the jury that appellant could be found to have been "in charge" of the facility so long as he had any supervisory control over the facility.

Appellant contends on appeal that this instruction was erroneous because (1) it extended the statutory reporting requirement to a relatively low-level employee, and (2) it allowed the jury to find that appellant was "in charge" so long as he exercised any control over the dumping. For the reasons stated below, we hold that the statutory reporting requirements were properly applied to appellant. We also hold that the jury instruction challenged on appeal, viewed as a whole, was not erroneous.

BACKGROUND

Appellant was a civilian employee at Fort Drum, an Army camp located in Watertown, New York. As a civilian employee at a military installation, he was supervised by Army officers. His position was that of maintenance foreman on the

Fort's firing range, and as part of his duties he assigned other civilian workers to various chores on the range. In May 1986, he directed several workers to dispose of old cans of waste paint in a small, man-made pit on the range; at that time, the pit had filled with water, creating a pond. On Carr's instructions, the workers filled a truck with a load of cans and drove to the pit. They backed the truck up to the water, and then began tossing cans of paint into the pond. After the workers had thrown in fifty or so cans, however, they saw that paint was leaking from the cans into the water, so they decided instead to stack the remaining cans of paint against a nearby target shed. At the end of the day, the workers told Carr of the cans leaking into the pond, and warned him that they thought that dumping the cans into the pond was illegal. Two truckloads of paint cans remained to be moved the next day, so Carr told the workers to place those cans alongside the target shed.

Approximately two weeks later, Carr directed one of the workers to cover up the paint cans in the pond by using a tractor to dump earth into the pit. Another worker, however, subsequently triggered an investigation by reporting the disposal of the cans to his brother-in-law, a special agent with the Department of Defense. A 43-count indictment was returned against appellant, charging him with various violations of federal environmental laws. The indictment included charges under the Resource Conservation and Recovery Act of 1976, 18 U.S.C. § 2 (Counts 1-4), the CERCLA charges here at issue (Counts 5-6), and multiple charges under the Clean Water Act of 1977. Appellant pleaded not guilty, and a 6-day trial before a jury began on October 3, 1988.

After the government had presented its evidence, it filed with the court various proposed jury instructions, including one regarding the definition of the term "in charge." Over appellant's objection, the district court gave the government's proposed instruction to the jury, essentially unchanged, as follows:

> There has been testimony that the waste paint was released from a truck assigned to the workers by the Defendant David Carr. The truck, individually, and the area of the disposal constitute facilities within the meaning of (CERCLA). So long as the Defendant had supervisory control or was otherwise in charge of the truck or the area in question, he is responsible under this law. The Defendant is not, however, required to be the sole person in charge of the area or the vehicle. If you find that he had any authority over either the vehicle or the area, this is sufficient, regardless of whether others also exercised control.

The jury acquitted appellant of all charges except Counts 5 and 6, the CERCLA charges. The district court imposed a suspended sentence of one year's imprisonment, and sentenced appellant to one year of probation. This appeal followed.

DISCUSSION
I. *The Meaning of "In Charge" Under Section 103*

Appellant raises two claims on this appeal, both of which arise out of the district court's instruction quoted above. The first claim turns on the meaning of the statutory term "in charge." Under section 103, only those who are "in charge" of a facility must report a hazardous release. There is, however, no definition of the term "in charge" within CERCLA. Appellant argues that the district court's instruction was erroneous because Congress never intended to extend the statute's reporting requirement to those, like Carr, who are relatively low in an organization's chain of command.

Our analysis of appellant's claim requires a review of the statute and its legislative history. The language of the statute itself sheds little light on the meaning of the term "in charge." *** The regulations implementing the statute fail to define the term "in charge." Since its meaning is unclear, we turn to the legislative history in an effort to determine the scope Congress intended the term "in charge" to have.

When CERCLA was enacted in late 1980, Congress sought to address the problem of hazardous pollution by creating a comprehensive and uniform system of notification, emergency governmental response, enforcement, and liability. The reporting requirements established by section 103 were an important part of that effort, for they ensure that the government, once timely notified, will be able to move quickly to check the spread of a hazardous release. The broad reporting requirements of section 103—which extend to anyone "in charge" of a facility—were part of the House and Senate bills from their inception, and were carried through, substantially intact, into the version of the bill finally passed into law.

The legislative history of CERCLA makes clear that Congress modeled the reporting requirements of section 103 on section 311 of the Clean Water Act. Like CERCLA's section 103, the reporting requirements of section 311 of the Clean Water Act require any person "in charge" of a facility to report a release of hazardous substances. Senator Jennings Randolph, one of the original sponsors of the Senate version of CERCLA, outlined the reasons for adopting the reporting requirements from section 311 of the Clean Water Act into CERCLA:

> Section 103 of (CERCLA) establishes the circumstances when notice must be given to the Government of a release of hazardous substances, including hazardous wastes. Notice of a release is the essential first step which enables the Government to respond quickly to the more significant releases, if the parties responsible fail to. The 8 years of experience with the spill response program established by section 311 of the Clean Water Act amply demonstrate the necessity of immediate notice if an emergency response program is to be effective in protecting public health, welfare, and the environment. The Government response program that would be established by this bill is modeled upon the experience with the Clean Water Act's spill response program.

126 Cong.Rec. 30,933 (1980). ***

Since CERCLA's use of the term "in charge" was borrowed from section 311 of the Clean Water Act, and the two sections share the same purpose, the parallel provisions can, as a matter of general statutory construction, be interpreted to be *in pari materia*. ***

Like CERCLA, however, neither the Clean Water Act nor its implementing regulations contain a definition of the term "in charge." In weighing appellant's claim regarding the term "in charge" in section 103 of CERCLA, we are able to borrow from the other constructions that have evolved concerning that term under section 311 of the Clean Water Act.

The legislative history of section 311 bears out appellant's argument that CERCLA's reporting requirements should not be extended to all employees involved in a release. "The term 'person in charge' (was) deliberately designed to cover only supervisory personnel who have the responsibility for the particular vessel or facility and not to include other employees." H.R.Conf.Rep. No. 940, 91st Cong., 2d Sess. 34 (1970). Indeed, as the Fifth Circuit has stated, "to the extent that legislative history does shed light on the meaning of 'persons in charge,' it suggests at the very most that Congress intended the provisions of (section 311) to extend, not to every person who might have knowledge of (a release) (mere employees, for example), but only to persons who occupy positions of responsibility and power." *United States v. Mobil Oil Corp.*, 464 F.2d 1124, 1128 (5th Cir.1972).

That is not to say, however, that section 311 of the Clean Water Act—and section 103 of CERCLA—do not reach lower-level supervisory employees. The reporting requirements of the two statutes do not apply only to owners and operators, but instead extend to any person who is "responsible for the operation" of a facility from which there is a release. As the Fifth Circuit noted in *Mobil Oil*, imposing liability on those "responsible" for a facility is fully consistent with Congress' purpose in enacting the reporting requirements. Those in charge of an offending facility can make timely discovery of a release, direct the activities that result in the pollution, and have the capacity to prevent and abate the environmental damage.

Appellant's claim that he does not come within the reporting requirements of section 103 fails because we believe Congress intended the reporting requirements of CERCLA's section 103 to reach a person—even if of relatively low rank—who, because he was in charge of a facility, was in a position to detect, prevent, and abate a release of hazardous substances. Appellant's more restrictive interpretation of the statute would only "frustrate congressional purpose by exempting from the operation of the [statute] a large class of persons who are uniquely qualified to assume the burden imposed by it." *Mobil Oil*, 464 F.2d at 1127.

II. *The Breadth of the Instruction Given*

Appellant's second claim focuses more closely on the specific instruction given by the district court. The district court instructed the jury that "[i]f you find that [Carr] had any authority over either the vehicle or the area, this is sufficient [to convict], regardless of whether others also exercised control." Appellant contends that the district court, by instructing the jury that it had only to find that appellant exercised "any authority" over the facility at issue, effectively broadened the statute to reach any employee working at the facility. As appellant points out, the district court itself acknowledged at a post-trial hearing that the use of the word "any" in the instruction was, in retrospect, a less than ideal choice of language.

* * *

A careful review of the challenged instruction indicates that the district court sought, through the charge, to explain two important principles to the jury: (1) that the appellant must have exercised supervisory control over the facility in order to be held criminally liable for his failure to report the release, but (2) that the appellant need not have exercised *sole* control over the facility. By taking the language of the instruction out of context—by focusing too narrowly on the district court's use of the word "any"—appellant ignores the broader point that the district court was attempting to make to the jury. The court had already explained that the appellant must have had "supervisory control" over the facility in order to be found guilty. The subsequent, challenged portion of the instruction was therefore not directed at the breadth of authority that appellant must have had, but instead was intended to make clear that the appellant need not have been the sole person in charge of the facility. Viewing the challenged language within the context of the charge as a whole rather than in "artificial isolation," see *Cupp v. Naughten*, 414 U.S. 141, 146-47 (1973), we hold that the instruction, though not ideal, was not erroneous.

CONCLUSION

We have reviewed all of appellant's other arguments on appeal, and consider them to be without merit. The judgment of the district court is, therefore, affirmed.

NOTES

1. It is important to keep in mind, particularly in light of the criminal sanctions, that the reporting obligations of CERCLA § 103(a) are entirely independent of the cleanup provisions. Indeed, reporting issues arise at many sites which neither the EPA, the state, nor indeed private parties would consider to be worthy of Superfund-scale cleanup activities. Reporting issues also arise when pre-existing contamination is discovered, for example by a new owner or operator of a facility, and a determination must be made whether the contamination need be reported, and by whom. Environmental consultants whose site inspection or sampling activities identify or confirm the contamination are often concerned whether they have a duty to report such contamination. What questions would you need answered in order to advise a consultant in that situation?

2. Is the abandonment of sealed containers of hazardous waste a "release" that triggers the reporting requirements? *See U.S. v. Freter*, 31 F.3d 783 (9th Cir. 1994), *cert. denied*, 513 U.S. 1048 (1994).

3. There is a dearth of case law construing the CERCLA § 103(c) reporting requirement, which required a one-time notification to the EPA in 1981 of the existence of certain hazardous substance facilities.

In 1993, the City of Toledo brought suit under CERCLA's citizen suit provision, § 310(a)(1), claiming that defendants, who had not complied with the § 103(c) reporting requirements in 1981, continued to be in violation. The defendants relied on a series of EPA internal memoranda stating that § 103(c) imposed a continuing reporting obligation. The court dismissed the claim, however, holding that § 103(c) imposed a one-time reporting requirement in 1981. Because the defendants' violation was wholly past, it could not be the subject of a citizen suit under CERCLA. *City of Toledo v. Beazer Materials and Services*, 833 F.Supp. 646 (N.D. Ohio 1993).

4. For an interesting analysis of the different reporting obligations—and disclosure prohibitions—governing attorneys and engineers, *see* David Richman and Donald B. Bauer, *Responsibilities of Lawyers and Engineers To Report Environmental Hazards and Maintain Client Confidences: Duties in Conflict*, 5 Toxics L. Rep. (BNA) 1458 (Apr. 17, 1991).

III
AREAS OF OVERLAP BETWEEN RCRA AND CERCLA

17 OVERLAPPING JURISDICTION OF RCRA/CERCLA CLEANUP PROGRAMS

Although RCRA and CERCLA operate independently, their cleanup programs are closely related. This chapter will highlight some points of intersection between them.

The two statutes actually encompass three cleanup programs that partially overlap: RCRA corrective action; RCRA § 7003; and CERCLA §§ 104, 106, and 107. They vary, first, in scope. RCRA's corrective action program applies to releases of hazardous waste (and, at least at Part B permitted facilities, hazardous constituents) at facilities that operate, or operated after November 19, 1980, as hazardous waste treatment, storage, or disposal facilities. RCRA § 7003 applies to solid waste as well as hazardous waste. And CERCLA applies to hazardous substances, encompassing all hazardous wastes and some, but not all, solid wastes.

Second, the three programs differ somewhat as to who may enforce them, and what remedies the various plaintiffs might obtain. Only the EPA (or an authorized state) may issue, or seek court issuance of, a RCRA corrective action order.[1] And only the EPA (not even a state) may issue, or seek court issuance of, a CERCLA § 106 cleanup order. Virtually anyone may bring an action under RCRA §§ 7002/7003—the EPA is so authorized under § 7003 and any other person is authorized under § 7002(a)(1)(B). Finally, anyone who incurs "response costs" may seek to recover some or all of their costs under CERCLA §§ 107 and/or 113(f).

A third difference is the cleanup standard applicable under each program. At one extreme, CERCLA cleanup actions must comply with all other federal, and more stringent state, standards that are applicable or relevant and appropriate. At the other extreme, RCRA § 7003 has no statutory or regulatory cleanup standards, relying heavily on the discretion of the EPA and, ultimately, the courts. In between is the RCRA corrective action program, which (at least in the proposed implementing regulations) has

---

[1] If a facility owner or operator is not complying with a government-issued corrective action order, then a citizen suit might be brought to remedy the violations. RCRA § 7002(a)(1)(A).

eschewed CERCLA's ARARs standard in favor of site-specific cleanup standards intended to be more sensitive to the actual and projected uses of each site.

Finally, the three programs ostensibly differ in the circumstances that trigger their application. The EPA may invoke RCRA's corrective action program and CERCLA's Superfund-financed cleanup program when there is a release of a hazardous waste or constituent (RCRA) or an actual or threatened release of a hazardous substance (CERCLA), regardless of whether the release poses an endangerment. In contrast, RCRA § 7003 and CERCLA § 106 (authorizing EPA- and court-issued cleanup orders) require circumstances that "may present" (RCRA § 7003) or "may be" (CERCLA § 106) an imminent and substantial endangerment. In practice, however, this difference is more superficial than substantive. *See, e.g., U.S. v. Waste Industries, Inc.,* 734 F.2d 159 (4th Cir. 1984)(excerpted in chapter 5.B, above).

Following are two cases addressing the overlapping jurisdiction between RCRA and CERCLA, and a third case where the Supreme Court used analogous provisions in CERCLA to construe RCRA § 7003.

CHEMICAL WASTE MANAGEMENT, INC. V. ARMSTRONG WORLD INDUSTRIES, INC.
669 F.Supp. 1285 (E.D.Pa. 1987)

CAHN, District Judge.

This action was brought under the liability provisions of the Comprehensive Environmental Response, Compensation, and Liability Act ("CERCLA"). Plaintiff, Chemical Waste Management, Inc. ("Chem Waste"), seeks to recover "response costs" incurred or to be incurred as a result of the release or threatened release of hazardous substances at the Lyncott Landfill in New Milford, Pennsylvania (the "Lyncott facility"). Defendants have moved for summary judgment, arguing that they cannot be responsible for Chem Waste's response costs.

* * *

I. FACTS

Chem Waste, its parent, Waste Management, Inc. ("Waste Management"), and several of Waste Management's wholly owned subsidiaries are engaged in the industrial, hazardous and chemical waste disposal business. Defendants, generators of hazardous waste, contracted with plaintiff and plaintiff's predecessor, the Stabatrol Corporation ("Old Stabatrol"), for the disposal of industrial waste material.

On November 14, 1980, Waste Management of Pennsylvania, Inc. ("WMPA"), a subsidiary of Waste Management, entered into an asset purchase agreement (the "Purchase Agreement") with Old Stabatrol, the owner and operator ("owner/operator") of the Lyncott facility, and the individual shareholders (the "Metzval parties") of 1533

North Fletcher Corporation, the sole shareholder of Old Stabatrol. WMPA acquired all the assets, rights, properties, and business of Old Stabatrol. These comprised, *inter alia,* all of the waste disposal contracts of Old Stabatrol, including those with the defendant generators, the business and trade name of "Stabatrol Corporation," all waste disposal facility permits and licenses, and all subsidiary corporations. After the sale, the Stabatrol Corporation became a wholly owned subsidiary ("New Stabatrol") of Chem Waste. Old Stabatrol changed its name to the Metzval Corporation and subsequently was dissolved.

* * *

During the negotiations and in the Purchase Agreement, Old Stabatrol represented that the Lyncott facility was operating in full compliance with state and federal laws. In addition, prior to the acquisition, Waste Management examined the waste disposal permits and engineering plans of the facility and conducted several on-site inspections. At the time of the purchase, construction on two of the three disposal vaults had not been completed, and substantial work remained to be completed on all vaults. The engineers of Waste Management concluded that, although there were some problems that might contribute to the operating costs, the design and construction of the facility appeared to be adequate.

Shortly after the acquisition, inspectors from the Pennsylvania Department of Environmental Resources ("DER") identified several violations of the DER permit and Pennsylvania environmental laws, including:

(1) On November 21, 1980, the DER observed damaged drums containing arsenic salts being placed in Vault 1, and observed arsenic waste spilled on the floor;

(2) On November 21, 1980, the DER observed that waste material in Vault 3 had been permitted to mix with water and flow from the vault over the surface soils;

(3) On December 4, 1980, the DER inspectors observed water in monitoring sumps; and

(4) On December 15, 1981 [sic], Chem Waste accepted wastes from Rockwell International, contrary to the DER's conditions of approval.

In March of 1981, the DER suspended the Lyncott facility's permit and ordered corrective action. Following the March order, DER inspectors continued to observe violations at the site, including Chem Waste's failure to implement all of the corrective actions ordered by the DER. The inspectors later concluded that the vaults were not constructed in accordance with the designs approved by the DER. The DER therefore issued a second order on September 4, 1981, which prescribed removal of all wastes from the site and submission of a Closure/Post-Closure Plan for the site. Chem Waste continued to refuse to comply with the DER orders. As a result, the DER suspended Chem Waste's hazardous waste transporter license and refused to approve permits and licenses for other Chem Waste waste disposal businesses in Pennsylvania. In August of 1982, the DER filed an action in state court to enforce its September 4, 1981 order. On September 28, 1984, Chem Waste entered into a settlement agreement with the DER whereby the DER agreed to discontinue denying permits and licenses to Chem Waste's other facilities if Chem Waste implemented the DER orders.

* * *

In March of 1985, Chem Waste commenced this action against defendants.

II. DISCUSSION
* * *

Chem Waste argues that [CERCLA] § 107 explicitly authorizes the recovery of response costs from defendants. There is, of course, no dispute that defendants are hazardous waste generators for the purposes of § 107(a)(3), or that Chem Waste is an owner/operator within the meaning of § 107(a)(1). Thus, unless defendants can present a viable defense to Chem Waste's claims, defendants' motion must fail.

In the face of CERCLA's expansive liability provisions, defendants have presented seven arguments why they should not be held liable for response costs incurred or to be incurred in connection with the Lyncott facility. The court shall address these arguments seriatim.

A.   *May the Owner and Operator of a RCRA Facility Recover CERCLA Response Costs?*

Defendants contend that, because the Lyncott facility was an "interim status facility" under § 3005(e) of the Resource Conservation and Recovery Act ("RCRA"), defendants cannot recover CERCLA response costs.   RCRA and regulations promulgated in connection with the statute require owners and operators of RCRA facilities, *inter alia*, to inspect and maintain the facility, remedy any deterioration or malfunction in the facility, and close the facility to prevent or minimize the escape of hazardous materials. Relying upon these regulations, which were applicable to Chem Waste in November 1980, defendants argue that Chem Waste may not recover CERCLA response costs because to permit such recovery would render RCRA a nullity. Defendants further contend that CERCLA's plain language, legislative history, and policy underpinnings support their position.

Although there is some merit to defendants' arguments, the court finds that the better-reasoned approach is that adopted by the court in *Mardan Corp. v. C.G.C. Music, Ltd.*, 600 F.Supp. 1049 (D.Ariz.1984), *aff'd*, 840 F.2d 1454 (9th Cir.1986), where the court held that RCRA does not preempt CERCLA. CERCLA's preemption provision, placed prominently at the beginning of the statute's liability provision, states that, subject to certain defenses not relevant here, liability shall attach "(n)otwithstanding any other provision or rule of law...." 42 U.S.C. § 9607(a).

Defendants argue further that Congress intended CERCLA to apply only to *abandoned* hazardous waste facilities and RCRA to apply only to *active* facilities. CERCLA's statutory language, however, belies such a contention. First, § 101(20)(A) of CERCLA differentiates between a "facility" and an "abandoned facility." By this language, Congress clearly evinced its intent that CERCLA apply to both active and abandoned facilities. Second, Congress distinguished RCRA sites when it deemed such differentiation important. In § 103(c) of CERCLA, for example, Congress exempted from notice requirements owner/operators who have been issued permits or been accorded interim status under RCRA. The liability provisions of CERCLA, however, which are at issue here, contain no exemption for RCRA owner/operators. Thus, defendants' statutory language argument must fail.

Finally, defendants argue that the policies underlying CERCLA mandate a decision in their favor. In urging their position, defendants explore a parade of horribles and conclude that a decision in Chem Waste's favor would detract from the statute's efficacy and would, in fact, spur a rash of *illegal* hazardous waste disposal. The court finds these arguments unpersuasive.

Defendants' policy arguments must fail because permitting RCRA owner/operators to recover CERCLA response costs from generators actually *promotes*, rather than detracts from, CERCLA's policies. First, an owner/operator that knows it can seek contribution from a generator will promptly cleanup a hazardous waste site. Defendants argue, though, that Chem Waste did not provide a prompt cleanup at the Lyncott facility, and that such inaction belies Chem Waste's argument that permitting owner/operators to recover response costs provides an incentive for prompt cleanup. Although it appears Chem Waste was less than diligent in its efforts at the Lyncott facility, defendants' argument is without merit: it was unclear at the time of the Lyncott cleanup that potentially responsible owner/operators could recover response costs from generators.   Defendants cannot argue that response costs are unavailable to owner/operators and in the same breath suggest that Chem Waste was dilatory even though response costs *were* available to owner/operators.   Second, permitting owner/operators to recover response costs from waste generators is consistent with CERCLA's goal of spreading the costs of environmental disasters. A theme running throughout CERCLA's legislative history is that all parties involved in hazardous waste disposal must share the costs thereof. Although parties may under certain circumstances "contract out" of CERCLA liability, *see* 42 U.S.C. § 9607(e)(2), an owner/operator presumably would take such a shifting of risks into account by charging waste generators a higher fee for hazardous waste disposal. Such an arrangement would fulfill Congress' intent that parties responsible for the release of hazardous substances bear the costs of response and costs of damage to natural resources.

In sum, the court holds that RCRA and its regulations do not preclude a RCRA owner/operator from recovering CERCLA response costs.

B.   *May a "Liable Party" Under CERCLA Maintain a Suit for Response Costs Under § 107 of CERCLA?*

In the face of statutory language that appears clearly to permit any person to recover its response costs from owners, operators, owner/operators, transporters, and generators, defendants argue that Chem Waste, as a potentially responsible party ("PRP"), may not recover such costs. Defendants base their argument on recent amendments to CERCLA, and it would seem, upon the equitable doctrine of "unclean hands."[7] The court finds both of these bases without merit and therefore holds upon this ground as well that Chem Waste may pursue its claim for response costs.

Defendants maintain that the Superfund Amendments and Reauthorization Act of 1986 ("SARA") clarify that a PRP may not maintain a suit to recover response costs. Rather than supporting defendants' position, however, amended § 113(f) makes quite clear that a PRP may maintain an action against another PRP. That section provides in pertinent part:

> *Any person* may seek contribution from *any other person who is liable* or potentially liable under Section 9607(a) of this title, during or following any civil action...under section 9607(a) of this title....Nothing in this subsection shall diminish the right of any person to bring an action for contribution in the absence of a civil action under section 106 or section 107.

42 U.S.C. § 9613(f)(1) (emphasis added). This subsequent statutory enactment gives the court guidance in construing the earlier statute and is therefore entitled to great weight. The clear significance of the word "other" in § 113(f) is that a PRP may maintain a suit for contribution against another person who is or may be liable for response costs. To read the statute in any other manner would be to read language out of the statute, an activity that this court must not undertake absent some direction from Congress.

*** Even assuming defendants' premises are correct, the court nevertheless holds that a PRP may recover response costs from another PRP. Defendants' arguments concerning "innocence" and "fault" are relevant only to the *amount* of response costs that Chem Waste may recover.[10]

---

[7] The court previously has stated that the "unclean hands" doctrine espoused in *Mardan Corp. v. C.G.C. Music, Ltd.*, 600 F.Supp. 1049, 1057 (D.Ariz.1984), *aff'd*, 804 F.2d 1454 (9th Cir.1986), has no place in CERCLA actions. To the extent defendants are attempting to resurrect their argument that Chem Waste's "unclean hands" bar it from pursuing CERCLA response costs, their contentions are rejected.

[10] Defendants argue, time and again, that Chem Waste would be made whole—or might even reap a profit—were it permitted to recover CERCLA response costs from defendants. Such an argument misses the mark: defendants assume that Chem Waste could recover all of its response costs from the waste generators. But, as the court has stated repeatedly, the degree of recovery by an owner/operator should depend on many factors. Thus, Chem Waste's alleged failure to comply with RCRA might substantially reduce its recovery of response costs; such failure should not, however, bar Chem Waste's cause of action ab initio.

The extent of an owner/operator's recovery of response costs should also depend upon: the owner/operator's relative fault, the volume of waste deposited, and the relative toxicity of such waste. See SARA § 113(f) ("In resolving contribution claims the court may allocate response costs among liable parties using such equitable factors as the court determines are appropriate.")

C.   *Is Chem Waste Precluded by Contract From Recovering Response Costs Under CERCLA?*

Defendants contend that Chem Waste assumed or succeeded to Old Stabatrol's liabilities for the Lyncott facility. Relying upon this contention, defendants then argue that Chem Waste is precluded by contract from recovering response costs under CERCLA.

　　　1. *Did Chem Waste Assume or Succeed to Old Stabatrol's Liabilities for the Lyncott Facility?*

Defendants argue that Waste Management and Chem Waste are responsible for Old Stabatrol's liabilities because: (a) Chem Waste expressly assumed Old Stabatrol's liabilities; and (b) the Old Stabatrol acquisition was a merger of Old Stabatrol into Chem Waste whereby Chem Waste continued Old Stabatrol's business and assumed Old Stabatrol's liabilities.

The court assumes for the purpose of this motion that Chem Waste did assume or succeed to Old Stabatrol's liabilities for the Lyncott facility. Based upon the analysis that follows, however, the court will deny defendants' motion on this point.

　　　2. *Is Chem Waste Precluded by Warranty or Indemnity from Recovering CERCLA Response Costs?*

Defendants contend that Chem Waste assumed Old Stabatrol's Waste Disposal Contracts and is precluded by the express and implied terms of those contracts from recovering response costs under CERCLA. Defendants also argue that Chem Waste itself contracted with generators, and that express and implied provisions of these contracts preclude Chem Waste's suit.

a. *Warranty*

Relying upon a tentative ruling of the court, defendants contend that Chem Waste may not recover response costs from its generators because the "essence" of the various waste disposal contracts was that the owner/operator would dispose of the hazardous waste in a safe, legal manner and would charge but a single fee for this service. According to defendants, Chem Waste's suit for response costs is an attempt to charge the generators a second fee for a service that Chem Waste and its predecessor performed improperly. Defendants argue that Chem Waste expressly and impliedly warranted the safe, legal disposal of the generators' waste, and that basic contract law therefore precludes Chem Waste from recovering CERCLA response costs from the generators.

Section 107(e)(2) of CERCLA provides that:

　　　Nothing in this subchapter, including the provisions of paragraph (1)
of this subsection, shall bar a cause of action that an owner or operator or

any other person subject to liability under this section, or a guarantor, has

or would have, by reason of subrogation or otherwise against any person.

42 U.S.C. § 9607(e)(2). Defendants contend this "language makes clear that the liability provisions of CERCLA do not abrogate contractual rights." Although it is debatable whether any provision of CERCLA is "clear," the court agrees that in this private suit for response costs, CERCLA's liability provisions do not abrogate the parties' contractual rights. Accordingly, the court shall first determine whether Chem Waste or its predecessor expressly warranted the safe, legal disposal of the generators' waste.

Defendant Armstrong argues that its contract, executed in February of 1981, precludes Chem Waste's recovery of response costs. Armstrong also asserts that it "had previously contracted with Old Stabatrol, and the Waste Management contract reaffirmed the terms of Armstrong's prior Agreement with Old Stabatrol." Defendants' Memorandum at 74. By not supplying a copy of its contract with Old Stabatrol, Armstrong apparently asks the court to assume that the terms of the contract were the same as those of the later contract, which Armstrong has provided the court. This we cannot do; there exists a clear issue of material fact, and summary judgment is therefore inappropriate. Summary judgment is no more proper with respect to waste disposed of pursuant to the February 1981 contract. In a cover letter to New Stabatrol, Armstrong stated that it had modified the proposed waste disposal agreement and that "(i)f you are in agreement, please send us a signed copy of the revised contract and a copy of this letter signed at the appropriate place below; upon receipt we will consider the contract to be effective." Defendants' Exhibit 54. If such a signed copy exists, Armstrong has not produced it for the court. Thus, it is unclear whether Armstrong even had a contract with New Stabatrol, and summary judgment is therefore inappropriate.

* * *

Defendants Vineland and CPS have submitted to the court no waste disposal agreements with Vineland and Chem Waste or its predecessor. Thus, the court cannot hold that Chem Waste or its predecessor expressly warranted to Vineland or CPS the safe, legal disposal of their hazardous waste.

In sum, defendants have failed to prove that their contracts with Chem Waste or its predecessor *expressly* preclude Chem Waste from recovering CERCLA response costs from defendants.

Defendants also argue that Chem Waste and its predecessor *impliedly* warranted the safe, legal disposal of defendants' waste. As noted previously, at argument on December 12, 1986, the court tentatively ruled that an owner/operator in the business of operating a hazardous waste facility could not recover CERCLA response costs from a waste generator that contracted with the owner/operator for disposal of hazardous waste.[14] Upon further reflection and research, however, the court has concluded that Congress intended that *all* parties involved in hazardous waste disposal be responsible

---

[14] The court's tentative ruling was based upon a common sense understanding of contract law: a party who provides a service for a fee may not extract a second fee from his client merely because the provider performed the service improperly and was held liable for damages as a result thereof.

for the cleanup of hazardous waste releases. In exceptionally broad language, Congress provided that owner/operators, generators, and transporters *"shall be liable for* ... any necessary costs of response incurred by *any other person* consistent with the national contingency plan...." 42 U.S.C. § 9607(a) (emphasis added). CERCLA's plain language thus permits an owner/operator to sue a generator of hazardous waste. As discussed *supra*, two of CERCLA's primary objectives are the prompt cleanup of leaking hazardous waste sites and the provision of effective incentives for the careful handling of hazardous wastes in the future. One means of achieving these objectives is to "spread the risks" of liability among *all* parties involved in hazardous waste disposal. Were the court to rule that implied in every waste disposal contract is a warranty by the owner/operator that it will not seek to recover CERCLA response costs from the waste generator, this court would engage in judicial legislation that would reshape CERCLA's liability scheme. This we cannot do. Accordingly, the court holds that, absent an express contractual provision to the contrary, an owner/operator in the business of operating a hazardous waste facility may recover from generators of waste deposited at the facility any necessary costs of response incurred or to be incurred by the owner/operator in connection with a release or threatened release of hazardous substances at the facility.

* * *

III. CONCLUSION

For the foregoing reasons, defendants' motion for summary judgment is denied. The court has concluded, however, that this matter involves a controlling question of law as to which there is a substantial ground for difference of opinion, and an immediate appeal may materially advance the ultimate termination of the litigation.

NOTES

1. The court rejects defendants' policy argument—that it would undermine RCRA to allow a permitted facility to obtain reimbursement from its customers for the costs of correcting its violations—by reference to CERCLA's policies of promoting prompt cleanup and spreading the costs thereof among all responsible parties. Is the court favoring CERCLA over RCRA? Can the objectives of both statutes be achieved in this case?

2. Consider the timing of Chemical Waste Management's business deal: it acquired the Lyncott facility, a state-permitted hazardous waste facility, in November 1980—just as the RCRA hazardous waste regulations were taking effect for the first time, and only weeks before Congress enacted CERCLA. Do you think Chemical Waste Management viewed RCRA as a liability or an opportunity? What about CERCLA?

3. This case highlights the breadth of CERCLA's jurisdiction. Although the "corrective action" ordered by the state preceded the addition of the corrective action provisions to RCRA in November 1984, it is well-settled that a party's motivation in

conducting a site cleanup (*e.g.*, to comply with RCRA provisions) is irrelevant to its ability to seek cost recovery or contribution under CERCLA. Thus, the numerous hazardous waste treatment, storage, and disposal facilities that are required to undertake corrective action programs under RCRA §§ 3004(u) or 3008(h) could use CERCLA to recover some (or all) of their costs if other PRPs are or were connected with the site, and if the corrective action is conducted in a manner consistent with the National Contingency Plan.

4. If a private party conducts a RCRA corrective action program, and the EPA expends money overseeing the work to ensure that it meets the EPA's requirements, can the EPA seek cost recovery under CERCLA for its oversight costs?

In *United States v. Rohm and Haas Co.*, 2 F.3d 1265 (3d Cir. 1993), the Third Circuit held that the fact that the work was done under RCRA's auspices does not preclude a cost recovery action under CERCLA.

> *** In the defendants' view, costs which would be removal costs if incurred under CERCLA are nevertheless not removal costs if incurred under RCRA. We are unpersuaded.
>
> Section 107(a) expressly stipulates that "all costs of removal...incurred by the Untied States Government" are recoverable, and neither it nor the definition of "removal" contains CERCLA specific language. *** [I]f a particular government action qualifies as a "removal action" under the definition contained in CERCLA, the government's costs are recoverable under the unambiguous language of § 107, regardless of what statutory authority was invoked by EPA in connection with its action.
>
> We find no support in the text of legislative history of CERCLA for the suggestion that identical oversight activity on the part of the government should be considered a removal if the government invokes CERCLA, but not a removal if other statutory authority is invoked. Moreover, given the similarity of the provisions of RCRA and CERCLA authorizing EPA to order private parties to conduct corrective activity, we fail to perceive any reason why Congress might have wished to make government oversight expenses recoverable if the government invoked CERCLA statutory authority, but not if it invoked RCRA.

Id. at 1274-75.

On the merits, the Third Circuit held that CERCLA provides no statutory authorization for the EPA to recover its oversight costs, except when private parties are conducting remedial investigations and feasibility studies pursuant to § 104(a)(1). In a slightly different context—a private cost recovery action where the plaintiff had already reimbursed the government for its oversight costs, the Tenth Circuit took a different view, and held that the oversight costs are recoverable response costs. *Atlantic Richfield Co. v. American Airlines, Inc.*, 98 F.3d 564 (10th Cir. 1996).

5. In the following case, the State of Colorado successfully invoked RCRA to circumvent the CERCLA § 113(h) bar on pre-enforcement review of CERCLA cleanup plans. Read this case in light of the § 113(h) cases in chapter 9.

UNITED STATES V. STATE OF COLORADO
990 F.2d 1565 (10th Cir. 1993)
cert. denied, 510 U.S. 1092 (1994)

Before BALDOCK and HOLLOWAY, Circuit Judges, and EARL E. O'CONNOR, Senior District Judge for the District of Kansas.
BALDOCK, Circuit Judge.

This case examines the relationship between the Resource Conservation and Recovery Act of 1976 ("RCRA"), and the Comprehensive Environmental Response, Compensation, and Liability Act of 1980 ("CERCLA"). At issue is whether a state which has been authorized by the Environmental Protection Agency ("EPA") to "carry out" the state's hazardous waste program "in lieu of" RCRA, is precluded from doing so at a hazardous waste treatment, storage and disposal facility owned and operated by the federal government which the EPA has placed on the national priority list, and where a CERCLA response action is underway.

I.

The Rocky Mountain Arsenal ("Arsenal") is a hazardous waste treatment, storage and disposal facility subject to RCRA regulation, which is located near Commerce City, Colorado in the Denver metropolitan area. The United States government has owned the Arsenal since 1942, and the Army operated it from that time until the mid-1980's. Without reiterating its environmental history, suffice it to say that the Arsenal is "one of the worst hazardous waste pollution sites in the country." *Daigle v. Shell Oil Co.,* 972 F.2d 1527, 1531 (10th Cir.1992). The present litigation focuses on Basin F which is a 92.7 acre basin located within the Arsenal where millions of gallons of liquid hazardous waste have been disposed of over the years.

A.

*** RCRA requires the EPA to establish performance standards, applicable to owners and operators of hazardous waste treatment, storage and disposal facilities "as may be necessary to protect human health and the environment." 42 U.S.C. § 6924(a). The EPA enforces RCRA standards by requiring owners and operators of facilities to obtain permits, and by issuing administrative compliance orders and seeking civil and criminal penalties for violations. The EPA may authorize states to "carry out" their own hazardous waste programs "in lieu of" RCRA and to "issue and enforce permits for the storage, treatment, or disposal of hazardous waste" so long as the state program meets the minimum federal standards. 42 U.S.C. § 6926(b). *** However, RCRA does not preclude a state from adopting more stringent requirements for the treatment, storage and disposal of hazardous waste. 42 U.S.C. § 6929. Once the EPA authorizes a state to carry out the state hazardous waste program in lieu of RCRA, "[a]ny action taken by [the] State [has] the same force and effect as action taken by the [EPA]...." 42 U.S.C.

§ 6926(d). The federal government must comply with RCRA or an EPA-authorized state program "to the same extent as any person...." 42 U.S.C. § 6961.

B.

Because RCRA only applied prospectively, it was "clearly inadequate" to deal with "the inactive hazardous waste site problem." H.R.Rep. No. 1016(I), at 17-18. Consequently, Congress enacted CERCLA in 1980 "to initiate and establish a comprehensive response and financing mechanism to abate and control the vast problems associated with abandoned and inactive hazardous waste disposal sites." *Id.* at 22.*** We note that Superfund monies cannot be used for remedial actions at federal facilities, 42 U.S.C. § 9611(e)(3), but CERCLA otherwise applies to the federal government "to the same extent, both procedurally and substantively, as any nongovernmental entity." *Id.* § 9620(a)(1).

II.

In November 1980, the Army, as the operator of the Arsenal, submitted to the EPA part A of its RCRA permit application which listed Basin F as a hazardous waste surface impoundment. By submitting the part A RCRA application, the Army achieved RCRA interim status. In May 1983, the Army submitted part B of its RCRA permit application to the EPA which included a required closure plan for Basin F, and the following month, the Army submitted a revised closure plan for Basin F. In May 1984, the EPA issued a notice of deficiency to the Army regarding part B of its RCRA permit application and requested a revised part B application within sixty days under threat of termination of the Army's interim status. The Army never submitted a revised part B RCRA permit application to the EPA; rather, in October 1984, the Army commenced a CERCLA remedial investigation/feasibility study ("RI/FS").[9]

Effective November 2, 1984, the EPA *** authorized Colorado to "carry out" the Colorado Hazardous Waste Management Act ("CHWMA") "in lieu of" RCRA. That same month, the Army submitted its part B RCRA/CHWMA permit application to the Colorado Department of Health ("CDH") which is charged with the administration and enforcement of CHWMA. Notably, the part B application was the same deficient application that the Army submitted to the EPA in June 1983. Not surprisingly, CDH found the application, specifically the closure plan for Basin F, to be unsatisfactory.

---

[9] While most of the President's CERCLA authority has been delegated to the EPA pursuant to 42 U.S.C. § 9615, the President delegated his CERCLA response action authority under § 9604(a-b) with respect to Department of Defense facilities to the Secretary of Defense. A RI/FS is the first step in a CERCLA remedial action in order "to assess site conditions and evaluate alternatives to the extent necessary to select a remedy." 40 C.F.R. § 300.430(a)(2). Interestingly, the Army initiated the RI/FS during the month preceding HSWA's effective date, which provided that RCRA interim status surface impoundments undertake corrective action in order to continue treating, storing and disposing of hazardous waste after November 1988. The Army has since maintained that its CERCLA response action precludes Colorado from enforcing its EPA-delegated RCRA authority at the Arsenal.

Consequently, in May 1986, CDH issued its own draft partial closure plan for Basin F to the Army, and in October 1986, CDH issued a final RCRA/CHWMA modified closure plan for Basin F and requested the Army's cooperation in immediately implementing the plan. The Army responded by questioning CDH's jurisdiction over the Basin F cleanup.

In response to the Army's indication that it would not implement CDH's closure plan for Basin F, Colorado filed suit in state court in November 1986. Colorado sought injunctive relief to halt the Army's alleged present and future violations of CHWMA and to enforce CDH's closure plan for Basin F. The Army removed the action to federal district court, and moved to dismiss Colorado's CHWMA enforcement action claiming that "CERCLA's enforcement and response provisions pre-empt and preclude a state RCRA enforcement action with respect to the cleanup of hazardous wastes at the Arsenal."

In June 1986, the Army announced that it was taking a CERCLA interim response action with respect to Basin F. In September 1986, the Army agreed with Shell Chemical Company[10] on an interim response action in which Shell would construct storage tanks with a total capacity of four million gallons to hold Basin F liquids. In June 1987, the Army, the EPA, Shell and Colorado agreed on a Basin F interim response action which required the Army to remove contaminated liquids to the temporary storage tanks and contaminated sludges and soils to a temporary holding area until determination of a final Arsenal-wide remedy. In August 1987, the Army requested that Colorado identify potential applicable or relevant and appropriate requirements ("ARAR's"), *see* 42 U.S.C. § 9621(d), for the Basin F interim response action, and, in October 1987, the Army requested comment on its plan; however, Colorado did not respond to either of these requests.

In October 1987, the Army advised Colorado that it was withdrawing its still pending part B RCRA/CHWMA permit application claiming that it was ceasing operations of all structures addressed in the application and that it intended to remediate Basin F pursuant to CERCLA. The Army indicated that it would, however, comply with RCRA and CHWMA in accordance with CERCLA's provisions at 42 U.S.C. § 9620(i) and § 9621(d)(2)(A)(i).

*** In January 1988, the Army issued its decision document for the Basin F interim response action. Thereafter, the Army began the Basin F interim response action, and, in December 1988, completed the removal of eight million gallons of hazardous liquid wastes from Basin F, relocating four million gallons to three lined storage tanks and four million gallons to a double-lined holding pond. In addition, the Army removed 500,000 cubic yards of contaminated solid material from Basin F, dried it, and placed it in a sixteen acre, double lined, capped wastepile. The Army also capped the Basin F floor.

In February 1989, the federal district court denied the Army's motion to dismiss Colorado's CHWMA enforcement action. The district court relied on several provisions

---

[10] From 1946 to 1982, Shell leased a portion of the Arsenal from the Army and disposed of hazardous wastes in Basin F.

of both RCRA and CERCLA, including CERCLA's provision for the application of state laws concerning removal and remedial action at federal facilities not listed on the national priority list. ***

In March 1989, *** the EPA added Basin F to the national priority list. The Army immediately moved for reconsideration of the district court's order in light of the EPA's listing of Basin F on the national priority list.

In September 1989, CDH, acting in accordance with the district court's February 1989 order, issued a final amended compliance order to the Army, pursuant to CDH's authority under CHWMA. The final amended compliance order requires the Army to submit an amended Basin F closure plan, as well as plans and schedules addressing soil contamination, monitoring and mitigation, groundwater contamination, and other identified tasks for each unit containing Basin F hazardous waste as required under CHWMA. The final amended compliance order also requires that CDH shall approve all plans and that the Army shall not implement any closure plan or work plan prior to approval in accordance with CHWMA.

As a result of the final amended compliance order, the United States filed the present declaratory action ***. The United States' complaint sought an order from the federal district court declaring that the final amended compliance order is "null and void" and enjoining Colorado and CDH from taking any action to enforce it. Colorado counterclaimed requesting an injunction to enforce the final amended compliance order. On cross motions for summary judgment, the district court relied on CERCLA's provision which limits federal court jurisdiction to review challenges to CERCLA response actions, *see* 42 U.S.C. § 9613(h), and held that "[a]ny attempt by Colorado to enforce CHWMA would require [the] court to review the [Army's CERCLA] remedial action ... prior to [its] completion" and that "[s]uch a review is expressly prohibited by [CERCLA] § 9613(h)." It is important to note that the district court distinguished its earlier order, which held that Colorado could enforce CHWMA despite the Army's CERCLA response action, based on the EPA's intervening listing of Basin F on the national priority list. In doing so, the district court appears to have implicitly relied on § 9620(a)(4), which provides for the application of state laws concerning removal and remedial action at federal facilities not listed on the national priority list, in addition to § 9613(h). Based on this reasoning, the district court granted summary judgment to the United States on its claims for declaratory and injunctive relief, denied Colorado's cross-motion for summary judgment, and enjoined Colorado and CDH from taking "any action to enforce the final amended compliance order."

III.
* * *

As this is a case of statutory construction, our job is to effectuate the intent of Congress. While our starting point is the statutory language, we must also look to the design of the statute as a whole and to its object and policy. When Congress has enacted two statutes which appear to conflict, we must attempt to construe their provisions harmoniously. Even when a later enacted statute is not entirely harmonious with an earlier one, we are reluctant to find repeal by implication unless the text or legislative history of the later statute shows that Congress intended to repeal the earlier statute and simply failed to do so expressly. ***

IV.

The district court focused on CERCLA's provision governing civil proceedings which grants federal courts exclusive jurisdiction over all actions arising under CERCLA. As the district court recognized, § 9613(h) expressly limits this grant of jurisdiction by providing, with exceptions not relevant here, that "[n]o Federal court shall have jurisdiction under Federal law ... to review any challenges to removal or remedial action selected under section 9604 of this title...." However, contrary to the district court's reasoning, § 9613(h) does not bar federal courts from reviewing a CERCLA response action prior to its completion; rather, it bars federal courts from reviewing any "challenges" to CERCLA response actions. This is a critical distinction because an action by Colorado to enforce the final amended compliance order, issued pursuant to its EPA-delegated RCRA authority, is not a "challenge" to the Army's CERCLA response action. To hold otherwise would require us to ignore the plain language and structure of both CERCLA and RCRA, and to find that CERCLA implicitly repealed RCRA's enforcement provisions contrary to Congress' expressed intention.

A.

Congress clearly expressed its intent that CERCLA should work in conjunction with other federal and state hazardous waste laws in order to solve this country's hazardous waste cleanup problem. CERCLA's "savings provision" provides that "[n]othing in [CERCLA] shall affect or modify in any way the obligations or liabilities of any person under other Federal or State law, including common law, with respect to releases of hazardous substances or other pollutants or contaminants." 42 U.S.C. § 9652(d). Similarly, CERCLA's provision entitled "relationship to other laws" provides that "[n]othing in [CERCLA] shall be construed or interpreted as preempting any State from imposing any additional liability or requirements with respect to the release of hazardous substances within such State." 42 U.S.C. § 9614(a). By holding that § 9613(h) bars Colorado from enforcing CHWMA, the district court effectively modified the Army's obligations and liabilities under CHWMA contrary to § 9652(d), and preempted Colorado from imposing additional requirements with respect to the release of hazardous substances contrary to § 9614(a).

As a federal facility, the Arsenal is subject to regulation under RCRA. More importantly, because the EPA has delegated RCRA authority to Colorado, the Arsenal is subject to regulation under CHWMA. *** Thus, Colorado has authority to enforce CHWMA at the Arsenal, and "[a]ny action taken by [Colorado] ... [has] the same force and effect as action taken by the [EPA]...." [42 U.S.C.] § 6926(d).

Notwithstanding Colorado's RCRA authority over the Basin F cleanup, and CERCLA's express preservation of this authority, § 9613(h), which was enacted as part of SARA, limits federal court jurisdiction to review challenges to CERCLA response actions. *** [T]he language of § 9613(h) does not differentiate between challenges by private responsible parties and challenges by a state. Thus, to the extent a state seeks to challenge a CERCLA response action, the plain language of § 9613(h) would limit a federal court's jurisdiction to review such a challenge.

Be that as it may, an action by a state to enforce its hazardous waste laws at a site undergoing a CERCLA response action is not necessarily a challenge to the CERCLA action. For example, CDH's final amended compliance order does not seek to halt the Army's Basin F interim response action; rather it merely seeks the Army's compliance with CHWMA during the course of the action, which includes CDH approval of the Basin F closure plan prior to implementation. Thus, Colorado is not seeking to delay the cleanup, but merely seeking to ensure that the cleanup is in accordance with state laws which the EPA has authorized Colorado to enforce under RCRA. In light of §§ 9652(d) and 9614(a), which expressly preserve a state's authority to undertake such action, we cannot say that Colorado's efforts to enforce its EPA-delegated RCRA authority is a challenge to the Army's undergoing CERCLA response action.

The United States relies principally on two cases to support its claim that § 9613(h) bars any action by Colorado to enforce the final amended compliance order. In *Schalk v. Reilly*, 900 F.2d 1091 (7th Cir.), *cert. denied*, 498 U.S. 981 (1990), the Seventh Circuit held that § 9613(h) barred private citizens from bringing a CERCLA citizen suit which challenged a consent decree between the EPA and a responsible party on the grounds that failure to prepare an environmental impact statement violated the National Environmental Policy Act. Responding to the citizens' argument that they were not challenging the remedial action but rather merely asking that certain procedural requirements be met, the court held that "challenges to the procedure employed in selecting a remedy nevertheless impact the implementation of the remedy and result in the same delays Congress sought to avoid by passage of the statute; the statute necessarily bars these challenges." *Id.* at 1097.

While we do not doubt that Colorado's enforcement of the final amended compliance order will "impact the implementation" of the Army's CERCLA response action, we do not believe that this alone is enough to constitute a challenge to the action as contemplated under § 9613(h). The plaintiffs in *Schalk* were attempting to invoke the federal court's jurisdiction under CERCLA's citizen suit provision. *See* 42 U.S.C. § 9659. While one of the exceptions to § 9613(h)'s jurisdictional bar is for CERCLA citizen suits, such suits "may not be brought with regard to a removal where a remedial action is to be undertaken at the site." *Id.* § 9613(h)(4). Thus, the CERCLA citizen suit in *Schalk* was jurisdictionally barred by the plain language of the statute. Unlike the plaintiffs in *Schalk*, Colorado has not asserted and need not assert jurisdiction under CERCLA's citizen suit provision to enforce the final amended compliance order; therefore, *Schalk*'s reasoning does not apply.

Nonetheless, the plain language of § 9613(h) bars federal courts from exercising jurisdiction, not only under CERCLA, but under *any* federal law to review a challenge to a CERCLA remedial action. In *Boarhead Corp. v. Erickson*, 923 F.2d 1011 (3d Cir.1991), the Third Circuit held that § 9613(h) barred the federal court from exercising federal question jurisdiction, under the National Historic Preservation Act, in an action which sought to stay the EPA's CERCLA response action pending determination of whether property qualified for historic site status.

Like *Schalk*, *Boarhead* is also distinguishable from the present case. First, the plaintiff in *Boarhead* was a responsible party under CERCLA; therefore, permitting the plaintiff's action to proceed would have been contrary to Congress' expressed intent in enacting § 9613(h). Moreover, the plaintiff's complaint in *Boarhead* sought to stay the CERCLA remedial action; thus, the plaintiff's action under the Preservation Act clearly constituted a challenge to the CERCLA remedial action. *** Most importantly, the *Boarhead* court's application of § 9613(h) to the facts of that case did not "affect or modify in any way the obligations or liabilities" of a responsible party "under other Federal or State law ... with respect to releases of hazardous substances," *see* 42 U.S.C. § 9652(d), and did not "preempt [the] state from imposing any additional liability or requirements with respect to the release of hazardous substances." *See id.* § 9614(a). In light of the plain language of §§ 9652(d) and 9614(a), and our responsibility to give effect to all of CERCLA's provisions, *Boarhead* cannot control this case.

B.

Not only is the district court's construction of § 9613(h) inconsistent with §§ 9652(d) and 9614(a) of CERCLA, it is also inconsistent with RCRA's citizen suit provision. *See* 42 U.S.C. § 6972. While CERCLA citizen suits cannot be brought prior to the completion of a CERCLA remedial action, RCRA citizen suits to enforce its provisions at a site in which a CERCLA response action is underway can be brought prior to the completion of the CERCLA response action.

RCRA's citizen suit provision permits any person to commence a civil action against any other person, including the United States government or its agencies, to enforce "any permit, standard, regulation, condition, requirement, prohibition, or order which has become effective pursuant to" RCRA. 42 U.S.C. § 6972(a)(1)(A). Such suits are prohibited if the EPA or the state has already "commenced and is diligently prosecuting" a RCRA enforcement action. *Id.* § 6972(b)(1)(B). ***

RCRA's citizen suit provision also permits any person to commence a civil action against any other person, including the United States government or its agencies, to abate an "imminent and substantial endangerment to health or the environment...." *Id.* § 6972(a)(1)(B). These types of RCRA citizen suits are prohibited, not only when the EPA is prosecuting a similar RCRA imminent hazard action pursuant to 42 U.S.C. § 6973, but also when the EPA is prosecuting a CERCLA abatement action pursuant to 42 U.S.C. § 9606; the EPA is engaged in a CERCLA removal action or has incurred costs to initiate a RI/FS and is "diligently proceeding" with a CERCLA remedial action pursuant to 42 U.S.C. § 9604; or the EPA has obtained a court order or issued an administrative order under CERCLA or RCRA pursuant to which a responsible party is conducting a removal action, RI/FS, or remedial action. *Id.* § 6972(b)(2)(B). Federal courts have jurisdiction over RCRA citizen imminent hazard suits and are authorized "to restrain any person who has contributed or who is contributing to the past or present handling, storage, treatment, transportation, or disposal of any solid or hazardous waste...." *Id.* § 6972(a).

By prohibiting RCRA citizen imminent hazard suits with respect to hazardous waste sites where a CERCLA response action is underway, while not prohibiting RCRA citizen enforcement suits with respect to such sites, Congress clearly intended that a CERCLA response action would not prohibit a RCRA citizen enforcement suit. Because the definition of "person" under RCRA includes a state, 42 U.S.C. § 6903(15), Colorado could enforce RCRA in federal court by relying on RCRA's citizen enforcement suit provision, provided that it complied with the requisite notice provisions. *** Because CHWMA became "effective" pursuant the EPA's delegation of RCRA authority to Colorado, and the final amended compliance order was issued pursuant to CHWMA, Colorado could arguably seek enforcement of the final amended compliance order in federal court pursuant to § 6972(a)(1). However, we need not decide this issue.   While Colorado's counterclaim sought enforcement of the final amended compliance order in the district court, Colorado asserted the counterclaim solely under CHWMA ***. Thus, we do not express any opinion on whether federal court jurisdiction over Colorado's counterclaim is proper under § 6972(a)(1)(A). Nonetheless, our discussion of this provision is relevant to our determination that Congress did not intend a CERCLA response action to bar a RCRA enforcement action, or an equivalent action by a state which has been authorized by EPA to enforce its state hazardous waste laws in lieu of RCRA.

C.

Rather than challenging the Army's CERCLA remedial action, Colorado is attempting to enforce the requirements of its federally authorized hazardous waste laws and regulations, consistent with its ongoing duty to protect the health and environment of its citizens. CERCLA itself recognizes that these requirements are applicable to a facility during the pendency of a CERCLA response action. *** While the decision to use CERCLA or RCRA to cleanup a site is normally a "policy question appropriate for agency resolution," *Apache Powder Co. v. United States*, 968 F.2d 66, 69 (D.C.Cir.1992), the plain language of both statutes provides for state enforcement of its RCRA responsibilities despite an ongoing CERCLA response action.   Thus, enforcement actions under state hazardous waste laws which have been authorized by the EPA to be enforced by the state in lieu of RCRA do not constitute "challenges" to CERCLA response actions; therefore, § 9613(h) does not jurisdictionally bar Colorado from enforcing the final amended compliance order.

V.

Even if an action by Colorado to enforce the final amended compliance order would be a "challenge" to the Army's CERCLA response action, the plain language of § 9613(h) would only bar a federal court from exercising jurisdiction over Colorado's action. Colorado, however, is not required to invoke federal court jurisdiction to enforce the final amended compliance order. Rather, Colorado can seek enforcement of the final amended compliance order in state court. Therefore, § 9613(h) cannot bar Colorado from taking "any" action to enforce the final compliance order.

The final amended compliance order was issued by CDH pursuant to its authority under CHWMA. CHWMA not only authorizes CDH to issue compliance orders, it also authorizes CDH to request the state attorney general to bring suit for injunctive relief or civil or criminal penalties. *** As the operator of a federal facility subject to regulation under CHWMA, the Army is subject to "process or sanction" of the Colorado state courts with respect to enforcement of CHWMA. 42 U.S.C. § 6961. Because Colorado may bring an enforcement suit in state court, § 9613(h) does not preclude Colorado from taking "any" action to enforce the final amended compliance order.

* * *

VII.

The United States alternatively contends that CERCLA's provision, which grants the President authority to select the remedy and allow for state input through the ARAR's process, bars Colorado from enforcing state law independent of CERCLA. This is a curious argument in light of §§ 9614(a) and 9652(d) which expressly preserve state RCRA authority, and we find it to be without merit.

A.

While the United States does not dispute that Congress intended states to play a role in hazardous waste cleanup, the United States argues that the states' role when a CERCLA response action is underway is confined to CERCLA's ARAR's process. Undoubtedly, CERCLA's ARAR's provision was intended to provide "a mechanism for state involvement in the selection and adoption of remedial actions which are federal in character." *Colorado v. Idarado Mining Co.*, 916 F.2d 1486, 1495 (10th Cir.1990), *cert. denied*, 111 S.Ct. 1584 (1991). *** Nonetheless, nothing in CERCLA supports the contention that Congress intended the ARAR's provision to be the exclusive means of state involvement in hazardous waste cleanup.

Contrary to the United States' claim, Colorado is not invading the President's authority to select a CERCLA remedial action. Rather, Colorado is merely insuring that the Army comply with CHWMA which §§ 9614(a) and 9652(d) of CERCLA expressly recognize is applicable. Sections 9614(a) and 9652(d) were included within CERCLA when it was originally enacted in 1980. However, the ARAR's provision was not enacted until the 1986 amendments to CERCLA. Certainly, Congress could not have intended the ARAR's provision to be the exclusive means of state involvement in hazardous waste cleanup as provided under §§ 9614(a) and 9652(d) when the ARAR's concept did not even come into being until six years after CERCLA was enacted.

Moreover, while the ARAR's provision requires the President to allow a state to participate in remedial planning and to review and comment on remedial plans, it only allows states to ensure compliance with state law at the completion of the remedial action. However, §§ 9614(a) and 9652(d) expressly contemplate the applicability of other federal and state hazardous waste laws regardless of whether a CERCLA response action is underway. Given that RCRA clearly applies during the closure period of a regulated facility, the ARAR's provision cannot be the exclusive means of state involvement in the cleanup of a site subject to both RCRA and CERCLA authority.

Contrary to the United States' claim, permitting state involvement in hazardous waste cleanup outside of CERCLA's ARAR's process, based on independent state authority, does not render the ARAR's process irrelevant. When a state does not have independent authority over the cleanup of a particular hazardous waste site, the ARAR's provision insures that states have a meaningful voice in cleanup. However, when, as here, a state has RCRA authority over a hazardous waste site, §§ 9614(a) and 9652(d) expressly preserve the state's exercise of such authority regardless of whether a CERCLA response action is underway.

* * *

NOTES

1. Precisely what is the basis of the court's conclusion that Colorado's action is not a "challenge" to the ongoing CERCLA remedial work? Do you agree? What arguments could you make that it is a challenge?

2. If this case had been brought by a citizens' group instead of the Colorado Department of Health, would the legal issues have been the same? Do you think that the outcome would have been the same?

3. Whereas in *Colorado* it could be said that RCRA encroaches on CERCLA, in the following case the provisions of CERCLA cabin RCRA's jurisdiction.

MEGHRIG V. KFC WESTERN, INC.
116 S.Ct. 1251 (1996)

Justice O'CONNOR delivered the opinion of the Court.

We consider whether § 7002 of the Resource Conservation and Recovery Act of 1976 (RCRA) authorizes a private cause of action to recover the prior cost of cleaning up toxic waste that does not, at the time of suit, continue to pose an endangerment to health or the environment. We conclude that it does not.

I

Respondent KFC Western, Inc. (KFC), owns and operates a "Kentucky Fried Chicken" restaurant on a parcel of property in Los Angeles. In 1988, KFC discovered during the course of a construction project that the property was contaminated with petroleum. The County of Los Angeles Department of Health Services ordered KFC to attend to the problem, and KFC spent $211,000 removing and disposing of the oil-tainted soil.

Three years later, KFC brought this suit under the citizen suit provision of RCRA, seeking to recover these cleanup costs from petitioners Alan and Margaret Meghrig.

KFC claimed that the contaminated soil was a "solid waste" covered by RCRA, that it had previously posed an "imminent and substantial endangerment to health or the environment," and that the Meghrigs were responsible for "equitable restitution" of KFC's cleanup costs under § 6972(a) because, as prior owners of the property, they had contributed to the waste's "past or present handling, storage, treatment, transportation, or disposal."

The District Court held that § 6972(a) does not permit recovery of past cleanup costs and that § 6972(a)(1)(B) does not authorize a cause of action for the remediation of toxic waste that does not pose an "imminent and substantial endangerment to health or the environment" at the time suit is filed, and dismissed KFC's complaint. The Court of Appeals for the Ninth Circuit reversed, over a dissent, finding that a district court had authority under § 6972(a) to award restitution of past cleanup costs, and that a private party can proceed with a suit under § 6972(a)(1)(B) upon an allegation that the waste at issue presented an "imminent and substantial endangerment" at the time it was cleaned up.

The Ninth Circuit's conclusion regarding the remedies available under RCRA conflicts with the decision of the Court of Appeals for the Eighth Circuit in *Furrer v. Brown*, 62 F.3d 1092, 1100-1101 (1995), and its interpretation of the "imminent endangerment" requirement represents a novel application of federal statutory law. We granted certiorari to address the conflict between the Circuits and to consider the correctness of the Ninth Circuit's interpretation of RCRA, and now reverse.

II

RCRA is a comprehensive environmental statute that governs the treatment, storage, and disposal of solid and hazardous waste. Unlike the Comprehensive Environmental Response, Compensation and Liability Act of 1980 (CERCLA), RCRA is not principally designed to effectuate the cleanup of toxic waste sites or to compensate those who have attended to the remediation of environmental hazards. RCRA's primary purpose, rather, is to reduce the generation of hazardous waste and to ensure the proper treatment, storage, and disposal of that waste which is nonetheless generated, "so as to minimize the present and future threat to human health and the environment." 42 U.S.C. § 6902(b) (1988 ed.).

Chief responsibility for the implementation and enforcement of RCRA rests with the Administrator of the Environmental Protection Agency (EPA), but like other environmental laws, RCRA contains a citizen suit provision, § 6972, which permits private citizens to enforce its provisions in some circumstances.

Two requirements of § 6972(a) defeat KFC's suit against the Meghrigs. The first concerns the necessary timing of a citizen suit brought under § 6972(a)(1)(B): That section permits a private party to bring suit against certain responsible persons, including former owners, "who ha[ve] contributed or who [are] contributing to the past or present handling, storage, treatment, transportation, or disposal of any solid or hazardous waste which *may present* an *imminent* and substantial endangerment to health or the environment." (Emphasis added.) The second defines the remedies a district court can award in a suit brought under § 6972(a)(1)(B): Section 6972(a) authorizes district courts "*to restrain* any person who has contributed or who is contributing to the past or present handling, storage, treatment, transportation, or disposal of any solid or hazardous waste ..., *to order such person to take such other action as may be necessary,* or both." (Emphasis added.)

It is apparent from the two remedies described in § 6972(a) that RCRA's citizen suit provision is not directed at providing compensation for past cleanup efforts. Under a plain reading of this remedial scheme, a private citizen suing under § 6972(a)(1)(B) could seek a mandatory injunction, *i.e.*, one that orders a responsible party to "take action" by attending to the cleanup and proper disposal of toxic waste, or a prohibitory injunction, *i.e.*, one that "restrains" a responsible party from further violating RCRA. Neither remedy, however, is susceptible of the interpretation adopted by the Ninth Circuit, as neither contemplates the award of past cleanup costs, whether these are denominated "damages" or "equitable restitution."

In this regard, a comparison between the relief available under RCRA's citizen suit provision and that which Congress has provided in the analogous, but not parallel, provisions of CERCLA is telling. CERCLA was passed several years after RCRA went into effect, and it is designed to address many of the same toxic waste problems that inspired the passage of RCRA. *** CERCLA differs markedly from RCRA, however, in the remedies it provides. CERCLA's citizen suit provision mimics § 6972(a) in providing district courts with the authority "to order such action as may be necessary to correct the violation" of any CERCLA standard or regulation. 42 U.S.C. § 9659(c) (1988 ed.). But CERCLA expressly permits the Government to recover "all costs of removal or remedial action," § 9607(a)(4)(A), and it expressly permits the recovery of any "necessary costs of response, incurred by any ... person consistent with the national contingency plan," § 9607(a)(4)(B). CERCLA also provides that "[a]ny person may seek contribution from any other person who is liable or potentially liable" for these response costs. See § 9613(f)(1). Congress thus demonstrated in CERCLA that it knew how to provide for the recovery of cleanup costs, and that the language used to define the remedies under RCRA does not provide that remedy.

That RCRA's citizen suit provision was not intended to provide a remedy for past cleanup costs is further apparent from the harm at which it is directed. Section 6972(a)(1)(B) permits a private party to bring suit only upon a showing that the solid or hazardous waste at issue "may present an imminent and substantial endangerment to health or the environment." The meaning of this timing restriction is plain: An endangerment can only be "imminent" if it "threaten[s] to occur immediately," Webster's New International Dictionary of English Language 1245 (2d ed.1934), and the reference to waste which "may present" imminent harm quite clearly excludes waste that no longer presents such a danger. As the Ninth Circuit itself intimated in *Price v. United States Navy*, 39 F.3d 1011, 1019 (1994), this language "implies that there must be a threat which is present now, although the impact of the threat may not be felt until later." It follows that § 6972(a) was designed to provide a remedy that ameliorates present or obviates the risk of future "imminent" harms, not a remedy that compensates for past cleanup efforts.

Other aspects of RCRA's enforcement scheme strongly support this conclusion. Unlike CERCLA, RCRA contains no statute of limitations, compare § 9613(g)(2) (limitations period in suits under CERCLA § 9607), and it does not require a showing that the response costs being sought are reasonable, compare §§ 9607(a)(4)(A) and (B) (costs recovered under CERCLA must be "consistent with the national contingency plan"). If Congress had intended § 6972(a) to function as a cost-recovery mechanism, the absence of these provisions would be striking. Moreover, with one limited exception, *** a private party may not bring suit under § 6972(a)(1)(B) without first giving 90 days' notice to the Administrator of the EPA, to "the State in which the alleged endangerment may occur," and to potential defendants, see §§ 6972(b)(2)(A)(i)-(iii). And no citizen suit can proceed if either the EPA or the State has commenced, and is diligently prosecuting, a separate enforcement action, see §§ 6972(b)(2)(B) and (C). Therefore, if RCRA were designed to compensate private parties for their past cleanup efforts, it would be a wholly irrational mechanism for doing so. Those parties with insubstantial problems, problems that neither the State nor the Federal Government feel compelled to address, could recover their response costs, whereas those parties whose waste problems were sufficiently severe as to attract the attention of Government officials would be left without a recovery.

Though it agrees that KFC's complaint is defective for failing properly to allege an "imminent and substantial endangerment," the Government (as *amicus*) nonetheless joins KFC in arguing that § 6972(a) does not in all circumstances preclude an award of past cleanup costs. The Government posits a situation in which suit is properly brought while the waste at issue continues to pose an imminent endangerment, and suggests that the plaintiff in such a case could seek equitable restitution of money previously spent on cleanup efforts. Echoing a similar argument made by KFC, the Government does not rely on the remedies expressly provided in § 6972(a), but rather cites a line of cases holding that district courts retain inherent authority to award any equitable remedy that is not expressly taken away from them by Congress.

RCRA does not prevent a private party from recovering its cleanup costs under other federal or state laws, see § 6972(f) (preserving remedies under statutory and common law), but the limited remedies described in § 6972(a), along with the stark differences between the language of that section and the cost recovery provisions of CERCLA, amply demonstrate that Congress did not intend for a private citizen to be able to undertake a clean up and then proceed to recover its costs under RCRA. As we explained in *Middlesex County Sewerage Authority v. National Sea Clammers Assn.*, 453 U.S. 1, 14 (1981), where Congress has provided "elaborate enforcement provisions" for remedying the violation of a federal statute, as Congress has done with RCRA and CERCLA, "it cannot be assumed that Congress intended to authorize by implication additional judicial remedies for private citizens suing under" the statute. ***

Without considering whether a private party could seek to obtain an injunction requiring another party to pay cleanup costs which arise after a RCRA citizen suit has been properly commenced, cf. *United States v. Price*, 688 F.2d 204, 211-213 (C.A.3

1982) (requiring funding of a diagnostic study is an appropriate form of relief in a suit brought by the Administrator under § 6973), or otherwise recover cleanup costs paid out after the invocation of RCRA's statutory process, we agree with the Meghrigs that a private party cannot recover the cost of a past cleanup effort under RCRA, and that KFC's complaint is defective for the reasons stated by the District Court. Section 6972(a) does not contemplate the award of past cleanup costs, and § 6972(a)(1)(B) permits a private party to bring suit only upon an allegation that the contaminated site presently poses an "imminent and substantial endangerment to health or the environment," and not upon an allegation that it posed such an endangerment at some time in the past. The judgment of the Ninth Circuit is reversed.

NOTES

1. Compare RCRA § 7002(a)(1)(B), governing citizen suits, with § 7003(a), authorizing governmental actions. After *Meghrig*, what if any arguments could the EPA make under RCRA § 7003 when it spends money to abate an imminent and substantial endangerment and then sues the contributors to the endangerment for reimbursement?

2. As discussed in chapter 14, CERCLA incorporates other federal statutes, where applicable or relevant and appropriate, in setting cleanup standards. Of prime importance to most CERCLA cleanups is the issue whether various RCRA provisions are applicable or relevant and appropriate. Although RCRA generator and TSD requirements are potential ARARs, often of greatest significance are RCRA's land ban provisions. Regulations addressing the hazardous waste status of contaminated media, and attendant land ban issues, are proposed as of the publication of this edition. (See chapter 2.B.) The ARARs aspect of these new RCRA regulations is undoubtedly a significant consideration in the EPA's decision-making process.

3. Because CERCLA clearly authorizes suits for reimbursement or cost recovery, whether under § 107(a) or § 113(f), *Meghrig* is of little moment in the context of hazardous substance releases. Where the material being released is not a hazardous substance—as in the case of petroleum product leaking from underground storage tanks—*Meghrig* effectively precludes any federal claim for cost recovery by parties (typically, current property owners) who are required by government order or business necessity to conduct a cleanup promptly, and cannot afford the time delay inherent in an injunction action seeking to force prior owners or operators to conduct the cleanup.

Underground tanks storing petroleum or hazardous substances are subject to RCRA Subtitle I, which was added to the statute in 1984. RCRA §§ 9001-9010, 42 U.S.C. §§ 6991-6991i. The Subtitle I program borrows provisions from both RCRA and CERCLA. Like RCRA, it establishes technical design and performance standards for the day-to-day operation of underground storage tanks. Tank owners and operators are required to demonstrate financial responsibility and to close out-of-service tanks in accordance with specified standards. In addition, state agencies may be, and most have been, authorized to administer the federal program within their states. Like CERCLA, the Subtitle I program has cleanup provisions (using the "corrective action" nomenclature of RCRA, rather than the "response action" phrase preferred by CERCLA). When there is a petroleum release from an underground storage tank, the EPA or authorized state may order the tank owner or operator to undertake corrective action, or they may use the Leaking Underground Storage Tank Trust Fund (a mini-Superfund) to conduct a governmental cleanup and then sue the owner and operator for cost recovery. Unlike under CERCLA, persons and entities other than the tank owner and operator are not subject to liability, there is no express imposition of liability on past owners and operators (except for the last owner of a tank taken out of use before Subtitle I was enacted), and there are no provisions for private cost recovery actions.

Detailed regulations implementing Subtitle I require tank owners or operators to utilize adequate leak detection methods and to ensure that their tanks are protected against corrosion, spills, and overfills. 53 Fed. Reg. 37082 (1988), *codified at* 40 C.F.R.Part 280. The regulations have applied to new tanks since being promulgated in 1988, and they required existing tanks to upgrade over a ten-year period, ending December 1998.

Problem #7: RCRA and CERCLA

TO: Assistant Regional Counsel for Solid Waste and Emergency Response

FROM: Regional Administrator

RE: High Priority Cleanup Site

Sleaze Publishing Co. ("Sleaze") is in the business of publishing "trashy" (but not RCRA hazardous) novels. Its corporate headquarters and sole printing facility are located at a picturesque, 150-acre site in Aardvark, Pennsylvania. Sleaze purchased the property in 1985 from Envirosure, an environmental consulting firm that had used the site as its corporate headquarters.

Notwithstanding Envirosure's outstanding world-wide reputation, its headquarters facility had an environmental problem of its own. In 1983, the large and attractive fishing pond on the site experienced a devastating fish kill. Envirosure ultimately traced the fish kill to the vindictive act of Zap, Inc., a former customer that was infuriated by the astronomical bills that Envirosure had racked up under its RCRA/CERCLA consulting contract with the company. Zap's fury was matched by its cunning, as it managed to circumvent Envirosure's elaborate security system to dump a sizeable volume of chloroform in the fish ponds late one night. Although the pond water was successfully treated and the pond restocked with fish, the chloroform quickly began seeping into the groundwater at the site.

Sleaze's printing operation uses 1,2-P, a (fictitious) chemical used widely in the printing industry. Sleaze generates some waste 1,2-P, which is a RCRA hazardous waste because it exhibits the characteristic of toxicity for lead when tested under the toxicity characteristic leaching procedure. Sleaze buys its 1,2-P from Chemmake Co., a specialty chemical manufacturer. In its chemical supply contracts, Chemmake offers to have ABC Transporter (the licensed hazardous waste transporter used routinely by Chemmake) pick up the customers' waste 1,2-P and deliver it to NIMBY, a RCRA-permitted hazardous waste landfill that is also used extensively by Chemmake. Sleaze has opted for this Chemmake-arranged transport and disposal service, as have most of Chemmake's customers.

Since Sleaze acquired the Aardvark site and commenced publishing operations there, it has shipped much of its waste 1,2-P off-site pursuant to the Chemmake contract. However, some of its waste 1,2-P has spilled and leaked onto the ground at various locations around the site, causing soil and groundwater contamination. The EPA had been unaware of this contamination, but I inadvertently discovered it when I toured the Sleaze facility last week while visiting relatives in the area. (You might as well know now that I have long been an avid fan of Sleaze's trashy novels.) I was greatly troubled to note extensive soil discoloration and to find only dead fish in the lovely fish pond. I promptly called in the top Region 3 environmental engineers, who determined that the soil, surface water, and groundwater at the Aardvark site had extensive concentrations of lead and chromium. They also informed me that the site is not on the National Priorities List.

We must ensure a complete cleanup of the Aardvark site. Please advise me promptly with respect to the following questions:

1. What options are available to the EPA under (a) RCRA and/or (b) CERCLA:
(a) to clean up the lead and chloroform contamination at the Aardvark site with government monies, and then seek reimbursement from responsible parties; or
(b) to require the responsible parties to clean it up?

2. Evaluate whether the EPA can name each of the following parties as defendants or respondents should we pursue the RCRA and CERCLA claims that you outlined above, and alert me to any defenses that each part might raise to attempt to avoid liability.
(a) Envirosure
(b) Zap
(c) Sleaze Publishing
(d) Chemmake.

18 ENVIRONMENTAL JUSTICE

Environmental and civil rights concerns have intersected in the area of environmental justice. Underlying this growing movement is the fact that minority and low-income communities bear a disproportionate share of the hazards associated with environmentally-sensitive activities, and enjoy fewer of the benefits of environmentally-protective activities. In the RCRA and CERCLA context, the greatest concerns have been that minority and low-income communities are more likely than other areas to contain RCRA TSD facilities and CERCLA sites. *See, e.g.,* COMMISSION FOR RACIAL JUSTICE, UNITED CHURCH OF CHRIST, TOXIC WASTES AND RACE (1987). Furthermore, the TSD facilities and CERCLA sites in minority and low-income communities are less likely to be the subject of aggressive enforcement and cleanup activities than facilities and sites in other areas. *See, e.g., Unequal Protection: The Racial Divide in Environmental Law,* NAT'L L. J., Sept. 21, 1992 (entire issue). Environmental justice advocates have thus been focusing on RCRA TSD permitting decisions, and on CERCLA cleanup decisions.

The environmental justice movement developed as a grass-roots response to site-specific decisions, such as the 1982 protest against the selection of Warren County, North Carolina as the disposal site for PCB-contaminated soil from numerous other locations in the state. Although the expression of environmental justice concerns can be traced to the early years of the RCRA and CERCLA programs, the movement did not gain national attention, or national momentum, until the publication in the late 1980's and early 1990's of several reports documenting disproportionate impacts.

Attempts to redress environmental justice complaints in legal fora focused initially on constitutional claims under the Equal Protection Clause of the Fourteenth Amendment. Such suits typically foundered on the difficulty of proving discriminatory intent, for example, in making TSD siting decisions. *See, e.g., East-Bibb Twiggs Neighborhood Ass'n v. Macon Bibb Planning & Zoning Comm'n,* 896 F.2d 1264 (11th Cir. 1990). In *R.I.S.E. v. Kay,* 768 F.Supp. 1144 (E.D. Va. 1991), *aff'd,* 977 F.2d 573 (4th Cir. 1992)(Table), 1992 WL 295129 (Oct. 15, 1992), the district court explained as follows in its Conclusions of Law:

2. The placement of landfills in King and Queen County from 1969 to the present has had a disproportionate impact on black residents.

3. However, official action will not be held unconstitutional solely because it results in a racially disproportionate impact. Such action violates the Fourteenth Amendment's Equal Protection Clause only if it is *intentionally* discriminatory.

4. The impact of an official action—in this case, the historical placement of landfills in predominantly black communities—provides "an important starting point" for the determination of whether official action was motivated by discriminatory intent. *Arlington Heights*, 429 U.S. at 266.

5. However, the plaintiffs have not provided any evidence that satisfies the remainder of the discriminatory purpose equation set forth in *Arlington Heights*. Careful examination of the administrative steps taken by the Board of Supervisors to negotiate the purchase of the Piedmont Tract and authorize its use as a landfill site reveals nothing unusual or suspicious. To the contrary, the Board appears to have balanced the economic, environmental, and cultural needs of the County in a responsible and conscientious manner.

* * *

7. [T]he Board was understandably drawn to the Piedmont Tract because the site had already been tested and found environmentally suitable for the purpose of landfill development.

8. The Board responded to the concerns and suggestions of citizens opposed to the proposed regional landfill by establishing a citizens' advisory group, evaluating the suitability of the alternative site recommended by the Concerned Citizens' Steering Committee, and discussing with landfill contractor BFI such means of minimizing the impact of the landfill on the Second Mt. Olive Church as vegetative buffers and improving access roads.

9. Both the King Land landfill and the proposed landfill spawned "Not In My Backyard" movements. The Board's opposition to the King Land landfill and its approval of the proposed landfill was based not on the racial composition of the respective neighborhoods in which the landfills are located but on the relative environmental suitability of the sites.

10. At worst, the Supervisors appear to have been more concerned about the economic and legal plight of the County as a whole than the sentiments of residents who opposed the placement of the landfill in their neighborhood. However, the Equal Protection Clause does not impose an affirmative duty to equalize the impact of official decisions on different racial groups. Rather, it merely prohibits government officials from intentionally discriminating on the basis of race. The plaintiffs have not provided sufficient evidence to meet this legal standard. ***

Id., 768 F.Supp. at 1149-50.

In light of the face of such equal protection claims, attention then turned to Title VI of the Civil Rights Act of 1964, which provides:

No person in the United States shall, on the ground of race, color, or national origin, be excluded from participation in, be denied the benefits of, or be subjected to discrimination under any program or activity receiving Federal financial assistance.

42 U.S.C. § 2000d. Although litigants proceeding directly under Title VI must also prove discriminatory intent, the Supreme Court has indicated that "actions having an unjustifiable disparate impact on minorities could be redressed through agency regulations designed to implement the purposes of Title VI." *Alexander v. Choate*, 469 U.S. 287, 293 (1985).

Pursuant to § 602 of the Act, which authorizes administrative agencies to issue implementing regulations, the EPA has promulgated regulations providing that "[a] recipient shall not use criteria or methods of administering its program which have the effect of subjecting individuals to discrimination because of their race, color, national origin, or sex." 40 C.F.R. § 7.35(b). In the first notable attempt to bring an environmental justice claim under the EPA's Title VI regulations, however, the district court held that individuals lack standing to sue under the EPA's regulations. *Chester Residents Concerned for Quality Living v. Seif*, 944 F.Supp. 413 (E.D. Pa. 1996), *appeal docketed*, No. 97-1125 (3d Cir. 1997). That decision appears to conflict with the practice in other circuits, where citizen suits seeking to enforce other agencies' regulations implementing Title VI have been maintained. *See, e.g., New York Urban League, Inc. v. State of New York*, 71 F.3d 1031 (2d Cir. 1995).

On the executive front, the White House and the EPA have begun addressing environmental justice concerns. In 1992, President Clinton issued the following Executive Order, requiring all federal agencies to develop and implement environmental justice strategies.

FEDERAL ACTIONS TO ADDRESS ENVIRONMENTAL JUSTICE IN MINORITY POPULATIONS AND LOW-INCOME POPULATIONS
Executive Order 12898
59 Fed. Reg. 7629 (1994)

By the authority vested in me as President by the Constitution and the laws of the United States of America, it is hereby ordered as follows:

Section 1-1. IMPLEMENTATION.

1-101. *Agency Responsibilities.* To the greatest extent practicable and permitted by law, *** each Federal agency shall make achieving environmental justice part of its mission by identifying and addressing, as appropriate, disproportionately high and adverse human health or environmental effects of its programs, policies, and activities on minority populations and low-income populations in the United States and its territories and possessions, the District of Columbia, the Commonwealth of Puerto Rico, and the Commonwealth of the Mariana Islands.

1-102. *Creation of an Interagency Working Group on Environmental Justice.* (a) Within 3 months of the date of this order, the Administrator of the Environmental Protection Agency ("Administrator") or the Administrator's designee shall convene an interagency Federal Working Group on Environmental Justice ("Working Group"). The Working Group shall comprise the heads of the following executive agencies and offices, or their designees: (a) Department of Defense; (b) Department of Health and Human Services; (c) Department of Housing and Urban Development; (d) Department of Labor; (e) Department of Agriculture; (f) Department of Transportation; (g) Department of Justice; (h) Department of the Interior; (i) Department of Commerce; (j) Department of Energy; (k) Environmental Protection Agency; (l) Office of Management and Budget; (m) Office of Science and Technology Policy; (n) Office of the Deputy Assistant to the President for Environmental Policy; (o) Office of the Assistant to the President for Domestic Policy; (p) National Economic Council; (q) Council of Economic Advisers; and (r) such other Government officials as the President may designate. The Working Group shall report to the President through the Deputy Assistant to the President for Environmental Policy and the Assistant to the President for Domestic Policy.

(b) The Working Group shall: (1) provide guidance to Federal agencies on criteria for identifying disproportionately high and adverse human health or environmental effects on minority populations and low-income populations;

(2) coordinate with, provide guidance to, and serve as a clearinghouse for, each Federal agency as it develops an environmental justice strategy as required by section 1-103 of this order, in order to ensure that the administration, interpretation and enforcement of programs, activities and policies are undertaken in a consistent manner;

* * *

1-103. *Development of Agency Strategies.* (a) Except as provided in section 6-605 of this order, each Federal agency shall develop an agency-wide environmental justice strategy, as set forth in subsections (b)-(e) of this section that identifies and addresses disproportionately high and adverse human health or environmental effects of its programs, policies, and activities on minority populations and low-income populations. The environmental justice strategy shall list programs, policies, planning and public participation processes, enforcement, and/or rulemakings related to human health or the environment that should be revised to, at a minimum: (1) promote enforcement of all health and environmental statutes in areas with minority populations and low-income populations; (2) ensure greater public participation; (3) improve research and data collection relating to the health of and environment of minority populations and low-income populations; and (4) identify differential patterns of consumption of natural resources among minority populations and low-income populations. In addition, the environmental justice strategy shall include, where appropriate, a timetable for undertaking identified revisions and consideration of economic and social implications of the revisions.

* * *

(e) Within 12 months of the date of this order, each Federal agency shall finalize its environmental justice strategy and provide a copy and written description of its strategy to the Working Group. During the 12 month period from the date of this order, each Federal agency, as part of its environmental justice strategy, shall identify several specific projects that can be promptly undertaken to address particular concerns identified during the development of the proposed environmental justice strategy, and a schedule for implementing those projects.

(f) Within 24 months of the date of this order, each Federal agency shall report to the Working Group on its progress in implementing its agency-wide environmental justice strategy.

* * *

1-104. *Reports to the President.* Within 14 months of the date of this order, the Working Group shall submit to the President *** a report that describes the implementation of this order, and includes the final environmental justice strategies described in section 1-103(e) of this order.

Sec. 2-2. FEDERAL AGENCY RESPONSIBILITIES FOR FEDERAL PROGRAMS. Each Federal agency shall conduct its programs, policies, and activities that substantially affect human health or the environment, in a manner that ensures that such programs, policies, and activities do not have the effect of excluding persons (including populations) from participation in, denying persons (including populations) the benefits of, or subjecting persons (including populations) to discrimination under, such programs, policies, and activities, because of their race, color, or national origin.

Sec. 3-3. RESEARCH, DATA COLLECTION, AND ANALYSIS.

3-301. *Human Health and Environmental Research and Analysis.* (a) Environmental human health research, whenever practicable and appropriate, shall include diverse segments of the population in epidemiological and clinical studies, including segments at high risk from environmental hazards, such as minority populations, low-income populations and workers who may be exposed to substantial environmental hazards.

(b) Environmental human health analyses, whenever practicable and appropriate, shall identify multiple and cumulative exposures.

(c) Federal agencies shall provide minority populations and low-income populations the opportunity to comment on the development and design of research strategies undertaken pursuant to this order.

3-302. *Human Health and Environmental Data Collection and Analysis.* To the extent permitted by existing law, including the Privacy Act: (a) each Federal agency, whenever practicable and appropriate, shall collect, maintain, and analyze information assessing and comparing environmental and human health risks borne by populations identified by race, national origin, or income. To the extent practical and appropriate, Federal agencies shall use this information to determine whether their programs, policies, and activities have disproportionately high and adverse human health or environmental effects on minority populations and low-income populations;

(b) In connection with the development and implementation of agency strategies in section 1-103 of this order, each Federal agency, whenever practicable and appropriate, shall collect, maintain and analyze information on the race, national origin, income level, and other readily accessible and appropriate information for areas surrounding facilities or sites expected to have a substantial environmental, human health, or economic effect on the surrounding populations, when such facilities or sites become the subject of a substantial Federal environmental administrative or judicial action. Such information shall be made available to the public, unless prohibited by law; and

(c) Each Federal agency, whenever practicable and appropriate, shall collect, maintain, and analyze information on the race, national origin, income level, and other readily accessible and appropriate information for areas surrounding Federal facilities that are: (1) subject to the reporting requirements under the Emergency Planning and Community Right-to-Know Act; and (2) expected to have a substantial environmental, human health, or economic effect on surrounding populations. Such information shall be made available to the public, unless prohibited by law.

Sec. 4-4. SUBSISTENCE CONSUMPTION OF FISH AND WILDLIFE.

4-401. *Consumption Patterns.* In order to assist in identifying the need for ensuring protection of populations with differential patterns of subsistence consumption of fish and wildlife, Federal agencies, whenever practicable and appropriate, shall collect, maintain, and analyze information on the consumption patterns of populations who principally rely on fish and/or wildlife for subsistence. Federal agencies shall communicate to the public the risks of those consumption patterns.

* * *

Sec. 5-5. PUBLIC PARTICIPATION AND ACCESS TO INFORMATION. (a) The public may submit recommendations to Federal agencies relating to the incorporation of environmental justice principles into Federal agency programs or policies. Each Federal agency shall convey such recommendations to the Working Group.

(b) Each Federal agency may, whenever practicable and appropriate, translate crucial public documents, notices, and hearings relating to human health or the environment for limited English speaking populations.

(c) Each Federal agency shall work to ensure that public documents, notices, and hearings relating to human health or the environment are concise, understandable, and readily accessible to the public.

(d) The Working Group shall hold public meetings, as appropriate, for the purpose of fact-finding, receiving public comments, and conducting inquiries concerning environmental justice. The Working Group shall prepare for public review a summary of the comments and recommendations discussed at the public meetings.

Sec. 6-6. GENERAL PROVISIONS.

* * *

6-609. *Judicial Review.* This order is intended only to improve the internal management of the executive branch and is not intended to, nor does it create any right, benefit, or trust responsibility, substantive or procedural, enforceable at law or equity by a party against the United States, its agencies, its officers, or any person. This order shall not be construed to create any right to judicial review involving the compliance or noncompliance of the United States, its agencies, its officers, or any other person with this order.

WILLIAM J. CLINTON

NOTES

1. How should the EPA's environmental justice strategy affect the implementation of RCRA and CERCLA? The EPA's strategy calls for early and ongoing public participation in facility siting and permitting decisions. It also requires demographic analyses of the surrounding areas to determine who is affected by newly-proposed sites. Environmental Justice Strategy: Executive Order 12898, EPA/200-R-95-002 (1995). *See* 60 Fed. Reg. 30871 (1995) (notice of availability of various federal agencies' environmental justice strategies).

Pursuant to its strategy, the EPA promulgated regulations expanding opportunities for public participation during all phases of RCRA TSD permitting. 60 Fed. Reg. 63417 (1995). The new requirements, which took effect in June 1996, added three steps to the permitting process: (1) the applicant must hold a public meeting even before it files its permit application; (2) the permitting agency must notify the public upon receipt of each permit application; and (3) if the permitting agency so requires, the applicant must establish an information repository regarding the proposed facility.

To guide the EPA in promoting environmental justice, the agency has created a National Environmental Justice Advisory Council and, internally, an Office of Environmental Justice.

2. Should states be required to adopt their own, comparable, environmental justice strategies in order to be eligible for EPA approval to administer the RCRA program within their states? Some states have begun addressing environmental justice issues under state law. *See generally,* Carol E. Dinkins, *Impact of the Environmental Justice Movement on American Industry and Local Government,* 47 ADMIN. L. REV. 337 (1995).

3. If you were the EPA's environmental justice ombudsman, what would you do to ensure that the EPA was complying with the Executive Order? If you were the in-house counsel of a hazardous waste treatment firm, what if any changes in your current and future operations might you expect as a result of the Executive Order and its implementation?

4. For an analysis of the environmental justice issue, and the interplay between environmental and civil rights laws, see Richard J. Lazarus, *Pursuing "Environmental Justice": The Distributional Effects of Environmental Protection*, 87 Nw. U. L. Rev. 787 (1993).

5. In the following case, the EPA's Environmental Appeals Board examines claims that the permitting of a hazardous waste landfill is inconsistent with the Executive Order.

In Re: Chemical Waste Management of Indiana, Inc.
1995 WL 395962 (EPA Env. App. Bd. June 29, 1995)

Before Environmental Appeals Judges Firestone, McCallum, and Reich.
Judge Reich.

On March 1, 1995, U.S. EPA Region V issued a final permit decision approving the application of Chemical Waste Management of Indiana, Inc. ("CWMII") for the renewal of the federal portion[1] of a Resource Conservation and Recovery Act ("RCRA") permit and a Class 3 modification of the same permit for its Adams Center Landfill Facility in Fort Wayne, Indiana. The Environmental Appeals Board has received three petitions challenging the Region's permit decision, one filed by the City of New Haven, one filed jointly by Cheryl Hitzemann and Deanna Wilkirson, and one filed by CWMII. ***

During the comment period on the draft permit and draft modification (collectively the "draft modified permit"), Petitioners and other commenters raised what the parties refer to as "environmental justice" concerns. More specifically, issues were raised as to whether the operation of CWMII's facility will have a disproportionately adverse impact on the health, environment, or economic well-being of minority or low-income populations in the area surrounding the facility. The gist of Petitioners' challenge is that the measures taken by the Region to address the environmental justice concerns failed to conform to the rules governing the permitting process, violated an Executive Order relating to environmental justice, resulted in factual and legal errors and an abuse of discretion, and raised an important policy issue warranting review. For the reasons set forth in this opinion, we conclude that Petitioners have failed to demonstrate that either the Region's permit decision or the procedures it used to reach that decision involved factual or legal errors, exercises of discretion, or policy issues that warrant review. Accordingly, we are denying review of the petitions.

---

[1] The State of Indiana has received authorization to administer its own RCRA program, pursuant to section 3006 of RCRA. Indiana has not, however, received authorization to administer the requirements contained in the Hazardous and Solid Waste Amendments to RCRA ("HSWA"). Consequently, when a RCRA permit is issued in Indiana, the State issues the part of the permit relating to the non-HSWA requirements and EPA issues the part of the permit relating to the HSWA requirements.

I. Background

* * *

During the pendency of CWMII's permit application, Executive Order 12898, relating to environmental justice, was issued. ***

In response to the environmental justice concerns raised during the comment period on the draft modified permit, the Region held what was billed as an "informational" meeting in Fort Wayne, Indiana, on August 11, 1994. The meeting was attended by concerned citizens, and representatives of CWMII, the Indiana Department of Environmental Management, and the Region. The purpose of the meeting was to "allow representatives of all parties involved to freely discuss Environmental Justice and other key issues, answer questions and gain understanding of each party's concerns." The Region also performed a demographic analysis of census data on populations within a one-mile radius of the facility. The Region ultimately concluded that the operation of the facility would not have a disproportionately adverse health or environmental impact on minority or low-income populations living near the facility.

It is the Region's efforts to address the environmental justice concerns raised during the comment period that Petitioners challenge on appeal. ***

II. Discussion

Under the rules governing this proceeding, the Regional administrator's permit decision ordinarily will not be reviewed unless it is based on a clearly erroneous finding of fact or conclusion of law, or involves an important matter of policy or exercise of discretion that warrants review. See 40 C.F.R. § 124.19; 45 Fed. Reg. 33,412 (May 19, 1980). *** For the reasons set forth below, we conclude that Petitioners have not carried their burden in this case.

We believe it is useful to begin by considering the precise nature of Petitioners' environmental justice claim in the context of this RCRA proceeding and the effect, if any, the issuance of Executive Order 12898 should have on the way in which the Agency addresses such a claim.

"Environmental justice," at least as that term is used in the Executive Order, involves "identifying and addressing, as appropriate, disproportionately high and adverse human health or environmental effects of [Agency] programs, policies, and activities on minority populations and low-income populations * * *." 59 Fed. Reg. at 7629. Some of the commenters also believe that environmental justice is concerned with adverse effects on the *economic* well-being of such populations. Thus, when Petitioners couch their arguments in terms of environmental justice, they assert that the issuance of the permit and the concomitant operation of the facility will have a disproportionately adverse impact not only on the health and environment of minority or low-income people living near the facility but also on economic growth and property values. The main support in the record for this assertion is an environmental impacts study submitted by the City of New Haven. That study purports to "evaluate the potential for human exposure to toxic chemicals derived from the treatment and disposal of chemicals at the Adams Center." It identifies "exposure pathways" by which citizens living near the facility may be exposed to pollutants from the facility, but its central conclusion is that more risk assessment needs to be done before the extent and probability of such exposure can be determined accurately.

Although it is not made explicit in the petitions, it is nevertheless clear that Petitioners do not believe that the threats posed by the facility can be addressed through revision of the permit. Rather, it is apparent that Petitioners believe that their concerns can be addressed only by permanently halting operation of the facility at its present location or, at a minimum, preventing the Phase IV Expansion of the facility. Thus, Petitioners challenge the permit decision, including the modification, in its entirety, rather than any specific permit conditions.

At the outset, it is important to determine how (if at all) the Executive Order changes the way a Region processes a permit application under RCRA. For the reasons set forth below, we conclude that the Executive Order does not purport to, and does not have the effect of, changing the substantive requirements for issuance of a permit under RCRA and its implementing regulations. We conclude, nevertheless, that there are areas where the Region has discretion to act within the constraints of the RCRA regulations and, in such areas, as a matter of policy, the Region should exercise that discretion to implement the Executive Order to the greatest extent practicable.

Permit Issuance Under RCRA: While, as is discussed later, there are some important opportunities to implement the Executive Order in the RCRA permitting context, there are substantial limitations as well. As the Region notes in its brief, the Executive Order by its express terms is to be implemented in a manner that is consistent with existing law. *** The Region correctly points out that under the existing RCRA scheme, the Agency is *required* to issue a permit to any applicant who meets all the requirements of RCRA and its implementing regulations. *** RCRA § 3005(c)(1). Thus, as the Region observes:

> Under federal law, public support or opposition to the permitting of a facility can affect a permitting decision if such support or opposition is based on issues relating to compliance with the requirements of RCRA or RCRA regulations or such support or opposition otherwise relate to protection of human health or the environment. RCRA does not authorize permitting decisions to be based on public comment that is unrelated to RCRA's statutory or regulatory requirements or the protection of human health or the environment.

The Region correctly observes that under RCRA and its implementing regulations, "there is no legal basis for rejecting a RCRA permit application based solely upon alleged social or economic impacts upon the community." Accordingly, if a permit applicant meets the requirements of RCRA and its implementing regulations, the Agency *must* issue the permit, regardless of the racial or socio-economic composition of the surrounding community and regardless of the economic effect of the facility on the surrounding community.

Implementing the Executive Order: Nevertheless, there are two areas in the RCRA permitting scheme in which the Region has significant discretion, within the constraints of RCRA, to implement the mandates of the Executive Order. The first of these areas is public participation. *** Part 124 already provides procedures for ensuring that the public is afforded an opportunity to participate in the processing of a permit application. The procedures required under part 124, however, do not preclude a Region from providing other opportunities for public involvement beyond those required under part 124. *** We hold, therefore, that when the Region has a basis to believe that operation of the facility may have a disproportionate impact on a minority or low-income segment of the affected community, the Region should, as a matter of policy, exercise its discretion to assure early and ongoing opportunities for public involvement in the permitting process.

A second area in which the Region has discretion to implement the Executive Order within the constraints of RCRA relates to the omnibus clause under section 3005(c)(3) of RCRA. Under the omnibus clause, if the operation of a facility would have an adverse impact on the health or environment of the surrounding community, the Agency would be required to include permit terms or conditions that would ensure that such impacts do not occur. Moreover, if the nature of the facility and its proximity to neighboring populations would make it impossible to craft a set of permit terms that would protect the health and environment of such populations, the Agency would have the authority to deny the permit. *** In that event, the facility would have to shut down entirely. Thus, under the omnibus clause, if the operation of a facility truly poses a threat to the health or environment of a low-income or minority community, the omnibus clause would require the Region to include in the permit whatever terms and conditions are necessary to prevent such impacts. This would be true even without a finding of disparate impact.

There is nothing in section 3005(c)(3) to prevent the Region from taking a more refined look at its health and environmental impacts assessment, in light of allegations that operation of the facility would have a disproportionately adverse effect on the health or environment of low-income or minority populations. Even under the omnibus clause some judgment is required as to what constitutes a threat to human health and the environment. It is certainly conceivable that, although analysis of a broad cross-section of the community may not suggest a threat to human health and the environment from the operation of a facility, such a broad analysis might mask the effects of the facility on a disparately affected minority or low-income segment of the community. (Moreover, such an analysis might have been based on assumptions that, though true for a broad cross-section of the community, are not true for the smaller minority or low-income segment of the community.) A Region should take this under consideration in defining the scope of its analysis for compliance with § 3005(c)(3).

*** [W]e hold that when a commenter submits at least a superficially plausible claim that operation of the facility will have a disproportionate impact on a minority or low-income segment of the affected community, the Region should, as a matter of policy, exercise its discretion under section 3005(c)(3) to include within its health and environmental impacts assessment an analysis focusing particularly on the minority or low-income community whose health or environment is alleged to be threatened by the facility. In this fashion, the Region may implement the Executive Order within the constraints of RCRA and its implementing regulations.

Petitioners' Challenge to the Region's Efforts to Implement the Executive Order: It is the Region's efforts to implement the Executive Order, described above, that are the basis of the Petitioners' challenges. Petitioners raise a number of points, all of which may be consolidated into the following three arguments: (1) The Agency has failed to promulgate a national environmental justice strategy, as it is required to do under the Executive Order, and the Region's effort to implement the Order in the absence of such a strategy or other national guidance and criteria was erroneous; (2) The Region's demographic study, the scope of which was restricted to a one-mile radius around the facility, was clearly erroneous and ignored evidence presented during the comment period concerning the racial and socio-economic composition of, and the facility's impact on, the community living both within and outside of the one-mile radius; (3) The Region based its decision on information obtained at the August 11 meeting, but the information was not part of the administrative record and the meeting did not conform to the rules in 40 C.F.R. part 124 governing public hearings.

Reviewing Challenges Based on the Executive Order: As a threshold matter, the Region suggests that claims relating to the implementation of the Executive Order are not subject to review. In support of this argument, the Region points out that the Executive Order itself expressly provides that it does not create any substantive or procedural rights that could be enforced through litigation. *** However, while the Region is correct that section 6-609 precludes *judicial* review of the Agency's efforts to comply with the Executive Order, it does not affect implementation of the Order *within* an agency. More specifically, it does not preclude the *Board*, in an appropriate circumstance, from reviewing a Region's compliance with the Executive Order as a matter of policy or exercise of discretion to the extent relevant under section 124.19(a). Section 124.19(a) authorizes the Board to review any condition of a permit decision (or as here, the permit decision in its entirety). Accordingly, the Board can review the Region's efforts to implement the Executive Order in the course of determining the validity or appropriateness of the permit decision at issue. With that in mind, we turn to the specific challenges raised by Petitioners in this case.

* * *

The Region's Demographic Study: Petitioners also question the Region's efforts to determine whether operation of the facility will have a disproportionate impact on a minority or low-income community. To assess whether there would indeed be a disproportionate impact on low-income or minority populations, the Region performed a demographic study, based on census figures, of the racial and socio-economic composition of the community surrounding the facility. The Region concluded that no minority or low-income communities will face a disproportionate impact from the facility. Petitioners argue that, in arriving at this conclusion, the Region erred by ignoring available census and other information submitted during the comment period that allegedly demonstrate a disproportionate impact of the facility on minority or low-income populations, particularly those at distances greater than one mile.

Petitioners particularly criticize the Region's decision to restrict the focus of its study to the community living within a one-mile radius of the facility. Petitioners contend that the facility adversely affects citizens who live further than one mile away from the facility. In its response to the petitions, the Region defends its decision to focus on a one-mile radius for its demographic study, as follows:

> [T]he Region 5 office of RCRA has chosen a one-mile radius for demographic evaluation of disproportionately high and adverse human health or environmental impacts of RCRA facilities upon minority populations and low- income populations, based upon a Comprehensive Environmental Response, Compensation and Liability Act, *** guidance developed for CERCLA sites without groundwater contamination; however, the demographic evaluation did not exclude the population located outside of the one-mile radius.

As explained above, the Region can and should consider a claim of disproportionate impact in the context of its health and environmental impacts assessment under the omnibus clause at section 3005(c)(3) of RCRA. The proper scope of a demographic study to consider such impacts is an issue calling for a highly technical judgment as to the probable dispersion of pollutants through various media into the surrounding community. This is precisely the kind of issue that the Region, with its technical expertise and experience, is best suited to decide. *** In recognition of this reality, the procedural rules governing appeals of permitting decisions place a heavy burden on petitioners who seek Board review of such technical decisions. To carry that burden in this case, Petitioners would need to show either that the Region erred in concluding that the permit would be protective of populations within one mile of the facility, or that, even if it were protective of such close-in populations, it for some reason would not protect the health or environment of citizens who live at a greater distance from the facility. We believe that Petitioners have failed to demonstrate that the Region erred in either of these respects.

The petition mentions two parts of the administrative record in support of its claim. First, it refers to the comments of Fort Wayne City Councilman Cletus Edmonds, who contends that the facility will adversely affect the economic growth and housing of some 13,500 of his African-American constituents. As noted above, however, neither RCRA nor its implementing regulations requires the Agency to consider the economic effects of a facility.

Second, the petition mentions an environmental impact study submitted by the City of New Haven. That study indicates that particulates from the facility "could" affect an African-American community living as far as two miles away from the facility:

> Since the predominant direction of the wind is westerly, residential areas may be exposed to high levels of particulates from the site. There is currently an Afro-American community approximately 2 miles west of the landfill site and they could be exposed to higher levels of particulates.

Stephanie Simstad and Dr. Diane Henshel, "Exposure Pathway Analysis and Toxicity Reviews for Selected Chemicals Present at the Adams Center Treatment, Storage, and Disposal Facility," at 8 (June 24, 1994). This conclusion, however, is stated in a very tentative fashion and provides no indication of the probabilities involved or the adverse effects, if any, increased exposure might cause. It does not show why the Region's conclusions as to the protectiveness of the permit were erroneous or why, if the population within one mile of the facility is protected (as the Region concludes), there would nonetheless be impacts beyond one mile cognizable under section 3005(c)(3). We conclude, therefore, that Petitioners have failed to carry their burden of demonstrating that the Region's technical judgment in this case does not deserve the same deference that the Board normally accords to such judgments. Review of this issue is therefore denied.

* * *

III. Conclusion

For all the foregoing reasons, we conclude that Petitioners have failed to carry their burden of demonstrating that either the Region's decision or the procedures it followed to reach that decision, involved a clear error, or an exercise of discretion or important policy consideration warranting review. Review of the petitions is therefore denied.

19 POLLUTION PREVENTION

The tremendous cost and complexity of the RCRA and CERCLA programs, combined with widely-felt frustration at what appears to be the slow pace of progress under both programs, have lead many to focus recently on pollution prevention. That is a generic term for a variety of efforts to reduce the volume and toxicity of waste that is generated in the first place, rather than focusing all attention on regulating waste after it is created or cleaning it up once it causes contamination. Pollution prevention and the broader, related concept of sustainable development, are central themes of environmental protection in the 1990s.

To the EPA and its state-level counterparts, to the regulated community and all others who have been exposed to Superfund liability, to environmentalists, and to the public at large, pollution prevention has many attractions. Preventing or minimizing the production of hazardous waste and hazardous substances appears, at least at first blush, to have the dual merits of being economically and environmentally sound. The costs to government of designing and implementing the RCRA and CERCLA programs—tasks not yet nearing completion nearly two decades after the inception of those programs—the costs to the regulated community of attempting (a) to understand the RCRA program and (b) to comply with its requirements, including land ban treatment requirements and corrective action cleanup requirements, and the costs to virtually every segment of society of addressing and remedying the thousands of Superfund sites across the nation, are enormous. Pollution prevention cannot and will not eliminate these programs and these categories of costs, but by reducing the volume and toxicity of hazardous waste and hazardous substances, it can reduce them—and protect the environment at the same time.

There has been considerable discussion and promotion of the merits of pollution prevention, a federal law (the Pollution Prevention Act of 1990) endorses the concept, a number of voluntary federal programs are in place to develop pollution prevention techniques, and a number of state laws encourage and/or require the implementation of pollution prevention strategies.

The concept of pollution prevention evolved in response to the medium-specific, end-of-the-pipe approach to pollution and waste control that characterized environmental law during the 1970s and 1980s. In 1990, occasioned by the twentieth anniversary of the EPA, and indeed of modern American environmental law, the EPA and its various constituencies stepped aside momentarily from the focused efforts to refine continually the individual environmental programs (clean air, clean water, hazardous waste, etc.). They searched in vain for a "big picture," a unifying theme, in the field of environmental law. They noted that efforts to clean up one medium often simply transfer pollution to another medium. And they seized upon pollution prevention as a means of integrating the independently-operating environmental programs with the unifying theme of focusing more on the front end, of changing raw materials, processes, etc. in order to produce less, and less toxic, waste from the start.

At the federal level, this new theme was articulated in at least three notable ways. First, the Science Advisory Board ("SAB"), which is comprised of a broad spectrum of interests and advises the EPA on issues of science, published a widely read and discussed report, "Reducing Risk: Setting Priorities And Strategies for Environmental Protection." The SAB made ten recommendations for reducing risk and highlighted pollution prevention:

> EPA should emphasize pollution prevention as the preferred option for reducing risk. By encouraging actions that prevent pollution from being generated in the first place, EPA will help reduce the costs, intermedia transfers of pollution, and residual risks so often associated with end-of-pipe controls.

Second, Congress passed the Pollution Prevention Act of 1990, 42 U.S.C. §§ 13101-13109. The Pollution Prevention Act is analogous to the first modern environmental law, the National Environmental Policy Act, in that it pronounces a new approach to environmental protection but is not accompanied by substantive means of implementing the new vision. Accordingly, the congressional findings and policy statement may be the most notable features of the Act:

> (a) Findings. The Congress finds that:
>
> (1) The United States of America annually produces millions of tons of pollution and spends tens of billions per year controlling this pollution.
>
> (2) There are significant opportunities for industry to reduce or prevent pollution at the source through cost-effective changes in production, operation, and raw materials use. Such changes offer industry substantial savings in reduced raw material, pollution control, and liability costs as well as help protect the environment and reduce risks to worker health and safety.
>
> (3) The opportunities for source reduction are often not realized because existing regulations, and the industrial resources they require for compliance, focus upon treatment and disposal, rather than source reduction; existing regulations do not emphasize multi-media management of pollution; and businesses need information and technical assistance to overcome institutional barriers to the adoption of source reduction practices.
>
> (4) Source reduction is fundamentally different and more desirable than waste management and pollution control. The

Environmental Protection Agency needs to address the historical lack of attention to source reduction.

(5) As a first step in preventing pollution through source reduction, the Environmental Protection Agency must establish a source reduction program which collects and disseminates information, provides financial assistance to States, and implements the other activities provided for in this subtitle.

(b) Policy. The Congress hereby declares it to be the national policy of the United States that pollution should be prevented or reduced at the source whenever feasible; pollution that cannot be prevented should be recycled in an environmentally safe manner, whenever feasible; and disposal or other release into the environment should be employed only as a last resort and should be conducted in an environmentally safe manner.

42 U.S.C. § 13101(a) and (b). The Pollution Prevention Act called upon the EPA to collect additional data about source reduction and recycling activities (by amending the annual toxic chemical release form under the Emergency Planning and Community-Right-to-Know Act, or EPCRA), to establish a clearinghouse for the exchange of information concerning pollution prevention techniques, and to provide grants to states for programs offering technical assistance to pollution prevention efforts.

Ironically (although not without precedent), Congress used the term "pollution prevention" in the title, findings, and policy statement, but then inexplicably switched to the term "source reduction" in the definitions and all other provisions. Because all activities under the Act are directed to "source reduction," the statutory definition is worth noting:

(A) The term "source reduction" means any practice which—

(i) reduces the amount of any hazardous substance, pollutant, or contaminant entering any waste stream or otherwise released into the environment (including fugitive emissions) prior to recycling, treatment, or disposal; and

(ii) reduces the hazards to public health and the environment associated with the release of such substances, pollutants, or contaminants.

The term includes equipment or technology modifications, process or procedure modifications, reformulation or redesign of products, substitution of raw materials, and improvements in housekeeping, maintenance, training, or inventory control.

(B) The term "source reduction" does not include any practice which alters the physical, chemical, or biological characteristics or the volume of a hazardous substance, pollutant, or contaminant through a process or activity which itself is not integral to and necessary for the production of a product or the providing of a service.

42 U.S.C. § 13102(5).

Third, the EPA published a pollution prevention strategy, aimed at encouraging voluntary efforts within particular industrial sectors to reduce the pollution they generate. 56 Fed. Reg. 7849 (1991). The EPA's Blueprint for National Pollution Prevention Strategy articulates its general principles as follows:

> Because EPA believes that pollution prevention can benefit both the environment and the economy, the Agency's policy will be designed to maximize private sector initiative by working with industry to achieve reasonable prevention goals. ***

> At the same time, EPA believes that there is a continuing need for a strong regulatory and enforcement program under existing statutory authorities and that these provide further incentives to prevent pollution. EPA will be working to coordinate its regulatory program to help industry identify the potential for multi-media prevention strategies that reduce end-of-the-pipe compliance costs.

The strategy announced the EPA's intention to identify and overcome regulatory obstacles to pollution prevention, to work with other federal agencies and the states to encourage voluntary efforts toward pollution prevention, and to "strengthen the ability of the existing regulatory framework to provide further incentives for [pollution] prevention," such as by issuing related regulations in clusters, integrating pollution prevention considerations into the EPA's permit programs, and encouraging the inclusion of pollution prevention conditions in enforcement settlements.

When the EPA issued its Pollution Prevention Strategy, it also promoted the first of several voluntary pollution prevention programs focused on specific industrial sectors. The first, the Industrial Toxics Project, invited the chemical manufacturing industry to reduce its releases to the environment of some 17 chemicals by 33 percent by the end of 1992 and by 50 percent by the end of 1995, using 1988 as the baseline and using the required toxic release inventory reports under EPCRA to measure progress toward these goals. The EPA followed up with the Green Lights Project, to encourage pollution prevention by utilities. In 1994, the EPA developed the Common Sense Initiative, a program designed to further depart from the current one-size-fits all approach, stressing common sense, innovation, and flexibility. In attempting to lessen the rigidity and complexity of current regulations, the program has created EPA subcommittees, comprised of representatives of industry, environmental groups and the government, to test and develop strategies for improving the regulatory process on an industry-specific, rather than a media-specific basis.

Illustrative of the EPA's attempt to increase the flexibility of environmental regulations is Project XL (representing "eXcellence and Leadership"), which is part of the agency's initiative to reinvent environmental regulation. Project XL encourages companies to undertake pollution prevention projects that they are not legally required to undertake in exchange for greater flexibility on the part of the EPA in the manner in which it administers the requirements that do apply. Regulatory Reinvention (XL) Pilot Projects, 60 Fed. Reg. 27282 (1995). This attempt to achieve superior environmental performance is facilitated by the EPA waiving certain regulatory requirements in exchange for the entity developing and testing alternative strategies to protect the environment in a "cleaner, smarter, cheaper" manner. Project XL mirrors the agency's increased use of Supplemental Environmental Projects, whereby enforcement penalties are reduced in consideration of substantial expenditures on pollution prevention projects that are not legally required. (See chapter 6.) Project XL encourages companies to enhance their pollution prevention efforts in an economically-attractive manner—before they face enforcement penalties.

Under Project XL, the EPA has invited proposals on four types of projects: facility specific projects; industry-wide projects; government agency projects; and community-based projects. *Ibid.* (regarding the first three types), and 60 Fed. Reg. 55569 (1995) (regarding community-based projects). An entity wishing to participate in the program must submit a proposal to the EPA detailing the project they wish to undertake, and the environmental benefits that will be realized. Initially, the EPA used eight criteria to determine whether to approve an XL project: superior environmental results; stakeholder support; cost savings and paperwork reduction; innovation/multi-media pollution prevention; transferability (of the project to other sites); feasibility; monitoring reporting and evaluation; and environmental justice concerns. EPA subsequently decided to place primary emphasis on the first three criteria. 62 Fed. Reg. 193325 (1997).

One of the first XL projects involving hazardous waste was HADCO Corporation's plan to enhance its reclamation of wastewater treatment sludge from its printed wiring board manufacturing process in exchange for the exemption of the sludge from hazardous waste status. In the absence of Project XL, RCRA requires HADCO to send the sludge, a listed hazardous waste (F006), to a RCRA-permitted facility to perform reclamation. After the waste is treated to meet RCRA standards, HADCO would dispose of it at a landfill, rather than extracting nonhazardous copper from the residue, because of the high cost associated with reclaiming the copper. Under Project XL, the EPA is expected to exempt the sludge from RCRA regulation and HADCO will use the savings it realizes to reclaim the nonhazardous copper. Project XL Draft Final Agreement for HADCO Corp., 62 Fed. Reg. 3508 (1997).

Project XL has been controversial. Because the EPA is merely promising not to enforce the regulations, and is not changing the law, industry representatives fear they will still face the possibility of citizen suits to enforce the regulations as written. Environmentalists fear that with a lack of substantive standards and a vague definition of "superior environmental performance" to judge potential projects, Project XL allows companies to gain advantages by trading decreased emissions of one class of pollutants for an increased emissions of another unrelated class, with the long term effects of these exchanges still unknown. Whether the EPA has the statutory authority to decide not to enforce certain provisions of the laws it administers is not entirely clear, as well. *See, e.g.,* Rena I. Steinzor, *Regulatory Reinvention and Project XL: Does the Emperor Have Any Clothes?* 26 Envtl. L. Rep. 10527 (1996).

In closing, it may be helpful to focus on the EPA's working definition of the term pollution prevention.

EPA is seeking to integrate pollution prevention as an ethic throughout its activities. ***

*** Pollution prevention requires a cultural change—one which encourages more anticipation and internalizing of real environmental costs by those who may generate pollution, and which requires EPA to build a new relationship with all of our constituents to find the most cost-effective means to achieve those goals.

*** [Pollution] prevention is our first priority within an environmental management hierarchy that includes: 1) prevention, 2) recycling, 3) treatment, and 4) disposal or release.

* * *

As EPA looks at the "big picture" in setting strategic directions for the decade ahead, it is clear that prevention is key to solving the problems that all our media programs face, including the increasing cost of treatment and cleanup. In the common-sense words of Benjamin Franklin, "an ounce of prevention is worth a pound of cure."

F.H. Habicht II, Memorandum on EPA Definition of Pollution Prevention (May 28, 1992).

Now that you are familiar with the hazardous waste "cures" known as RCRA and CERCLA, perhaps you, too, agree with Ben Franklin.